INFORMATION TECHNOLOGY PROJECT MANAGEMENT

THIRD EDITION

INFORMATION TECHNOLOGY PROJECT MANAGEMENT

THIRD EDITION

Providing Measurable Organizational Value

Jack T. Marchewka

WILEY

John Wiley & Sons, Inc.

VICE PRESIDENT & EXECUTIVE PUBLISHER   Don Fowley
EXECUTIVE EDITOR   Beth Golub
ASSOCIATE EDITOR   Jen Devine
SENIOR EDITORIAL ASSISTANT   Maria Guarascio
MARKETING MANAGER   Carley DeCandia
DESIGN DIRECTOR   Harry Nolan
SENIOR DESIGNER   Kevin Murphy
SENIOR PRODUCTION EDITOR   Patricia McFadden
SENIOR MEDIA EDITOR   Lauren Sapira
PRODUCTION MANAGEMENT SERVICES   Pine Tree Composition

This book was set in 10.5/12 Times Roman by Laserwords Private Limited, Chennai, India and printed and bound by Hamilton Printing. The cover was printed by Phoenix Color.

The book is printed on acid free paper. ∞

To order books or for customer service please, call 1-800-CALL WILEY (225-5945).

ISBN-13   978-0-470-37193-0

Printed in the United States of America

10 9 8 7 6 5 4 3

The first two editions were dedicated to the memory of my mother, Josephine. And also to Beth, Bill, Tim, Kellie Ann, Matt, and to my father, Ted.

This edition is dedicated to the memory of:

Gayle Dubowski
Julianna Gehant
Catalina Garcia
Ryanne Mace
Daniel Parmenter

Forward, Together Forward

And also in memory of

Don Scully
John Scully
Katherine Coleman
Adel Antkowiak

BRIEF CONTENTS

CONTENTS

ix

CHAPTER 4   The Human Side of Project Management   100

CHAPTER 7   **The Project Schedule and Budget 180**

CHAPTER 10 IT Project Quality Management 263

CHAPTER 11   **Managing Organizational Change, Resistance, and Conflict 299**

CHAPTER 12   **Project Procurement Management and Outsourcing 324**

PREFACE

Welcome to *Information Technology Project Management—Providing Measurable Organizational Value 3e*. This book was written to help you understand the processes, tools, techniques, and areas of knowledge needed to successfully manage information technology (IT) projects.

The idea of project management has been around for a long time. In fact, it was around before the great pyramids of Egypt were created. Today, project management has emerged as its own field, supported by a body of knowledge and research across many disciplines. Although still relatively new, the fields of management information systems (MIS) and software engineering have their own bodies of knowledge that include various tools, techniques, and methods supported by a continually growing base of research.

Unfortunately, the track record for IT projects has not been as successful as one might expect, although the situation appears to be improving. One reason for this improvement has been a greater focus on a project management approach to support the activities required to develop and deliver information systems. Just as building a system is more than sitting down in front of a computer and writing code, project management is more than just creating fancy charts or diagrams using one of the more popular project management software packages.

We can, however, build a system that is a technical success but an organizational failure. Information systems—the products of IT projects—are planned organizational change. Information technology is an enabler for new products, services, and processes that can change existing relationships between an organization and its customers or suppliers, as well as among the people within the organization.

This change can represent a threat to many groups. Therefore, people may not always be receptive to a new IT solution regardless of how well it was built or whether cutting edge technology, tools, and techniques are used. On the other hand, people in an organization may rightfully resist an information system that does not function properly or meet their envisioned needs. Therefore, we must take an approach that does not consider the technical side over the organizational side or vice versa. Attention to both the technical and organizational sides of IT projects must be balanced in order to deliver a successful project.

APPROACH

In writing this book, I have tried to create a balance between concept and application. Many project management books tend to cover a broad set of topics with little practical application. Others tend to focus on the tools and techniques, but fall short in showing how everything ties together.

This book was written with the student in mind. Many years ago—more than I would care to admit—when I was a student, one of my instructors said that the problem with many textbooks was that they were written by professors for other professors. That statement stuck with me over the years. When I began writing this text, I wanted to be sure that it was written with the student in mind.

Learning and understanding how to apply new concepts, tools, and techniques can be challenging enough without being made more complex by obscure writing. As you will find out, learning concepts is relatively easy when compared to putting them into good practice. This book is intended for both undergraduate and graduate students. While it has no specific prerequisites, you should have at least an introductory class in information systems or programming under your belt. You should find that the concepts of IT project management will complement courses in systems analysis and design.

Those of you who are undergraduates will not be thrust into the role of a project manager immediately after graduation. My goal is to help prepare you for the next several progressions of your career. For example, your first assignment may be to work on a project as a programmer or analyst. The knowledge that you will gain from this text will give you a good idea of how your work fits into the big picture so that you can be a more valuable project team member. More challenging and interesting assignments and opportunities for advancement will follow as you continue to gain more knowledge and experience. Eventually, this may lead to a leadership role where your knowledge and experience will be put to the optimal test.

On the other hand, you may have already acquired some experience and now find yourself in the role of a project manager. This text will provide you not only with the big picture, but also with a foundation for applying directly the tools, processes, and methods to support the management and delivery of a successful IT project.

This book follows a generic information technology project methodology (ITPM). Most students who read this book will never have been on a real IT project. I have written this book based on a flexible methodology that attempts to bridge the questions: How do I get started?, What do I do next?, How do we know when we're finished? This methodology provides a structure for understanding how projects are initiated, conceptualized, planned, carried out, terminated, and evaluated. This methodology will take you through the different phases of the project life cycle and introduce the concepts and tools that are appropriate for each specific phase or stage of the project. In addition, you will find the methodology and central theme of this text is that IT projects should provide measurable value to organizations.

The text provides an integrated approach to IT project management. It incorporates the nine areas outlined in the Project Management Institute's Project Management Body of Knowledge (PMBOK®). The concepts associated with information systems management and software engineering when integrated with PMBOK® provide an important base of knowledge that builds a foundation for IT project management. This integration helps to distinguish IT projects from other types of projects such as construction or engineering.

The text also integrates a knowledge management approach. The area of knowledge management is an area of growing interest and development. Knowledge management is a systematic process for acquiring, creating, synthesizing, sharing, and using information, insights, and experiences to create business value. Here, the concept of learning cycles provides a unique approach for defining and creating new knowledge in terms of lessons learned. These lessons learned can be stored in a repository and made available throughout the organization. Best practices can be developed from the lessons learned and integrated or made a part of an organization's IT project methodology. Over time, the generic ITPM introduced in this text can evolve and become a valuable asset to an organization as it becomes aligned with the organization's culture and business. In turn, this evolving process will provide the organization with increased capability and maturity that hopefully will increase the likelihood of successful projects.

CHAPTER OVERVIEWS

The material in each chapter provides a logical flow in terms of the phases and processes required to plan and manage an IT project. The text begins with a call for a better way to manage IT projects and then focuses on the deliverables and processes required to initiate a project. Once a decision to approve and fund an IT project is made, the project must be planned at a detailed level to determine the schedule and budget. The planning and subsequent execution of the project's plan are supported by the project management and information technology bodies of knowledge.

- *Chapter 1: The Nature of Information Technology Projects* includes defining what a project is and the discipline of project management. The concepts of the project life cycle and systems development life cycle are also introduced, as well as IT project governance and the project selection process.

- *Chapter 2: Conceptualizing and Initializing the IT Project* introduces an information technology project management methodology (ITPM) and the concept of measurable organizational value (MOV), which will provide a foundation for this text. In addition, the first phase of this methodology, conceptualizing and initializing the project, and the first deliverable of this methodology, the business case, are described and discussed.

- *Chapter 3: Developing the Project Charter and Baseline Project Plan* introduces project integration management and a project planning framework to support the development of the project plan.

- *Chapter 4: The Human Side of Project Management* describes the formal and informal organization so that the project manager and team can conduct a stakeholder analysis to better understand the organizational landscape. Project team selection and the roles of the project manager are discussed, as is the concept of learning cycles to support a knowledge management approach to IT project management.

- *Chapter 5: Defining and Managing Project Scope* introduces and describes the project management knowledge area called project scope management. The project's scope defines what the team will and will not deliver to the sponsor or client. Scope management processes also ensure that the scope is properly defined and that controls are in place in order to manage scope throughout the project.

- *Chapter 6: The Work Breakdown Structure and Project Estimation* describes the project management tool called the work breakdown structure (WBS), which breaks up the project's scope into work packages that include specific deliverables and milestones. Several traditional project estimation approaches will be introduced, as will several software engineering techniques and metrics for software estimation.

- *Chapter 7: The Project Schedule and Budget* introduces several project management tools, including Gantt charts, activity on the node (AON), critical path analysis, program evaluation and review technique (PERT), and precedence diagramming, that can be used to develop the project schedule. A budget can then be developed based upon the activities defined in the WBS, the schedule, and the cost of the resources assigned or required.

■ *Chapter 8: Managing Project Risk* describes the concept of risk management and introduces a framework for defining and understanding the integrative nature of risks associated with an IT project. Several qualitative and quantitative approaches and tools will be introduced for analyzing and assessing risks so that appropriate risk strategies can be formulated.

■ *Chapter 9: Project Communication, Tracking, and Reporting* focuses on developing a communication plan for reporting the project's progress to various project stakeholders. This chapter includes an introduction to the concept of earned value and several common project metrics to monitor and control the project.

■ *Chapter 10: IT Project Quality Management* provides a brief history of the quality movement, the people involved, and their philosophies and teachings as an underpinning to support the project quality objective. Several quality systems to support IT project quality will also be discussed. These include the International Standards Organization (ISO), Six Sigma, and the capability maturity model (CMM). Together, the concepts, teachings, philosophies, and quality system approaches provide a basis for developing the IT project quality plan.

■ *Chapter 11: Managing Organizational Change, Resistance, and Conflict* describes the nature and impact of change associated with the delivery of an information system on the people within an organization. Several organizational change theories will be introduced so that a change management plan can be formulated and executed in order to ease the transition from the current system to the system that will be implemented.

■ *Chapter 12: Project Procurement Management and Outsourcing* introduces several project procurement management processes. This PMBOK® knowledge area focuses on contract management and the processes needed to administer relationships with outside suppliers and vendors as well as clients or customers. In addition, outsourcing of organizational and project components has received a great deal of attention. This chapter describes the various types of outsourcing relationships as well as how an outsourcing relationship should be managed.

■ *Chapter 13: Leadership and Ethics* describes some modern approaches to leadership and the relationship with ethics. Some common ethical dilemmas that may be encountered on projects are introduced along with a process for making sound ethical decisions. Moreover, several challenges and issues associated with managing multicultural projects are discussed as more organizations attempt to diversify their workforce or conduct business across the globe.

■ *Chapter 14: Project Implementation, Closure, and Evaluation* describes the tactical approaches for installing and delivering the project's product—the information system. In addition, the processes for bringing closure to the project and evaluating the project team and the project's MOV are discussed.

■ *Appendix: An Introduction to Function Point Analysis* provides a more detailed discussion on counting function points than is provided in Chapter 6.

WHAT'S NEW IN THE THIRD EDITION

- An update of the state of IT project management that includes the latest Chaos studies and studies conducted in 2007 by Tata Consultancy Services and the author
- New material on IT project governance and the project management office
- Updated material on project management process and project integration management
- New material on critical chain project management
- Added material on Monte Carlo simulation for risk management
- New Quick Thinking exercises that are short cases that can be useful classroom discussion tools
- New medium-length cases at the end of each chapter that can be used either as classroom discussion tools or student assignments

ORGANIZATION AND SUPPORT

For each chapter there is a Web-based practicum that includes a set of integrated hands-on case assignments. The case assignments allow the student to play the role of a project team member who has been hired by a newly formed consulting firm. The Web site provides all the background for the company. The cases lead the student through the various stages of planning an IT project for a client. They include several deliverables such as the project charter, project plan, scope management plan, risk plan, and implementation plan, and they require the student to apply the concepts and techniques covered in the book. One case from this Web site, Pilot Angels, can be found at the end of each chapter.

More specifically, each case assignment will include both a hands-on and a critical thinking component. For example, the hands-on component of the case assignment may ask students to develop a project plan using Microsoft Project®. However, the student would then be asked to answer questions about how specific concepts discussed in the book relate to the hands-on component. The hands-on component allows students to develop a particular skill, while the critical thinking component allows them to reflect upon how their actions may affect the project in different ways.

The end of each chapter includes a case story that describes a particular situation faced by a project manager and team undertaking an IT project. This scenario will set the stage for the concepts and tools introduced in the chapter and make the learning of the material more meaningful. From a student's perspective, this will attempt to answer the "so what?" and "why do I have to know this?" questions that should be addressed.

In addition, the Web site will host various student support materials. For example, it links to various IT and project management-related Web sites and articles to support the material included in the text.

An instructor's manual, test bank, and presentation slides are available through the Wiley Web site.

A 60-day trial edition of Microsoft Project is packaged with every new textbook. Note that Microsoft has designed the trial version to be installed only once. If you have purchased a used book and a prior user has installed the software, you will not be able to install it. Also, please be aware that Microsoft has changed their policy and no longer offers the 120-day trial available with previous editions of this textbook.

Another option now available to education institutions adopting this Wiley textbook is a free 3-year membership to the **MSDN Academic Alliance**. The MSDN AA is designed to provide the easiest and most inexpensive way for academic departments to make the latest Microsoft software available in labs, classrooms, and on student and instructor PCs.

Microsoft Project 2007 software is available through this Wiley and Microsoft publishing partnership, free of charge with the adoption of any qualified Wiley textbook. Each copy of Microsoft Project is the full version of the software, with no time limitations, and can be used indefinitely for educational purposes. Contact your Wiley sales representative for details. For more information about the MSDN AA program, go to http://msdn.microsoft.com/academic/.

ACKNOWLEDGMENTS

I would like to thank my editor Beth Lang Golub, as well as Maria Guarascio, Trish McFadden, and Sunitha Arun Bhaskar for all their hard work. Also, I would like to thank the following reviewers who provided useful and insightful comments:

Wita Wojtkowski   *Boise State*
Anthony Scime   *SUNY Brockport*
Phyllis Chasser   *Nova Southeastern*
Narayanan Perumal   *IUPUI*

ABOUT THE AUTHOR

Jack T. Marchewka is a professor of Management Information Systems at Northern Illinois University. He received his Ph.D. from Georgia State University's department of Computer Information Systems in 1994 and was a former faculty member at Kennesaw State University. Prior to entering academia, Dr. Marchewka was a vice president of MIS for a healthcare company in Atlanta, Georgia.

Dr. Marchewka has taught a number of courses at both the undergraduate and graduate levels and has been a guest lecturer at the Rotterdam School of Management, Erasmus University in the Netherlands. His current research interests include IT project management, electronic commerce, knowledge management, and organizational security and business continuity. His articles have appeared in journals such as *Information Resources Management Journal, Information Technology & People, Journal of International Technology and Information Management*, and *Information Management*.

Jack Marchewka is also a black belt in Kajukenbo and an instrument-rated commercial pilot who enjoys his family, karate, fishing, playing guitar, good BBQ, riding his motorcycle, and a good laugh.

1

The Nature of Information Technology Projects

CHAPTER OBJECTIVES

Chapter 1 provides an overview of information technology project management (ITPM). After studying this chapter, you should understand and be able to:

- Describe the dominant eras of information systems called the electronic data processing (EDP) era, the micro era, the network era, and the globalization era, and understand how managing IT projects has evolved during these eras.
- Understand the current state of IT project management and how successfully managing IT projects remains a challenge for most organizations.
- Explain the value-driven, socio-technical, project management, and knowledge management approaches that support ITPM.
- Define what a project is and describe its attributes.
- Define the discipline called project management.
- Describe the role and impact IT projects have on an organization.
- Identify the different roles and interests of project stakeholders.
- Describe some common approaches to structured systems development and iterative systems development.
- Describe the project life cycle (PLC), the systems development life cycle (SDLC), and their relationship.
- Describe Extreme project management.
- Identify the Project Management Body of Knowledge (PMBOK®) core knowledge areas.

INTRODUCTION

Information technology (IT) projects are organizational investments. When an organization builds or implements an IT solution, it often commits considerable time, money, and resources to the project with an expectation of receiving something of value in return. To improve the chances of success, you will be introduced to a relatively new discipline called information technology project management (ITPM). Some may argue that managing an IT project is like managing any other project, so all we need to do is apply the processes, tools, and techniques of traditional project management. This may be true to some degree, but a one-size-fits-all approach has not served us all that well in the past. Moreover, building an information system is different from building a house, a bridge, or a rocket for space travel. Although many of the project processes are similar, an entirely different approach to engineering each of these examples is needed. By combining the body of knowledge of modern-day project management with the body of knowledge of management information systems (in particular, software engineering and systems analysis and design), we can craft a better philosophy and method for planning and managing IT projects. This will provide a foundation for a logical and repeatable approach that improves the likelihood of IT project success.

Modern-day project management is often credited to the U.S. Navy, with its initiation of the Polaris missile project as a way to deter potential Soviet nuclear aggression in the early 1950s. The Polaris project was complex and risky, but the Navy used a project management approach to take the project from concept to deployment. This approach was viewed as a great success, and other organizations in various industries began to adopt project management as a way to define, manage, and execute work to achieve a specific objective.

Today, project management is viewed as an effective approach that addresses a wide variety of organizational opportunities and challenges. Project management focuses on reducing costs and product cycle times and provides an important link between an organization's strategy and the deployment of that strategy. In turn, this will have a direct impact on an organization's bottom line and competitiveness.

The field of information systems also evolved in parallel with the field of modern project management. According to Richard Nolan, a consultant and Harvard business professor, the use of the business computer has gone through a series of three dominant eras: the electronic data processing (EDP) era, the micro era, and the network era. However, some people believe that we are entering into a new era called globalization. We can look at each of the first three eras to understand how technology supported organizations and the approaches used to manage these projects. As we enter a new era of globalization, many projects can benefit from a foundation built upon past experience and knowledge, but new ways will be needed to overcome many of the challenges and issues that will be encountered.

The EDP era began in the early 1960s and is characterized by the purchase of the first centralized mainframe or a minicomputer by large organizations. The IT projects during this era focused generally on automating various organizational transactions such as general accounting tasks, inventory management, and production scheduling. The manager of this technology resource was often called the data processing (DP) manager and usually reported to the head accounting or financial manager. The goal of using technology was to improve efficiency and reduce costs by automating many of the manual or clerical tasks performed by people. As Richard Nolan (2001) points out, software programmers applied computer technology similar to the ways that farmers or engineers applied steam engine technology to mechanize agriculture. The process remained relatively unchanged, while the means for realizing the process became more efficient. Subsequently, IT projects during this era were generally structured, and therefore a structured approach for managing these projects could be used. Since the requirements or business processes were fairly stable, changing requirements were not a major issue and large, multiyear projects were common.

Unfortunately, in many cases these legacy systems created information silos, as projects supported specific business functions that often employed different technology platforms and programming languages.

In the early 1980s, the IBM personal computer (PC) and its subsequent clones signaled the beginning of the micro era. However, the transition or integration from a centralized computer to the PC did not happen immediately or without conflict. The often uncontrolled proliferation of the PC in many organizations challenged the centralized control of many MIS managers. For example, the first PCs cost less than $5,000 and many functional department managers had the authority to bypass the MIS manager and purchase these machines directly for their department. This often led to the rise of user-developed, independent systems that replicated data throughout the organization. Security, data integrity, maintenance, training, support, standards, and the sharing of data became a rightful concern. The organization often had an IT resource that was split between a centralized computer and a collection of decentralized user-managed PCs.

The organization needed to regain control of its IT resource while using IT strategically. Many organizations created the new position called the chief information officer (CIO) to expand the role of IT within the organization. While the DP manager often reported to the head accounting or financial manager, the CIO often reported to the chief executive officer (CEO). Therefore, IT increasingly became viewed as more than just a tool for automating low-level transactions and more of a tool for supporting the knowledge worker. Shoshana Zuboff (1988) coined the term "infomate" to describe the role of computers in this era.

The computer no longer remained under the direct control of the IT function and its spread throughout the various levels of the organization made IT ubiquitous. IT projects had to take more of an organizational view so that policies, standards, and controls become a part of all systems in order for existing mainframe or minicomputer applications to coexist or integrate with a growing surge of PCs. Moreover, a project manager and team could no longer rely on stable business processes, requirements, or technology that would allow for longer project schedules; otherwise, they would face the risk of implementing an obsolete IT solution. Shorter project horizons that crossed functional lines became the norm, while software development methodologies attempted to shorten the development life cycle.

Meanwhile, in the late 1960s and early 1970s, a defense project called ARPANET allowed university researchers and scientists to share information with one another even in the event of a nuclear war. By the mid-1980s, this network of computers became known as the Internet and led to the network era that began around 1995. In the network era, IT projects focused primarily on the challenge of creating an IT infrastructure to support many partners, strategic alliances, vendors, and customers. The network architecture had to be scalable so that potentially thousands of networked computers could function in an efficient and timely manner. Moreover, *digital convergence* or the integration of data, voice, graphics, and video allowed for new and innovative ways to deliver new products and services to customers. While the micro era focused on creating an internal network within the organization, the thrust of the network era was to extend this network externally. Network era projects not only faced the challenge of coordination and control, but also how to support a dynamic business strategy and new organizational structures. IT project members not only needed to understand the technology, but the organization and its competitive environment. As witnessed by the rise and fall of many dot com businesses in the late 1990s, the benefits and risks of managing IT projects were much higher than the two previous eras.

With the new millennium, IT received a great deal of attention in the media and the boardroom. Some people at the end of the century emptied their bank accounts and stockpiled food and water for fear that computers would crash and civilization would fall into mass confusion. Fortunately, the reported Y2K computer-related problems were few and not too critical. But what made the Y2K problem fascinating was that just about everyone was in it together and the project had an immovable deadline. To fix the Y2K date problem in the millions of lines of code, many organizations took advantage of cheaper wage rates and outsourced the rewriting of its code overseas to such countries as India.

After Y2K, it appeared that organizations now had the time and money to start on the IT projects that had been put on hold. Electronic commerce, enterprise resource planning (ERP) and customer relationship management (CRM) systems were at the top of the IT project list for many organizations. Together with large, global investments in fiber optics and the rise of the dot coms, the demand for skilled IT professionals and IT project managers to head up these new initiatives had never been stronger. Recruiters couldn't hire experienced professionals and university graduates fast enough to meet the demand.

Unfortunately, this golden time for IT did not last, especially in the United States. The tragic events of September 11, 2001 had a profound impact on the world and the global economy. As a result, many organizations were forced to make some difficult choices in order to survive. Seasoned IT professionals and new graduates who once commanded high salaries and choice assignments found themselves facing a tough job market. The bubble had burst. People learned that things can change quickly and without warning.

According to Richard Nolan, people, organizations, and even society goes through a period of discontinuity whereby people try to make sense of the changes created by the transition from one era to the next. Some people such as Thomas L. Friedman (2007) suggest that we may be entering into a new era called globalization. According to Friedman, the combination of technology and lowering of political barriers has flattened the world so that it is possible for people and organizations to work with almost anyone in any place and at any time. Moreover, the real IT revolution is just beginning as the global competitive playing field becomes leveled for everyone.

What does this mean for you? As a project manager or member of a project team you will be involved in projects that are more dynamic, geographically dispersed, and ethnically or culturally diverse than ever before. The risk and rewards will be greater than the previous eras. Therefore, a solid set of technical, nontechnical, and project management skills founded upon past experience and adapted to this new environment will be needed to manage IT projects successfully.

In both good times and bad, senior management will make a certain level of funding available for IT projects. The budgeted amount will depend on such things as the economy, competitors' actions within the industry, and the organization's strategic plan. Regardless whether an organization's budget for IT projects shrinks or grows, the resources available for any given period will be relatively fixed. Quite often the total funding requests for proposed projects will be greater than the available budget. As a result, any project that receives funding will do so at the expense of another project. The competition for funding IT projects proposed by the various business units or departments within an organization will be especially keen when the budget is tight. Projects that do not receive any funding will either have to wait or fall by the wayside. Therefore, the decision to fund a specific project will always be an important management decision because it will have a major impact on the organization's performance.

The decision to fund or invest in an IT project should be based on the value that the completed project will provide the organization. Otherwise, what is the point of spending all that time, effort, and money? Although senior management must make the difficult decision as to which IT projects receive funding and which ones do not, others must plan and carry out the project work. Which situation is worse: successfully building and implementing an information system that provides little or no value to the organization, or failing to implement an information system that *could have* provided value to the organization, but was developed or managed poorly? It's probably a moot point: In either situation everyone with a direct or indirect interest in the project's success loses.

The Purpose of This Book

The goal of this book is to help you to plan and manage information technology projects. We will focus on a number of different theories, but the main emphasis will be on applying the methods, tools, techniques, and processes for planning and managing an IT project from start to finish. If you are a project manager (or will be one soon), this book will help you to understand and apply project management principles in order to better manage your IT project. If you are just starting out in the field, this book will help you to understand the big picture of what an IT project is all about. This knowledge will help you to become a better team member and prepare you for the next several progressions in your career.

Many of the principles of project management can be applied to just about any project, but IT projects are unique in several ways. Throughout the text, we will discuss what makes IT projects different from other types of projects and how the principles and methods of system development can be integrated to define the IT project management discipline. Although many of the concepts for developing an information system will be integrated throughout, this is not a systems analysis and design text. More specifically, we will not delve too deeply into the systems analysis and design techniques that are used during systems development. We will leave that for other books and classes.

The remainder of this book provides a foundation for understanding project planning processes, methods, and tools. We will begin by understanding the nature of IT projects and then follow the project life cycle from project initiation through implementation and closure. Throughout the book you will be introduced to a number of project management knowledge areas and related software engineering concepts. While the goal of this book is not to prepare you for a professional certification in project management, it will provide a solid base to help you in your career and later on should you choose to become a certified project manager.

THE STATE OF IT PROJECT MANAGEMENT

Although IT is becoming more reliable, faster, and less expensive, the costs, complexity, and risks of managing IT projects continues to be a challenge for many organizations. Although IT projects have experienced challenges since the DP era, a survey conducted by the Standish Group of 365 IT managers in 1994 drew attention to what many called the *software crisis*. The study was called *CHAOS* and reported that only 16 percent of the application development projects were successful in terms of being completed on time and within budget. Moreover, about 31 percent of the projects were canceled before completion, while 53 percent were completed but

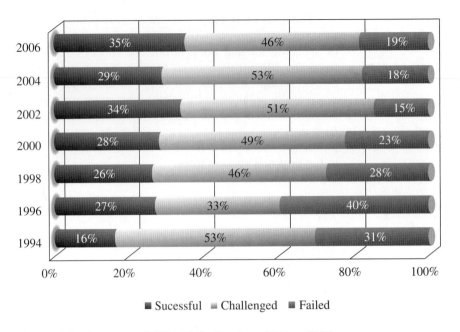

Figure 1.1   Summary of *CHAOS* Studies from 1994 to 2006

SOURCE: http://www.infoq.com/articles/Interview-Johnson-Standish-CHAOS.

over budget, over schedule, and not meeting original specifications. The average cost overrun for a medium-size company surveyed was about 182 percent of the original estimate, while the average schedule overrun was about 202 percent. That is, the results of the survey suggest that a medium-size project estimated to cost about $1 million and take a year to develop actually cost about $1.8 million, took just over two years to complete, and only included about 65 percent of the envisioned features and functions. Many took this to mean that IT project management was in a state of crisis, especially since 48 percent of the IT managers surveyed believed that there were more failures at the time than five or ten years earlier.

The 1994 *CHAOS* study has become one of the most cited, and Robert Glass (2005) raises the issue that people tend to quote the original 1994 figures while ignoring the fact that the Standish Group has updated the *CHAOS* reports every two years. A key reason may be that the 1994 study is free and easily attainable from the Standish Group, while the later studies must be purchased and thus are an expensive barrier for many researchers and practitioners. Fortunately, a summary of the later studies can be found using a good Internet search engine. The findings of these studies from 1994 through 2006 are summarized in Figure 1.1. Overall, it appears that IT projects are showing a higher success rate. For example, the latest study in 2006 reports that 35 percent of the IT projects were classified as successful in terms of being completed on time, within budget, and including all of the features or requirements envisioned. The Standish Group attributes this continuing improvement to better project management tools and processes, smaller projects, improved communication, more skillful IT project managers, and iterative development.

Interestingly, the *CHAOS* studies also report factors for successful and unsuccessful projects. Table 1.1 provides a summary of key factors for successful projects for three different time periods. It appears that successful projects have a strong nontechnical component in terms of executive support and user involvement that may

Table 1.1 Summary of *CHAOS* Study Factor Rankings for Successful Projects

Rank	1994	2001	2006
1	User involvement	Executive support	User involvement
2	Executive management support	User involvement	Executive management support
3	Clear statement of requirements	Experienced project manager	Clear business objectives
4	Proper planning	Clear business objectives	Optimizing scope
5	Realistic expectations	Minimized scope	Agile process
6	Smaller project milestones	Standard software infrastructure	Project management expertise
7	Competent staff	Firm basic requirements	Financial management
8	Ownership	Formal methodology	Skilled resources
9	Clear vision & objectives	Reliable estimates	Formal methodology
10	Hard-working, focused team	Other	Standard tools and infrastructure

SOURCE: Adapted from the Standish Group, *CHAOS* (West Yarmouth, MA: 1995) and http://www.infoq.com/articles/Interview-Johnson-Standish-CHAOS.

lead to clearly defined requirements and project objectives, while the technology, tools, and methods play an important, but lesser, role.

However, a study of 800 senior IT managers from the U.K., United States, France, Germany, India, Japan, and Singapore conducted by Tata Consultancy Services (2007) reports dire results similar to the *CHAOS* studies:

- sixty-two percent of the IT projects failed to meet their schedules
- forty-nine percent experienced budget overruns
- forty-seven percent experienced higher than expected maintenance costs
- forty-one percent failed to deliver the expected business value and return on investment (ROI)

A recent study of 114 IT professionals by Marchewka (2007) looked at perceived project performance and customer satisfaction over the past three years. A segment of this study's results are summarized in Table 1.2. A majority of respondents reported that their organization's ability to meet project schedules, budgets, and requirements has gotten better or much better in the past three years. Similarly, only a minority of the IT professionals surveyed believe that internal or external customer satisfaction has become worse over the past three years.

All studies have strengths and weaknesses. More research over time and broader samples will allow us to better understand the state of IT project management. While we will never be able to achieve a 100 percent success rate for all projects, we should strive to understand why certain projects are successful and others are not. While some people may argue that the success rate for IT projects is getting better, there is still ample room for improvement.

Why IT Projects Fail

One reason for high failure rates in the *CHAOS* studies may be the way we define "success" and "failure." For example, Robert Glass (2005) asks, How should a project be classified if it is "functionally brilliant" but is over budget and over schedule by 10 percent? According to the *CHAOS* definition, this would be considered a failure, while in reality, it could be a success for the organization. However, no matter what value a project brings to an organization, a project that continues to exceed its budget

Table 1.2   Project Performance and Internal/External Customer Satisfaction

		Much Worse	Worse	Same	Better	Much Better
IT project performance over the past 3 years	Ability to meet project schedules	0.0%	12.3%	40.4%	41.2%	6.1%
	Ability to meet project budgets	1.8%	10.5%	44.7%	37.7%	5.3%
	Ability to complete project scope or system requirements	2.6%	7.0%	41.2%	41.2%	7.9%
Customer satisfaction over the past 3 years (customers can be internal, e.g., HR department; or external, e.g., a particular client)	Overall satisfaction of the customer	1.8%	13.2%	34.2%	39.5%	11.4%
	Perceived value of the delivered product to the customer	0.0%	9.6%	39.5%	38.6%	12.3%
	Potential for future work with the customer	0.9%	3.5%	42.1%	38.6%	14.9%

SOURCE: J.T. Marchewka (2007); $n = 114$.

and schedule will eventually exceed any potential or real value it can bring to the organization.

The *CHAOS* studies also provide some interesting insight as to why some projects fail. For example, Table 1.3 summarizes the project factors for not-so-successful projects to see what might be happening. Lack of user input or involvement ranks at or near the top in factors listed under challenged or failed (impaired) projects. One can almost picture that chain of events. Without close support of key users, the team will have a difficult time understanding and defining the requirements of the project. As a result, suspicion and conflicts may arise, and there can easily be an "us versus them" situation between the developers and the users. Without effective communication and a clear direction, changes to the project's requirements always seem to appear, and both the users and developers may set unrealistic expectations. Management then begins to find fewer reasons to support an unpopular project, and more and more resources may be diverted from it. The project is barely successful, if not a failure.

More recently, however, according to a Web-based poll conducted by Computing Technology Industry Association (CompTIA), nearly 28 percent of the more than

Table 1.3   Summary of Factor Rankings for Challenged and Failed (Impaired) Projects

Rank	Factors for Challenged Projects	Factors for Failed (Impaired) Projects
1	Lack of user input	Incomplete requirements
2	Incomplete requirements	Lack of user involvement
3	Changing requirements & specifications	Lack of resources
4	Lack of executive support	Unrealistic expectations
5	Technology incompetence	Lack of executive support
6	Lack of resources	Changing requirements & specifications
7	Unrealistic expectations	Lack of planning
8	Unclear objectives	Didn't need it any longer
9	Unrealistic time frames	Lack of IT management
10	New technology	Technology illiteracy

SOURCE: Adapted from the Standish Group, *CHAOS* (West Yarmouth, MA: 1995).

1,000 respondents said that poor communication is the number one reason for project failure, followed by insufficient resources (18 percent), and unrealistic schedule deadlines (13.2 percent) (Rosencrance, 2004). Communication is an important component throughout the project in terms of setting project expectations, requirements, as well as schedule and budget constraints. As seen in Table 1.3, a number of factors relating to challenged and failed projects can be attributed directly or indirectly to poor communication.

Insufficient resources can be tied closely to poor communication. All projects require resources in terms of people, technology, and facilities. Communication is important in understanding the appropriate number of people that will be needed, what skill sets they will need, the training that may be necessary, and the tools to do the job.

Moreover, executive sponsors may accept schedule commitments from developers who offer no evidence that they can meet those commitments, while developers may accept schedules that are unrealistic. Not getting the right resources when they are needed may risk that the schedule will not be met. Unrealistic schedules may doom the project before it even starts. According to the CompTIA poll, other factors that contribute to project failure include poor project requirements, lack of stake-holder buy-in/support, undefined project success/closure criteria, unrealistic budget, insufficient or no risk planning, and lack of control/change process.

One can look at troubled projects to identify whether there are any signs of impending failure. These warning signs may include strained relationships among the project team members or between the project team and the client or users, excessive overtime, lost confidence, threats of legal action by the customer or client, and low project stakeholder moral.

What becomes interesting is how many people have accepted IT project problems and failure as the status quo. Figure 1.2 provides a summary of Tata Consultancy

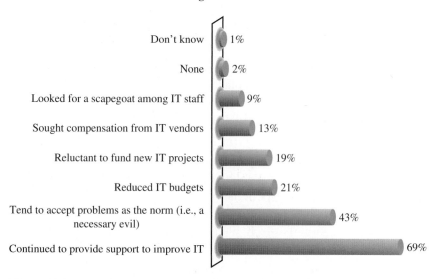

When IT projects have gone wrong, what has been the reaction from the business managers and the Board of Directors?

Don't know — 1%
None — 2%
Looked for a scapegoat among IT staff — 9%
Sought compensation from IT vendors — 13%
Reluctant to fund new IT projects — 19%
Reduced IT budgets — 21%
Tend to accept problems as the norm (i.e., a necessary evil) — 43%
Continued to provide support to improve IT — 69%

Figure 1.2 Reaction to Failed IT Projects by Business Managers and Board of Directors

SOURCE: http://www.tcs.com/pdf/Board%20research%20statistical%20factsheet.pdf.

Services survey in terms of how business managers and board of directors view IT project failure and problems.

Improving the Likelihood of Success

How can we improve the chances for IT project success and avoid repeating past mistakes? Here are four approaches that will be focal points throughout this book.

A Value-Driven Approach   Plain and simple: IT projects must provide value to the organization. Many people and organizations define project success in terms of the project being completed on time and within budget. While schedule and budget are important, they are not sufficient definitions of project success. For example, if an organization sets a mandate that a particular customer relationship management (CRM) package must be up and running within eight months and cost no more than $1 million to implement, would the project be considered unsuccessful if it required an extra day and an extra dollar to complete? You may think this is trivial, but at exactly what point in terms of schedule or budget does the project become unsuccessful?

We can also turn things around and ask whether finishing a project early and under budget necessarily makes the project successful. Of course, any organization would like to spend less money and have its system delivered early, but what if the system does not perform as expected? More specifically, what value will the organization receive by spending six months and $1 million on this particular project? If IT projects are investments, what measurable value will it receive to offset the time, money, and opportunity cost of purchasing and implementing the CRM system? This value could come in terms of better customer service, more efficient business processes, lower costs, or expanded market share. Therefore, success should not be measured in terms of schedule or budget, but in terms of value. This will put less pressure on project stakeholders to set unrealistic schedules and budget, since the value of the project will be the true measure of success.

A Socio-Technical Approach   In the past, organizations have attempted to improve the chances of IT project success by focusing on the tools, techniques, and methodologies of IT development. A purely technical approach, however, focuses attention on the technology. We can easily end up developing an application that no one asked for or needs. Applications to support electronic commerce, supply chain management, and integration require that at least equal attention be paid to the organizational side. The days of being good order takers are over. We can no longer be content with defining a set of user requirements, disappearing for several months, and then knocking on the user's door when it is time to deliver the new system. IT professionals must understand the business and be actively creative in applying the technology in ways that bring value to the organization. Similarly, the clients must become stakeholders in the project. This means actively seeking and encouraging their participation, involvement, and vision. The successful application of technology and the achievement of the project's goal must be an equal responsibility of the developers and users.

A Project-Management Approach   One suggestion of the *CHAOS* study was the need for better project management. But, isn't building an information system a project? Haven't organizations used project management in the past? And aren't they

QUICK THINKING —HOTTEST IT SKILLS

A recent article in *Computerworld* highlights a distinct and growing shortage of IT skills. This shortage is being augmented by dramatic declining enrollments in university computer science and information systems programs and the start of the baby boomers heading for retirement. According to CW's Vital Signs survey, the skill sets that will be in most demand are:

1. *Programming/application development*—The demand for people knowledgeable in AJAX, .Net, and PHP is going to be red hot as organizations continue to expand deeper into Web-enabling their existing applications.

2. *Project management*—There is an increased demand for people who can oversee complex projects that deliver clear business benefits.

3. *Help desk/technical support*—The demand for help desk and technical support will grow as organizations expand their applications portfolios. Much more of this expertise will remain in house, with only a small part of the work being contracted offshore.

4. *Security*—While there will always be a demand for people with security knowledge in intrusion detection, database and wireless security projects will drive that demand even higher.

5. *Data centers*—Many organizations and government agencies have begun to upgrade or relocate their data centers to take advantage of recent data automation and efficiency gains such as virtualization. Moreover, the demand for data centers is also increasing due to expanding data management and storage requirements as a result of regulations such as Sarbanes-Oxley and Health Insurance Portability and Accountability Act (HIPPA). Subsequently, individuals experienced in mainframe and database technologies will be needed as organizations place greater reliance on large, open systems to run mission-critical applications.

6. *Business knowledge*—Information technology must align closely with the business side of the organization so there will be a strong demand for IT professionals who have a solid understanding of the business.

7. *Networking and telecommunications*—All types of networking skills are in demand, including general network administration, network convergence, wireless, and network security as organizations move from voice and data networks to wireless and voice-over-IP technologies.

1. Do any of the hottest skills listed above surprise you? Why or why not?

2. Why do you think project management is one of the hottest skills?

3. If you were a project manager, how might the shortage of skilled IT professionals affect your project?

using project management now? While many organizations have applied the principles and tools of project management to IT projects, many more—even today—build systems on an ad hoc basis. Success or failure of an IT project depends largely on who is, or is not, part of the project team. Applying project management principles and tools across the entire organization, however, should be part of a **methodology**—the step-by-step activities, processes, tools, quality standards, controls, and deliverables that are defined for the entire project. As a result, project success does not depend primarily on the team, but more on the set of processes and infrastructure in place. A common set of tools and controls also provides a common language across projects and the ability to compare projects throughout the organization.

In addition, other reasons for project management to support IT projects include:

■ *Resources*—When developing or purchasing an information system, all IT projects are capital projects that require cash and other organizational resources. Projects must be estimated accurately, and cost and schedules must be controlled effectively. Without the proper tools, techniques, methods, and controls in place, the project will drain or divert resources away from other projects and areas of the organization. Eventually, these uncontrolled costs could impact the financial stability of the organization.

- *Expectations*—Today, organizational clients expect IT professionals to deliver quality products and services in a professional manner. Timely status updates and communication, as well as sound project management practices, are required.

- *Competition*—Internal and external competition has never been greater. An internal IT department's services can easily be outsourced if the quality or cost of providing IT services can be bettered outside the organization. Today, competition among consultants is increasing as they compete for business and talent.

- *Efficiency and effectiveness*—Peter Drucker, the well-known management guru, defined **efficiency** as doing the thing right and **effectiveness** as doing the right thing. Many companies report that project management allows for shorter development time, lower costs, and higher quality. Just using project management tools, however, does not guarantee success. Project management must become accepted and supported by all levels within the organization, and continued commitment in terms of training, compensation, career paths, and organizational infrastructure must be in place. This support will allow the organization to do the right things and do them right.

A Knowledge-Management Approach   A socio-technical approach and a commitment to project management principles and practices are important for success. However, excellence in IT project management for an individual or an organization takes time and experience. **Knowledge management** is a systematic process for acquiring, creating, synthesizing, sharing, and using information, insights, and experiences to transform ideas into business value. Although many organizations today have knowledge management initiatives under way, and spending on knowledge management systems is expected to increase, many others believe that knowledge management is just a fad or a buzzword.

What about learning from experience? Experience can be a great teacher. These experiences and the knowledge gained from these experiences, however, are often fragmented throughout the organization. Chances are that if you encounter what appears to be a unique problem or situation, someone else in your organization has already dealt with that problem, or one very similar. Wouldn't it be great to just ask that person what they did? What the outcome was? And, would they do it again the same way? Unfortunately, that person could be on the other side of the world or down the hall—and you may not even know!

Knowledge and experience, in the form of lessons learned, can be documented and made available through the technologies accessible today, technologies such as the World Wide Web or local versions of the Web called intranets. **Lessons learned** that document both reasons for success and failure can be valuable assets if maintained and used properly. A person who gains experience is said to be more mature. Similarly, an organization that learns from its experiences can be more mature in its processes by taking those lessons learned and creating **best practices**—simply, doing things in the most efficient and effective manner. In terms of managing IT projects, managing knowledge in the form of lessons learned can help an organization develop best practices that allow all of the project teams within the organization to do the right things and then to do them right. As summarized in the *CHAOS* report:

> There is one aspect to be considered in any degree of project failure. All success is rooted in either luck or failure. If you begin with luck, you learn nothing but arrogance. However, if you begin with

QUICK THINKING—TOP IT PROJECTS

Rank	2005	2006	2007
1	Application integration	Voice-over-IP	Business process improvement
2	Business analytics	Outsourcing	Customer relationship management
3	Enterprise portals	Data networking	Business analytics/business intelligence
4	Customer relationship management	Customer relationship management	Desktop/laptop upgrades
5	Intrusion detection & prevention	Collaboration	Web services
6	Financial reporting	Supply chain management	Disaster planning/recovery
7	Application consolidation	Desktop upgrades	Intrusion detection & prevention
8	Data management	Application performance management	Server upgrades
9	Voice-over IP	Business analytics	Enterprise system planning
10	Desktop upgrades	Compliance tracking	Financial reporting

The following was compiled from Baseline's Top IT Project surveys from 2005, 2006, and 2007. Organizations can spend a few thousand to a few million dollars on a project, while some projects can take a few weeks to a few years to complete.

1. Choose one of the projects from the table for consideration. How might this particular IT project meet a business or organizational need?

2. What factors might lead to an unsuccessful project?

failure and learn to evaluate it, you also learn to succeed. Failure begets knowledge. Out of knowledge you gain wisdom, and it is with wisdom that you can become truly successful (Standish Group 2002, 4).

 # THE CONTEXT OF PROJECT MANAGEMENT

What Is a Project?

Although the need for effectively managing projects has been introduced, we still require a working definition of a project and project management. The Project Management Institute (PMI), an organization that was founded in 1969, has grown to become the leading nonprofit professional association in the area of project management. In addition, PMI establishes many project management standards and provides seminars, educational programs, and professional certification. It also maintains the *Guide to the Project Management Body of Knowledge (PMBOK® Guide)*. The *PMBOK® Guide* (Project Management Institute, 2004) provides widely used definitions for **project** and **project management.**

A *project* is a temporary endeavor undertaken to accomplish a unique product, service, or result. (5)
Project management is the application of knowledge, skills, tools and techniques to project activities to meet project requirements.... Managing a project includes:

■ Identifying requirements

- Establishing clear and achievable objectives
- Balancing the competing demands for quality, scope, time, and cost
- Adapting the specifications, plans, and approaches to the different concerns and expectations of the various stakeholders (8)

Attributes of a Project   Projects can also be viewed in terms of their attributes: time frame, purpose, ownership, resources, roles, risks and assumptions, interdependent tasks, organizational change, and operating in an environment larger than the project itself.

Time Frame   Because a project is a temporary endeavor, it must have a definite beginning and end. Many projects begin on a specific date and the date of completion is estimated. Some projects, on the other hand, have an immovable date when the project must be completed. In this case, it is necessary to work backwards to determine the date when the project must start. Keep in mind that your career should not consist of a single project, but a number of projects.

Purpose   Projects are undertaken to accomplish something. An IT project can produce any number of results—a system, a software package, or a recommendation based on a study. Therefore, a project's goal must be to produce something tangible and of value to the organization. A project must have a goal to drive the project in terms of defining the work to be done, its schedule, and its budget, and to provide the project team with a clear direction.

Because it sets expectations that will directly influence the client's level of satisfaction, the project's goal must be clearly defined and agreed on. A better definition for project management suggests that project activities *must meet or exceed stakeholder needs and expectations.* Expectations and needs, however, cannot be met if the project's goal is not achieved. It is, therefore, important to keep in mind that a project should only be undertaken to provide some kind of value to the organization. Moreover, a specific and measurable project goal can be evaluated after the project is completed.

Ownership   The project must provide something of value to an individual or group who will own the project's product after it is completed. Determining who owns this product is not always easy. For example, different groups may fight over who does or does not own the system, the data, the support, and the final cost of implementing and maintaining the system. Although a project may have many **stakeholders** (i.e., people or groups who have a vested interest in the project's outcome), a project should have a clearly defined sponsor. The **sponsor** may be an executive, the end user, customer, or the client who has the ability and desire to provide direction, funding, and other resources to the project.

Resources   IT projects require time, money, people, and technology. Resources provide the means for achieving a project's goal and also act as a constraint. For example, the project's **scope,** or work to be accomplished, is determined directly by the project's goal—that is, if we know what we have to accomplish, we can then figure out how to accomplish it. If the project sponsor asks that an additional feature be added to the system, however, this request will undoubtedly require additional resources in terms of more work on the part of the project team. The use of a project resource has an associated cost that must be included in the overall cost of the project.

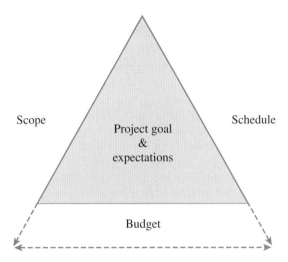

Figure 1.3 The Scope, Schedule, and Budget Relationship—the Triple Constraint

In the past, computer technology was relatively more expensive than the labor needed to develop a system. Today, the labor to build a system is relatively more expensive than the technology. As IT salaries increase, the cost of IT projects will become even more expensive. Therefore, if team members must do additional work, their time and the costs associated with time spent doing unscheduled work must be added to the project's schedule and budget. In other words, if the scope increases, then the schedule and budget of a project must increase accordingly. If the project's schedule and resources are fixed, then the only way to decrease the cost or schedule of the project may be to reduce the project's scope. Scope, schedule, and budget must remain in a sort of equilibrium to support a particular project goal. This relationship, sometimes referred to as the **triple constraint,** is illustrated in Figure 1.3. It should be a consideration whenever making a decision that affects the project's goal, scope, schedule, or budget.

Roles Today, IT projects require different individuals with different skill sets. Although these skills may be different on different projects, a typical project may include the following:

- *Project manager or leader*—The project manager or team leader is responsible for ensuring that all of the project management and technical development processes are in place and are being carried out within a set of specific requirements, defined processes, and quality standards.

- *Project sponsor*—The project sponsor may be the client, customer, or organizational manager who will act as a champion for the project and provide organizational resources and direction when needed.

- *Subject matter expert(s) (SME)*—The subject matter expert may be a user or client who has specific knowledge, expertise, or insight in a specific functional area needed to support the project. For example, if the organization wishes to develop a system to support tax decisions, having a tax expert on the project team who can share his/her knowledge will be more productive than having the technical people try to learn everything about tax accounting while developing the system.

- *Technical expert(s) (TE)*—Technical expertise is needed to provide a technical solution to an organizational problem. Technical experts can include systems analysts, network specialists, programmers, graphic artists, trainers, and so forth. Regardless of their job title, these individuals are responsible for defining, creating, and implementing the technical and organizational infrastructure to support the product of the IT project.

Risks and Assumptions All projects have an element of risk, and some projects entail more risk than others. Risk can arise from many sources, both internal and external to the project team. For example, **internal risks** may arise from the estimation process or from the fact that a key member of the project team could leave in the middle of the project. **External risks,** on the other hand, could arise from dependencies on other contractors or vendors. **Assumptions** are a form of risk that we introduce into the project in terms of forecasts or predictions. They are what we use to estimate scope, schedule, and budget and to assess the risks of the project. There are many unknown variables associated with projects, and it is important to identify and make explicit all of the risks and assumptions that can impact the IT project.

Interdependent Tasks   Project work requires many interdependent tasks. For example, a network cannot be installed until the hardware is delivered, or certain requirements cannot be incorporated into the design until a key user is interviewed. Sometimes the delay of one task can affect other subsequent, dependent tasks. The project's schedule may slip, and the project may not meet its planned deadline. In addition, projects are also characterized by **progressive elaboration.** This means that many of the project tasks will be conducted in steps or increments. For example, the features and functionality of an information system will be defined at a higher or abstract level early on in the project, but will eventually be defined at a much greater level of detail later on. Progressive elaboration will result as part of the systems development process or as the project manager and team gain a deeper understanding of the project or as new information becomes available.

Organizational Change   Projects are planned organizational change. Change must be understood and managed because implementation of the IT project will change the way people work. The potential for resistance, therefore, exists, and a system that is a technical success could end up being an organizational failure.

Operating in an Environment Larger Than the Project Itself   Organizations choose projects for a number of reasons, and the projects chosen can impact the organization (Laudon and Laudon 1996). It is important that the project manager and team understand the company's culture, environment, politics, and the like. These organizational variables will influence the selection of projects, the IT infrastructure, and the role of IT within the organization. For example, a small, family-owned manufacturing company may have a completely different corporate culture, strategy, and structure than a start-up electronic commerce company. As a result, the projects selected, the technical infrastructure, and the role of IT for each organization will be different. The project team must understand both the technical and organizational variables so that the project can be aligned properly with the structure and strategy of the organization. Moreover, understanding the organizational variables can help the project team understand the political climate within the organization and identify potential risks and issues that could impede the project.

THE PROJECT LIFE CYCLE AND IT DEVELOPMENT

The **project life cycle (PLC)** is a collection of logical stages or phases that maps the life of a project from its beginning to its end in order to define, build, and deliver the product of a project—that is, the information system. Each phase should provide one or more deliverables. A **deliverable** is a tangible and verifiable product of work (i.e., project plan, design specifications, delivered system, etc.). Deliverables at the end of each phase also provide tangible benefits throughout the project and serve to define the work and resources needed for each phase.

Projects should be broken up into phases to make the project more manageable and to reduce risk. **Phase exits, stage gates**, or **kill points** are the phase-end review of

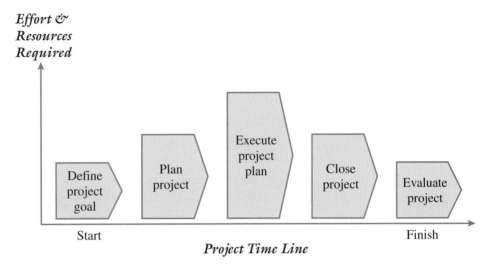

Figure 1.4 Generic Project Life-Cycle

key deliverables that allow the organization to evaluate the project's performance and to take immediate action to correct any errors or problems. Although the deliverables at the end of a stage or phase usually are approved before proceeding to the next stage, **fast tracking** or starting the next phase before approval is obtained can sometimes reduce the project's schedule. Overlapping of phases can be risky and should only be done when the risk is deemed acceptable.

Just like living things, projects have life cycles where they are born, grow, peak, decline, and then terminate (Gido and Clements 1999; Meredith and Mantel 2000). Although project life cycles may differ depending on the industry or project, all project life cycles will have a beginning, a middle, and an end (Rosenau 2007; Gido and Clements 1999). Figure 1.4 provides a generic life cycle that describes the common phases or stages shared by most projects.

Define Project Goal

Defining the project's overall goal should be the first step. This goal should focus on providing business value to the organization. A well defined goal gives the project team a clear focus and drives the other phases of the project. The project goal should also answer the question: How will we know if this project is successful given the time, money, and resources invested? In addition, most projects seem to share the following characteristics:

- The effort, in terms of cost and staffing levels, is low at the start of the project, but then increases as the project work is being done, and then decreases at the end as the project is completed.

- Risk and uncertainty are the highest at the start of a project. Once the goal of the project is defined and the project progresses, the probability of success should increase.

- The ability for stakeholders to influence the scope and cost of the project is highest at the beginning of the project. The cost of changing the scope and correcting errors becomes more expensive as the project progresses.

Plan Project

Once the project's goal has been defined, developing the project plan is a much easier task. A project plan essentially answers the following questions:

- What are we going to do?
- Why are we going to do it?
- How are we going to do it?
- Who is going to be involved?
- How long will it take?
- How much will it cost?
- What can go wrong and what can we do about it?
- How did we estimate the schedule and budget?
- Why did we make certain decisions?
- How will we know if we are successful?

In addition, the deliverables, tasks, resources, and time to complete each task must be defined for each phase of the project. This initial plan, called a **baseline plan,** defines the agreed upon scope, schedule, and budget and is used as a tool to gauge the project's performance throughout the life cycle.

Execute Project Plan

After the project's goal and plan have been defined, it's time to put the plan into action. As work on the project progresses, scope, schedule, budget, and people must be actively managed to ensure that the project achieves its goal. Progress must be documented and compared to the baseline plan. In addition, project performance must be communicated to all of the stakeholders. At the end of this phase, the team implements or delivers a completed product to the organization.

Close Project

As mentioned previously, a project should have a definite beginning and end. The closing phase ensures that all of the work is completed as planned and as agreed to by the team and the sponsor. Therefore, there should be some kind of formal acknowledgment by the sponsor that they will accept (and pay for!) the product delivered. This closure is often capped with a final project report and presentation to the client that documents that all promised deliverables have been completed as specified.

Evaluate Project

Sometimes the value of an IT project is not readily known when the system is implemented. For example, the goal of a project to develop an electronic commerce site should be to make money—not to build or install hardware, software, and Web pages on a particular server platform. The technology and its subsequent implementation are only a means to an end. Therefore, the goal of the electronic commerce site may be to produce $250,000 in revenue within six months. As a result, evaluating whether the project met its goal can be made only after the system has been implemented.

However, the project can be evaluated in other ways as well. The project team should document its experiences in terms of lessons learned—those things that it would do the same and those things it would do differently on the next project, based on its current project experiences. This post mortem should be documented, stored electronically, and shared throughout the organization. Subsequently, many of these experiences can be translated into best practices and integrated into future projects.

In addition, both the project team and the project itself should be evaluated at the end of the project. The project manager may evaluate each team member's performance in order to provide feedback and as part of the organization's established merit and pay raise processes and procedures. Often, however, an outside third party, such as a senior manager or partner, may audit the project to determine whether the project was well managed, provided the promised deliverables, followed established processes, and met specific quality standards. The team and project manager may also be evaluated in terms of whether they acted in a professional and ethical manner.

The Systems Development Life Cycle (SDLC)

Although projects follow a project life cycle, information systems development follows a product life cycle. The most common product life cycle in IT is the **systems development life cycle (SDLC),** which represents the sequential phases or stages an information system follows throughout its useful life. The SDLC establishes a logical order or sequence in which the system development activities occur and indicates whether to proceed from one system development activity to the next (McConnell 1996). Although there are variations of the SDLC, the life cycle depicted in Figure 1.5 includes the generally accepted activities and phases associated with systems development. Keep in mind that these concepts are generally covered in great detail in system analysis and design books and courses. For some, this may be a quick review, while for others it will provide a general background for understanding how IT project management and information system development activities support one another.

Planning, analysis, design, implementation, and maintenance and support are the five basic phases in the systems development life cycle.

Planning   The planning stage involves identifying and responding to a problem or opportunity and incorporates the project management and system development processes and activities. Here a formal planning process ensures that the goal, scope, budget, schedule, technology, and system development processes, methods, and tools are in place.

Analysis   The analysis phase attempts to delve into the problem or opportunity more fully. For example, the project team may document the current system to develop an "as is" model to understand the system currently in place. In general, systems analysts will meet with various stakeholders (users, managers, customers, etc.) to learn more about the problem or opportunity. This work is done to identify and document any problems or bottlenecks associated with the current system. Generally,

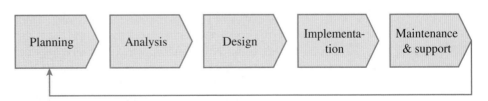

Figure 1.5   Systems Development Life Cycle

the "as is" analysis is followed by a requirements analysis. Here the specific needs and requirements for the new system are identified and documented. Requirements can be developed through a number of means—interviewing, joint applications development (JAD), conducting surveys, observing work processes, and reading company reports. Using process-oriented, data-oriented, and/or object-oriented modeling techniques, the current system, user requirements, and logical design of the future system called the "to be" system are represented and documented (Dennis and Haley 2000).

Design   During the design phase, the project team uses the requirements and "to be" logical models as input for designing the architecture to support the new information system. This architecture includes designing the network, hardware configuration, databases, user interface, and application programs.

Implementation   Implementation includes the development or construction of the system, testing, and installation. In addition, training, support, and documentation must be in place.

Maintenance and Support   Although maintenance and support may not be a true phase of the current project, it is still an important consideration. Once the system has been implemented, it is said to be in production. Changes to the system, in the form of maintenance and enhancements, are often requested to fix any discovered errors (i.e., bugs) within the system, to add any features that were not incorporated into the original design, or to adjust to a changing business environment. Support, in terms of a call center or help desk, may also be in place to help users on an as-needed basis.

Eventually, the system becomes part of the organizational infrastructure and becomes known as a legacy system. At this point, the system becomes very similar to a car. Let's say you buy a brand new car. Over time, the car becomes less and less new, and parts have to be replaced as they wear out. Although a system does not wear out like a car, changes to the system are required as the organization changes. For example, a payroll system may have to be changed to reflect changes in the tax laws, or an electronic commerce site may have to be altered to reflect a new line of products that the company wishes to introduce. As the owner of an older or classic car, you may find yourself replacing part after part until you make the decision to trade in the old junker for something newer and more reliable. Similarly, an organization may find itself spending more and more on maintaining a legacy system. Eventually, the organization will decide that it is time to replace this older system with a newer one that will be more reliable, require less maintenance, and better meets its needs. Subsequently, a new life cycle begins.

Implementing the SDLC

There are a number of ways to implement the SDLC. The chosen method or approach depends on the size and complexity of the project, as well as the experience and skills of the project team. A particular method will not only define the software processes and tools needed, but will also be a critical factor for developing the project plan in terms of defining project phases, deliverables, tasks, and resources that will be used to estimate the project's schedule and budget. Today, an IT project will follow a structured development approach or an iterative development approach.

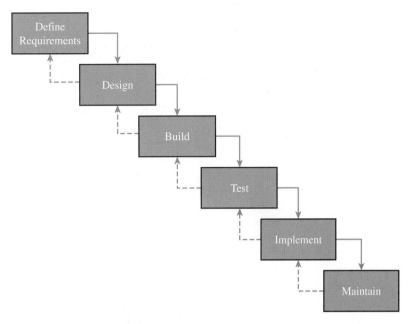

Figure 1.6 Waterfall Model

Structured Approach to Systems Development A structured approach to systems development has been around since the 1960s and 1970s, when large mainframe applications were developed. The **waterfall model** illustrated in Figure 1.6 was developed as a simple and disciplined method that follows the SDLC closely in a very sequential and structured way. The idea of a waterfall is a metaphor for a cascading of activities from one phase to the next where one phase is completed before the next phase is started.

The waterfall model stresses a sequential and logical flow of software development activities. For example, design activities or tasks begin only after the requirements are defined completely. Subsequently, the building or coding activities will not start until the design phase is complete. Although there is some iteration where the developers can go back to a previous stage, it is not always easy or desirable.

One characteristic of the waterfall model is that a great deal of time and effort is spent in the early phases getting the requirements and design right because it is more expensive to fix a bug or add a missing requirement in the later phases of the project.

An advantage of the waterfall model is that it allows us to plan each phase in detail so that the project schedule and budget can be computed by summing the time and cost estimates for all the tasks defined in each phase. In theory, the project will be completed on time and within budget if each phase is completed according to our estimates.

This approach is still used today, especially for large government systems and by companies that develop *shrink-wrap* or commercial software packages (NASA 2004). A structured approach is suitable when developing large, more complex systems where one assumes, or at least hopes, that the requirements defined in the early phases do not change very much over the remainder of the project. In addition, because it will provide a solid structure that can minimize wasted effort, the waterfall model may work well when the project team is inexperienced or less technically competent (McConnell 1996).

Iterative Systems Development   Critics of the structured approach to systems development argue that it takes too long to develop systems and that it does not embrace the idea that changing requirements are inevitable. Inexperienced developers often have the false belief that if they ask the users what they want, they will be rewarded with a set of clear, accurate, and complete requirements. In truth, most users do not know or are unable to articulate their needs early on in the project. And if they do, those requirements will most likely change later on. Over the years, a number of iterative approaches to systems development have been proposed. The central theme focuses on shortening the SDLC and embracing the idea that requirements are difficult to define and will change. Iterative methods tend to emphasize working software to measure progress and are rely heavily on face-to-face communication. Subsequently, a different approach to project planning will be needed. While a bottom-up planning approach tends to work best for software development using a structured approach, a box of time (e.g., two weeks) is generally allocated for each version or iterative cycle. The following summarize some common iterative approaches for systems development:

- *Rapid applications development (RAD)*—RAD was proposed by James Martin in the early 1990s as a less formal way to expedite the SDLC. RAD attempts to compress the analysis, design, build, and test activities of the SDLC into a series of short iterations or development cycles. For example, a small team of users and developers would work closely together to develop a set of system requirements during a workshop. Using tools such as computer-aided software engineering (e.g., CASE) or visual development environments (e.g., .NET), the developers would then work with the users to develop a functional or usable version of the system that might include only 25 percent of the total requirements. The development cycle would continue with a second usable version that would include the next 25 percent of the requirements. Subsequent iterations would continue until all of the requirements are included in the system.

- *Prototyping*—Similar to RAD, prototyping is an iterative approach to systems development where the user and developer work closely together to develop a partially or fully functional system as soon as possible. Often, however, a prototype may be developed to discover or refine system requirement specifications that can be used as a model for developing a real system. For example, a team may develop a nonfunctional user interface on a personal computer as a model to define the look, feel, and features of a large, multi-user system.

- *Spiral development*—Another way to expedite the SDLC is the spiral approach first proposed by Barry Boehm (1988). The spiral model breaks up a software project into a number of miniprojects that address one or more major risks until all the risks have been addressed (McConnell 1996). A risk, for example, could be a poorly understood requirement or a potential technical problem or system performance issue. The basic idea is to begin development of a system on a small scale where risks can be identified. Once identified, the development team then develops a plan for addressing these risks and evaluates various alternatives. Next, deliverables for the iteration are identified, developed, and verified before planning and committing to the next iteration. As a result, the completion of each iteration brings the project closer to a fully functional system.

■ *Agile systems development*—Agile methods are becoming an increasingly popular approach to systems development and include various methodologies such as SCRUM, dynamic systems development method (DSDM), and adaptive software development (ASD). However, one of the most commonly known agile methodologies is *eXtreme programming (XP)*, which was introduced by Kent Beck in the mid-1990s. Under XP, the system is transferred to the users in a series of versions called releases. A release may be developed using several iterations that are developed and tested within a few weeks or months. Each release is a working system that includes only one or several functions that are part of the full system specifications. XP includes a number of activities where the user requirements are first documented as a user story. The user stories are then documented using an object-oriented model called a class diagram. A set of acceptance tests is then developed for each user story. Releases that pass the acceptance tests are then considered complete. Small teams of developers often work in a common room where workstations are positioned in the middle and a workspace for each team member is provided around the perimeter. In addition, XP often incorporates team programming, where two programmers work together on the same workstation. Developers often are prohibited from working more than 40 hours a week in order to avoid burnout and the mistakes that often occur because of fatigue (Satzinger, Jackson, & Burd 1998).

The PLC and the SDLC

The project life cycle (PLC) focuses on the phases, processes, tools, knowledge and skills for managing a project, while the system development life cycle (SDLC) focuses on creating and implementing the project's product—the information system. It bears worth mentioning again that how a project team chooses to implement the SDLC will directly affect how the project is planned in terms of phases, tasks, estimates, and resources assigned.

As illustrated in Figure 1.7, the SDLC is really part of the PLC because many of the development activities occur during the execution phase of the PLC. The last two

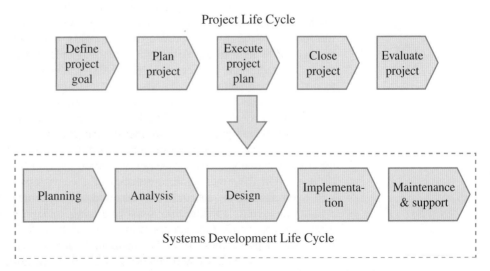

Figure 1.7   PLC and SDLC

phases of the PLC, close project and evaluate project, occur after the implementation of the information system.

The integration of project management and systems development activities is one important component that distinguishes IT projects from other types of projects. A methodology presented in Chapter 2 will illustrate how the project life cycle and systems development life cycle can be combined to plan and manage the processes and product of an IT project. This methodology will provide a foundation for the concepts, processes, tools, and techniques throughout the text.

EXTREME PROJECT MANAGEMENT

Prototyping, spiral development, and extreme programming provide three approaches for implementing and shortening the SDLC. Similarly, eXtreme project management (XPM) is becoming increasingly popular as a new approach and philosophy for managing projects.

Doug DeCarlo (2004) defines XPM as:

> The art and science of facilitating and managing the flow of thoughts, emotions, and interactions in a way that produces valued outcomes under turbulent and complex conditions: those that feature high speed, high change, high uncertainty, and high stress (p. 34).

This definition certainly characterizes many of today's IT projects that exemplify speed, uncertainty, changing requirements, and high risks. According to DeCarlo, a traditional approach to project management often employs an orderly approach that attempts to fit "reality" to the project tools and processes, while XPM embraces the reality that projects are often chaotic and unpredictable. Since most projects are not stable or predictable, an XPM approach does not try to change that reality; rather, it attempts to deal with it through increased flexibility and adaptability.

XPM also differs from a more traditional approach to project management in that XPM takes a more holistic view of planning and managing projects. For example, a key principle of XPM is that requirement changes are inevitable so planning becomes a self-correcting and iterative process. Another important principle of XPM focuses on innovation—not only creative ideas for new products or services, but innovative processes, methods, and tools for managing the project. Therefore, people are vital to the success of the project because their thoughts, emotions, and interactions become a catalyst for new ideas. Although organizing, planning, and control are the focal points of traditional project managers, XPM leadership focuses on enabling people to discover best solutions and self-correct themselves as needed.

At this point, it is important for you to understand that, just like developing information systems, there are a number of approaches to managing projects. Each approach or paradigm has its advantages and disadvantages, proponents and critics. In this book, we will not take a pure, traditional approach to project management, even though many of the processes, methods, and tools could be considered "traditional." On the other hand, a number of the processes, methods, and tools you will learn about later on could be classified as "eXtreme" project management. We will try to avoid labeling things as belonging under one paradigm or the other. That gets too confusing, and learning and applying only one paradigm can lead to missed opportunities since we might fall into the trap of viewing reality in a certain way. Instead, we will take the view that we have an IT project management toolbox before us. Right now, the toolbox may not have a lot in it, but as we learn about a new tool or idea, we can begin to fill this toolbox so that we can choose the right tool for the right job. While we need to be open and receptive to new ideas and approaches, we still should have an understanding of past approaches and ways so that we can begin to build on a solid foundation. This text provides a beginning. You'll continue to fill this toolbox throughout your professional career.

THE PROJECT MANAGEMENT BODY OF KNOWLEDGE (PMBOK®)

As was mentioned earlier, the *Guide to the Project Management Body of Knowledge* is a document available from the Project Management Institute (PMI)—an international, nonprofit, professional organization with more than 55,000 members worldwide. The original document was published in 1987, and the updated version provides a basis for identifying and describing the generally accepted principles and practices of project management. However, as the *PMBOK® Guide* is quick to point out, "generally accepted" does not mean these principles and practices work the same way on each and every project. It does mean that many people over time believe that these principles and practices are useful and have value. Determining what is appropriate is the responsibility of the team and comes from experience. (Perhaps experiences that can be documented and shared?)

This text will use the *PMBOK® Guide* as a foundation but will also integrate a number of concepts and ideas that are part of the body of knowledge that makes up the field of information systems. Ideally, you will then understand not only what many IT project managers and organizations throughout the world think are important, but also the language and the processes.

PMI provides a certification in project management through the Project Management Professional (PMP) certification exam. This text can also help you prepare for the PMP certification exam. To pass, you must demonstrate a level of understanding and knowledge about project management, satisfy education and experience requirements, and agree to and adhere to a professional code of ethics.

Project Management Knowledge Areas

The *PMBOK® Guide* defines nine knowledge areas for understanding project management. These nine knowledge areas are illustrated in Figure 1.8 and will be covered in more detail in later chapters.

- *Project integration management*—Integration focuses on coordinating the project plan's development, execution, and control of changes.

- *Project scope management*—A project's scope is the work to be completed by the project team. Scope management provides assurance that the project's work is defined accurately and completely and that it is completed as planned. In addition, scope management includes ways to ensure that proper scope change procedures are in place.

- *Project time management*—Time management is important for developing, monitoring, and managing the project's schedule. It includes identifying the project's phases and activities and then estimating, sequencing, and assigning resources for each activity to ensure that the project's scope and objectives are met.

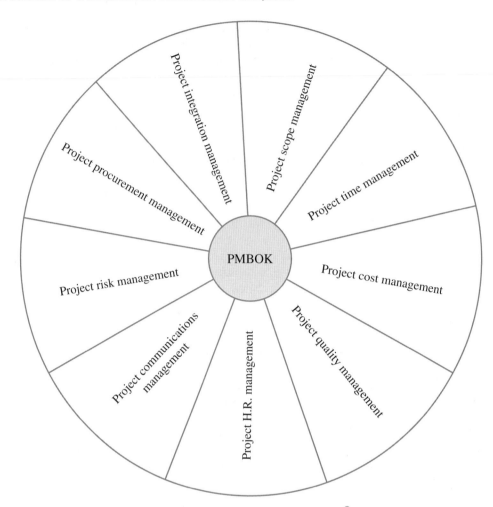

Figure 1.8 Project management body of knowledge (PMBOK®)

- *Project cost management*—Cost management assures that the project's budget is developed and completed as approved.

- *Project quality management*—Quality management focuses on planning, developing, and managing a quality environment that allows the project to meet or exceed stakeholder needs or expectations.

- *Project human resource management*—People are the most important resource on a project. Human resource management focuses on creating and developing the project team as well as understanding and responding appropriately to the behavioral side of project management.

- *Project communications management*—Communication management entails communicating timely and accurate information about the project to the project's stakeholders.

- *Project risk management*—All projects face a certain amount of risk. Project risk management is concerned with identifying and responding appropriately to risks that can impact the project.

- *Project procurement management*—Projects often require resources (people, hardware, software, etc.) that are outside the organization. Procurement management makes certain that these resources are acquired properly.

CHAPTER SUMMARY

This chapter provides an introduction to the text and to the area of information technology project management (ITPM). The field of information systems (IS) has evolved in parallel with the field of modern day project management. Since the 1960s the use of the business computer has gone through a number of eras: the electronic data processing (EDP) era, the micro era, and the network era. Some propose, however, that we have entered into a new era called globalization. Each era brings new challenges and issues for organizations and society, as well as for managing IT projects. As evidenced by a number of studies since the mid-1990s, successfully managing IT projects continues to be a challenge for many organizations. Although many factors contribute to a project's success or failure, the project and product processes associated with developing an IS must be managed actively. This includes (1) a value-driven approach, (2) a socio-technical approach, (3) a project management approach, and (4) a knowledge management approach.

The *Guide to the Project Management Body of Knowledge (PMBOK® Guide)* defines a project as a temporary endeavor undertaken to accomplish a unique purpose and project management as the application of knowledge, skills, tools, and techniques to project activities in order to meet or exceed stakeholder needs and expectations. Projects can also be viewed in terms of their attributes. These attributes include the project's time frame, purpose, ownership, resources, roles, risks and assumptions, tasks, and the impact the project will have on the organization. Projects also operate in an environment larger than the project itself. The company's culture, environment, politics, strategy, structure, policies, and processes can influence the selection of projects, the IT infrastructure, and the role of IT within the organization. Similarly, the selection of projects, the IT infrastructure, and the role of IT within the organization can influence the organizational variables.

The project life cycle (PLC) is a collection of logical stages or phases that maps the life of a project from its beginning to its end. It also helps in defining, building, and delivering the product of a project. Projects are broken up into phases to make the project more manageable and to reduce risk. In addition, each phase should focus on providing a deliverable—a tangible and verifiable product of work. A generic project life cycle was introduced. Its phases included (1) defining the project goal, (2) planning the project, (3) executing or carrying out the project, (4) closing the project, and (5) evaluating the project. Although projects follow a project life cycle, information systems development follows a product life cycle.

The Systems Development Life Cycle (SDLC) represents the sequential phases or stages an information system follows throughout its useful life. The SDLC described in this chapter includes the following phases: (1) planning, (2) analysis, (3) design, (4) implementation, (5) maintenance and support. In addition, the SDLC can be implemented using a structured approach (the Waterfall model) or by means of more iterative approaches. By following a rapid applications development (RAD) approach, systems developers can combine different approaches, tools, and techniques in order to shorten the time needed to develop an information system. The SDLC is really a component of the PLC, and choice of a particular approach for systems development will influence the activities, their sequence, and the estimated time to complete. In turn, this will directly impact the project's schedule and budget.

eXtreme project management (XPM) is a new approach to project management that is becoming increasingly popular. XPM focuses on the human element of projects and embraces the reality that projects often operate in an uncertain and high-speed environment. XPM also takes a more holistic view of planning and managing projects in which changing requirements are inevitable; planning thus becomes an iterative and self-correcting process that supports innovation.

The *PMBOK® Guide* outlines nine knowledge areas for understanding project management. These nine areas include: (1) project integration management, (2) project scope management, (3) project time management, (4) project cost management, (5) project quality management, (6) project human resources management,

(7) project communications management, (8) project risk management, and (9) project procurement management. Along with a number of concepts and principles that make up the body of knowledge for information systems, these nine PMBOK areas will be integrated in the chapters throughout this text.

REVIEW QUESTIONS

1. Describe the EDP era in your own words.
2. Describe the micro era in your own words.
3. Describe the network era in your own words.
4. Describe the globalization era in your own words.
5. How can a value-driven approach improve the likelihood of IT project success?
6. What is the socio-technical approach to systems development?
7. What are the benefits of using a project management approach to developing information systems?
8. What is a methodology? What are the advantages of following a methodology when developing an information system?
9. How does sharing experiences in the form of lessons learned lead to best practices in managing and developing information systems?
10. What is a project?
11. What is project management?
12. What are the attributes of a project?
13. Describe the relationship among scope, schedule, and budget.
14. Describe the different roles and skill sets needed for a project.
15. Describe three risks that could be associated with an IT project.
16. Why should assumptions associated with a project be documented?
17. Discuss the statement: Projects operate in an environment larger than the project itself.
18. Describe the project life cycle.
19. What are phase exits, stage gates, and kill points? What purpose do they serve?
20. What is fast tracking? When should fast tracking be used? When is fast tracking not appropriate?
21. Describe the systems development life cycle (SDLC).
22. Describe the waterfall model for systems development. When should the waterfall model be used?
23. Describe the prototyping approach to systems development. When is prototyping appropriate?
24. Describe the spiral approach for iterative development. What advantages does this model have in comparison with the waterfall model?
25. Describe extreme programming (XP). How does XP accelerate the SDLC?
26. Describe extreme project management. How does XPM differ from a more traditional approach to project management?
27. What is knowledge management? Although many people believe knowledge cannot be managed, why do you think many companies are undertaking knowledge management initiatives?
28. Although the *Guide to the Project Management Body of Knowledge* describes the generally accepted principles and practices of project management, why wouldn't these principles and practices work for every project?

EXTEND YOUR KNOWLEDGE

1. Using the Web or library, find an article that describes either a successful or an unsuccessful IT project. Discuss whether any of the project factors listed in Table 1.1 had any bearing on the project.
2. Design a template that could be used by a project team to document its experiences and lessons learned. Describe or show how these experiences could be catalogued and shared with other members and other teams.
3. Using the Web or library as a resource, write a one-page position paper on knowledge management. You should provide a definition of knowledge management and your opinion as to whether an organization should invest in a knowledge management initiative.

GLOBAL TECHNOLOGY SOLUTIONS

Tim Williams placed the phone gently back in its cradle. He sat for a moment, not sure whether he felt excitement or sheer terror. Or, could it be he was feeling both? Kellie Matthews, his partner in Global Technology Solutions (GTS), had just told Tim that Husky Air, a business air charter company, was very interested in having them develop an information system. This was the moment Tim had been waiting for—their first client! Before Husky Air will sign a contract, however, they need to know what GTS will deliver, how much it will cost, and when the project will be completed.

As the project's manager, Tim knows that getting this contract is important. Husky Air would be the company's first and, so far, only client. Tim also understands that a successful project could lead to other work with Husky Air. Moreover, a verbal or written recommendation would provide additional credibility to help GTS get its foot in the door with other potential clients.

While working together in the information services department at a large company, Tim and Kellie decided that a small, independent consulting firm could be successful developing smaller IT-based systems. The lure of being their own bosses and the potential for financial and personal rewards were too great to resist. Tim and Kellie cashed in their stock options, and GTS was born. They decided that Kellie would develop new business and manage the day-to-day operations of GTS, while Tim would deliver and manage the projects. New employees with specific skill sets would be hired as needed to support particular projects.

Although both Tim and Kellie had worked in IT for several years, neither of them had ever managed a consulting project before. Aside from the questions posed by Husky Air (What will you deliver? How much will it cost? How long will it take?), Tim felt a bit overwhelmed because he knew the success or failure of this project would have an immediate impact on the viability of the new firm.

Things to Think About

1. If you were in Tim's shoes, what feelings do you think you would experience?
2. What questions would you have?
3. What might help reduce your anxiety and uncertainty as an inexperienced project manager?
4. What steps would you take to begin a new project?

 ## HUSKY AIR—PILOT ANGELS

Background

Husky Air opened for business in January 2008 when L. T. Scully and several other investors pooled their life savings and secured a rather large loan from a Chicago bank.

Located at DeKalb Taylor Municipal Airport (DKB) in DeKalb, Illinois, Husky Air is a fixed base operator (FBO) facility that offers a full range of services to the growing demands for business and private aviation. Currently, the company has 23 employees composed of pilots, mechanics, and office staff.

As a FBO, Husky Air provides:

- Business jet, propjet, helicopter, and propeller aircraft charter
- Refueling
- Airframe, engine, propeller, and avionics maintenance
- Aircraft rental
- Flight instruction
- Pilot supplies

Although FBOs at other airports offer similar services, Husky Air has been receiving increased attention throughout the Midwest for its charter service, maintenance, and flight instruction.

Pilot Angels

In addition, Husky Air coordinates a charitable service called Pilot Angels. Working with hospitals, health care agencies, and organ banks, Husky Air matches volunteer private pilots, willing to donate their time and aircraft, with needy people whose health care problems require them to travel to receive diagnostic or treatment services. In addition, Pilot Angels also will provide transportation for donor organs, supplies, and medical personnel. All flights are free of charge and the costs are paid for by the volunteer pilots who use their own aircraft.

The pilots who volunteer for the Pilot Angel program need no medical training and offer no medical assistance. The planes do not carry any medical equipment and do not have to accommodate any stretchers. Patients, however, must be medically stable and able to enter and exit the aircraft with no or little assistance. The Pilot Angel passengers typically travel to or from a hospital or clinic for diagnosis, surgery, or some other treatment. Travel companions, such as a relative, friend, or nurse, are common.

Currently, a pool of pilot volunteers is kept in a file folder. If a hospital or person with a medical or financial hardship contacts Husky Air, the name of the traveler, the destination, dates/times, and the number of travel companions are requested. Because of limited weight restrictions in small aircraft, the weights of the passengers and their luggage are needed as well.

After the initial information is provided, Husky Air contacts the volunteer pilots to determine their availability. Although a volunteer pilot may be willing and available for a Pilot Angel flight, the plane may not have the range or weight-carrying requirements. This may be an inefficient use of time since many pilots may have to be contacted until a pilot and suitable plane can be found.

The Project Description

Husky Air would like to have a computer-based system to keep track of all its Pilot Angel volunteers. Basic information about the pilots may include their name, address, phone number, and so forth, as well as their total hours,

certifications, and ratings. Moreover, specific information about a volunteer's aircraft would be useful. Such information should include the type of plane, aircraft identification number (called the N number), whether single or multi-engine, and its capacity for carrying passengers and cargo. Some pilots own more than one plane.

Husky Air also wants to know more about the people, hospitals, clinics, and organ banks who request the Pilot Angel service. In addition, they also would like basic information about the patients, their passengers, and specific needs to help match volunteers with the request for transport. Finally, Husky Air wants a list of all the Pilot Angel flights in order to recognize specific volunteers for their contributions. This would include:

- The pilot who flew the flight
- The passengers on board
- The plane that was used
- The total time of the flight
- The distance and destination of the flight
- The date and time of the flight
- The total fuel used

 ## HUSKY AIR ASSIGNMENT

The Team Charter

Congratulations! You have been hired as a consultant to work with a new client called Husky Air. The objective of your first assignment is to organize teams for completing the various Husky Air assignments. Your instructor will either assign you to a team or allow you to select your team.

Please provide a professional-looking document that includes the following:

- *Team name*—You should come up with a name for your team. This will give you an identity.
- *Team members*—Please list the names of your team members and their phone numbers and email addresses. This will provide a directory for your team later on.
- *Agreed-on meeting times*—You and your team should compare schedules so that you can agree on a time or set of times that allow you to meet as a group to work on these assignments. If you discover any conflicts, you should reevaluate whether you should be a team. You may want to think about using a software collaboration tool or other available technology to help reduce the dependency on same place/same time meetings.

- *A list of team rules and expectations*—In the past, you probably have all worked with at least one other person. As a team, share some of those experiences and discuss whether they were positive or negative. Based on your discussion, define a set of team rules and expectations. For example, how should the team resolve conflicts? What happens if someone misses a meeting? Two meetings? Three? How will the team deal with someone who does not contribute equally? Each member of your team should agree to these rules. Do not take this lightly. You may also want to discuss and document how the team may change its charter if needed later on.
- *A code of ethics*—A project team has a responsibility to themselves and their client or sponsor. You may want to start by developing a list of values that you and your team members feel are important. Based on that list, create a statement or itemized list that summarizes those values to guide your team's ethical behavior.
- *Signatures*—Each member of your team should sign the team charter. This will indicate that each member has read, understands, and agrees to the rules and expectations of the team.

CASE STUDIES

Project Ocean—The Troubled Water Billing System

The city of Philadelphia entered into an agreement with Oracle Corporation to replace its antiquated, custom-built, 30-year-old water billing system that fails to collect all the revenue it should. After three years and spending $18 million on "Project Ocean," the project was two years behind schedule and at almost twice the cost originally envisioned. Moreover, the new billing system still had not been deployed to support its 500,000 customers.

Philadelphia Chief Information Officer (CIO) Dianah Neff cited technical complexity, administrator turnover, and Oracle's inexperience building such a system as the reasons for Project Ocean's problems. Alan Butkovitz, the City Controller, said that his office is currently reviewing what happened with Oracle, but that it is too soon to speculate as to what went wrong with Project Ocean. An official at Oracle has said that they would deliver on their promise to complete the project and that implementation is "still in progress, and Oracle believes that the work performed to date conforms with the current agreement."

Project Ocean is currently on hold until the Mayor's Office of Information Services (MOIS) and other city officials can reach an agreement with Oracle to put Project Ocean back on track. Neff stated that she believes a workable solution can be delivered within 18 months to protect the city's investment.

Former City Water Commissioner Kumar Kishinchand was a vocal critic of Project Ocean since before leaving the commission after 12 years. Kishinchand believes that Project Ocean was doomed from the start. "One reason is that they picked a company that had never done a water billing system. Oracle had only done viable customer service systems with a small portion for billing purposes. Municipal billing systems tend to be tremendously complex. The off-the-shelf components of such systems have to be heavily modified, a complex and time-consuming effort."

Kishinchand also believes that the project managers did not have much to lose if Project Ocean failed because the city's Finance Department was in charge of the project—not the Water Department, which is the main operator and user of the system. He believes that Neff and the MOIS were interested in building empires because the water billing system takes in over $300 million in revenues a year. Kinshinchand also accused city officials of "putting all of their eggs in one basket [Oracle], without consulting the Water Department."

In rebuttal, Neff contends that MOIS chose the Oracle Enterprise Resources Planning E-Business suite for a number of city uses that include human resources and that the Finance Department made the decision to make water billing the first application. MOIS was then brought in to implement the system once the decision was made. As Neff contends, "it [the water billing system] was a big system,

very complicated with very unique features. Hindsight is 20/20 and ERP is difficult anyway."

In addition, the system was designed to be run by a number of city departments, but there was constant turnover among executive sponsors. Neff contemplated "Continuity was a problem, and we could have had better-defined business processes. Problems came up between the contractor and business people. As we put it, it was a project that 'washed ashore' for IT to handle."

About 12 months ago, MOIS was assigned to review the work completed on Project Ocean so far. This led to a work stoppage and the suspension of several consultants, Oracle employees, and a private contractor who had been indicted by a federal grand jury in Connecticut on unrelated charges that she had paid a state senator to help her win consulting contracts.

While negotiations between the city of Philadelphia and Oracle continue, Neff is preparing to start a new job as a consultant in another city. After five years as CIO, Neff maintains that her impending departure is unrelated to Project Ocean.

1. Do you believe that the trouble with Philadelphia's water billing system is a technical problem or a people problem? Why?

2. What factors contributed to the problems associated with Project Ocean?

3. Compare the different views the city's MOIS and Oracle may have when negotiating a new agreement that will continue that project.

4. Can this project be saved? If so, what should the new agreement include? If not, can Philadelphia and Oracle come to an agreement that satisfies both parties? Or would this end up being a "win/lose" situation?

Source: Adapted From Matt Hamblen, Philly CIO: Troubled Water Billing System Can Still Work, *Computerworld*, August 10, 2006.

The FBI's Virtual Case File

After the tragic events of September 11, 2001, the Federal Bureau of Investigation (FBI) recognized the need to modernize its largely paper-based system for gathering intelligence. After years of developing information systems without an overarching organizational view, the agency found itself with an "improvised" IT infrastructure with more than 50 independent application systems written in different programming languages and running on disparate platforms. The result was a shortfall of knowledge management that became even more apparent after September 11th. The FBI concluded that it was losing intelligence as fast as it could gather it.

Robert Chiaradio, an agent in charge of the field office in Tampa, Florida, was requested by FBI Director Robert Mueller to help push a three-part modernization project called Trilogy that was started by former Director Louis Freeh. The project centered on upgrading the agency's desktops and servers, Web-enabling a number of the most important investigative database systems, and, most importantly, an automated case file system.

As the new CIO, Chiaradio was in charge of the entire IT operation for the Bureau, and one of four officials who reported to Mueller. Recognizing that there was no time to waste, Mueller instructed that the year schedule for the project had to be put into overdrive so that the Trilogy project could completed "as soon as technically possible." After a meeting at 6:00 AM on October 1, 2001, Chiaradio quickly developed the concept for the Virtual Case File system.

The Virtual Case File was envisioned to help FBI agents efficiently share data about cases in progress, especially terrorist investigations. The system would also enable agents anywhere in the United State quickly to search various documents and allow them to connect possible leads from different sources. In addition, the Virtual Case File would include a case management system, an evidence management system, and a records management system. The intention was to eliminate the need for FBI employees to scan hard-copy documents into computer files. A custom-developed system was needed since no existing commercial software packages were available that meet the agency's needs when the project began in 2001. Development of the Trilogy Project was contracted to Science Applications International Corp. (SAIC) in San Diego, California and was to be completed by late 2003.

After 18 months, Robert Chiaradio left the FBI to take a new position as managing director of homeland security at BearingPoint Inc. in McLean, Virginia. By the end of 2004, SAIC had delivered only about 10 percent of what the FBI had envisioned and didn't include many of the enhancements that were recommended by a second contractor.

In January 2005, the FBI was faced trying to salvage the $170 million project and appease a growing number of critics who believed that the four-year-old project was a waste of taxpayer money. Moreover, Robert Mueller confided to reporters that while the Virtual Case File project has not been scrapped, the FBI has asked another contractor to look for commercial or government off-the-shelf software packages that could be used instead.

The project's lack of progress drew public criticism from Senator Patrick Leahy (D-Vt.), who said "the FBI's long-anticipated Virtual Case File has been a train wreck in slow motion, at a cost of $170 million to American taxpayers and an unknown cost to public safety." To the contrary, Duane Andrews, SAIC's chief operating officer, said "The FBI modernization effort involved a massive technological and cultural change, agency wide. To add to

that complexity, in the time that SAIC has been working on the Trilogy project, the FBI has had four different CIOs and 14 different managers. Establishing and setting system requirements in this environment has been incredibly challenging."

One FBI official remarked that this experience has led to a number of lessons learned in contract management, and this particular contract has led the agency to change its IT contracting practices and develop an IT roadmap. The official also added, "It's definitely not fair to say we haven't gotten anyplace. We haven't gotten the overarching program we wanted, but we're going to take these lessons and move forward with it."

In March 2005, the FBI officially terminated the Virtual Case File and announced that it would develop a new case management system called Sentinel. This announcement was made by Robert Mueller during his testimony before a subcommittee of the U.S. House Appropriations Committee. Mueller said "I am disappointed that we did not come through with Virtual Case File." However, he added that he sees the decision to cancel the project as an opportunity to use off-the-shelf software to create a more up-to-date system that will allow FBI agents to share information about cases more easily.

An FBI official who wished to remain anonymous said that agency will begin to evaluate software packages next month in order to develop a more firm direction. In addition, the FBI will be conducting a test of SAIC's most recent version of the system. Although the system developed by SAIC does not meet the agency's requirements, "we needed to evaluate what they had given us as far as user capability and usability" was concerned.

Interestingly, Jared Adams, a spokesman for SAIC, contends that the FBI hasn't formally killed the Virtual Case File project. Ongoing tests are proof that a final decision has not yet been made. He added, "When the tests are done at the end of March, I think then a decision will be made."

Robert Mueller stated that the new case management system will be implemented in four phases and should take about 39 months to complete. He was unwilling, however, to estimate how much the new system will cost.

The House Appropriations Committee said that it would open a formal investigation as to why the project failed.

1. A Computerworld article by Paul Glen[1] lists a number of ways to detect disaster projects. Discuss how the following may apply to the FBI's failed Virtual Case File.

   a. No real plan—No baseline to work from, so no one really knows that a project is late.

[1] From Paul Glen, Opinion: Detecting Disaster Projects, *Computerworld*, February 06, 2006.

b. **Excessive optimism**—Many times there's a perpetual optimism that just because a project is behind there's no reason why things can't get caught up.

c. **Fear of admission**—When a project is in trouble, no one wants to go to senior management and admit it, because that may be uncomfortable. And maybe things will get better.

d. **Poor team morale**—Although this may not be a leading cause of project failure, it may be a leading indicator.

e. **Poorly understood team roles**—People may not be clear as to what their role should be or how they should be interacting with others.

f. **Absent sponsors**—If sponsors can't be bothered with investing time in the project up front, chances are they won't like what they get in the end.

g. **Not enough methodology**—If the project team doesn't have a common and well understood approach to completing the work, it is likely to have trouble doing so.

h. **Too much methodology**—A methodology is a tool for completing the work, but not a guarantee that everything will go smoothly. A team can become overburdened with a methodology where the means become more important than the ends, or become a process to further political goals.

i. **Meager management**—An inexperienced or unskilled manager can doom a project to failure.

j. **Lacking leadership**—Good leadership may be difficult to define, but we often know it when we see it. A project must have good leadership to succeed.

k. **Inadequate technical skills**—While not the most common cause for project failure, it can happen if we assign people to projects without the requisite skills, or training, or when we assign people because they are available at the time.

l. **Too many meetings**—Project team members who spend an inordinate amount of time in meetings may be trying to make up for inadequate planning. Since they may not have thought things out in advance, they are forced to coordinate on the fly.

SOURCE: Adapted from:

Dan Verton, FBI Has Made Major Progress, Former IT Chief Says, *Computerworld,* April 18, 2004.

Grant Gross, FBI Trying to Salvage $170 million Software Package: Its Virtual Case File Project is under Fire for Not Working as Planned, *Computerworld*, January 14, 2005.

Linda Rosencrance, FBI Scuttles $170 million System for Managing Investigations, *Computerworld*, March 14, 2005.

Frank Hayes, FBI on the Move, *Computerworld*, May 30, 2005.

BIBLIOGRAPHY

Boehm, B. W. 1988. A Spiral Model of Software Development and Enhancement. *Computer* (May): 61–72.

DeCarlo, D. 2004. *eXtreme Project Management: Using Leadership, Principles, and Tools to Deliver Value in the Face of Volatility*. San Francisco: Jossey-Bass.

Dennis, A. and W. B. Haley. 2000. *Systems Analysis and Design: An Applied Approach*. New York: John Wiley.

Friedman, T. L. 2007. *The World Is Flat: A Brief History of the Twenty-first Century*. New York: Picador.

Gido, J. and J. P. Clements. 1999. *Successful Project Management*. Cincinnati, OH: South-Western College Publishing.

Glass, R. L. 2005. IT Failure Rates—70% or 10–15%? *IEEE Software* (May/June): 109–112.

Hoffman, T. and J. King. 2000. Y2K Freeze Melts in January Thaw. *Computerworld*, January 17. http://www.computerworld.com/home/print.nsf/all/000117E04A.

Laudon, K. C. and J. P. Laudon. 1996. *Management Information Systems: Organization and Technology*. Upper Saddle River, NJ: Prentice Hall.

McConnell, S. 1996. *Rapid Development: Taming Wild Software Schedules*. Redmond, WA: Microsoft Press.

Meredith, J. R. and S. J. Mantel, Jr. 2000. *Project Management: A Managerial Approach*. New York: John Wiley.

Marchewka, J. T. 2007. An application of the deming management model for information technology projects. *Journal of International Technology and Information Management* 16(2) 57–71.

NASA. 2004. http://web.archive.org/web/20040403211247/http://asd-www.larc.nasa.gov/barkstrom/public/The_Standard_Waterfall_Model_For_Systems_Development.htm

Nolan, R. L. 2001. Information Technology Management from 1960–2000. *Harvard Business School*. June 7.9-301-147.

Project Management Institute (PMI). 2004. *A Guide to the Project Management Body of Knowledge (PMBOK® Guide)*. Newtown Square, PA: PMI Publishing.

Rosencrance, L. 2007. Survey: Poor Communciation Causes Most IT Project Failures. *Computerworld* (March 9). http://www.computerworld.com/action/article.do?command=viewArticleBasic&articleId=9012758.

Rosenau, M. D. J. 1998. *Successful Project Management*. New York: John Wiley.

Satzinger, J. W., R. B. Jackson, and S. D. Burd. 2002. *Systems Analysis and Design in a Changing World*. Boston: Course Technology.

Standish Group. 1995. *CHAOS*. West Yarmouth, MA: The Standish Group.

Tata. 2007. http://www.tcs.com/AboutUs/Research_survey.html

Zuboff, S. 1988. *In the Age of the Smart Machine: The Future of Work and Power*. New York: Basic Books.

2

Conceptualizing and Initializing the IT Project

CHAPTER OVERVIEW

Chapter 2 describes how IT projects are conceptualized and initialized. After studying this chapter, you should understand and be able to:

- Define what a methodology is and describe the role it serves in IT projects.
- Identify the phases and infrastructure that make up the IT project methodology introduced in this chapter.
- Develop and apply the concept of a project's measurable organizational value (MOV).
- Describe and be able to prepare a business case.
- Distinguish between financial models and scoring models.
- Describe the project selection process as well as the Balanced Scorecard approach.
- Describe IT governance and how it helps to ensure that investments in IT projects align with organizational strategies and provide the returns originally envisioned.
- Describe the role of the project management office (PMO) in organizations.

INTRODUCTION

This chapter will introduce a framework for an IT project methodology that will be integrated throughout this text. A methodology provides a game plan for planning and managing the IT project and recommends the phases, steps, tools, and techniques to be followed and used throughout the project life cycle. All projects, however, are unique. A project methodology must be flexible in order to be useful. Moreover, a methodology should evolve to include the best practices that are derived from an organization's lessons learned. Over time, the methodology will better fit the organization and may even provide a competitive advantage.

After the IT project methodology is introduced, the remainder of this chapter will focus on conceptualizing and initializing the project. Through high-level strategic planning, the overall project goal is defined. Defining this goal (and getting agreement) may be the most difficult part of the methodology and the project itself. The project's goal, if achieved, should provide direct and measurable value to the organization. A project, however, will have specific objectives that support this overall goal. These objectives, in terms of a project's scope, schedule, budget, and product quality, are important, but not necessarily sufficient, conditions for defining the project's success or lack of success. A project should have only one goal, but may have several objectives.

Once the project's goal is defined, the IT project methodology introduced in this chapter recommends that the project team develop a **business case.** A business case is a deliverable that documents the project's goal, as well as several alternatives or options. The feasibility, costs, benefits, and risks for each alternative are analyzed and compared, and a recommendation to approve and fund one of the alternatives is made to senior management. The first phase of the IT project methodology, as in all of its phases, ends with a review of the project by the client or sponsor.

Most organizations have limited resources, and a particular project may have to compete with other projects within the organization for those scarce resources. As a result, only a limited number of projects can be selected and funded to make up the IT project portfolio. Therefore, many organizations are adopting a form of IT governance to select and measure the performance of IT projects. This chapter will introduce a general framework for IT governance and some common techniques and tools for selecting IT projects. A project that has a clear and measurable goal that brings value to the organzation will have a greater likelihood of being selected. The development and subsequent process to approve the business case provides a form of IT governance to ensure that selected IT projects align with the organization's strategy. Approval of the business case then provides the authority to proceed to the next phase of the methodology. This next phase focuses on developing a project charter and plan that details the organization of the project as well as its detailed schedule and budget.

AN INFORMATION TECHNOLOGY PROJECT METHODOLOGY (ITPM)

A **methodology** provides a strategic-level plan for managing and controlling IT projects. Think of a methodology as a template for initiating, planning, and developing an information system. Although information systems may be different, it is the product, and not necessarily the process, of managing the project that makes them different. As you can see in Figure 2.1, the methodology recommends the phases, deliverables, processes, tools, and knowledge areas for supporting an IT project. The key word is *recommends* because different types of projects, such as electronic commerce (EC), customer relations management (CRM), or data warehousing applications, may require different tools and approaches.

Methodologies provide the project team with a game plan for implementing the project and product life cycles. The team can then focus on the tasks at hand, instead of always worrying about what they are supposed to do next. In addition, a methodology provides a common language that allows the project team, project sponsor, and others within the organization to communicate more effectively. By standardizing a methodology throughout the organization, management can compare different projects more objectively because each project's planned and actual progress is reported the same way. Ideally, this will allow management to make better informed and more objective decisions with respect to which

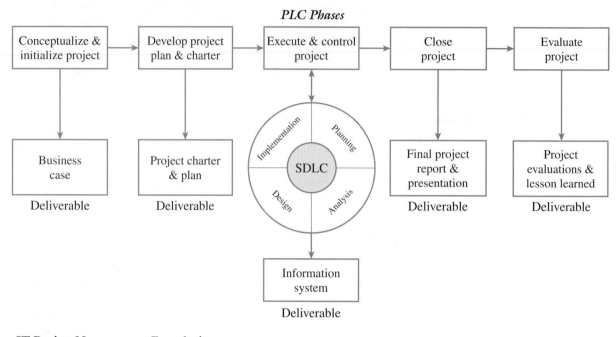

PLC Phases

IT Project Management Foundation

PM process groups:	Initiating, planning, executing, controlling, closing
PM objectives:	Scope, schedule, budget, quality
Tools:	Project management, information systems development
Infrastructure:	Organizational, project, technical
PMBOK areas:	Integration management, scope management, time management, cost management, quality management, HR management, communications management, risk management, procurement management

Figure 2.1 An Information Technology Project Methodology

projects get selected and whether funding should continue to support a particular project.

A good methodology should be flexible and adapt to the needs of the project organization over time. For example, whether a structured or an iterative development approach is used depends upon the project and application system. During the analysis and design phases of the systems development life cycle, a team may use one modeling approach or a combination (i.e., process modeling, data modeling, or object-oriented modeling).

The development and modeling approach used, however, depends on a number of factors. These factors may include the organization's experiences, the knowledge and skill sets of the project team, the IT and organizational infrastructure to support the development effort and the application, and the nature of the project itself—that is, the project's size, degree of structure, development time frame, and role within the organization. Many IS development methodologies have been proposed, but most focus on the *product* of the development effort. As discussed in Chapter 1, whether or not an organization follows a formal IS development methodology, the development effort should fit within, or be part of, an overall project management methodology.

Although many IT projects fail or experience significant challenges, a methodology can incorporate the experiences of and lessons learned by the project team members. Developing and implementing an IT product then becomes more predictable and the likelihood of success increases. Over time, an organization's methodology incorporates a set of best practices that fits the organization and the projects it undertakes. These best practices should lead to fewer wasted resources and projects that provide true value to the organization. The organization will find more opportunities for competitive advantage as efficiency and effectiveness increase.

Phase 1: Conceptualize and Initialize

The first stage of the IT project methodology focuses on defining the overall goal of the project. A project is undertaken for a specific purpose, and that purpose must be to add tangible value to the organization. Defining the project's goal is the most important step in the IT project methodology. As you will see, the project's goal aids in defining the project's scope and guides decisions throughout the project life cycle. It will also be used at the end of the project to evaluate the project's success.

Alternatives that would allow the organization to meet its goal must be identified. Then, the costs and benefits, as well as feasibility and risk, of each alternative must be analyzed. Based on these analyses, a specific alternative is recommended for funding. Finally, the project's goal and the analysis of alternatives that support the goal are summarized in a deliverable called the business case. Senior management will use the business case during the selection process to determine whether the proposed project should be funded. The details of developing the project goal and business case will be discussed in more detail later in this chapter.

Phase 2: Develop the Project Charter and Detailed Project Plan

The **project charter** is a key deliverable for the second phase of the IT project methodology. It defines how the project will be organized and how the project alternative that was recommended and approved for funding will be implemented. The project charter provides another opportunity to clarify the project's goal and defines the project's objectives in terms of scope, schedule, budget, and quality standards. In addition, the project charter identifies and gives authority to a project manager to begin carrying out the processes and tasks associated with the systems development life cycle (SDLC). The **project plan** provides all the tactical details concerning who will carry out the project work and when. The project charter and plan answer the following questions:

- Who is the project manager?
- Who is the project sponsor?
- Who is on the project team?
- What role does everyone associated with the project play?
- What is the scope of the project?
- How much will the project cost?
- How long will it take to complete the project?
- What resources and technology will be required?
- What approach, tools, and techniques will be used to develop the information system?

- What tasks or activities will be required to perform the project work?
- How long will these tasks or activities take?
- Who will be responsible for performing these tasks or activities?
- What will the organization receive for the time, money, and resources invested in this project?

In addition, the project's scope, schedule, budget, and quality objectives are defined in detail. Although some may wish to combine the business case with the project charter and plan, the IT project methodology presented in this text recommends that the business case and project charter/plan remain separate. There are a number of reasons to justify separation.

First, much time and effort must be devoted to understanding the "big picture." This process involves high-level strategic planning. Defining and agreeing to the project's goal and making a recommendation are not easy, nor is getting agreement on which projects should be funded. However, once the project's goal and recommended strategy are defined and agreed to, this will help define the details of the project, that is, who does what and when. The focus of the *conceptualize and initialize phase* is to determine whether a proposed project should and can be done. This is more strategic in terms of assessing how well the project aligns with the organization's business strategy.

The second reason is that the project charter and plan are the products of tactical planning. Here, the details will define how the project's goal will be achieved, by defining the approach and tasks to support the SDLC. Combining strategic planning with tactical planning can confuse the project's goal and objectives with how they should be achieved. It then becomes easy for people to fall into a trap where they worry too much about how they are going to get someplace when they have not even decided where they are going!

The third reason to separate the phases is time. It is better to pull the plug on a project with a high probability of failure or without the expected business value as early as possible. Why spend the time, money, and resources on developing a detailed plan for a project that should not be undertaken? Therefore, a project should be *doable* and *worth doing* before an organization spends resources determining *how* the project should be done. Reviews at the end of each phase provide the decision-making controls to ensure that resources are committed appropriately.

Phase 3: Execute and Control the Project

The third phase of the IT project methodology focuses on execution and control—carrying out the project plan to deliver the IT product and managing the project's processes to achieve the project's goal. It is during this phase that the project team uses a particular approach and set of systems analysis and design tools for implementing the systems development life cycle (SDLC).

In addition, the project manager must ensure that the environment and infrastructure to support the project includes:

- Acquisition of people with the appropriate skills, experience, and knowledge
- The technical infrastructure for development
- IS development methods and tools
- A proper work environment
- Scope, schedule, budget, and quality controls

- A detailed risk plan
- A procurement plan for vendors and suppliers
- A quality management plan
- A change management plan
- A communications plan
- A testing plan
- An implementation plan
- A human resources system for evaluation and rewards

Phase 4: Close Project

After the information system has been developed, tested, and installed, a formal acceptance should transfer control from the project team to the client or project sponsor. The project team should prepare a final project report and presentation to document and verify that all the project deliverables have been completed as defined in the project's scope. This gives the project sponsor confidence that the project has been completed and makes the formal approval and acceptance of the project go more smoothly.

At this time, the final cost of the project can be determined. Subsequently, the consultant may invoice the client for any remaining payments, or the accounting department may make any final internal charges to appropriate accounts. In addition, the project manager and team must follow a set of processes to formally close the project. These processes include such things as closing all project accounts, archiving all project documents and files, and releasing project resources.

Phase 5: Evaluate Project Success

The final phase of the methodology should focus on evaluating four areas. First, a "postmortem," or final project review, should be conducted by the project manager and team. This review should focus on the entire project and attempt to assess what went well and what the project team could have done better. Subsequently, the lessons learned from the project team's experience should be documented and made available to others throughout the organization. In addition, the project manager and team should identify best practices that can be institutionalized throughout the organization by incorporating them into the methodology. As a result, the methodology evolves and better suits the organization's processes, culture, and people.

The second type of evaluation should take place between the project manager and the individual project team members. Although this performance review may be structured in terms of the organization's performance and merit review policies and procedures, it is important that each member of the team receive honest and useful feedback concerning his or her performance on the project. Areas of strength and opportunities for improvement should be identified so that plans of action can be developed to help each person develop to his or her potential.

In addition, an outside third party should review the project, the project manager, and project team. The focus of this review should be to answer the following questions:

- What is the likelihood of the project achieving its goal?
- Did the project meet its scope, schedule, budget, and quality objectives?

- Did the project team deliver everything that was promised to the sponsor or client?

- Is the project sponsor or client satisfied with the project work?

- Did the project manager and team follow the processes outlined in the project and system development methodologies?

- What risks or challenges did the project team face? And how well did they handle those risks and challenges?

- How well did the project sponsor, project team, and manager work together? If there were any conflicts, how well were they addressed and managed?

- Did the project manager and team act in a professional and ethical manner?

Lastly, the project must be evaluated in order to determine whether the project provided value to the organization. The goal of the project should be defined in the first phase of the project. In general, the value an IT project brings to the organization may not be clearly discernable immediately after the project is implemented. Therefore, it may be weeks or even months before that value is known. However, time and resources should be allocated for determining whether the project met its intended goal or not.

IT Project Management Foundation

The box under the phases in Figure 2.1 defines the IT project management foundation. This includes the project management processes, objectives, tools, infrastructure, and knowledge areas that are needed to support the IT project.

Project Management Process Group   According to the Project Management Body of Knowledge (PMBOK®), a **process** is a series of activities that produce a result. **Project management processes** describe and help organize the work to be accomplished by the project, while **product-oriented processes** focus on the creation and delivery of the product of the project. These management and product-oriented processes tend to overlap and are integrated throughout the project's life cycle. Each phase of the methodology should include the following:

- *Initiating processes*—To start or initiate a project or phase once commitment is obtained

- *Planning processes*—To develop and maintain a workable plan to support the project's overall goal

- *Executing processes*—To coordinate people and other resources to execute the plan

- *Controlling processes*—To ensure proper control and reporting mechanisms are in place so that progress can be monitored, problems identified, and appropriate actions taken when necessary

- *Closing processes*—To provide closure in terms of a formal acceptance that the project or a project's phase has been completed satisfactorily

Project Objectives   In addition to an overall goal, a project will have several objectives. These objectives support the overall goal and may be defined in terms of the project's scope, schedule, budget, and quality standards. Separately, each of these objectives cannot define success; however, together they must support the project's goal. This relationship is illustrated in Figure 2.2.

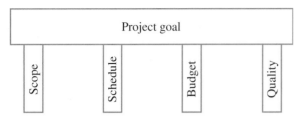

Figure 2.2   Project Objectives

Tools   Tools support both the processes and product of the project. These project management tools include tools and techniques for estimation, as well as tools to develop and manage scope, schedule, budget, and quality. Similarly, tools support the development of the information system. For example, computer aided software engineering (CASE) tools and models support the analysis and design phases of development.

Infrastructure   Three infrastructures are needed to support the IT project. These include:

1. *An organizational infrastructure*—The organizational infrastructure determines how projects are supported and managed within the organization. The organizational infrastructure influences how project resources are allocated, the reporting relationships of the project manager and the project team members, and the role of the project within the organization.

2. *A project infrastructure*—The project infrastructure supports the project team in terms of the project environment and the project team itself. It includes:

   ■ *The project environment*—The physical workspace for the team to meet and work.

   ■ *Roles and responsibilities of the team members*—This determines the reporting relationships, as well as the responsibilities and authorities of the individual team members.

   ■ *Processes and controls*—Processes and controls provide support for managing all aspects of the project. They ensure that the project's goal and objectives are being met.

3. *A technical infrastructure*—The technical infrastructure provides the hardware and software tools to support the project team. It may include such things as project management software, e-mail, voice mail, word processing, access to the Internet, and so on. The technical infrastructure allows the project team to do its work.

Project Management Knowledge Areas   The Project Management Body of Knowledge (PMBOK®) encompasses nine areas generally accepted as having merit for effectively managing projects. These nine areas support both the project processes and product by providing a foundation of knowledge for supporting projects within a particular organization.

As an organization gains more experience with projects over time, the lessons learned from every project contribute to each of these nine areas. Ideally, these lessons will lead to an IT project management knowledge base that can be used to identify best practices that adapt the IT project methodology to an organization's needs, culture, and IT project environment. This base of knowledge can then be institutionalized throughout the organization and its projects.

THE BUSINESS CASE

What Is a Business Case?

Although organizations have increasingly turned to information technology to improve effectiveness and levels of efficiency, many projects have been undertaken without a thorough understanding of their full costs and risks. As a result, numerous IT projects have failed to return benefits that compensate adequately for the time and resources invested.

A business case provides the first deliverable in the IT project life cycle. It provides an analysis of the organizational value, feasibility, costs, benefits, and risks of several proposed alternatives or options. However, a business case is *not* a budget or the project plan. The purpose of a business case is to provide senior management with all the information needed to make an informed decision as to whether a specific project should be funded (Schmidt 1999a).

For larger projects, a business case may be a large, formal document. Even for smaller projects, however, the process of thinking through why a particular project is being taken on and how it might bring value to an organization is still useful.

Because assumptions and new information are sometimes used to make subjective judgments, a business case must also document the methods and rationale used for quantifying the costs and benefits. Different people who work independently to develop a business case can use the same information, tools, and methods, but still come up with different recommendations. Therefore, it is imperative that decision makers who read the business case know and understand how it was developed and how various alternatives were evaluated.

One can also think of a business case as an investment proposal or a legal case. Like an attorney, the business case developer has a large degree of latitude to structure arguments, select or ignore evidence, and deliver the final presentation. The outcome depends largely on the ability to use compelling facts and logic in order to influence an individual or group with decision-making authority. Thus, a good IT business case should be (1) thorough in detailing all possible impacts, costs, and benefits; (2) clear and logical in comparing the cost/benefit impact of each alternative; (3) objective through including all pertinent information; and (4) systematic in terms of summarizing the findings (Schmidt 1999a).

Developing the Business Case

The purpose of a business case is to show how an IT solution can create business value. Although IT projects can be undertaken for any number of reasons, organizational value generally focuses on improving effectiveness and/or efficiency. For example, an IT project may be undertaken to:

- Reduce costs
- Create a new product or service
- Improve customer service
- Improve communication
- Improve decision making
- Create or strengthen relationships with suppliers, customers, or partners

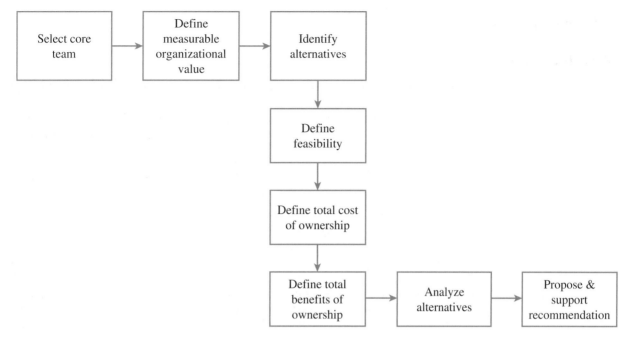

Figure 2.3 The Process for Developing a Business Case

- Improve processes
- Improve reporting capabilities
- Support new legal requirements

Although these are just some of the reasons for proposing an IT project, it is up to management to evaluate, select, and fund projects on the basis of the value they bring to the organization. Therefore, the business case must show explicitly how an investment in IT will lead to an increase in business value. Figure 2.3 depicts a process for developing a business case.

Step 1: Select the Core Team Rather than have one person take sole responsibility for developing the business case, a core team should be recruited. If possible, developing a business case should include many of the stakeholders affected by the project or involved in its delivery. The core team should, therefore, include managers, business specialists, and users who understand the requirements to be met, as well as IT specialists who understand the opportunities, limitations, and risks associated with IT. The core team for developing the business case most likely will be different from the project team that will carry out the project work if the project is accepted and funded. In general, there are several advantages for having a core team develop the business case (Schmidt 1999b):

- *Credibility*—A team made up of individuals from various organizational areas or departments can provide access to critical expertise and information that may not be readily accessible to others outside that particular area. Moreover, a team can provide different points of view and provide a check for important items that an individual may overlook.

- *Alignment with organizational goals*—Higher level managers can help connect the business case with the organization's long-term strategic plan and mission. This alignment may be beneficial in understanding and presenting how the expected business value of the IT project will support the overall goals and mission of the organization. Moreover, it may facilitate prioritizing, legitimizing, and assigning value of the IT project to the organization's strategic business objectives. In other words, the business case should outline how the successful completion of the proposed project will help the organization achieve its overall mission, goals, and objectives.

- *Access to the real costs*—Core members with certain expertise or access to important information can help build more realistic estimates in areas such as salaries, overhead, accounting and reporting practices, training requirements, union rules and regulations, and hiring practices.

In addition, the core team that develops the business case can play a crucial role when dealing with various areas or departments within the organizational boundary. The advantages include:

- *Ownership*—A cross-functional team can spread a sense of ownership for the business case. A project that includes other areas from the outset has a better chance of reducing the political problems associated with territorial domains.

- *Agreement*—If you develop a business case in isolation, it is very likely that you will have to defend your assumptions and subjective judgments in a competitive or political setting. However, if a core team develops the business case, the critics may be more apt to argue the results rather than the data and methods used.

- *Bridge building*—The core team may serve as an effective tool for handling critics of the business case. One tactic may be to include critics on the core team or to at least allow recognition and consideration for their positions. This may lead to fewer surprises and attacks later on.

Step 2. Define Measurable Organizational Value (MOV) The core team's objective should be to define the problem or opportunity and then identify several alternatives that will provide direct and measurable value to the organization. To provide real value to an organization, however, IT projects must align with and support the organization's goals, mission, and objectives. Therefore, any recommended alternative by the core team must have a clearly defined purpose and must map to the goals and strategy of the organization. The goal of the project then becomes the project's measure of success (Billows 1996; Smith 1999). In the IT project management methodology, the project's overall goal and measure of success is referred to as the project's **measurable organizational value (MOV)**. As the name implies, the MOV must:

- *Be measurable*—Measurement provides focus for the project team in terms of its actions. Instead of implementing an information system, the project team attempts to achieve a specific performance target. Moreover, an MOV provides a basis for making decisions that affect the project through its remaining phases. Why do additional work or make decisions that affect the project if they do not help you achieve the MOV?

- *Provide value to the organization*—Resources and time should not be devoted to a project unless they provide some kind of value to the organization. Keep

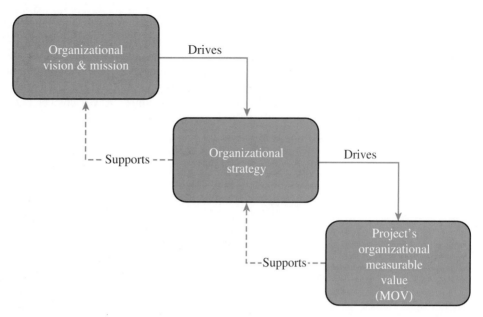

Figure 2.4   The IT Value Chain

in mind that information technology in itself cannot provide value. Technology is only an enabler—that is, IT enables organizations to do things.

- *Be agreed on*—A clear and agreed on MOV sets expectations for the project stakeholders. It is important that all project stakeholders understand and agree to the project's MOV. It is not easy to get everyone to agree to the project's goal so early; but it will be well worth the time and effort in the later stages of the project (Billows 1996).

- *Be verifiable*—At the end of the project, the MOV must be verified to determine if the project was a success.

The MOV guides all the decisions and processes for managing the IT project and serves as a basis for evaluating the project's achievements. In other words, a project cannot be properly planned or evaluated unless the goal of the project is clearly defined and understood. An organization should not undertake projects that are not clearly linked to its overall mission.

The IT value chain depicted in Figure 2.4 suggests that an organizational goal leads to or defines an organizational strategy. In turn, a project's measurable organizational value then supports this organizational strategy. This mapping shows how a project's goal aligns with an organization's strategy and goal. At the end of the project, the project's actual achievements can be compared to its initial MOV to determine whether the project was successful. If the project is a success (i.e., it either met or exceeded its MOV), then one can see explicitly how that project will support the organization.

For example, if we follow Michael Porter's competitive forces model (Porter 1980; Porter 1985), one organizational goal may be to prevent customers from leaving or switching to a competitor. Therefore, an organizational strategy to support this goal may be to develop tight linkages with customers. To support this organizational strategy and goal, the organization may consider developing a business-to-business (B2B) application that will allow customers to check inventory status, place orders, track shipments, receive an invoice, pay an invoice, and receive various reports online.

Will the installation of hardware and a network mean that the B2B application was a success? Moreover, will the development and implementation of the application software mean that the project was successful? What if the project is completed not only on time, but also within budget? A yes answer here is only partially correct. Although all of these achievements are important, they cannot be true measures of a project's success.

More specifically, installing hardware and a network are activities. Having them in place is a necessary, but not sufficient, condition for success. In other words, hardware and software can be in place, but unless they support the organizational goal and strategy, their mere installation does not bring much value to the organization. One can also view budget and schedule in the same light. You can have a project that is finished on time and within budget, but unless it brings value to the organization in terms of supporting a goal and strategy, it will not be of much use.

But what if a project goes over schedule and over budget? How will that impact the project's value to the organization? The answer is that it depends. A project that is late and over budget certainly can impact the project's value to the organization, but success or failure really depends on the amount of value a project will provide. For example, should a project that is one day late and a dollar over budget be considered unsuccessful? Probably not. What about a project that is one week late and $1,000 over budget? That depends on how these overruns compare to the original schedule and budget. If the original schedule and budget were two years and $1 million, then most people would agree that the schedule and cost variation is no big deal.

What's more important is the value the project brings to the organization. A consultant friend once told a story of a CEO who was ecstatic because an e-commerce project the company was taking on was only one year late and only $12 million over budget. In this case, schedule and cost did not matter all that much because once the e-commerce site was up and running the company would make the deficit up within six months. The moral of the story is that business value is the most important criterion for IT projects.

A project's MOV should be based on the organization's goal and strategy. An excellent example of an MOV is the following statement that John F. Kennedy made back in the 1960s: "Our goal is to land a man on the moon and return him safely by the end of the decade."

This simple yet powerful statement mobilized an entire nation and fueled the space race with the then Soviet Union. What is interesting about this statement is how clear and measurable the goal becomes:

- A human being is to land on the moon—not an unmanned spacecraft or a spacecraft with a chimpanzee.
- We will not just get a human to the moon or get that person back just halfway. This person must make the whole trip and come back safely.
- This will all be done before 1970.

What is equally interesting is that Kennedy never told anyone *how* to do this. That was NASA's job, not his. The goal was to beat the Soviets to the moon, and the project's MOV defined this explicitly.

But how do we go about developing a project's MOV? There are six basic steps. Let's follow that process using as an example a company that would like to develop and implement a business-to-consumer (B2C) electronic commerce application that it hopes will allow it to expand its current bricks and mortar operations.

Table 2.1 Potential Areas of Impact for IT Projects

Potential Area	Examples of Desired Impact
Strategic	■ Penetration of new markets ■ Transformation of the terms of competition within the market ■ Increased market share
Customer	■ Customers have more choices of products or services ■ Customers receive better products or services ■ Transaction processes are more efficient or effective
Financial	■ Increased profit ■ Increased margins
Operational	■ Lower costs due to streamlined operations ■ Increased operational effectiveness ■ Improvements to supply chain
Social	■ Education ■ Health ■ Safety ■ Environment

SOURCE: Adapted from *CIO* magazine's Enterprise Value Awards Application Form and Elaine M. Cummings, "Judgment Call," *CIO*, February 2, 2000, http://www.cio.com/awards/eva/index.html.

Identify the Desired Area of Impact   The first step involves identifying the desired impact the IT project will play in supporting the organization. One approach might be to adapt the criteria used by *CIO* magazine's Enterprise Value Awards.[1] The guidelines summarized in Table 2.1 are used by the judges to define IT value and provide a good starting point for developing the MOV and business case. You should feel free to adapt these areas of impact as needed. The important question to answer at this point is why we are thinking of doing this project.

In our B2C example, the project manager would meet with the project sponsor and first determine how the idea for the project came about. Although the reasons could be broad and numerous (i.e., all of our competitors are doing it, it is part of our long-term strategy, we think we can make a lot of money, B2C will make our company look hip), identifying them will provide a background for understanding how and why decisions are made by the sponsor's organization. In this example, we will say that the reasons for considering this project are both strategic and financial because the company wants to expand its current brick and mortar operations. The idea is not to neatly categorize the project, but to understand the nature of the project and how it will impact the organization.

Identify the Desired Value of the IT Project   Once the desired area of impact is identified, the next step involves determining the desired value the IT project will bring to the organization. This area can be tricky, but having a process helps. In simplest terms, we can identify the value of an IT project by providing answers to the following four questions:

- *Better*—What does the organization want to do better? (For example, improve quality or increase effectiveness?)
- *Faster*—What does the organization want to do faster? (Increase speed, increase efficiency, or reduce cycle times?)
- *Cheaper*—What does the organization want to do cheaper? (Reduce costs?)
- *Do more*—What does the organization want to do more than it is currently? (Growth or expansion?[2])

[1] Since 1993, *CIO* magazine has conducted a competition to identify and honor organizations that create enterprise value through the innovative use of IT. Entrants must submit an entry following contest guidelines. A team made up of *CIO* editors and consultants selects finalists. Entries are judged on the value of the achievement that an IT investment provides and how it serves the organization's mission.

[2] Value to an organization may also result by doing *less* of something. For example, a Company may develop a safety program to reduce the number of accidents. Reducing accidents can be viewed as negative growth or as an increase in safety as a result of doing something better (i.e., quality). It just depends on one's viewpoint.

The key words to identifying the value an IT project will provide an organization are *better, faster, cheaper*, and *do more*. The first three criteria—better, faster, and cheaper—focus on quality, effectiveness, and efficiency, while doing more of something focuses on growth. For example, if an organization has identified increasing profits as its desired area of impact, it makes sense that it would like to make more money than it currently does. Therefore, value to this organization would be in the form of growth. On the other hand, another organization may be faced with high inventory costs as a result of having too much inventory in its warehouse. The value that an IT project would bring to this organization would not be from growth; it does not want to do more of what it is currently doing. The value comes from doing something better (e.g., improved quality to reduce waste or rework), faster (e.g., fewer manufacturing bottlenecks or reduced cycle times), or even cheaper (e.g., lower overhead costs).

While the question in the first step focuses on why an organization wants to take on the project, this second step focuses on the question "how will this project help us achieve what we want to achieve as an organization?" At this point, the project manager and client should identify one or two value areas to emphasize. If all four of the value areas appear important, it is a good idea to rank them in order of importance. Keep in mind, however, that not having a clear idea of the desired impact or value of the project may well mean that the problem or opportunity is not clearly understood. The project team may end up treating the symptoms rather than the real problem.

Following our example of the B2C project, the value critical to the organization may be doing more through the project's ability to enable the organization to expand its current operations. Value from improved customer service and improved operations could also support the organization in doing things better, faster, and cheaper as well. This step provides an excellent vehicle for all project stakeholders to discuss and identify the expected value of the project.

Develop an Appropriate Metric   Once there is agreement as to the value the IT project will bring to the organization, the next step is to develop a metric or set of metrics that (1) provides the project team with a target or directive, (2) sets expectations among all stakeholders, and (3) provides a means for evaluating whether the project is a success later on. In general, tangible benefits to the organization are easier to define than intangible ones; however, this can be done with some creativity. For example, knowing whether profits increased should be fairly straightforward, but customer satisfaction may require surveys or interviews. Often evaluation requires benchmarking so that a before and after comparison can be made.

To develop a metric, the project manager and sponsor should agree on a specific number or range of numbers. When not obvious, the target metric should indicate whether an increase or decrease from the organization's current state is desired. The metrics may be expressed as dollars, percentages, or numbers. For example, an organization that wishes to increase profits may state this as a 20 percent increase or an increase of $1 million from the last month, quarter, or fiscal year. On the other hand, an organization that would like to grow its customer base may set a goal of one hundred new customers. Therefore, the metrics to support an MOV may be one or a combination of the following:

- Money (in dollars, euros, etc.)   (increase or decrease)
- Percentage (%)   (increase or decrease)
- Numeric value   (increase or decrease)

The company in our example would like to grow strategically, that is, expand its current base of operations. There are a number of relevant metrics that could be used. The question is how will this company determine whether this project is a success. Keep in mind that the organization will make a significant investment by the time the project is completed. Will the B2C application be successful when the Web site is finished and anyone with an Internet connection can view the site? It is important to have a working Web site, but that alone will not make up for the investment and subsequent maintenance and support for keeping the site up and running. What about using a hit counter so that the organization can tell how many times the B2C site was visited? Having traffic to the Web site is also important, but people who just visit will not keep the company in business, nor will visitors justify the investment and cost of keeping the B2C Web site up and running.

It should now be obvious that the company must make money from its B2C Web site. Only a profit can justify the time, effort, and resources needed to develop and support the application. The questions then become: How much profit? Are there any other metrics that should be considered? Assume that management has determined that a 20 percent return will be adequate for covering all expenses and for providing the desired return. Also assume that management is interested in developing new customers. Therefore, the company has set a target of 500 new customers. Why a 20 percent return and 500 new customers? Those numbers are not developed by the project manager or project team on their own. The 20 percent return and 500 new customers' metrics can only be determined by the project sponsor. The project manager and project team only guide the process.

Set a Time Frame for Achieving the MOV Once you have agreement on the target metrics that will provide the desired impact to the organization, the next step is to agree on a specific time frame. For example, a company may focus on increasing profits or reducing costs, but the question is: When will these results be achieved? Keep in mind that the scheduled completion of the project is not the same thing as the agreed upon time frame for achieving the MOV. Scope, schedule, budget, and quality are project objectives. The MOV is the project goal. Rarely will the installation of an information system provide the desired or expected value right away. A project with an immovable deadline may, however, have a specific date as part of the MOV. For example, there may be cause for putting a deadline date in the MOV in 01/01/10000, when all the dates in computers, or whatever they are using then, have to be changed once more.

The project manager and sponsor should also agree on how and when the project's MOV will be evaluated. Continuing with the example, let's say that management would like to see a 20 percent return and 500 new customers within one year after the system goes online. But what happens after the first year? Perhaps the company would like to maintain this growth annually over the useful life of the system. There is, however, no reason why different targets cannot be set for different time periods. For example, a 20 percent return and 500 new customers may be sufficient for the first year, but these targets may change as word spreads and more and more people know about the B2C Web site. Therefore, the company may establish a target of a 25 percent return and 1,000 new customers in the second year, while a 30 percent return with 1,500 new customers is set for the third year. The MOV should be flexible to accommodate the expectations and needs of the project sponsor.

Verify and Get Agreement from the Project Stakeholders The next step in developing the MOV is to ensure that it is accurate and realistic. In short, will the successful completion of this project provide the intended value to the organization? And is the MOV realistic? The development of the MOV requires a close working relationship between the project manager and the sponsor. The project manager's responsibility is to guide the process, while the sponsor must identify the value and target metrics. This joint responsibility may not always be easy, especially when several sponsors or individuals need to agree on what will make an IT project successful or what exactly will bring value to the organization. Still, it is better to spend the time arguing and getting consensus now rather than during later phases of the project. While the project manager is responsible for guiding the process, he or she needs to be confident that the MOV can be achieved. Being challenged is one thing; agreeing to an unrealistic MOV is another. The latter can be detrimental to your career, the project team, and everyone's morale.

Summarize the MOV in a Clear, Concise Statement or Table Once the impact and value to the organization are verified and agreed upon by all the project stakeholders, the MOV should be summarized in a single statement or table. Summarizing the MOV (1) provides an important chance to get final agreement and verification, (2) provides a simple and clear directive for the project team, and (3) sets explicit expectations for all project stakeholders. The easiest way to summarize the MOV in a statement form is to complete the following statement:

This project will be successful if_____.

For example, using a single statement format, the MOV would be:

> ***MOV: The B2C project will provide a 20 percent return on investment and 500 new customers within the first year of its operation.***

However, if the MOV includes a growth component, a table format may be clearer. For example, the project's MOV over three years could be summarized as shown in Table 2.2.

Notice that the MOV does not include any explicit statements about technology. More specifically, it does not mention that a particular relational database vendor's product will be used or that the system will be programmed in a particular language. It is up to the project team to figure out how to build the system and determine what technology will be employed to achieve the project goal. At this point in the project, we are concerned with the organization—not with the technology!

The project team's directive will be to achieve the MOV, not just develop and implement a B2C Web site. Although information technology will play an important role, the designers and developers of the information system cannot be expected to know everything or be solely responsible for achieving the project goal.

In the past, purely technical approaches were often applied to organizational problems. A system would be built, but did it really support or have a significant, positive impact on the organization? Judging from the *CHAOS* studies, IT projects have not lived up to management's expectations. In short, the technical people may understand and be very good at working with the technology, but achieving this MOV will also require an organizational approach and commitment. A cross-functional project team that includes a number of nontechnical experts will be required so that the burden of achieving this MOV does not rest squarely on the shoulders of the technical experts. Therefore, the selection of the project team becomes a crucial project management decision.

Table 2.2 Sample MOV Using Table Format

Year	MOV
1	20% return on investment
	500 new customers
2	25% return on investment
	1,000 new customers
3	30% return on investment
	1,500 new customers

Step 3: Identify Alternatives Since no single solution generally exists for most organizational problems, it is imperative to identify several alternatives before dealing directly with a given business opportunity. The alternatives, or options, identified in the business case should be strategies for achieving the MOV.

It is also important that the alternatives listed include a wide range of potential solutions as well as a **base case alternative** that describes how the organization would perform if it maintained the status quo—that is, if it did not pursue any of the options described in the business case. In some situations, maintaining the status quo may be the best alternative. It is important to be open to and objective on all viable options.

The base case should also delve into the realistic costs of maintaining the current system over time. Include such things as increased maintenance costs of hardware and software, as well as the possibility for more frequent system failures and downtime. However, if the demand for service decreases, maintaining a legacy system may be a more viable alternative than a proposed new system.

On the other hand, other options may provide the best solution. These options should consider a spectrum of choices that include:

- Changing the existing business processes without investing in IT
- Adopting or adapting an application developed by a different area or department within the organization
- Reengineering the existing system
- Purchasing an off-the-shelf application package from a software vendor
- Custom building a new application using internal resources or outsourcing the development to another company

Step 4: Define Feasibility and Assess Risk Each option or alternative must be analyzed in terms of its feasibility and potential risk. **Feasibility** should focus on whether a particular alternative is *doable* and *worth doing*. **Risk,** on the other hand, focuses on *what can go wrong* and *what must go right*. Analyzing the feasibility and risk of each alternative at this point may act as a screening process for ruling out any alternatives that are not worth pursuing. Feasibility may be viewed in terms of:

- *Economic feasibility*—Although a cost/benefit analysis will be conducted to look at the alternatives in greater depth, some alternatives may be too costly or simply not provide the benefits envisioned in the problem statement. At this point, an organization may evaluate an alternative in terms of whether funds and resources exist to support the project. For example, although you may be in a market for a new car, the reality of your limited income rules out the fancy sports car. Conducting an economic feasibility should serve as a reality check for each option or alternative.
- *Technical feasibility*—Technical feasibility focuses on the existing technical infrastructure needed to support the IT solution. Will the current infrastructure support the alternative? Will new technology be needed? Will it be available? Does the current IT staff have the skills and experience to support the proposed solution? If outsourcing, does the vendor or company have the skills and experience to develop and implement the application?
- *Organizational feasibility*—Organizational feasibility considers the impact on the organization. It focuses mainly on how people within the organization

QUICK THINKING—MEASURING THE IMMEASURABLE

According to Douglas Hubbard, the *IT value measure problem* is common in many companies today. Often business managers hear their IT departments say that the value of IT can't be measured because the benefits of IT are too intangible. Moreover, IT investments are fundamentally different from other types of investments. For example, accounting departments don't have to justify their budgets, and IT is just as basic to the business as accounting. So the logic is that the IT budget should likewise be exempt from justification. While this position may be popular among some IT executives because it gets them off the hook, Hubbard believes that many business managers are no longer buying it. Unlike most accounting departments, IT's budget is often large and growing. Given that many IT departments have had a few high-profile failures, business managers have the right to question the value of their organization's IT investments. On the other hand, many believe that only pseudo measurements are possible and that many of the benefits of IT are intangible and therefore immeasurable. Hubbard believes that the value of IT is measurable. He challenges the attendees of his seminars to come up with the most difficult or even impossible IT measurement problems they can think of. No matter how difficult it seemed at first, no suggested intangible has taken more than 20 minutes to solve. Hubbard believes that "immeasurability" is an illusion caused by the concept or intangible thing to be measured and the techniques or methods of measurement available not being well understood. For example, an organization may wish to measure something like employee empowerment, customer relationships, or strategic alignment. Organizations may consider these things as being intangibles because they don't fully grasp what they mean. Hubbard contends that specific, unambiguous measures can underlie these ambiguous concepts. After thinking through an intangible, we can find that our lack of understanding was the only barrier to creating a meaningful measure. He also suggests that IT managers should conduct simple random samples or controlled experiments to measure the quality of interest. Moreover, IT people rarely consider simple scientific observation as a valid technique, although the basic elements are often used in market research, actuarial science, and operations research. Hubbard suggests that no matter how difficult a measurement problem seems, the first step requires changing your initial assumption that something is an immeasurable intangible and instead assume that it is tangible and therefore measurable.

1. The intangible concept of user friendliness is an often used and widely cited requirement for many information systems. Come up with some measurements that could be used to represent the concept of user friendliness.

2. Using a scientific method such as direct observation, controlled experiment, or survey, come up with a way for measuring or assessing the user friendliness of a spreadsheet software package.

SOURCE: Adapted from Douglas Hubbard, Everything is Measurable, *CIO Magazine.* May 23, 2007.

---

will adapt to this planned organizational change. How will people and the way they do their jobs be impacted? Will they accept this change willingly? Will business be disrupted while the proposed solution is implemented?

- *Other feasibilities*—Depending on the situation and the organization, a business case may include other issues, such as legal and ethical feasibility.

Risk should focus on:

- *Identification*—What can go wrong? What must go right?
- *Assessment*—What is the impact of each risk?
- *Response*—How can the organization avoid or minimize the risk?

Step 5: Define Total Cost of Ownership The decision to invest in an IT project must take into account all of the costs associated with the application system. **Total Cost of Ownership (TCO)** is a concept that has gained widespread attention and generally refers to the total cost of acquiring, developing, maintaining, and supporting the application system over its useful life. TCO includes such costs as:

- *Direct or up-front costs*—Initial purchase price of all hardware, software, and telecommunications equipment, all development or installation costs, outside consultant fees, etc.

- *Ongoing costs*—Salaries, training, upgrades, supplies, maintenance, etc.

- *Indirect costs*—Initial loss of productivity, time lost by users when the system is down, the cost of auditing equipment (i.e., finding out who has what and where), quality assurance, and post-implementation reviews.

It is important to note that TCO goes beyond the original purchase or development costs. In fact, the TCO is really an organized list of all possible cost impacts. When preparing the business case, it is also important to document all data sources, assumptions, and methods for determining the various costs.

Step 6: Define Total Benefits of Ownership   Similarly, the **Total Benefits of Ownership (TBO)** must include all of the direct, ongoing, and indirect benefits associated with each proposed alternative. The TBO should address the benefits of an alternative over the course of its useful life. Benefits can arise from:

- *Increasing high-value work*—For example, a salesperson may spend less time on paperwork and more time calling on customers

- *Improving accuracy and efficiency*—For example, reducing errors, duplication, or the number of steps in a process

- *Improving decision making*—For example, providing timely and accurate information

- *Improving customer service*—For example, new products or services, faster or more reliable service, convenience, and so on

Tangible benefits associated with an IT project are relatively easy to identify and quantify. They will usually arise from direct cost savings or avoided costs. On the other hand, intangible benefits may be easy to identify, but they are certainly more difficult to quantify. It is important to try and quantify all the benefits identified. One way to quantify intangible benefits is to link them directly to tangible benefits that can be linked to efficiency gains. For example, a corporate telephone directory on an intranet not only improves communication, but can cut paper, printing, and labor costs associated with creating and distributing a paper-based telephone book.

Another way to quantify intangible benefits is to estimate the level of service. For example, one could determine how much someone is willing to pay for a particular service or compare prices of products or services that have or do not have a particular feature. Moreover, if an electronic data interchange (EDI) application allows an organization to collect its accounts receivable more quickly, it can estimate the value of this benefit by determining the return it could earn by investing that money.

Step 7: Analyze Alternatives   Once costs and benefits have been identified, it is important that all alternatives be compared with each other consistently. Understanding the financial and numeric tools and techniques required by financial people and senior management is critical, even for the technically savvy. Being able to communicate effectively using their terms and tools increases one's credibility and the chances of getting projects approved and funded. There are several ways to analyze the proposed alternatives. The most common are financial models and scoring models.

Financial models focus on either profitability and/or cash flows. Cash flow models focus on the net cash, may be positive or negative, and are calculated by subtracting the cash outflows from the cash inflows. In general, one could view the benefits associated with a particular alternative as a source of cash inflow and the costs as the source of outflows. Using a tool such as an electronic spreadsheet application, one could conduct a sensitivity analysis to view how changes in the initial investment or net cash flows would impact the risk of a particular project alternative.

The most commonly used cash flow models include **payback, breakeven, return on investment, net present value,** and **scoring.**

Payback   The payback method determines how long it will take to recover the initial investment. For example, if a company spends $100,000 developing and implementing an application system and then receives a net cash return of $20,000 a year, the payback period for that investment would be:

$$\text{Payback Period} = \frac{\text{Initial Investment}}{\text{Net Cash Flow}}$$
$$= \frac{\$100,000}{\$20,000}$$
$$= 5 \text{ years}$$

Although the payback period is fairly straightforward to calculate and understand, it does not consider the time value of money or cash flows beyond the payback period. Still, the payback period is useful for highlighting the risk of a particular investment because a riskier investment will have a longer payback period than a less risky investment. Depending on the situation and the organization's policy, net cash flow may be either before tax or after tax.

Breakeven   Similar to the payback method, the breakeven method attempts to determine the point at which a project would begin to recoup its original investment. This method is useful if a certain number of transactions allow the original investment to be recovered. For example, let's say that you would like to create a Web site to sell golf putters that you manufacture. If you spent $100,000 to create the site, how many golf putters would you have to sell to break even if you sell each putter for $30? To determine this point, you have to look at the cost of selling a putter. These costs may include the following:

Materials (putter head, shaft, grip, etc.)	$12.00
Labor (0.5 hours at $9.00/hr)	$ 4.50
Overhead (rent, insurance, utilities, taxes, etc.)	$ 8.50
Total	$25.00

If you sell a golf putter for $30 and it costs $25 to make it, you have a profit margin of $5. The breakeven point is computed as follows:

$$\text{Breakeven Point} = \frac{\text{Initial Investment}}{\text{Net Profit Margin}}$$
$$= \frac{\$100,000}{\$5}$$
$$= 20,000$$

Therefore, you would have to sell 20,000 putters over your Web site to break even.

Like the payback period method, the breakeven method is generally easy to compute and can provide a measure of risk. In general, riskier project alternatives will have a higher breakeven point than less risky project alternatives.

Return on Investment   In a strict financial sense, **return on investment (ROI)** is an indicator of a company's financial performance. From a project management point of view, ROI provides a measure of the value expected or received from a particular alternative or project. It is calculated by dividing the net income, or return, of a project alternative by its total cost. So, if a project alternative, for example, is expected to cost $100,000 but provides $115,000 in expected benefits, its ROI would be:

$$\text{Project ROI} = \frac{\text{Total Expected Benefits} - \text{Total Expected Costs}}{\text{Total Expected Costs}}$$
$$= \frac{\$115,000 - \$100,000}{\$100,000}$$
$$= 15\%$$

The above formula shows the expected ROI for a project alternative; a completed project's ROI would use the actual costs and benefits derived and can be compared to its expected ROI to provide a comparison at the end of the project. The usefulness of a project's ROI depends on two important assumptions. First, there must be the ability to define accurately the total costs and benefits expected or realized. Second, the returns must arise as a direct result of the initial investment. For example, if you purchased a lottery ticket for $1 and won $1 million, you can determine the ROI directly because the $1 million return can be related to the $1 lottery ticket you purchased. Even though the chances of winning a lottery are pretty slim, the ROI calculated as ($1,000,000 − $1) ÷ $1 = 99,999,900 percent would be quite acceptable for most people. In complex business situations, however, ROI analysis may be difficult because intervening variables and conditions may have an indirect influence.

Regardless, with ROI one can see the relationship between a project's costs and benefits. A project's ROI will increase as the benefits increase and/or the expected costs decrease. When comparing two or more projects or alternatives, those with the higher ROI would be the most desirable (all other things being equal). Many organizations even have a required ROI, whereby no project or alternative may be considered unless a certain ROI value can be achieved. The idea is that it is not worth investing time and resources in a project that does not provide a certain level of value to the organization and its shareholders.

Net Present Value   **Net Present Value (NPV)** focuses on the time value of money. For example, if you borrow $20 today, you may have to agree to pay back the original $20 plus another $2 at the end of the month. Someone may also be willing to give you either $18 today or $20 at the end of the month. If you could take the $18 and invest it, ending up with $20 at the end of the month, you might feel indifferent as to whether you collected $18 today or $20 at the end of the month. The point here is that there is a cost associated with time when it comes to money.

It is going to take time and resources (i.e., costs) before any particular project or alternative is completed and provides the returns we originally envisioned. NPV takes this into account by discounting streams of cash flows a particular alternative or project returns in the future so that we can determine if investing the time, money, and resources is worth the wait. Very simply put, only a project or alternative with a positive NPV should be considered. Let's say that one alternative is an application system that is expected to cost $200,000 and will be completed in the current year (Year 0). In addition, over the following four years the project's benefits will provide inflows of cash, while the costs to build, maintain, and support this application will require outflows of cash. The expected cash flows for the next five years may look something like:

	Year 0	*Year 1*	*Year 2*	*Year 3*	*Year 4*
Total Cash Inflows	$0	$150,000	$200,000	$250,000	$300,000
Total Cash Outflows	$200,000	$85,000	$125,000	$150,000	$200,000
Net Cash Flow	($200,000)	$65,000	$75,000	$100,000	$100,000

To discount the net cash flows, a **discount rate** is required. This rate is sometimes called a **cutoff rate** or **hurdle rate** because it basically defines the organization's required rate of return. In short, the discount rate is the minimum return a company would expect from a project if the company were to make an equivalent investment in an opportunity of similar risk. This discount rate is usually set by management. The NPV is calculated using the formula:

$$NPV = -I_O + \sum \left(\frac{\text{Net Cash Flow}}{(1+r)^t} \right)$$

Where:
I = total cost (or investment) in the project
r = discount rate
t = time period

Therefore, if we use a discount rate of 8 percent, we can discount the net cash flow for each period and add them up to determine the NPV.

Time Period	*Calculation*	*Discounted Cash Flow*
Year 0	($200,000)	($200,000)
Year 1	$65,000 \div (1 + .08)^1$	$60,185
Year 2	$75,000 \div (1 + .08)^2$	$64,300
Year 3	$100,000 \div (1 + .08)^3$	$79,383
Year 4	$100,000 \div (1 + .08)^4$	$73,503
Net Present Value (NPV)		**$77,371**

This alternative would be acceptable because a NPV of $77,371 is positive. One can compare the NPV for different alternatives and projects. In general, the project or alternative with a higher NPV would be more desirable. Remember, increasing the discount rate will decrease the NPV.[3]

---

[3]Closely related to the concept of net present value is the popular concept called internal rate of return (IRR). The IRR focuses on streams of cash flows and is the discount rate where the total present value of future cash flows equals the cost of the investment. In short, it is the rate where the NPV is equal to zero. Therefore, alternatives or projects with higher IRR are more desirable. Management may set a minimum desired IRR that an alternative or project must meet in order to be considered. IRR can be readily computed with a financial calculator or by using specific spreadsheet or program functions; otherwise, the exact IRR must be interpolated.

Scoring models provide a method for comparing alternatives or projects based on a weighted score. Scoring models also allow for quantifying intangible benefits or for different alternatives using multiple criteria. Using percentage weights, one can assign values of importance to the different criteria. The weights must sum to 100 percent, and when multiplied by a score assigned to each criterion they allow a composite score that is the weighted average. For example, one could compare several alternatives using the following formula:

$$\text{Total Score} = \sum_{i=1}^{n} w_i c_i$$

Where:
w_i = criterion weight
c_i = criterion score
$0 \leq w_i \leq 1$

Table 2.3 compares three project alternatives using this system. The scoring model in Table 2.3 highlights several important ideas:

- *The scoring model can combine both qualitative and nonqualitative items—* Whether one assigns more weight to intangible or intangible criteria depends on the philosophy of management or the client.

- *Weights and scores can be largely subjective—*This scoring is a two-edged sword. People use their judgment, or gut feelings, in assigning weights and scores, but may not necessarily have the same judgments. Thus, getting agreement among individuals may be difficult. One suggestion is to have different individuals assign weights and scores to the different criteria and then average these individual responses to create a composite score. Even if people don't agree, at least they have an opportunity to express their opinions. Another suggestion would be to use a relative score whenever possible. For example, let's say that the NPVs for the three alternatives were as follows:

Alternative

	A	B	C
NPV	$200	$400	$1,000

Since Alternative C has the highest NPV, we can determine a relative score (on a basis of 0 to 10) for each alternative as follows:

Alternative	*NPV*	*Calculation*	*Relative Score*
A	$1,000	($1,000 ÷ $1,000) × 10	10
B	$400	($400 ÷ $1,000) × 10	4
C	$200	($20 ÷ $1,000) × 10	2

The scores used in this example range from 0 to 10; but there is nothing sacred about this range. One could use a scale of 0 to 100. Consistency rather than any particular scale is the key.

- *Financial models can be biased toward the short run.* Although financial models are important and should be considered, they focus solely on the periods used in discounting cash flows. Scoring models go beyond this limitation because they allow for multicriteria (Meredith and Mantel 2000).

Table 2.3 Comparison of Project Alternatives

Criterion		Weight	Alternative A	Alternative B	Alternative C
Financial	ROI	15%	2	4	10
	Payback	10%	3	5	10
	NPV	15%	2	4	10
Organizational	Alignment with strategic objectives	10%	3	5	8
	Likelihood of achieving project's MOV	10%	2	6	9
Project	Availability of skilled team members	5%	5	5	4
	Maintainability	5%	4	6	7
	Time to develop	5%	5	7	6
	Risk	5%	3	5	5
External	Customer satisfaction	10%	2	4	9
	Increased market share	10%	2	5	8
Total Score		**100%**	**2.65**	**4.85**	**8.50**

Note: Risk scores have a reverse scale—that is, higher scores for risk imply lower levels of risk.

■ *Some criteria can be reverse-scored.* In our example, higher scores for certain criteria make sense. For instance, higher financial performance measures inherently have higher scores. However, a criterion such as risk can be reverse-scored with lower risk alternatives having higher scores. If you reverse-score any criterion, it is beneficial to note these assumptions conspicuously for the reader.

■ *Past experience may help create a more realistic business case.* As mentioned before, many of the weights and scores are subjective. Instead of relying on guesswork, past experience with past projects can provide guidelines and a reference for ensuring that the selection models are relevant and realistic. Although the business situation, technology, and data will change over time, the process or method of preparing a business case and analyzing alternatives will remain much the same. Learning from past experience can improve the process and product associated with business cases and thus improves the likelihood of a project being approved and funded.

Step 8: Propose and Support the Recommendation Once the alternatives have been identified and analyzed, the last step is to recommend one of the options. It is important to remember that a proposed recommendation must be supported. If the analysis was done diligently, this recommendation should be a relatively easy task. The business case should be formalized in a professional-looking report. Remember that the quality and accuracy of your work will be a reflection on you and your organization. A potential client or project sponsor may not give you a second chance. Figure 2.5 provides a template for developing a business case.

PROJECT SELECTION AND APPROVAL

The objective of the business case is to obtain approval and funding for a proposed alternative. However, a proposed project may have to compete against several others.

The following provides a suggested outline for developing and writing a business case:

Cover Page

- Title and subtitle
- Author and address
- Date

Executive Summary

- Brief description of the problem or opportunity
- Brief description of organization's goal and strategy
- Brief description of project's MOV and how it ties to the organizational goal and strategy
- Brief description of each option or alternative analyzed
- Brief explanation of which alternative is being recommended and why

Introduction

- Background
- Current situation
- Description of the problem or opportunity
- Project's measurable organizational value

- How achieving the project's MOV will support the organization's goal and strategy
- Objectives of writing this business case

Alternatives

- Description of alternative 1 (Base Case)
- Description of alternative 2…
- Description of alternative N

Analysis of Alternatives

- Methodology of how alternatives will be analyzed
  - Data collection methods
  - Metrics used and explanation why they are relevant

- Presentation of results that compares each alternative
  - Metrics
  - Sensitivity analysis
  - Risks
  - Assumptions
- Proposed recommendation

Figure 2.5   Business Case Template

The criteria for selecting a **project portfolio,** a set of projects that an organization may fund, are very similar to the analysis and subsequent selection of the proposed project alternatives. Similar to portfolio theory in finance, an organization may wish to select a portfolio of IT projects that have varying levels of risk, technological complexity, size, and strategic intent (McFarlan 1981; Marchewka and Keil 1995). An IT project portfolio mainly composed of projects with low risk or those that do not attempt to take advantage of new technology may lead to stagnation. The organization may not move ahead strategically and the IT employees may fail to grow professionally due to lack of challenge. On the other hand, an organization that focuses too heavily on risky projects employing cutting-edge technology may end up in a precarious position if the IT projects experience serious problems and failures. Learning from mistakes can be useful, unless the same mistakes are repeated over and over. Thus, an organization should attempt to balance its IT project portfolio with projects that have varying degrees of risk, cutting-edge technologies, and structure.

Unfortunately, as Harold Kerzner (Kerzner 2000, 120) points out, "What a company wants to do is not always what it can do." He contends that companies generally have a number of projects that they would like to undertake, but because of limited resources, they must prioritize and fund projects selectively. Depending on the demand for IT professionals or the state of the economy, it is not always feasible to hire new employees or to have them trained in time.

The IT Project Selection Process

Although each organization's selection process is different, this section describes the general process for selecting and funding a given project. The selection process determines which IT projects will be funded in a given period. This period can be for a quarter, year, or a time frame used by the organization. In order to weed out projects that have little chance of being approved, many organizations use an initial screening process in which business cases submitted for review are compared with a set of organizational standards that outline minimum requirements.

Projects that meet the minimum requirements are then forwarded to a decision-making committee of senior managers who have the authority to approve and provide the resources needed to support the project. On rare occasions an individual might make such decisions, but most organizations of any size prefer to use committees. The committee may compare several competing projects based on the costs, benefits, and risks to projects currently under development and to those already implemented. Projects selected should then be assigned to a project manager who selects the project team and then develops a project charter and detailed plan.

The Project Selection Decision

Even though each project proposal should be evaluated in terms of its value to the organization, it is important to reiterate that IT projects should not be undertaken for technology's sake. The decision to approve an IT project requires a number of conditions be met:

- The IT project must map directly to the organization's strategies and goals.
- The IT project must provide measurable organizational value that can be verified at the completion of the project.
- The selection of an IT project should be based upon diversity of measures that include:
  - Tangible costs and benefits
  - Intangible costs and benefits
  - Various levels throughout the organization (e.g., individual, process, department, and enterprise)

One way to select an IT project portfolio is to use the same methods that were used and discussed when analyzing the project alternatives in the business case. Today, however, there are several ways to measure the expected and realized value of IT to an organization. One method that is becoming increasingly popular is the **Balanced Scorecard** approach that was introduced by Robert S. Kaplan and David Norton in a 1992 *Harvard Business Review* article. Instead of focusing solely on the financial impact of a decision, the Balanced Scorecard approach helps balance traditional financial measures with operational metrics across four different perspectives: finance, customer satisfaction, internal business processes, and the organization's ability to innovate and learn (Kaplan and Norton 1992, 1993).

An organization that utilizes the Balanced Scorecard approach must create a set of measurements, or key performance indicators, for each of the perspectives illustrated in Figure 2.6. In turn, these measures are used to create a report or scorecard for the organization that allows management to track, or keep score, of the organization's performance. The four perspectives provide a balanced approach in terms of

Figure 2.6   A Balanced Scorecard Approach

tangible and intangible benefits and long- and short-term objectives, as well as how each perspective's desired outcomes and drivers impact the other perspectives.

- *Financial perspective*—The balanced scorecard approach encourages managers to consider measures other than traditional financial measures for strategic success. Most financial measures are useful for understanding how an organization performed in the past, and some have likened this to steering the ship by watching the wake. Traditional financial measures, however, are still important and can be a cornerstone for ensuring that an organization's strategies are being implemented properly. More importantly, the balanced scorecard approach provides a means for linking financial performance with customer focused-initiatives, internal operations, and investments in employees and the infrastructure to support their performance. Although traditional financial measures that include operating income—ROI, NPV, IRR, and so forth—are still useful, many organizations are now using new financial measures as well. One financial measure that has been receiving a great deal of attention and scrutiny recently is **economic value added (EVA)**. EVA is a measurement tool to determine if an organization is earning more than its true cost of capital. Supporters of EVA believe it provides a clearer picture on whether management is creating or destroying shareholder wealth. EVA is calculated by considering the cost of debt (e.g., the interest rate a bank would charge) and the cost of equity (e.g., what shareholders could earn elsewhere). Subsequently, a positive EVA indicates that positive wealth has been created.

- *Customer perspective*—How an organization performs in its customers' eyes largely determines customer satisfaction. In turn, satisfied customers can mean repeat business and referrals for new business. As a result, measures or targets for customer satisfaction can be linked to financial rewards. They create a value chain for establishing customer-focused initiatives that can be linked to financial performance. Customer-based measurements may focus on areas that determine the level of satisfaction with the products and services of the company and how well those products and services are delivered.

- *Internal process perspective*—The internal process perspective focuses on the processes—both long term and short term—that an organization must excel at in order to achieve its customer and financial objectives. Customer satisfaction can be achieved through improved operational activities by the organization, which in turn leads to improved financial performance. Therefore, internal-based measurements should focus on the efficiency and effectiveness of the organization's processes.

- *Innovation and learning perspective*—The abilities, capabilities, and motivations of the people within an organization determine the outcomes of the operational activities, financial performance, and levels of customer satisfaction within the organization. Thus, an organization relies heavily on its people not only to support the other three perspectives, but also to provide continuous improvements in these areas. An organization's ability to innovate and learn at the individual level is critical for supporting the organization as a whole. Therefore, the balanced scorecard approach gives considerable support to the importance of investing in the future by investing in people and makes investing in human infrastructure at least as important as investing in technical and physical infrastructures. Measures for the innovation and learning perspective may include training, certifications, and employee satisfaction and retention.

By measuring the value of an IT project across these four areas, the scorecard approach compels an organization's management to consider the impact and context of a project from an organization-wide view. It also limits the potential for overemphasizing traditional financial measurement at the expense of perspectives that include both tangible and intangible benefits. Still, the balanced scorecard can fail for a number of reasons (Schneiderman 1999):

- The nonfinancial measurement variables are incorrectly identified as the primary drivers for stakeholder satisfaction.
- Metrics are not properly defined.
- Goals for improvements are negotiated and not based on stakeholder requirements, fundamental process limits, or capabilities.
- No systematic way to map high-level goals with subprocess levels where the actual improvement activities reside.
- Reliance on trial and error as a methodology for improvement.
- There is no quantitative linkage between the nonfinancial and expected financial results.

The balanced scorecard approach is an overall performance management system that is useful for selecting all projects in an organization, monitoring their progress, and then evaluating their overall contribution. As illustrated in Figure 2.7, the MOV concept introduced earlier supports the balanced scorecard approach.

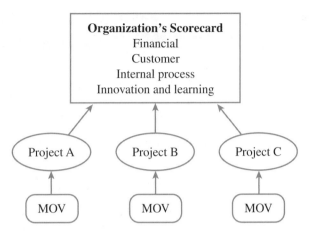

Figure 2.7   MOV and the Organization's Scorecard

The MOV can be developed and reviewed in terms of how it supports the four balanced scorecard perspectives. However, the MOV concept can also support organizations that use other means of identifying a project's value to the organization.

IT GOVERNANCE AND THE PROJECT MANAGEMENT OFFICE

> I.T. project decisions, and the ways they are made, inevitably shape our destiny. Get them right and we boost business success. Get them wrong and we preside over investment disasters. Jack Keen, *CIO Magazine*, May 15, 2003.

Governance focuses on the processes that coordinate and control an organization's resources, actions, and decisions to help prevent people from making bad investments, acting unethically, or doing something illegal (Meyer 2005). For example, a human resources (HR) department doesn't manage each employee individually, but defines and communicates plans, policies, and procedures so that all of the organization's employees are managed well (Cramm 2001). The idea of IT governance has been gaining popularity in many organizations. For many organizations IT governance was driven by the need to comply with regulations like the Sarbanes-Oxley Act of 2002 which mandated openness and audit trails in financial reporting (Hildreth 2005). Karen Schwartz (2007) defines IT governance as:

> ... putting structure around how organizations align IT strategy with business strategy ensuring that companies stay on track to achieve their strategies and goals, and implementing good ways to measure IT's performance. It makes sure that all stakeholders' interests are taken into account and that processes provide measurable results. An IT governance framework should answer some key questions such as how the IT department is functioning overall, what key metrics management needs and what return IT is giving back to the business from the investment it's making.

The level of detail of IT governance will depend on the organization's size and industry. In general, more sophisticated IT governance structures are more common in

QUICK THINKING—THE ELEVATOR PITCH

Just about every IT project starts off as a written proposal or business case that was sold to a high-level executive. A poorly written proposal rarely results in a funded project. To make your project compelling, Alan Horowitz suggests that you first presell your proposal by having conversations with senior executives to gauge their reactions and listen to their concerns. Preselling also helps to create a strong partnership with the business units involved. Credibility and a business focus are key ingredients for selling the proposal. It should be tied to the organization's mission and management's current hot buttons. Unfortunately, IT often takes a narrow view. For example, a CRM system may save a salesperson 30 minutes a day, but a successful proposal should go beyond the immediate user and explain how it can impact the rest of the organization like manufacturing or human resources. People like things summarized, and most people focus on the executive summary, a short summary that explains why you are asking for the money, what you will do with it, and how it will benefit the organization in a paragraph or two. After the executive summary, the proposal will contain much more detail as to what you plan to do and how you plan to do it. A million dollar project may be 8 to 10 pages long, while a $10,000 project may need only 2 or 3 pages. If you take more than 10 pages to explain a project, you probably don't understand it as well as you think you do. An "elevator pitch" (a.k.a.

elevator speech) can be a useful technique for your pre-selling an idea and sharpening presentation skills. As the name implies, you need to state your case or sell an idea to someone in the time it takes to ride in an elevator from the ground to the top floor. Many times key decision makers will ask people to present an elevator speech to weed out bad ideas. It is important that you consider what people are interested in. For example, a chief financial officer (CFO) is going to be interested in different metrics than the director of manufacturing. And if your proposal gets shot down? You can still gain credibility if you've taken a leadership role and show an organization's managers that there are opportunities at hand.

1. Prepare an elevator pitch to the director of human resources as if you were riding from the lobby to the 35th floor (say, 60 seconds) to presell a project proposal. The proposed project will be an addition to the company's current Web site and will allow potential candidates to view and apply for available jobs online. Feel free to make assumptions, but unrealistic assumptions will not pass the scrutiny of an astute executive.

SOURCE: Adapted from Alan Horowitz, The IT Business Case: It's Not War and Peace, *Computerworld*, March 29, 2004.

larger organizations that are in highly regulated industries. However, any organization regardless of size and industry should ensure that IT supports the organization's mission and strategies (Schwartz 2007).

For many organizations, IT governance started with project management, but today it also includes change management, application life-cycle management, asset and resource management (i.e., IT investment/project approval), portfolio management, and security management (Hildreth 2005). Based on a study of large multibusiness unit firms in the United States and Europe, Peter Weill and Richard Woodham (2002) found that an effective IT governance structure is the single most important predictor of receiving value from IT.

Four IT governance best practices include (Dragoon 2003):

1. *Identify strategic value.* Organizations are often faced with a stack of potential IT projects, so it is important to compare them in terms of their business value as well as their costs and potential risks. To focus on the factors that matter the most, many organizations have developed their own tools for evaluating and ranking competing projects. For example, GE Industrial systems use a cause and effect matrix to decide which projects GE will fund. Business managers first identify important strategic focuses such as customer centricity, business simplification, improved productivity, or inventory reduction. Project proposals must then categorize the potential

project as having a low, medium, or high impact for each strategic initiative on the matrix. GE also uses an algorithm to analyze payback, strategic value, and the proposing team's success of delivering promised value on time and within budget in order to compute a score between 1 and 100. An investment council then decides which projects receive funding.

2. *Top business managers should set IT priorities.* Many organizations rely on a committee of business and IT leaders to determine how the IT budget will be spent. Giving business managers control over the IT budget helps IT align with organizational objectives and increases shared accountability in terms of project success and failure. For example, at Farmers Insurance a group of high-level executives make up the IT Governance Board that meets every quarter and outlines an overall strategic direction for IT. Funding decisions are then made by another committee called the Capital Appropriations Committee (CAC), which includes the IT Governance Board and some of their key direct reports. The CAC meets every two weeks and reviews all funding requests with a total cost of ownership greater than $50,000. Requests are detailed documents that outline the project's purpose and cost/benefit analysis. After a project is approved, a Business and Technology Integration (BTI) committee made up of line vice presidents from IT and the lines of business meet weekly with the project management office (PMO) to review each project's progress. Farmers Insurance believes that these governance practices have helped achieve its goal of cutting expenses and improving capacity 5 percent annually.

3. *Communicate priorities and progress clearly.* The priorities defined by the top IT and business managers must be communicated clearly to the rest of the organization. Effective communication ensures that everyone in the organization is aware of and understands how the governance process works. For example, the insurance and financial services company, MONY Group, posts companywide priorities each month, as well as the name of the individual responsible. An employee's incentive compensation is then tied to meeting 90 percent of the monthly priorities and achieving a score of at least 3 out 5 on customer satisfaction for those priorities. MONY has also adopted a shared services model for IT that allows the lines of business to choose to go outside and outsource a particular IT service. Since each line of business has a choice, an IT scorecard is posted each month to track innovative ideas, project execution (whether key projects are implemented on time, within budget, and have a 90 percent customer satisfaction rating of 3 or better), operational excellence (the goal to meet 90 percent of companywide monthly priorities), and IT transformation (how much progress IT has made in moving from a corporate IT mindset to a full-service IT bureau).

4. *Monitor projects regularly.* Once projects are selected to receive funding and launched, an organization needs to track each project's progress on a regular basis to protect the value of its investment. This may include monthly "traffic reports" that summarize key project metrics and spotlight any potential issues or problems early on so that corrective actions can be taken before they become major challenges. For example, the CIO at MONY reviews about 20 monthly dashboard documents for all the projects. A one-page dashboard document summarizes a project's progress against milestones, resource usage, user involvement, and issues or barriers using green, yellow, or red traffic lights to indicate a project's status at a glance.

The Project Management Office (PMO)

The establishment of a project management office (PMO) can be a critical component for supporting the idea of IT governance. In the past, many organizations did not follow a project management approach in the development of IT systems, and as a result, many IT projects did not align well with business strategy and were late and over budget. Today, many organizations are trying to create a project management culture and governance structure, and establishing a project management office is one way of developing that culture while improving process and control. In fact, Forrester Research, Inc. in Cambridge, Massachusetts, conducted a study of 30 companies that suggests the mission of PMOs is "to bring order out of the *CHAOS* of project management." The study also suggests that the biggest challenges focus on managing multiple projects, cross-functional projects, global projects, overlapping projects, interdependent projects, project resource allocation, politics, sponsorship, and culture.

The role of a PMO is to provide support and collect project-related data while providing tools and methodologies. Collecting information about projects across the organization gives the PMO a means to study the organization's portfolio of IT projects. Eventually, this historical information can be used as an audit trail to conform to regulatory requirements and as a basis for estimating and conducting reality checks for projects. A PMO can become center of excellence for project management. Kathleen Melymuka (1999) describes several benefits of PMOs that include:

- Pointing out minefields in project processes, such as time and cost estimation
- Enforcing priorities and/or controls that keep the project on track
- Coordinating cross-functional projects that may stumble as a result of organizational politics that often arise when intraorganizational boundaries are crossed
- Providing a standardized way for all projects to be planned, managed, and reported
- Showing the real value of projects by comparing projected costs and benefits with actual results
- Coordinating more and larger projects than the organization could handle in the past
- Allowing IT to support its requests for additional staff or resources

 CHAPTER SUMMARY

A methodology provides a blueprint or template for planning, managing, and controlling a project throughout its life cycle. Although the products of information systems projects are different, many of the processes are the same. In this chapter, a framework for an IT project methodology was introduced. This framework will be used throughout the remainder of this text and provides a basic foundation that will allow organizations to adapt it to their particular needs and from their lessons learned.

In addition, the concept of a project's measurable organizational value or MOV was introduced because it is an important tool for defining a project's goal and value to the organization. The MOV becomes the project's measure of success and must be measurable, agreed upon, and verifiable at the end of the project. A project's MOV must align with the organization's goals and strategies in order to provide value to the organization.

A business case defines the problem or opportunity, MOV, feasibility, costs, and benefits of several alternatives that an organization may choose in order to achieve its goals and strategies. Based on the analysis of the alternatives identified, a recommendation is made to approve and fund a specific project.

The business case is formalized in a report to senior management who may review several proposed projects. The decision to fund a particular project and add it to the organization's project portfolio depends largely on the resources available and the value of the project to the organization. One increasingly popular method for defining value to an organization is the balanced scorecard approach. This approach focuses on four perspectives—financial, customer, internal processes, and innovation and learning. Regardless of the selection approach, an organization should make the project selection decision based on a diverse set of measures and in terms of how well the project supports the goals and strategies of the organization.

IT governance provides a framework of processes and controls to help organizations make the right IT investment decisions. It creates a structure to ensure that IT projects align with organizational strategy and then stay on track so that investments provide the measurable value originally envisioned. In addition, many organizations are creating a project management office (PMO) as a part of IT governance to support project management processes, tools, methods, and culture so that the right projects are selected and then managed well to increase the likelihood of success.

REVIEW QUESTIONS

1. What are the advantages of having and following a project methodology?
2. Describe the five phases of the IT project methodology.
3. Why is it important to have deliverables for each phase of the IT project methodology?
4. How can the experiences of and lessons learned by past project team members be incorporated into a project methodology?
5. Describe the conceptualize and initialize phase of the IT project methodology.
6. What is a project charter?
7. What are the advantages of developing a detailed project plan after a project has been approved for funding?
8. Describe the "execute and control phase" of the IT project methodology.
9. Describe the "close project phase" of the IT project methodology.
10. Describe the "evaluate project success" phase of the IT project methodology.
11. Describe the five project management processes.
12. Why can a project that is developed under budget and before its deadline still not be considered successful?
13. What kinds of tools would be needed to support an IT project?
14. How does an organizational infrastructure support a project?
15. What is a project infrastructure?
16. Describe a technical infrastructure that would be needed to support a consulting team working at a client site.
17. Discuss how the project management knowledge areas support the IT project methodology.
18. What is a business case?
19. Why should an organization develop a business case?
20. What is the purpose of selecting a core team to develop a business case?
21. What is a project's measurable organizational value (MOV)?
22. Develop a MOV for an organization that is contemplating developing a corporate intranet.
23. Why must a project's MOV be agreed upon?
24. Describe how a project's MOV can support an organization's goals and strategies.
25. Describe how an IT project can bring value to an organization.
26. What is a base case alternative? Why should a business case even consider a base case alternative?
27. Describe economic feasibility.
28. Describe technical feasibility.
29. Describe organizational feasibility.
30. What other types of feasibility issues should an organization consider?
31. How should the risk of each business case alternative be analyzed?

32. What is total cost of ownership?
33. What is total benefits of ownership?
34. What is the difference between tangible and intangible benefits? Give an example of each.
35. What are some ways of quantifying intangible benefits?
36. Describe the payback method. What are some advantages and disadvantages of this method?
37. Describe the breakeven method. What are some advantages and disadvantages of this method?
38. Describe the ROI method. What are some advantages and disadvantages of this method?
39. Describe the NPV method. What are some advantages and disadvantages of this method?
40. What effect does increasing the discount rate have on a project's NPV?
41. What are the advantages of using a scoring model when comparing several project alternatives? Any disadvantages?
42. What is an IT project portfolio?

43. Why shouldn't an organization always take on less challenging projects?
44. Describe the criteria that should be used to make a project selection decision.
45. Describe the balanced scorecard approach.
46. Describe the financial perspective of the balanced scorecard approach.
47. Describe the customer perspective of the balanced scorecard approach.
48. Describe the internal process perspective of the balanced scorecard approach.
49. Describe the innovation and learning perspective of the balanced scorecard approach.
50. How does the concept of MOV support the balanced scorecard approach?
51. What is the purpose of IT governance?
52. What role does project management play in IT governance?
53. What is a PMO? And what is the role of a PMO in organizations?

EXTEND YOUR KNOWLEDGE

1. Using the Web or the library as a resource, write a one-page position paper on the balanced scorecard approach. Why does this approach seem to be gaining popularity?
2. Determine the total cost of ownership (TCO) and total benefits of ownership (TBO) for purchasing, maintaining, and supporting a personal computer of your choice over the next three years. You may want to use a spreadsheet package to conduct your analysis.
3. Analyze the TCO and TBO that you conducted in Question 2 using the payback, ROI, and NPV methods.
4. Create a scoring model to analyze whether to purchase a new car. Your alternatives are: keep your current mode of transportation, purchase a used car, or purchase a new car. Be sure to include both tangible and intangible costs and benefits.
5. Develop a balanced scorecard for an organization contemplating an Internet-based application that would allow its customers to look up their order status online.
6. Suppose a bank's goal is to gain competitive advantage by developing tighter relationships with its customers. Its strategy is to create focused differentiation through a customer relationship management (CRM) system. Develop project MOV and discuss how this MOV supports the goal and strategy of this organization.

GLOBAL TECHNOLOGY SOLUTIONS

Tim Williams sat across from Kellie Matthews as the waiter brought their orders and refilled the water glasses. After the waiter left, Tim handed a folder with GTS embossed on the cover to Kellie. "I've been giving this a great deal of thought," Tim said as he reached for the peppershaker. Kellie began to look over the contents of the folder while Tim waited.

"It's a methodology that I'm working on to help us organize the Husky Air project," Tim explained. "In fact," he added, "I think we can use it as a blueprint for all of our projects. Of course, I'm trying to make it flexible so we can add to it or change it over time as we learn better ways of doing things."

Kellie thought for a moment. "Will it restrict the project team's creativity?" she asked. "Husky Air's management is counting on us to come up with some innovative solutions for them. I know I've always hated the feeling of being constrained by too many rules."

Tim was ready with his answer: "Think of this methodology as a road map. If you were planning a trip, the first thing you would have to do is decide on a destination based on your interests. For our purposes, that would be similar to defining the project's goal. Once you decide where you're going, you then need to figure out how to get there and how much it will cost."

"Some kind of plan?" Kellie interjected.

"Exactly!" exclaimed Tim. "A travel plan would help you figure out whether to drive, fly, take a train, or use a combination to get to your destination. It really depends on where you're going and how much you want to spend."

Kellie reflected for a moment. "But when I'm on vacation, I like to be spontaneous!" she said. "Planning every minute of a vacation takes the fun out of it."

"Aha!" Tim replied. "You see, that's the difference between a methodology and a plan. The methodology would help you to plan your plan."

"What?" said Kellie, "Are you playing a game with words?"

Tim grinned. "No, not really," he answered. "Let's say you went on vacation and had a terrible time. And maybe you even spent more than you budgeted for your vacation."

"I've had a few of those experiences," Kellie reflected.

"So the next time you decide to take a vacation, you might want to do things differently," Tim explained. "What you might do is organize the way you plan your vacation. First, you may try to come up with a better way of choosing a vacation spot. Then, you go about

picking a mode of travel and reserve your accommodations. Finally, you figure out what you want to see and do while on your vacation. You may schedule your vacation by the minute, or you can have a list of places to visit or see while you're there—it really depends on what would make your vacation enjoyable."

The waiter returned and refilled their water glasses. Kellie thought for a moment. "I guess we really owe it to our client to have a game plan," she said. "After all, we can't really just wander in any direction and hope we'll somehow end up at our destination. They're paying us by the hour, and time is money. Besides, we owe it to them to meet their needs in the most efficient and effective way possible. So, what's our first step? We're meeting with Husky Air's management tomorrow morning."

"Glad you asked," Tim smiled. "If you take a look at the methodology, you'll see that the first thing we need to do is prepare a business case. That's where we'll figure out our destination—I mean, the overall goal of this project. Once we know where we're headed, we can identify several options for Husky Air. After one is approved, we'll develop a project charter and plan that defines the detailed schedule and budget. That will tell us what needs to be done, when, by whom, and how much it will cost. In addition, the methodology will help make sure that our plan is being followed, or changed when necessary."

"Sounds good," said Kellie, "But there's just one more thing."

"What's that?" asked Tim.

Kellie grinned. "It's your turn to buy lunch."

Things to Think About

1. What are the advantages of having and following a project methodology?

2. Why should a methodology be flexible?

3. What perceptions might a client have if GTS has a methodology in place? If they don't?

 # HUSKY AIR ASSIGNMENT—PILOT ANGELS

The Business Case

A business case is the first deliverable defined in the IT Project Methodology. It provides an analysis of the business value, several alternatives for achieving the project's MOV, the feasibility of the alternatives, as well as their costs, benefits, and risks. The business case is *not* a budget or the project plan; however, it does provide

all the information necessary for senior management to make a decision whether a specific project should be undertaken.

The following is a suggested outline for developing your business case. Because this is a fictitious case, you will not be able to meet with your client. Subsequently, you will have to make a number of assumptions about the case and your project. Feel free to do so—just be sure that you document these assumptions in your business case.

Please provide a professional-looking document that includes the following:

1. **Project name**—You came up with a name for your project team when you developed your team charter. Now you need to name your project.

2. **Project team**—At this point you should have your project team in place. Be sure to identify your team by its name and list all team members.

3. **Project description**—Provide a brief description of the project. A project description should be written so that anyone unfamiliar with the project can read and understand what the project is about. Include a brief description of the organization and the problem or opportunity that led to initiating the project.

4. **Measurable organizational value (MOV)**—The MOV is the goal of the project and is used to define the value that your project will bring to your client. It will also be used to evaluate whether your project was a success later on. In reality, you would work very closely with your client in developing an MOV. Your responsibility would be to lead the process, while the client would commit to specific areas of impact, metrics, and time frames. Once the MOV is defined, it becomes the responsibility of all the project stakeholders to agree whether the MOV is realistic and achievable. For the purposes of this assignment, you will have to come up an MOV on your own. You are free to be creative, but please strive to make the MOV realistic. For our purposes, learning how to develop an MOV is an important process. Use the following steps to define your project's MOV:

    a. **Identify the desired area of impact**—At this point, what areas do you think are the most important to your client, Husky Air? Based on Table 2.1, rank the following areas in terms of their importance:
       - Strategic
       - Customer
       - Financial
       - Operational
       - Social

    b. **Identify the desired value of the IT project**—Value to an organization can come from doing something better, faster, or less expensively (i.e., cheaper). On the other hand, it can come from growth by doing more of something that the organization is currently doing (e.g., increase market share). The next step in developing an MOV is to identify the project's

potential value to the organization. In general, an IT project should focus on delivering one or two of the following types of value.

    - *Better?* Does Husky Air want to do something better? For example, is improving quality important to your client?
    - *Faster?* Does Husky Air want to do something faster? For example, does your client want to increase speed, efficiency, or reduce cycle times?
    - *Cheaper?* Does Husky Air want to reduce costs? For example, is cutting costs important to your client?
    - *Do More?* Does Husky Air want to do more of something? For example, does your client want to continue the growth of something that they are currently doing?

    c. **Develop an appropriate metric**—Once you have identified the desired area of impact and value to the organization, the next step is to develop a metric that sets a target and expectation for all of the project stakeholders. For example, if an organization desires to do more of something that is strategic to the organization (i.e., increase market share of a particular product or service), then the organization's management may feel that an IT project will bring value to the organization if they can grow their current market share from 10 to 25 percent. On the other hand, a bank may be able to process a loan request within 10 days. By developing and implementing a proposed information system, the bank's management may believe that it can reduce the cycle time of processing a loan to 24 hours or less. This would allow the company to do something faster operationally. Therefore, it is important to come up with a quantitative target. This target should be expressed as a metric in terms of an increase or decrease of money (dollars, euros, etc.), percent, or a specific numeric value.

    d. **Set a time frame for achieving the MOV**—Once you have identified the area of impact, value to the organization, and an appropriate metric, you need to set a time frame for achieving the MOV. Keep in mind that this time frame may not coincide with the scheduled completion of the project work. For example, reducing the time to process a loan within 24 hours may be achievable once the system is implemented, but instant growth of market share from 10 to 25 percent may take a few months. Setting the time frame for achieving the MOV can be determined by asking the question: When do we want to achieve this target metric?

e. **Summarize the MOV in a clear, concise statement or table**—Once the area of impact, value, metrics, and time frame are agreed on, the MOV should be summarized so that it can be clearly communicated to all of the project stakeholders. The MOV can be summarized in a statement by completing the statement: This project will be successful if_____? On the other hand, a table format may be more appropriate for summarizing the MOV if it has a growth component over two or more time periods. Keep in mind that the MOV should tell everyone *what* the project will achieve, not *how* it will be achieved. The MOV should focus on the organization, not the technology that will be used to build or support the information system.

5. **A comparison of alternatives**—To keep things simple, you may consider only three alternatives for your client: maintain the status quo (i.e., do nothing), purchase a software package, or build a custom system. Using the Web or library, determine whether any software packages currently exist that you think may support Husky Air's requirements. If more than one exists, then select one that you feel may be the best option for your client. Compare each of the alternatives based on the following criteria:

a. **Total cost of ownership (TCO)**—This can be only a rough estimate at this time. Later on, you will develop a detailed project schedule and budget that can be compared to your ballpark estimate now. Currently, Husky Air has a manual, paper-based system. If Husky Air purchases a software package or builds a system, they will need three workstations that will be networked to a server. Determine any other hardware and software that the company may

need. This will require a reasonable amount of research using the Web, library, or company catalogs to estimate the cost of the hardware and software and to support your initial estimate. Keep in mind that total cost of ownership should include:

- All direct or upfront costs
- Indirect costs
- Ongoing support and maintenance costs

b. **Total benefits of ownership (TBO)**—Total benefits of ownership should include all of the direct, indirect, and ongoing benefits for each proposed alternative. It should focus on:

- Increasing high-value work
- Improving accuracy and efficiency
- Improved decision making
- Improving customer service

6. **A recommendation**—At this point you may have more questions than answers and feel that you are being forced to make many assumptions. This is common for many real project teams and consultants at this stage of the project. You'll gain confidence from experience, doing good research, and paying attention to the details. Now you are ready to make a recommendation to your client and support it. Given the limited amount of information and time, you should still be confident that your recommendation provides the best value to the organization and that the benefits outweigh the costs. Be sure that you not only recommend one of the three alternatives, but that you provide support based on your analysis to back it up. The client will make a decision whether to continue to the next phase of the project. If the project continues, a detailed schedule and budget will provide a clearer picture of the project's true costs, and another decision whether to fund and support the project in the next phase will be made.

 # CASE STUDIES

Data Mining to Prevent Terrorism

Data mining is becoming an important IT tool for the intelligence community. It combines statistical models, powerful processors, and artificial intelligence to find valuable information that can be buried in large amounts of data. Retailers have relied on data mining to understand and predict the purchasing habits of customers, while credit card companies have relied on data mining to detect fraud. After 9/11, the U.S. government concluded that data

mining could be a valuable tool for preventing future terrorist attacks.

There are two basic types of data mining: subject-based and pattern-based. A subject-based data mining application could be used to retrieve data that could help an agency analyst follow a particular lead. Pattern-based or link analysis can be used to look for suspicious behaviors through nonobvious associations or relationships between seemingly unconnected people or activities. For example, a pattern-based data mining analysis could identify two terrorists who use the same credit card to book a flight or who share the same address.

Pressure to prevent another catastrophic terrorist attack has led to a proliferation of data mining projects. A 2004 report by the General Accountability Office (GAO) reported that federal agencies were engaged in or planning almost 200 data mining projects. Former deputy director of the Information Awareness Office at the Defense Advanced Research Projects Agency, Robert Popp, says "There is a real fear of not going down this path, because if there is value you don't want to be on the side that opposed [a data mining project]." It comes as no surprise that agency heads have been approving data mining projects almost as fast as they are conceived. However, such media outlets as *The New York Times* and *USA Today* have uncovered top secret programs that collect and look for patterns in phone records, emails, and other personal information. Although many government officials and politicians defend this as being critical to the war on terror, a growing number of people have expressed their concerns for ensuring privacy.

A number of experts are questioning whether an IT strategy with no clear goals and unlimited scope, budget, and schedule will best serve its end. Given the government's poor track record for IT projects, many people are concerned that projects could drag on for years and that good projects could be overlooked because some bad projects may have serious privacy and civil liberties issues. IT projects, no matter how vital, tend to experience serious problems when controls are nonexistent or drop to the wayside when organizations face a crisis. This is a problem that all organizations face and this can lead to overly ambitious projects, an unwillingness to change the original vision, and overlooking signs when something is not working. Moreover, some experts believe that the government's eagerness to apply IT to antiterrorism could backfire and disrupt the crime-fighting process if users view the system as an obstacle for getting their work done. They will rebel or simply not use it.

According to Steve Cooper, former CIO of the Department of Homeland Security, "No one [in the government] has looked at data mining from an IT value perspective. I couldn't figure out [the value of data mining] when I was in DHS, and I can't figure it out now. But that didn't stop us from using it." In short, no one has done a business case to determine whether the government was getting any return on its investment—just a rationalization that a project would be worth the investment if it could catch just one terrorist.

However, a number of projects have gotten the ax. For example, Congress pulled the plug on a project to create a large database that would include everything and anything that could identify a terrorist. Moreover, after 9/11 the government decided to replace the Computer Assisted Passenger Pre-Screening System (CAPPS), which focused on passenger information (names, credit card numbers, addresses) collected by the airlines, with CAPPS II, which would also include information purchased from data brokers such as ChoicePoint and LexisNexis. In 2003, a controversy was created when Northwest Airlines and JetBlue gave passenger information to the Transportation Security Administration (TSA) in order to test the new system. Outcries of critics that privacy safeguards were virtually nonexistent led to Congress withholding funds for CAPPS II until a study completed by the GAO could determine how the TSA could protect people's privacy. After spending over $100 million on CAPPS II, TSA cancelled the project in 2004 and proposed a new system called Secure Flight. This new system was very similar to its predecessor, CAPPS II, in that both systems would combine passenger information with purchased information from commercial databases.

In 2005, a group of data mining and privacy experts made up the Secure Flight Working Group and were asked to review the project. After nine months they submitted a confidential report that became available on the Internet within a week. The report was highly critical and read, "First and foremost, TSA has not articulated what the specific goals of Secure Flight are." Moreover, it also reported, "Based on the limited test results presented to us, we cannot assess whether even the general goal of evaluating passengers for the risk they represent to aviation security is a realistic or feasible one or how TSA proposes to achieve it."

According to Jim Dempsey, policy director of the Center for Democracy and Technology who was part of the Secure Flight Working Group, "TSA was never willing to reevaluate the scope of the project. So now, five years after 9/11, we still don't have an automated system for matching passenger names with names on the terror watch list. Civil liberties had nothing to do with that."

Bruce Schneier, a security expert and another member of the working group, views CAPPS II and Secure Flight as examples that show how a poor understanding of what the systems must achieve can damage antiterror IT efforts. Schneier argues that even if a data mining system could be developed to scour through phone records or credit card transactions and identify terrorists with 99 percent accuracy, it still would not be of much use to investigators. More specifically, if 300 million Americans make just 10 phone calls or other identifiable transactions per day, that would produce over 1 trillion pieces of data each year that the government would have to mine. Even with a 99 percent accuracy rate, that would produce a billion false positives a year, or about 27 million a day. This would still mean missing transactions that would be made by terrorists. It came to no surprise to Schneier when *The New York Times* reported that hundreds of FBI agents were looking into thousands of data mining leads each month, with just about all of them turning out to be dead ends.

Despite the failures of CAPPS II, there is still a belief that data mining can be an effective tool against terrorism. One antiterrorism data mining that has been deemed successful is a link analysis system that has been used by investigators at Guantanamo Bay to determine which detainees were likely terrorists. The Army's Criminal Investigative Task Force (CITF) used a commercially available tool and reliable data about detainees such as where they were captured, who they associated with, and other details about their relationships and behaviors to construct a chart of all the detainees. Using a system called Proximity—a system developed by the University of Massachusetts—the CITF was able to calculate a probability that a given detainee was a terrorist or just a person in the wrong place at the wrong time.

The Guantanamo system was viewed as having a high accuracy rate because it had a limited scope and reliable data that was gathered by human investigators. It was a specific application used to solve a specific problem. Valdis Krebs, an IT consultant who developed a map connecting the 9/11 hijackers (after the fact) says that link analysis projects are useful only if they have a narrow scope. According to Krebs, "If you're just looking at the ocean, you'll find a lot of fish that look different. Are they terrorists or just some species you don't know about? If the government searched for only the activities mentioned above—emails, checks and plane tickets—without the added insight that one of the network's members was a terrorist, investigators would be more likely to uncover a high school reunion than a terrorist plot."

1. Why should the government consider developing a business case for antiterrorist data mining projects?

2. Could instituting IT governance save taxpayers money, improve the likelihood of success, and ensure privacy or civil liberties?

3. Develop an MOV for a link analysis data mining application that could be used to identify a terrorist traveling on an airline within the United States. Use the process for developing an MOV that was outlined in this chapter.

Adapted from Ben Worthen, IT Strategy: IT Versus Terror, *CIO Magazine, August 01, 2006.*

Wal-Mart's RFID Supply Chain

In 2003, Wal-Mart of Bentonville, Arkansas announced its vision for an RFID-enabled transparent supply chain. By January 1, 2005 the company decreed that its suppliers would be required to have a system in place for attaching radio frequency identification tags to a portion of its products destined for Wal-Mart stores. Unfortunately, as the deadline grew closer many of the company's suppliers knew that they were not going to be able to meet that deadline.

One supply chain executive, who wished to remain anonymous, said that his company would stick RFID tags on just enough pallets to satisfy Wal-Mart's mandate, but he's not even sure that those tags would work upon arrival because of technical problems. According to Patrick Sweeney, CEO of ODIN Technologies—a software and integration company working with several of Wal-Mart's top 100 suppliers—there are two camps. About 30 percent of Wal-Mart's suppliers will integrate RFID fully into their infrastructures now, while the rest will follow the practice of "slap and ship" like the supply chain executive mentioned above. As a result, the efficiencies Wal-Mart envisioned for the RFID supply chain may not be realized any time in the near future.

In addition, the mandate by Wal-Mart has become a moving target. Originally, only Wal-Mart's top suppliers were required to put RFID tags on all products shipped to specific distribution centers in Texas. Wal-Mart now wants its suppliers to attach tags to only 65 percent of their products. Several suppliers have confided that the percentage of their products shipped with RFID tags would be much lower—about 10 percent. The method of slap and ship will involve only a small percentage of products shipped to Texas, minimal data integration, and leave the supply chain blind to the movement of product. Not surprisingly, Simon Langford, Wal-Mart's manager of RFID strategy, says "[The slap and ship method] is something we sort of cringe at."

The anonymous supply chain executive also said, "We don't have a business case for RFID. Because the standards are not complete, the equipment isn't developed. And because the equipment isn't developed, I can't fulfill Wal-Mart's demand." In addition, Christine Overby, an RFID analyst at Forrester Research said, "Many of these consumer-packaged goods companies are really struggling with the business case. These are really costly projects, and they're hard to do with a technology that's a moving target."

The failure of the January 1 deadline for RFID could mean more bad press for the retail giant when it could use some positive publicity. Wal-Mart's reputation has recently become blemished because of allegations of unfair wage practices, hiring illegal immigrants, and discriminating against female employees. Many believe that Wal-Mart made a critical mistake when it imposed a top-down mandate on its suppliers before the technology and business needs matured to the point where RFID technology made good sense for Wal-Mart and its suppliers and customers.

Founded in 1999, MIT's Auto-ID Center began to look at how RFID technology could help organizations track and manage products using embedded sensors. The center proposed an electronic product code (EPC) that replaces bar codes by utilizing radio frequencies to identify computer chips placed in tags. In a controlled environment, RFID works quite well. Although tags can vary in size and shape, they can be affixed to cases and pallets as stickers or labels, or like thin plastic wrist bands. Each tag contains a small antenna and a chip with a unique string of numbers to identify each product. Active tags contain a battery, while the more common passive tags acquire their energy from a reader and are less expensive. Readers are antenna devices that identify the tags as they pass by. The tag transmits its digital electronic product code to the reader and then to a computer system.

The promise of RFID is to help reduce the number of products that are misplaced or misdirected in a supply chain. According to Paul Fox, director of external relations at Gillett, "There are countless millions of dollars tied up in warehousing because of the inefficiencies in the supply chain." He believes that RFID technology will tell Gillett "where the product is in our warehouses, what the product is and how much of it we have. No manual counting, no driving around, no question of mispicks, no order number mistakes. Once you get an accurate understanding of inventory position, that information becomes invaluable."

Before the year 2000, the price of RFID tags was about $1 to $2 apiece. Recently, the cost became as low as 25 to 75 cents, depending on the volume of the purchase. However, many suppliers contend that the price of an RFID tag must be even lower before they make economic sense. Assuming a cost of 40 cents per tag, a supplier that ships 15.6 million cases and pallets to Wal-Mart per year would spend about $7.6 million in RFID tags. Adding to the problem is Wal-Mart's one-size-fits all strategy, where there is no difference between such consumer products as razor blades, tires, or computers. Each pallet will require an RFID tag when shipped. Kara Romanow, an RFID analyst at AMR Research, calls this the "toilet paper and toothpaste problem." She says, "If you look at TVs, DVDs, and video games, the price tag doesn't matter. But when you're talking about TP and toothpaste, there is no tag cost at the case and pallet level that makes the numbers work."

Another problem with RFID is that no standard for the technology currently exists. Not all tags and readers are compatible. As a result, Wal-Mart may need more than one reader in its warehouses to read different tags. Moreover, the radio waves that are the foundation for the technology have not lived up to expectation in several pilots. One RFID technology provider wasn't getting a good read rate so their engineer kept increasing the power and adding more antennas. The read-rate still never got higher than 50 percent and one reader kept drowning out another reader. Radio frequency also tends to act abnormally when it's near certain elements like liquids, metals, or porous objects. Many believe that the next generation of tags that will supposedly be available in two years will overcome many of these problems. Unfortunately, no one is sure how much they will cost.

According to Wal-Mart executive vice president and CIO Linda Dillman, the business case is, "[RFID] will help us increase customer satisfaction in the near term, and ultimately pay an important role in helping us control costs and continue offering low prices. Moreover, Simon Langford believes that the RFID payback for Wal-Mart's suppliers will be twofold: First, it will help Wal-Mart's suppliers reduce their inventory, and second, sales will improve because Wal-Mart will always have its products in stock.

Some of Wal-Mart's suppliers need to consider some unpleasant alternatives. If they wait for RFID to mature, they can lower the costs of developing an RFID system that meets Wal-Mart's demands. However, by waiting they may jeopardize their relationship with Wal-Mart and open the door for their competitors to slip into their place. As a result, some are complying with the mandate via slap and ship. And what if many suppliers can't meet the deadline? Will this turn into more bad press for Wal-Mart?

1. How would having a clear MOV and business case help Wal-Mart and its suppliers decide whether an RFID supply chain makes good sense for everyone?

Adapted from Thomas Wailgum, Tag, You're Late, *CIO Magazine*, November 15, 2004.

 # BIBLIOGRAPHY

Billows, D. 1996. *Project and Program Management: People, Budgets, and Software*. Denver: The Hampton Group, Inc.

Cramm, S. (2001). Why You Should Follow the Fiduciary Model of IT Management. *CIO Magazine*. March 15.

Dragoon, A. (2003). Four Governance Best Practices. *CIO Magazine*. August 15.

Hildreth, S. (2005). IT Governance: Business in the Driver's Seat. *Computerworld*. October 17.

Kaplan, R. S. and D. Norton. 1992. The Balanced Scorecard: Measures that Drive Performance. *Harvard Business Review* (January–February): 71–79.

Kaplan, R. S. and D. Norton. 1993. Putting the Balanced Scorecard to Work. *Harvard Business Review* (September–October): 134–147.

Kerzner, H. 2000. *Applied Project Management: Best Practices on Implementation*. New York: John Wiley.

Marchewka, J. T. and M. Keil 1995. A Portfolio Theory Approach for Selecting and Managing IT Projects. *Information Resources Management Journal* 8: 5–14.

McFarlan, F. W. 1981. Portfolio Approach to Information Systems. *Harvard Business Review* (September–October).

Meredith, J. R. and S. J. Mantel, Jr. 2000. *Project Management: A Managerial Approach*. New York: John Wiley.

Melymuka, K. (1999). Here Comes the Project Office. *Computerworld*. August 2.

Meyer, D. (2005). What Does Governance Mean? *CIO Magazine*. February 28.

Porter, M. 1980. *Competitive Strategy*. New York: Free Press.

Porter, M. 1985. *Competitive Advantage*. New York: Free Press.

Project Management Institute (PMI). 2004. *A Guide to the Project Management Body of Knowledge (PMBOK® Guide)*. Newtown Square, PA: PMI Publishing.

Schmidt, M. J. 1999a. *The IT Business Case: Keys to Accuracy and Credibility*. Solution Matrix, Ltd.: www.solutionmatrix.com.

Schmidt, M. J. 1999b. *What's a Business Case? And Other Frequently Asked Questions*. Solution Matrix, Ltd.: www.solutionmatrix.com.

Schneiderman, A. M. 1999. Why Balanced Scorecards Fail. *Journal of Strategic Performance Management* (January): 6–12.

Smith, D. K. 1999. *Make Success Measurable*. New York: John Wiley.

Schwartz, K. D. (2007). ACB: An Introduction to IT Governance. *CIO Magazine*. May 22.

Weill, P. and Woodham, R. (2002). Don't Just Lead, Govern: Implementing Effective IT Governance. Center for Information Systems Research, Sloan School of Management. CISR WP No. 326 and 4247-02.

C H A P T E R

3

Developing the Project Charter and Baseline Project Plan

CHAPTER OBJECTIVES

Chapter 3 focuses on developing the project charter and project plan. After studying this chapter, you should understand and be able to:

- Describe the five project management processes and how they support each phase of the project life cycle.
- Define the project management knowledge area called project integration management and describe its role in project plan development, project plan execution, and overall change control.
- Develop a project charter and describe its relationship to the project plan.
- Identify the steps in the project planning framework introduced in this chapter and describe how this framework links the project's measurable organizational value (MOV) to the project's scope, schedule, and budget.

INTRODUCTION

Up to this point, we have looked at IT project management from a very high or strategic level. The first phase of the IT project management methodology focuses on conceptualizing and initializing the project. The primary deliverable or work effort of this phase is the development of a business case. The business case defines the project's goal and value to the organization and includes an analysis and feasibility of several alternatives. Moreover, the business case plays an important role in the project selection process by providing sufficient, reliable information to senior management so that a decision whether the organization should support and fund the project can be made.

The basic question when conceptualizing and initializing the project is, What is the value of this project to the organization? Making the right decision is critical. Abandoning a project that will provide little real value to an organization at this early stage will save a great deal of time, money, and frustration. On the other hand, failure to fund a project that has a great deal of potential value is an opportunity lost.

The development of the business case and its subsequent approval represents closure for the first phase of the IT project methodology and the beginning of the next. This second phase, Develop the Project Charter and Plan, requires the planning, creating, review, and acceptance of another project deliverable before considerable time, resources, and energy are committed. This requires a subtle yet important transition from a strategic mindset to a more tactical one that integrates a number of subplans to identify, coordinate, authorize, manage, and control the project work.

These subplans are separate plans for managing the project's scope, schedule, budget, quality, risk, and people. Together with the processes, methods, and tools defined in the project's methodology, all these areas come together to make up a project governance framework or project infrastructure. Unfortunately, the knowledge, tools, processes, and techniques required to develop a complete project plan cannot be presented in a single chapter. Therefore, the next several chapters will focus on human resources management, scope management, time management, cost management, and so forth that are integrated into a larger and more complete project plan.

Before we get to the details, this chapter provides an overview of the project planning process. This overview will include a more detailed discussion of the five project processes that were briefly introduced in Chapter 2 as part of the IT project methodology. More specifically, it explains how these processes are integrated with the various project management knowledge areas in order to support the development of the project's tactical plan. In fact, it will concentrate on one of the nine knowledge areas called project integration management.

The project charter and detailed project plan make up the project's tactical plan. The project charter defines the project infrastructure and identifies the project manager, the project team, the stakeholders, and the roles each will play within the project. In addition, the project charter formalizes the project's MOV, scope, supporting processes and controls, required resources, risks, and assumptions. This project infrastructure provides the foundation for developing a detailed project plan that answers four major questions: How much will the project cost? When will the project be finished? Who will be responsible for doing the work? And, what will we ultimately get at the end of the project?

In addition, a project planning framework will be introduced in this chapter that links the project's MOV to the project's scope, schedule, and budget. This framework outlines the steps necessary to create a detailed project plan so that management can determine whether the project's budget aligns with the cost analysis conducted in the business case. If the budget exceeds the overall cost envisioned in the business case, iterations to change the plan may be necessary to bring the project's scope, schedule, and budget in line. Cost cutting measures may require using less expensive resources or trade-offs in terms of reducing the scope and schedule. If the total cost of the project exceeds the expected organizational value, then the decision to cancel the project may be appropriate before more time, money, energy, and resources are committed to the next phase. However, once the project plan is approved, it then becomes the project's baseline plan that will be executed and used to benchmark actual progress.

PROJECT MANAGEMENT PROCESSES

The *PMBOK Guide*® defines a **process** as "a set of interrelated actions and activities that are performed to achieve a pre-specified set of products, results, or services" (38). In other words, a process is something you do to achieve a result. It may

QUICK THINKING—CREATING A PROJECT MANAGEMENT CULTURE

In many organizations, the project manager is held visibly accountable for ensuring that the project is delivered on time and within budget. In many cases, however, the project manager is not given any real authority over the project's resources. For example, many of the resources needed by the project manager may be controlled by several departments or business functions that will be released to the project on an as-needed basis. Without any formal authority, the project manager's power over these resources becomes de facto. The project manager's authority becomes pushed to the limit when the project team is distributed over multiple geographic locations. Many outsourcing projects face the same challenge.

In such cases, the project manager must rely on negotiation, persuasion, and team building, as well as the occasional use of threats or intimidation to make sure things get done. Supervisors or sponsors can fail to meet their project commitments and promises, but the project manager often is held accountable. This can be a challenge for even the most seasoned project managers. Inexperienced project managers often don't stand a chance.

These challenges require a cultural commitment to quality project management and delivery excellence. A project management culture is an environment where all of the project stakeholders share a commitment to the project's success and exhibit a healthy respect for the time and dollars spent on a project. Keane, Inc. developed six principles of productivity management for managing projects, regardless of project size or complexity. The six principles include:

1. *Define the job in detail*—The project manager must be able to draw a boundary around the project in order to define the personnel needed and their roles and responsibilities.

2. *Get the right people involved*—Project managers rarely get all the right people they need. Often the assignment of people to a project team is not a matter of their skill sets, but their availability. To overcome this issue, a project team must understand their responsibilities and assigned roles, but,

more importantly, they must believe that the success of the project is in their best interests.

3. *Estimate the time and costs*—In many projects, someone provides a short description of the project and then asks, How much will it cost? And how long will it take? These questions are often answered without really understanding what the project is all about or what resources are available. Therefore, dialog is important for setting realistic expectations that include various risks that can impact the project's estimates.

4. *Break the job down*—The project can be broken down into smaller jobs, with each job defining an area of difficulty, uncertainty, or opportunity in a document called the statement of work (SOW). The SOW then becomes a critical component of the project management culture as it functions as a contract between the project sponsor and project manager that specifies all promises and commitments.

5. *Establish a change procedure*—This should include rules and guidelines for managing and funding changes. This principle also holds people accountable for changes made when promises documented in the SOW are not kept.

6. *Agree on acceptance criteria*—This principle focuses on rules and guidelines for accepting work products or deliverables throughout the project. This can help avoid unpleasant surprises along the way, and the final acceptance of a finished and successful project becomes straightforward.

1. How do the six principles help establish a project management culture in an organization?

2. How can a project charter help define a project manager's authority over resources not under his or her direct control?

SOURCE: Adapted from Bob Wyatt, Building a Project Management Culture, *Computerworld*, October 4, 2004.

involve some kind of input as well as directions, tools, or techniques to change the input to the desired output or result. For example, if you wanted to bake a cake, you would need specific inputs (ingredients such as flour, eggs, etc.), tools (oven, mixing bowls, mixer, etc.), and directions (a recipe). This whole process could be subdivided into subprocesses such as a mixing process, baking process, measuring process, and decorating process. If this was the first time you had baked a cake, you might follow the recipe directions to the letter in terms of mixing the ingredients and

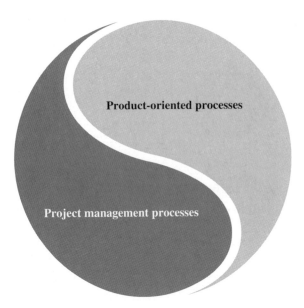

Figure 3.1   Project Processes

baking time. However, with experience you may experiment with the ingredients to produce a cake that is more to your liking and learn when the cake should come out of the oven—a little early or when it needs just another minute or two.

Similarly, processes are an integral component of project management. They support all of the activities necessary to plan, create, and manage all of the project activities. **Project management processes** help initiate, plan, execute, monitor and control, and close a project as well as interact with the project management knowledge areas. In Chapter 2, for example, you were introduced to a project management process for developing a business case and another for developing a project's MOV. If you were a caterer hired to bake a wedding cake, project management processes would be needed to define, plan, estimate the cost, and deliver a cake that meets your customer's expectations, budget, and needs while being profitable for you.

On the other hand, **product-oriented processes** can be thought of as development processes that focus on the tangible results of the project. For an IT project, this would be all of the processes required to design, build, test, document, and implement an application system. Just like baking a cake, product-oriented processes require specific domain knowledge, tools, and techniques to complete the work. Otherwise, this could result in a poor cake or an information system that is a technical failure.

An emphasis or sole focus on project management processes does not provide an ability to develop a quality product, regardless of whether it is a cake or information system. However, focusing on the product-oriented processes may not provide the management or controls to ensure that the delivered cake or information system meets the expectations or needs of the intended customer or user. As Figure 3.1 illustrates, there must be a balance or harmony between project management processes and product-oriented processes in order to complete a project successfully. As one's experience grows, processes may not have to be applied the same way on all projects. The situation at hand will dictate the appropriateness of how each process should be applied.

Project Management Process Groups

While the project life and systems development life cycles define the phases of a project, five process groups define appropriate processes for managing the project by function or the kind of work that needs to be done. As illustrated in Figure 3.2, the process groups overlap within and between the phases of the project as the output of one process group within a phase becomes the input for a process group in the next phase.

Initiating   The initiating process group signals the beginning of the project or a phase. For example, an organization may initiate a project by requiring the development of a business case as part of its IT governance or as part of its IT project methodology. During this phase, a set of project management processes would define how the project and the first phase of the methodology should be initiated. The

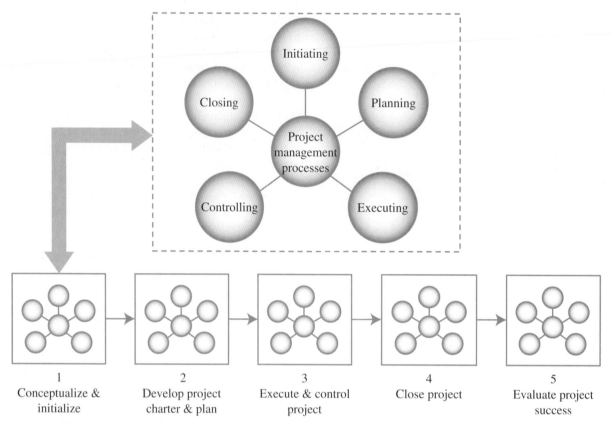

Figure 3.2 Project Management Processes and ITPM Phases

approval of the business case would then provide an authorization to start another set of processes to begin the second phase of the IT project methodology in order to develop the project charter and plan. Although all of the phases of the project should have some type of initiating process, the first phases of the IT project methodology would require the most detail and attention.

Planning   The planning process group supports planning of the entire project and each individual phase. Supporting project management processes may include scope planning, activity planning, resource planning, cost estimating, schedule estimating, and procurement planning. The planning process should be in line with the size and complexity of the project—that is, larger, more complex projects may require a greater planning effort than smaller, less complex projects. Planning processes are most important during the second phase of the IT project methodology when the project charter and plan are developed. However, planning processes can be important for each phase whereby objectives and activities may need to be defined or refined as new information becomes available. In addition, planning is often an iterative process. A project manager may develop a project plan, but senior management or the client may not approve the scope, budget, or schedule. Or circumstances may arise that warrant changes to the project plan. This could happen as the result of a competitor's actions or legislation (external), or even changes to the project team or sponsor (internal).

Executing Once a project phase has been approved and planned, the executing process group focuses on integrating people and resources to carry out the planned activities of the project plan or phase. During the execute and control phase of the IT project methodology, the product-oriented processes play an important role in developing the IT solution. For example, software engineering processes, tools, and methods for developing and/or implementing a system become critical for delivering the project's end result. Project management processes such as quality assurance, risk management, and team development play an important supporting role. Although executing processes are part of every project phase, the majority of executing processes will occur during the execute and control phase of the IT project methodology.

Monitoring and Controlling The monitoring and controlling process group allows for managing and measuring progress toward the project's MOV and scope, schedule, budget, and quality objectives. Monitoring and controlling processes also allow the project manager and team to measure and keep an eye on project variances between actual and planned results so that appropriate corrective actions can be taken when necessary. Supporting project management processes include scope control, change control, schedule control, budget control, quality control, and a communications plan. The emphasis of monitoring and controlling processes will occur during the execution and control phase of the IT project methodology.

Closing The closing process group provides a set of processes for formally accepting the project's product, service, or end result so that the project or phase can be brought to an orderly close. The project manager or team must verify that all deliverables have been satisfactorily completed before the project sponsor accepts a phase's deliverable or the project's end product. Closure of a project may include processes for *contract closure* and *administrative closure*. Contract closure ensures that all of the deliverables and agreed upon terms of the project have been completed and delivered so that the project can end. It allows resources to be reassigned and settlement or payment of any account. Administrative closure, on the other hand, involves documenting and archiving all project documents. It also includes processes for evaluating the project in terms of whether it achieved its MOV. Lessons learned should be documented and made available to other teams. Although each phase must include closing processes, the major emphasis on closing processes will occur during the close project and evaluate project success phases of the IT project methodology.

PROJECT INTEGRATION MANAGEMENT

The *PMBOK Guide®* views project integration management as one of the most important knowledge areas because it coordinates the other eight knowledge areas and all of the project management processes throughout the project life cycle. As Rita Mulcahy (2005) points out, it is the project team's responsibility to focus on completing the project work while the project sponsor should be protecting the project from unnecessary changes and loss of resources. However, the project manager or leader's role should be "to put all the pieces of the project together in a cohesive whole that gets the project done faster, cheaper, and with fewer resources while meeting project objectives" (85). According to the *PMBOK Guide®*:

> Integration, in the context of managing a project, is making choices
> about where to concentrate resources and effort on any given day,

anticipating potential issues, dealing with these issues before they become critical, and coordinating work for the overall project good. The integration effort also involves making trade-offs among competing objectives and alternatives. (77)

In many ways, integration is the job of the project manager. For example, let's say that you estimate that a database analyst assigned to your project will require two weeks to create a set of tables. However, right before the analyst is to begin her assigned task, she decides to take a job in another city. Your role as the project manager is to ensure that the project stays on track. This may entail recruiting another database analyst (human resource management), who will be paid a higher salary (cost management) and will now take four weeks (time management) to complete the assignment (Very few individuals are "plug and play." They will need time to assimilate in their new job and surroundings). Hopefully, their work will meet specific database design standards (quality management), but then this could all be overly optimistic (risk management). As you can see, project management processes and knowledge areas are interdependent. An experienced project manager knows there is no single way to manage a project. Project management knowledge, skills, and processes must be combined and applied in different ways in order to meet the project's goal and objectives.

Therefore, an understanding of the integrative nature of projects is especially critical in developing the project plan when all the knowledge areas and project and product-oriented processes must be brought together in order to produce a realistic and usable project plan. The *PMBOK Guide®* outlines seven processes for Project Integration Management:

1. *Develop the project charter*—The project charter is a document that formally authorizes the project and gives specific authority to the project manager to apply organizational resources to the project tasks or activities. In fact, the *PMBOK Guide®* stresses that a project cannot be started without a project charter. Although the project manager may not have been assigned when the business case was proposed, it is critical that he or she be named in the project charter.

2. *Develop the preliminary scope statement*—Think of the preliminary scope statement as the first iteration or draft of what the project must deliver. This may include project deliverables such as the project plan and the high-level features and functionality of the application system. The preliminary scope statement can be provided by the project sponsor or by having the project team interview key project stakeholders. At this point, the project team needs to "size" the project, i.e., is this a big project? Or a little project? Or something in between? Detailed features of the system (such as should the date be on the left or right hand side of the screen?) are not needed at this point. Those details will be specified when the project team completes the analysis of the detailed user requirements later on when implementing the SDLC. At this point, only enough detail is needed to plan the project activities in order to derive a project schedule and budget.

3. *Develop the project management plan*—The project management plan is a document that details how the project will be executed, monitored, controlled, and closed. Although the project plan may evolve and change over the course of the project life cycle, it becomes the day-to-day tool that outlines how the project goal and objectives will be met. All subsidiary plans

such as a scope management plan, risk management plan, and communications plan are integrated into the project management plan.

4. *Direct and manage project execution*—The project manager accomplishes the project management plan by integrating all of the project processes into one coordinated effort. Here the project work is carried out to complete the project's scope.

5. *Monitor and control project work*—During the execution process, effort and resources will be expended to accomplish the project goal and objectives. Therefore, *corrective actions* may be necessary from time to time when the project's performance strays from the project management plan. On the other hand, *preventive actions* are sometimes necessary when the project team thinks or believes deviations from the project plan are likely. Corrective actions are reactive, while preventive actions are proactive. In addition, *defect repair* and rework may be necessary when project deliverables or processes do not meet quality standards.

6. *Integrated change control*—Change is inevitable during the entire project life cycle. Some approaches to project management and systems development embrace change, while other approaches may not embrace change as well. Regardless, change control processes must be in place so that all proposed changes can be documented, reviewed, and decided upon. Then corrective, preventive, or defect repairs can be made effectively and efficiently. In most circumstances, proposed changes will impact the project's scope, schedule, budget, and quality objectives. As a result, changes should be incorporated into the project management plan.

7. *Close the project*—As described in the previous section, this includes both administrative and contract closure procedures to ensure that closure is brought to the project or project phase. Regardless of whether a project ends as planned or prematurely, a project should be closed out using the close project process.

In the next section, you will learn how the project process groups and project integration knowledge area combine to create the project charter.

THE PROJECT CHARTER

The **project charter** and baseline project plan provide a project governance framework for carrying out or executing the IT project. More specifically, the project charter serves as an agreement or contract between the project sponsor and project team—documenting the project's MOV, defining its infrastructure, summarizing the project plan details, defining roles and responsibilities, showing project commitments, and explaining project control mechanisms.

- *Documenting the project's MOV*—Although the project's MOV was included in the business case, it is important that the MOV be clearly defined and agreed upon before developing or executing the project plan. At this point, the MOV must be cast in stone. Once agreed upon, the MOV for a project should not change. As you will see, the MOV drives the project planning process and is fundamental for all project-related decisions.

- *Defining the project infrastructure*—The project charter defines all of the people, resources, technology, methods, project management processes, and knowledge areas that are required to support the project. In short, the project charter will detail everything needed to carry out the project. Moreover, this infrastructure must not only be in place, but must also be taken into account when developing the project plan. For example, knowing who will be on the project team and what resources will be available to them can help the project manager estimate the amount of time a particular task or set of activities will require. It makes sense that a highly skilled and experienced team member with adequate resources should require less time to complete a certain task than an inexperienced person with inadequate resources. Keep in mind, however, that you can introduce risk to your project plan if you develop your estimates based upon the abilities of your best people. If one of these individuals should leave sometime during the project, you may have to replace them with someone less skilled or experienced. As a result, you will either have to revise your estimates or face the possibility of the project exceeding its deadline.

- *Summarizing the details of the project plan*—The project charter should summarize the scope, schedule, budget, quality objectives, deliverables, and milestones of the project. It should serve as an important communication tool that provides a consolidated source of information about the project that can be referenced throughout the project life cycle.

- *Defining roles and responsibilities*—The project charter should not only identify the project sponsor, project manager, and project team, but also when and how they will be involved throughout the project life cycle. In addition, the project charter should specify the lines of reporting and who will be responsible for specific decisions.

- *Showing explicit commitment to the project*—In addition to defining the roles and responsibilities of the various stakeholders, the project charter should detail the resources to be provided by the project sponsor and specify clearly who will take ownership of the project's product once the project is completed. Approval of the project charter gives the project team the formal authority to begin work on the project.

- *Setting out project control mechanisms*—Changes to the project's scope, schedule, and budget will undoubtedly be required over the course of the project. But, the project manager can lose control and the project team can lose its focus if these changes are not managed properly. Therefore, the project charter should outline a process for requesting and responding to proposed changes.

In general, the project charter and project plan should be developed together—the details of the project plan need to be summarized in the project charter, and the infrastructure outlined in the project charter will influence the estimates used in developing the project plan. It is the responsibility of the project manager to ensure that the project charter and plan are developed, agreed upon, and approved. Like the business case, the project charter and plan should be developed with both the project team and the project sponsor to ensure that the project will support the organization and that the goal and objective of the project are realistic and achievable.

What Should Be in a Project Charter?

The framework for a project charter should be based on the project management knowledge areas. Although the formality and depth of developing a project charter

QUICK THINKING—THE PROJECT SPONSOR

According to Gopal Kapur, president of the Center for Project Management, "Sponsorship is not a spectator sport." A project sponsor should be an executive or manager with financial authority, political clout, and a personal commitment to the project. An effective sponsor is critical to the success of an IT project. Although no formal job description exists for a project sponsor, most agree that the project sponsor must provide leadership and direction, as well as political protection and problem-resolution skills. The project sponsor "champions" by:

- Empowering the project manager
- Ensuring sustained "buy in" from other project stakeholders
- Clearing political and organizational roadblocks
- Ensuring the availability of resources
- Reviewing the project's progress
- Approving plans, schedules, budgets, and deliverables
- Ensuring that the project's goal is realized

However, as Gopal Kapur explains, "Of all the items that can go wrong on a project, the one the project manager has the least control over is the sponsorship." Often when an IT project experiences problems, there's a good chance the sponsor is to blame.

1. Why is a good project sponsor or champion so important to the success of an IT project?
2. How could a project manager or team handle a situation where the project sponsor leaves the organization to take a job with another company?
3. How should a project manager handle a project sponsor who is either incompetent or loses interest in the project and withdraws?

SOURCE: Adapted from Bart Perkins, Executive Sponsors: What They Really Do, *Computerworld*, September 12, 2005; Kathleen Melymuka, Project Management: Surviving the Sponsor Exit, *Computerworld*, February 16, 2004; Kathleen Melymuka, Firing Your Project Sponsor *Computerworld*, February 23, 2004.

will most likely depend on the size and complexity of the project, the fundamental project management and product-development processes and areas should be addressed and included for all projects. This section presents an overview of the typical areas that may go into a project charter; however, organizations and project managers should adapt the project charter based on best practices, experience, and the project itself.

Project Identification It is common for all projects to have a unique name or a way to identify them. It is especially necessary if an organization has several projects underway at once. Naming a project can also give the project team and stakeholders a sense of identity and ownership. Often organizations will use some type of acronym for the project's name. For example, instead of naming a project something as mundane as the Flight Reservation System in 1965, American Airlines named its system Semi-Automated Business Research Environment (SABRE). Today, SABRE has become a well recognized product that connects travel agents and online customers with all of the major airlines, car rental companies, hotels, railways, and cruise lines.

Project Stakeholders It is important that the project charter specifically name the project sponsor and the project manager. This reduces the likelihood of confusion when determining who will take ownership of the project's product and who will be the leader of the project. In addition, the project team should be named along with their titles or roles in the project, their phone numbers, and email addresses. This section should describe who will be involved in the project, how they will be involved, and when they will be involved. Formal reporting relationships can be specified and may be useful on larger projects. In addition, including telephone numbers and email addresses can provide a handy directory for getting in touch with the various participants.

Project Description   The project charter should be a single source of information. Therefore, it may be useful to include a description of the project to help someone unfamiliar with the project understand not only the details, but the larger picture as well. This may include a brief overview or background of the project as to the problem or opportunity that became a catalyst for the project and the reason or purpose for taking on the project. It may also be useful to include the vision of the organization or project and how it aligns with the organization's goal and strategy. Much of this section could summarize the total benefits expected from the project that were described in the business case. It is important that the project description focus on the business and not the technology.

Measurable Organizational Value (MOV)   The MOV should be clear, concise, agreed on, and made explicit to all of the project stakeholders. Therefore, the project's MOV should be highlighted and easily identifiable in the project charter.

Project Scope   The project's scope is the work to be completed. A specific section of the project charter should clarify not only what will be produced or delivered by the project team, but what will not be part of the project's scope. This distinction is important for two reasons. First, it provides the foundation for developing the project plan's schedule and cost estimates. Changes to the project's scope will impact the project's schedule and budget—that is, if resources are fixed, expanding the amount of work you have to complete will take more time and money. Therefore, the creation of additional work for the project team will extend the project's schedule and invariably increase the cost of the project. Formal procedures must be in place to control and manage the project's scope. Secondly, it is important for the project manager to manage the expectations of the project sponsor and the project team. By making the project's scope explicit as to what is and what is not to be delivered, the likelihood of confusion and misunderstanding is reduced.

For example, the project team and several users may have several discussions regarding the scope of a project. One user may suggest that the system should allow for the download of reports to a wireless personal digital assistant (PDA). After discussing this idea in depth, management may decide that the cost and time to add this wireless PDA capability would not be in the organization's best interest. In this case, it would be a good idea to state explicitly in the project charter that wireless PDA capability will not be part of the project's scope. Although *you* may be clear on this issue, others may still have different expectations. The project's scope should, therefore, define key deliverables and/or high-level descriptions of the information system's functionality. The details of the system's features and functionality will, however, be determined later in the systems development life cycle when the project team conducts an information requirements analysis.

At this point, a first attempt is made to define the project's scope and is based on information provided by the project sponsor. Only enough detail is needed to plan the project so that estimates for the project schedule and budget can be defined. This may include a high-level view of the project and product deliverables and the criteria for their acceptance by the project sponsor. Detailed system requirements will be specified later on during the execution phase of the project when the SDLC is carried out.

The scope defined in the project charter can take the form of a narrative description of the products or services produced by the project. This narrative is often called the **statement of work** (SOW). The SOW can be developed by the project sponsor or by interviewing key stakeholders conducted by the project team.

Project Schedule   Although the details of the project's schedule will be in the project plan, it is important to summarize the detail of the plan with respect to the expected start and completion dates. In addition, expected dates for major deliverables, milestones, and phases should be highlighted and summarized at a very high level.

Project Budget   A section of the project charter should highlight the total cost of the project. The total cost of the project should be summarized directly from the project plan.

Quality Issues   Although a quality management plan should be in place to support the project, a section that identifies any known or required quality standards should be made explicit in the project charter. For example, an application system's reports may have to meet a government agency's requirements.

Resources   Because the project charter acts as an agreement or contract, it may be useful to specify the resources required and who is responsible for providing those resources. Resources may include people, technology, or facilities to support the project team. It would be somewhat awkward for a team of consultants to arrive at the client's organization and find that the only space available for them to work is a corner table in the company cafeteria! Therefore, explicitly outlining the resources needed and who is responsible for what can reduce the likelihood for confusion or misunderstanding.

Assumptions and Risks   Any risks or assumptions should be documented in the project charter. Assumptions may include things that must go right, such as a particular team member being available for the project, or specific criteria used in developing the project plan estimates. Risks, on the other hand, may be thought of as anything that can go wrong or things that may impact the success of the project. Although a risk management plan should be in place to support the project team, the project charter should summarize the following potential impacts:

- *Key situations or events that could significantly impact the project's scope, schedule, or budget*—These risks, their likelihood, and the strategy to overcome or minimize their impact should be detailed in the project's risk plan.

- *Any known constraints that may be imposed by the organization or project environment*—Known constraints may include such things as imposed deadlines, budgets, or required technology tools or platforms.

- *Dependencies on other projects internal or external to the organization*—In most cases, an IT project is one of several being undertaken by an organization. Subsequently, dependencies between projects may exist, especially if different application systems or technology platforms must be integrated. It may also be important to describe the project's role in relation to other projects.

- *Impacts on different areas of the organization*—As described in Chapter 1, IT projects operate in a broader environment than the project itself. As a result, the development and implementation of an IT solution will have an impact on the organization. It is important to describe how the project will impact the organization in terms of disruption, downtime, or loss of productivity.

- *Any outstanding issues*—It is important to highlight any outstanding issues that need further resolution. These may be issues identified by the project sponsor, the project manager, or the project team that must be addressed and agreed upon at some point during the project. They may include such things as resources to be provided or decisions regarding the features or functionality of the system.

Project Administration   Project administration focuses on the knowledge areas, processes, and controls that will support the project. These are actually separate subplans or strategies that make up the project management plan. Administration may include:

- A *communications plan* that outlines how the project's status or progress will be reported to various stakeholders. This plan also includes a process for reporting and resolving significant issues or problems as they arise.
- A *scope management plan* that describes how changes to the project's scope will be submitted, logged, and reviewed.
- A *quality management plan* that details how quality planning, assurance, and control will be supported throughout the project life cycle. In addition, a plan for testing the information system will be included.
- A *change management and implementation plan* that will specify how the project's product will be integrated into the organizational environment.
- A *human resources plan* for staff acquisition and team development.

Acceptance and Approval   Since the project charter serves as an agreement or contract between the project sponsor and project team, it may be necessary to have key stakeholders sign off on the project charter. By signing the document, the project stakeholder shows formal acceptance of the project and, therefore, gives the project manager and team the authority to carry out the project plan.

References   In developing the project charter and plan, the project manager may use a number of references. It is important to document these references in order to add credibility to the project charter and plan, as well as to provide a basis for supporting certain processes, practices, or estimates.

Terminology   Many IT projects use certain terms or acronyms that may be unfamiliar to many people. Therefore, to reduce complexity and confusion, it may be useful to include a glossary giving the meaning of terms and acronyms, allowing all the project's stakeholders to use a common language. Figure 3.3 provides a template for a project charter. Feel free to adapt this template as needed.

PROJECT PLANNING FRAMEWORK

In this section, a project planning framework will be introduced. This framework is part of the IT project methodology and provides the steps and processes necessary to develop the detailed project plan that will support the project's MOV.

Project Name or Identification

Project Stakeholders

- Names
- Titles or roles
- Phone numbers
- E-mail addresses

Project Description

- Background
- Description of the challenge or opportunity
- Overview of the desired impact

Measurable Organizational Value (MOV)

- Statement or table format

Project Scope

- What will be included in the scope of this project
- What will be considered outside the scope of this project

Project Schedule Summary

- Project start date
- Project end date
- Timeline of project phases and milestones
- Project reviews and review dates

Project Budget Summary

- Total project budget
- Budget broken down by phase

Quality Issues

- Specific quality requirements

Resources Required

- People

- Technology
- Facilities
- Other
- Resources to be provided
    - Resource
    - Name of resource provider
    - Date to be provided

Assumptions and Risks

- Assumptions used to develop estimates
- Key risks, probability of occurrence, and impact
- Constraints
- Dependencies on other projects or areas within or outside the organization
- Assessment project's impact on the organization
- Outstanding issues

Project Administration

- Communications plan
- Scope management plan
- Quality management plan
- Change management plan
- Human resources plan
- Implementation and project closure plan

Acceptance and Approval

- Names, signatures, and dates for approval

References

Terminology or Glossary

Appendices (as required)

Figure 3.3   Project Charter Template

A project plan attempts to answer the following questions:

- *What* needs to be done?
- *Who* will do the work?
- *When* will they do the work?
- *How long* will it take?
- *How much* will it cost?

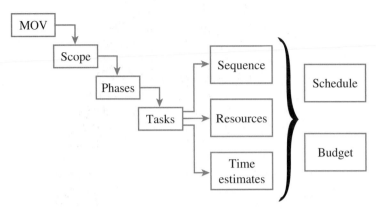

Figure 3.4   The Project Planning Framework—Defining the MOV

The project planning framework illustrated in Figure 3.4 consists of several steps and processes. We will now focus on each of these steps to show how the project's schedule and budget are derived.

The MOV

The first step of the project planning framework entails finalizing the definition of and agreement on the project's measurable organizational value, or MOV. Although an indepth discussion of a project's MOV was provided in Chapter 2, it is important here to focus on a few salient points. First, the project's MOV must be defined and agreed on before proceeding to the other steps of the project planning framework. The project's MOV provides a direct link to the organization's strategic mission; however, as Figure 3.4 illustrates, a project's MOV links directly to the project plan. Therefore, a project's MOV acts as a bridge between the strategic mission and objectives of the organization and the project plans of individual projects it undertakes. The MOV guides many of the decisions related to scope, schedule, budget, and resources throughout the project's life cycle.

Define the Project's Scope

Once the project's MOV has been defined and agreed upon, the organization must make a commitment, in terms of time and resources, to define the project's scope in order to estimate the project's schedule and budget. Scope includes the products or services to be provided by the project and includes all of the project deliverables. One can think of scope as the work that needs to be completed in order to achieve the project's MOV. Project scope management is covered in more detail in the next chapter; however, the basic processes include:

- *Planning*—The project team must develop a detailed scope statement that defines the work to be included, as well as the work not to be included in the project plan. The scope statement will be used to guide future project-related decisions and to set stakeholder expectations.

- *Definition*—The project's scope must be organized into smaller and more manageable packages of work. These work packages will require resources and time to complete. This may include more detail than the preliminary scope statement in the project charter.

- *Verification*—Once the project's scope has been defined, the project team and stakeholders must verify it to ensure that the work completed will in fact support the project in achieving its MOV.

- *Change Control*—Controls must be in place to manage proposed changes to the project's scope. Scope changes can either move the project closer to its MOV or result in increased work that drains the project's budget and causes the project to exceed its scheduled deadline. Proper scope control procedures can ensure that the project stays on track.

Subdivide the Project into Phases

Once the project's scope has been defined and verified, the work of the project can be organized into phases and subphases in order to complete all of the project's deliverables. **Phases** are logical stages that organize the project work to reduce complexity and risk. In many cases, it is easier to focus and concentrate the project team's effort on the pieces instead of the whole; however, it is important to keep an eye on the big picture.

Each phase of the project should focus on providing at least one specific project **deliverable**—that is, a tangible and verifiable piece of work. Examples of deliverables include the business case, the project plan, and, most important, the project's product—the information system to be developed or software package to be implemented. In addition, a **milestone** is a significant event or achievement that provides evidence that the deliverable, phase, or subphase has been completed and accepted by the project sponsor.

Phases are largely determined by the project methodology and the approach chosen for carrying out the systems development life cycle (SDLC). As discussed in Chapter 1, the SDLC can be implemented by using a more structured approach, such as the waterfall method, or by using a more iterative approach. The selection of an approach to implement the SDLC is an important decision that will affect not only how the system will be developed and implemented, but to a large degree outline the phases, deliverables, and tasks defined in the project plan. The appropriate decision depends on how quickly the system needs to be delivered as well as how well defined and stable the requirements of the system will remain throughout the project life cycle (DeCarlo 2004). For example, the waterfall model would be more appropriate for a project where the requirements are well understood and complex, but it would not be appropriate for a project following the eXtreme project management paradigm (DeCarlo 2004; McConnell 1996). On the other hand, an iterative approach for carrying out the SDLC would be more appropriate where the project is characterized by uncertainty, change, and tight deadlines.

Tasks—Sequence, Resources, and Time Estimates

Once the project is divided into phases, tasks are then identified. A **task** may be thought of as a specific activity or unit of work to be completed. Examples of some tasks in an IT project may be to interview a particular user, write a program, or test links in a Web page. When considering tasks, it is important to consider sequences, resources, and time.

Sequence Some tasks may be linear—that is, have to be completed in a particular sequence—while others can be completed in parallel—that is at the same time.

Performing parallel tasks often provides an opportunity to shorten the overall length of the project. For example, assume that a project has two tasks—A and B. Task A will require only one day to complete; task B requires two days. If these tasks are completed one after the other, the project will finish in three days. On the other hand, if these tasks are performed in parallel, the length of the project will be two days. In this case, the length of the project is determined by the time it takes to complete the longest task (i.e., task B). This simple example illustrates two important points: (1) A project is constrained by the longest tasks, and (2) any opportunity to perform tasks in parallel can shorten the project schedule.

Resources   Resources on an IT project may include such things as technology, facilities (e.g., meeting rooms), and people. Tasks require resources, and there is a cost associated with using a resource. The use of a resource may be accounted for by using a per-use charge or on a prorated basis—that is, a charge for the time you use that resource. For example, a developer earns $50,000 a year and is assigned to work on a task that takes one day to complete. The cost of completing that particular task would be prorated as $191 (assuming an eight-hour, five-day work week).

Time   It will take a resource a specific amount of time to complete a task. The longer it takes a resource to complete a specific task, however, the longer the project will take to finish and the more it will cost. For example, if we plan on assigning our developer who earns $50,000 a year to a task that takes two days, then we would estimate the cost of completing that task to be approximately $400. If the developer completes the task in one-half the time, then the cost of doing that task will be about $200. Moreover, if the developer were then free to start the next task, our schedule would then be ahead by one day. Unfortunately, the reverse is true. If we thought the task would take two days to complete (at a cost of $400) and it took the developer three days to complete, the project would be one day behind schedule and $200 over budget. However, if two tasks could be performed in parallel, with our developer working on Task A (one day) and another $50,000/year-developer working on Task B (two days), then even if Task A takes two days, our project schedule would not be impacted—as long as the developer working on Task B completes the task within the estimated two days. While this parallel work may save our schedule, our budget will still be $200 over budget because task A took twice as long to complete. Understanding this relationship among tasks, resources, and time will be important when developing the project plan and even more important later if it is necessary to adjust the project plan in order to meet schedule or budget constraints.

Schedule and Budget—The Baseline Plan

The detailed project plan is an output of the project planning framework. Once the tasks are identified and their sequence, resources required, and time to complete estimated, it is a relatively simple step to determine the project's schedule and budget. All of this information can be entered into a project management software package that can determine the start and end dates for the project, as well as the final cost.

Once completed, the project plan should be reviewed by the project manager, the project sponsor, and the project team to make sure it is complete, accurate, and, most important, able to achieve the project's MOV. Generally, the project plan will go through several iterations as new information becomes known or if there are compromises with respect to scope, schedule, and budget. In addition, many of the details of the project plan are summarized in the project charter in order to provide a clearer picture as to how the plan will be carried out. Once the project plan is approved, it becomes the baseline plan that will serve as a benchmark to measure and gauge the project's progress. The project manager will use this baseline plan to compare the actual schedule to the estimated schedule and the actual costs to budgeted costs.

THE KICK-OFF MEETING

Once the project charter and project plan are approved, many organizations have a **kick-off meeting** to officially start work on the project. The kick-off meeting is useful for several reasons. First, it brings closure to the planning phase of the project and signals the initiation of the next phase of the IT project methodology. Second, it is a way of communicating to everyone what the project is all about. Many kick-off meetings take on a festive atmosphere in order to energize the stakeholders and get them enthusiastic about working on the project. It is important that everyone start working on the project with a positive attitude. How the project is managed from here on will determine largely whether that positive attitude carries through.

CHAPTER SUMMARY

Processes are important to project management because they support all of the activities needed to develop and manage the development of an IT solution. Product-oriented processes focus on the development of the application system itself and require specific domain knowledge, tools, and techniques. On the other hand, project management processes are needed to manage and coordinate all of the activities of the project. A balance of both product-oriented processes and project management processes is needed; otherwise, the result may be a solution that is a technical success but an organizational failure. In addition, five project management process groups were introduced that support both the project and each phase of the project. These include: (1) initiating, (2) planning, (3) executing, (4) controlling, and (5) closing.

Project integration management is one of the most important Project Management Body of Knowledge areas. Its purpose is to coordinate and integrate the other knowledge areas and project processes. Project integration management processes focus on (1) develop project charter, (2) develop preliminary project scope statement, (3) develop project management plan, (4) direct and manage project execution, (5) monitor and control project work, (6) integrated change control, and (7) close project.

The project charter serves as an agreement and as a communication tool for all of the project stakeholders. The project charter documents the project's MOV and describes the infrastructure needed to support the project. In addition, the project charter summarizes many of the details found in the project plan. A well written project charter should provide a consolidated source of information about the project and reduce the likelihood of confusion and misunderstanding. In general, the project charter and project plan should be developed together—the details of the project plan need to be summarized in the project charter, and the infrastructure outlined in the project charter will influence the estimates used to develop the project plan.

The project plan provides the details of the tactical plan that answers these questions: What needs to be done? Who will do the work? When will they do the work? How long will it take? How much will it cost?

A project planning framework was introduced and recommended a series of steps to follow in order to develop a detailed project plan. The details with respect to carrying out these steps will be the focus of subsequent chapters. Once the project charter and plan are approved, the project plan serves as a baseline plan that will allow the project manager to track and access the project's actual progress to the original plan. A kick-off meeting usually brings closure to the second phase of the IT project methodology and allows the project team to begin the work defined in the plan.

REVIEW QUESTIONS

1. What are project management processes? Give one example.

2. What are product-oriented processes? Give one example.

3. Why must a balance exist between project management processes and product-oriented processes?

4. Describe the initiating processes. Give one example of an initiating process to support a particular phase of the IT project methodology.

5. Describe the planning process. Give one example of a planning process to support a particular phase of the IT project methodology.

6. Describe the executing process. Give one example of an executing process to support a particular phase of the IT project methodology.

7. Describe the controlling process. Give one example of a controlling process to support a particular phase of the IT project methodology.

8. Describe the closing process. Give one example of a closing process to support a particular phase of the IT project methodology.

9. Describe how the output of project management process groups in one phase becomes the input or catalyst for the process group in the next phase. Provide an example.

10. What is the difference between contract closure and administrative closure?

11. Describe project integration management and its relationship to the other Project Management Body of Knowledge areas.

12. Describe project plan development and its importance to the second phase of the IT project methodology.

13. Describe project plan execution and its importance to project plan development.

14. Describe overall change control and its importance to the project team.

15. What is the purpose of a project charter?

16. Why can a project charter serve as an agreement or a contract?

17. Why is a project charter a useful communication tool?

18. Why should the project charter and project plan be developed together?

19. How does the project charter support the project plan?

20. How does the project plan support the project charter?

21. Describe the project planning framework.

22. Why is it important that the project's MOV be cast in stone?

23. Describe how the project's MOV supports the development of the project's scope, schedule, and budget.

24. What is a project's scope?

25. Why should a project be divided into phases?

26. What is a deliverable? What is the relationship between phases and deliverables?

27. What is a milestone? Why are milestones useful?

28. What is a task? Provide three examples of some typical tasks in an IT project.

29. What impact can the sequence of tasks have on a project's schedule?

30. How can resources impact the schedule of a project?

31. What is a baseline plan? What purpose does it serve once the project team begins to execute the project plan?

32. What is a kick-off meeting? What purpose does it serve?

EXTEND YOUR KNOWLEDGE

1. You have just been hired by a local swim team to develop a Web site. This Web site will be used to provide information to boys and girls between the ages of 6 and 18 who are interested in joining the team. In addition, the Web site will provide information about practices and the swim meet schedule for the season. The team would also like to be able to post the meet results. The head coach of the swim team is the project sponsor. He would also like the Web site to include pictures of the three assistant coaches and of the different swimmers at swim meets and practice. The swim team is

supported largely by an association of parents who help run the swim meets and work the concession stand. Several of the parents have asked that a volunteer schedule be part of the Web site so that the parent volunteers can see when they are scheduled to work at a particular meet. The head coach, however, has told you that he believes this functionality can wait and should not be part of the Web site now. Two people will be helping you on the project. One is a graphic artist; the other is a person who is very familiar with HTML, Java, Active Server Pages (ASP), and several Web development tools. Based upon the information provided, develop the basics of a project charter. Although you will not be able to develop a complete project charter at this point, you can get started on the following:

a. Come up with a name for the project.

b. Identify the project stakeholders, their roles, and their titles.

c. Provide a brief description of the project.

d. Develop a MOV for this project.

e. Specify the project's scope in terms of the high-level features or functionality that should be included in the Web site.

f. Specify what should not be included in the project's scope.

g. Specify the resources that will be required and provide an estimated cost for each resource. (Be sure to include a reference or sound basis to justify the cost for each resource.)

h. Identify some of the risks associated with this project.

i. You are free to make assumptions as needed, but be sure to document them!

2. Suppose a company is interested in purchasing a call center software package to improve its customer service. Describe the project management processes that would be needed to support the first two phases of the IT project methodology.

3. Plan a kick-off meeting for a project team.

 # GLOBAL TECHNOLOGY SOLUTIONS

The quiet drive back to the office was a welcome respite for Tim Williams, even though he was catching the tail end of rush hour traffic. Traffic was moving well below the speed limit, so the time alone gave him a chance to reflect on the activities of the last few weeks. The business case for Husky Air was complete, and Tim had presented it to the company's senior management not more than 30 minutes ago.

Just as Tim was about to turn on the car's radio, his cell phone rang and he was immediately brought back to reality. Tim answered, and heard his business partner Kellie Matthews ask, "So, how did it go?"

"Not bad!" Tim replied. "In fact, senior management approved our recommendation and is willing to make funds available for us to go on to the next step."

Kellie laughed and teased, "I guess that means we can pay the office rent next month. So what's our next step?"

The traffic had now come to a complete stop, so Tim didn't feel that talking on his cell phone would distract him. "Now that we've completed the business case and Husky Air gave us the approval and funds, I would say that the first phase of our project methodology is complete," he said. "The next thing we need to do is develop a project charter and baseline plan that will outline what we're going to do, how we're going

to do it, when we're going to do it, and how much it will cost."

"Wow," exclaimed Kellie, "I thought that was all outlined in the business case."

"The business case was a strategic plan, the project charter and baseline project plan are going to be our tactical plan," Tim explained. "This will also be a reality check to make sure that we can deliver the application to our client within the guidelines that were specified in the business case."

"Will this require another approval by Husky Air's management?" asked Kellie.

"Actually, there will be several more," answered Tim. "In fact, the CEO was pleased that our methodology has approval or review points throughout the project life cycle. He said that Husky Air hired a consulting firm a few years ago to develop an inventory system. The consultants didn't keep senior management informed after the project was approved. So the CEO was surprised to find out that the project was only half complete when the agreed upon project deadline arrived. Husky Air's management had only two choices: Cancel the project and take the loss, or bite the bullet and continue funding a project that would cost twice as much as originally planned. Needless to say, they intend never to hire that consulting firm again."

"Well if the client is happy then we should be happy as well," Kellie said.

The traffic started moving again, and Tim said "I'll see you in the office tomorrow morning. We have a lot of work ahead of us."

Kellie agreed, and they both said goodbye before hanging up. Tim relaxed as the traffic started to move again. Even though there was still much work to be done before the actual work on the system would begin, he felt good that they had cleared the first hurdle. "What the heck," he thought. He turned off at the next exit and headed for his favorite Italian restaurant. "It's important to celebrate the small but important successes along the way," he told himself. "Pizza is perfect."

Things to Think About

1. Why is it important to have several status review and decision points throughout the project's life cycle?

2. Aside from *reality checks*, what other purposes do status reviews and decision points throughout the project's life cycle provide?

3. How does a business case differ from the project charter/project plan?

4. Why is it important to celebrate the small but important successes?

 ## HUSKY AIR ASSIGNMENT—PILOT ANGELS

Defining the Project Infrastructure

Husky Air's management has decided that building a custom information system will provide the most value to their organization. Your team has been asked to continue with the project and develop this system.

The first step before planning the details of the project's schedule and budget requires that you define an infrastructure for your project. The infrastructure is the foundation for the project charter. Knowing what resources you need or are available and their associated cost will directly influence your schedule and budget estimates. This will entail defining the stakeholders of the project and the resources that will be required.

Please provide a professional-looking document that includes the following:

1. **The project name, project team name, and the names of the members of your project team**

2. **A brief project description**

3. **The project's MOV** (This should be revised or refined if necessary.)

4. **A list of the resources needed to complete the project**—This should include:

   a. **People (and their roles)**—Your team is responsible for planning the project. However, the project may need additional individuals

with both technical and nontechnical expertise to develop the system.

   b. **Technology**—In the previous assignment, you estimated the hardware, network, and software needs for a system to support your client. You will also need various hardware, network, software, and telecommunication resources to support the project team.

   c. **Facilities**—Husky Air has limited space. The project team will have to do most of its project and development work at a different site.

   d. **Other**—for example, travel, training, and so on.

5. **An estimate for the cost of each resource**—Use the Web, trade journals, newspaper advertisements, and so forth as a basis. For example, if you need to hire a programmer, then you could use want ads or salary surveys as a basis for an annual base salary or hourly wage. The people who work on the project (including you and your team) will be paid a base salary or hourly wage plus benefits. Therefore, the cost of any people on your team will be a base salary (the person's gross income) plus an addition 25 percent paid out in benefits. Be sure to include a reference for all the sources you use.

 ## CASE STUDIES

People, Processes, and Tools

People, processes, and tools play an important role in projects. People provide value to projects because of their creativity. A person's ability to create is not something easily replaced by a machine even though the dream of

artificial intelligence has been around for decades. Projects start with a goal or need and creativity allows us make conceptual leaps that allow us to come up with new ideas to solve a problem or overcome a challenge. In addition, creativity often is prompted by another inherently human trait called vision, or our ability to see what is not yet there—that is, to imagine. Projects often start out as someone's vision that becomes a guide for the project work to be done and motivation for creative energy. Lastly, the combination of creativity and vision provides a unique outlet for our intellect. We carry around a number of facts in our heads, but intellect is more than what we know. Intellect is our ability to use those facts to uncover relationships and is the enabler of creativity.

Unfortunately, people are not perfect. Although people are essential to projects, people are also a main reason why projects experience problems and even fail. Another human trait is our ability to make mistakes. For example, we would most likely trust a compiler because we expect it to compile a program correctly, but we may not have the same degree of trust in a program that someone wrote that wasn't properly tested, reviewed, examined, and retested. People can make errors that impact a project significantly. Time, effort, and money must be spent fixing those errors. Moreover, people can also forget things. While we can all forget facts and information, we can also forget to do things. An activity may require a number of steps, and a person may omit one or more steps if they aren't familiar with the activity or when their attention is diverted. Regardless, omissions often result in someone having to go back and filling in the missing work or redoing what was already done. Another human shortfall is that people can be imprecise. A systems analyst, for example, may fail to document fully the requirements of a system. The programmer may make assumptions to fill in the blanks, resulting in a system that may not satisfy the user's needs.

Since people bring unique abilities to a project, it is important that we seek opportunities to enhance their value while mitigating their shortcomings. This is the basic reason for processes and tools. Recently, the topic of processes has been a controversial issue. Many people believe that processes get in the way or stifle creativity. The truth is that we follow processes in many of our day-to-day routines. These routines that we repeat regularly help us get through the day without having to stop and think through every step each time we do something. This frees up our minds so that we can focus on things that require our conscious attention; for example, each of us has a morning routine (i.e., process) for getting up and getting to work or school.

Processes fail when they do not meet the needs of the people who must follow them. A process becomes unconscious when it meets our needs and doesn't get in the way. People complain about ineffective processes when they fail to meet our needs or when they become a waste of our time and effort.

Processes provide value when they compensate for our human shortcomings in terms of helping us compensate for errors, omissions, or imprecision. They get in the way when they impede creativity, vision, or intellect.

For example, a morning routine that includes checking the weather and traffic reports can help us choose the best time to leave or the best route for our commute. Therefore, a process should help us do all the things we're supposed to do and do them in the right order and with the right amount of detail or precision required. Since not every error, omission, or imprecision can be avoided, processes also provide necessary checks and balances to detect and correct mistakes before they become problems. Moreover, a process that is followed inconsistently will produce inconsistent results, while a process followed consistently will provide consistent results. Often processes are undocumented, but the need for documentation increases as more people become involved in a process. This helps new staff learn the rules and what is expected of them.

Tools, on the other hand, can improve efficiency by magnifying or leveraging a person's efforts or by replacing the human effort. For example, a long time ago programmers wrote code that ran by stringing together the 1s and 0s or bits so the computer's processor could directly execute the program. Compliers replaced the task of programmers having to write code directly to the processor while magnifying their work by allowing them to write higher level abstractions using a programming language. A human could therefore spend time analyzing a problem and applying creativity and intellect to solve it, while the compiler translates each line of this source code into the language the computer could understand.

Tools are appropriate when people spend a great deal of time working on processes that do not involve a great deal of creativity. A tool should help them spend less time on mundane activities and more time on the challenging aspects of their work. This can improve the quality of their work-life as they spend more time on interesting and challenging work.

However, adoption of a tool often necessitates a process change. For example, a code repository tool may require a process change that now requires programmers to check code out to work on it and then check it back in when they are done. While this may be a small change, one should consider whether a tool should be adopted if it changes the process so significantly that it then becomes a hindrance or waste of time and effort. Tools should make people and processes more efficient and effective. Tools and processes that reduce efficiency and effectiveness are not worth adopting.

1. Discuss the relationship between people, processes, and tools. When is this relationship most effective? When is it least effective?

2. Can good people make up for poor processes? Can good processes make up for incompetent people?

3. We've all encountered a process that we felt wasted our time and/or money. This could be in our job, waiting in line trying to renew our driver's license, or at a fast food restaurant. Describe an inefficient

process that you may have performed as part of a job (past or present) or a process you encountered in your day-to-day life. How did this process stifle a person's intellect or ability to be creative? Could the process be improved? Could a tool be used to free a person from the mundane tasks and improve the quality of their work life?

SOURCE: Adapted from a three-part series by Alan Koch, The People Premium, Processes for People, and The Role of Tools, *Projects@Work*, October 6, 2005, December 1, 2005, and February 2, 2006.

The Project Battlefield

Daniel Starr tells an interesting story that compares an ancient parable to a modern-day confrontation. If he had lived 2000 years before with his Celtic ancestors, the story might have unfolded something like:

> Summoned was I, summoned to the stronghold of mine enemy. There he stood, a great brute of a man, brandishing an immense spear and shouting epithets in his foul tongue. My heart did sink as he advanced, for I knew my own short blade was no match for such a great weapon. And so, summoning up all of my courage and that of my ancestors, I removed my helmet, released the buckles that held my armor and let it fall to the ground. There I stood, unprotected, exposing my breast to his attack. With a mighty roar he charged toward me, and when his spear-tip was inches away I ducked to the side, reached out with my left arm and grasped his weapon, taking a grievous wound to the hand, and held on with all my might. Unwilling to release his spear, mine enemy attempted to pull the spear away from my grasp. This I fought, and slowly drew him closer until, when our eyes were but a hand's breadth apart, I took the small dagger I had hidden in my right hand and slid it through the chink in his armor and then between his ribs. He fell away gasping and bleeding, and while I did not kill him, this enemy never troubled me again.

Since Daniel was born in 20th century America, the story happens in a different way. He was project manager for a small software development team who had "plenty of responsibility and no official authority." He describes his reputation in the organization as "the hairy wild man genius in the software department."

On a Wednesday morning, his phone rang. It was the executive secretary asking him to attend a meeting in conference room 2. When he arrived, Daniel found a group of executives and Ted, a middle manager who for some reason had never quite liked him. Perhaps it could be Daniel's long hair, casual dress, or the fact that he rode a motorcycle to work.

With the manner of a prosecuting attorney, Ted held up a piece of paper and read a description of a bug that his people had found in some software Daniel's team was responsible for. Daniel thought it was odd that he had not heard about this issue through the formal trouble-reporting system. After reading the charges, Ted asked, "What do you have to say about this?"

Daniel asked politely to see the report, and with some disdain Ted handed it to him. While reading the report, several defenses crossed Daniel's mind: "Why hadn't the report been formally reported?" "Could Ted's people have been misusing the software again?" Or a number of excuses came to mind like "The system is still a prototype."

After about 30 seconds, Ted spoke up and said "Well!!?"

Daniel replied, "I guess I messed up." A murmur began among the executives. Daniel added calmly, "It's a simple mistake. I should have a patch by tomorrow and a complete fix for Friday's release."

The attitude among the executives began to change, and Daniel suddenly realized that no one was looking at him anymore—all eyes were now on Ted. The expression on their faces said "Why are you wasting our time?!" After an awkward moment of silence, one of the executives turned to Daniel and excused him from the meeting.

Daniel saw Ted later that afternoon. Although Ted didn't say anything to him, he did have a pained expression on his face. Daniel had to work late on Thursday to get the fix into Friday's release as promised, but Ted never bothered him again.

As Daniel philosophizes, "Some things don't change. Whether it's fought with swords and shields or words and processes, life is still a battle, decided by weaponry and armor."

For example, we all develop our personal suits of armor that fit us so well that we may not even know we're wearing them. This personal armor could be in the form of nicknames (e.g., Buzzsaw Bob), policies (e.g., "please put that in writing"), reputations (e.g., "he's the only one who knows how the system works"), the way we use email or voice mail, and so on. Although the list is endless, the purpose is to deflect or absorb words, actions, changes, problems, or anything that might threaten our sense of comfort or safety. On projects, this may include added processes, standards, control of communication channels or information, checklists, audits, etc. to protect our projects from unpredictable and hostile environments.

In Daniel's battle with Ted, his armor included his reputation, the rules regarding bug reporting, the manual he wrote describing how the software was and wasn't to be used, and the understanding that the system was still a prototype so a certain number of problems could be expected.

Although armor can protect you (it can let you get work done), in many cases it can slow you down, limit your agility, and consume your strength. Moreover, a particular piece of armor is effective against some weapons while ineffective against others. For example, chain mail made up of interlocking steel rings can be effective against a sword, but useless against poison-tipped darts. Subsequently, armor evolves. Armor designed to protect a person from arrows and swords is now on display in museums. Modern armor is designed to protect soldiers from bullets and shrapnel.

In summary, Daniel Starr suggests that people be aware of their armor in terms of its value and limitations. We often build our personal armor unconsciously in response to attacks we suffer or threats we perceive. To become a more effective project leader or even a better person, one should take an inventory of their personal armor. The questions then become: How well does this armor protect me? What is the cost in terms of losing agility and flexibility? What pieces of armor need replacing or repair?

1. Daniel's first-century counterpart took a "grievous wound to the hand" when he deflected his opponent's spear. How did Daniel take a similar wound when he admitted that he made a mistake? How did this change the situation with Ted?

2. What armor might a project manager wear when he or she develops the project charter and project plan? When would this personal armor be useful? How could it become more of a hindrance than offering protection to the project manager and team?

SOURCE: Adapted from Daniel Starr, Choosing Your Armor, *Projects@Work*, November 3, 2005.

 # BIBLIOGRAPHY

DeCarlo, D. 2004. *eXtreme Project Management: Using Leadership, Principles, and Tools to Deliver Value in the Face of Volatility*. San Francisco: Jossey-Bass.

McConnell, S. (1996). *Rapid Development: Taming Wild Software Schedules*. Redmond, WA: Microsoft Press.

Mulcahy, R. 2005. *PMP® Exam Prep for the PMBOK® Guide*, 5th ed. Minneapolis, MN: RMC Publications, Inc.

Project Management Institute (PMI) 2004. *A Guide to the Project Management Body of Knowledge (PMBOK® Guide)*. Newtown Square, PA: PMI Publishing.

4

The Human Side of Project Management

CHAPTER OVERVIEW

Chapter 4 focuses on the human side of project management. After studying this chapter, you should understand and be able to:

- Describe the three major types of formal organizational structures: functional, pure project, and matrix.
- Discuss the advantages and disadvantages of the functional, pure project, and matrix organizational structures.
- Describe the informal organization.
- Develop a stakeholder analysis.
- Describe the difference between a work group and a team.
- Describe and apply the concept of learning cycles and lessons learned as a basis for knowledge management.

INTRODUCTION

The key ingredients to IT project management are people, processes, and technology. Technology is a tool, while processes provide a structure and path for managing and carrying out the project. The success of a project, however, is often determined by the various project stakeholders, as well as who is (or who is not) on the project team.

In this chapter, we will discuss the human side of project management. According to the *PMBOK Guide*®, the processes under the knowledge area of project human resources management entail:

- *Human resource planning*—The creation of a staffing management plan. Includes identifying and documenting the various project roles, responsibilities, and reporting relationships.
- *Acquiring the project team*—Members of the project team with required skills and experience need to be recruited, hired, or acquired from within or outside

the organization. The objective for every project manager is to staff a project with the best available people. Effective staffing involves having policies, procedures, and practices to guide the recruitment of appropriately skilled and experienced staff. This may include negotiating for people from other functional areas within the organization.

- *Developing the project team*—Often the technical, organizational, or interpersonal skills of the project team members may have to be augmented through training and so forth in order to improve their competencies and interactions as a team. Team development also involves creating an environment to develop and support the individual team members and the team itself.

- *Managing the project team*—Today, this can become a real challenge, as project teams may be spread across geographic locations, time zones, and even organizations when components of the project work are subcontracted or outsourced to subteams. Regardless, each team member's performance must be tracked so that issues can be resolved quickly and changes to the project work can be coordinated. Each person's quality of work and contribution to the project should be documented so that feedback in the form of performance reviews can help each member of the project team grow both professionally and personally.

This chapter will expand upon three PMBOK® concepts and integrate several relatively recent concepts for understanding the human side of IT project management. In the next section, we will focus on project and organizational planning. Three primary organizational structures—the **functional, project,** and **matrix**—will be described. In addition, the various opportunities and challenges for projects conducted under each structure will be discussed. As a project manager or project team member, it is important to understand an organization's structure since this will determine authorities, roles, responsibilities, communication channels, and availability of resources.

While the formal organizational structure defines official roles, responsibilities, and reporting relationships, informal relationships will exist as well. It is important to understand why these informal structures and relationships exist and how they can influence the relationships among the different project stakeholders. In addition, understanding both the formal and informal organizations will help you to understand not only who makes certain decisions, but also why certain decisions are made.

We will also focus on the various roles of the project manager. In general, one of the greatest responsibilities of the project manager is the selection and recruitment of the project team. Once the project team is in place, the project manager must also ensure that the project team members work together to achieve the project's MOV. Therefore, the language and discipline of *real teams* versus *work groups* will be introduced. These concepts will provide the basis for understanding the dynamics of the project team.

Once the project team is in place, it is important that the project team members learn from each other and from past project experiences. Thus, the idea of learning cycles will be introduced as a tool for team learning and for capturing lessons learned that can be documented, stored, and retrieved using a knowledge management system.

In the last section of this chapter, we will focus on the project environment. In addition to staffing the project, the project manager must create an environment to support the project team. If necessary, this includes appropriating a suitable place for the team to work and ensuring that the team has the proper tools and supplies needed to accomplish their work.

ORGANIZATION AND PROJECT PLANNING

The performance of an organization or a project is influenced largely by how well its resources are organized. In general, structures are created within an organization to manage the input, processing, and output of resources. For example, departments or areas based on the specialized skills needed to manage a particular resource are created—that is, accounting and finance manages the money resources, personnel manages the human resources, and information systems manages the information resource. As a result, many organizations adopt a structure based upon function. Other organizations may adopt a structure based on the products it sells or its customers. These structures may use brand management or geographical divisions.

However, the structure of an organization must fit its strategy, and since organizations may follow different strategies, it makes sense that no single structure can work well for every organization. Therefore, there are different organizational structures and ways to efficiently and effectively manage not only the organizational resources but the work and processes involved. As long as the firm performs well, a particular structure and strategy will exist. On the other hand, when a firm performs poorly, a change in structure and/or strategy may be required.

Projects are part of an organization and can be thought of as micro organizations that require resources, processes, and structure. Moreover, these resources, processes, and structures are determined largely by the organizational structure of the supporting or parent organization, which may determine or influence the availability of resources, reporting relationships, and project roles and responsibilities. Therefore, it is important to understand how the project interfaces with the host or parent organization and how the project itself will be organized. In this section, we will focus on three formal structures that tie projects explicitly to the organization. Each structure provides distinct opportunities and challenges, and choosing and implementing the correct structure can have a major impact on both the project and the organization.

The Formal Organization

An organization's structure reveals the formal groupings and specializations of activities. Generally, these groupings and activities are documented in an organizational chart to clarify and portray the lines of authority, communication, reporting relationships, and responsibilities of individuals and groups within the organization. Although an organization's formal structure does not tell us anything about the informal lines of communication among its subunits, it does provide us with an indication of how a project will interface with the parent or supporting organization. In other words, the formal organizational structure will determine how resources are allocated, who has authority over those resources, and who is really in charge of the project.

Figure 4.1 illustrates the three most common structures—the functional, matrix, and project-based organization. Keep in mind that these organizations are not exhaustive—they represent a continuum of approaches that may evolve over time or as the result of a unique situation. An organization may choose to combine these forms any number of ways to create a hybrid organization such as a **functional matrix** or **project matrix.**

The Functional Organization   The functional organizational structure may be thought of as the more traditional organizational form. This particular structure is

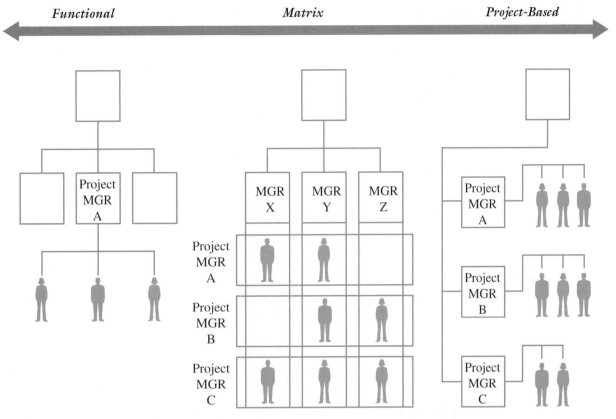

Figure 4.1   Organizational Structures

based upon organizing resources to perform specialized tasks or activities in order to attain the goals of the organization. As Figure 4.2 illustrates, individuals and subunits (i.e., groups of individuals) perform similar functions and have similar areas of expertise. Subsequently, projects are managed within the existing functional hierarchy.

Projects in a functional organization are typically coordinated through customary channels and housed within a particular function. For example, a project to install a new machine would be a self-contained project within the manufacturing function because the expertise required for the project would reside within the manufacturing subunit. The project manager would most likely be a senior manufacturing manager, and the project team would be made up of individuals from the engineering and production areas. As a result, the manufacturing subunit would be responsible for managing the project and for supplying and coordinating all of the resources dedicated to the project.

However, a project may cross functional boundaries. In the case of an information technology project, the knowledge and expertise to design and develop an application may reside in the information systems subunit, while the domain or functional knowledge resides in one of the functional subunits. As a result, the project team may consist of individuals from two or more functional areas. There are two main issues that must be resolved at the outset of a project: Who will be responsible for the project? What resources will each subunit provide?

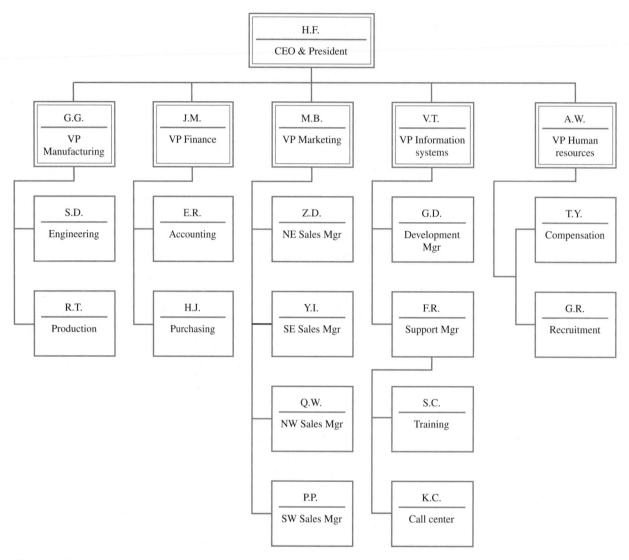

Figure 4.2 Functional Organizational Structure

There are a number of advantages for projects sponsored by organizations with functional structures. These include:

- *Increased flexibility*—Subject matter experts and other resources can be assigned to the project as needed. In addition, an individual can be part of the project team on a full-time or part-time basis. Once the project is completed, the project team members can return to their respective functional units.

- *Breadth and depth of knowledge and experience*—Individuals from a particular subunit can bring a wealth of knowledge, expertise, and experience to the project. This knowledge can be expanded even further as a result of their experiences with the project. As a result, the project experience may lead to greater opportunities for career advancement within the subunit. If the project crosses functional areas, an opportunity exists for these individuals to learn from each so that a less parochial solution can be developed.

■ *Less duplication*—Coordination of resources and activities can lead to less duplication of resources across projects since specialization of skills and resources are housed within a functional area. The project also tends to be more focused because a primary functional area is responsible for and ultimately takes ownership of the project.

There are, however, several disadvantages associated with projects sponsored by organizations with functional structures. These include:

■ *Determining authority and responsibility*—As was mentioned previously, determining who has authority and responsibility for a project must be resolved at the outset, especially when the project involves more than one functional area. For example, in an IT project, will the project manager be from the IS department or from the functional area? A project manager from the IS area may have knowledge and expertise with respect to the technology, but lack critical knowledge about the business. On the other hand, a project manager from the functional area may understand the business, but lack an understanding of the technology. Furthermore, there is a chance that the project manager will have an insular view of the project—that is, the project manager's allegiance and loyalty to a particular functional area may lead her or him to focus primarily on the interests of that area. The likelihood of this happening increases when the project expands across several functional boundaries. Other functional areas may begin to ask if there is anything in it for them and withhold resources unless their needs and expectations are met. The project manager may not have the authority for acquiring and providing the resources, but will certainly be accountable for the failure of the project.

■ *Poor response time*—The normal lines of authority and communication delineated by the functional structure determine who makes specific decisions. Projects may take longer if important decisions have to pass through several layers of management and across several functional areas. Unfortunately, what's important to you may not be important to me if a particular functional unit has a dominant role or interest in a project. Due to the potential for parochial interests, problem resolution may break down because of finger pointing or trying to place blame for the problem rather than focusing on problem resolution.

■ *Poor integration*—The culture of the organization may encourage functional areas to insulate themselves from the rest of the organization as a way to avoid many of these parochial issues. However, this can result in two problems. First, the individuals in a functional area may act in their own best interests instead of taking a holistic or organizational view of the project. Second, the functional area may attempt to become self-sufficient by acquiring knowledge, expertise, and technology outside of its normal area of specialization. While specialization of skills and resources can *reduce* duplication of activities and resources, the functional structure can also *increase* this duplication. It may lead to an organization of warring tribes as functional areas compete for resources and blur lines of responsibility.

The Project Organization   At the other end of the spectrum from the functional organization is the project organization (see Figure 4.3). Sometimes referred to

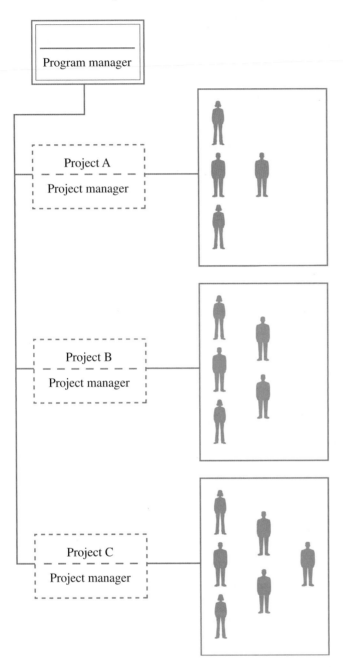

Figure 4.3 The Project Organization

as the *pure project organization*, this organizational structure supports projects as the dominant form of business. Typically, a project organization will support multiple projects at one time and integrate project management tools and techniques throughout the organization. Each project is treated as a separate and relatively independent unit within the organization. The project manager has sole authority over and responsibility for the project and its resources, while the parent or supporting organization provides financial and administrative controls. Both the project manager and the project team are typically assigned to a particular project on a full-time basis.

There are advantages and disadvantages associated with projects supported by the project organization. Advantages include:

■ *Clear authority and responsibility*— Unlike the projects in a functional organization, the project manager here is fully in charge. Although he or she must provide progress reports and is ultimately responsible to someone who has authority over all the projects (e.g., a program manager), the project manager has full authority over and responsibility for the assigned project. Moreover, the project team reports directly to the project manager, thus providing clear unity of command. This structure may allow the project team to better concentrate on the project.

■ *Improved communication*—A clear line of authority results in more effective and efficient communication. In addition, lines of communication are shortened because the project manager is able to bypass the normal channels of distribution associated with the functional organizational structure. This structure thus results in more efficient communication and fewer communication problems.

■ *High level of integration*—Since communication across the organization is increased, the potential for a higher level of cross integration across the organization exists. For example, the project team may include experts with technical skills or knowledge of the business. Fewer conflicts over resources arise since each project has resources dedicated solely to it.

Projects supported by project organization structures face several disadvantages. These disadvantages include:

- *Project isolation*—Since each project may be thought of as a self-contained unit, there is the potential for each project to become isolated from other projects in the organization. Unless a project management office or program manager oversees each project, inconsistencies in policies and project management approaches may occur across projects. In addition, project managers and project teams may have little opportunity to share ideas and experiences with other project managers and project teams, thus hindering learning throughout the organization.

- *Duplication of effort*—While the potential for conflicts over resources is reduced, various projects may require resources that are duplicated on other projects. Project managers may try to stockpile the best people and other resources that could be shared with other projects. Each project must then support the salaries of people who are part of the dedicated project team but whose services are not needed at all times. There is then the problem of what to do with these people when the project is completed and they have not been assigned to another project. Many consulting firms, for example, refer to people who are between projects as being on *the beach* or *on the bench*. While awaiting the next assignment, consultants are often sent to training in order to make the most of their idle time.

- *Projectitis*—Projectitis sometimes occurs when the project manager and project team develop a strong attachment to the project and to each other. As a result, these individuals may have a difficult time letting go, and the project begins to take on a life of its own with no real end in sight (Meredith and Mantel 2000). The program manager or project office must ensure that proper controls are in place to reduce the likelihood of this happening.

The Matrix Organization   The third type of organizational form is the matrix structure. The matrix organization is a combination of the vertical functional structure and the horizontal project structure (see Figure 4.4). As a result, the matrix organization provides many of the opportunities and challenges associated with the functional and project organizations.

The main feature of the matrix organization is the ability to integrate areas and resources throughout an organization. Moreover, people with specialized skills can be assigned to the project either on a part-time or on a more permanent basis. Unfortunately, **unity of command** is violated since each project team member will have more than one boss, leading to the possibility of confusion, frustration, conflict, and mixed loyalties. The functional manager will be responsible for providing many of the people and other resources to the project, while the project manager is responsible for coordinating these resources. In short, the project manager coordinates all the project activities for the functional areas, while the functional areas provide the wherewithal to carry out those activities.

The matrix organization can take on various forms that can create **hybrid organizations.** The most common forms include:

- *Balanced matrix*—In the balanced matrix form, the project manager focuses on defining all of the activities of the project, while the functional managers determine how those activities will be carried out.

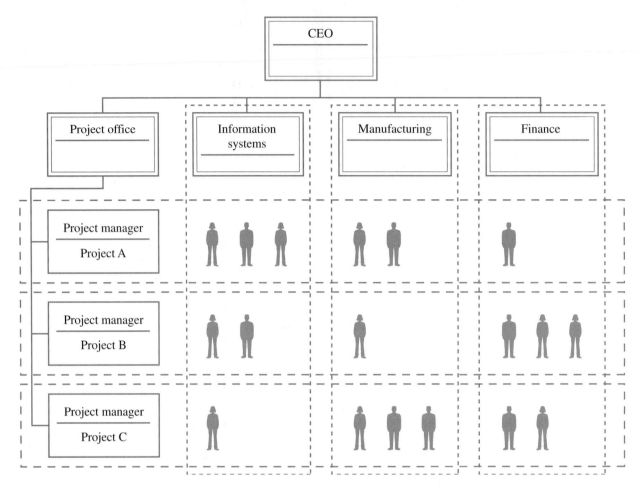

Figure 4.4 Matrix Organization

■ *Functional matrix*—The functional matrix organization tends to take on more of the qualities of a functional organization. Here the project manager focuses on coordinating the project activities, while the functional managers are responsible for completing those activities that are related to their particular area.

■ *Project matrix*—It follows, then, that a project matrix structure would take on more of the qualities of a project organization. In this case, the project manager has most of the authority and responsibility for defining and completing the project activities, while the functional managers provide guidance and resources, as needed.

There are several advantages and disadvantages for projects supported by a matrix organization. The advantages include:

■ *High level of integration*—The cross-functional nature of the matrix structure allows for the access and sharing of skilled people and resources from across the organization, and people within the organization can be assigned to more than one project. This ability to share can result in less duplication of resources and activities.

- *Improved communication*—Due to the high level of integration, communication channels are more efficient and effective. As a result, problems and issues can be addressed by the project manager and functional managers, and decisions can be made more quickly than in a functional organization.

- *Increased project focus*—Because a project under the matrix organization has improved communication channels and access to a repository of resources and skilled expertise, the project team can focus on the activities of the project. This ability to focus should increase the likelihood of projects being completed on time and meeting the needs of the organization better.

On the other hand, there are several disadvantages for projects supported by the matrix organization. These include:

- *Higher potential for conflict*—Since power is distributed, project team members may wonder who really is their boss. They may receive conflicting orders, especially if the project and functional area managers have different goals or are fighting over scarce resources. In general, power may depend on which manager has the fewest direct reports to the chief executive office. The project manager may be required to be a skillful mediator and negotiator in order to keep the project on track.

- *Poorer response time*—Because the concept of unity of command is violated in a matrix structure, there can be confusion, mixed loyalties, and various distributions of power. Communication can become bogged down, and decisions may require agreement from individuals who are in conflict with each other. As a result, the project may stall and the project team may begin to experience low morale, little motivation, and the pressure to pick sides.

Which Organizational Structure Is Best?   Unfortunately, there are no simple answers. It really depends on factors such as the nature of the organization's products and services it provides, the business environment, and its culture—that is, the personality of the organization. Projects supported under a functional organizational structure may work best when the organization focuses on a few internal projects. On the other hand, a project organizational structure may work better if an organization takes on a large number of external projects. Subsequently, most consulting firms follow the project organization structure. On the other hand, the matrix organizational structure may work best when an organization takes on projects that require a cross-functional approach.

There has been some research in this area. For example, Larson and Gobeli (1988) surveyed more than 1,600 project management professionals. The results of their study suggest that both project and functional managers have a strong preference for the project or project matrix organization. The functional and functional matrix organizational structures were viewed as the least effective, and the balanced matrix structure was seen as only marginally effective. Larson and Gobeli suggest that the success of a project is linked directly to the project manager's degree of autonomy and authority.

The success of large, complex projects may require a concentrated project focus that can be best supported by the project or project-matrix organization. On the other hand, the matrix organizational structure may work well when an organization cannot dedicate scarce staff and resources to a project or when a cross-functional focus is needed. If a project is undertaken within one specific area of the organization, then a functional-matrix structure would be effective. Although there is little evidence to support the effectiveness of projects supported under a functional organization, it would make sense that the best organizational structure would balance the needs of the project with those of the organization (Gray and Larson 2000).

The Informal Organization

The formal organization is the published structure that defines the official lines of authority, responsibilities, and reporting relationships. While the formal structure tells us how individuals or groups within an organization *should* relate to one another, it does not tell us how they *actually* relate (Nicholas 1990). In many cases the informal organization bypasses the formal lines of communication and authority because of the inevitable positive and negative relationships that occur over time in any organization. While communication in the formal organization is supposed to flow through published channels, it can flow in any direction and at a much faster pace through the network of informal relationships—the famous grapevine. Power in an organization, therefore, is not only determined by one's place in the hierarchy, but also how well one is connected in the informal network. A person's degree of connectedness in the informal organization largely determines what information is received or not received.

Stakeholders   Stakeholders are individuals, groups, or even organizations that have a stake, or claim, in the project's outcome. Often we think of stakeholders as only those individuals or groups having an interest in the successful outcome of a project, but the sad truth is that there are many who can gain from a project's failure. While the formal organization tells us a little about the stakeholders and what their interests may be, the informal organization paints a much more interesting picture.

Stakeholder Analysis   A published organizational chart is usually fairly easy to acquire or create. The informal organization may be more difficult to understand or explain, even for those well connected individuals. To help the project manager and project team understand the informal organization better, one can develop a stakeholder analysis as a means of determining who should be involved with the project and understanding the role that they must play. To develop a stakeholder analysis, one may start with the published organizational chart and then add to it as the complexities of the informal organization become known. Since the purpose of the stakeholder analysis is to understand the informal organization, it may be best to view this as an exercise rather than a formal document to be made public. The following steps provide a process for developing a stakeholder analysis:

1. Develop a list of stakeholders. Include individuals, groups, and organizations that must provide resources to the project or who have an interest in the successful or unsuccessful outcome of the project.

2. Next to each stakeholder, identify the stakeholder's interest in the project by giving the stakeholder a "+1" if they have an positive interest in the project's outcome or a "–1" if they have a negative interest. Neutral individuals or groups can be given a "0." If you are not sure, then give a stakeholder a "?".

3. Next, it may be useful to gauge the amount of influence each stakeholder has over the project. One can use a scale from 0 to 5, with 0 meaning no influence and 5 meaning extremely high influence—that is, this person or group could terminate the project.

4. After determining each stakeholder's degree of influence, the next step involves assessing whether potential conflict among the different stakeholders exists. An IT project is planned organizational change, and some stakeholders may act in their own self-interest. This self-interest can often be in conflict with the self-interest of other stakeholders. For example, an individual or group may want to increase the functionality of the system. This increase in functionality will require more time and resources that may be in conflict with another individual or group that wants to limit the project's budget or shorten the project's schedule.

5. This step involves defining a role for each of the stakeholders. For example, every project should have a champion or someone prominent within the organization who will be a public supporter of the project. In addition, it is important to identify the owner of the project. This list may include an individual, group, or organization that will accept the transfer of the project's product. Other roles may include consultant, decision maker, advocate, ally, rival, foe, and so forth. Use adjectives or metaphors that provide a clear meaning and picture of the stakeholder.

6. Once you determine who has an interest in the project, what that interest is, and what influence they may have, it may be useful to identify an objective for each stakeholder. This may include such things as providing specific resources, expertise, or guidance navigating through the political waters of the organization. In the case of potential adversarial stakeholders, this may require getting their acceptance or approval concerning certain aspects of the project.

7. Lastly, it is important to identify various strategies for each stakeholder. These strategies may require building, maintaining, improving, or reestablishing relationships. This list should include a short description of how the objective could be attained.

The exercise for developing a stakeholder analysis can be conducted and summarized in a table as illustrated in Figure 4.5.

THE PROJECT TEAM

The word *team* has different meanings for each of us. As a result of past experiences with teams, those meanings probably have both positive and negative connotations. Information technology projects require various resources; but people are the most valuable resource and have the greatest influence on the project's outcome. Indeed, the human resource of a systems development project will consume up to 80 percent of its budget (McLeod and Smith 1996). It is important, then, that the project manager and project team members be chosen wisely. In addition, people must be sure to support the project team so that project success is not a random event.

The Roles of the Project Manager

One of the most critical decisions in project management is selecting a project manager or team leader. The project manager is usually assigned to the project at the earliest stages of the project life cycle, but a new one may be brought in as replacement in the later stages of a project.

Stakeholder	Interest	Influence	Potential Conflicts	Role	Objective	Strategy
Hirem N.Firem	(+1)	5	Competition for resources with other functional managers	Project sponsor and champion	Provide resources, approvals, and public support for the project	To maintain open communication so that political landmines can be avolded
Dee Manitger	+1	3	Resources not made available as promised by functional managers	Project Manager	Lead and manage the project so that it achieves its MOV	Work closely with project stakeholders and project team
Project Team	+1	2	This project will change a number of business processes. Affected users may resist change by withholding information	*Steve Turner-* Network Administrator *Shedelle Bivits-* Systems Analyst *Corean Jenkins-* Programmer/DBA *Myra Dickens-* Inventory Analyst	Provide expertise to complete the project work	Support project team with adequate resources while minimizing distractions
Will Sellit	−1	4	As the marketing manager, Sellit is not pleased that this project was chosen over his proposed project. May withhold promised resources.	Foe	Build and maintain best possible relationship to minimize attempts to divert resources	Maintain open communication, use project sponsor's influence as necessary

Figure 4.5 Example Stakeholder Analysis Chart

The project manager must play many roles. First, the project manager must play a managerial role that focuses on planning, organizing, and controlling. The project manager, for example, is responsible for developing the project plan, organizing the project resources, and then overseeing execution of the plan. The project manager must also perform many administrative functions, including performance reviews, project tracking and reporting, and other general day-to-day responsibilities.

Although this work sounds fairly simple and straightforward, even the best thought out plans do not always go the way we expect. Thus, the project manager must know when to stay the course and when to adapt or change the project plan by expediting certain activities or acting as a problem solver.

The success of the project, of course, depends not only on the project team, but also on the contributions and support of all project stakeholders as well. Therefore, the project manager must build and nurture the relationships among the various stakeholders. To do this effectively, the project manager must play a strong leadership role. While the managerial role focuses on planning, organizing, and controlling, leadership centers on getting people motivated and then headed down the right path toward a common goal.

Choosing a project manager for a project is analogous to hiring an employee. It is important to look at his or her background, knowledge, skill sets, and overall strengths and weaknesses. Some attributes of a successful project manager include:

- *The ability to communicate with people*—A project manager must have strong communication skills. A project manager need not to be a great motivational speaker, but should have the ability to connect with people, share a common vision, and get everyone to respond or head in the right direction.

- *The ability to deal with people*—Aside from being a good communicator, a project manager must have the soft skills for dealing with people, their egos, and their agendas. The project manager must be a good listener, hearing what people say and understanding what they mean. This skill allows the project manager to get below the surface of issues when people are not being completely honest or open without being annoying or alienating them. A project manager must also have a sense of humor. Often, project managers and project teams are expected to perform during stressful situations, and a sense of humor can make these situations more manageable. Although a project manager does not have to be everyone's best friend, people should feel that they are at least approachable and should be comfortable talking with him or her. In addition, the project manager must also be willing to share knowledge and skills with others and be willing to help each individual develop to her or his fullest potential.

- *The ability to create and sustain relationships*—A good project manager must be able to build bridges instead of walls. Acting as a peacemaker or negotiator among the project client or sponsor, top management, the project team, customers, suppliers, vendors, subcontractors, and so forth may be necessary. In addition, the project manager should be a good salesperson. An effective project manager must continually sell the value of the project to all of the stakeholders and influence others over whom he or she has no direct authority.

- *The ability to organize*—A project manager must be good at organizing—developing the project plan, acquiring resources, and creating an effective project environment. The project manager must also know and understand both the details and the big picture, which requires a familiarity with the details of the project plan and also an understanding of how contingencies may impact the plan.

Team Selection and Acquisition

Another critical task of a project manager is selecting and staffing the project. Staffing involves recruiting and assigning people to the project team. Selecting the right mix of people, with both technical and nontechnical skills, is a decision that can influence the outcome of the project. Although a project manager should strive to acquire the brightest and the best, project team members should be chosen based on the following skills:

- *Technology skills*—Depending upon the nature of the project, members with specific technology skill sets—programmers, systems analysts, network specialists, and so forth—will be required.

- *Business/organization skills*—Although technology skills are important in IT projects, it is also important to have people or access to people with domain knowledge. These skills include knowledge or expertise within a specific domain (e.g., compensation planning) as well as knowledge of a particular organization or industry (e.g., healthcare) to augment the technical skill requirements.

■ *Interpersonal skills*—The ability to communicate with other team members and other stakeholders is an important skill for team members. It is important not only for the team members to understand one another, but for the project team to understand the project sponsor's needs. Due to the nature of many projects, other desirable characteristics should include creativity, a tolerance for ambiguity, acceptance of diversity, flexibility in adapting to different roles, and the capacity to take calculated risks.

The size or scope of the project will determine the size of the project team. Although smaller teams have the potential to work faster and develop a product in a shorter time, larger teams can provide a larger knowledge base and different perspectives. Unfortunately, there is also a tendency for larger teams to function more slowly. One solution to this latter problem may be creating subgroups to make the project more manageable and to facilitate communication and action.

The project manager may recruit project team members internally or externally. For example, in the functional or matrix organization, people may be acquired from the functional areas. In a project organization, a project manager may recruit people who are currently in between projects or who will be soon *rolling off* an existing project. The project manager may have to negotiate with other managers for specific individuals with specific skills or areas of expertise. On the other hand, a project manager may have to hire individuals from outside the organization. In either case, for a particular project, training may be required. Therefore, the timing of when a particular individual can begin work on the project is a significant factor that can impact the project's schedule.

Team Performance

The project team has a direct influence on the outcome of the project. Therefore, it is important that the team's performance be of the utmost concern to the project manager. In *The Wisdom of Teams*, Jon R. Katzenbach and Douglas K. Smith (1999) provide an insightful and highly usable approach for understanding the language and discipline of teams. In refining the language of teams, they provide a distinction between work groups and several types of teams.

Work Groups   The work group is based on the traditional approach where a single leader is in control, makes most of the decisions, delegates to subordinates, and monitors the progress of the assigned tasks. Therefore, the performance of a work group depends greatly on the leader.

A work group can also include members who interact to share information, best practices, or ideas. Although the members may be interested in each other's success, work groups do not necessarily share the same performance goals, do not necessarily provide joint work-products, and are not necessarily held mutually accountable. A study group is an example of a work group. You and several members of a class may find it mutually beneficial to study together for an exam, but each of you (hopefully!) will work on the exam individually. The grade you receive on the exam is not a direct result of the work produced by the study group, but rather of your individual performance on the exam. In an organizational context, managers may form work

QUICK THINKING—PROJECTS AS SOCIAL NETWORKS

Simply storing and disseminating information will not encourage individuals assigned to a project to share ideas or become involved as a team. A project social network is an influential mapping of people and ideas.

Managing a project is more than just a set of project plans, tools, and assignment to activities. It's also about people. An effective project manager understands that people assigned to a project enter with a set of self-interests and expectations so it's important to know what makes them tick. For example, a newbie might try to over-achieve and impress, while a more seasoned veteran may believe that he or she has seen it all, and a negative neutron may find all kinds of reasons why nothing will work. As a result, a social network is created as each person shows and communicates a strong set of self-interests that, in turn, inform and influence the people they work with. Command-and-control techniques or a one-size-fits-all approach will not get people to work together. The project manager must understand the signals each person is sending out and how interests and events can be aligned to create a basis for a successful project.

The available resource pool is an important input for acquiring a project team. Unfortunately, many project managers don't consider fully a person's previous experience, interests, and characteristics when negotiating for or assigning people to a project team. Project managers should not just staff a project, but staff the social network in their favor.

In addition to getting the right people, the project manager adds to the social network by creating a sense of belonging that goes beyond a celebratory project kick-off. This may include thanking people for being part of the project or by bringing them into the loop by asking them what they think about the project charter, scope, or plan. The project manager can create an environment where people want to belong to the project. By meeting with each person individually, the project manager can get a realistic sense of each person's involvement and commitment.

The project manager should craft a shared vision that is a collection of the expectations and interests of each of the team members. A constancy of purpose should tie everyone together and make everyone feel as though they've been heard. However, one of the most important criteria for creating a social network is a candid, approachable, and likeable project manager.

1. Why are project social networks important?
2. What other aspects should a project manager consider when developing a social network for the project?
3. Why is it important that a project team believe that the project manager is managing a project and not their work?

SOURCE: Adapted from Sainath Nagarajan, The Project Social Network, *Project@Works*, November 29, 2007.

---

groups to share information and help decide direction or policy, but performance will ultimately be a reflection of each manager and not the group. Work groups or single leader groups are viable and useful in many situations.

Real Teams   In cases where several individuals must produce a joint work product, teams are a better idea. More specifically, Katzenbach and Smith (1999) define a team as:

> a small number of people with complimentary skills who are committed to a common purpose, performance goals, and approach for which they hold themselves mutually accountable. (45)

Moreover, calling a group of people a team does not make it one nor does working together make a group a team. Teamwork focuses on performance, not on becoming a team. Subsequently, there are several *team basics* that define a real team:

- *A small number of people*—Ideally, a project team must be between two and twelve people. Although a large number of people can become a team, a large team can become a problem in terms of logistics and communication. As a result, a large team should break into subteams rather than try to function as one large unit.

- *Complementary skills*—For achieving the team's goal, a team must have or develop the right mix of skills that are complementary. These skills include:
  - Technical or functional expertise
  - Problem-solving or decision-making skills
  - Interpersonal skills—that is, people skills

- *Commitment to a common purpose and performance goals*—Katzenbach and Smith distinguish between activity goals (e.g., install a local area network) and performance goals (e.g., ship all orders within 24 hours of when they are received). The concept of a performance goal is similar to the concept of the MOV and sets the tone and aspirations of the team while providing a foundation for creating a common team purpose. As a result, the team develops direction, momentum, and commitment to its work. Moreover, a common performance goal and purpose inspires pride because people understand how their joint work product will impact the organization. A common goal also gives the team an identity that goes beyond the individuals involved.

- *Commitment to a common approach*—Although teams must have a common purpose and goal, they must also develop a common approach to how they will work together. Teams should spend as much time developing their approach as they do defining their goal and purpose. A common work approach should focus not only on economic and administrative issues and challenges, but also on the social issues and challenges that will shape how the team works together.

- *Mutual accountability*—A group can never become a team unless members hold themselves mutually accountable. The notion that "we hold ourselves accountable" is much more powerful than "the boss holds me accountable." Subsequently, no team can exist if everyone focuses on his or her individual accountability. Mutual accountability requires a sincere promise that each team member makes to herself or himself and to the other members of the team. This accountability requires both commitment and trust because it counters many cultures' emphasis on individualism. In short, it can be difficult for many people to put their careers and reputations in the hands of others. Unless a common approach and purpose has been forged as a team, individuals may have a difficult time holding themselves accountable as a team.

Based on their in-depth study of several teams, Katzenbach and Smith provide several commonsense findings:

- *Teams tend to flourish on a demanding performance challenge.* A clear performance goal is more important to team success than team-building exercises, special initiatives, or seeking team members with ideal profiles.

- *The team basics are often overlooked.* The weakest of all groups is the pseudo team, which is not focused on a common performance goal. If a team cannot shape a common purpose, it is doomed to achieving mediocre results. We cannot just tell a group of individuals to be a team.

- *Most organizations prefer individual accountability to team accountability.* Most job descriptions, compensation plans, and career paths emphasize individual accomplishments and, therefore, tend to make people uncomfortable trusting their careers to outcomes dependent on the performance of others.

Katzenbach and Smith provide some *uncommonsense* findings as well:

■ *Strong performance goals tend to spawn more real teams.* A project team cannot become a real team just because we call them a team or require them to participate in team-building activities or exercises. However, their findings suggest that real teams tend to thrive as a result of clearly defined performance-based goals.

■ *High performance teams are rare.* In their study of teams, Katzenbach and Smith identified high performance teams. These are real teams that outperform all other teams and even the expectations given. This special type of team requires an extremely high level of commitment to other team members and cannot be managed.

■ *Real teams provide the basis of performance.* Real teams combine the skills, experiences, and judgments of the team members to create a synergy that cannot be achieved through the summation of individual performance. Teams are also the best way to create a shared vision and sense of direction throughout the organization.

■ *Teams naturally integrate performance and learning.* Performance goals and common purposes translate into team members developing the skills needed to achieve those goals. As a result of open communication and trust, the members of a team are more apt to share their ideas and skills so that they may learn from one another. Moreover, successful teams have more fun, and their experiences are more memorable for both what the team accomplished and in terms of what each member learned as a result of the team process.

Project Teams and Knowledge Management

The primary challenge of real teams is to develop shared performance goals and a common purpose. For project teams following the IT project methodology, this challenge requires defining and getting agreement on the project's MOV. It also requires that the team members learn from each other and from other project teams' experiences.

In *The Radical Team Handbook*, John Redding (2000) describes a fundamentally new and different form of teamwork based on learning. Based on a study of 20 teams, Redding suggests that traditional teams tend to:

■ *Accept background information at face value.* In short, most teams accept the project challenge as it is first defined and do not challenge preconceived notions about the problem or opportunity and what they must do.

■ *Approach projects in a linear fashion.* Projects have a beginning and end, and the project plan outlines all of the steps needed to complete the project on time and within budget. Traditional teams tend to focus on the project's schedule and, therefore, base project success on completing the project on time and within budget.

■ *Provide run-of-the-mill solutions.* Since the team focuses on the challenge as it was handed to them (i.e., the way the challenge was originally framed), they never really understand the challenge and subsequently provide a solution that has minimal impact on the organization. In other words, the team may focus on a symptom and, therefore, never focus on the real problem or opportunity since the solutions remain within the original *frame* or how the challenge was originally presented to them.

In contrast, Redding describes a radical team as a team that is able to get to the root or fundamental issue or challenge. In general, radical teams do not accept the original performance challenge at its face value. The core objective of a radical team is to question and challenge the original framing of the problem or challenge at hand.

The way the problem or challenge is defined may very well be the problem. Too often a team is handed a performance challenge that is framed by a senior manager. For example, the team may be told by a senior manager that the company is losing money and, therefore, the team should focus on cutting costs. If the team accepts this framing of the challenge, they will develop a solution aimed at saving money. If, however, a team challenges this original frame, they may find out that the real reason why the organization is losing money is because customers are leaving due to poor service. Unless the project team understands the real problem in this case, its solution to cut costs will have little impact on the organization and the organization will continue to lose money.

Learning Cycles and Lessons Learned

Learning cycle theory was originally proposed by John Dewey in 1938 and used to describe how people learn (Kolb 1984). More recently, the concept of **learning cycles** has been applied to project teams and knowledge management. More specifically, learning cycles provide a way to resolve ambiguous situations through the repeated pattern of thinking through a problem (Dewey 1938). Figure 4.6 illustrates a team learning cycle.

Redding (2000) suggests that a team learning cycle has four phases:

1. *Understand and frame the problem.* It is important that a project team not accept the issues and challenges presented to them at face value. Assumptions must be surfaced and tested because the problem or issue as it is originally framed may not be the real problem after all. Thus, the project team must get to the root of the problem. At the beginning of a project, the team members' understanding may be quite general, or they may feel that they really do not understand the challenge assigned to them. Unfortunately, few people are willing to admit that they do not have all the answers or that their understanding of the team's challenge is limited. On the other hand, other members of the team may approach the project with a high degree of certainty—that is, they may act as though they know what the solution is and, therefore, the team just needs to work out the details of how to go about implementing the solution. Opinions are often accepted without question and can result in erroneous assumptions that lead the project team in the wrong direction or keep the team from getting at the real problem. Moreover, there is often pressure for the team to take immediate action so that the project can be completed on time and within budget. In either case, the team runs the risk of not getting to the root of the problem and may propose solutions that have minimal impact on the organization.

   For example, a project team may meet with a project sponsor who tells them that the company has an inventory problem. More specifically, the

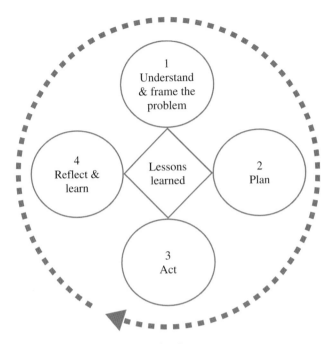

Figure 4.6 A Learning Cycle

SOURCE: The Radical Team Handbook, John Redding, Jossey-Bass 2000.
Reprinted by permission of John Wiley & Sons, Inc.

company has too much inventory on hand, and the cost to warehouse this inventory is becoming too costly. After touring the warehouse, the project team can see for themselves that the company's product takes up just about all the available floor space and is stacked to the ceiling. The project sponsor tells them that an information system would increase efficiency and therefore provide a solution for reducing inventory. Without questioning the problem (and solution) as it was handed to them, they may focus on solving the project just as it was handed to them.

Therefore, the project team must come to understand two things: Preconceived solutions are likely to produce run-of-the-mill results, and teams should encourage open humility. In other words, it is all right for team members to recognize and admit that they do not have all the answers, especially at the beginning of a project. As a result, team members may feel more comfortable admitting they have more questions than answers and the potential for preconceived ideas leading to mediocre solutions is reduced.

2. *Plan.* To help teams understand and reframe the problem, teams should create a shared understanding of the problem or opportunity. This understanding includes defining what the team is trying to accomplish and how they are going to go about it.

The team can brainstorm what they know (the facts), what they think they know (assumptions), and what they don't know (questions to be answered). Early in the project, a team may have more questions and assumptions than facts. That is to be expected because the team may not really understand the problem or challenge fully. Assumptions are ideas, issues, or concepts that must be tested (e.g., "The users will never agree to this," or "Senior management will never spend the money"). Often, a person can make an assumption sound like a fact, especially if she or he says it with enough conviction or authority. Therefore, it is every team member's responsibility to separate the facts (proof, evidence, or reality) from assumptions (theories, opinions, or guesses). On the other hand, if the team identifies (or admits) things it does not know, these can be classified as questions to be answered.

Figure 4.7 shows an example of a team learning record. After meeting with the sponsor and touring the warehouse, the team may list the facts, assumptions, and questions to be answered. The first column lists all the facts or evidence from their tour of the warehouse. The second column attempts to separate the sponsor's opinion from fact so the team does not fall into the trap of solving the wrong problem or just a symptom of the problem. The third column provides an opportunity to admit that no one has all the answers at this time, but answers can be found.

Once the project team identifies what it knows, what it thinks it knows, and what it needs to find out, it can create a plan of action. Team members can volunteer or be assigned to specific tasks that require testing assumptions

What we know (Facts)	What we think we know (Assumptions)	What we don't know (Questions to be Answered)
Company has too much inventory on hand	It may be an efficiency problem	Why are inventory levels so high?
Cost of maintaining current inventory is becoming prohibitive	Management believes a new information system will improve efficiency and therefore lower inventory levels	What are the current levels of inventory?
Inventory turnover needs to be increased		What is the desired level of inventory?

Figure 4.7   An Example of a Team Learning Record

SOURCE: Adapted from, *The Radical Team Handbook*, John Redding, Jossey-Bass 2000. Reprinted by permission of John Wiley & Sons, Inc.

or learning answers to questions. Documenting who does what by when also provides a tool for accountability. An example of a plan of action is illustrated in Figure 4.8.

3. *Act.* The key to team learning is carrying out the actions defined in the team's action plan. Team members can work on their own or together to test out assumptions, try out hunches, experiment, or gather and analyze data. The purpose of these actions should be to generate knowledge and test assumptions, not to complete a series of tasks like a to-do list. Thus, the purpose of these actions is to confirm or disconfirm assumptions and learn answers to questions the team does not know. Redding suggests that what teams do outside of meetings is just as important as the meeting itself because only by acting do teams have the opportunity to learn.

4. *Reflect and learn.* After the team has had a chance to carry out the action items in the action-learning plan, the team should meet to share its findings

Who?	Does What?	By When?
Shedelle and Steve	Interview sales team to understand past, current, and future trends for the company's product	Tuesday
Myra	Provide a detailed count of the current physical inventory on hand	Thursday
Corean	Research potential inventory management system commercial packages	Thursday
Steve	Research average inventory levels for the industry	Wednesday

Figure 4.8   An Example of an Action Plan for Team Learning

SOURCE: Adapted from, *The Radical Team Handbook*, John Redding, Jossey-Bass 2000. Reprinted by permission of John Wiley & Sons, Inc.

and reflect upon what everyone has learned. To be effective, this reflection must take place in an environment of openness, honesty, and trust. Once the team has a chance to meet and reflect on the information it has acquired, the team can document what it has learned. One format Redding suggests is for the team to answer the following questions:

- What do we know now that we didn't know before?
- Have we encountered any surprises? Have we gained any new insights? If so, what were they?
- What previous assumptions have been supported or refuted by what we have learned so far?
- How does the team feel the project is progressing at this point?
- How effective has the team been so far?

Following our example, the team may find out that the real reason why inventory levels are so high is because the company's product is obsolete or no longer in style. If the team had followed blindly the sponsor's recommendation that an information system would reduce inventory levels through efficiency, only modest improvements would have resulted. Remember: Many times the problem may be the way the problem is handed to you.

Another approach for documenting **lessons learned** is the United States Army's After Action Review (AAR). The format for an AAR is:

- *What was the intent?* Begin by going back and defining the original purpose and goal of the action.
- *What happened?* Describe as specifically and objectively as possible what actually occurred.
- *What have we learned?* Identify key information, knowledge, and insights that were gained as a result.
- *What do we do now?* Determine what will be done as a result of what has been learned, dividing actions into three categories: short-term, mid-term, and long-term.
- *Take action.*
- *Tell someone else.* Share what has been learned with anyone in the organization who might benefit.

The team learning cycles and lessons learned can be documented and shared with other project teams. However, the completion of a team's lessons learned marks the ending of one learning cycle and the beginning of another. Based on the learning that has transpired, the team can focus once again on understanding and reframing the problem and then repeat the plan, act, reflect and learn phases again. Figure 4.9 illustrates this concept.

As shown in Figure 4.9, an entire project can be viewed as a series of learning cycles. An initial team meeting can examine the original problem or challenge assigned to the team. During that meeting, the team can develop an initial action plan. Between meetings, the members of the team can then carry out their assigned tasks for testing assumptions or gathering information. At the next meeting, the team can reflect on what it has learned, document the lessons learned, and then start the beginning of a new cycle. Each cycle should be used to challenge the framing of the problem and create new opportunities for learning.

Teams do not always begin and end learning cycles at each meeting. Some learning cycles may take longer, and some can be accomplished in a shorter time if

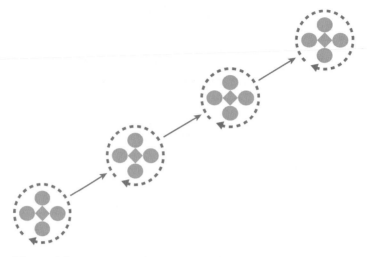

Figure 4.9   Team Learning Cycles over the Project Life Cycle

SOURCE: *The Radical Team Handbook*, John Redding, Jossey-Bass 2000. Reprinted by permission of John Wiley & Sons, Inc.

face-to-face meetings are not needed. Redding suggests, however, that three dimensions can be used to assess team learning: speed, depth, and breadth.

- *Speed*—First, a team should follow a learning cycle approach rather than a traditional, linear approach. Second, speed refers to the number of learning cycles completed. Therefore, the opportunity to learn can be increased if a team can complete more cycles in a given amount of time.

- *Depth*—Just increasing the number of learning cycles does not guarantee that teams will increase their learning. Subsequently, depth of learning refers to the degree to which a team can deepen its understanding of the project from cycle to cycle. This learning includes challenging the framing of the problem and various assumptions. In short, depth focuses on how well the team is able to dig below the surface in order to get to the root of the problem. Redding suggests that a team can measure depth by asking the question: Was the team's conception of the project at the end any different from what it was in the beginning? (47)

- *Breadth*—The breadth of learning refers to the impact the project has on the organization. It also focuses on whether the learning that has taken place within the team stays within the team or is shared and used throughout the organization. If a team can uncover complex relationships, it can develop a solution that impacts the whole organization. For example, what originally was thought to be a marketing problem could very well cross several functional or departmental boundaries.

THE PROJECT ENVIRONMENT

The project manager is responsible for many things. In addition to acquiring human resources, the project manager must also focus on the project environment. The project environment includes not only the physical space where the team will work, but the project culture. More specifically, the project environment includes:

- *A place to call home*—It may seem obvious, but a project team must have adequate space to work and meet. If the project team is internal to the organization, a work area may already be available. However, consultants often are found camped out in a conference room or even the organization's cafeteria because no other space is available. Therefore, the project manager should make sure that the team has a place to call home and a place to meet as a team for the duration of the project.

- *Technology*—In addition to having an adequate work area, the team will also need adequate technology support. Support may include a personal computer and appropriate software, Internet access, electronic mail, and a telephone. In addition, many teams today are geographically dispersed. Technology provides a means for teams to collaborate when they cannot meet at the same time in the same place. Collaboration tools not only can improve communication, but can increase the speed of the team's learning cycles by allowing the team to store and share minutes of team meetings, action plans, and lessons learned.

- *Office supplies*—Aside from technology resources, the team will need various office supplies, such as paper, pens, pencils, staplers, and so forth.

- *Culture*—Each organization has its own culture, but a project team should have its own culture as well. Culture reflects the values and norms of the team. One way of establishing a culture for the project team is to have the project team develop a team charter early on in the project. The team charter allows the team to agree on a set of values and expectations that will help define the project team culture. This charter includes:

  - What is expected from each member?
  - What role will each team member play?
  - How will conflicts be resolved?

Figure 4.10 provides an example of an actual team charter. Because many organizations operate globally today, many projects teams are made up of people from different backgrounds and cultures. The project manager and the project team members must be sensitive to these cultural differences.

Expectations and Team Values
- Everybody's ideas and opinions count
- Everyone must learn something new technically and with the business
- Work hard, but have fun
- Produce necessary, quality periodic deliverables throughout the course of the product
- Add values to clients' organization
- Heavy team commitment
- Show up for team meetings
- Team coordination
- Accountability
- Assistance
- Communication with clients and team

- No such thing as a stupid question
- *RESPECT for everyone*
- Research: expanding knowledge base as well as comfort zone
- Extend ourselves (Leave our comfort zones)
- Punctuality and group attendance
- Equal contributions from members
- Be prepared for meetings: check e-mail and team web site before every meeting
- Trust one another

Grievance Resolution
- Try to resolve issue with each team member first

Figure 4.10 Project Team Charter

QUICK THINKING—LEARNING FROM FAILURE

Michael Hugos says that he often learns more from failure than success. He concedes, "When I succeed, it just confirms what I already know—I'm a genius. When I fail, I have an opportunity to learn, if I can bring myself to take an objective look at what happened. This is hard, but then making the same mistakes over again is even harder. So failure can be a great opportunity to learn."

Hugos also provides some lessons learned from what he calls "one of the greatest learning experiences in his career" when he was a development leader on a systems development project that turned into a multimillion-dollar disaster. Since then, he has delivered many new systems successfully, and much of that success is due to the lessons he learned from the failure of this project. The following is a summary of what happened and some of the lessons learned from his experiences on that project.

- Although the project started out with great fanfare and enthusiasm, there were no clearly defined goals or objectives. The basic idea behind the system was to empower the sales force to grow revenues by $1 billion. *Lesson: Be wary when projects start out with wild enthusiasm and unclear goals. This can lead to the "bandwagon effect," where intelligent people do dumb things.*

- The first six months of the project was spent investigating technology and dreaming up ideas. The development team put together a slide show and a short demonstration of some of the technology. Senior management liked what it saw and approved major funding for the project. *Lesson: Getting lots of ideas and money can commit a team to unrealistic expectations. A better approach may be to focus on only a few realistic ideas that cost less money.*

- Four teams were working together on the project. One team was responsible for programming and hardware selection, while the other three worked on design specifications. Although all four teams were supposed to work together, the design teams began to duplicate each others' work. No single person was in charge of the entire project. Team members became confused, tempers flared, and feelings were hurt. *Lesson: Teams should have clear and nonoverlapping assignments, and a project leader should resolve disputes to keep the project on track.*

- After six months and hundreds of pages of specifications the design was still incomplete, but pressure mounted to start programming. Regardless, the design was handed over to the programming team who were overwhelmed by the volume and complexity of the specifications. *Lesson: Spending more time designing a system will result in greater complexity. It may be better to design and build smaller components of the system in short, iterative steps.*

- To cope with the pressure, the programmers began to change the specifications and cut out features they didn't understand. In addition, new hardware and software releases kept coming out, so the programmers rewrote many of the programs to take advantage of the new technology releases. It took about a year to program and reprogram the system. *Lesson: System specifications must be clear and complete. Developers should stick to them and not redesign the system while building it. New features can be added in future releases.*

- Beta testing resulted in a slow system that crashed often. *Lesson: After almost two years and such high expectations, the performance of the tests seriously damaged the credibility of the project.*

- Support for the system began to fade as the programmers scrambled to fix the bugs. Senior management began to question the constantly increasing budget and cancelled the project—writing off millions of dollars. *Lesson: Dividing a large project into smaller subsystems or projects is better than trying to deliver one large system in a few years. Smaller systems are easier to debug and can show a return to the organization more quickly.*

1. Should a project team wait until the end of a project to document its lessons learned?

2. How can lessons learned be documented and made available to other project teams?

3. What lessons have you learned from your experiences and applied them?

SOURCE: Adapted from Michael Hugos, Lessons Learned from a Major Project Failure, *Computerworld.* August 21, 2006.

CHAPTER SUMMARY

Organizations create a specific structure to support a particular strategy. If the organization performs poorly, then the firm will often develop a new strategy and/or formal organizational structure. Three different formal organizational structures were discussed in this chapter: the functional organization, the project organization, and the matrix organization. These organizational structures represent a continuum of possible structures, and an organization can create structures that are between functional and matrix organizations or matrix and project organizations.

Each organizational structure presents opportunities and challenges for projects in terms of flexibility, knowledge and expertise available, and authority and responsibilities. While the formal organization, in terms of an organizational or hierarchical chart, defines the official line of authority and communication, the informal organization includes the informal relationships and internetworking of people within the organization that develops over time. Understanding the formal and informal sides of an organization is important because it will help the project manager and project team better understand the politics and culture of the organization and provide greater insight into the decision-making process.

The project manager is a key position that should be filled at the earliest stages of the project. The project manager plays many important roles that include not only the traditional roles of a manager, but roles specific to the nature of projects. Therefore, the project manager must be a skillful communicator, negotiator, organizer, and relationship builder. In addition, the project manager must perform several critical tasks, including selecting and acquiring members of the project team and creating the project environment.

Two relatively new approaches to managing project teams were introduced in this chapter. First, *The Wisdom of Teams* by Jon R. Katzenbach and Douglas K. Smith (1999) provides a new language and discipline for project teams. For example, a work group can follow a traditional approach where a single leader or boss is in control, makes most of the decisions, and delegates to subordinates who work independently from each other. Or a work group can include several individuals who come together to share information or set policy, but work independently from one another and do not necessarily share the same performance goals or work products. On the other hand, real teams are a

special type of team, with a few individuals with complimentary skills who focus on a performance-based goal and share a common purpose and approach. Based on their study of teams, Katzenbach and Smith found that real teams consistently outperform work groups.

Project team members must learn from each other and from other project team experiences if they are to provide a solution that gets to the root of the problem and not just a symptom. Learning cycle theory has been around since 1938, but has recently been applied to team learning and knowledge management. In *The Radical Team Handbook*, John Redding (2000) provides an interesting approach for teams based on learning cycles. Here, it is important that a team not accept the problem or challenge as it is originally presented to them. Following a learning cycle, the team follows four phases: (1) understand and frame the problem, (2) plan, (3) act, and (4) reflect and learn. The conclusion of a learning cycle and the beginning of the next is marked by the documentation of lessons learned.

Instead of developing a solution prematurely, the project team is to encourage open humility by acknowledging that it does not have all the answers, especially at the beginning of a project. Therefore, the project team is encouraged to discuss and separate facts from assumptions or opinions. The team then creates an action plan to research questions and test assumptions. When the team meets, the members reflect on and learn from the information collected. Surprises, insights, and confirmed (or disconfirmed) assumptions are then documented as lessons learned. A team's learning can be assessed using three dimensions: (1) speed or the number of learning cycles, (2) depth or the degree to which the team deepened its understanding of the project, and (3) breadth or the impact of the team's proposed solution on the organization.

Although the project manager is responsible for overseeing many project activities, it is his or her responsibility to ensure that the project team has an adequate work environment. A suitable workspace and the technology to support the team are necessary. In addition, each project should define its own culture. It is helpful to have the team develop a team charter that outlines the roles, values, expectations, and methods for resolving conflict in order to set proper expectations.

REVIEW QUESTIONS

1. What is the relationship between an organization's strategy and organizational structure?
2. What is meant by the formal organization?
3. Why is it important for a project manager to understand the formal organization?
4. Describe the functional organizational structure.
5. What are some challenges for IT projects under the functional organizational structure?
6. What are some opportunities for IT projects under the functional organizational structure?
7. Describe the project organizational structure.
8. What are some challenges for IT projects under the project organizational structure?
9. What are some opportunities for IT projects under the project organizational structure?
10. Describe the matrix organizational structure.
11. What are some challenges for IT projects under the matrix organizational structure?
12. What are some opportunities for IT projects under the matrix organizational structure?
13. What is projectitis? When might you expect to encounter projectititis? How could an organization minimize the likelihood of projectititis?
14. Describe the balanced matrix, functional matrix, and project matrix organizational structures.
15. Describe what is meant by the informal organization. Why should the project manager or project team be concerned with understanding the informal organization?
16. What is a stakeholder?
17. How does conducting a stakeholder analysis help the project manager and project team understand the informal organization?
18. Why would the project manager and project team not want to make a stakeholder analysis public to the entire organization?
19. In conducting a stakeholder analysis, why is it important not only to identify those who will gain from the project's success, but also those who may gain from its failure?
20. What is the purpose of defining a role and objective for each stakeholder identified in the stakeholder analysis?
21. Describe the roles of a project manager.
22. What qualities are required for a good project manager? Can you come up with any on your own?
23. What skills or qualities are important in selecting a project team?
24. What is the difference between a work group and a real team?
25. What is the difference between a performance-based goal and an activity-based goal? Give an example of each.
26. Why is focusing on a performance-based goal, such as a project's MOV, more important than having the team go through a series of team-building exercises?
27. Why do you think many teams accept the project opportunity at face value and never question the way the project was originally framed?
28. Describe the concept of a learning cycle.
29. What purpose does creating a lesson learned at the end of a learning cycle provide?
30. What advantage does a team have when it encourages open humility instead of trying to solve the problem or provide a solution as soon as possible?
31. What is meant by the speed of learning cycles? How is speed associated with team learning?
32. What is meant by depth of learning cycles? How is depth associated with team learning?
33. What is meant by breadth of learning cycles? How is breadth associated with team learning?
34. What is the project environment? Why must a project manager ensure that a proper project environment is in place?

EXTEND YOUR KNOWLEDGE

1. Develop and write a job description for hiring a project manager to manage an Enterprise Resource Planning (ERP) project. Once the job description is complete, describe how you might go about finding this person externally. What sources would you use?

2. If you are working on a semester assignment with other individuals in your class, complete a stakeholder analysis using the Stakeholder Analysis Chart in Figure 4.5.

3. If you are working with other students on a semester project assignment, do you consider yourselves more of a work group or a team? Why? How effectively has this worked for you? What would you like to change? What would you like to leave the same?

4. If you are working with a team on a class project, go through a learning cycle as a team.

   ■ Write down the problem or challenge assigned to your team as you originally understood it. What is the MOV (i.e., performance-based goal) that your team is trying to achieve?

   ■ Using the following table as a guide, write down what you know (facts), what you think you know (assumptions), and what you don't know (questions to be answered). Be sure to challenge any opinions or assumptions before concluding they are facts.

What We Know (Facts)	What We Think We Know (Assumptions)	What We Don't Know (Questions to be Answered)

   ■ Once you and your team members finish brainstorming facts, assumptions, and questions, develop an action plan and assign responsibilities for each member of the team using the following table as a guide. Agree on a meeting day and time so that each member has a chance to complete his or her assignment and so that the team can meet to discuss these findings.

Who?	Does What?	By When?

   ■ After everyone has had a chance to complete his or her action-learning assignments, the team should meet to share this information. Each member should take a turn presenting what he or she found. While a team member is presenting what they found, the other members must listen carefully and not challenge any of the information presented. Clarification questions are fine. After each member has had a chance to present her or his findings, the team should focus on the following questions:

   a. Is there anything we know now that we didn't know before?

   b. Were there any surprises? Have we gained any new insights? If so, what are they?

   c. What assumptions have been supported and not supported?

   d. How well is the team progressing?

   e. The answers to these questions should be documented. Once documented, the team has completed one full learning cycle. The next step is to start over and reframe the project challenge as you did in Part a.

GLOBAL TECHNOLOGY SOLUTIONS

Tim Williams thought he was going to be the first one to arrive at the office, but as he turned into the parking lot, he could see Kellie Matthews' car in its usual spot. Tim parked his car next to Kellie's and strode into the GTS office. This was going to be an exciting and busy day because several new employees were going to report for their first day of work at GTS. He wanted to get to the office early so he could greet them and prepare for their day of orientation.

As Tim walked through the office door, he made a beeline for the small kitchen area where a fresh pot of coffee was waiting. The smell brought a smile to his face as he poured the dark liquid into his favorite coffee mug. Tim turned around as Kellie entered the kitchen area. "Good morning!" Kellie exclaimed. Tim never had been a morning person, and he wondered to himself how anyone could be so cheerful this early. He tried to be as cheerful as possible given that he hadn't had his first cup of coffee. "Good morning to you, too." Tim could see that Kellie was at least one cup of coffee ahead of him, which gave him some consolation. "Care for another cup?" Tim asked as he offered to pour a cup for Kellie. "Sure, thanks," said Kellie as she held the cup out.

As Tim poured the coffee for Kellie, she smiled and said, "After you left yesterday, I received a phone call from Sitaramin. He said that he would accept our offer and join us at GTS next week." That news seemed to wake Tim up. "That's great!" Tim exclaimed.

Both Tim and Kellie have been busy during the last two weeks interviewing and negotiating with a number of candidates to join GTS. With the addition of Sitaramin, the team for the Husky Air project would be complete.

Kellie sipped her coffee and said, "Well, our budget for salaries is going to be slightly higher than we had planned, but I guess that can be expected given the job market for information systems professionals and the fact that we had to pay a premium because we're a start-up company. But if all goes well, I'm pretty sure that the Husky Air project will still be profitable for us. We can develop a detailed project plan and use the latest software metrics for planning the project schedule and budget, but the success of this project rests largely on how well this team performs."

Tim agreed, looked at his watch and said, "We have about an hour before our new employees arrive. I suggest we go over the details of the day's agenda one more time." Tim refilled his coffee mug and Kellie's before they made their way to the conference room where the orientation would be held. As they walked down the hall, Tim thought about what Kellie had said. He knew that it was going to be a challenge to form a cohesive and high-performance team from people who would meet for the first time in less than an hour.

Things to Think About

1. What feelings might a new employee have when starting a new job?

2. What could GTS do to help new employees transition successfully to their new jobs?

3. Why does the success of a project rest largely on the performance of the team?

4. How can a group of individuals become a cohesive and high-performing team?

 ## HUSKY AIR ASSIGNMENT—PILOT ANGELS

Developing a Stakeholder Analysis

To become more familiar with the project environment, you will conduct a stakeholder analysis. Use the following grid and information about each stakeholder to complete your analysis.

1. Create a list of project stakeholders. The following will provide a basis for your analysis.

- **L. T. Scully** is the president and CEO of Husky Air. He hired Global Technology Services (GTS), the consulting firm, to work on the Pilot Angels project. He believes that this project will allow Husky Air to increase the number of charitable flights significantly but in a cost-effective manner. L. T. has the authority to authorize all payments for the project.

Stakeholder	Interest	Influence	Potential Conflicts	Role	Objective	Strategy

- **Alma Coleman** currently schedules and coordinates all Pilot Angel flights using a manual system. She has been with Husky Air from the beginning, but has worked for various organizations over the past 40 years. She has mentioned to various individuals that she is apprehensive about using a computer and will consider retiring if the new computer system is "just too hard to learn." Alma just about knows all of the volunteer pilots and healthcare organization contacts on a first-name basis, and believes that an automated system will depersonalize these relationships. Although she maintains meticulous care of all the paper files and folders, she has been accommodating but not enthusiastic when she has had to interact with any of the GTS project team members.

- **Tim Williams** is the project manager and one of the co-owners of GTS. Aside from contributing to the bottom line of GTS, this project, if successful, can lead to additional projects with Husky Air.

- **Sitaramin, Yan, and Pat** are employed by GTS and members of the project team who will be involved in the design, development, and delivery of the new Pilot Angels system. Sitaramin and Yan are experienced and knowledgeable systems analysts who have the requisite database and programming skills. Pat is a network specialist with several technical certifications.

- **Volunteer pilots** provide the means for transporting patients, organs, or medical personnel. They donate their time and use of their aircraft.

- **Passengers** include patients, their family, caregivers, or other medical personnel.

- Review the case at the end of Chapter 1 to come up with any other stakeholder whom you think should be included.

2. Complete the analysis:
   - Determine each stakeholder's interest in the project. For example, you could represent a positive interest with (+1), a negative interest with (−1), or neutral interest with (0).
   - Define each stakeholder's degree of influence. Use a scale of 0 (no influence) to 5 (high influence).
   - Describe any potential conflicts with other stakeholders.
   - Develop a metaphor for each stakeholder to reflect his or her role in the project (e.g., project champion, leader, ally, etc.).
   - Identify an objective for each stakeholder that will make the best use of the stakeholder if he or she has a positive interest in the project's outcome, help to overcome any potential conflicts with other stakeholders, or gain the acceptance or approval of any stakeholders who may have a negative interest in the project's success.
   - Develop a strategy that outlines how each stakeholder may be involved in the project. This should focus on attaining the objective you set for each stakeholder.

 # CASE STUDIES

Choosing the Right Team

Bill was a novice attending his first meeting with other project managers to pick people for their upcoming projects. He felt like the other project managers stepped all over him when he ended up with all the "leftovers." He vowed that he would never let that happen again when his project didn't go all that well.

The next time, Bill thought he was better prepared. Before the meeting, he approached the top-skilled people and sold them on the project so their managers agreed to let them work on Bill's project. According to Bill, "I got all the people I wanted. And it turned out to be a terrible project."

Bill picked his team for their technical skills and ended up with a team of prima donnas who couldn't work together. Bill learned a few things over the years. First, a great project team requires more than just great technical skills. It takes the right mix of "soft" skills, personalities, and attitudes to make a team gel.

Unfortunately, many project managers fall back on some of the most common questions used in interviews to help select people for their projects. Some of them can be downright dumb. Examples include:

- *"Where do you see yourself in five years?"* Few organizations can guarantee you a job for five years so a career path is even more difficult to predict. You can always answer that you hope to be "happy and productive working in a job you love for a company that values your talents."

- *"What would you do if I gave you an elephant (or insert here: some other ridiculous object)?"*

Sometimes interviewers ask this ridiculous question to new graduates because they think it's cute and because it's supposed to test how they think.

■ *"What are your weaknesses?"* The stock answer to this question is "I'm a perfectionist" even though you're really thinking that it's putting up with people who ask dumb questions.

This is just an example of some of the questions people ask. The objective of an interview is not to make the candidate squirm, or to be a psychology exam. Some interview questions can be illegal if they deal with age, family responsibilities, and lifestyle. Some examples include:

■ *Can you work overtime, evenings, and weekends?*

■ *What child care arrangements have you made?*

■ *How old are you?*

■ *Where were you born?*

■ *What is your marital status?*

■ *Are you living with anyone?*

■ *Do you plan on having more children?*

■ *What are your religious beliefs?*

■ *Have you ever filed a lawsuit against an employer?*

So what questions should you ask to help you make the right decision? Questions should help make the right decision and give some insight as to how well someone will perform on the project. This requires being specific, since a decision to hire or bring someone on the project team can be very difficult to undo.

■ *Ask for real examples of what the person has accomplished.* A resume will tell you something about a person, but you really need to find out what they can do. Looking at someone's work is a good method for understanding a person's capabilities. Ask them to provide you with a sample of their work.

■ *Use the review of their work as a guide to prepare specific questions.* In a follow-up interview, you can ask the candidate to take you through how they developed the sample of the work they left with you. You can ask them to critique it first by asking them what they liked and then didn't like about it. Ask them how they made certain choices and then ask your prepared questions concerning what else you'd like to know about their work.

■ *Give them a deliverable like a program, database design, or project plan to critique.* A few days before, forward a good, but not great, deliverable, to the candidate. This could be something that has some things that could be improved. Ask questions regarding what works

or doesn't work. What could be improved? Or what would they have done differently?

■ *Scenarios and case studies can be used as an interview exercise.* Real and project situations that someone could reasonably expect to encounter can be a useful interview too. Examples could include handling a change request, or a risk that needs to be addressed, or dealing with conflicts. It is important to give the candidate enough time to think about a response and have a specific response in mind.

■ *Have the candidate meet with the team members he or she will work with.* This can provide an invaluable sense of how the candidate might interact with the project team. The team members should have some specific questions in mind when talking with the candidate, and you should have questions in mind when talking with the team afterwards. The focus should be on how the candidate and team interact—not on the skills.

These suggestions will not guarantee that you always will pick the perfect team; however, they may help get a better sense of who you will be dealing with and how they may react in certain situations. As Mark Mullaly points out, "Sure, you can just ask someone what their strengths and weaknesses are. For my money, though, it's far more valuable to get them to show you."

1. Suppose you are the project manager for a small project that will be based in Chicago. At this point, you have four other project team members on board. All you need to do is hire a C++ programmer. Later today you will be interviewing Mary, who recently graduated from a large university nearby. Develop a interview plan that includes an itinerary and set of interview questions. Mary is schedule to arrive at 10 AM and will be available until 4 PM.

SOURCE: Adapted from:

Kathleen Melymuka, How to Pick a Project Team, *Computerworld*, April 12, 2004.

Mark Mullaly, Deadly Questions for the Killer Candidate, *Gnatthead.com*, August 11, 2005.

Liz Ryan, Stupid Interview Questions, *Business Week*, September 21, 2005.

Ronald L. Krannich, 38 Illegal, Sensitive, and Stupid Interview Questions . . . and How to Respond, Washingtonpost.com, April 11, 2003.

The Project Manager Career Path

There are basically three career paths for project managers: corporate project managers, consultant project managers, and the independent project manager. Each type of project manager works in a distinct environment with its own unique advantages, disadvantages, opportunities, and challenges.

The *corporate project manager* is an employee of an organization assigned either to manage an internal project or oversee the installation of the company's product or service for a client or customer.

Advantages

- The organization may have a project management office (PMO) that has a standardized project methodology in place.
- An enterprise-level software system is often available to help manage projects and project resource availabilities and skill sets.
- The project manager usually has a high level of authority because of a strong link between project team members' performance and compensation and/or career progression.
- The corporate project manager generally has input in choosing his or her project team.
- Project procurement, financial, and other major project functions are managed by a central organizational function like the accounting department.
- Key project team members on an internal project would be from the same organization as the project manager so everyone would share similar knowledge of the organization and industry, as well as organizational culture.

Disadvantages

- The corporate project manager may have to deal with more organizational politics, controls, or bureaucracy.
- Senior management's priorities may change, resulting in weak sponsorship and resources diverted to other projects.
- Project managers may become protective of their resources and thereby limit the exchange of resources among other projects.
- A project manager can become typecast or so focused in a particular industry or product line that moving to another project environment may be difficult. Often the project manager is too busy to be released for training.
- Often the most talented project managers are called in to take over a failing project even when a successful recovery is improbable.

The *consultant project manager* manages a project as part of a contractual engagement for a client. In many cases, the consultant project manager begins the project after the requirements and objectives are locked down in a signed contract. Although one could make the case that all project managers are essentially consultants, the consultant project manager is transplanted to a new project environment rather than the project coming into the project manager's environment.

Advantages

- The consulting organization may have its own proven project methodology or solution to support the consulting team.
- A consulting firm may have many successful and experienced project managers with diverse skills and experiences to assist other project managers with peer advice, mentoring, or coaching.
- Often a client will call upon a consultant when they need experienced or expert help. Depending on the consulting organization's reputation, the consultant's advice can carry a great deal of credibility initially. Subsequently, the consultant project manager usually has the freedom to use new ideas, technologies, or methods when creative solutions are needed.

Disadvantages

- Typically, the client sponsor reserves and defines project management authority before the outside consultant is selected, so the consultant project manager may have little or no input to select team members from the client side.
- The consultant project manager may work with a project team made up of consultants from the same firm, the client organization, and even consultants from competitor organizations.
- Scope, schedule, and time estimates may be unrealistic if the project manager was not involved with the original project planning. Subsequently, the project manager and team may be locked into a project doomed from the beginning.
- Some clients may have the "Not invented here" or "You're not experienced enough" attitude or perception that can be difficult to overcome.
- It is not uncommon for employment to be discontinued at the close of the project.

The *independent project manager* works as an independent contractor or practitioner. He or she is a company of one.

Advantages

- As a self-employed project management consultant, the independent project manager has the freedom to refuse undesirable projects.

- Work and life outside of work may be planned with more balance and control.

- Often the independent contractor has built a reputation for service or expertise in a very specific area. Clients may therefore perceive this person as someone who is more cost effective than hiring someone with similar skills and experience, or hiring a consulting firm.

- This project environment can provide a direct relationship between the independent contractor and the client.

- Delivering a specialized, high-quality product or service can be extremely rewarding.

Disadvantages

- Developing the business (e.g., developing marketing materials, maintaining a Web site, writing proposals, billing and collecting for services) can be time consuming and requires additional skills and resources.

- The independent contractor must be aware of tax status and financial reporting requirements.

- Clients can come up with surprises that must be dealt with in an efficient and professional manner.

- Changes in the marketplace can have an immediate and detrimental impact if the majority of a contractor's client base is in one area.

- Clients may expect more travel and tighter deadlines. Or if the contractor only has one client, the client may feel solely leased to the project.

1. Which project manager model appeals most to you? Why?

2. Why is it important that you manage your own career while your knowledge and experience as a project manager grows?

3. What does a person need to consider if he or she was a corporate or consultant project manager and desires to become an independent project manager/contractor? What skills would be transferable? What skills would have to be acquired?

SOURCE: Adapted from Ann Sachs, Whose Grass is Greener?, *Projects@Work*, January 31, 2008.

BIBLIOGRAPHY

Dewey, J. 1938. *Logic: The Theory of Inquiry*. New York: Holt, Rinehart, and Winston.

Gray, C. F. and E. W. Larson 2000. *Project Management: The Managerial Process*. Boston: Irwin McGraw-Hill.

Katzenbach, J. R. and D. K. Smith 1999. *The Wisdom of Teams*. New York: HarperCollins Publishers.

Kolb, D. 1984. *Experiential Learning*. Upper Saddle River, N.J.: Prentice Hall.

Larson, E. W. and D. H. Gobeli 1988. Organizing for Product Development Projects. *Journal of Product Innovation Management* 5: 180–190.

McLeod, G. and D. Smith 1996. *Managing Information Technology Projects*. Danvers, Mass: Boyd & Fraser Publishing Company.

Meredith, J. R. and S. J. Mantel, Jr. 2000. *Project Management: A Managerial Approach*. New York: John Wiley.

Nicholas, J. M. 1990. *Managing Business and Engineering Projects: Concepts and Implementation*. Upper Saddle River, N.J.: Prentice Hall.

Project Management Institute (PMI) 2004. *A Guide to the Project Management Body of Knowledge (PMBOK® Guide)*. Newtown Square, PA: PMI Publishing.

Redding, J. C. 2000. *The Radical Team Handbook*. San Francisco: Jossey-Bass.

5

Defining and Managing
Project Scope

CHAPTER OVERVIEW

Chapter 5 focuses on developing a scope management plan to define and manage the project and product deliverables of the project. After studying this chapter, you should understand and be able to:

- Identify the five processes that support project scope management. These processes, defined in the *PMBOK Guide®*, include scope planning, scope definition, create work breakdown structure (WBS), scope verification, and scope control.
- Describe the difference between product scope (i.e., the features and functions that must support the IT solution) and project scope (i.e., the deliverables and activities that support IT project methodology).
- Apply several tools and techniques for defining and managing the project's scope.

INTRODUCTION

This chapter focuses on defining and managing the work that must be accomplished by the project team over the course of the project. The term **scope** is used to define the work boundaries and deliverables of the project so what needs to get done, gets done—and only what needs to get done, gets done. Therefore, it is important to define not only what *is* part of the project work, but also what *is not* part of the project work. Any work not part of the project is considered to be outside of the project's scope.

Project Scope Management Processes

The *Guide to the Project Management Body of Knowledge (PMBOK Guide®)* defines five project processes that support the knowledge area called project scope management. These processes are summarized in Table 5.1. This process group begins with

Table 5.1   Scope Management Processes

Scope Management Process	Description
Scope planning	The development of a scope management plan that defines the project's scope and how it will be verified and controlled throughout the project
Scope definition	A detailed scope statement that defines what work will and will not be part of the project and will serve as a basis for all future project decisions
Create work breakdown structure	The decomposition or dividing of the major project deliverables into smaller and more manageable components
Scope verification	Confirmation and formal acceptance that the project's scope is accurate, complete, and supports the project's MOV
Scope control	Ensuring that controls are in place to manage proposed scope changes once the project's scope is set. These procedures must be communicated and understood by all project stakeholders

scope planning once the project sponsor gives the project manager the authority and resources to develop a scope management plan. Scope planning lays out all the processes, tools, and techniques that will be used by the project team to define and manage the project's scope. This plan can be a large, formal document, depending on the size and complexity of the project.

Scope definition and **create work breakdown structure (WBS)** both help to determine what is and is not included in the project work. This sets the work boundary for the project and identifies the project deliverables (as defined in the IT Project Methodology) and the product deliverables (the features and functionality of the IT solution). The WBS organizes and defines all the work to be completed by the project team in terms of a hierarchical decomposition of all of the project's deliverables. In this text, we will begin the introduction of the WBS by introducing several tools that will lead to a more formal WBS that will be described in the next chapter. These tools include the Deliverable Definition Table (DDT) and the Deliverable Structure Chart (DSC) for defining the project-oriented deliverables, as well as the Context Data Flow Diagram (DFD) and Use Case Diagram (UCD) that can be used for defining the product-oriented deliverables. Accurate definition of these deliverables is critical for the next step when we plan and estimate the project's schedule and budget.

Once the scope is defined, the process of **scope verification** confirms that the scope is complete and accurate. The project team and sponsor must agree to all of the project deliverables. This not only sets expectations, but also focuses the project team on what needs to get done and what is outside the scope of the project. The project's scope should be considered complete if it supports the project's MOV.

Time and resources will be wasted needlessly if the scope of the project is never defined accurately or agreed upon. However, changes to the scope may be inevitable as new information becomes available or if the needs of the organization change. Therefore, a process called **scope change control** is needed to handle these changes so that if a scope change is appropriate, the change can be approved in order to amend the project's schedule and budget accordingly. In addition, scope change control procedures also protect the scope boundary from expanding as a result of *increasing featurism*, requests by project stakeholders to keep adding additional features and functions (i.e., bells and whistles) to the project once the scope has been set. Remember that the scope, schedule, and budget relationships suggest that increasing the project's scope (i.e., expanding the scope boundary) will generally require an increase in schedule and budget. Therefore, adding additional work to the project's scope will ultimately lead to a project that misses its deadline and costs more than originally estimated. Subsequently, once the project's scope has been set, approved changes to the project's scope must be reflected in the project's baseline plan.

Together, the processes and techniques for defining and managing scope make up the **scope management plan**. Depending on the size and nature of the project, this plan can be separate and/or summarized in the project charter. Regardless, the procedures for defining and managing the scope of a project must be communicated and understood by all of the project's stakeholders to minimize the likelihood of misunderstandings. Moreover, the project's scope must align and support the project's MOV. Why spend time and resources to perform work that will not add any value to the organization or help the project achieve its MOV? Again, work that does not add value consumes valuable time and resources needlessly. Figure 5.1 summarizes the components and processes of a scope management plan.

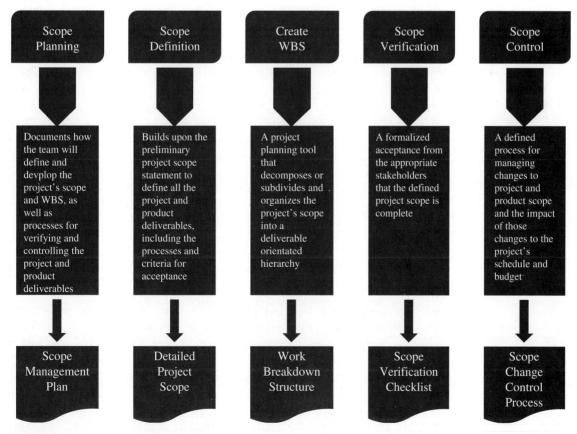

Figure 5.1 Scope Management Plan

SCOPE PLANNING

> Failure to define what is part of the project, as well as what is not, may result in work being performed that was unnecessary to create the product of the project and thus lead to both schedule and budget overruns.
>
> Olde Curmudgeon, *PM Network Magazine*, 1994

Scope planning begins with a process that formally authorizes the project manager and team to develop the scope management plan. In terms of the IT project methodology, this authorization is given after the project is formally accepted and funds are committed to developing the project charter and plan by the project sponsor or client. The business case provides important information about the project's description, MOV, risks, assumptions, and feasibility. In addition, the business case provides information about the background of the project in terms of why it was proposed and how it aligns with the organization's overall strategic plan.

Scope planning, however, is a process for defining and documenting the project work. More specifically, a project's scope defines all the work, activities, and deliverables that the project team must provide in order for the project to achieve its MOV. It is an important step in developing the project plan since one must know what work must be done before an estimate can be made of how long it will take and how much it will cost. The scope management plan documents how the scope will be defined, verified, and controlled, as well as how the work breakdown structure will be defined and created.

Scope Boundary

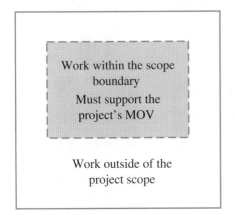

Figure 5.2   Scope Boundary

Defining the scope boundary is the first step to establishing what is, and what is not, part of the project work to be completed by the project team. Think of the scope boundary as a fence designed to keep certain things in and other things out. As Figure 5.2 illustrates, any work within the scope boundary should include only the work or activities that support the project's MOV. This work is what we want to capture and keep within our fence. On the other hand, a project team can spend a great deal of time doing work and activities that will not help the project achieve its MOV. As a result, the project will consume time and resources with very little return. Therefore, the scope boundary must protect the scope from these activities once it is set and agreed upon by the project stakeholders. Having a clear and agreed-upon definition of the project MOV is critical for defining and managing the scope boundary.

The Scope Statement

One way to define the scope boundary is to create a more detailed **scope statement** that documents the project sponsor's needs and expectations. This can be based on the preliminary scope statement developed in the project charter. For example, let's say we are outside consultants hired to develop an electronic commerce application for a bank. After developing and presenting a business case to our client, we have been given the authority to develop the project charter and plan. Although the business case provides a great deal of relevant information, we will still set up several meetings and interviews with key stakeholders in the bank. Based upon these meetings and interviews, we create a scope statement.

Scope Statement

1. Develop a proactive electronic commerce strategy that identifies the processes, products, and services to be delivered through the World Wide Web.

2. Develop an application system that supports all of the processes, products, and services identified in the electronic commerce strategy.

3. Integrate the application system with the bank's existing enterprise resource planning system.

It is just as important to clarify what work is not to be included, that is, what work is outside the scope of the project. Often the scope of a project is defined through interviews, meetings, or brainstorming sessions. Stakeholders often suggest ideas that are interesting, but not feasible or appropriate for the current project.

Let's say that in our example a certain bank vice president pushed for a customer relationship management (CRM) and a data mining component to be included in the application system. The bank's president, however, has decided that the time and effort to add these components cannot be justified because launching the Web site in eight months is vital to bank's competitive strategy. Let's also assume that conducting technology and organizational assessments of our client's current environment is an important piece of our project methodology. But because the bank would like to control some of the costs of this project, we agree that its IT department will conduct that study. The results of this study will then be documented and provided to us.

In this case, it is critical that we define explicitly both what is and what is not part of the project scope. Individuals from both organizations may believe that specific project work (i.e., the assessment study), system features, or functionality (i.e., CRM and data mining) will be part of this project. These beliefs may result in misunderstandings that lead to false expectations or needless work. To manage these expectations, it is useful to list explicitly what is *not* part of the project's scope.

Out of Scope for This Project

1. Technology and organizational assessment of the current environment

2. Customer resource management and data mining components

Setting the scope boundary for the project not only sets expectations, but also can define the constraints of the project and how the product of the organization fits within the organization, that is, the system must integrate with the organization's existing systems.

The scope statement provides a very general and high-level view of the project work and provides only a starting point for defining the scope of our project. At the beginning of a project, our understanding of the project's scope may be limited. However, as we work more closely with our client, more information is uncovered and our understanding of the project increases. Subsequently, the project scope will evolve from being very general and high level to more detailed and defined.

PROJECT SCOPE DEFINITION

Developing a scope statement is a useful first step for defining the scope of the project and setting a boundary. A project's scope, however, should also be defined in terms of the deliverables that the team must provide. These deliverables can be divided into project-oriented deliverables and product-oriented deliverables. This separation gives the team a clearer definition of the work to be accomplished and improves the likelihood of accurately assigning resources and estimating the time and cost of completing the work. Moreover, a clear definition of the project's deliverables sets unambiguous expectations and agreement among all of the project stakeholders. This will provide the important details needed to create the work breakdown structure.

Project-Oriented Scope

Project-oriented deliverables, or **scope**, support the project management and IT development processes that are defined in the information technology project methodology (ITPM). Project scope includes such things as the business case, project charter, and project plan and defines the work products of the various ITPM phases. Project-oriented deliverables also include specific deliverables such as a current systems study, requirements definition, and the documented design of the information system. These are deliverables supported by the systems development life cycle (SDLC) component of the overall ITPM.

Project-oriented deliverables require time and resources and, therefore, must be part of the overall project schedule and budget. Their role is to ensure that the project processes are being completed so that the project's product (i.e., the information system) achieves the project's MOV and objectives. Project-oriented deliverables also provide tangible evidence of the project's progress (or lack of progress). Finally, they allow the project manager to set a baseline for performance and quality control because they usually require some form of approval before work on the next project phase or deliverable begins.

Project-Oriented Scope Definition Tools   All of the project deliverables must have a clear and concise definition. One way to communicate the project's deliverables is to create a **deliverable definition table (DDT)**. An example of a DDT for our bank's electronic commerce system is illustrated in Table 5.2.

The purpose of the DDT is to define all of the project-oriented deliverables to be provided by the project team. Each deliverable should have a clear purpose. In addition, it is important to define the structure of the deliverable. For example, a deliverable could be a document (paper or electronic), prototype, presentation, or the application system itself. This sets the expectation of what will be *delivered* by the project team. Moreover, the standards provide a means to verify whether the deliverable was produced correctly. These standards could be defined within the IT Project methodology, controlling agency (e.g., International Organization for Standardization), or through various quality standards established by the organization. In general, each deliverable must be verified and approved by the project sponsor and/or the project manager. It is important that the responsibility for approving a deliverable be clearly defined as well. Once a deliverable is approved, the project team is authorized to begin work on the next deliverable. This provides authorization control as well as a basis for logically sequencing the work. Finally, it is important that the resources required to complete the deliverable be defined.

Table 5.2 Deliverable Definition Table

Deliverable	Structure	Standards	Approval Needed By	Resources Required
Business case	Document	As defined in the project methodology	Project sponsor	Business case team & office automation (OA) tools
Project charter & project plan	Document	As defined in the project methodology	Project sponsor	Project manager, project sponsor, & OA tools
Technology & organizational assessment	Document	As defined in the project methodology	Project manager & project sponsor	Bank's systems analysts users, case tool, and OA tools
Requirements definition	Document	As defined in the project methodology	Project manager	System analyst, users, case tool, & OA tools
User interface	Prototype	As defined in the user interface guidelines	Project sponsor	System analyst, programmer, users, & integrated development environment (IDE)
Physical & technical design	Document	As defined in the project methodology	Project manager & project sponsor	System analyst, programmer, & case tool
Application system	Files & database	As defined in the project methodology	Project sponsor	Programmers, system analysts, network specialists, program development tools, and relational database management system
Testing plan	Document	As defined in the project methodology	Project manager	System analysts & OA tools
Testing results	Document	As defined in the test plan	Project manager	Programmers, system analysts, & OA tools
Change management and implementation plan	Document	As defined in the project methodology	Project manager	Systems analysts & OA tools
Training program	User documentation & training class	As defined in the implementation plan	Project manager & project sponsor	Trainers, documentation writers, & OA tools
Final report & presentation	Document	As defined in the project methodology	Project sponsor	Project sponsor, project manager, & OA tools
Project evaluations & lessons learned	Document	As defined in the project methodology	Project manager & senior	Project team, knowledge management system

SOURCE: Inspired by Graham McLeod and Derek Smith, *Managing Information Technology Projects* (San Francisco: Boyd & Fraser, 1996), 51–52.

This will provide the foundation for determining not only what resources will be needed for the project, but also for estimating the time and cost in completing each deliverable.

Once the deliverables have been defined in the DDT, a **deliverable structure chart (DSC)** can be developed as an interim step to define detailed work packages that will be used to estimate the project schedule and budget. Later on, these work packages will be used to create a **work breakdown structure (WBS)**—a tool used to help create the project plan. Figure 5.3 provides an example of a deliverable structure chart that maps the project life cycle and systems development life cycle phases to the deliverables defined in the DDT.

QUICK THINKING—SINKING A PROJECT

The trade magazine *Computerworld* contains a section called *Sharkbait* that allows people to submit real stories about their professional experiences. An anonymous writer described a situation where an IT manager decided to add a "cool new feature" to the next release of an internal software application. The new feature was added to the scope of the project, and the developers developed and tested it at an additional cost of about $50,000. When the application was given to the users for acceptance testing, they were surprised to find the new functionality. Immediately, they sent the application back to the developers and informed them that they would not pay for something they did not ask for or need. The IT manager was soon transferred to another position.

1. Were the users justified in rejecting the application even though it contained a "cool new feature"?

2. What lessons can we learn from this experience?

SOURCE: Adapted from "Scope Creep?", *Computerworld*, 10/29/2007, http://sharkbait.computerworld.com/node/1774.

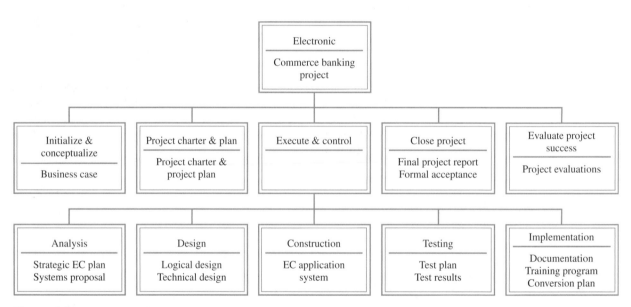

Figure 5.3 Deliverable Structure Chart (DSC)

Product-Oriented Scope

Although the electronic commerce application system is listed as a project-oriented deliverable, we really do not have a clear idea what exactly will be delivered to the client at this point in our project. In general, the application system will be the largest project deliverable and will, therefore, require the most time and resources to complete. Identifying the features and functionality of the application system (and their complexity) will be pivotal for estimating the time and cost of producing this deliverable.

Product-Oriented Scope Definition Tools **Product scope** therefore focuses on identifying the features and functionality of the information system to be implemented. A useful tool for refining the scope boundary and defining what the system must do is a modeling tool called a context level **data flow diagram (DFD)**. A DFD is a process model that has been available for quite some time and is often taught in systems analysis and design courses. A context level DFD, however, presents a high-level representation of the system that has one process (i.e., a circle or rounded rectangle that represents the system as a whole) and depicts all the inflows and outflows of data and information between the system and its external entities. The external entities are usually represented by a square and can be people, departments, or other systems that provide or receive flows of data. Arrows represent the directional flow of data between external entities and the system. Each arrow and entity should be labeled appropriately. Lower level DFDs can be developed later to model the processes and flows of data in greater detail. An example of a context level DFD for our banking electronic commerce system is provided in Figure 5.4. As you can see, the high level features and functionality of the system focus on what the system must do.

Another useful tool for defining the product scope is the **use case diagram**, which has been used in the object-oriented world as part of the Unified Modeling Language (UML). While Jacobson (Jacobson, Cristerson et al. 1992) introduced the use case as a tool for software development, a use case diagram can provide a high level model for defining, verifying, and reaching agreement upon the product scope.

The use case diagram is a relatively simple diagram in terms of symbols and syntax, but it is a powerful tool for identifying the main functions or features of the system and the different users or external systems that interact with the system. At this early stage of the project, the use case can provide a high level diagram that can be further refined and detailed during requirements analysis later in the project.

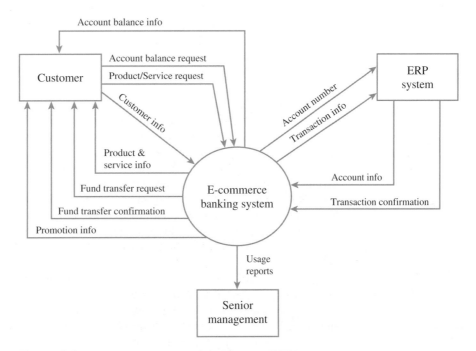

Figure 5.4 Context Level Data Flow Diagram (DFD)

Actors are people (users, customers, managers, etc.) or external systems (i.e., the bank's ERP system) that interact, or *use*, the system. Think of actors in terms of roles (e.g., customer) instead of as specific individuals (e.g., Tom Smith). A **use case**, on the other hand, depicts the major functions the system must perform for an actor or actors. When developing a use case diagram, actors are identified using stick figures, while use cases are defined and represented using ovals. Figure 5.5 provides an example of a use case diagram for the bank example.

As you can see in Figure 5.5, the use case diagram provides a simple yet effective overview of the functions and interactions between the use cases and the actors. The box separating the use cases from the actors also provides a system boundary that defines the scope boundary. Use cases inside the boundary are considered within the scope of the project, while anything outside of the boundary is considered outside the scope of the project. Listing the actors provides an opportunity to identify various stakeholders and can be useful for understanding the needs of the organization as a whole. It can be useful not only for addressing competing needs among various stakeholders, but for identifying security issues as well (Fowler and Scott 1997). The development of a use case diagram is an iterative process that can be developed during a **joint application development (JAD)** session. JAD is a group-based method where the users and systems analysts jointly define the system requirements or design the system (Turban, Rainer, and Potter 2001).

The use case diagram used to define the product scope can be used to refine the level of detail and functionality later on in our project. Following our example, the use case diagram in Figure 5.5 identifies the customer actor as using the system to transfer payments. However, a scenario or set of scenarios could be developed during the analysis and design phases of our project to determine how a customer would transfer funds successfully, while another scenario might focus on what happens when a customer has insufficient funds in their account. This level of detail is more suited to the requirements definition rather than the scope definition. At this point, it is more important to identify that the system must allow a customer to transfer funds than to identify how the funds may be transferred. Later on, the product scope can be compared or measured against the detailed requirements. These detailed requirements will be defined during the SDLC component of the ITPM.

But what is the appropriate level of detail for defining the product scope? Knowing the right level of detail is more an art than a science. The right level allows the project manager to estimate the time it will take to produce the application system accurately. As the next chapter shows, estimating the time and effort to produce the application system deliverable depends on the size of the application, the number of features incorporated, and their level of complexity. Therefore, the quality of the estimates will be greatly influenced by our understanding of the information system to be delivered.

The time and resources committed to developing the project charter and plan may limit the amount of time and energy we can devote to defining the details of the information system. Thus, the objective during this planning stage of the project should be to secure enough detail about the information system to allow us to estimate the time and effort needed to produce this deliverable. During the analysis and design phases, we can commit more time and resources to increasing our understanding and to documenting the level of detail needed to build and deliver the system.

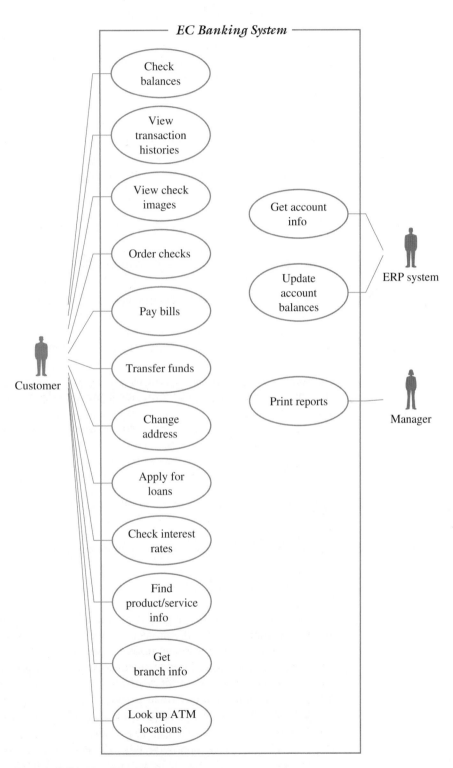

Figure 5.5 Use Case Diagram

PROJECT SCOPE VERIFICATION

Once the project's scope has been defined, it must be verified and formally accepted by the project sponsor and other appropriate stakeholders. **Project scope verification** is the scope management process that provides a mechanism for ensuring that the project deliverables are completed according to the standards described in the DDT. Gray and Larson (2000) provide a project scope checklist for ensuring that the deliverables are completed—and completed correctly. This checklist has been adapted to include the MOV concept.

- *MOV*—Is the project's MOV clearly defined and agreed upon? Failure to define and agree upon the MOV could result in scope changes later in the project, which can lead to added work impacting the project's schedule and budget.

- *Deliverables*—Are the deliverables tangible and verifiable? Do they support the project's MOV?

- *Quality standards*—Are controls in place to ensure that the work was not only completed, but completed to meet specific standards?

- *Milestones*—Are milestones defined for each deliverable? Milestones are significant events that mark the acceptance of a deliverable and give the project manager and team the approval to begin working on the next deliverable. In short, milestones tell us that a deliverable was not only completed, but reviewed and accepted.

- *Review and acceptance*—Are both sides clear in their expectations? The project's scope must be reviewed and accepted by the project stakeholders. The project sponsor must formally accept the boundary, product to be produced, and the project-related deliverables. The project team must be clear on what it must deliver. In both cases, expectations must be realistic and agreed upon.

SCOPE CHANGE CONTROL

According to the *PMBOK® Guide*, **scope change control** is concerned with managing actual changes to the project's scope as and when they occur, to ensure that any changes to the project's scope will be beneficial. Scope control is also concerned with:

- *Scope grope*—Scope grope is a metaphor that describes a project team's inability to define the project's scope. This situation is common early in a project when the project team and sponsor have trouble understanding what the project is supposed to accomplish. Scope grope can be minimized by having a clearly defined MOV and by following or applying the processes, concepts, and tools described in this chapter.

- *Scope creep*—Scope creep refers to *increasing featurism*, adding small yet time- and resource-consuming features to the system once the scope of the project has been approved. For example, a project sponsor may try to add various bells and whistles to the project scope. Yet, scope creep does not always come from the project sponsor side. The project team itself may come across interesting or novel ideas as the project work progresses. Its enthusiasm for

QUICK THINKING—GOING FULL CIRCLE

A programmer is approached by the company's engineer to "whip up a small database to track issues on the manufacturing line as tests are run." The programmer agrees, but a newly hired engineer who hears about the project convinces the programmer's manager that what's really needed is a more robust system that will not only track test results but run the manufacturing line. Consultants are brought in and the engineer is wined and dined. Before long, it is decided that to have a really good system a new network will have to be installed on the line, additional coding will be necessary so that orders can be taken from the company's mainframe, and new equipment will be needed to replace some of the older equipment on the line. The engineer travels across the country to look at new equipment, and after a year of research and $100,000 spent

on consultants, the engineer presents his recommendation to the company's president. The cost of the system will be just over $2 million to install with an addition of four new full-time staff to run things. The president shoots the proposal down, and the engineer resigns to go work for the consulting company. A week after the engineer leaves, the programmer is approached by the original engineers and is asked to create the database they wanted originally. A week later they have their database and are happy.

1. How could something like this have gotten so far?
2. Is there any way to avoid this situation?

SOURCE: Adapted from *Who are You Calling a Scope Creep?*, *Computerworld*, December 5, 2007.

---

adding these ideas can divert its attention or add features and functions to the system that the project sponsor did not ask for and does not need. Scope creep must be identified and controlled throughout the project because it will lengthen the project schedule and, in turn, lead to cost overruns.

- *Scope leap*—If scope creep is caused by increasing featurism, scope leap suggests a fundamental and significant change in the project scope. For example, the original scope for the bank's electronic commerce project was to provide new products and services to its customers. Scope creep may be adding a new feature, such as a new product or service, not originally defined in the project's scope. Scope leap, on the other hand, is an impetus to change the project so that the electronic commerce system would allow the bank to obtain additional funding in the open market. Adding this activity would dramatically change the entire scope and focus of the project. Scope leap can occur as a result of changes in the environment, the business, and the competitive makeup of the industry. Scope leap entails changing the MOV and, therefore, requires that the organization rethink the value of the current project. If this change is critical, the organization may be better off pulling the plug on the current project and starting over by conceptualizing and initiating a new project.

Scope Change Control Procedures

A scope change procedure should be in place before the actual work on the project commences. It can be part of, or at least referenced in, the project charter so that it is communicated to all project stakeholders. This procedure should allow for the identification and handling of all requested changes to the project's scope. Scope change requests can be made, and each request's impact on the project can be assessed. Then, a decision whether to accept or reject the scope change can be made.

A scope change procedure may include a scope change request form. An example of a scope change request form is illustrated in Figure 5.6. Regardless of the format for a scope change request form, it should contain some basic information. First, the description of the change request should be clearly defined so that the project manager and project team understand fully the nature and reason for the scope change. Second, the scope change should be justified, which separates the *would likes* from the *must haves*. In addition, several alternatives may be listed in order to assess the impact on scope, schedule, resources, and cost. Often a trade-off or compromise will be suitable if the impact of the scope change is too great. The project sponsor must understand and approve these impacts because the baseline project plan will have to be adjusted accordingly. Alternatives may include reducing functionality in other areas of the project, extending the project deadline, or adding more resources in terms of staff, overtime, or technology. Finally, all scope changes must be approved so that additional resources can be committed to the project.

However, nothing can be more frustrating than making a request and then not hearing anything. Too often requests fall through the cracks, leading to credibility concerns and accusations that the project manager or project team is not being

Scope change request form

Requestor name: _____   Request date: _____

Request title: _____   Request number: _____

Request description:

Justification:

Possible alternatives:

Impacts	*Alternative 1*	*Alternative 2*	*Alternative 3*
Scope			
Schedule			
Resources required			
Cost			

Recommendation:

Authorized by   *Date*

_____   _____

Figure 5.6   Scope Change Request Form

Request Number	Request Title	Date of Request	Requested by	Priority (L, M, H)	Authority to Approve Request	Expected Response Date	Scope Change Approved? (Y/N)

Figure 5.7   Scope Change Request Log

responsive to the client's needs. Therefore, a scope change control procedure should be logged with the intention that each request will be reviewed and acted upon. As seen in Figure 5.7, an example of a Change Request Log includes information as to who has the authority to make the scope change decision and when a response can be expected.

Although this may seem like the beginning of a bureaucracy, it is really designed to protect all project stakeholders. Too often the project manager and project team feel the pressure to say yes to each and every scope change request because their refusal may be interpreted as being uncooperative. Unfortunately, introducing scope creep will impact the schedule and budget. As the deadline passes or as costs begin to overrun the budget, the project manager and team then may come under fire for not controlling the project objectives.

Still, a project manager and team should not say no to every scope change request. Some changes will be beneficial and warranted as the project proceeds. The question then becomes: What should be the basis for making a scope change decision?

As you have seen, the project's MOV guides the project planning process. Similarly, the project's MOV can also guide scope change decisions. A scope change request should be approved if—and only if—the scope change can bring the project closer to achieving its MOV; otherwise, why bother adding additional work, resources, time, and money to activities that will not bring any value to the organization?

Benefits of Scope Control

The most important benefit of scope change control procedures is that they keep the project manager in control of the project. More specifically, they allow the project manager to manage and control the project's schedule and budget. Scope control procedures also allow the project team to stay focused and on track in terms of meeting its milestones because it does not have to perform unnecessary work.

CHAPTER SUMMARY

Although scope is the work to be performed on the project, a project's scope can be defined as the boundary and deliverables that the project team will provide to the project sponsor. A scope boundary acts as a fence to ensure that what needs to get done, gets done—and only what needs to get done, gets done. Performing work that does not help the project achieve its MOV needlessly consumes valuable time and resources.

Therefore, the project's boundary helps the project team define the limits of the project and how it will interact with its environment. In addition, deliverables are tangible units of work that ensure that the project is on track. Deliverables may be product oriented or project oriented. Product-oriented deliverables focus on the high level features and functionality of the application system—the project's product. On the other hand, project-oriented deliverables focus on the project's processes as defined in the IT project methodology.

The *Project Management Body of Knowledge Guide®* identifies five processes that support project scope management: scope planning, scope definition, create work breakdown structure, scope verification, and scope control.

Scope grope is a common occurrence in the early stages of the project. Often the project team struggles to define what the project is all about and what work must be done. By applying the concept of an MOV and the tools introduced in this chapter, the time a project team spends searching for these answers should be reduced.

Scope creep, on the other hand, is a common occurrence in many projects. It entails adding additional features or functions to the scope once the scope has been set and approved. This phenomenon can increase the schedule and budget, causing the project to miss its deadline and budget targets. Scope creep can be managed by (1) verifying that the scope is accurate and complete by using a scope verification checklist, and (2) ensuring that appropriate scope changes are approved and reflected in the baseline plan by having scope change procedures. The MOV concept can guide this decision process. For example, scope changes that move the project closer to achieving its MOV should be approved, while those that do not merely waste time and resources. Lastly, scope leap entails a major and fundamental change to the project scope. It may be the result of a changing business environment or the competitive makeup of the industry. Such a radical departure from the original business case may require the project stakeholders to rethink the viability of the current project.

REVIEW QUESTIONS

1. What is meant by project scope?
2. Briefly describe the five scope management processes.
3. Briefly describe the scope planning process.
4. Briefly describe the scope definition process.
5. Briefly describe the scope verification process.
6. Briefly describe the scope change control process.
7. Describe the scope management plan in Figure 5.1.
8. Why is it important to define the project's scope accurately and completely?
9. What is a scope boundary? What purpose does it serve?
10. What is the difference between product-oriented deliverables and project-oriented deliverables?
11. How does a project's scope support the MOV concept?
12. What is a scope statement? What purpose does it serve?
13. What is a context dataflow diagram (DFD)? What purpose does it serve?
14. How does a use case diagram help to define the project's scope?
15. What is a deliverable definition table (DDT)? What purpose does it serve?
16. What is a deliverable structure chart (DSC)? How does it map to a deliverable definition table (DDT)?
17. What is a work breakdown structure (WBS)? How does it map to the DDT and DSC?
18. Briefly describe what must be included in a scope verification checklist.
19. What is the purpose of verifying a project's scope?
20. What is the purpose of scope change control procedures?
21. Briefly describe scope grope.
22. Briefly describe scope creep.
23. Briefly describe scope leap.
24. What are the benefits of having scope control procedures?
25. Briefly describe what should be included on a scope change request form.
26. What is the purpose of a scope change request log?

EXTEND YOUR KNOWLEDGE

1. Using the Web or library, find an article about an unsuccessful IT project. Discuss whether poor scope management had any bearing on the project's being unsuccessful.

2. Discuss the statement: Failing to define what is not part of the project is just as important as failing to define what is part of the project.

3. Choose a company that sells a product or service on the Web. Using this Web site as a guide, develop the following (even though the application is already in existence). You may make assumptions where necessary, but be sure to document them.

   a. Scope statement

   b. Context level DFD

   c. Use case diagram

GLOBAL TECHNOLOGY SOLUTIONS

On Friday evening Tim Williams and Kellie Matthews were still at the GTS office, working on the project charter and project plan for Husky Air. Rubbing her eyes, Kellie asked, "I know we defined the goal of the project by developing the MOV, but what about the work that has to be done to get us there?"

"Glad you asked," Tim said as he put down his personal digital assistant on the desk in front of him. "I think we're ready to start defining the scope of the project, which will help us define all of the deliverables and activities that support the MOV."

"I remember working on a project that never seemed to end," she replied. "The users always wanted to add more bells and whistles to the system, and the project ended up missing its deadline and costing a lot more than we had planned."

Tim thought for a moment, then asked. "So, what can we learn from that experience?"

Kellie smiled. "First of all," she said. "I think we need to have a plan in place to make sure that the scope of the project is well defined. I think part of our problem was that we never really got a clear idea of the project's goal, so we never defined the scope of the project properly. And secondly, we should've had some kind of process in place to control scope changes once we started the project."

Tim agreed. "That sounds like an excellent idea. But why not just say no to any scope change requests?"

Kellie sat back in her chair. "The way I see it, if we say yes to each and every scope change request, we run the risk of escalating the project's schedule and, in turn, the project's budget. On the other hand, if we say no to all scope change requests, we run the risk of missing some opportunities or appearing nonresponsive to our client's needs."

"Good point, but how do you know when to say yes to a scope change and when to say no?" asked Tim.

"I guess we could let the project's MOV be our guide," she answered. "If a scope change supports the MOV, then it's worth doing. Otherwise, if it doesn't support the MOV, then the scope change isn't worth the time or money. Besides, the client has to make the decision whether the change in scope is worth the increase in schedule and cost. All we can do is keep the schedule and budget under control and then point out to them how any requested scope change will impact the project."

Tim stood up, saying "I think what we need is a scope management plan that can be part of the project charter. It's also important that we let everyone involved with the project know about it. Let's call it a day and get started on it first thing Monday morning."

Kellie agreed. "That's the best idea I've heard all day. Why don't you go ahead? I'll lock up after I make a few phone calls."

Things to Think About

1. What is the importance of ensuring that the scope of a project has been defined completely and accurately?

2. What is the relationship between the project's MOV and its scope?

3. What is the importance of having scope control procedures in place?

4. Why should a scope control process be communicated to all of the stakeholders of a project?

HUSKY AIR ASSIGNMENT—PILOT ANGELS

The Scope Management Plan

Your client, Husky Air, has given your team the authority to develop the project's scope. The project's scope defines the project work. It includes the work boundaries and deliverables that you will deliver to your client.

Please provide a professional-looking document that includes the following:

1. **Project name, project team name, and the names of the members of your project team**
2. **A brief project description**
3. **The project's MOV**—(This should be revised or refined if necessary.)
4. **A Deliverable Structure Chart (DSC)**—This should be based on the project life cycle and the systems development life cycle. You should begin by creating a hierarchical chart that defines all of the project and system development phases. The system development phases will depend largely on the development approach you use (waterfall, rapid applications development, etc.). After you have identified all project phases, the next step in developing a DSC is to identify at least one project or product deliverable for each phase.
5. **A use case diagram (UCD)**—A UCD defines the high-level features and functionality that the application system should include. Although Figure 5.5 provides an example of a use case, you can build one:
   a. Draw a box to represent the system boundary.
   b. Draw stick figures to represent the actors of the system. Actors can be users, managers, customers, or even other systems that will interact with or *use* the application system. Actors should be drawn on the outside of the system boundary. Be sure to label each actor with a descriptive name to describe the actor's role.
   c. A use case is a particular function that the application system will perform. Draw an oval inside the system boundary for each function and label the oval with a descriptive name. Examples of use cases are: update customer information, print employee overtime report, create new vendor record, and so forth. This important step during your project necessitates a great deal of interaction with your client. Unfortunately, you will not have access to a real client, so you can be creative. Keep in mind, however, that additional (and often unused) functionality will require more time and resources to build the system, thus adding to the project's schedule and budget. You and your team need to be aware that any features and functionality of the system should help the organization achieve its MOV.
   d. Draw a connecting line to identify the actors who will make use of a particular use case.
6. **A scope change process**—Together, the DSC and UCD define what will and what will not be part of the project scope. In short, the project team is responsible for delivering everything that is listed in the DSC and UCD. Unfortunately, items may be overlooked and often needs will change. Adding deliverables or functionality to the system is an important decision. Therefore, develop a logical process that your client and team will follow for identifying, cataloging, managing, and responding to a scope change request. Be sure to include templates or examples of any forms or logs that will be used to support the scope change process.

 CASE STUDIES

Just Say No?

Many project managers agree that "half-baked" or "hare-brained" ideas becoming projects and excessive scope creep are two key causes of challenged and failed projects. And a half-baked idea that turns into a project with excessive scope creep can be a nightmare for the project manager and team.

Top management is often under pressure to develop new and innovative products and services that move the organization toward profitability and competitive leadership. However, many times these ideas include a number of less than stellar ideas that get turned into projects.

This can occur as a result of "management by magazine," when a manager reads an article and forms a new vision. Unfortunately, many project managers fail to object because the organization may have a culture where such things aren't questioned or a belief that senior management could never be wrong.

Moreover, scope creep can be a key challenge, especially when the customer or sponsor has unreasonable or unrealistic expectations. Many project managers may feel they don't have the ability, experience, or power to just say no. Their only option may be to do as they're told and comply begrudgingly even though they know that the likelihood of their project's success is small.

Gopal Kapur believes that this is where the idea of intelligent disobedience can come into play. Intelligent disobedience is a quality taught to guide dogs for the blind. For example, a blind person may initiate the move to cross a busy street by giving a signal to the guide dog to move forward. If traffic blocks the crosswalk, the guide dog will disobey the command. This failure to comply with an unsafe command is intelligent disobedience, and the dog owner must learn to trust the guide dog.

A project manager can apply the concept of intelligent disobedience by saying no to demands that can be detrimental to the project or the organization. This, however, requires trust and empowerment, as well as the project manager's ability to read the danger signals when a project is a half-baked idea or when scope creep becomes excessive. On the other hand, the project sponsor or customer must trust and respect the project manager's judgment.

1. What determines whether a project manager will react with intelligent disobedience or begrudging compliance?

2. How can half-baked ideas that turn into projects and excessive scope creep be minimized?

3. The vice president of marketing read an article on a plane that interactive marketing on the World Wide Web is the hottest trend. Subsequently, she believes that your organization should develop an interactive marketing Web site or else your organization will be at a competitive disadvantage. After meeting with her, you find that this is really more of a half-baked idea than a real project. She also says not to worry, that "We'll firm up the project as we go along." If you were asked to be the project manager, how would you handle this situation?

Adapted from Gopal K. Kapur, Intelligent Disobedience, *Computerworld*, August 30, 2004.

The Vasa

The Vasa was a Swedish warship built in 1628 for King Gustavus Adolphus. On her maiden voyage, the ship floundered and keeled over in a light wind after sailing less than a nautical mile. Wives and children of the 125 crew were invited to take part in the festivities; however, around 50 perished in the tragedy.

In the 17th century, Sweden rose to become one of the most powerful states in the Balkan Sea. Gustavus Adolphus became Sweden's king at the age of 17 in 1611 and was considered a born leader of great intellect and bravery. A decade later, Sweden was involved with a war with Poland, and looking at the possibility of war with Germany. This required a strong navy, but several setbacks during the 1620s weakened Sweden's military dominance: a Swedish squadron of 10 shops ran aground in 1625 and was wrecked by a bitter storm while two large warships were outmaneuvered by the Polish navy and defeated in 1627; in 1628, three more ships were lost within a month.

In January 1625, the king ordered Admiral Fleming to sign a contract with Henrik Hybertson and his brother Arend to build four ships, two smaller ones with keels of 108 feet (33 m) and two larger ones of 135 feet (41 m). After losing the 10 ships in a storm, the king sent a concerned letter to Admiral Fleming instructing him to tell Henrik Hybertson that the schedule for the two smaller ships must be expedited. The king also requested that these ships have 120 foot (37 m) keels and include two enclosed gun decks so that they could carry more armament. This presented a dilemma for Hybertson because the timber had already been cut for the specifications outlined in the contract for one smaller ship and one larger ship. Moreover, no one had built a ship with two gun decks before. Hybertson tried to convince the king to follow the original specifications, but the king demanded that the ships be built according to his new measurements. Master Shipwright Hybertson soon became ill in 1625 and died in the spring of 1627, never seeing the Vasa completed. The project was handed over to Hybertson's assistant, Hein Jacobsson, who had very little management experience and no detailed records or plans from which to work.

In 1628, Admiral Fleming ordered a test of the Vasa's stability. This consisted of having 30 sailors running from one side of the ship to the other to assess how the ship would rock. The test was aborted only after three runs; otherwise the ship would have keeled over. The two shipbuilders, Jacobsson and his assistant Johan Isbrandsson, were not present for the test. A member of the crew was heard to make a remark about the ship's instability, but the admiral replied that "The master shipbuilder surely has built ships before, so there is no need to have worries of that kind." No doubt the admiral, captain, and crew had wished the king were present, but he was fighting in Poland and sending a stream of messages instructing that the ship be launched immediately.

During the stability test, the ship's armament was being produced and artists were working feverishly to complete the decorations. The number and types of armaments to be carried by the redesigned Vasa went through a number of revisions as well. The original design called for 32 24-pound guns, but the 135-foot version was to carry 36 24-pound guns, 24 12-pound guns, eight 48-pound mortars, and 10 smaller guns. After further revisions, the king finally ordered the Vasa to carry 64 24-pound guns (32 on each deck) and as many as 60 24-pound guns. The idea was to arm the Vasa with powerful guns and a high stern that could act as a firing platform in boarding actions for the 300 soldiers the ship was to carry.

Moreover, it was customary for warships to be decorated ornately with hundreds of gilded and painted sculptures of Biblical, mythical, and historical themes to glorify the authority and power of the king and to frighten or taunt the enemy. The 500 sculptures added considerably to the effort and cost of the ship as well as raising the ship's center of gravity and contributing to its instability. During this period, no methods for calculating the ship's center of gravity, heeling characteristics, and stability existed, so shipbuilders and captains had to design and learn how a ship handled through trial and error.

On August 10, 1628 Captain Sofring Hansson ordered the Vasa to set sail on its maiden voyage. The wind was relatively calm with only a light breeze from the southwest. The gun ports were open so that a salute could be fired as the ship left her shipyard in Stockholm. Suddenly, a gust of wind filled her sails and the ship heeled to port. The ship slowly righted herself, but another gust pushed the ship again to her port side where water began to flow through her open gun ports. The Vasa heeled even further, until she sank in about 100 feet of water not far from shore. The ship sank in front of hundreds or even thousands of people who had come to see the ship sail on her first voyage. Survivors clung to debris while many boats rushed to

their aid. Despite heroics and the short distance to shore, records indicate that as many as 50 people perished with the ship.

The king was notified of the Vasa's fate by letter. He wrote a reply that "imprudence and negligence" must have been the cause and that the guilty parties would be punished. Captain Hansson survived and was imprisoned immediately to await trial. The captain and crew were interrogated regarding the handling of the ship as well as the sobriety of the captain and crew. Crew members and contractors blamed each other and everyone swore that they had done their job without fault. When asked why the ship was built to be so narrow and so unstable, the shipwright Jacobsson said that he had simply followed orders as directed by the long dead and buried Henrik Hybertsson, who had followed the king's orders. In the end, no one was sent to prison or found guilty of negligence. The disaster was explained as an act of God, but the sinking of the Vasa ended up being a major economic disaster for a small country.

1. What were some of the major problems associated with this project?
2. What lessons can we learn from the sinking of Vasa that can be applied to IT projects?

SOURCE: Vasa (ship) Wikipedia.com; Richard E. Fairley and Mary Jane Willshire, Why the Vasa Sank: 10 Problems and Some Antidotes for Software Projects, IEEE Software, March/April 2003, 18–25.

BIBLIOGRAPHY

Fowler, M. and K. Scott 1997. UML Distilled: Applying the Standard Object Modeling Language. Reading, MA: Addison-Wesley.

Gray, C. F. and E. W. Larson 2000. Project Management: The Managerial Process. Boston: Irwin McGraw-Hill.

Jacobson, I., M. Cristerson, P. Jonsson, and G. Overgaard 1992. Object-Oriented Software Engineering: A Use-Case Driven Approach. Reading, MA: Addison-Wesley.

Project Management Institute (PMI) 2004. *A Guide to the Project Management Body of Knowledge (PMBOK® Guide)*. Newtown Square, PA: PMI Publishing.

Turban, E., R. K. Rainer, Jr., and R. E. Potter 2001. Introduction to Information Technology. New York: John Wiley.

6

The Work Breakdown Structure and Project Estimation

CHAPTER OVERVIEW

Chapter 6 focuses on developing the work breakdown structure, as well as on introducing a number of project estimation approaches, tools, and techniques. After studying this chapter, you should understand and be able to:

- Develop a work breakdown structure.
- Describe the difference between a deliverable and a milestone.
- Describe and apply several project estimation methods. These include the Delphi technique, time boxing, top-down estimation, and bottom-up estimation.
- Describe and apply several software engineering estimation approaches. These include lines of code (LOC), function point analysis, COCOMO, and heuristics.

INTRODUCTION

In the last chapter, you learned about defining and managing the project's scope—the work to be done in order to achieve the project's MOV or goal. Defining and understanding what you have to do is an important first step to determining how you're going to do the work that has to be done. In this chapter, we will focus on defining the tasks or activities that need to be carried out in order to complete all of the scope-related deliverables as promised. Moreover, we need to estimate or forecast the amount of time each activity will take so that we can determine the overall project schedule.

The Project Management Body of Knowledge (PMBOK®) area called **project time management** focuses on the processes necessary to develop the project schedule and to ensure that the project is completed on time. As defined in the *PMBOK Guide®*, project time management includes:

- *Activity definition*—Identifying what activities must be completed to produce the project scope deliverables

153

- *Activity sequencing*—Determining whether activities can be completed sequentially or in parallel and any dependencies that may exist among them
- *Activity resource estimation*—Identifying the type of resources (people, technology, facilities, etc.) and the quantity of resources needed to carry out project activities
- *Activity duration estimation*—Estimating the time to complete each activity
- *Schedule development*—Based on the availability of resources, the activities, their sequence, and time estimates, a schedule for the entire budget can be developed
- *Schedule control*—Ensuring that proper processes and procedures are in place in order to control changes to the project schedule

In this chapter, we will concentrate on two of these processes: activity definition and activity estimation. These are key processes that deserve special attention because they are required inputs for developing the project network model that will determine the project's schedule and budget. In the next chapter, you will see how we put this all together to develop the detailed project plan.

The remainder of this chapter will introduce several important tools, techniques, and concepts. A **work breakdown structure (WBS)** is discussed first. It provides a hierarchical structure that outlines the activities or work that needs to be done in order to complete the project scope. The WBS also provides a bridge or link between the project's scope and the detailed project plan that will be entered into a project management software package.

Today, most project management software packages are relatively inexpensive and rich in features. It is almost unthinkable that anyone would plan and manage a project without such a tool. Project success, however, will not be determined by one's familiarity with a project management software package or the ability to produce nice looking reports and graphs. It is the thought process that must be followed before using the tool that counts! Thinking carefully through the activities and their estimated durations first will make the use of a project management software package much more effective. You can still create nice looking reports and graphs, but you'll have more confidence in what those reports and graphs say.

Once the project activities are defined, the next step is to forecast, or estimate, how long each activity will take. Although a number of estimation methods and techniques are introduced here, estimation is not an exact science. It is dependent upon a number of variables—the complexity of the activity, the resources (i.e., people) assigned to complete the activity, and the tools and environment to support those individuals working on the activity (technology, facilities, etc.). Moreover, confidence in estimates will be lower early in the project because a full understanding of the problem or opportunity at hand is probably lacking. However, as we learn and uncover new information from our involvement in the project, our understanding of the project will increase as well. Although estimates may have to be revised periodically, we should gain more confidence in the updated schedule and budget. Even though no single estimation method will provide 100 percent accuracy all of the time, using one or a combination of methods is preferable to guessing.

THE WORK BREAKDOWN STRUCTURE (WBS)

In the last chapter, you learned how to define and manage the project's scope. As part of the scope definition process, several tools and techniques were introduced.

For example, the deliverable definition table (DDT) and deliverable structure chart (DSC) identify the deliverables that must be provided by the project team.

Once the project's scope is defined, the next step is to define the activities or tasks the project team must undertake to fulfill the scope deliverable requirements. The work breakdown structure (WBS) is a useful tool for developing the project plan and links the project's scope to the schedule and budget. According to Gregory T. Haugan (2002),

> The WBS represents a logical decomposition of the work to be performed and focuses on how the product, service, or result is naturally subdivided. It is an outline of what work is to be performed (17).

The WBS provides a framework for developing a tactical plan to structure the project work. PMBOK® views the WBS as a hierarchical decomposition of the project's scope that the project team will deliver over the course of the project. The total scope of the project is divided and subdivided into specific deliverables that can be more easily managed. This includes both product and project-oriented deliverables. In short, the WBS provides an outline for all of the work the project team will perform.

Work Packages

The WBS decomposes, or subdivides, the project into smaller components and more manageable units of work called **work packages.** Work packages provide a logical basis for defining the project activities and assigning resources to those activities so that all the project work is identified (Haugan 2002). A work package makes it possible to develop a project plan, schedule, and budget and then later monitor the project's progress.

As illustrated in Figure 6.1, a work package may be viewed as a hierarchy that starts with the project itself. The project is then decomposed into phases, with each phase having one or more deliverables as defined in the deliverable definition table and deliverable structure chart. More specifically, each phase should provide at least one specific deliverable—that is, a tangible and verifiable piece of work. Subsequently, activities or tasks are identified in order to produce the project's deliverables.

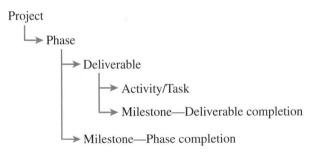

Figure 6.1 Work Package

Deliverables and Milestones

One departure from most traditional views of a WBS is the inclusion of milestones. A **milestone** is a significant event or achievement that provides evidence that that deliverable has been completed or that a phase is formally over.

Deliverables and milestones are closely related, but they are not the same thing. Deliverables can include such things as presentations or reports, plans, prototypes, and the final application system. A milestone, on the other hand, must focus on an achievement. For example, a deliverable may be a prototype of the user interface, but the milestone would be a stakeholder's formal acceptance of the user interface.

Only the formal acceptance or approval of the user interface by the project sponsor would allow the project team to move on to the next phase of the project.

In theory, if a project team succeeds in meeting all of its scheduled milestones, then the project should finish as planned. Milestones also provide several other advantages. First, milestones can keep the project team focused. It is much easier to concentrate your attention and efforts on a series of smaller, short-term deliverables than on a single, much larger deliverable scheduled for completion well into the future. On the other hand, if milestones are realistic, they can motivate a project team if their attainment is viewed as a success. If meeting a milestone signifies an important event, then the team should take pleasure in these successes before gearing up for the next milestone.

Milestones also reduce the risk of a project. The passing of a milestone, especially a phase milestone, should provide an opportunity to review the progress of the project. Additional resources should be committed at the successful completion of each milestone, while appropriate plans and steps should be taken if the project cannot meet its milestones.

Milestones can also be used to reduce risk by acting as **cruxes** or proof of concepts. Many times a significant risk associated with IT projects is the dependency on new technology or unique applications of the technology. A crux can be the testing of an idea, concept, or technology that is critical to the project's success. For example, suppose that an organization is building a data warehouse using a particular vendor's relational database product for the first time. A crux for this project may be the collection of data from several different legacy systems, cleansing this data, and then making it available in the relational database management system. The team may ensure that this can be accomplished using only a small amount of test data. Once the project team solves this problem on a smaller scale, they have proof that the concept or technique for importing the data from several legacy systems into the data warehouse can be done successfully. This breakthrough can allow them to incorporate what they have learned on a much larger scale. Subsequently, solving this crux is a milestone that would encourage the organization to invest more time and resources to complete the project.

Milestones can also provide a mechanism for quality control. Continuing with our example, just providing the users with an interface does not guarantee that it will be acceptable to them. Therefore, the completion of user interface deliverable should end only with their acceptance; otherwise, the team will be forced to make revisions. In short, the deliverable must not only be done, but must be done right.

Developing the WBS

Developing the WBS may require several versions until everyone is comfortable and confident that all of the work activities have been included. It is also a good idea to involve those who will be doing the work—after all, they probably know what has to be done better than anyone else.

The WBS can be quite involved, depending upon the nature and size of the project. To illustrate the steps involved, let's continue with our electronic commerce project example from the last chapter. As you may recall, we created a DDT and DSC to define the scope of the project. To make things easier to follow, let's focus on only one portion of the project—creating a document called the test results report. Figure 6.2 provides the DSC that we developed in Chapter 5. As you can see, two deliverables—the test plan and test results report—are to be completed and delivered during the testing phase of the project.

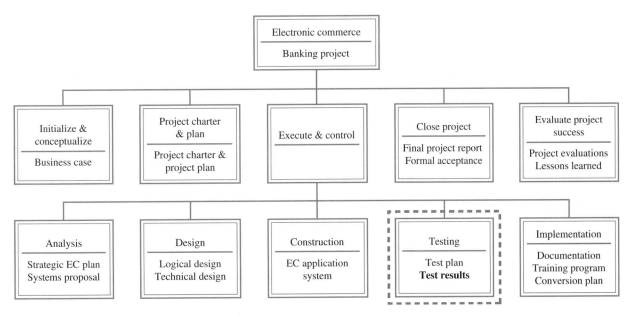

Figure 6.2 Deliverable Structure Chart (DSC) for EC Example

The DSC defines the phases and deliverables for our project. Now we can subdivide the project work into lower levels of detail or components that represent a verifiable product, service, or result. After a team meeting, let's say that we have identified and discussed several activities that we need to do in order to produce the test results document:

- Review the test plan with the client so that key stakeholders are clear as to what we will be testing, how we will conduct the tests, and when the tests will be carried out. This review may be done as a courtesy or because we need specific support from the client's organization and, therefore, must inform them when that support will be required.
- After we have informed the client that we will test the system, we basically carry out the tests outlined in the test plan.
- Once we have collected the test results, we need to analyze them.
- After we analyze the results, we will need to summarize them in the form of a report and presentation to the client.
- If all goes well, then the client will approve or sign off on the test results. Then we can move on to the implementation phase of our project. If all does not go well, we need to address and fix any problems. Keep in mind that the test phase is not complete just because we have developed a test plan and created a test report. The client will sign off on the test results only if the system meets certain predetermined quality standards.

Figure 6.3 provides an example of a WBS with the details shown for only the testing phase of the project. As you can see, the WBS implements the concept of a work package for the project, phase, deliverable, task/activity, and milestone components that were illustrated in Figure 6.1. This particular WBS follows an outline format with a commonly used decimal numbering system that allows for

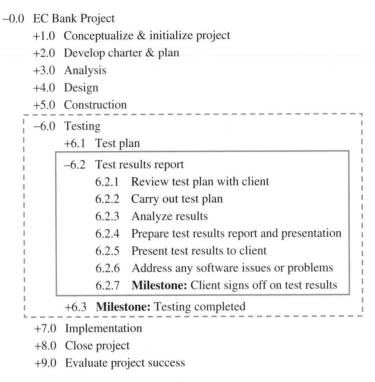

−0.0   EC Bank Project
+1.0   Conceptualize & initialize project
+2.0   Develop charter & plan
+3.0   Analysis
+4.0   Design
+5.0   Construction
−6.0   Testing
    +6.1   Test plan
    −6.2   Test results report
        6.2.1   Review test plan with client
        6.2.2   Carry out test plan
        6.2.3   Analyze results
        6.2.4   Prepare test results report and presentation
        6.2.5   Present test results to client
        6.2.6   Address any software issues or problems
        6.2.7   **Milestone:** Client signs off on test results
    +6.3   **Milestone:** Testing completed
+7.0   Implementation
+8.0   Close project
+9.0   Evaluate project success

Figure 6.3   Work Breakdown Structure

continuing levels of detail.[1] If a software package is used to create the WBS, signs in front of each item can either hide or show the details. For example, clicking on "−6.2 Test Results Report" would roll up the details of this work package into "+6.2 Test Results Report." Similarly, clicking on any item with a "+" in front of it would expand that item to show the details associated with it.

The skills to develop a useful WBS generally evolve over time with practice and experience. Everyone, experienced or not, should keep in mind the following points when developing a WBS.

The WBS Should Be Deliverable Oriented   Remember, the focus of a project should be to produce something, not merely on completing a specified number of activities. Although the WBS does not provide for any explicit looping, some activities may have to be repeated until the milestone is achieved. For example, software testing may uncover a number of problems or bugs that make the software system unacceptable to the client. As a result, these problems will have to be addressed and fixed and the same tests may have to be conducted again. This process may be repeated a number of times (while consuming the project schedule and budget) until the quality standards are met.

The WBS Should Support the Project's MOV   The WBS should include only tasks or activities that allow for the delivery of the project's deliverables. Before continuing with the development of the project plan, the project team should ensure

---

[1] Many people prefer to develop a WBS using a chart format, and the DSC in Figure 6.3 could be easily adapted by adding the work package levels. Although a graphic WBS can be visually appealing, it can also become extremely complex and confusing as more detail is added. Feel free to experiment with the WBS. The correct form will depend on the situation or your preference.

that the WBS allows for the delivery of all the project's deliverables as defined in the project's scope. In turn, this will ensure that the project is more likely to achieve its MOV. Haugan (2002) also suggests that the **100 percent rule** is the most important criterion in developing and evaluating the WBS. The rule states: "The next level decomposition of a WBS element (child level) must represent 100 percent of the work applicable to the next higher (parent) element." (17) In other words, if each level of the WBS follows the 100 percent rule down to the activities, then we are confident that 100 percent of the activities will have been identified when we develop the project schedule. Moreover, 100 percent of the costs or resources required will be identified when we create the budget for our project.

The Level of Detail Should Support Planning and Control The WBS provides a bridge between the project's scope and project plan—that is, the schedule and budget. Therefore, the level of detail should support not only the development of the project plan but allow the project manager and project team to monitor and compare the project's actual progress to the original plan's schedule and budget. The two most common errors when developing a WBS are too little or too much detail. Too little detail may result in a project plan that overlooks and omits important activities and tasks. This will lead to an overly optimistic schedule and budget. On the other hand, the WBS should not be a to-do list of one-hour tasks. This excessive detail results in micromanagement that can have several adverse effects on the project. First, this may impact the project team's morale because most people on projects are professionals who do not want someone constantly looking over their shoulders. Second, the progress of each and every task must be tracked. As a result, the project plan will either not be updated frequently or clerical staff will have to be hired (at a cost to the project) just to keep everything current.

Developing the WBS Should Involve the People Who Will Be Doing the Work
One way to ensure that the WBS has the appropriate level of detail is to ensure that the people who do the work are involved in its development. A person who has experience and expertise in a particular area probably has a better feel for what activities need to be performed in order to produce a particular project deliverable. Although the project manager is responsible for ensuring that a realistic WBS is developed, the people who must carry out the activities and tasks may be more committed to the plan if they are involved in its development. However, confusion and misunderstanding can occur when different people work on different parts of the WBS. Therefore, the various work packages can be described in a **WBS dictionary**. Information included in the WBS dictionary may include a code or account identifier, a description of the work, a list of the project team members assigned to carry out the work, contract information, quality standards, and resources required.

Learning Cycles and Lessons Learned Can Support the Development of a WBS
By using the concept of learning cycles, the project team can focus on what they know (the facts), what they think they know (assumptions), and what they need to find out (research) in order to develop a more useful WBS. Lessons learned from previous projects can be helpful in ensuring that the WBS and subsequent project plan are realistic and complete.

PROJECT ESTIMATION

Once the project deliverables and activities have been defined, the next step in developing the project schedule and budget is to estimate each activity's duration. One of the most crucial—and difficult—activities in project management is estimating the time it will take to complete a particular task. Since a resource generally performs a particular task, a cost associated with that particular resource must be allocated as part of the time it takes to complete that task. The time estimated to complete a particular task will have a direct bearing on the project's budget as well. As T. Capers Jones (Jones 1998) points out:

> The seeds of major software disasters are usually sown in the first three months of commencing the software project. Hasty scheduling, irrational commitments, unprofessional estimating techniques, and carelessness of the project management function are the factors that tend to introduce terminal problems. Once a project blindly lurches forward toward an impossible delivery date, the rest of the disaster will occur almost inevitably (120).

In this section, we will review several estimation techniques—guesstimating, Delphi, top-down and bottom-up estimating.

Guesstimating

Estimation by guessing or just picking numbers out of the air is not the best way to derive a project's schedule and budget. Unfortunately, many inexperienced project managers tend to **guesstimate,** or guess at the estimates, because it is quick and easy. For example, we might guesstimate that testing will take two weeks. Why two weeks? Why not three weeks? Or ten weeks? Because we are picking numbers out of thin air, the confidence in these estimates will be quite low. You might as well pick numbers out of a hat. The problem is that guessing at the estimates is based on feelings rather than hard evidence.

However, many times a project manager is put on the spot and asked to provide a ballpark figure. Be careful when quoting a time frame or cost off the record, because whatever estimates you come up with often become on the record.

People are often overly optimistic and, therefore, their guesstimates are overly optimistic. Underestimating can result in long hours, reduced quality, and unmet client expectations. If you ever find yourself being pressured to guesstimate, your first impulse should be to stall until you have enough information to make a confident estimate. You may not, however, have that luxury, so the best approach is to provide some kind of confidence interval. For example, if you think something will probably take three months and cost $30,000, provide a confidence interval of three to six months with a cost of $30,000 to $60,000. Then quickly offer to do a little more research to develop a more confident estimate. Notice that even though three months and $30,000 may be the most likely estimate, an estimate of two to six months was not made. Why? Because people tend to be optimists and the most likely case of finishing in three months is probably an optimistic case.

Delphi Technique

The **Delphi technique** involves multiple experts who arrive at a consensus on a particular subject or issue. Although the Delphi technique is generally used for group decision making, it can be a useful tool for estimating when the time and money warrant the extra effort (Roetzheim and Beasley 1998).

To estimate using the Delphi technique, several experts need to be recruited to estimate the same item. Based upon information supplied, each expert makes an estimate and then all the results are compared. If the estimates are reasonably close, they can be averaged and used as an estimate. Otherwise, the estimates are distributed back to the experts, who discuss the differences and then make another estimate.

In general, these rounds are anonymous and several rounds may take place until a consensus is reached. Not surprisingly, using the Delphi technique can take longer and cost more than most estimation methods, but it can be very effective and provide reasonable assurance when the stakes are high and the margin for error is low.

Time Boxing

Time boxing is a technique whereby a *box* of time is allocated for a specific activity or task. This allocation is based more on a requirement than just on guesswork. For example, a project team may have two (and only two) weeks to build a prototype. At the end of the two weeks, work on the prototype stops, regardless of whether the prototype is 100 percent complete.

Used effectively, time boxing can help focus the project team's effort on an important and critical task. The schedule pressure to meet a particular deadline, however, may result in long hours and pressure to succeed. Used inappropriately or too often, the project team members become burned out and frustrated.

Top-Down Estimating

Top-down estimating involves estimating the schedule and/or cost of the entire project in terms of how long it *should* take or how much it *should* cost. Top-down estimating is a very common occurrence that often results from a mandate made by upper management (e.g., Thou shalt complete the project within six months and spend no more than $500,000!).

Often the schedule and/or cost estimate is a product of some strategic plan or because someone *thinks* it should take a certain amount of time or cost a particular amount. On the other hand, top-down estimating could be a reaction to the business environment. For example, the project may have to be completed within six months as a result of a competitor's actions or to win the business of a customer (i.e., the customer needs this in six months).

Once the target objectives in terms of schedule or budget are identified, it is up to the project manager to allocate percentages to the various project life cycle phases and associated tasks or activities. Data from past projects can be very useful in applying percentages and ensuring that the estimates are reasonable. It is important to keep in mind that top-down estimating works well when the target objectives are reasonable, realistic, and achievable.

When made by people independent from the project team, however, these targets are often overly optimistic or overly aggressive. These unrealistic targets often lead to what Ed Yourdon (1999) calls a *death march* project:

> I define a death march project as one whose "project parameters" exceed the norm by at least 50 percent. This doesn't correspond to the "military" definition, and it would be a travesty to compare even the worst software project with the Bataan death march during the Second World War, or the "trail of tears" death march imposed upon Native Americans in the late 1700s. Instead, I use the term as a metaphor, to suggest a "forced march" imposed upon relatively innocent victims, the outcome of which is usually a high casualty rate (2).

Project parameters include schedule, staff, budget or other resources, and the functionality, features, performance requirements, or other aspects of the project. A death march software project means one or more of the following constraints has been imposed (Yourdon 1999):

- The project schedule has been compressed to less than 50 percent of its original estimate.
- The staff originally assigned or required to complete the project has been reduced to less than 50 percent.
- The budget and resources needed have been reduced by 50 percent or more.
- The functionality, features, or other performance or technical requirements are twice what they should be under typical circumstances.

On the other hand, top-down estimating can be a very effective approach to cost and schedule analysis (Royce 1998). More specifically, a top-down approach may force the project manager to examine the project's risks more closely so that a specific budget or schedule target can be achieved. By understanding the risks, trade-offs, and sensitivities objectively, the various project stakeholders can develop a mutual understanding that leads to better estimation. This outcome, however, requires that all stakeholders be willing to communicate and make trade-offs.

Bottom-Up Estimating

Most real-world estimating is made using **bottom-up estimating** (Royce 1998). Bottom-up estimating involves dividing the project into smaller modules and then directly estimating the time and effort in terms of person-hours, person-weeks, or person-months for each module. The work breakdown structure provides the basis for bottom-up estimating because all of the project phases and activities are defined.

The project manager, or better yet the project team, can provide reasonable time estimates for each activity. In short, bottom-up estimating starts with a list of all required tasks or activities and then an estimate for the amount of effort is made. The total time and associated cost for each activity provides the basis for the project's target schedule and budget. Although bottom-up estimating is straightforward, confusing effort with progress can be problematic (Brooks 1995).

Continuing with our earlier example, let's assume that after meeting with our software testers, the following durations were estimated for each of the following activities:

6.2   Test results report
      6.2.1. Review test plan with client   1 day
      6.2.2. Carry out test plan   5 days
      6.2.3. Analyze results   2 days
      6.2.4. Prepare test results report and presentation   3 days
      6.2.5. Present test results to client   1 day
      6.2.6. Address any software issues or problems   5 days

If we add all of the estimated durations together, we find that creating the test results report will take 17 days. How did we come up with these estimates? Did we guesstimate them? Hopefully not! These estimates could be based on experience—the software testers may have done these activities many times in the past so they know what activities have to be done and how long each activity will take. Or, these estimates could be based on similar or analogous projects. **Analogous estimation** refers to developing estimates based upon one's opinion that there is a significant similarity between the current project and others (Rad 2002).

Keep in mind that estimates are a function of the activity itself, the resources, and the support provided. More specifically, the estimated duration of an activity will first depend upon the nature of the activity in terms of its complexity and degree of structure. In general, highly complex and unstructured activities will take longer to complete than simple, well structured activities.

The resources assigned to a particular activity will also influence an estimate. For example, assigning an experienced and well trained individual to a particular task should mean less time is required to complete it than if a novice were assigned. However, experience and expertise are only part of the equation. We also have to consider such things as a person's level of motivation and enthusiasm.

Finally, the support we provide also influences our estimates. Support may include technology, tools, training, and the physical work environment.

These are just some of the variables that we must consider when estimating. You can probably come up with a number of others. Subsequently, estimates will always be a forecast; however, by looking at and understanding the big picture, we can increase our confidence in them.

SOFTWARE ENGINEERING METRICS AND APPROACHES

The discipline of **software engineering** focuses on the processes, tools, and methods for developing a quality approach to developing software (Pressman 2001). **Metrics,** on the other hand, provide the basis for software engineering and refers to a broad range of measurements for objectively evaluating computer software.

The greatest challenge for estimating an IT project is estimating the time and effort for the largest deliverable of the project—the application system. Maintenance projects and the installation of packaged software can experience similar difficulties.

QUICK THINKING—MORE PEOPLE = MORE PROBLEMS

The classic book, *The Mythical Man-Month*, by Fredrick P. Brooks was first published in 1975 with an anniversary edition published 20 years later (due to the fact that some things have not changed). Brooks worked at IBM as the manager of a large project that developed the OS/360 operating system. Although the OS/360 operating system was eventually a successful product for IBM, the system was late, and cost several times more than originally estimated. In fact, the product did not perform well until after several releases. Based on his experience, Brooks wrote a number of essays that were embodied in his book. One timeless insight became known as **Brooks' Law:**

> Adding manpower to a late software project makes it later.

More recently, a study conducted by Quantitative Software Management (QSM) reports having a larger team on

a software project can add millions of dollars to the cost of the project while only reducing the schedule by a few days. The study suggests that larger teams tend to create more defects or "bugs," and the additional rework detracts from any potential schedule benefits that may arise from having more people.

1. Why would adding more people to an already late IT project make it even later?
2. Many projects tend to be overstaffed during the planning and requirements gathering stages of the project. Why would having a smaller or leaner project team be a better approach?

SOURCE: Adapted from Frederick P. Brooks, *The Mythical Man-Month: Essays on Software Engineering*, 2nd ed., 1975; More People, More Bugs, from *Projects@Work*, October 6, 2005.

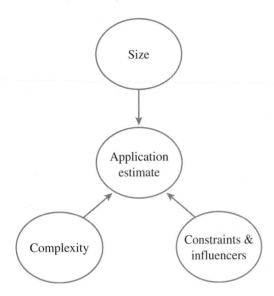

Figure 6.4 Software Engineering Estimation Model

SOURCE: Adapted from Garmus and Herron 1996; Jones 1998, Royce 1998.

The challenge lies in trying to estimate something that is logical, rather than physical, and that is not well defined until the later stages of the project life cycle. Scope definition can only provide a high-level view of what is and what is not within the scope boundary of the project. Specific requirements, in terms of features and functionality, are generally not defined until later, during the design phase. In addition, the complexity and technical challenges of implementing those features are either unknown or optimistically glossed over in the early stages of the project. As a result, estimating an IT project can be like trying to hit a moving target—hitting either one accurately requires continuous adjustments.

As illustrated in Figure 6.4, the first step to accurately estimating an IT application is determining its size (Jones 1998). How big is the application? Without getting into too much detail at this point, it should be intuitive that it takes more effort (i.e., in terms of schedule, resources, and budget) to build a larger system than a smaller system. However, the size of the application is only one piece of the estimation puzzle. A good portion of time and effort will be spent on features and functionality that are more complex. As a result, the greater the complexity, the more time and effort spent. Constraints and various influencers will also affect the time and effort needed to develop a particular application. These constraints could be attributes of the application (Jones 1998) or include the processes, people, technology, environment, and required quality of the product as well (Royce 1998). Once the resources and time estimates are known, the specific activities or tasks can be sequenced in order to create the project's schedule and budget.

Lines of Code (LOC)

Counting the number of lines of code in computer programs is the most traditional and widely used software metric for sizing the application product. It is also the most controversial.

Although counting lines of code seems intuitively obvious—a 1,000 LOC Java program will be ten times larger than a 100 LOC Java program—counting LOC is not all that straightforward. First, what counts as LOC? Do we include comments? Maybe we should not, because a programmer could artificially boost productivity by writing one hundred comment lines for every line of code that actually did something. On the other hand, comments are important because they tell us what the code should be doing. This makes it easier to debug and for others to understand what sections of code in the program are doing.

What about declaring variables? Do they count as LOC? In addition, experienced programmers tend to write *less* code than novice programmers. After all, an experienced programmer can write more efficient code, code that does the same thing in fewer lines than a novice programmer would use. The same can be said for different programming languages. Writing a program in Assembler requires a great deal more code than writing a similar program in C++. In fact, one could argue that counting LOC could encourage programmers to write inefficient code, especially when LOC are used as a productivity metric. Finally, it is much easier to count the lines of code after a program is written than it is to estimate how many lines of code will be required to write the program.

Function Points[2]

The inherent problems of LOC as a metric for estimation and productivity necessitated the need for a better software metric. In 1979, Allan Albrecht of IBM proposed the idea of function points at a conference hosted by IBM in Monterey, California (Albrecht 1979). **Function points** are a synthetic metric, similar to ones used every day, such as hours, kilos, tons, nautical miles, degrees Celsius, and so on. However, function points focus on the *functionality* and *complexity* of an application system or a particular module. For example, just as a 20 degree Celsius day is warmer than a 10 degree Celsius day, a 1,000 function point application is larger and more complex than a 500 function point application.

The good thing about function points is that they are independent of the technology. More specifically, functionality and the technology are kept separate so we can compare different applications that may or may not use different programming languages or technology platforms. That is, we can compare one application written in COBOL with another application developed in Java. Moreover, function point analysis is reliable—that is, two people who are skilled and experienced in function point analysis will obtain function point counts that are the same, that is, within an acceptable margin of error.

Counting function points is fairly straightforward; however, the rules can be complex for the novice. It is recommended that anyone serious about learning function point analysis become certified. Although several function point organizations exist, the two main ones are the International Function Point Users Group (IFPUG) and the United Kingdom Function Point Users Group (UFPUG). Both of these nonprofit organizations oversee the rules, guidelines, standards, and certifications for function point analysis. In addition, there are resources at the end of the chapter if you are interested in learning more about function points.

The key to counting function points is having a good understanding of the user's requirements. Early on in the project, a function point analysis can be conducted based on the project's scope. Then a more detailed analysis of the user's requirements can be made during the analysis and design phases. Then function point analysis can and should be conducted at various stages of the project life cycle. For example, a function point analysis conducted based on the project's scope definition can be used for estimation and developing the project's plan. During the analysis and design phases, function points can be used to manage and report progress and for monitoring scope creep. In addition, a function point analysis conducted during or after the project's implementation can be useful for determining whether all of the functionality was delivered. By capturing this information in a repository or database, it can be combined with other metrics useful for benchmarking, estimating future projects, and understanding the impact of new methods, tools, technologies, and best practices that were introduced.

Function point analysis is based on an evaluation of five data and transactional types that define the application boundary as illustrated in Figure 6.5.

- *Internal logical file (ILF)*—An ILF is a logical file that stores data within the application boundary. For example, each entity in an Entity-Relationship Diagram (ERD) would be considered an ILF. The complexity of an ILF can

---

[2]A more thorough discussion of function point analysis is provided in Appendix A.

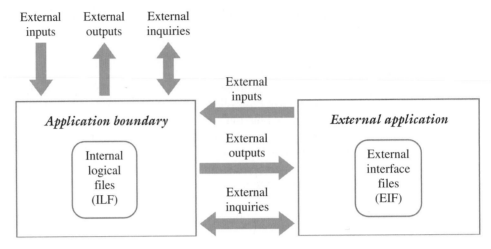

Figure 6.5   The Application Boundary for Function Point Analysis

be classified as low, average, or high based on the number of data elements and subgroups of data elements maintained by the ILF. An example of a subgroup would be new customers for an entity called customer. Examples of data elements would be customer number, name, address, phone number, and so forth. In short, ILFs with fewer data elements and subgroups will be less complex than ILFs with more data elements and subgroups.

- *External interface file (EIF)*—An EIF is similar to an ILF; however, an EIF is a file maintained by another application system. The complexity of an EIF is determined using the same criteria used for an ILF.

- *External input (EI)*—An EI refers to processes or transactional data that originate outside the application and cross the application boundary from outside to inside. The data generally are added, deleted, or updated in one or more files internal to the application (i.e., internal logical files). A common example of an EI would be a screen that allows the user to input information using a keyboard and a mouse. Data can, however, pass through the application boundary from other applications. For example, a sales system may need a customer's current balance from an accounts receivable system. Based on its complexity, in terms of the number of internal files referenced, number of data elements (i.e., fields) included, and any other human factors, each EI is classified as low, average, or high.

- *External output (EO)*—Similarly, an EO is a process or transaction that allows data to exit the application boundary. Examples of EOs include reports, confirmation messages, derived or calculated totals, and graphs or charts. This data could go to screens, printers, or other applications. After the number of EOs are counted, they are rated based on their complexity, like the external inputs (EI).

- *External inquiry (EQ)*—An EQ is a process or transaction that includes a combination of inputs and outputs for retrieving data from either the internal files or from files external to the application. EQs do not update or change any data stored in a file. They only read this information. Queries with different processing logic or a different input or output format are counted as a single EQ. Once the EQs are identified, they are classified based on their complexity

Table 6.1 Computing UAF

	Complexity			
	Low	Average	High	Total
Internal logical files (ILF)	$3 \times 7 = 21$	$2 \times 10 = 20$	$1 \times 15 = 15$	56
External interface files (EIF)	__ $\times 5 =$ __	$2 \times 7 = 14$	__ $\times 10 =$ __	14
External input (EI)	$3 \times 3 = 9$	$5 \times 4 = 20$	$4 \times 6 = 24$	53
External output (EO)	$4 \times 4 = 16$	$2 \times 5 = 10$	$1 \times 7 = 7$	33
External inquiry (EQ)	$2 \times 3 = 6$	$5 \times 4 = 20$	$3 \times 6 = 18$	_44_
Total unadjusted function points (UAF)				200

as low, average, or high, according to the number of files referenced and number of data elements included in the query.

Once all of the ILFs, EIFs, EIs, EOs, and EQs, are counted and their relative complexities rated, an unadjusted function point (UAF) count is determined. For example, let's say that after reviewing an application system, the following was determined:

- *ILF:* 3 Low, 2 Average, 1 Complex
- *EIF:* 2 Average
- *EI:* 3 Low, 5 Average, 4 Complex
- *EO:* 4 Low, 2 Average, 1 Complex
- *EQ:* 2 Low, 5 Average, 3 Complex

Using Table 6.1, the (UAF) value is calculated.

Table 6.2 GSC and Total Adjusted Function Point

General System Characteristic	Degree of Influence
Data communications	3
Distributed data processing	2
Performance	4
Heavily used configuration	3
Transaction rate	3
On-line data entry	4
End user efficiency	4
Online update	3
Complex processing	3
Reusability	2
Installation ease	3
Operational ease	3
Multiple sites	1
Facilitate change	2
Total degrees of influence (TDI)	40
VALUE ADJUSTMENT FACTOR $\text{VAF} = (\text{TDI} * 0.01) +.65$	VAF = (40 *. 01) +.65 = 1.05
Total adjusted function points = FP = UAF * VAF	FP = 200 * 1.05 = 210

SOURCE: Adapted from Dennis and Haley (2000).

The next step in function point analysis is to compute a Value Adjustment Factor (VAF). The VAF is based on the Degrees of Influence (DI), often called the Processing Complexity Adjustment (PCA), and is derived from the fourteen General Systems Characteristics (GSC) shown in Table 6.2. To determine the total DI, each GSC is rated based on the following scale from 0 to 5:

- 0 = not present or no influence
- 1 = incidental influence
- 2 = moderate influence
- 3 = average influence
- 4 = significant influence
- 5 = strong influence

Continuing with our example, let's say that after reviewing the application, the degrees of influence shown in Table 6.2 were determined to produce 210 total adjusted function points (TAFP). So what do we do with the total adjusted function point number? Once a total adjusted function point count is calculated, the function point count can be transformed into development estimates. The first approach focuses on productivity—i.e., a person, such as a programmer, can produce a certain number of function points in a given amount of time, such as in a day, a week, or a month. Once again, creating a repository of function point information and other metrics allows an organization to compare various projects and support more realistic estimates.

The second approach focuses on converting the function point count into an equivalent number of lines of code. Continuing with our example, we can determine how many lines of code will be required for several different programming languages. Table 6.3 provides an example that approximates the number of lines of code per function point for some of the more popular programming languages. As you can see, the number of lines of code depends on the programming language. An application or module that has 210 total unadjusted function points would require, for example, 134,440 lines of code if programmed in machine language, but only 6,090 lines of code using Visual Basic 5. Again, these estimates not only provide an estimate for the size of the application, but also for the complexity of the application.

In addition, T. Capers Jones has conducted extensive research and has come up with a technique called **backfiring,** which allows direct conversion from an application's source code to an equivalent function point count. Individual programming styles can create variation in the number of LOC so the accuracy of backfiring is not very high. It can, however, provide an easy way to create a function point inventory of an organization's project portfolio if LOC are readily available.

COCOMO

COCOMO is an acronym for COnstructive COst MOdel, which was first introduced in 1981 by Barry Boehm in his book *Software Engineering Economics*. Based on LOC estimates, it is used to estimate cost, effort, and schedule (Boehm 1981). The original COCOMO model received widespread interest and is an open model, meaning that all of the underlying equations, assumptions, definitions, and so on are available to the public. The original COCOMO model was based on a study of 63 projects and is a hierarchy of estimation models.

Table 6.3 Function Point Conversion to LOC

Language	*Average Source LOC per Function Point*	*Average Source LOC for a 210 FP Application*
Basic	107	22,470
Visual Basic 5	29	6,090
C	128	26,880
C++	53	11,130
COBOL	107	22,470
Java	53	11,130
Machine Language	640	134,440
1st Generation (default)	320	67,200
2nd Generation (default)	107	22,470
3rd Generation (default)	80	16,800
4th Generation (default)	20	4,200
5th Generation (default)	5	1,050

SOURCE: Original: http://www.theadvisors.com/langcomparison.htm. A more recent programming language table can be found at http://www.qsm.com/FPGearing.html

COCOMO is an example of a *parametric model* because it uses dependent variables, such as cost or duration, based upon one or more independent variables that are quantitative indices of performance and/or physical attributes of the system. Often, parametric models can be refined and fine-tuned for specific projects or projects within specific industries (Rad 2002).

Estimating with COCOMO begins with determining the type of project to be estimated. Project types can be classified as:

- *Organic*—These are routine projects where the technology, processes, and people are expected all to work together smoothly. One may view these types of projects as the easy projects, where few problems are expected.

- *Embedded*—An embedded project is viewed as a challenging project. For example, it may be a system to support a new business process or an area that is new ground for the organization. The people may be less experienced, and the processes and technology may be less mature.

- *Semi-Detached*—If organic projects are viewed as easy and embedded as difficult or challenging, then semi-detached fall somewhere in the middle. These projects may not be simple and straightforward, but the organization feels confident that its processes, people, and technology in place are adequate to meet the challenge.

The basic COCOMO model uses an equation for estimating the number of person-months needed for each of these project types. A person-month can be thought of as a one-month effort by one person. In COCOMO, a person-month is defined as 152 hours. Once the project type is defined, the level of effort, in terms of person-months, can be determined using the appropriate equation:

- Organic: Person-Months $= 2.4 \times KDSI^{1.05}$
- Semi-Detached: Person-Months $= 3.0 \times KDSI^{1.12}$
- Embedded: Person-Months $= 3.6 \times KDSI^{1.20}$

Where: KDSI = Thousands of delivered source instructions, i.e., LOC

Let's suppose that we are developing an application that we estimated to have 200 total adjusted function points. Using Table 6.3, we can convert function points into lines of code. If our application is going to be developed in Java, this would require approximately 10,600 lines of code. If we assume that our project will be of medium difficulty, then the semi-detached equation would be appropriate.

$$Person-Months = 3.0 \times KDSI^{1.12}$$
$$= 3.0 \times (10.6)^{1.12}$$
$$= 42.21$$

In summary, our 200 function point project will require about 10,600 lines of code and take just over 42.21 person-months to complete. Once we have estimated the effort for our project, we can determine how many people will be required. Subsequently, this will determine the time estimate and associated cost for developing our application system.

As Frederick Brooks (1995) points out, people and months are not always interchangeable. More people may complicate communication and slow things down. Therefore, duration is determined using one of the following formulas:

- Organic: Duration $= 2.5 \times Effort^{0.38}$

- Semi-Detached: Duration $= 2.5 \times \text{Effort}^{0.35}$
- Embedded: Duration $= 2.5 \times \text{Effort}^{0.32}$

Since our semi-detached project requires 42.21 person-months, the duration of development will be:

$$\begin{aligned} \text{Duration} &= 2.5 \times \text{Effort}^{0.35} \\ &= 2.5 \times (42.21)^{0.35} \\ &= 9.26 \text{ months} \end{aligned}$$

Subsequently, we can determine how many people should be assigned to the development effort:

$$\begin{aligned} \text{People Required} &= \text{Effort} \div \text{Duration} \\ &= 42.21 \div 9.26 \\ &= 4.55 \end{aligned}$$

Therefore, we need 4.55 people working on the project. Okay, so it is pretty tough getting .55 of a person, so we probably will need either four or five people. One could even make an argument that four full-time people and one part-time person will be needed for this project.

The example shows how the basic COCOMO model can be used. There are, however, two other COCOMO models: intermediate COCOMO and advanced COCOMO. Intermediate COCOMO estimates the software development effort as a function of size and a set of 15 subjective cost drivers that include attributes of the end product, the computer used, the personnel staffing, and the project environment. In addition, advanced COCOMO includes all of the characteristics of intermediate COCOMO but with an assessment of the cost driver's impact over four phases of development: product design, detailed design, coding/testing, and integration/testing.

Today, COCOMO II is available and is more suited for the types of projects being developed using 4GLs or other tools like Visual Basic, Delphi, or Power Builder. However, for more traditional projects using a 3GL, the original COCOMO model can still provide good estimates and is often referred to as COCOMO 81.

Another estimating model that you should be aware of is SLIM, which was developed in the late 1970s by Larry Putnam of Quantitative Software Management (Putnam 1978; Putnam and Fitzsimmons 1979). Like COCOMO, SLIM uses LOC to estimate the project's size and a series of 22 questions to calibrate the model.

Heuristics

Heuristics are rules of thumb. Heuristic approaches rely on the fact that the same basic activities will be required for a typical software development project and these activities will require a predictable percentage of the overall effort (Roetzheim and Beasley 1998). For example, when estimating the schedule for a software development task one may, based on previous projects, assign a percentage of the total effort as follows:

- 30 percent planning
- 20 percent coding
- 25 percent component testing
- 25 percent system testing

In his book *Estimating Software Costs*, T. Capers Jones provides a number of heuristics or rules of thumb for estimating software projects based on function points. Some of these rules include:

- Creeping user requirements will grow at an average rate of 2 percent per month from the design through coding phases.

- Function points raised to the 1.25 power predict the approximate defect potential for new software projects.

- Each formal design inspection will find and remove 65 percent of the bugs present.

- Maintenance programmers can repair eight bugs per staff month.

- Function points raised to the 0.4 power predict the approximate development schedule in calendar months.

- Function points divided by 150 predict the approximate number of personnel required for the application.

- Function points divided by 750 predict the approximate number of maintenance personnel required to keep the application updated.

Jones makes an important observation: Rules of thumb are easy, but they are not always accurate. As Garmus and Herron point out (Garmus and Herron 1996):

> Accurate estimating is a function of applying a process and recognizing that effort must be expended in creating a baseline of experience that will allow for increased accuracy of that process. Estimating does not require a crystal ball; it simply requires commitment (142).

Automated Estimating Tools

A number of automated tools can be used for cost, schedule, and resource estimation. These tools include spreadsheets, project management tools, database management systems, software cost estimating, and process or methodology tools. Many of these tools not only help estimate, but also allow the organization to create a database or repository of past projects. In fact, it was found that estimates usually have an accuracy of between 5 and 10 percent when historical data was accurate. Moreover, automated estimating tools are generally more conservative when they are not accurate, as opposed to manual methods that are generally optimistic (Jones 1998).

As the complexity of software development projects increases, the market for software estimation tools will increase as well. Some of the automated tools available include COCOMO II, SLIM, CHECKPOINT, Knowledge Plan, and Cost*Xpert. Research suggests that projects that use a formal estimating tool have a better chance of delivering a system that is on time and within budget.

WHAT IS THE BEST WAY TO ESTIMATE IT PROJECTS?

Unfortunately, no single method or tool is best for accurately estimating IT projects. It may be a good idea to use more than one technique for estimating. You will, however, very likely have two different estimates.

If the estimates from different estimating techniques are fairly close, then you can average them with a fairly high degree of confidence. If the estimates vary

QUICK THINKING—POLITICS AND ESTIMATES

Very often project estimates are political. A project manager must not only come up with project estimates that are reasonable, but also acceptable to the project client or sponsor. Subsequently, political games ensue when the project manager attempts to "sell the right estimate." One game, for example, is to pad or inflate an estimate when one believes that it will be cut in some way. Therefore, the project manager may try to make an estimate high enough so that whatever is left over after the cut is adequate to carry out the project. Similarly, one may inflate an estimate with the idea that it is better to deliver ahead of schedule or below budget than to go over. Here the project manager will try to make him- or herself look better by consistently beating the estimates. On the other hand, a strategy of

low-balling or basing an estimate on what we feel others want to hear is rooted in human psychology. We often go to great lengths to tell people in power what they want to hear—not necessarily what they should hear.

1. Why would the project manager and project sponsor/client have different political interests in project estimates?

2. Why is neither padding or low-balling project estimates a reasonable strategy?

3. As a project manager, how could you ensure that your project estimates do not put you and the project client/sponsor at political odds?

widely, then you should probably be skeptical of one or both estimates and review the data that was collected (Roetzheim and Beasley 1998).

Your initial estimates probably will have to be adjusted up or down based on past experience or data from past projects. Many times, however, the initial estimates are negotiated by upper management or the client. For example, you may come up with an estimate that the project will take twelve months and cost $1.2 million. Unless you can substantiate your estimates, upper management may counter and mandate that the project be completed in eight months and cost no more than $750,000. This counter may be a result of a real business need (i.e., they really do need it in eight months and can not spend more than $750,000) or their belief that you inflated the schedule and budget and some of the fat can be trimmed from your estimates. As a result, you may end up working on a death march project.

It basically comes down to whether the project can or cannot be delivered earlier. It is up to the project manager not only to arrive at an estimate, but to support the estimates. Otherwise, the project's schedule and budget can be very unrealistic. Working long hours and under intense pressure will surely have a negative impact on the project team. A project manager's team must always come first, and protecting them by having a realistic deadline and adequate resources as defined by the project's schedule and budget is the first step.

 ## CHAPTER SUMMARY

Although defining a project's scope in terms of project-oriented and product-oriented deliverables provides an idea of what must be done, the project manager and team must still develop a tactical approach that determines what needs to be done, when it will be done, who will do the work, and how long will it take. The work breakdown structure (WBS) is an important and useful tool for bridging the project's scope with the detailed project plan. More specifically, the WBS pro-

vides a logical hierarchy that decomposes the project scope into work packages. Work packages focus on a particular deliverable and include the activities required to produce the deliverable. In addition, milestones provide a mechanism for ensuring that project work is not only done, but done right.

Once the work packages have been identified, projected durations must be made. Instead of guesstimating, or guessing at the estimates, a number of project estimation methods and techniques were introduced. Traditional approaches to estimating include:

- *The Delphi technique*—This approach involves multiple experts who arrive at a consensus after a series of round-robin sessions in which information and opinions are anonymously provided to each expert.

- *Time-boxing*—A technique where a box of time is allocated to a specific task. For example, a team may be given two weeks (and only two weeks) to develop a prototype of a user interface.

- *Top-down estimating*—This system involves estimating a schedule or budget based upon how long the project or an activity should take or how much it should cost. For example, the project manager may be told that the project must be completed in six months. The project manager then schedules or estimates the project and activities backwards so that the total duration of the activities adds up to six months or less. Although this approach may be used when competitive necessity is an issue, unrealistic expectations can lead to projects with very little chance of meeting their objectives.

- *Bottom-up estimating*—Most real-world estimating uses this approach. The WBS outlines the activities that must be completed, and an estimate is made for each of the activities. The various durations are then added together to determine the total duration of the project. Estimates may be analogous to other projects or based on previous experience. These estimates are also a function of the activity itself (degree of complexity, structuredness, etc.), the resources assigned (a person's knowledge, expertise, enthusiasm, etc.) and support (technology, tools, work environment, etc.).

In addition, several software engineering approaches were introduced for estimating the software development effort. These included:

- *Lines of code (LOC)*—Although counting or trying to estimate the amount of code that must be written may appear intuitively pleasing, there are a number of deficiencies with this approach. The number of LOC may provide an idea of the size of a project, but it does not consider the complexity, constraints, or influencers that must be taken into account.

- *Function points*—Function points were introduced by Allen Albrecht of IBM in 1979. They are synthetic measures that take into account the functionality and complexity of software. Because function points are independent of the technology or programming language used, one application system can be compared with another.

- *COCOMO*—The COnstructive COst MOdel was introduced by Barry Boehm in 1981. Estimates for a software systems effort are determined by an equation based on the project's complexity. More specifically, a software project may be classified as organic (relatively simple and straightforward), embedded (difficult), or semi-detached (somewhere in the middle). Once the effort, in terms of person-months, is calculated, a similar procedure using another model can estimate the project's duration.

- *Heuristics*—Heuristics are rules of thumb that are applied to estimating a software project. The basic premise is that the same activities will be repeated on most projects. This approach may include assigning a specific percentage of the project schedule to specific activities or using other metrics such as function points.

Estimating the effort and duration of an IT project is not an exact science. No single method or technique will provide 100 percent accuracy. Using a combination of approaches may help triangulate an estimate, which provides a confidence greater than when merely guessing or using a single estimation technique. To be realistic, estimates should be revised as understanding of the project increases and new information is acquired.

■ WEB SITES TO VISIT

- **www.softwaremetrics.com**: Articles and examples for learning more about function point analysis
- **www.spr.com**: The site for Software Productivity Research. Capers Jones articles and information about software estimation and planning tools for IT projects
- **www.ifpug.org**: International Function Point Users Group
- **sunset.usc.edu/research/COCOMOII/index.html**: The latest version and information about COCOMO

REVIEW QUESTIONS

1. Describe the PMBOK® area of project time management.
2. What is a WBS? What purpose does it serve?
3. Discuss why a project's scope must be tied to the WBS.
4. What is a work package?
5. What is the difference between a deliverable and a milestone?
6. What purpose do milestones serve?
7. What are some advantages of including milestones in the WBS?
8. What is a crux? Why should the project manager and project team identify the cruxes of a project?
9. What is the proper level of detail for a WBS?
10. Why should the WBS be deliverable oriented?
11. Explain why people who do the work on a project should be involved in developing the project plan.
12. How does the concept of knowledge management support the development of the project plan?
13. How is estimating an IT project different from estimating a construction project?
14. What makes estimating an IT project challenging?
15. What is guesstimating? Why should a project manager not rely on this technique for estimating a project?
16. Describe the potential problems associated with providing an off-the-record estimate?
17. What is the Delphi technique? When would it be an appropriate estimating technique for an IT project?
18. What is time boxing? What are some advantages and disadvantages of time boxing project activities?
19. Describe top-down estimating. What are some advantages and disadvantages of top-down estimating?
20. Describe bottom-up estimating. What are some advantages and disadvantages of bottom-up estimating?
21. What is a death march project? What situations in project planning can lead to a death march project?
22. Discuss why adding people to a project that is already behind schedule can make it later.
23. What is software engineering?
24. Why is counting lines of code (LOC) a popular method for estimating and tracking programmer productivity? What are some problems associated with this method?
25. What is a function point? What advantages do function points have over counting lines of code?
26. How can function point analysis be used to help manage scope creep?
27. What is backfiring? How could an organization use backfiring to improve the accuracy of estimating IT projects?
28. What is COCOMO?
29. Under the COCOMO model, describe the organic, semi-detached, and embedded models.
30. What are heuristics? Discuss some of the advantages and disadvantages of using heuristics for estimating IT projects.
31. What can lead to inaccurate estimates? How can an organization improve the accuracy of estimating IT projects?
32. What is the impact of consistently estimating too low? Too high?

EXTEND YOUR KNOWLEDGE

1. Develop a deliverable-oriented WBS for a surprise birthday party for a friend or relative (perhaps even your instructor?). Be sure to define a measure of success for this party and include milestones.

2. Using the following phases as a guide, develop a WBS for an IT project that will allow Husky Air to keep track of all scheduled maintenance for its chartered aircraft. For each phase, define a deliverable, several activities or tasks, and a milestone.

1.0 Conceptualize and Initialize Project
2.0 Develop Project Charter and Plan
3.0 Analysis
4.0 Design
5.0 Construction
6.0 Testing
7.0 Implementation
8.0 Close Project
9.0 Evaluate Project Success

3. Using the information below, complete a function point analysis in order to use the basic COCOMO model to estimate the duration and number of people needed to develop an application using C++. Assume that the project is relatively simple and straightforward and that the project team is familiar with both the problem and technology. You can perform the calculations by hand, but feel free to use an appropriate software tool.

	Complexity			
	Low	*Average*	*High*	*Total*
Internal logical files (ILF)	__× 7 = __	__× 10 = __	__× 15 = __	
External interface files (EIF)	__× 5 = __	__× 7 = __	__× 10 = __	
External input (EI)	__× 3 = __	__× 4 = __	__× 6 = __	
External output (EO)	__× 4 = __	__× 5 = __	__× 7 = __	
External inquiry (EQ)	__× 3 = __	__× 4 = __	__× 6 = __	

	Complexity		
	Low	*Average*	*High*
Internal logical files (ILF)	4	2	0
External interface files (EIF)	0	1	0
External input (EI)	3	2	0
External output (EO)	5	7	3
External inquiry (EQ)	2	5	2

Language	*Average Source LOC per Function Point*
Basic	107
C	128
C++	53
COBOL	107
Delphi	29
Java	53
Visual Basic 5	29

General System Characteristic	*Degree of Influence*
Data communications	2
Distributed data processing	3
Performance	3
Heavily used configuration	4
Transaction rate	4
On-line data entry	2
End user efficiency	2
Online update	2
Complex processing	2
Reusability	3
Installation ease	2
Operational ease	2
Multiple sites	1
Facilitate change	1

 # GLOBAL TECHNOLOGY SOLUTIONS

The white board in the GTS conference room was filled with multicolor markings reflecting the ideas and suggestions from the Husky Air team. Several empty pizza boxes were piled neatly in the corner. It had been an all-day working session for the Husky Air project team. Although it was late in the day, the energy in the room was still high. Everyone felt they were drawing closer to a first draft of the project plan.

Tim Williams stood up and walked over to the electronic white board. Addressing the group, he said, "It looks like we have just about everything we need, but I would like to make sure all the activities or tasks in the systems testing phase are defined more clearly. Let's start out by identifying what deliverables we need to produce as a result of the testing phase."

Sitaramin paged through his notes and said that the team had identified a test plan and a test results report as part of the project scope defined in the Deliverable Structure Chart. Yan, the project's database administrator, suggested that the test report summarize not only the results of the system tests, but what was tested and how the tests were conducted. The rest of the team agreed, and Tim wrote *TESTING PHASE* in capital letters on the board and then *Deliverable: Test Results Report* underneath it. Yan then suggested that the phase needed a milestone. Sitaramin said that the testing phase would not be completed when the report was finished, but only when the test results were acceptable to the client. The rest of the team agreed and Tim wrote *Milestone: Client signs off on test results*.

Tim then asked what specific activities or tasks the team would have to undertake to create the test results report. For the next ten minutes, the entire team brainstormed ideas. Tim dutifully wrote each idea on the board without judgment and only asked for clarification or help spelling a particular word. After working together for just a short time, the team had already adopted an unwritten rule that no one was to evaluate an idea until after they had finished the brainstorming activity. They had found that this encouraged participation from everyone and allowed for more creative ideas.

After a few minutes, the frequency of new ideas suggested by the team started to slow. Tim then asked if any of these ideas or suggestions were similar—that is, did they have the same meaning, or could they be grouped? Again, everyone had ideas and suggestions, and Tim rewrote the original list until the team agreed on a list of activities that would allow them to develop the test results plan.

"This looks pretty good!" exclaimed Tim. Then he added, "But do all of these activities have to be followed one after the other? Or can some of these activities be completed in parallel by different team members?"

Once again, the team began making suggestions and discussing ideas of how to best sequence these activities. This only took a few minutes, but everyone could see how the testing phase of the project was taking shape. Tim paused, took a few steps back, and announced, "OK, it looks like we're headed in the right direction. Now who will be responsible for completing these tasks and what resources will they need?"

Since everyone on the team had a specific role, the assigning of team members to the tasks was pretty straightforward. Some of the tasks required only one person, while others needed two or more. The team also identified a few activities where the same person was assigned to tasks scheduled at the same time. The team's discussion also identified an important activity that was overlooked and needed to be added.

Tim joked that he was glad they were using a white board that could easily be erased as he carefully updated the activities and assignments. Then he smiled and said, "Our work breakdown structure is almost complete. All we need to do now is estimate how long each of these testing activities will take. Once we have these estimates, we can enter the work breakdown structure into the project management software package we're using to get the schedule and budget. I think we'll need to review our project plan as a team at least one more time before we present it to our client. I'm sure we'll have to make some changes along the way, but I would say the bulk of our planning work is almost complete."

It was getting late in the day, and the team was starting to get tired. Ted, a telecommunications specialist, suggested that they all meet the next day to finalize the time estimates for the testing phase activities. He also asked that before they adjourned, the team should once again develop an action plan based upon facts the team knew to be true, any assumptions to be tested, and what they would need to find out in order to estimate each of the testing phase activities.

The rest of the team agreed, and they began another learning cycle.

Things to Think About

1. What are some advantages of a project team working together to develop the project plan? What are some disadvantages?

2. Why should the project team members not be too quick to judge the ideas and suggestions provided during a brainstorming session?

3. How can the concept of learning cycles support the project planning process?

HUSKY AIR ASSIGNMENT—PILOT ANGELS

The Work Breakdown Structure (WBS)

Now that you have defined the project's scope, it's time to start the process of determining how the work will be accomplished. This will require that you draw upon work you did in several previous assignments.

Please provide a professional-looking document that includes the following:

1. **Project name, project team name, and the names of the members of your project team**

2. **A brief project description**

3. **The project's MOV** (This should be revised or refined if necessary.)

4. **The phases of your project**—Using a spreadsheet, word processor, or Microsoft Project®, list all of the project life cycle and systems development life cycle phases and the associated deliverables that you defined in the Project Scope assignment.

5. **Milestones for each phase and deliverable**—Achieving a milestone will tell everyone associated with the project that the phase or deliverable was completed satisfactorily.

6. **Activities/Tasks**—Define a set of activities or tasks that must be completed to produce each deliverable.

7. **Resource Assignments**—Assign people and other appropriate resources to each activity. This will be based on the people and resources that you identified when you completed the project infrastructure assignment. Keep in mind that adding resources to an activity may allow the activity to be completed in a shorter amount of time; however, it may increase the cost of completing that task or activity.

8. **Estimates for Each Activity/Task**—Based on the tasks or activities and the resources assigned, develop a time estimate for each task or activity to be completed. For the purposes of this assignment, you should use a combination of estimation techniques such as time-boxing and bottom-up estimation.

 # CASE STUDIES

Extreme Programming at Sabre

Extreme programming (XP) was first introduced by Kent Beck when he was the project leader on a large, long-term project to rewrite Chrysler Corporation's payroll system. He later outlined this development methodology in a book titled *Extreme Programming Explained: Embrace Change*. Some of the main concepts of XP include using small teams, using simple code, reviewing it frequently, testing it early and often, and working no more than a 40 hour work week. XP is often referred to as a lightweight methodology because it does not emphasize lengthy requirements definition and extensive documentation.

Instead, XP focuses on having the end user or customer develop user stories that describe what the new system must do. Beck suggests that project teams have no more than 12 developers working in pairs that work side by side on a single assignment. He believes that this approach leads to better quality code that takes less time to test and debug. Close communication between the developers and users/customers is key, as the user stories provide a basis for prioritizing the applications' most important functionality and estimating code releases that are tested and shared among the development team.

Sabre Airline Solutions for many years relied on a large modeling and forecasting software package called AirFlite Profit Manager to make flight schedules more profitable. In 2000, Release 8 of the software system contained approximately 500,000 lines of code and was four months late, with 300 known bugs or defects identified in final system testing. Moreover, a Sabre customer found 26 bugs in the first three days of acceptance testing, with an additional 200 bugs uncovered after the system was joint tested by Sabre and the customer.

Since then, the company has adopted XP and claims that XP has dramatically improved the quality and productivity of its 300 developers. More specifically, only 100 bugs were found 16 months after Release 10 of AirFlite Profit Manager was shipped to its airline customers. Even more impressive was that Release 10 required just 3 developers to support 13 customers, while Release 8 required 13 people to support 12 customers. On another project, Sabre converted the user interface of its AirServ airline cabin provisioning optimization system from C++ to a Web-based Java application over a two-year period that required rewriting about 100 GUI programs. After the development team changed over to XP halfway through the project, Sabre reported that programmer productivity—as measured by the number of labor hours required for each screen—still increased by 42 percent.

Other success stories include a Host Access Tool project that provides a common application programming interface for accessing legacy host systems. This system had over 15,000 lines of code and was developed from the outset using the XP methodology. Twenty months after its ship date, the software has remained defect free. In addition, only four bugs have shown up after 15 months in another software system called Peripheral Manager, a system that manages interactions between host systems and peripheral devices, and contains about 28,000 lines of code.

With XP as its new approach to development, Sabre Airline Solutions customers defined features in terms of user stories that are expressed in user terms and simple enough to be coded, tested, and integrated in two weeks or less. Developers define criteria for automated test units, while customers define a broader set of criteria for acceptance testing. Both unit and acceptance testing are written before a feature or user story is coded. An inability to write a test usually means that the feature is not well defined or understood.

The coding is accomplished in an open lab in pairs by teams of developers to promote collective ownership of the code. The developers can sign up for the tasks they want to work on and/or the person they want to work with. Each team also has an "XP coach" and an "XP customer" who is a subject matter expert and prioritizes product features, writes user stories, and signs off on the test results. Developers are encouraged to refactor code—i.e., rewrite code not just to fix bugs or add features, but to make it more efficient and easier to maintain. Customers see new releases in one to three months.

According to Brad Jensen, senior vice president for airline product development at Sabre, the quality improvements come directly from XP's continuous testing and integration. He says: "Every two weeks what you've completed has got to be production-ready. You code as you test. You actually write an automated unit test before you code the unit, so if bugs do creep in, you find out about it right then."

Moreover, Damon Hougland, director of airline products and services, believes that paired programming can be a difficult sell at first because many think it will double programming costs. However, he believes that XP actually reduces costs because the extra time to write a line of code is more than offset by effort to test, fix, and maintain the code. He also explains, "Everyone on the team works on every part of the system. You have the weaker people paired with the stronger people, and the business knowledge and coding knowledge are transferred very quickly."

However, XP does not include all the processes and practices a software development organization must follow. As Hougland contends, "XP really focuses on what [programmers] do. It doesn't cover the traditional project management you have to do with customers, such as customer communications, and a lot of the testing we do is not covered in XP. A lot of people try XP and fail because they assume that XP will do everything for a development methodology."

Suppose you have been hired as a consultant by a company that is interested in exploring XP as a development methodology. In the past, the company has developed systems using more traditional project management and development approaches, so the current IT staff has little or no knowledge of XP. The CIO has asked you to provide some insight into the following questions:

1. How should the company introduce XP? More specifically, should the company just jump right into it and attempt to use XP on a large, upcoming project that is mission critical to the company? Or should it experiment with a smaller, less critical project?

2. Can traditional project management tools such as a work breakdown structure (WBS) be used in XP?

3. What methods for estimation would be most appropriate when following an XP approach?

4. If the company's developers have always followed a more traditional approach to IT projects, what impacts might introducing XP have on them?

SOURCE: Adapted from Lee Copeland, "Extreme Programming," *Computerworld*, December 03, 2001; Gary Anthes, "Sabre Takes Extreme Measures," *Computerworld*, March 29, 2004.

Improving Productivity

In the United States, the H-1B is a nonimmigrant visa that allows a U.S. employer to hire foreign workers in a specialty occupation. A specialty occupation is a job that requires the theoretical and practical application of a body of highly specialized knowledge such as medicine, engineering, education, law, and software development. The foreign worker generally must possess at least a bachelor's degree or its equivalent, and the person authorized to work under the H-1B visa is strictly limited to employment with the sponsoring organization.

However, a study of U.S. Department of Labor records released by the Center for Immigration Studies reports that H-1B visa IT workers earn on average $13,000 less than their American counterparts. For example, the study found that the average wage for a H-1B programmer in 2003 was $49,258, while the average U.S. wage salary was $65,000. Even though H-1B workers are paid less, they are required by law to receive the same prevailing wages.

Subsequently, an H-1B worker's ability to seek better wages by changing employers can be limited. The H-1B visa is valid for six years but then allows the foreign worker to apply for permanent residency.

Some believe that the H-1B visa program has been a catalyst for moving jobs offshore, while others like John Miano, a former chairman of the Programmers Guild, argue that productivity improvements, not hiring programmers at lower wages, can reduce software development costs. According to Miano, "It's my personal view that we have twice as many software developers in this country as we need." He believes that improvements in development tools, processes, and better work environments can reduce development costs. Such simple things as getting rid of cubicles and replacing them with enclosed offices can reduce distractions and improve productivity.

1. Would a software developer be more productive if he/she worked in an enclosed office?

2. What are some common distractions in an office environment? What impact do they have on employees? How could many of these distractions be minimized?

3. According to William Duncan, project estimates are an "informed assessment of an uncertain event." Therefore, when you make an estimate regarding the effort required to perform a particular task or deliver a particular work product, you are assuming that a particular resource (e.g., person) will be available, have the requisite skills and experience, motivation, and support (technology, work environment, etc.) available. Therefore, productivity is a key component in determining whether an estimate can be met. Other than an enclosed office, what are some other ways for improving developer productivity?

SOURCE: Adapted from: Patrick Thibodeau, H-1B Workers Earn Less Than American Counterparts, Report Says, *Computerworld*, January 03, 2006;

William Duncan, The Mechanics of Estimating, *Computerworld Blog*, January 04, 2006;

Patrick Thibodeau, Do Cubicles Hurt Productivity?, *Projects@Work*, March 10, 2005.

BIBLIOGRAPHY

Albrecht, Allan J. 1979. *Measuring Application Development Productivity*. Proceedings SHARE/GUIDE IBM Applications Development Symposium, Monterey, Calif., October 14–17, 1979.

Boehm, B. W. 1981. *Software Engineering Economics*. Englewood Cliffs, NJ: Prentice Hall.

Brooks, F. P. 1995. *The Mythical Man-Month*. Reading, MA: Addison Wesley.

Dennis, A. and Haley, H. B. (2000). *Systems Analysis and Design: An Applied Approach*. New York: John Wiley.

Garmus, D. and D. Herron. 1996. *Measuring the Software Process*. Upper Saddle River, NJ: Prentice Hall PTR.

Haugan, G. T. 2002. *Efffective Work Breakdown Structures*. Vienna, VA: Management Concepts, Inc.

Jones, T. C. 1998. *Estimating Software Costs*. New York: McGraw-Hill.

Pressman, R. S. 2001. *Software Engineering: A Practitioner's Approach*. Boston: McGraw-Hill.

Project Management Institute (PMI) 2004. *A Guide to the Project Management Body of Knowledge (PMBOK® Guide)*. Newtown Square, PA: PMI Publishing.

Putnam, L. H. 1978. General Empirical Solution to the Macro Software Sizing and Estimating Problem. *IEEE Transactions Software Engineering* SE 4(4): 345–361.

Putnam, L. H. and A. Fitzsimmons. 1979. Estimating Software Costs. *Datamation* 25 (Sept–Nov): 10–12.

Rad, P. F. 2002. *Project Estimating and Cost Management*. Vienna, VA: Management Concepts, Inc.

Roetzheim, W. H. and R. A. Beasley. 1998. *Software Project Cost and Schedule Estimating: Best Practices*. Upper Saddle River, NJ: Prentice Hall.

Royce, W. 1998. *Software Project Management: A Unified Framework*. Reading, MA: Addison Wesley.

Yourdon, E. 1999. *Death March*. Upper Saddle River, NJ: Prentice Hall.

CHAPTER

7

The Project Schedule and Budget

CHAPTER OVERVIEW

Chapter 7 focuses on developing the project schedule and budget and introduces a number of project management tools for developing the project plan. After studying this chapter, you should understand and be able to:

- Describe the Project Management Body of Knowledge (PMBOK®) area called project cost management.
- Develop a Gantt chart.
- Develop a project network diagram using a technique called activity on the node (AON) technique.
- Identify a project's critical path and explain why it must be controlled and managed.
- Develop a PERT diagram.
- Describe the concept of precedence diagramming and identify finish-to-start, start-to-start, finish-to-finish, and start-to-finish activity relationships.
- Describe the concept of critical chain project management (CCPM).
- Describe the various types of costs that make up the project's budget.
- Define what is meant by the baseline project plan.

INTRODUCTION

The last several chapters have been leading up to the development of the project schedule and budget. Chapter 3 introduced the project planning framework (see Figure 7.1). To support this framework, subsequent chapters introduced several Project Management Body of Knowledge (PMBOK®) areas, including project integration management, human resources management, project scope management, and project time management. In this chapter, you will be introduced to another knowledge area called project cost management, which will bring all of the concepts, tools, and techniques covered in the last several chapters together so that the project plan can be developed.

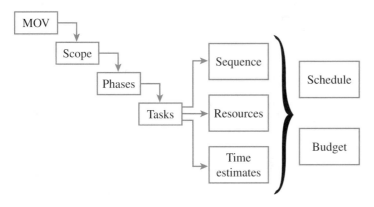

Figure 7.1   The Project Planning Framework

The project plan contains all of the details of the project's schedule and budget. It will be used to guide the project team and monitor the project's progress throughout the project life cycle. Project time management was introduced in the last chapter; however, our focus was on two important processes: Activity definition and activity duration estimation. These two processes are key ingredients for developing the work breakdown structure (WBS) that links the project's scope to the project plan. The development of a project plan, however, requires a schedule and budget. The project schedule builds upon the WBS by identifying the sequence of activities as well as the interdependencies and relationships. Once the activities, their expected durations, and sequence are identified, various project management tools can be used to map a network of activities to yield the project schedule. This information, in turn, can be entered into a project management software package to make developing the project plan more efficient and to provide a means to monitor and control the project schedule and budget as the plan is executed.

The project budget is determined by the project schedule, the cost of the resources assigned to each of the tasks, and by any other direct or indirect costs and reserves. In addition, a PMBOK® area called **project cost management** focuses on the processes, procedures, and techniques to develop and manage the project budget. According to PMBOK®, project cost management includes:

- *Cost estimating*—Based upon the activities, their time estimates, and resource requirements, an estimate can be developed.

- *Cost budgeting*—Once the time and cost of each activity is estimated, an overall cost estimate for the entire project can be made. Once approved, this estimate becomes the project budget.

- *Cost control*—Ensuring that proper processes and procedures are in place to control changes to the project budget.

Once the project schedule and budget are determined, the total time and cost of each activity can be summed using a bottom-up approach to determine a target deadline and budget. The schedule and budget must, however, be reviewed and accepted by the project sponsor or client. This may require several revisions and possible trade-offs before the scope, schedule, and budget relationship is reasonable and acceptable to *all* of the project stakeholders. Once the schedule and budget are approved by the sponsor or client, the plan becomes the baseline project plan. This milestone is an important achievement that marks the completion of the second phase of the IT project methodology and gives the project manager and team the authority to begin carrying out the activities outlined in the plan.

DEVELOPING THE PROJECT SCHEDULE

Overeager new manager promises his boss a thirty-day schedule for a project to automate passwords on company's mainframe, midrange, and desktop systems. "We can't do that," desktop support pilot fish tells manager when he sees the project plan. "Have you confirmed that the mainframe and midrange support groups can do the product evaluation in the three days you've allotted?" fish asks. "No," says manager, "but if they don't meet the plan, then it'll be their fault it fails, not mine."

From Shark Tank: That's One Way to Look at It, May 20, 2002. http://www .computerworld.com/careertopics/careers/training/story/0,10801,71293,00.html.

The WBS identifies the activities and tasks that must be completed in order to provide the project scope deliverables. Estimates provide a forecasted duration for each of these activities and are based upon the characteristics of the activity, the resources assigned, and the support provided to carry out the activity. Project networks, on the other hand, support the development of the project schedule by identifying dependencies and the sequencing of the activities defined in the WBS. The project network also serves as a key tool for monitoring and controlling the project activities once the project work begins.

In this section, several project management tools and techniques will be introduced to create a project network plan that defines the sequence of activities throughout the project and their dependencies. These tools include Gantt charts, activity on the node (AON), critical path analysis, PERT, and the precedence diagramming method (PDM). Many of these tools are integrated into most project management software packages; however, it is important to have a fundamental understanding of how these various project management tools work in order to make the most of an automated tool.

Gantt Charts

Working with the U.S. Army during World War I, Henry L. Gantt developed a visual representation that compares a project's planned activities with actual progress over time. Although **Gantt charts** have been around for a long time, they are still one of the most useful and widely used project management tools.

Figure 7.2 shows how a basic Gantt chart can be used for planning. Estimates for the tasks or activities defined in the WBS are represented using a bar across a horizontal time axis. Other symbols, for example, diamonds, can represent milestones to make the Gantt chart more useful.

The Gantt Chart in Figure 7.2 depicts the general sequence of activities or work tasks. In this project example, there are five tasks of varying durations and the project should be completed in 15 time periods (e.g., days). In addition, the two shaded diamonds following tasks C and E indicate milestone events.

Gantt charts can also be useful for tracking and monitoring the progress of a project. As shown in Figure 7.3, completed tasks can be shaded or filled in, and one can get an accurate picture of where the project stands for a given status or reporting date. In Figure 7.3, tasks A and B have been completed, but it looks like Task C is somewhat behind schedule.

Although Gantt charts are simple, straightforward, and useful for communicating the project's status, they do not show the explicit relationships among tasks or activities. For example, we can see from Figure 7.3 that task C is somewhat behind schedule; however, the Gantt chart does not tell us whether there will be an impact on tasks D or E and whether this impact will push back the project's original deadline. The Gantt chart introduced in this section follows a more traditional form. As you will see, the Gantt chart used in most project management software packages today has been modified to overcome these limitations.

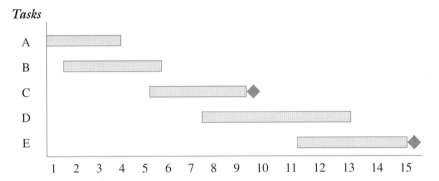

Figure 7.2   Gantt Chart for Planning

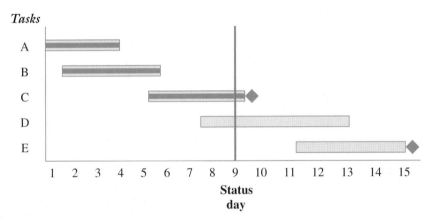

Figure 7.3   Gantt Chart Reporting Project's Progress

Project Network Diagrams

Project network diagrams include several useful tools for planning, scheduling, and monitoring the project's progress. Similar to Gantt charts, project network diagrams use the WBS as a basis to provide a visual representation of the workflow of activities and tasks. However, project network diagrams also provide valuable information about the logical sequence and dependencies among the various activities or tasks. Subsequently, a completion date or project deadline should be developed based on a sound estimating process rather than guesstimating a target date or a date set arbitrarily by upper management or the client.

In addition, project network diagrams provide information concerning when specific tasks must start and finish, and what activities may be delayed without affecting the deadline target date. In addition, the project manager can make decisions regarding scheduling and resource assignments to shorten the time required for those critical activities that will impact the project deadline.

Activity on the Node (AON)   An activity or task focuses on producing a specific project deliverable, generally takes a specific amount of time to complete, and requires resources. **Activity on the node (AON)** is a project network diagramming tool that graphically represents all of the project activities and tasks, as well as their

QUICK THINKING—PROJECT RUNWAY

Atlanta's Hartsfield-Jackson International Airport is one of the world's busiest, with over 88 million travelers in 2005 and an estimated 120 million by 2010. In 2003, Dwight Pullen, a civil engineer for H. J. Russel & Company in Atlanta, Georgia, was named project manager for a $1.28 billion construction project to build a fifth runway. With only 13 years' experience, a friend joked that Pullen was the youngest person in the country to manage a billion dollar project. He may have been right.

The 9,000 foot expansion runway project was built over a two-lane highway, Interstate 285, which loops around the city of Atlanta. This included building a 1,264 foot tunnel for the highway and building the runway on top of the tunnel to accommodate large planes like the Boeing 747 and Airbus A-380 that can weigh up to 1 million pounds. The project was expected to provide a financial boom that would save the airline industry an estimated $5 million a week in delay costs and was considered a project of national significance. Pullen says that "getting the project done on time and on budget were absolutely essential to the credibility of everyone involved in the project." The project was completed 11 days ahead of schedule and at $100 million under budget.

Pullen said that the biggest challenge of the project was dealing with the various stakeholders, which included Atlanta city council members, airport executives, the Federal Aviation Administration, the Georgia Department of Transportation, environmental groups, contractors, engineers, and architects. This required building and maintaining strong relationships with all of them. Although Pullen said that he didn't have to make best friends or go golfing with these people, he relied on these relationships to help with negotiations and to keep his team focused on milestones. According to Pullen, "Some of my colleagues aren't that good with the relationship side, and I think that causes projects to fail, be delayed, or go over budget. Contractors will hold up your project if they don't like you—they're notorious for that!"

The project plan entailed about as much time in the planning phase as it did in the construction phase. Moreover, the design phase was the shortest phase in the master project schedule and included more than 15,000 scheduled activities. These activities were input into a project management software tool called Primavera®. Pullen contends that the work breakdown structure was critical to this project because it served as a "common language" for everyone working on the project and a best practice that allowed him to be successful in analyzing, forecasting, scheduling, and base-lining.

Pullen believes one of his keys to success was the idea of project celebrations to keep morale up and mark the completion of milestones along the way. For example, he instituted cake and ice cream parties for "employee of the quarter," project team awards, groundbreakings, and safety records. At the end of the successful project, Pullen explains, "We went out and had dinner at the end of the runway, then we got up on top of the runway while the lights were on. It's absolutely beautiful to see that up close, so that was a phenomenal moment. Then we put the whole team in company trucks and raced all the way down the nearly two miles of runway like an airplane would. It was thrilling and even though the celebration was inexpensive, everybody appreciated it." In addition, the project team also got to take a ten-minute flight around the city on a 767 that took off and landed on the new runway.

1. What is the importance of using project management software for managing a large-scale project?

2. A project will not fail because of a project manager's inability to use a particular project management software tool. What is the significance of relationships among the various project stakeholders and the project's schedule and budget?

SOURCE: Adapted from Karen Klein, A Runway Success, *Projects@Work*, April 5, 2007.

---

logical sequence and dependencies. Using AON, activities are represented as boxes (nodes) and arrows indicate precedence and flow.

To construct an AON network diagram, one begins with the activities and tasks that were defined in the WBS. Estimates for each activity or task defined in the WBS should have an associated time estimate. The next step is to determine which activities are **predecessors, successors,** or **parallel.** Predecessor activities are those activities that must be completed *before* another activity can be started—for example, a computer's operating system must be installed before loading an application package. On the other hand, successor activities are activities that must follow a particular

Table 7.1   Activity Analysis for AON

Activity	Description	Estimated Duration (Days)	Predecessor
A	Evaluate current technology platform	2	None
B	Define user requirements	5	A
C	Design Web page layouts	4	B
D	Set up server	3	B
E	Estimate Web traffic	1	B
F	Test Web pages and links	4	C, D
G	Move Web pages to production environment	3	D, E
H	Write announcement of intranet for corporate newsletter	2	F, G
I	Train users	5	G
J	Write report to management	1	H, I

activity in some type of sequence. For example, a program must be tested and then documented after it is compiled. A parallel activity is an activity or task that can be worked on at the same time as another activity. Parallel activities may be thought of as an opportunity to shorten the project schedule; however, they also can be a trade-off since doing more than one thing at the same time can have a critical impact on project resources. The activities, time estimates, and relationships for developing a simple corporate intranet can be summarized in a table similar to Table 7.1.

Once the relationships and time estimates for each activity or task in the WBS have been developed, an AON project network diagram can be created, as in Figure 7.4.

The work in an AON flows from left to right. An activity cannot begin until all of its predecessor activities have been completed. For example, Activity F cannot begin until Activities C and D are done.

Critical Path Analysis   At this point we have a visual road map of our project. Moreover, the time estimates for each of the activities determines the project schedule and tells us how long our project will take to complete. This is determined by looking at each of the possible paths and computing the total duration for each path, as shown in Table 7.2.

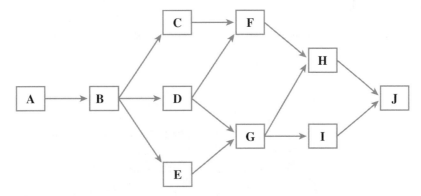

Figure 7.4   Activity on the Node (AON) Network Diagram

Table 7.2 Possible Activity Paths

Possible Paths	Path	Total
Path 1	A + B + C + F + H + J	18
	2 + 5 + 4 + 4 + 2 + 1	
Path 2	A + B + D + F + H + J	17
	2 + 5 + 3 + 4 + 2 + 1	
Path 3	A + B + D + G + H + J	16
	2 + 5 + 3 + 3 + 2 + 1	
Path 4	A + B + D + G + I + J	19*
	2 + 5 + 3 + 3 + 5 + 1	
Path 5	A + B + E + G + I + J	17
	2 + 5 + 1 + 3 + 5 + 1	

*Critical Path

As can be seen in Table 7.2, the longest path in the AON network diagram is 19 days. This number is significant for two reasons. First, this tells us that our project is estimated to take 19 days (i.e., the project deadline will be 19 days after the project starts). Second, and perhaps more importantly, Path 4 is also our **critical path.** The critical path is the longest path in the project network and is also the shortest time in which the project can be completed.

Identifying the critical path is a major concern to the project manager because any change in the duration of the activities or tasks on the critical path will affect the project's schedule. In other words, the critical path has zero **slack** (or **float**). Slack, which is sometimes called float, is the amount of time an activity can be delayed, that is, take longer than expected, before it delays the project. For example, Activity E is not on the critical path. In fact, the only path that includes Activity E is Path 5. Subsequently, the start of Activity E could be delayed for two days or take up to three days to complete before the project schedule is affected. On the other hand, Activities A, B, D, G, I, and J have no float because delaying their start or taking longer to complete than we estimated will increase the total duration of the project by the same amount.

As a result, knowing the critical path can influence a project manager's decisions. For example, a project manager can **expedite,** or **crash,** the project by adding resources to an activity on the critical path to shorten its duration. The project manager may even be able to divert resources from certain activities, for example, Activity E because this activity has some slack or float. Diverting resources can reduce the overall project schedule, but keep in mind that there may be a trade-off—shortening the schedule by adding more resources may inflate the project's budget.

Another way to shorten the project schedule is to look for parallel activity opportunities. Doing two, or several, activities that were originally planned to be completed in sequence at the same time can shorten the critical path. It is known as **fast tracking** the project.

Can the critical path change? The answer is, absolutely! As a result, it is imperative that the project manager not only identify the critical path, but monitor and manage it appropriately. In fact, it is very possible for a project to have more than one critical path.

PERT The **program evaluation and review technique (PERT)** was developed in the late 1950s to help manage the Polaris submarine project. At about the same time, the critical path method (CPM) was developed. The two methods are often combined and called PERT/CPM.

PERT uses the project network diagramming technique to create a visual representation of the scheduled activities that expresses both their logical sequence and interrelationships. PERT also uses a statistical distribution that provides probability for estimating when the project and its associated activities will be completed. This probabilistic estimate is derived by using three estimates for each activity: optimistic, most likely, and pessimistic.

An optimistic estimate is the minimum time in which an activity or task can be completed. This is a best-case scenario where everything goes well and there is little or no chance of finishing earlier. A most likely estimate, as the name implies, is the normally expected time required to complete the task or activity. A pessimistic

Table 7.3 Activity Analysis for PERT

Activity	Predecessor	Optimistic Estimates (Days) a	Most Likely Estimates (Days) b	Pessimistic Estimates (Days) c	Expected Duration $\frac{(a + 4b + c)}{6}$
A	None	1	2	4	2.2
B	A	3	5	8	5.2
C	B	2	4	5	3.8
D	B	2	3	6	3.3
E	B	1	1	1	1.0
F	C, D	2	4	6	4.0
G	D, E	2	3	4	3.0
H	F, G	1	2	5	2.3
I	G	4	5	9	5.5
J	H, I	.5	1	3	1.3

estimate is a worst-case scenario and is viewed as the maximum time in which an activity can or should be completed.

One can use the following equation to compute a mean or weighted average for each individual activity that will become the PERT estimate:

$$\text{Activity Estimate} = \frac{\text{Optimistic Time} + (4 \times \text{Most Likely Time}) + \text{Pessimistic Time}}{6}$$

The total expected time to complete the project can be easily found by summing each of the individual activity estimates or:

$$\text{Total Expected Time of Project} = \sum_{i=1}^{n} \text{Activity Estimates}$$

For example, on our project used earlier, a project manager and team came up with the estimates presented in Table 7.3.

Analyzing the various paths using PERT provides the critical paths presented in Table 7.4. As can be seen in Table 7.4, the critical path is still Path 4 and the expected completion date of the project is 20.5, or 21 days if we round up. In this

Table 7.4 Possible PERT Activity Paths

Possible Paths	Path	Total
Path 1	A + B + C + F + H + J	18.8
	2.2 + 5.2 + 3.8 + 4.0 + 2.3 + 1.3	
Path 2	A + B + D + F + H + J	18.3
	2.2 + 5.2 + 3.3 + 4.0 + 2.3 + 1.3	
Path 3	A + B + D + G + H + J	18.6
	2.2 + 5.2 + 3.3 + 4.0 + 2.3 + 1.3	
Path 4	A + B + D + G + I + J	20.5*
	2.2 + 5.2 + 3.3 + 3.0 + 5.5 + 1.3	
Path 5	A + B + E + G + I + J	18.2
	2.2 + 5.2 + 1.0 + 3.0 + 5.5 + 1.3	

*Critical Path

case, the deadline increased from 19 days using the AON method to 21 days using the statistical technique associated with PERT. In the first case, the most likely estimates were used, while PERT took into account not only the most likely estimates, but optimistic and pessimistic estimates as well. PERT is well suited for developing simulations whereby the project manager can conduct a sensitivity analysis for schedule planning and risk analysis. But, like any planning and scheduling tool, its usefulness is highly correlated to the quality of the estimates used.

Precedence Diagramming Method (PDM)   Another tool that is useful for understanding the relationships among project activities is the **precedence diagramming method (PDM).** This tool is similar to the AON project diagram technique and is based on four fundamental relationships shown in Figure 7.5.

- *Finish-to-start (FS)*—A finish-to-start relationship is the most common relationship between activities and implies a logical sequence. Here, activity or task B cannot begin until task A is completed. For example, a program is tested after it is written. Or, in other words, the code is written and then tested. This relationship is similar to the successor and predecessor relationships used in the AON method.
- *Start-to-start (SS)*—A start-to-start relationship between tasks or activities occurs when two tasks can or must start at the same time. Although the tasks start at the same time, they do not have to finish together—that is, the tasks can have different durations. A start-to-start relationship would be one type of parallel activity that can shorten a project schedule.
- *Finish-to-finish (FF)*—Another type of parallel activity is the finish-to-finish relationship. Here, two activities can start at different times, have different durations, but are planned to be competed at the same time. Once both of the FF activities are completed, the next activity or set of activities can be started, or if no more activities follow, the project is complete.

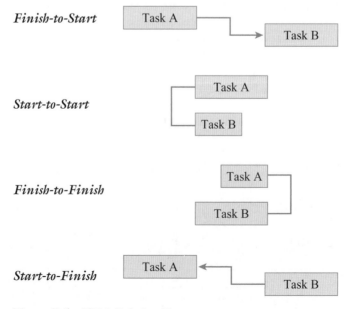

Figure 7.5   PDM Relationships

- *Start-to-finish (SF)*—The start-to-finish relationship is probably the least common and can be easily confused with the finish-to-start relationship. A SF relationship, as illustrated in Figure 7.5, is exactly the opposite of an FS relationship. In addition, an SF relationship means that task A cannot end until task B starts. An example of an SF relationship in real life might be a nurse working at a hospital. This person may have to work until relieved by another nurse who arrives to start the next shift.

An advantage of using PDM is that the project manager can specify **lead** and **lag** times for various activities. More specifically, lead time allows for the overlapping of activities. For example, a project plan may have two activities or tasks that have been identified as a finish-to-start relationship. These two activities may be the setup of computers in a lab followed by the installation of an operating system on those computers. If we had two people, one to set up the computers and one to install the operating systems on each computer, the project plan might specify a finish-to-start relationship where the installation of the operating systems cannot begin until all of the computers have been set up in the lab. Based on this project plan, the person who installs the operating system must wait and watch while the other person works.

Let's assume, however, that it takes about half the time to install an operating system as it does to set up a computer. Furthermore, there is no reason why the software person cannot begin installing the operating system when the hardware person has about half of the computers set up. In this case, both tasks will finish about the same time, and we have created an opportunity to shorten the project schedule. By scheduling the task of installing the operating systems when the task of setting up the computers is 50 percent complete, we have used the concept of lead time to our advantage.

On the other hand, let's suppose further that before our hardware person starts setting up the computers in the lab, we want the lab walls to be painted. This would be another finish-to-start relationship because we would like to schedule the painting of the lab before we start installing the computers. Using lead time in this case, however, would not make sense because we do not want the hardware person and painters getting in each other's way. In this case, we may even want to give the freshly painted walls a chance to dry before we allow any work to be done in the lab. Therefore, we would like to schedule a lag of one day before our hardware person starts setting up the computers. Another way of looking at this is to say we are going to schedule a negative lead day in our project schedule.

Critical Chain Project Management (CCPM)

Critical chain project management (CCPM) may be one of the most important recent developments in modern project management. CCPM was introduced in a 1997 book called *Critical Chain* by Eliyahu Goldratt and is based on his previous work called the *Theory of Constraints*.

CCPM is based on the idea that people often inflate or add cushioning to their time estimates in order to give themselves a form of "safety" to compensate for uncertainty. People may build safety into each task for three basic reasons. First, you may inflate an estimate if your work is dependent upon the work of someone else. For example, you may add a cushion to your time estimates if you believe there's a good chance your work will be delayed if the person you are depending upon will not finish their task or work on time. Second, you may increase an estimate of an activity because of pessimism arising from a previous experience where things did not go as planned. Third, the project sponsor or customer may not be happy with a proposed schedule and therefore decides to cut the schedule globally by, say, 20 percent. If you know this is going to happen, you may inflate your estimates by 25 percent just to guard against the cut.

If people tend to build safety into each task, then why do projects still finish late? The answer is mainly human nature. More specifically, many people tend to wait until the last minute before they begin to work on a task. This is often referred to as "student's syndrome," as many students procrastinate and then begin working on an assignment right before it's due—regardless of how much time is available. If things don't go exactly as planned, the task or assignment ends up being late.

The second reason why projects are still late has to do with Parkinson's law. This law states that work expands to fill the time available. For example, an individual or team assigned to complete a particular task will rarely report finishing early because there is no incentive to do so. They may be afraid that management will cut their estimates next time or the individual or team waiting for them to complete their task won't be ready. As a result, the safety built into an estimate disappears. Any time saved by completing a task early is wasted while any overruns get passed along.

A third reason why added safety does not ensure that projects are completed on time has to do with the multitasking of resources. Goldratt calls this resource contention, whereby a project team member often is assigned to more than one project. In addition, this person may be required to attend meetings, training, or be pulled off one project task to work on another. As a result, this person can become a constraint to the project because they are no longer able to devote time and energy to tasks on the critical path. Subsequently, the task takes longer, and so does the project.

CCPM follows a completely different assumption: Instead of adding safety to each task, put that safety in the form of buffers where needed the most. This would be in the form of feeding buffers, resource buffers, and a buffer at the end of the project. Figure 7.6 provides a comparison of a traditional project network schedule and a CCPM schedule. The top diagram illustrates a project schedule that would have safety built into each estimate. The project has five tasks, with each task estimated to be completed in ten days. The critical path would be Tasks A, B, C, and E, so the project schedule is 40 days.

However, CCPM begins by asking each person or team assigned to a task to provide an estimate that would have a 50 percent chance of being completed. For our example, let's say that each task will have a 50 percent chance of being completed in five days. Instead of adding safety to each task, we place buffers where needed. More specifically, we add a buffer to the end of the project by taking one-half of the time saved from the individual tasks. In this example, we saved a total of 20 days from our critical path tasks A, B, C, and E. Therefore, one-half of 20 equals 10 days, and that becomes our project buffer. In addition, task D requires a "feeder" buffer, since the work completed in Task D will be an input to Task C. This is important because a bottleneck can occur when a task acts as a feeder to any task on the critical path. If Task D is delayed or takes longer than planned, it will impact when Task C can either start or finish.

As a result, this will have an impact on the critical path of the project. To minimize the chance of this happening, a feeder buffer is added to Task D that is one-half of the time saved (i.e., 2.5 days).

However, the critical chain is different from the critical path in that it also takes into account resource contention. Continuing with our example, let's say that each project task is to be completed by a different resource (i.e., person or team). Task C is on the critical path but is also part of the critical chain because of its potential to

Project Schedule with Safety in Each Task

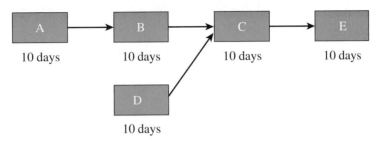

Critical Chain Project Schedule

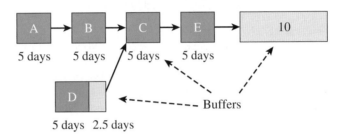

Figure 7.6 The Critical Chain Project Schedule

become a bottleneck if the resource assigned to this task must multitask by working on different projects. If this is the case, the CCPM approach takes a more project portfolio view and would suggest that other projects begin or start so that the person or team working on Task C can be dedicated to work solely on this particular task for this project.

Therefore, CCPM proposes that a resource buffer be created so that the resource working on this task can dedicate time and effort to complete the task with a 50 percent probability in five days. In this case, the critical path and critical chain are the same; however, our project under the CCPM approach is expected to be completed in 30 days.

The CCPM approach requires that everyone understand that since each project task has a 50 percent chance of being completed as scheduled that approximately half of the tasks will be late. This is fine since this is the reason for having the project buffer. Instead of tracking each task individually, we become more concerned with the project buffer. In other words, the project will be late only if it uses more than the ten days allotted in the project buffer. Instead of penalties for being late, the organization may have to provide bonuses or other incentives for completing tasks early.

PROJECT MANAGEMENT SOFTWARE TOOLS

A number of software tools are available to make project planning and tracking much easier. In fact, it would be almost unthinkable to plan and manage even a small project without the aid of such a tool. In this section, you will see some examples of how these software tools incorporate and integrate the project management tools

QUICK THINKING—THE MAP IS NOT THE TERRITORY

Project planning is a critical activity regardless of whether one follows an agile or traditional approach to project management. Too often projects deviate from plans, and the project manager simply assumes that the project needs to be brought back on track. Unfortunately, this may be the result of a poor initial plan or because software is intangible and requirements can be difficult to specify.

Traditional approaches to project management tend to emphasize planning early in the project life cycle when not enough is known about the problem, business environment, or team dynamics. On the other hand, agile methods tend to embrace the realities of IT projects and focus on making planning a more visible and iterative component of the project life cycle. However, a project sponsor will require some indication of how long a project will take and how much it will cost so some sort of schedule and budget will be needed at the beginning of a project. This will require planning the entire project at a high level that outlines an overall timeline and iteration boundaries, but none of the details about individual features should be included in each iteration. Detailed iteration plans that include use cases or user stories are developed from meetings between the developers and customers for each iteration. The high-level plan is then updated to include new details, and velocity. Instead of trying to develop large, detailed plans that quickly deviate from reality and become difficult to maintain, Mike Griffiths of Quandras Development suggests that we are better off leveraging each team member's ability to manage complexity locally by creating lightweight plans that embrace inevitable changes. Moreover, this supports the PMBOK® guideline to encourage planning throughout the project lifecycle in terms of "rolling wave planning" and "progressive elaboration." Rolling wave planning is defined as an iterative approach to where planning is ongoing, while progressive elaboration involves developing a plan in steps and continuing increments. Unfortunately, many project managers focus the bulk of their planning too early in the project and therefore create large plans that are difficult to change, so that these two ideas are rarely implemented.

1. Alfred Korzybski is credited with the quote, "*The map is not the territory*." How does this quote reflect the realities of project planning?

2. Does an agile approach to project planning better support the PMBOK® concepts of rolling wave planning and progressive elaboration than a traditional approach to project planning where the project manager tries to develop a detailed project plan early in the project life cycle? How could these two concepts be implemented better when a more traditional approach is followed?

SOURCE: Adapted from Mike Griffiths, Extreme Planning, *Ganthead.com*, January 22, 2007.

and concepts described in the previous section. The overview is intended to show you what these tools do, rather than tell you how to use them.

As you can see in Figure 7.7, the Gantt chart view integrates not only the Gantt chart, but the project network diagram and PDM techniques. Tasks A and B show a finish-to-start relationship, while Tasks B and C show a start-to-start relationship. Tasks D and E show a finish-to-finish relationship. The task Project Complete has a duration of zero days and, therefore, represents a milestone. The Network Diagram View in Figure 7.8 then highlights the project's critical path. One of the most useful tools for scheduling and planning a project is a simple calendar. Figure 7.9 illustrates a Calendar View of the project.

Developing the project schedule and budget is an important planning process that requires that we sometimes define and estimate a large number of activities several months into the future. But, of course, predicting the future is difficult, and detailed project plans will have to be changed frequently to be useful. A technique called **rolling wave** planning is becoming common to help deal efficiently with project planning. Instead of developing a large, detailed project plan requiring frequent updates, the project manager can prepare an overall summary plan, or master schedule, and then develop detailed schedules for only a few weeks or a few months at a time (Haugan 2002).

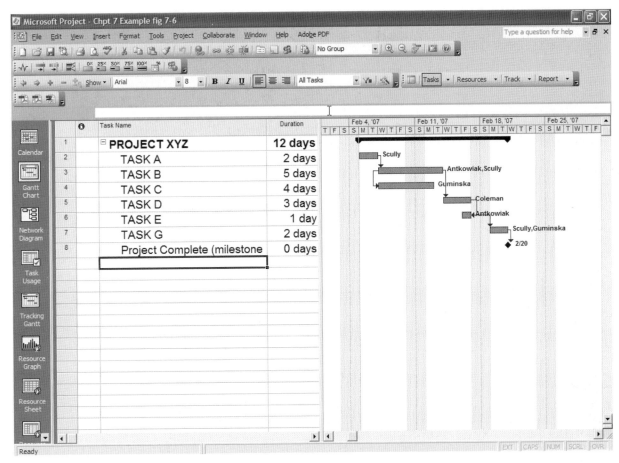

Figure 7.7   Microsoft Project® Gantt Chart View

DEVELOPING THE PROJECT BUDGET

The project's budget is a function of the project's tasks or activities, the duration of those tasks and activities, their sequence, and the resources required. In general, resources used on a project will have a cost, and the cost of using a particular task or activity must be included in the overall project budget. Unless these costs are accounted for, the project manager and the organization will not know the true cost of the project.

Cost Estimation

Estimating the cost of a particular activity or task with an estimated duration involves five steps:

1. Defining what resources will be needed to perform the work
2. Determining the quantity of resources that are needed

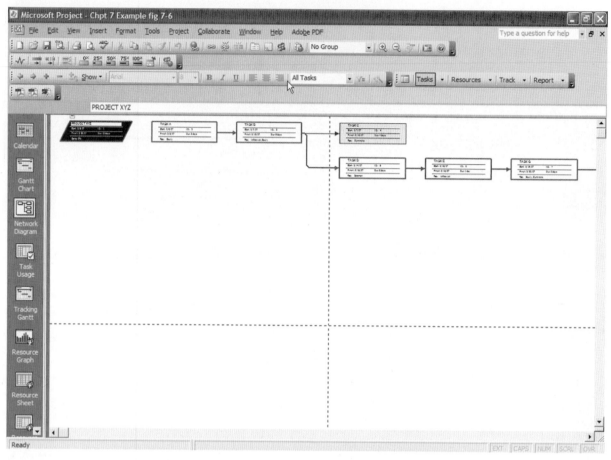

Figure 7.8   Microsoft Project® Network Diagram View and Critical Path

3. Defining the cost of using each resource

4. Calculating the cost of the task or activity

5. Ensuring that the resources are leveled—that is, not overallocated. An example of an overallocated resource would be assigning a project team member to two tasks scheduled at the same time.

For example, let's suppose that we have identified a particular task and estimated that it will take one day to complete and requires one project team member. Let's also assume, for simplicity, that no other resources are needed.

This estimate may require that we define a cost for using this particular resource. For example, if our team member earns $20 an hour, that sum is what our employee sees on his or her paycheck (before taxes and other deductions). The organization, however, may also provide certain benefits to the employee (health care, life insurance, and so forth) that should be included in the cost for using this particular resource. Since these costs are going to vary from organization to organization, let's assume that our friends in the accounting department have conducted a cost accounting analysis for us and that the true cost of using this particular employee (i.e., hourly

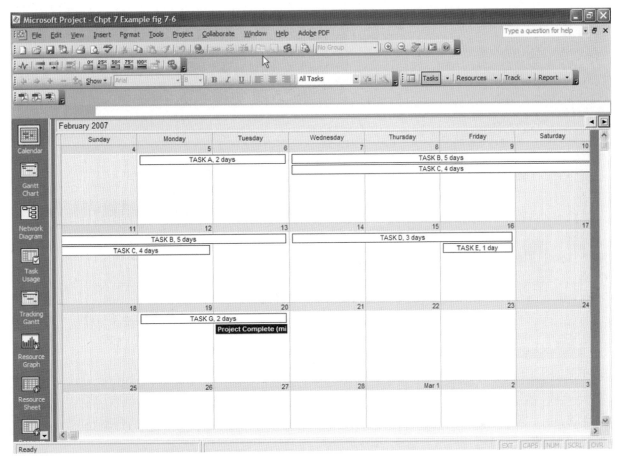

Figure 7.9   Microsoft Project® Calendar View

wage plus benefits) is $25 an hour. Subsequently, if we pay our employee for one day's work (i.e., an eight-hour day), the cost of completing this particular task is:

$$\textbf{Cost of task} = \text{Estimated duration} \times \text{True cost of the resource}$$
$$= 8\ \text{hours} \times \$25/\text{hour}$$
$$= \$200$$

We can even estimate the cost of a salaried employee by prorating her or his salary. This just means that we assign a portion of that salary to the task at hand. For example, let's say that the fully loaded, or true annual, cost to the organization is $65,000. If this employee works a five-day work week, the associated true cost to the organization would be for $5 \times 52 = 260$ days a year. Therefore, the prorated cost per day would be $65,000 \div 260$ workdays = $250 a day.

However, this whole process can be greatly simplified if we use a project management software tool. We still have to identify the tasks and accurately estimate their durations, but determining the costs of a particular task and for the whole project becomes painless. Figure 7.10 shows how resources can be assigned to specific tasks on a project.

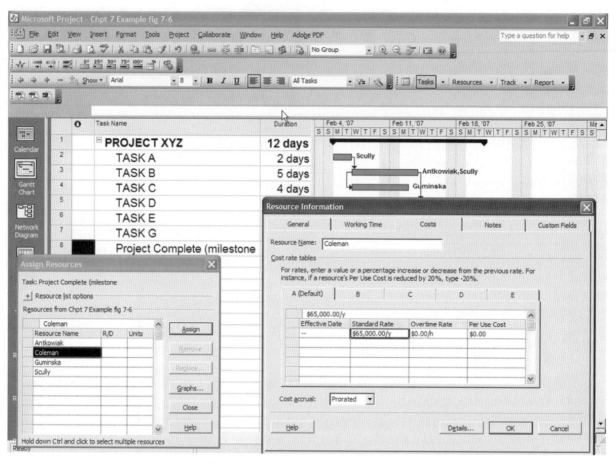

Figure 7.10 Using Microsoft Project® to Assign Resources to Tasks

The project's total budget is computed using a bottom-up approach by summing the individual costs for each task or activity. As shown in Figure 7.11, the basic budget for this project is $5,203.85.

Other Costs

It is important to keep in mind that our example has only considered **direct costs,** or the cost of labor for using this resource directly. In addition to direct labor, resource costs include indirect labor, materials, supplies, and reserves (Kinsella 2002). To determine the total project's budget, we need to include other costs as well. These costs include:

- *Indirect costs*—These costs include such things as rent, utilities, insurance, and other administrative costs. For example, a consulting firm may charge a client $150 an hour per consultant. Included in that hourly fee would be the salary and benefits of the consultant and enough margin to help cover the administrative and operation costs needed to support the consulting office.

- *Sunk costs*—Sunk costs are costs that have been incurred prior to the current project. For example, a previous attempt to build an application system may have ended in failure after three months and $250,000. This $250,000 would

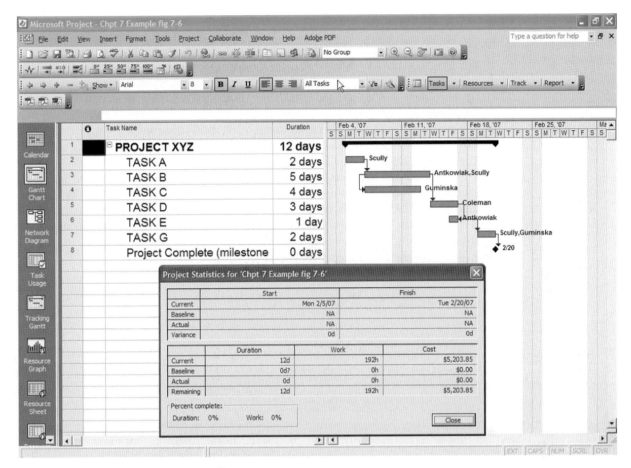

Figure 7.11   Using Microsoft Project® to Compute the Basic Budget

be considered a sunk cost, regardless of whether any work from the previous project is salvageable or of use to the current project.

- *Learning curve*—Often we have to "build one and throw it away" in order to understand a problem or use a new technology effectively. In addition, inexperienced people will make mistakes and new technology will usually require a steep learning curve in the beginning. As a result, time and effort can be wasted. This time to learn should be considered in either the project schedule or budget.

- *Reserves*—Reserves provide a cushion when unexpected situations arise. **Contingency reserves** are based on risk and provide the project manager with a degree of flexibility. On the other hand, a project budget should have some management contingencies built in as well. Of course, reserves are a trade-off. Upper management or the client will view these as fat that can be trimmed from the project budget; however, the wise project manager will ensure that a comfortable reserve is included in the project's budget. For example, it would be sad to think that the project's budget would not allow the project manager to buy pizza or dinner for the team once in a while as a reward for working late to meet an important milestone.

Resource Allocation

Once the resources have been assigned to the project, it is important that the project manager review the project plan to ensure that the resources are level. In other words, resources cannot be overallocated—that is, most resources cannot be assigned to more than one task at the same time. Although the project manager may catch these mistakes early on, it is important that the level of resources be reviewed once the project schedule and resource assignments have been made. Not catching these mistakes early can have a demoralizing effect on the team and lead to unplanned (i.e., unbudgeted) costs.

A project management tool such as Microsoft Project® provides the means for identifying overallocated resources. Figure 7.12 provides an example of the resource allocation view, where a project team member has been assigned to two tasks at the same time. A project manager has the choice of creating a new relationship for these tasks (e.g., FS) or reassigning another resource to one of the tasks. In addition, many software management tools can level resources automatically for the project manager.

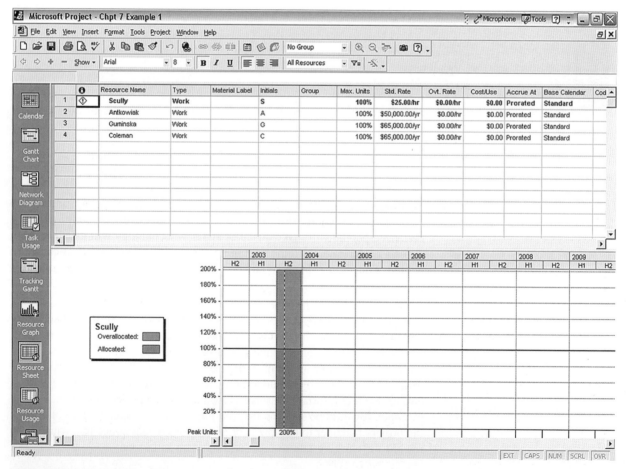

Figure 7.12   Example of Resource Overallocation

FINALIZING THE PROJECT SCHEDULE AND BUDGET

The project schedule and budget may require several iterations before it is acceptable to the sponsor, the project manager, and the project team. In addition, it is important that the project manager document any and all assumptions used to come up with duration and cost estimates. For example, this documentation may include estimating the salary of a database administrator (DBA) who will be hired at a future date. Instead of allocating a cost of what the project manager *thinks* a DBA will cost (or worse yet, what upper management would like to pay), he or she could use salary surveys or salary information advertised in classified advertisements as a base cost estimate. So, the project manager should document the source of this cost in order to give the cost estimates greater credibility. In addition, the project plan may include several working drafts. Having assumptions documented can help keep things organized as well.

Once the project schedule and project plan are accepted, the project plan becomes the **baseline plan** that will be used as a yardstick, or benchmark, to track the project's actual progress with the original plan. Once accepted, the project manager and project team have the authority to execute or carry out the plan. As tasks and activities are completed, the project plan must be updated in order to communicate the project's progress in relation to the baseline plan. Any changes or revisions to the project's estimates should be approved and then reflected in the plan to keep it updated and realistic.

CHAPTER SUMMARY

Once project activities or tasks are identified and activity durations are estimated, the sequencing of these activities will help determine the project schedule and estimated completion date. Several techniques were introduced in this chapter. The use of project management software tools can help simplify the development of the project schedule. In addition, these tools can help the project manager identify and monitor activities that are on the critical path. They can help the project manager make decisions with respect to allocation of resources or the rescheduling of activities. In addition, these tools provide a useful information system capable of communicating the actual progress of the project to the original baseline plan.

In general, if a project uses a resource, the cost associated with that resource must be included in the

project's budget and must be accounted for as a cost to the project. Project costs are both directly and indirectly related to the resources needed to complete a particular task or activity or support other resources that do. It is important that the right resources and the right quantity of resources be assigned to the project activities.

Together, the approved project schedule and project budget make up the baseline project plan. Approval of this plan by the project client or upper management gives the project manager and team the authority to carry out this plan. Actual progress is then compared to this plan to determine whether the project is on track, ahead of plan, or behind the plan. In order to keep the plan realistic, revisions or changes to the plan should be approved and made.

REVIEW QUESTIONS

1. Describe the PMBOK® area of project cost management.
2. Discuss why no project ever failed because of someone's inability to draw a nice looking project network diagram.
3. What are some advantages project network diagrams have over traditional Gantt charts?
4. Define predecessor, successor, and parallel activities. Give a real world example of each.

5. How can parallel activities help shorten the project schedule? Are there any trade-offs?

6. What is meant by slack (or float)?

7. What is the difference between *crashing* and *fast tracking* a project's schedule?

8. What is the difference between AON and PERT?

9. Define the following and give a real world example of each (other than the ones described in this book): finish-to-start; start-to-start; finish-to-finish; start-to-finish

10. What is the difference between lead and lag? Give real world examples (other than the ones used in this book) of how a project manager may use lead and lag in a project schedule.

11. Why do many people inflate their estimates?

12. Does adding safety to each task or activity ensure that the project will be completed as scheduled? Why or why not?

13. In the context of critical chain project management, what is resource contention?

14. In the context of CCPM, what is the purpose of buffers?

15. What is the critical chain? How is it different from the concept of a critical path?

16. Describe the steps necessary for estimating the cost of a particular activity or task that has an estimated duration.

17. What does prorating the cost of a resource mean?

18. Why should the project manager ensure that the project resources are leveled?

19. Why should assumptions used in estimating be documented?

20. What is a baseline plan?

21. When does the project manager or team have the authority to begin executing the project plan?

EXTEND YOUR KNOWLEDGE

1. Develop a network diagram using the AON technique and calculate the critical path using the information in the table.

2. Enter the information from the table into a project management software package. What is the critical path?

Task/Activity	Estimated Duration	Predecessor
A	1 day	None
B	3 days	A
C	4 days	B
D	2 days	B
E	1 day	C
F	3 days	C, D
G	3 days	E
H	1 day	F
I	2 days	G, H
J	5 days	I

GLOBAL TECHNOLOGY SOLUTIONS

Kellie Matthews stopped in the doorway of Tim Williams' office. Tim was just finishing a conversation on his cell phone, and he motioned for her to come in and sit down. After pressing the end button, he asked "How did your meeting go this morning?"

Kellie sat back in her chair. "I think it went well," she said. "It was with a local textbook distributor interested in purchasing and implementing a call center software package. There are a number of software packages available from different vendors, but the company is not really sure which one best suits its needs. Its information systems department is stretched pretty thin working on several projects already, so it is considering outsourcing

this project. I have another meeting with management later this week, so keep your fingers crossed. We may have another client."

"I will," Tim said. "That might stretch things around here a little bit, but we'll cross that bridge when we come to it."

Kellie agreed. "So how are things going with the Husky Air project? Have you finished the schedule and budget?"

Tim chuckled and said, "I knew that you were going to ask that. Actually, we are making good progress. The phone call that I just finished was with Husky Air's CEO. He's pretty anxious to find out how much the project will cost and how long it will take to complete. We have a meeting next week to present the project charter and plan to him and several other senior managers."

"Will you be ready?" Kellie asked.

Tim picked up his coffee mug from his desk, took a sip, and then said, "We completed the work breakdown structure yesterday. That helped us to identify all of the tasks or activities, the resources that will be required, and each activity's estimated duration. Right now, we're trying to determine which activities need to be completed sequentially and which can be completed in parallel. That will help us develop a project network of activities that will allow us to develop a schedule and budget once we enter everything into the project management software package. To finally answer your question, I'm pretty confident that we'll have a draft of the project plan ready by next week."

Kellie leaned forward in her chair and asked, "That sounds reasonable. So what do you hope happens at next week's meeting?"

"If this were a perfect world, I'd hope that our client would approve everything and we could get started right away," he said, laughing. "But I know that's not likely to happen. I'm sure that once we present the schedule and budget to them next week, we'll have to make some changes. But, I'm confident that we're close to the original estimates outlined in the business case, so we should only have to make some minor modifications. Once approved, we then have our baseline project plan and we can get started on the real project work."

Kellie stood up to leave. "I have to return a few phone calls before lunch, but please keep me informed and let me know if I can help out," she said.

Tim was grateful and knew that he could count on Kellie's help. As Kellie was walking through the doorway and back to her office, Tim was turning to his computer to answer the six e-mails that had arrived in his inbox since he had last checked 30 minutes ago.

Things to Think About

1. How does the work breakdown structure (WBS) link the project's scope to the schedule and budget?

2. Why might a project manager expect a project plan to go through a number of iterations before being accepted by the project sponsor or client?

3. What role does project management software play in developing the project schedule and budget?

 ## HUSKY AIR ASSIGNMENT—PILOT ANGELS

The Project Schedule and Budget

Now that you have defined the project's scope, it's time to start the process of determining how the work will be accomplished. This will require that you draw upon work you did in several previous assignments.

Please provide a professional-looking document that includes the following:

1. **Project name, project team name, and the names of the members of your project team**

2. **A brief project description**

3. **The project's MOV** (This should be revised or refined if necessary.)

4. **A detailed project plan**

   a. If you used a spreadsheet to create your work breakdown structure (WBS), you may want to cut and paste the phases, deliverables, milestones, and activities into Microsoft Project®.

   b. Add and assign the resources that you identified in your WBS to each activity or task. Be sure to assign a cost for each resource.

   c. Link the tasks. Look for opportunities for shortening the project schedule by performing tasks in parallel (i.e., start-to-start or finish-to-finish).

5. **Answers to the following questions:**

   a. What are beginning and end dates for your project? How many days will it take to complete the project?

   b. Does your project have a single critical path or multiple critical paths? What is the importance of the critical path?

   c. Does your project have any over allocated resources? If so, be sure to level your resources.

6. **An electronic copy of your project plan—** Depending on what your instructor tells you, submit your project plan on disk or electronically.

CASE STUDIES

Planning for Success

Chris Morris is a senior IT project manager for Agere Systems, Inc. with over 2,000 projects in his portfolio. A few years ago, major IT initiatives at Agere were in trouble. According to Morris, "Everybody had Microsoft Project® on their desktop and Gantt charts on their wall. The problem was that we weren't making project decisions based on what was affordable or good for the company." Project plans ended up being more historical records than future projections. Moreover, there was no clear way to see interdependencies among projects.

Agere decided to take advantage of a project management software package called Primavera®, establish a dedicated project management office, and apply lessons learned and methodologies to every IT project. The results have been more predictable and accurate project schedules and budgets, as well as IT projects that better meet business goals that are achieved for less money. Morris acknowledges that success was not quick or easy.

Based in Allentown, Pa., Agere is a leading manufacturer of integrated chips for wireless devices, disk drives, and network equipment. The company has approximately 7,000 employees and about $2 billion in revenues. The company was spun off from Lucent Technologies in 2001 as the technology industry encountered major challenges and drastic belt tightening. Not surprisingly, Agere's IT budget was slashed from $270 million in 2001 to about $94 million in 2003.

However, before the spinoff from Lucent, Agere made the decision to implement Oracle's enterprise resource planning (ERP) system. As Morris explains, "The company had close to 550 business applications that we were executing the business on. It became clear that an integrated package was needed." To support this project, Agere chose Primavera®, but the IT department wasn't taking full advantage of this project management software tool. More specifically, project teams weren't creating project plans that provided accurate schedules and budgets. Even worse, IT was trying to support every project requested by the business units. Morris further explains, "We were doing too many things outside the concept of business benefits. We stopped making good business decisions."

The high-risk ERP project was in trouble due to divisional conflicts, disjointed planning, and poor resource control. Morris admits, "After a year of execution the project was still essentially at square one. From a pure planning perspective, the project plan was useless as a guide for completion."

The project needed to be jumpstarted. The project team began by conducting a thorough understanding of Primavera® 's features and functions so they could have a better idea of how the software tool could be better utilized.

As Morris points out, "By discovering what Primavera® could do, and why it did what it did, we were really able to understand program management." The team was able to turn the project around and get it back on track before Agere was spun off from Lucent.

Morris outlines seven steps for program management success:

1. **Block and tackle**—By clearly identifying the remaining work for the ERP project, the project team was able to develop a realistic and logical plan that focused on the critical path. The schedule became like a police officer, while variance reports acted as an auditor.

2. **Move beyond the basics**—As the team became more knowledgeable in its approach to project management, it began using the resource profile and loading reports to analyze resource demand and increase the accuracy of the project plan. The team also ran "what if" scenarios to understand the impact scope changes would have on the schedule and resource load. As a result, the team improved the accuracy of the project plan and could plan for multiple possible project paths. Shortly, thereafter, the team started meeting commitments.

3. **Repeat and extend**—This next step became critical as a project management approach was extended to all major IT projects. All projects now had a sound project plan with extended resource loading moving beyond the view of only a single project. Most importantly, Agere created a program management office (PMO) charged with developing standards, identifying cross-project constraints, providing consistent project management support for key initiatives, and measuring the success of the project portfolio. The PMO could then provide commit dates for all projects based on resource projections with respect to consumption and capacity. Primavera® was a key component for having this ability. As Morris points out, "We were able to use the functionality in Primavera® as a guide for developing methods and standards. We're now able to model 100 percent of our activities and make project decisions based on the financial and human resources available."

4. **Involve the business units**—Due to the tightening of budgets, the PMO had to prioritize projects and justify their value to the organization. The best way to do this was to involve the business units. This included the formation of a portfolio review board that included senior management representation from each of the business units. The board

makes decisions regarding work prioritization and the allocation of financial and human resources. This resulted in a shared ownership and accountability for the IT portfolio.

5. **Integrate with financial management**—Unfortunately, to some degree project management still took place in a vacuum. Therefore, it was important that each project budget be integrated with financial management. The PMO began tracking project costs and comparing them with the planned budget. This was accomplished through the use of project codes.

6. **Decentralize project management**—In terms of plan accuracy and decision-making effectiveness, the PMO was still viewed with skepticism even after two years since its inception. Therefore, a decision was made to decentralize some of the project management processes such as time reporting. As Morris says, "That has a few key advantages. To be able to report on work, the work had to be planned. You can then track how good you are at making estimates versus actual."

7. **Simplify project management**—As management of the project portfolio becomes more broadly distributed, it becomes accessible to more individuals. For example, Primavera Methodology Manager® allows for consistent and simplified planning for lower level projects. According to Morris, "We built a series of templates that ask questions and, based on the answer, construct a plan. Users don't have to apply codes and resources, they just use the Methodology Manager and validate the data."

Two factors were critical for Agere's ability to transform IT project management. The first was unwavering support of multiple senior managers. The second was an effective project management solution. As Morris states, "Primavera® provided the only tool with the complete functionality we needed. This includes the ability to operate across all Agere locations, the ability for multiple users to work with a project plan simultaneously, and robust, role-based security." In addition, Morris believes Primavera® provided some tangible benefits, "The biggest benefit was the ability to reduce our budget. We could not have gone from a $270 million to a $94 million budget in 18 months without the ability to understand what our project load is and where our resources are." A recent analysis of the 11 largest projects indicated that all were on time and within budget.

1. How is managing IT projects from a project portfolio view different from a single-project view? What are the advantages? What are some challenges?

2. With a tightening of budgets for IT projects, what was the significance of Agere involving the business units in making decisions about work prioritization and resource allocation?

3. Chris Morris believes that Agere will view project management the way IT sees it: as a core competency. Do you believe project management should be a core competency for most organizations?

4. Should all projects be planned using a project management software tool?

Adapted from Eric Shoeniger, From Chaos to Competency, *Projects@Work*, June 17, 2004.

Poor Baseline Plans Lead to Federal Waste of IT

According to a survey of 104 U.S. government IT executives, an estimated $12 billion dollars was wasted on IT projects in 2007. The study, called *A Cracked Foundation*, was conducted by Price Systems, a provider of program affordability management solutions.

The study suggests that 46 percent of the failed (cancelled, over-budget) projects could have been avoided if project baseline plans were more realistic, thus saving an estimated $5.5 billion annually. According to Larry Reagan, a vice president at Price Systems, "Agencies require stronger foundations upon which to base government IT program structures in order to avoid the continued rate of collapse. Better baselines can help fill in these structural cracks—arming agency personnel with the tools, training, and historical data necessary to build projects on solid rock." The study found that only 18 percent of the government IT executives expressed confidence in their IT budgets, with about 69 percent reporting that they usually begin to notice problems about halfway through their projects.

In addition, the study also reports:

- Seventy-eight percent believe they have inadequate cost estimating training.

- Seventy-seven percent believe they have inadequate risk identification and management training.

- Seventy-three percent believe they have inadequate initial baseline development training.

- Sixty-seven percent believe they have inadequate project management training.

- Sixty percent believe they do not have the necessary methodologies to collect historical data to produce realistic estimates when a baseline changes.

- Fifty-eight percent believe they do not have the necessary historical data to produce realistic estimates.

■ Fifty-four percent believe that they have inadequate tools to manage the cost estimating, control, and reporting processes for IT programs.

The respondents contend that the main reasons why projects are over budget include poor project management, scope creep, the lack of proper baselines, and late understanding of risk. Moreover, the IT executives surveyed reported that the most important tool for ensuring that IT projects are on budget is a fully coordinated baseline, followed by training, project management tools, and defined risk management.

Similarly, the IT executives identified schedule management, cost management, and risk management as being the most challenging baseline elements for their organizations. The study also reports why project managers fail to establish effective baselines. More specifically, 64 percent attributed this to a lack of personnel to perform the functions effectively, 47 percent stated a lack of training, 47 percent stated that timelines were too short, and 34 percent claimed that projects teams were not given appropriate tools and data for establishing accurate baseline plans up front.

Reagan claims, "In these days of heightened federal fiscal accountability, our government is not in a position to waste billions of dollars that could be redirected toward any number of programs. Supported by stronger structural foundations—including assigning responsibility for program affordability management; integrating cost estimating, project control, and knowledge management into a single team; providing effective training and certification; implementing a methodology for regularly scheduled, independent baseline reviews; and establishing the consistent use of a resusable knowledge-based framework—better baselines can empower agencies to achieve project and program objectives, effectively enabling them to better deliver upon their missions."

1. Do you agree that improving IT project baseline plans will help avoid failed projects?

2. Consider Larry Reagan's statement in the last paragraph. Do you agree with his assessment? Is there anything you would add that could be done to improve project success, not only for the federal government but for any type of organization?

SOURCE: Adapted from:

Larry Reagan, A Cracked Foundation: A Critical Look at the Role of Baselining in Government IT Project Management.

Vice President—Government Solutions, and Robert W. Young—Executive Director, Price Systems, Poor Baselines Cause of Federal IT Waste, Study Finds, *Projects@Work*, November 30, 2006.

BIBLIOGRAPHY

Goldratt, E. M. 1997. *Critical Chain*. Great Barrington, MA: The North River Press.

Haugan, G. T. 2002. *Project Planning and Scheduling*. Vienna, VA: Management Concepts.

Kinsella, S. M. 2002. Activity-Based Costing: Does It Warrant Inclusion in *A Guide to the Project Management Body of Knowledge (PMBOK Guide)*? *Project Management Journal* 33(2): 49–55.

Project Management Institute (PMI) 2004. *A Guide to the Project Management Body of Knowledge (PMBOK® Guide)*. Newtown Square, PA: PMI Publishing.

C H A P T E R

8

Managing Project Risk

CHAPTER OVERVIEW

Chapter 8 focuses on project risk management. After studying this chapter, you should understand and be able to:

- Describe the project risk management planning framework introduced in this chapter.
- Define risk identification and the causes, effects, and the integrative nature of project risks.
- Apply several qualitative and quantitative analysis techniques that can be used to prioritize and analyze various project risks.
- Describe the various risk strategies, such as insurance, avoidance, or mitigation.
- Describe risk monitoring and control.
- Describe risk evaluation in terms of how the entire risk management process should be evaluated in order to learn from experience and to identify best practices.

INTRODUCTION

In the last chapter you learned how to develop a baseline project plan. This project plan is based on a number of estimates that reflect our understanding of the current situation, the information available, and the assumptions we must make. The fact that we must estimate implies a degree of uncertainty in predicting the outcome of future events. Although no one can predict the future with 100 percent accuracy, having a solid foundation, in terms of processes, tools, and techniques, can increase our confidence in these estimates.

Unfortunately, things seldom go according to plan because the project must adapt to a dynamic environment. Project risk management is becoming an important sub-discipline of software engineering. It focuses on identifying, analyzing, and developing strategies for responding to project risk efficiently and effectively (Jones 1994). It is important, however, to keep in mind that the goal of risk management is not to avoid risks at all costs, but to make well informed decisions as to what risks are worth taking and to respond to those risks in an appropriate manner (Choo 2001).

Project risk management also provides an early warning system for impending problems that need to be addressed or resolved. Although risk has a certain negative connotation, project stakeholders should be vigilant in identifying opportunities. Although many associate uncertainty with threats, it is important to keep in mind that there is uncertainty when pursuing opportunities, as well.

It is unfortunate that many projects do not follow a formal risk management approach (Jones 1994). Because of their failure to plan for the unexpected, many organizations find themselves in a state of perpetual crisis characterized by an inability to make effective and timely decisions. Many people call this approach *crisis management* or *fire fighting* because the project stakeholders take a reactive approach or only address the project risks after they have become problems. Several common mistakes in managing project risk include:

- *Not understanding the benefits of risk management*—Often the project sponsor or client demands results. They may not care how the project team achieves its goal and objectives—just as long as it does! The project manager and project team may rely on aggressive risk taking with little understanding of the impact of their decisions (Lanza 2001). Conversely, project risks may also be optimistically ignored when, in reality, these risks may become real and significant threats to the success of the project. Unfortunately, risks are often schedule delays, quality issues, and budget overruns just waiting to happen (Wideman 1992). Risks can result in sub-par productivity and higher than average project failure rates (Kulik 2000).

- *Not providing adequate time for risk management*—Risk management and the ensuing processes should not be viewed as an add-on to the project planning process, but should be integrated throughout the project life cycle (Lanza 2001). The best time to assess and plan for project risk, in fact, is at the earliest stages of the project when uncertainty for a project is the highest. Catastrophic problems or surprises may arise that require more resources to correct than would have been spent earlier avoiding them (Choo 2001). It is better to reduce the likelihood of a risk or be capable of responding to a particular risk as soon as possible in order to limit the risk's impact on the project's schedule and budget.

- *Not identifying and assessing risk using a standardized approach*—Not having a standardized approach to risk management can overlook both threats and opportunities (Lanza 2001). Consequently, more time and resources will be expended on problems that could have been avoided; opportunities will be missed; decisions will be made without complete understanding or information; the overall likelihood of success is reduced; and catastrophic problems or surprises may occur without advanced warning (Choo 2001). Moreover, the project team may find itself in a perpetual crisis mode. Over time, crisis situations can have a detrimental effect on team morale and productivity.

Capers Jones (1994) suggests that effective and successful project risk management requires:

- *Commitment by all stakeholders*—To be successful, project risk management requires a commitment by all project stakeholders. In particular, the project sponsor or client, senior management, the project manager, and the project team must all be committed. For many organizations, a new environment and commitment to following organizational and project processes may be required. For many managers, the first impulse may be to shortcut or sidestep many of these processes at the first sign that the project is in trouble. A firm commitment to a risk management approach will not allow these impulses to override the project management and risk management processes that the organization has in place.

■ *Stakeholder responsibility*—It is important that each risk have an owner. This owner should be someone who will be involved in the project, who will take the responsibility to monitor the project in order to identify any new or increasing risks, and who will make regular reports to the project sponsor or client. The position may also require the risk owner to ensure that adequate resources be available for managing and responding to a particular project risk. Ultimately, however, the project manager is responsible for ensuring that appropriate risk processes and plans are in place.

■ *Different risks for different types of projects*—In a study that looked at IT project risks, Jones (1994) found that patterns of risk are different across different types of IT projects. The implication is that each project has its own unique risk considerations. To attempt to manage all projects and risks the same way may spell disaster.

The remainder of this chapter will incorporate many of the processes and concepts outlined in the Project Management Body of Knowledge (PMBOK®) that define the processes of risk management. More specifically, these processes include:

■ *Risk management planning*—Determining how to approach and plan the project risk management activities. An output of this process is the development of a risk management plan.

■ *Risk identification*—Deciding which risks can impact the project. Risk identification generally includes many of the project stakeholders and requires an understanding of the project's goal, as well as the project's scope, schedule, budget, and quality objectives.

■ *Qualitative risk analysis*—Focusing on a qualitative analysis concerning the impact and likelihood of the risks that were identified.

■ *Quantitative risk analysis*—Using a quantitative approach for developing a probabilistic model for understanding and responding to the risks identified.

■ *Risk response planning*—Developing procedures and techniques to reduce the threats of risks, while enhancing the likelihood of opportunities.

■ *Risk monitoring and control*—Providing an early warning system to monitor identified risks and any new risks. This system ensures that risk responses have been implemented as planned and had the effect as intended.

IT PROJECT RISK MANAGEMENT PLANNING PROCESS

To manage risk, we first need to have a definition of *risk*. Although Webster's dictionary defines risk as *"hazard; peril; or exposure to loss or injury,"* the *PMBOK*® *Guide* defines **project risk** as:

> An uncertain event or condition that, if it occurs, has a positive or negative effect on the project objectives (238).

QUICK THINKING—SEND IN THE RESERVES

The project's baseline budget should be based on realistic time and cost estimates as well as a reserve amount set aside for contingencies. Once the project plan is executed, the cost of each individual task and cumulative cost of the project should be monitored regularly to ensure that the project is kept under control. However, flawed estimates, anomalies, and permanent or minor variances can create budget issues.

- *Flawed estimates*—Original estimates can present a budget risk because they simply can be wrong. As a result, new estimates should identify how much more money will be needed to complete the project as well as how much has been spent to date. It may be useful to note any lessons learned so that these errors can be avoided in the future.

- *Anomalies*—These are risks that can come out of nowhere and take everyone by surprise because they are often one-time events that can significantly impact the project's budget. This type of risk is difficult to plan for ahead of time so you end up dealing with them after the fact. A large anomaly can be a project killer, while smaller anomalies can usually be absorbed by the reserve.

- *Permanent variances*—These are variances that are expected to be typical for the rest of the project. For example, a project team member assigned to a number of tasks may not be as competent or skilled as expected. As a result, the budgeted amount for these tasks will increase if this team member requires more time to complete the work than originally estimated. As a project manager, you may accept these variances for the duration of the project, provide additional training, or bring in other people or contractors to help. Regardless, the project reserve will be consumed.

- *Minor variances*—These normally occur in projects and are the reason for having a reserve in the first place. A reserve can be created for each project phase or deliverable. Since minor variances are expected, a threshold for "minor" can be determined so that everyone is clear as to what minor means in terms of a budget variance. For example, a variance would be considered minor if a task does not exceed its budgeted amount by more than 5 percent. However, the reserve must be closely monitored because it can become quickly consumed if a number of tasks exceed their budgeted amount by 5 percent.

1. How does having a reserve help manage project risks?

2. Can a project reserve become a risk if funds are too low or even too high?

3. Suppose you are a project manager and you've ordered ten new servers. The servers arrive one at a time and your team unpacks each one and begins to install them. After five of the servers are set up and installed, each one begins to fail because of a manufacturing problem. The vendor agrees to replace them immediately and assures you that it won't happen again, but you've spent half of your budget setting up and installing defective servers. You have a choice of reinstalling the new servers whereby your project will be late and use up your entire project's reserve, or subcontracting with another IT consulting firm that will ensure that the project is delivered on time but will exceed your reserve by 100 percent. How would you handle this situation?

SOURCE: Adapted from Susan Snedaker, Changes to Your Budget, *Projects@Work*, June 1, 2006.

The *PMBOK® Guide* definition provides an important starting point for understanding risk. First, project risk arises from uncertainty. This uncertainty comes from our attempt to predict the future based on estimates, assumptions, and limited information. Although project risk has a downside resulting from unexpected problems or threats, project risk management must also focus on positive events or opportunities. Therefore, it is important that we understand what those events are and how they may impact the project beyond its objectives. It is also important that we understand not only the nature of project risks but also how those risks interact and impact other aspects of the project throughout the life of a project.

The PMBOK® defines **project risk management** as:

Project risk management includes the processes concerned with conducting risk management planning, identification, analysis, responses, and monitoring and control of a project; most of these processes are updated throughout the project. The objectives of project risk management are to increase the probability and impact of positive events, and decrease the probability and impact of events adverse to the project (237).

This *PMBOK® Guide* definition of risk management suggests that a systematic process is needed to manage effectively the risk of a project. In this section, an approach for risk management planning is introduced. It is illustrated in Figure 8.1.

The framework presented in Figure 8.1 outlines seven steps for managing IT project risk. Each of these steps will be discussed in more detail throughout the chapter.

Risk Planning

Risk planning is the first step and begins with having a firm commitment to the entire risk management approach from all project stakeholders. This commitment ensures that adequate resources will be in place to plan properly for and manage the various

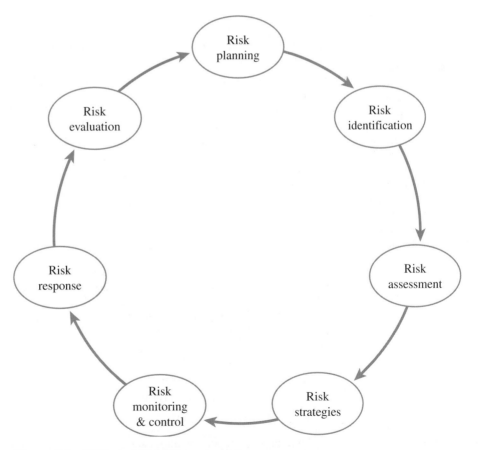

Figure 8.1 IT Project Risk Management Processes

risks of the IT project. These resources may include time, people, and technology. Stakeholders also must be committed to the process of identifying, analyzing, and responding to threats and opportunities. Too often plans are disregarded at the first sign of trouble, and instinctive reactions to situations can lead to perpetual crisis management. In addition to commitment, risk planning also focuses on preparation. It is important that resources, processes, and tools be in place to adequately plan the activities for project risk management. Systematic preparation and planning can help minimize adverse effects on the project while taking advantage of opportunities as they arise.

Risk Identification

Once commitment has been obtained and preparations have been made, the next step entails identifying the various risks to the project. Both threats and opportunities must be identified. When identifying threats to a project, they must be identified clearly so that the true problem, not just a symptom, is addressed. Moreover, the causes and effects of each risk must be understood so that effective strategies and responses can be made. A framework for understanding the sources and nature of IT project risks will be introduced in the next section; however, it is important to keep in mind that project risks are rarely isolated. Risks tend to be interrelated and affect the project and its stakeholders differently.

Risk Assessment

Once the project risks have been identified and their causes and effects understood, the next step requires that we analyze these risks. Answers to two basic questions are required: What is the likelihood of a particular risk occurring? What is the impact on the project if it does occur? Risk assessment provides a basis for understanding how to deal with project risks. To answer the two questions, qualitative and quantitative approaches can be used. Several tools and techniques for each approach will be introduced later. Assessing these risks helps the project manager and other stakeholders prioritize and formulate responses to those risks that provide the greatest threat or opportunity to the project. Because there is a cost associated with responding to a particular risk, risk management must function within the constraints of the project's available resources.

Risk Strategies

The next step of the risk planning process is to determine how to deal with the various project risks. In addition to resource constraints, an appropriate strategy will be determined by the project stakeholders' perceptions of risk and their willingness to take on a particular risk. Essentially, a project risk strategy will focus on one of the following approaches:

- Accept or ignore the risk.
- Avoid the risk completely.
- Reduce the likelihood or impact of the risk (or both) if the risk occurs.
- Transfer the risk to someone else (i.e., insurance).

In addition, triggers or flags in the form of metrics should be identified to draw attention to a particular risk when it occurs. This system requires that each risk have an owner to monitor the risk and to ensure that resources are made available in order to respond to the risk appropriately. Once the risks, the risk triggers, and strategies or responses are documented, this document then becomes the **risk response plan.**

Risk Monitoring and Control

Once the salient project risks have been identified and appropriate responses formulated, the next step entails scanning the project environment so that both identified and unidentified threats and opportunities can be followed, much like a radar screen follows ships. Risk owners should monitor the various risk triggers so that well informed decisions and appropriate actions can take place.

Risk Response

Risk monitoring and control provide a mechanism for scanning the project environment for risks, but the risk owner must commit resources and take action once a risk threat or opportunity is made known. This action normally follows the planned risk strategy.

Risk Evaluation

Responses to risks and the experience gained provide keys to learning. A formal and documented evaluation of a risk episode provides the basis for lessons learned and lays the foundation for identifying best practices. This evaluation should consider the entire risk management process from planning through evaluation. It should focus on the following questions:

- How did we do?
- What can we do better next time?
- What lessons did we learn?
- What best practices can be incorporated in the risk management process?

The risk planning process is cyclical because the evaluation of the risk responses and the risk planning process can influence how an organization will plan, prepare, and commit to IT risk management.

IDENTIFYING IT PROJECT RISKS

Risk identification deals with identifying and creating a list of threats and opportunities that may impact the project's goal and/or objectives. Each risk and its characteristics are documented to provide a basis for the overall risk management plan.

An IT Project Risk Identification Framework

Identifying and understanding the risks that will impact a project is not always a straightforward task. Many risks can affect a project in different ways and during different phases of the project life cycle. Therefore, the process and techniques used to identify risks must include a broad view of the project and attempt to understand a particular risk's cause and impact among the various project components. Figure 8.2

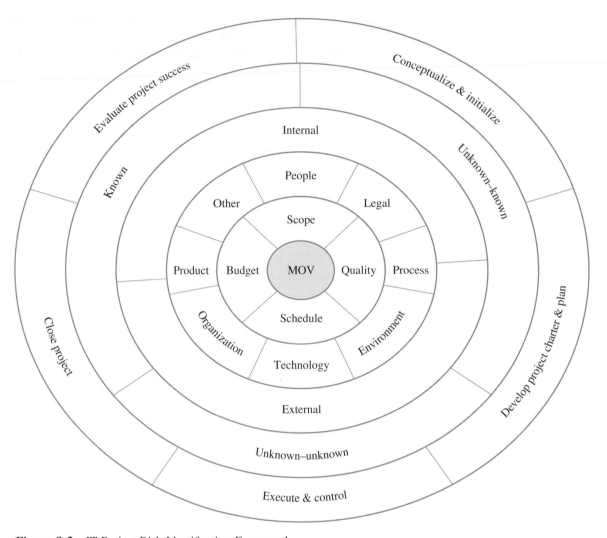

Figure 8.2   IT Project Risk Identification Framework

provides a framework for identifying and understanding the sources and impacts of IT project risks.

At the core of the IT project risk framework is the MOV, or measurable organizational value. The MOV is the goal of the project that defines the measurable value the organization expects from the project. It is both a measure and definition of project success.

The next layer of the framework includes the project objectives in terms of scope, quality, schedule, and budget. Although these objectives are not by themselves sufficient conditions for success, together they do play a critical role in supporting the MOV.

The third layer focuses on the sources of IT project risk. Risks can arise as a result of the various people or stakeholders associated with a project, legal considerations, the processes (project and product), the environment, the technology, the organization, the product, and a catchall category called *other*.

The next layer focuses on whether the sources of risk are internal or external to the project. It is important to make this distinction because a project manager is responsible and accountable for all project risks internal to the project. For example, if a project team member is not adequately trained to use a particular technology, then the project's objectives—scope, schedule, budget, and quality—may be impacted. In turn, this lack of training may inhibit the project from achieving its goal or MOV. Once this project risk has been identified along with its impact, the project manager can avoid or mitigate the risk by sending this particular project team member to training or by assigning certain critical tasks to a more experienced or skillful team member. On the other hand, a project manager may not be responsible for external risks. For example, a project manager would not be responsible or accountable if the project were cancelled because the organization sponsoring the project went bankrupt.

The distinction between internal and external risks is not always clear. For example, even though a particular hardware or software vendor may be external to the project, the project manager may still be responsible if that vendor is unable to deliver required technology resources. If the project manager chose that particular vendor, he or she would then be responsible or accountable for that risk. In short, a project manager will (or should) have control over internal risks, but not external risks. That distinction does not mean the project manager can ignore external risks. These risks can have a significant impact on the project, as well as the project manager's employment!

The fifth layer of the IT project risk management framework includes three different types of risks: **known risks, known-unknown risks**, and **unknown-unknown risks**. Wideman (1992) defines known risks as events that are going to occur. In short, these events are like death and taxes—they will happen and there is no uncertainty about it. On the other hand, known-unknowns are of identifiable uncertainty. For example, if you own a home or rent an apartment, you know that you will receive a bill next month for the utilities you use. The precise amount you will owe the utility company will be unknown until you receive the actual bill. Unknown-unknown risks are residual risks or events that we cannot even imagine happening. For example, it was not too long ago that people had never even heard about the Internet. How could they comprehend the impact it would have on many of us? Unknown-unknown risks are really just a way to remind us that there may be a few risks remaining even after we think we have identified them all. In general, these are the risks that we identify after they have occurred.

The outer layer provides a time element in terms of the project life cycle. It may help us determine or identify when risks may occur, but remind us that they may change over the life of the project. Although risk management is an important concern at the beginning of a project, the IT project risk management framework reminds us that we must be vigilant for opportunities and problems throughout the project life cycle.

Applying the IT Project Risk Identification Framework

To better understand how to apply the IT project risk identification framework summarized in Figure 8.1, let's use an example. A consulting firm has been hired by a client to develop a data warehouse that will include business intelligence to identify and better serve its more loyal customers. The project is still in the early stages, with the baseline project plan and charter almost finalized. Unfortunately, the client has been hit hard by a lawsuit and is ordered to pay significant legal fees and fines.

The client is now strapped and must cut costs to survive. Not surprisingly, a number of the client's managers are suggesting that the data warehouse project be cancelled. However, due to the expected value the project can bring to this organization, it is decided that the product's scope will be cut in half in order to create two projects—one that will provide minimum functionality and another project that will add the remaining features and functions once the company becomes more financially stable. The contract between the consulting firm and the client will be renegotiated. The project's new scope will be reduced in order to reduce the budget and schedule as well. The risk faced by this team could be defined as:

- A threat that occurred in the Develop Project Charter and Project Plan Phase.
- It was an unknown-unknown risk because it was identified after it occurred and, therefore, caught the project team off guard.
- It was an external risk, and the project manager and project team should not be held responsible for the economic downturn experienced by the client.
- The sources of risk to the project include environment (economic), organizational (the client) and people (if you would like to argue that management was responsible for this problematic event).
- The impact on the project was significant because it would affect the project's scope, schedule, and budget. Since the consulting firm was able to renegotiate the contract based on a trimmed scope, we can assume that quality would not be an issue. But if the client's management insisted on maintaining the original scope, schedule, and budget, chances are good that quality would become an issue, especially if, for example, the scheduled testing time had to be shortened in order to meet the scheduled deadline.
- It is likely that the project's MOV would change as well because the project team would not complete the scope as originally planned. A revised MOV would determine the revised scope, schedule, and budget for the project.

This example shows how a risk can be understood after it occurs. The framework can also be used to proactively identify IT project risks. For example, a project team could begin with the project phases defined in the outer core of the framework. Using the project's work breakdown structure (WBS) and the individual work packages, the team could identify the risks for each of the work packages under the various project phases. Again, it is important that both threats and opportunities be identified. These risks could be classified as either known risks or known-unknown risks. The category of unknown-unknown risks should serve as a reminder to keep asking the question, What other threats or opportunities have we not thought about? Hopefully, the project team will do a more thorough job of identifying risks early in the project and reduce the likelihood of being surprised later.

The risks identified by the team can then be categorized as external or internal to the project. The internal risks are the direct responsibility of the project manager or team, while external risks may be outside their control. Regardless, both external and internal risks must be monitored and responses should be formulated.

The next step involves identifying the various sources of risk. Instead of trying to neatly categorize a particular risk, it may be more important to understand how the sources of risk are interrelated with each other. In addition, it may be a situation where precise definitions get in the way of progress. Instead of arguing or worrying about the exact source of a particular risk, it is more important the stakeholders understand the complex nature of a risk. Each risk-source category may mean different things to different stakeholders. Depending on the project, the stakeholders should be free to develop their own definitions and interpretations for each risk source category. They should also feel free to add categories, as needed.

After identifying the nature and characteristics of a particular risk, the project team can assess how a particular risk will impact the project. At this point, the team should focus on the project objectives that would be impacted if a particular risk occurred and, in turn, whether the project's MOV or goal would be impacted. Later on, these risks can be assessed to determine how the objectives will be impacted.

The example shows how, working from the outside and then inward toward the center of the model, risks can be identified using the IT project risk framework. This procedure works well as a first pass and when using the project plan or WBS as a source of input. Many threats and opportunities may, however, be overlooked when relying only on the WBS.

The project team could start with the inner core of the IT risk framework and work outward. For example, the project team could identify how the MOV may be affected in terms of threats or opportunities that affect the project's scope, schedule, budget, or quality. Working away from the center, the team could identify possible sources of risk and then categorize whether the risk is internal or external, known, known-unknown, or unknown-unknown (i.e., did we miss something?), and when during the project life cycle this particular risk might occur.

Tools and Techniques

Identifying risks is not always easy. Risks tend to be interrelated and identifying each and every risk may not be possible or economically feasible. People may not want to admit that potential problems are possible for fear of appearing incompetent. As a result, stakeholders may deny or downplay a particular risk. Still, people and organizations have different tolerances for risk, and what may be considered a normal risk for one stakeholder or organization may be a real concern for another. So, the stakeholders may concentrate on a particular risk (that may or may not occur) at the expense of other risks that could have the same impact on the project.

It is, therefore, important that the project manager and team guide the risk management process. Risk identification should include the project team and other stakeholders who are familiar with the project's goal and objectives. Using one or more of the following tools, the IT project risk framework introduced earlier in this section can provide direction for identifying the threats and opportunities associated with the project:

- *Learning cycles*—The concept of learning cycles was introduced in Chapter 4. The project team and stakeholders can use this technique, whereby they identify facts (what they know), assumptions (what they think they know), and research (things to find out), to identify various risks. Using these three categories, the group can create an action plan to test assumptions and conduct research about various risks. Based on the team's findings, both risks and lessons learned can then be documented.

- *Brainstorming*—Brainstorming is a less structured activity than learning cycles. Here the team could use the IT risk framework and the WBS to identify risks (i.e., threats and opportunities) starting with the phases of the project life cycle and working towards the framework's core or MOV or working from the MOV outward toward the project phases. The key to brainstorming is encouraging contributions from everyone in the group. Thus, initially ideas must be generated without being evaluated. Once ideas are generated by the group as a whole, they can be discussed and evaluated by the group.

- *Nominal group technique (NGT)*—The NGT is a structured technique for identifying risks that attempts to balance and increase participation (Delbecq and Van de Van 1971). Using the NGT:

  a. Each individual silently writes her or his ideas on a piece of paper.

  b. Each idea is then written on a board or flip chart one at a time in a round-robin fashion until each individual has listed all of his or her ideas.

  c. The group then discusses and clarifies each of the ideas.

  d. Each individual then silently ranks and prioritizes the ideas.

  e. The group then discusses the rankings and priorities of the ideas.

  f. Each individual ranks and prioritizes the ideas again.

  g. The rankings and prioritizations are then summarized for the group.

- *Delphi technique*—If the time and resources are available, a group of experts can be assembled—without ever having to meet face to face. Using the Delphi technique, a group of experts are asked to identify potential risks or discuss the impact of a particular risk. Initially, in order to reduce the potential for bias, the experts are not known to each other. Their responses are collected and made available anonymously to each other. The experts are then asked to provide another response based upon the previous round of responses. The process continues until a consensus exists. The advantage of using the Delphi technique is the potential for getting an insightful view into a threat or opportunity; but the process takes time and may consume a good portion of the projectresources.

- *Interviewing*—Another useful technique for identifying and understanding the nature of IT project risks is to interview various project stakeholders. This technique can prove useful for determining alternative points of view; but the quality of the information derived depends heavily on the skills of the interviewer and the interviewees, as well as the interview process itself.

- *Checklists*—Checklists provide a structured tool for identifying risks that have occurred in the past. They allow the current project team to learn from past mistakes or to identify risks that are known to a particular organization or industry. One problem with checklists is that they can lead to a false sense of security—i.e., if we check off each of the risks on the list, then we will have covered everything. Table 8.1 provides an example of items that may be included in a project risk checklist.

- *SWOT analysis*—SWOT stands for Strengths, Weaknesses, Opportunities, and Threats. Brainstorming, NGT, or the Delphi technique could be used to identify and understand the nature of IT project risks by categorizing risks using the framework illustrated in Figure 8.3. The usefulness of using SWOT analysis is that it allows the project team to identify threats and opportunities as well as their nature in terms of project or organizational strengths and weaknesses.

Table 8.1   Example of an IT Project Check List

Risk Checklist

✓ Funding for the project has been secured.

✓ Funding for the project is sufficient.

✓ Funding for the project has been approved by senior management.

✓ The project team has the requisite skills to complete the project.

✓ The project has adequate manpower to complete the project.

✓ The project charter and project plan have been approved by senior management or the project sponsor.

✓ The project's goal is realistic and achievable.

✓ The project's schedule is realistic and achievable.

✓ The project's scope has been clearly defined.

✓ Processes for scope changes have been clearly defined.

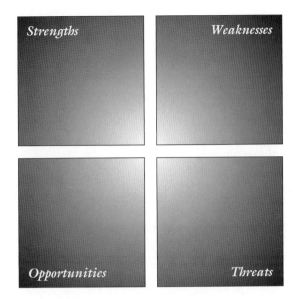

Figure 8.3   SWOT Analysis—Strengths, Weaknesses, Opportunities, and Threats

- *Cause-and-effect diagrams*—The most widely known and used cause-and-effect diagram is the fishbone, or Ishikawa, diagram developed by Kaoru Ishikawa to analyze the causes of poor quality in manufacturing systems. The diagram can also be used for understanding the causes or factors of a particular risk, as well as its effects. An example of an Ishikawa diagram is illustrated in Figure 8.4. The diagram shows the possible causes and effects of a key member of the team leaving the project. This technique itself can be used individually or in groups by taking the following steps:

  a. Identify the risk in terms of a threat or opportunity.

  b. Identify the main factors that can cause the risk to occur.

  c. Identify detailed factors for each of the main factors.

  d. Continue refining the diagram until satisfied that the diagram is complete.

- *Past projects*—One of the themes in this text has been the integration of knowledge management to support the project management processes. Lessons learned from past projects can provide insight and best practices for identifying and understanding the nature of IT project risks. The usefulness of these lessons takes time and a commitment by the organization and project team to develop a base of knowledge from past projects. The value of this knowledge base will increase as the base does, allowing project teams to learn from the mistakes and successes of others.

RISK ANALYSIS AND ASSESSMENT

The framework introduced in the previous section provides tools for identifying and understanding the nature of risks to IT projects. The next step requires that those risks be analyzed to determine what threats or opportunities require attention or a response. Risk analysis and assessment provide a systematic approach for evaluating the risks that the project stakeholders identify. The purpose of **risk analysis** is to determine each identified risk's probability and impact on the project. **Risk assessment,** on the other hand, focuses on prioritizing risks so that an effective risk strategy can be formulated. In short, which risks require a response? To a great degree, this will be determined by the project stakeholders' tolerances to risk.

There are two basic approaches to analyzing and assessing project risk. The first approach is more qualitative in nature because it includes subjective assessments based on experience or intuition. Quantitative analysis, on the other hand, is based on mathematical and statistical techniques. Each approach has its own strengths and weaknesses when dealing with uncertainty, so a combination of qualitative and quantitative methods provides valuable insight when conducting risk analysis and assessment.

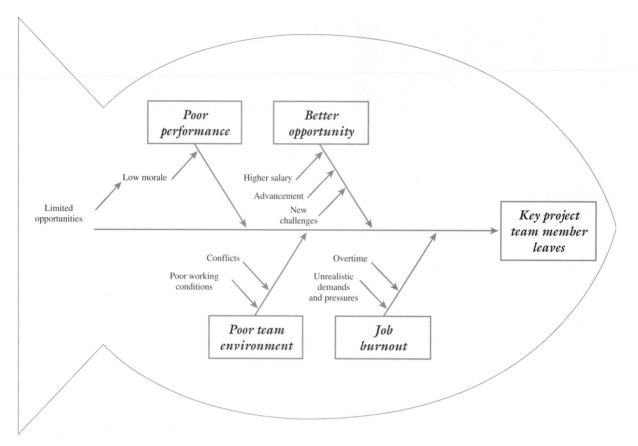

Figure 8.4 Cause and Effect Diagram

Qualitative Approaches

Qualitative risk analysis focuses on a subjective analysis of risks based upon a project stakeholder's experience or judgment. Although the techniques for analyzing project risk qualitatively can be conducted by individual stakeholders, it may be more effective if done by a group. This group process allows each stakeholder to hear other points of view and supports open communication among the various stakeholders. As a result, a broader view of the threats, opportunities, issues, and points of view can be discussed and understood.

Expected Value   The concept of **expected value** provides the basis for both qualitative and quantitative risk analysis. Expected value is really an average, or mean, that takes into account both the probability and impact of various events or outcome. For example, let's assume that a project manager of a consulting firm would like to determine the expected return or payoff associated with several possible outcomes or events. These outcomes or events, in terms of possible schedule scenarios, determine the return or profit the project will return to the consulting firm. The project manger believes each outcome has a probability of occurring and an associated payoff. The project manager's subjective beliefs are summarized in a **payoff table** in Table 8.2.

As you can see from Table 8.2, the project manager believes that the project has a small chance of finishing 20 days early or 20 days late. The payoff for finishing

Table 8.2 Expected Value of a Payoff Table

Schedule Risk	A Probability	B Payoff (in thousands)	A · B Prob · Payoff (in thousands)
Project completed 20 days early	5%	$ 200	$ 10
Project completed 10 days early	20%	$ 150	$ 30
Project completed on schedule	50%	$ 100	$ 50
Project completed 10 days late	20%	$ —	$ —
Project completed 20 days late	5%	$ (50)	$ (3)
	100%		$ 88

the project early is quite high, but there appears to be a penalty for completing the project late. As a result, the expected value or return to the consulting firm is $88,000. Since each event is mutually exclusive (i.e., only one of the five events can occur), the probabilities must sum to 100 percent.

Decision Trees Similar to a payoff table, a **decision tree** provides a visual, or graphical, view of various decisions and outcomes. Let's assume that a project is going to overrun its schedule and budget. The project manager is contemplating reducing the time allocated to testing the application system as a way of bringing the project back within its original schedule and budget objectives.

The project manager, then, is faced with a decision about whether the project team should conduct a full systems test as planned or shorten the time originally allocated to testing. The cost of a full test will be $10,000; but the project manager believes that there is a 95 percent chance the project will meet the quality standards set forth by the client. In this case, no additional rework will be required and no additional costs will be incurred. Since there is only a 5 percent chance the system will not meet the standards, the project manager believes that it would only require a small amount of rework to meet the quality standards. In this case, it will cost about $2,000 in resources to bring the system within standards.

On the other hand, the shortened test will cost less than the full test and bring the project back on track. But, if the project team limits the testing of the system, it will very likely lower the probability of the system meeting the quality standards. Moreover, a failure will require more rework and cost more to fix than if these problems were addressed during a full testing of the system. As you can see from Figure 8.5, a limited testing of the system will cost only $8,000, but the chances of the system failing to meet the quality standards increase. Moreover, the time and cost to complete the rework will be higher.

Even though the project manager still has a difficult decision to make, it now becomes a more informed decision. If the project team continues with the testing activities as planned, there is a very good chance that the system will not require a great deal of rework. On the other hand, reducing the time to test the system is more of a gamble. Although there is a 30 percent chance the limited testing will save both time and money, there is a high probability that the system will not pass or meet the quality standards. As a result, the required rework will make the project even later and more over its budget. If you were the project manager, what decision would you make?

Risk Impact Table We can create a **risk impact table** to analyze and prioritize various IT project risks. Let's use another example. Suppose a project manager has identified seven risks that could impact a particular project.

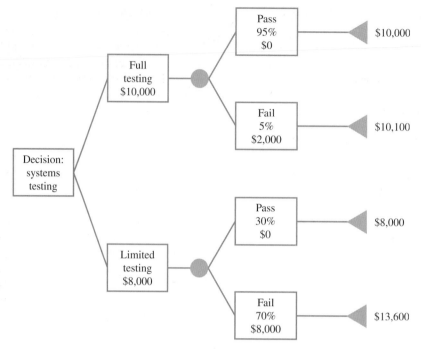

Figure 8.5 Decision Tree Analysis

The left-hand column of Table 8.3 lists the possible risks that were identified using the IT project risk framework introduced in the last section. For simplicity, we will focus only on risks in terms of threats, but opportunities could be analyzed and assessed using the same technique.

The second column lists the subjective probabilities for each of the risks. In this case, the probabilities do not sum to 100 percent because the risks are not mutually exclusive. In other words, none, some, or all of the risk events could occur. A probability of zero indicates that a probability has absolutely no chance of occurring, while a probability of 100 percent indicates an absolute certainty that the event will occur. The next column provides the potential impact associated with the risk event occurring. This also is a subjective estimate based on a score from 0 to 10, with zero being no impact and ten having a very high or significant impact on the project.

Table 8.3 IT Project Risk Impact Analysis

Risk (Threats)	0–100% Probability	0–10 Impact	P · I Score
Key project team member leaves project	40%	4	1.6
Client unable to define scope and requirements	50%	6	3.0
Client experiences financial problems	10%	9	0.9
Response time not acceptable to users/client	80%	6	4.8
Technology does not integrate with existing application	60%	7	4.2
Functional manager deflects resources away from project	20%	3	0.6
Client unable to obtain licensing agreements	5%	7	0.4

Table 8.4 Risk Rankings

Risk (Threats)	Score	Ranking
Response time not acceptable to users/client	4.8	1
Technology does not integrate with existing application	4.2	2
Client unable to define scope and requirements	3.0	3
Key project team member leaves project	1.6	4
Client experiences financial problems	0.9	5
Functional manager deflects resources away from project	0.6	6
Client unable to obtain licensing agreements	0.4	7

Once a probability and an impact are assigned to each risk event, they are multiplied together to come up with a risk score. Although this score is based on the subjective opinions of the project stakeholders, it does provide a mechanism for determining which risks should be monitored and which risks may require a response. Once a risk score is computed for each risk, the risks can be prioritized as in Table 8.4.

Table 8.4 shows that "Response time not acceptable to users/client" and "Technology does not integrate with existing application" are the two most significant risks to this project. The risk scores for all of the risks include the stakeholders' risk tolerances and preferences since the subjective probabilities and impacts will reflect these tolerances and preferences.

The risk scores can be further analyzed using a risk classification scheme introduced by Robert Tusler (Tusler 1998). Figure 8.6 shows how the risk analysis can be used to classify the different risks.

As you can see in Figure 8.6, each risk from Table 8.4 is plotted against its probability and potential impact. Tusler suggests that risks can be classified according to the four quadrants:

- *Kittens*—Risks that have a low probability of occurring and a low impact on the project. These risks are rarely a source of trouble and, therefore, a great deal of time and resources should not be devoted to responding to these threats. Similarly, these types of opportunities are not worth pursuing since they offer little payback and have little chance of fruition.

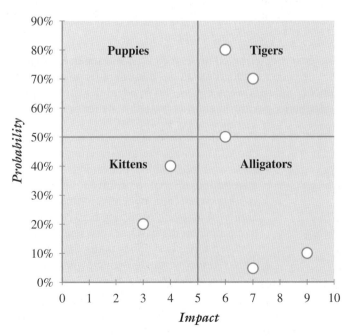

Figure 8.6 Tusler's Risk Classification Scheme

- *Puppies*—Puppies are similar to kittens, but can become a source of problems very quickly because they have a high probability of occurring. Like the risks that they represent, puppies can grow into large troublesome dogs unless they are trained properly. Similarly, these types of risks must be watched so that corrective action can be taken before they get out of hand.

- *Tigers*—These types of risks have a high probability of occurring and a high impact. Similar to the dangerous animals they represent, they must be neutralized as soon as possible.

- *Alligators*—Alligators are not a problem if you know where they are; otherwise, they can be. These risks have a low probability of occurring, but a high impact if they do. These types of risks can be avoided with care.

Quantitative Approaches

Quantitative approaches to project risk analysis include mathematical or statistical techniques that allow us to model a particular risk situation. At the heart of many of these models is the probability distribution. Probability distributions can be continuous or discrete.

Discrete Probability Distributions **Discrete probability distributions** use only integer or whole numbers where fractional values are not allowed or do not make sense. For example, flipping a coin would allow for only two outcomes—heads or tails. If you wanted to find the probability of flipping a fair coin into the air and having the outcome of the coin landing with the heads side up, just divide the number of favorable events (heads) by the number of total outcomes (heads or tails). This results in a $1/2$ or 50 percent probability of the coin coming up heads. Since these events (heads or tails) are mutually exclusive and exhaustive (one and only one of these events will occur), the probability of tails is 50 percent (i.e., 100 percent − 50 percent = 50 percent). Probabilities must be positive and the sum of all of the event probabilities must sum to one.

If you were to flip a coin repeatedly a few hundred times and then record the outcomes, you would end up with a distribution similar to Figure 8.7.

Continuous Probability Distributions **Continuous probability distributions** are useful for developing risk analysis models when an event has an infinite number of possible values within a stated range. Although in theory there are an infinite number of probability distributions, we will discuss three of the more common continuous probability distributions used in modeling risk. These include the **normal distribution**, the **PERT distribution**, and the **triangular distribution**. A quick overview shows how these distributions may be used to develop models for simulation or sensitivity analysis.

One of the most common continuous probability distributions is the normal distribution, or bell curve. Figure 8.8 provides an example of a normal distribution. The normal distribution has the following properties:

■ The distribution's shape is determined by its mean (μ) and standard deviation (σ). In Figure 8.8, this particular distribution has a mean of 0 and a standard deviation of 1. Other combinations of means and standard deviations will result in normal distributions with shapes that are either flatter or taller.

■ Probability is associated with area under the curve. Therefore, the total area under the curve and the baseline that extends from negative infinity (− ∞) to positive infinity (+ ∞) is 100 percent. Subsequently, to find the probability of an event occurring between any two points on the baseline, just find the area between those two points under the curve. This is done by standardizing a given value for X using the formula: $z = (X - \mu) \div \sigma$ to obtain a z score. A table with the various z scores is then used to compute the probability for the area between any two z scores.

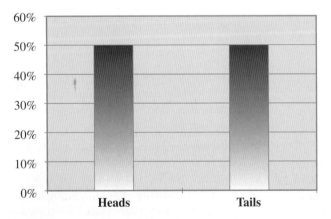

Figure 8.7   Binomial Probability Distribution

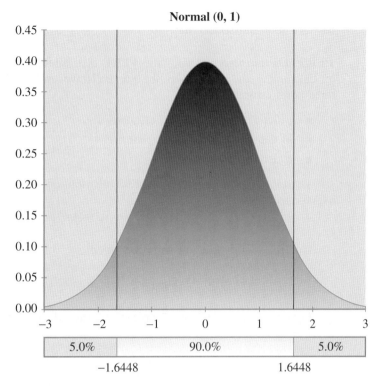

Figure 8.8 Normal Distribution

- Since the normal distribution is symmetrical around the mean, an outcome that falls between $-\infty$ and the mean, μ, would have the same probability of falling between the mean, μ, and $+\infty$ (i.e., 50 percent).
- Since the distribution is symmetrical, the following probability rules of thumb apply:
    - About 68 percent of all the values will fall between $\pm 1\sigma$ of the mean.
    - About 95 percent of all the values will fall between $\pm 2\sigma$ of the mean.
    - About 99 percent of all the values will fall between $\pm 3\sigma$ of the mean.

Therefore, if we know or assume that the probability of a risk event follows a normal distribution, we can predict an outcome with some confidence. For example, let's say that a particular project task has a mean duration of ten days. Moreover, over time we have been able to determine that this particular task has a standard deviation of two days. The mean tells us that if we were to complete this particular task over and over again, we would expect to complete this task, on average, in ten days. If we always completed the task in ten days, there would be no variability and the standard deviation would be zero. If, however, the task sometimes took anywhere between six and fifteen days to complete, we would have some variability, and the standard deviation would be a value greater than zero. The more variability we have, the larger the computed standard deviation.

Using the rules of thumb described above, we could estimate, for example, that we would be about 95 percent certain that the project's task would be complete within six to fourteen days ($\mu \pm 2\sigma = 10 \pm 2 \times 2$). In addition, we could also say that we would be about 99 percent confident that the task would be completed between four and sixteen days ($\mu \pm 3\sigma = 10 \pm 3 \times 2$).

PERT Distribution Using the PERT distribution, one can find a probability by calculating the area under the curve. However, the PERT distribution uses a three-point estimate where:

- *a* denotes an optimistic estimate.
- *m* denotes a most likely estimate.
- *b* denotes a pessimistic estimate.

Therefore, the mean for the PERT distribution is computed using a weighted average as follow:

$$\text{PERT Mean} = (a + 4m + b) \div 6$$

And the standard deviation is computed:

$$\text{PERT Standard Deviation} = (b - a) \div 6$$

Figure 8.9 provides an example of a PERT distribution where $a = 2$, $m = 4$, and $b = 8$.

Triangular Distribution Lastly, the triangular distribution, or TRIANG, also uses a three-point estimate similar to the PERT distribution where:

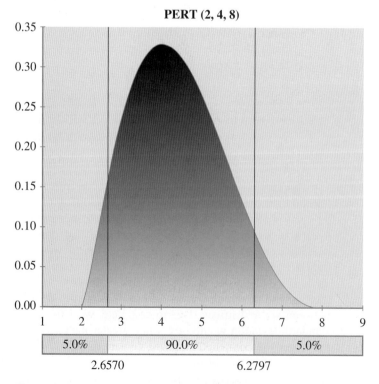

Figure 8.9 Example of a PERT Distribution

- *a* denotes an optimistic estimate.
- *m* denotes a most likely estimate.
- *b* denotes a pessimistic estimate.

However, the weighting for the mean and standard deviation are different.

$$\text{TRIANG Mean} = (a + m + b) \div 3$$
$$\text{TRAING Standard Deviation} = [((b - a)^2 + (m - a)(m - b)) \div 18]^{1/2}$$

Figure 8.10 provides an example of a triangular distribution where $a = 4$, $m = 6$, and $b = 10$.

Simulations In general, when people want to study a particular phenomenon, they pick a random sample. For example, if you wanted to know more about customer satisfaction or consumer tastes, you could survey a certain number of randomly selected customers and then analyze their responses. On the other hand, if you wanted to study projects, you might randomly select a certain number of projects and then collect data about certain attributes in order to make comparisons. This same approach can be used to analyze and understand how different input variables (e.g., task durations) can impact some output variable (e.g., project completion date).

Monte Carlo simulation is a technique that randomly generates specific values for a variable with a specific probability distribution. The simulation goes through a specific number of iterations or trials and records the outcome. For example, instead of flipping a coin 500 times and then recording the outcome to see whether we

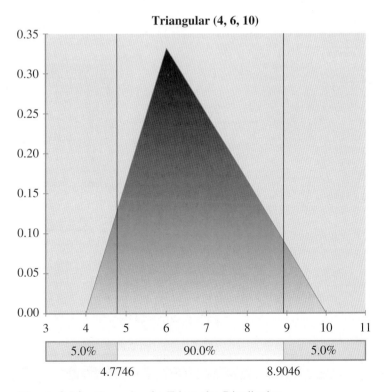

Figure 8.10 Example of a Triangular Distribution

get about the same number of heads as we do tails, a Monte Carlo simulation can literally flip the coin 500 times and record the outcome for us. We can perform a similar simulation using almost any continuous or discrete probability distribution.

If we would like to apply our knowledge of probability distributions to risk analysis, there are a number of software tools available to model our project and develop simulations. One tool is an add-on to Microsoft Project® called @Risk™. As an example of a Monte Carlo simulation, let's say that we are interested in modeling a section of the work breakdown structure that was used in Figure 6.3. In our example, we have identified six tasks to complete a deliverable called a test results report. The WBS, time estimates, and assumed probability distributions are illustrated in Figure 8.11.

As you can see, the project is estimated to be completed in 155 days, while the deliverable, the test results report, is expected to take 17 days. All of these estimates were entered as point estimates that do not take into consideration any variability or risk.

On the right side of Figure 8.11 is a message box that shows a probability distribution for each of the tasks for completing the test results report. These probabilities would be defined based on data collected from past projects or based on statistical theory that would help define an appropriate distribution for a particular task, or an

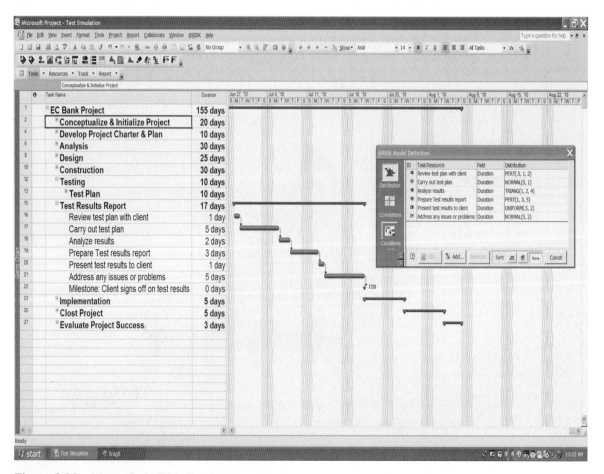

Figure 8.11   Monte Carlo Risk Simulation

assumption the project manager or team is willing to make. In our example, we'll make an assumption that the "Review test plan with client" follows a PERT distribution with an optimistic estimate of .5 days, a most likely estimate of 1 day, and a pessimistic estimate of 2 days. On the other hand, we make an assumption that the task "Carry out test plan" follows a normal distribution and has a mean of 5 and a standard deviation of 1.

Since the variability of these tasks can be modeled using various probability distributions, a Monte Carlo simulation will allow us to assess the probability of the test results report deliverable being completed in 17 days. A Monte Carlo simulation was set to run 500 iterations or trials. In short, instead of flipping a coin 500 times, the software will simulate the running of our project 500 times according to the probability distributions we defined for each of the tasks and record the results. A histogram for the tasks associated with the test results report deliverable is shown in Figure 8.12. As can be seen, the mean time to complete this deliverable is about 17.75214 days, with a 90.4% chance that the project will be completed between 13.8 and 21.71 days.

Figure 8.13 provides an alternative view for assessing the likelihood that the test results report will be finished in 17 days. A cumulative probability distribution shows that the deliverable has approximately a 40 percent chance of being completed in 17 days.

In addition, the project manager can conduct a sensitivity analysis to determine the tasks that entail the most risk. Figure 8.14 illustrates a **tornado graph**, which summarizes the tasks, with the most significant risks at the top. As the risks are ranked from highest to lowest, the bars of the graph sometimes resemble a tornado. The tornado graph allows us to compare the magnitudes of impact for each of the

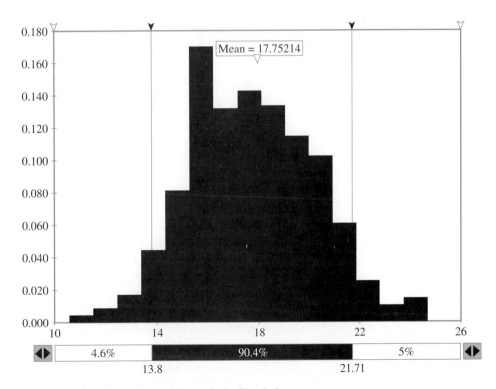

Figure 8.12   Output From Monte Carlo Simulation

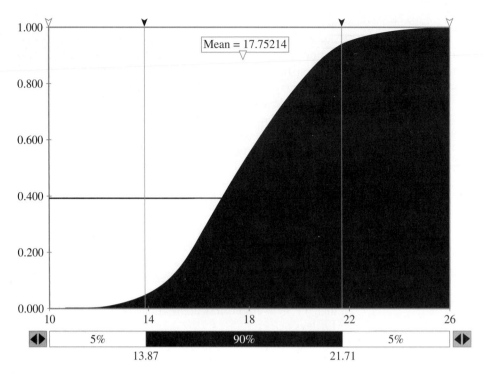

Figure 8.13 Cumulative Probability Distribution

tasks by comparing the size of each bar. As you can see in Figure 8.14, the task "Address any issues or problems" has the greatest potential for impacting the project's schedule because of risk or uncertainty. Although this example used one component of the WBS, the same risk analysis could be conducted for each component, as well as the entire project.

RISK STRATEGIES

The purpose of risk analysis and assessment is to determine what opportunities and threats should be addressed. It is not feasible or advisable to respond to each and every threat or opportunity identified because avoiding all threats or chasing after every opportunity requires resources to be diverted from the real project work. Therefore, the risk strategy or response to a particular risk depends on:

- *The nature of the risk itself*—Is this really a threat to or opportunity for the project? How will the project be affected? At what points during the project life cycle will the project be affected? What are the triggers that would determine if a particular risk is occurring? Why should the risk be taken?

- *The impact of the risk on the project's MOV and objectives*—A risk has a probability and an impact on the project if it occurs. What is the likelihood of this occurring? And if this risk occurs, how will the project be affected? What can be gained? What could be lost? What are the chances of success or failure?

- *The project's constraints in terms of scope, schedule, budget, and quality requirements*—Can a response to a particular threat or opportunity be made

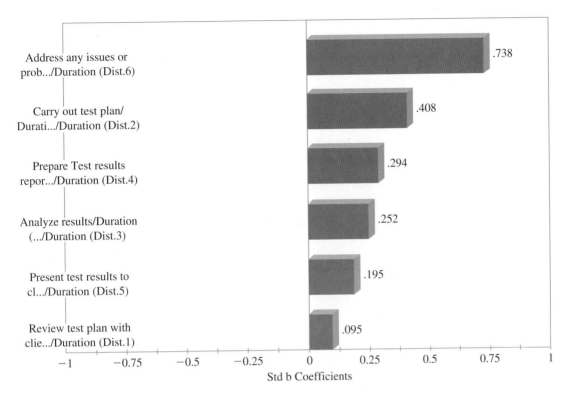

Figure 8.14 Sensitivity Analysis Using a Tornado Graph

within the available resources and constraints of the project? Will additional resources be made available if a particular risk occurs? Can certain contractual obligations be waived or modified? What will happen if the desired result is not achieved?

■ *Risk tolerances or preferences of the various project stakeholders*—Is a risk for one stakeholder a risk for another? How much risk is each stakeholder willing to tolerate? How committed is each stakeholder to the risk management process? Is the potential reward worth the effort?

A response to a particular risk may follow one of the following strategies:

■ *Accept or ignore*—Choosing to accept or ignore a particular risk is a more passive approach to risk response. The project stakeholders can either be hopeful that the risk will not occur or just not worry about it unless it does. This can make sense for risks that have a low probability of occurring or a low impact. However, reserves and contingency plans can be active approaches for risks that may have a low probability of occurring but with a high impact.

■ *Management reserves*—These are reserves that are controlled and released by senior management at its discretion. These reserves are not usually included in the project's budget, but provide a cushion for dealing with the unexpected.

■ *Contingency reserves*—A contingency reserve is usually controlled and released within specific guidelines by the project manager when a particular risk occurs. This reserve is usually included in the project's budget.

Risk	Trigger	Owner	Response	Resources Required

Figure 8.15   Template for a Risk Response Plan

- *Contingency plans*—Sometimes called an alternative plan, or *plan B*, this plan can be initiated in the event a particular risk occurs. Although these types of plans are viewed as plans of last resort, they can be useful in a variety of ways. For example, a project team should have a disaster recovery plan in place should a natural disaster, such as a hurricane or earthquake, occur. This plan may have procedures and processes in place that would allow the project team to continue to work should its present workplace become unusable or unavailable. This type of disaster recovery plan is only useful if it is up to date and communicated to the various project stakeholders.

- *Avoidance*—The avoidance strategy focuses on taking steps to avoid the risk altogether. In this case, an active approach is made to eliminate or prevent the possibility of the threat occurring.

- *Mitigate*—The term *mitigate* means to lessen. Therefore, a mitigation risk strategy focuses on lessening the probability and/or the impact of threat if it does occur.

- *Transfer*—A transfer strategy focuses on transferring ownership of the risk to someone else. This transfer could be in the form of purchasing insurance against a particular risk or subcontracting a portion of the project work to someone who may have more knowledge or expertise in the particular area. As a result, this strategy may result in a premium, or added cost, to managing and responding to the risk.

Once the project risks and strategies are identified, they can be documented as part of the **risk response plan**. This plan should include the following:

- The project risk
- The trigger that flags whether the risk has occurred
- The owner of the risk (i.e., the person or group responsible for monitoring the risk and ensuring that the appropriate risk response is carried out)
- The risk response based on one of the four basic risk strategies

The risk response plan can be developed using a template, such as the one illustrated in Figure 8.15.

RISK MONITORING AND CONTROL

Once the risk response plan is created, the various risk triggers must be continually monitored to keep track of the various IT project risks. In addition, new threats and opportunities may present themselves over the course of the project, so it is important that the project stakeholders be vigilant.

Risk monitoring and control should be part of the overall monitoring and control of the project. Monitoring and control focus on metrics to help identify when a risk occurs, and also on communication. The next chapter addresses how important it is to have a good monitoring and control system that supports communication among the various stakeholders and provides information essential to making timely and effective decisions.

Risk monitoring and control are analogous to a radarscope, as Figure 8.16 shows. Threats and opportunities present themselves at different times. Some are on the horizon, while others are closer to affecting the project's MOV and objectives.

Various tools exist for monitoring and controlling project risk. These include:

- *Risk audits*—A knowledgeable manager or group can be useful for auditing the project team from time to time. The audit should focus on ensuring that the project manager and team have done a good job of identifying and analyzing project risks and on ensuring that proper procedures and processes are in place. Risk audits should be conducted by people outside the project team. Using outsiders provides a fresh perspective; the project team may be too close to the project and miss significant threats or opportunities.

- *Risk reviews*—Risk audits should be conducted by individuals outside the project team; but risk reviews can be conducted internally. Throughout the project life cycle, the project stakeholders should hold scheduled, periodic risk reviews. These reviews should be part of each team meeting and part of the project team's learning cycles.

- *Risk status meetings and reports*—Similar to risk reviews, a monitoring and control system should provide a formal communication system for monitoring and controlling project risks.

Figure 8.16   Project Risk Radar

RISK RESPONSE AND EVALUATION

The risk triggers defined in the risk response plan provide risk metrics for determining whether a particular threat or opportunity has occurred. A system for monitoring and controlling risk provides a mechanism for monitoring these triggers and for supporting communication among the various risk owners. The risk owners must be vigilant in watching for these triggers.

When a trigger occurs, the project risk owner must take appropriate action. In general, the action is responding to the risk as outlined in the risk response plan. Adequate resources must be available and used to respond to the risk.

QUICK THINKING—RISKY MANAGEMENT

Many project managers are uncomfortable with the probabilistic and speculative nature of risk management and therefore tend to avoid it. On the other hand, a project manager and team may sit down and identify project risks with sticky notes on the wall, estimate their probability and impact, and then log them into an Excel® spreadsheet with strategies for dealing with these risks. A reserve is then created by arbitrarily tacking on a percentage markup to the project's budget for contingencies. Unfortunately, the project plan, risk spreadsheet log, and reserve have little to do with each other. Too often the risk plans become forgotten or ineffective. Moreover, management or the project sponsor can easily cut the project's reserve when it becomes isolated from the project plan or just gets added as a line item to the project's budget.

Tom Westcott suggests that a risk plan should be integrated into the project plan so that a risk budget or reserve becomes part of the project's schedule and budget. For example, let's say that you are the project manager for a project to build a custom application for the human resources department. Upon reviewing the WBS, you and the team identify the task "load data" as a major risk. More specifically, the HR department is responsible for providing your team with the data but in the past this department has often given your team corrupt, improperly formatted, and incomplete data. Since "bad data" is viewed as a risk, you and your team look for ways to mitigate this risk. A team member suggests holding a meeting with the HR department to discuss data requirements, responsibilities, and processes for ensuring that the data is usable, but this does not ensure that the risk will not occur on the day the data is scheduled to be loaded. Therefore, it is decided that that a member of your team will be assigned the task of extracting, cleaning, formatting, and validating the data. This will require additional time and cost, but only in the event that the HR department does not provide good data. The main point is that instead of logging this risk into a

spreadsheet and then adding a percentage markup to the schedule and budget as a contingency, you can actually build these actions into your project plan.

To incorporate this risk, your project plan would have three additional tasks: (1) hold data meeting with HR, (2) validate the data, and (3) clean the data. The first two tasks are tasks that would actually be done, so 100 percent of their time and cost would be included in the plan. However, the third task, clean the data, would be performed only if the risk occurs. Since this risk may or may not occur, we can assign a percentage of the estimated schedule and budget based on the probability of the risk occurring that we estimated during our risk management process. We can then multiply the impact of this contingency task (i.e., its cost, effort, and duration) by the probability of the risk's occurrence to get an expected monetary value (EMV). The risk reserve or contingency budget then becomes the sum of all the EMV's for all the contingency tasks in the project plan. Although the EMV for a particular contingency task may not be enough to cover a particular risk when it occurs, it is unlikely that all of the risks on the project will occur.

1. Contingency plans are not executed until after a risk occurs and often involve cleanup, rework, added resources, waste, and damage. Is an investment made in prevention less expensive than executing a contingency strategy?

2. Will incorporating prevention and risk management into a project plan lessen the chances of management or the project sponsor arbitrarily slashing the project's budget?

3. What other advantages can you see in having a more holistic project plan?

SOURCE: Adapted from Tom R. Westcott, The Risk in Risk Management, *Projects@Work*, March 9, 2006.

The outcome of the risk response will either be favorable or unfavorable. Therefore, a great deal can be learned about the entire process of risk management (i.e., the preparedness of risk planning, identifying risks, analyzing and assessing risks, risk responses, and so forth). Lessons learned can lead to the identification of best practices that can be shared throughout the project organization. In summary, lessons learned and best practices help us to:

- Increase our understanding of IT project risk in general
- Understand what information was available to managing risks and for making risk-related decisions
- Understand how and why a particular decision was made
- Understand the implications not only of the risks but also the decisions that were made
- Learn from our experience so that others may not have to repeat our mistakes

 CHAPTER SUMMARY

This chapter introduced the processes and concepts of project risk management. Risk is an inherent component of IT projects because the project plan is based on a number of estimates that reflect our understanding of the current situation, the information available, and the assumptions that must be made. But, events seldom go according to plan, so the project must adapt to an ever-changing environment. Our inability to predict the future with 100 percent accuracy coupled with a dynamic environment create degrees of uncertainty or risk that must be addressed and managed throughout the project life cycle.

Although risk implies a negative connotation, project stakeholders must be vigilant in identifying opportunities presented by risk. The Project Management Body of Knowledge (*PMBOK® Guide*) points out that project risk management provides a systematic process for identifying, analyzing, and responding to project risks. A project risk management approach should focus on maximizing the probability and impacts of positive events while minimizing the probability and impacts of negative events.

In this chapter, two IT risk management frameworks were introduced. The first framework focused on the IT project risk management processes. These seven steps or processes include risk planning, risk identification, risk assessment, risk strategies, risk monitoring and controlling, risk response, and risk evaluation.

Risk planning begins with a firm commitment by all the project stakeholders to a risk management approach. A great deal of this commitment should be in terms of commitments to following the processes and to provide adequate resources when responding to risk events.

Risk identification should include identifying both threats and opportunities. Since most risks are interrelated and can affect the project in different ways, the project stakeholders should take a broad view of project risks. A second framework was introduced in this section to help understand the nature and influence of various IT project risks. This IT project risk framework is illustrated in Figure 8.2. It helps the project stakeholders identify and understand the nature and influence of various risks.

Risk assessment allows the project stakeholders to determine what risks require a response. The goal of project risk management is not to avoid each and every risk at all costs, but to make well informed decisions as to which risks are worth taking and which risks require a response. A well informed decision requires an analysis of the probability of a particular risk occurring and its likely impact. Several qualitative and quantitative approaches were introduced to help in analysis. It is, however, important to keep in mind that there is a cost associated with responding to a particular risk, so risk management must function within the project's available resources.

Risk strategies define how the project stakeholders will respond to risk. In general, risk strategies include (1) accepting or ignoring the risk, (2) avoiding the risk, (3) mitigating or reducing the likelihood and/or impact of the risk, and (4) transferring the risk to someone else. A set of risk metrics should be defined to act as triggers, or flags, when a particular risk event occurs. The risks, the risk triggers, risk owners, and strategies should be formalized in a risk response plan.

Once the risk response plan has been completed and the project is underway, the various risks identified must be monitored and controlled. This process should include vigilance on the identified and unidentified threats and/or opportunities. As these risks present themselves, project risk owners should make resources available and respond to risk (risk response) in an appropriate manner, as outlined in the risk response plan.

Risk evaluation provides a key to learning and identifying best practices. A formal and documented evaluation of a risk response or episode can help an organization evaluate its entire risk management approach and provide insight for future project teams that may have to deal with a similar risk in the future.

WEB SITES TO VISIT

- **www.palisade.com:** Palisade Corp. provides many project risk management software tools. Free trial versions can be downloaded and evaluated.

- **www.decisioneering.com:** Decisioneering provides a risk management tool called Crystalball™. Free trial versions of several of its products can be downloaded and evaluated.

- **http://perso.wanadoo.fr/courtot.herve/links.htm:** Project Risk Management Sites of Interest.

- You can download a copy of this tool without cost from two Web sites, **www.iceincUSA.com** (Integrated Computer Engineering) and **www.spmn.com** (Software Program Managers Network): Integrated Computer Engineering, Inc. (ICE) provides Risk Radar™ (Version 2.02) as a free software product.

REVIEW QUESTIONS

1. What leads to uncertainty in an IT project?

2. How does a project risk management approach provide an early warning signal for impending problems or issues?

3. What is meant by crisis management? And why do many organizations find themselves in this mode?

4. Describe some of the common mistakes in project risk management.

5. Briefly describe what is required for effective and successful project risk management.

6. What is project risk?

7. What is project risk management?

8. What are the seven IT project risk management processes?

9. What types of commitment are necessary for risk planning?

10. Why can identifying IT project risks be difficult?

11. What is a "known" risk? Give an example of one.

12. What is a "known-unknown" risk? Give an example of one.

13. What is an "unknown-unknown" risk? Give an example of one.

14. What is the difference between an internal and external risk? Give an example of each.

15. Describe some of the tools and techniques that can be used to identify IT project risks.

16. Describe the nominal group technique and how it can be applied to identifying IT project risks.

17. Describe how learning cycles can be used to identify IT project risks.

18. What is the Delphi technique? How can this technique be used to identify IT project risks?

19. How can interviewing be used as a technique for identifying IT project risks? What are some of the advantages and disadvantages of using this technique?

20. How do checklists help in identifying IT project risk? Discuss the pros and cons of using this technique.

21. What is SWOT analysis? How can this technique be used to identify IT project risks?

22. What is a fishbone (Ishikawa) diagram? How can this tool be used to identify IT project risks?

23. What is the purpose of risk analysis and assessment?

24. What is the difference between qualitative and quantitative risk analysis?

25. Describe the concept of expected value.

26. What is the purpose of a decision tree? What are the advantages and disadvantages of using a decision tree?

27. What is the purpose of a risk impact table?

28. What is the difference between a discrete probability distribution and a continuous probability distribution?

29. What are the rules of thumb that can be applied to a normal distribution?

30. Compare and contrast the normal distribution, the PERT distribution, and the triangular distribution.

31. What is a simulation? What value do simulations provide when analyzing and assessing IT project risks?

32. What is a Monte Carlo simulation? Describe a situation (other than the one used in this chapter) that could make good use of a Monte Carlo simulation.

33. Define and discuss the four risk strategies described in this chapter.

34. What is the difference between a management reserve and a contingency reserve?

35. What is a contingency plan?

36. Why can't a project team respond to all project risks?

37. What is a risk response plan? What should be included?

38. What are risk triggers or flags?

39. Why is having a risk owner a good idea? What role does a risk owner play?

40. What is risk monitoring and control?

41. Describe the three risk monitoring tools that were discussed in this chapter.

42. What is the purpose of evaluating a response to a particular risk?

 EXTEND YOUR KNOWLEDGE

1. Using the Internet or the library, find an article about an IT project that failed. Using the IT project risk framework (Figure 8.2), identify the explicit or implicit risks that may have impacted this project.

2. Plan a trip to a show or a sporting event in another city. Define how you will get there and estimate how long it will take. Then define the risks that you might encounter and construct a risk impact table. Afterwards, rank the risks and come up with a risk strategy for the three most significant risks.

 GLOBAL TECHNOLOGY SOLUTIONS

The Husky Air project team filed into the GTS conference room, and everyone took a seat at the conference table. No one seemed to know why this urgent meeting had been called, but they knew from Tim Williams' email that they were about to hear some interesting news.

Tim walked into the room and shut the door behind him. Everyone could tell by the expression on his face that the news was not going to be good. Tim took a seat at the head of the table. "Thank you for being here on such short notice," he said. "As you all know, I had a meeting with our client this morning to go over the project plan we prepared." The look on Tim's face grew more serious, and the tension began to mount. He paused, then continued, "Husky Air's management has informed me that they are feeling the effects of the downturn in the economy. The company is getting hit from two sides. First, there has been an increase in

fuel costs. Second, with the continuing demand for airline pilots, several of its more experienced charter pilots have left to take jobs with the scheduled airlines. With costs up and revenues down, cash flow is a concern."

The project team members looked at each other with puzzled expressions. Sitaramin spoke up, "Tim, how will this affect *our* project?"

Tim looked down at faces of the team members gathered around the table. "When I met with them this morning, a few of the managers were inclined to cancel the project," he said. "However, because we focused on the value that this project is expected to bring to the organization, they decided that the project was too valuable just to cancel outright. But because cash flow is a problem, they need to reduce the cost of the project. After much discussion, it was agreed that we would trim the project's scope in order to decrease the project's budget. The good news is that Husky Air's management believes that the increase in fuel costs will be temporary and they are in the process of recruiting new pilots. However, it may be a few months before they are back on solid financial ground. If that happens, they want us to complete the rest of the scope as we had originally planned. In the meantime, we'll have to get back to work and come up with a revised schedule and budget."

Ted, the project's telecommunication specialist, asked, "What about our contract with Husky Air? Can't we hold them to the contract they signed?"

"I just got off the phone with our company's lawyer," Tim answered. "She said that our contract allows either party to cancel the project if they cannot fulfill the terms of the agreement. There's a significant financial penalty, of course, but Kellie and I decided that it was in everyone's best interest to renegotiate the contract based on a newly defined scope. We feel legal action is not the best way to build and maintain a good, long-term relationship with our client. Kellie did a quick financial analysis and believes we can still make a profit without having to downsize our project team. Besides, we have leads for several other projects with new clients so all of our eggs are not in one basket."

"Well, at least I can still make the payments on my new car!" joked Pat. Everyone in the room laughed.

Sitaramin interjected, "Tim, maybe we should think seriously about what else could affect our project?"

Tim looked around the table at the other team members. They seemed to be in agreement with the suggestion. Pat spoke up, "Sitaramin's right. What we need to do is come up with a risk management plan."

Tim laughed, "Okay, it looks like we're in for another brainstorming session. I just hope we have enough color markers. Any suggestions as to how we should get started?"

Even though the team had received bad news just a few minutes earlier, they were energized by the thought of tackling another problem together. Yan suggested they focus on identifying different risks and the potential impact they might have on the project. This process would help them come up with strategies for handling risks and reduce the likelihood of surprises. Then, the team could develop a learning cycle to identify the facts, assumptions to be tested, and things to find out. The lessons learned could be documented and made part of the GTS knowledge base. Pat thought that was a good idea, and he suggested that they also identify triggers or flags that warn them when a particular risk might be imminent. This system would allow them to monitor the project's risk throughout the project life cycle and reduce the likelihood of being surprised again.

Tim rolled up his sleeves and walked over to the whiteboard. "Okay, everyone, slow down so I can write these ideas down," he said. "Now, how do you propose we get started?" Tim grinned and thought to himself how much he enjoyed working with this group of people.

Things to Think About

1. Was the financial downturn of Husky Air a problem that the GTS team could have foreseen and avoided?

2. Can all risks to a project be identified and managed?

3. In addition to identifying threats, why should project stakeholders also look for opportunities?

 # HUSKY AIR ASSIGNMENT—PILOT ANGELS

The Risk Management Plan

After reviewing your project plan, Husky Air's management has decided that the project's schedule needs to be cut by 10 percent and the project budget must be reduced by 20 percent. For example, if your original project plan estimated that the project would be completed in 100 days, you need to revise your plan so that the project will now be completed within 90 days. If the project budget was estimated to be $50,000, it now has to be revised so that the project does not cost more than $40,000.

Before you begin, be sure to make a backup copy of your original project plan!

Please provide a professional-looking document that includes the following:

1. **Project name, project team name, and the names of the members of your project team**

2. **A brief project description**

3. **The project's MOV** (This should be revised or refined if necessary.)

4. **A printout of the Project Summary Report (original project plan)**—Include a copy of your original project schedule and budget. This is a canned Microsoft Project® Report. (From the View

menu, choose Reports, Overview, and then Project Summary.) This will provide a baseline for revising your project plan.

5. **A printout of the Project Summary Report (revised project plan)**—Modify your project plan so that your project schedule is reduced by 10 percent and the project budget by 20 percent. Provide a printout of the Project Summary report to show that the project schedule and budget now meet your client's needs. Conduct a discussion about how you reduced the schedule and budget and logically support why you feel this strategy will not create a serious risk to your project. If your logic suggests that your original estimates were padded (i.e., you were overly "conservative"), then you can expect that Husky Air's management will ask you to revise your project schedule and budget even further.

6. **A project risk analysis and plan**

   a. Using the IT Risk Framework in Figure 8.2 as a basis, identify a total of five risks to your project. More specifically, identify one risk for each of the five phases of the IT project methodology depicted in the outer ring of the framework. Then, use the framework for analyzing each risk by moving from the outer ring to the center.

   b. For each of the five risks identified, assign an owner to each risk and describe a strategy for managing each particular risk.

 ## CASE STUDIES

Probabilities—Not Ones and Zeros

Montserrat is an island in the Caribbean West Indies that covers just 39 square miles. Its air and water temperatures rarely fall below 78 degrees Fahrenheit. With beautiful mountains, lush rain forests, and groves of mangoes, bananas, and coconuts, it is easy to call Montserrat a paradise. Unfortunately, Montserrat also is home to the Soufriere Hills Volcano, which first erupted in 1995 and continues to be a threat today. Approximately two-thirds of the island is now uninhabitable, and Montserrat's population has fallen to 4,000 from 11,000 since 1995. In 1997, 20 people perished and the island's economy, which relies mainly on tourism, has suffered. A recording studio owned by former Beatles producer George Martin allowed rock stars like Sting, the Rolling Stones, and Paul McCartney to record their music, but is now buried by volcanic ash.

Montserrat is now a dichotomy where one side of the island is paradise and the other uninhabitable part is called the Exclusion Zone. However, the island has become a excellent laboratory for conducting risk analysis. Based on probabilities, scientists know that there's only a 3 percent chance that the volcano will become dormant in the next six months. Moreover, they also know that there's a 10 percent chance that someone will be injured from the volcano on the border of the Exclusion Zone. Scientists are able to draw an imaginary line across the island where the risk from the volcano is the same as the risk from hurricanes and earthquakes. According to Willy Aspinall, while a large computer was needed to do this type of statistical analysis 30 years ago, the same risk analysis can be accomplished using a laptop and spreadsheet software package.

As Scott Berinato explains, "If this type of risk analysis is good enough for Aspinall, it ought to be good enough for CIOs, especially now that they're working in an economic environment looming ominously over their businesses as Soufriere Hills looms over Montserrat. For the most part, though, CIOs have not adopted statistical analysis tools to analyze and mitigate risk for software project management."

Many experts agree that statistical risk analysis is an important tool in managing individual projects as well as the project portfolio. Rebecca Rhoads is the CIO at Raytheon and believes that risk management has lowered the rate of project failure and helped Raytheon achieve cost-performance goals. Although she may be ahead of the curve, Rhoads has yet to use sophisticated statistical analysis like the scientists studying the Soufriere Hills Volcano. In addition, Robert Sanchez, senior vice president and CIO at Ryder, admits that statistical analysis is welcome but yet to be used to its fullest potential. He explains, "Have we really embraced it completely and understood it in all its detail? No, we haven't. But we will."

One challenge to utilizing fully such tools as Monte Carlo Simulation and decision tree analysis may be common sense. For example, simple tasks like choosing a route when driving to work or school may involve a risk assessment that can be easily done in your head. Though the cost of being late may be high, the risk of encountering a new construction zone can be low and easily mitigated by tuning into a local radio station to get a traffic report. Steve Snodgrass is the CIO of a construction materials supplier called Granite Rock that literally straddles the San Andreas Fault. He doesn't need a sophisticated risk analysis tool to tell him that an earthquake could be devastating to his company's IT operations. Common sense dictates that he should have a backup site far from the fault line.

Authors Tom DeMarco and Timothy Lister believe that this type of common sense can impede doing real risk analysis. As Lister points out, "It's been very frustrating to see a best practice like statistical analysis shunned in IT. It seems there's this enormously strong cultural pull in IT to avoid looking at the downside." Art Misyan is the director of foreign exchange at Merck and is also baffled by IT's laissez-faire attitude toward risk management. He believes that IT needs to think in terms of probabilities, not ones and zeros. In addition, the best way to start is to have a formalized risk process that starts with identifying and managing risks. Research or brainstorming sessions are common techniques for identifying risks. Once project risks are identified, statistical tools can be applied.

Berinato believes that it is important that CIOs and IT project managers become familiar with two statistical tools that are becoming the workhorses of risk analysis: Monte Carlo simulation and decision tree analysis. As he points out, "Probabilities figure heavily into both, which means risk has to be quantified. CIOs must draw their own line between the Exclusion Zone, where it's too risky to venture, and the beaches, rain forests, and coconut groves, where the living is easy and the threats are manageable."

Monte Carlo Simulation was a technique developed in the 1940s for the Manhattan Project and is used today for myriad applications, like oil well drilling or compacting garbage at a waste treatment facility. It is based on the idea that if you roll a die (hence the name) 100 times and record the results, each face will come up about one-sixth of the time. This may not happen exactly due to randomness, but the results will come closer the more times you roll the die.

Each side of the die can represent a risk that is predictable and evenly distributed. So, for example, the probability of rolling a 2 has a one-sixth probability of occurring and a five-sixth probability of not occurring. A die could then represent a project risk and each side could represent a possible outcome of that risk. So for example, rolling a die could represent a key member of the project team leaving the project, while rolling a 1 could represent that the project will be 1 week late, a 2 two weeks late, and so on. On the other hand, a project manager may believe that a particular program being written will have a 50 percent chance of passing a quality test and a 50 percent chance that it won't, resulting in a one-week delay of the project. A die could be rolled whereby an even number represents the program passing the quality test and an odd number represents the week's delay.

A Monte Carlo simulator allows for "rolling the dice" according to predefined probability distribution and then recording the results. This can help determine a project's risk profile so that additional resources or attention can help mitigate a particular risk. Vitro is a $2.6 billion glass company in Monterrey, Mexico and requires that a Monte Carlo simulation be conducted for all projects valued at more than $20,000. Gustavo Benitez, Vitro's IT supply chain managers, says "No one wanted to measure at first because measuring makes you accountable. We're not that deep into it; we only use best case, worst case, and most likely, and already it helps. It helps you see different scenarios."

Decision tree analysis is the other risk analysis tool that can be applied to IT projects. While Monte Carlo is excellent for understanding what happens to a project when many risks can come to play at once, a decision tree is most useful for mapping either-or situations and the sequential risks that can follow. For example, a program can either pass a quality test or it doesn't. Either decision or action is a branch with a probability. Each branch can then lead to other branches that represent the risks associated with the original branch. A main advantage of a decision tree is that it shows that probabilities compound. Anne Rogers of Waste Management likes decision trees because they can often show that good risk decisions can be counterintuitive when you follow the branches. She explains, "I'll give some outlandish choice, like rewiring your office or building a new one. Everyone thinks they know which one is less risky, but you watch the risks compound over time and guess what, it's not nearly as risky as you think to build a new office in certain situations."

It often takes time to get used to risk analysis. For example, a weather forecast may say there's a 90 percent chance of sunshine tomorrow, but it rains. The analysis may have been correct—there was a 10 percent chance of rain and it did. Therefore, risk analysis does not provide solid answers. It won't tell a CIO which project to do, and it won't tell a project manager whether a key employee will leave the project team. It will, however, tell you which risks have a certain level of threat and payoff.

1. Why aren't risk analysis tools like Monte Carlo simulation and decision tree analysis more common in analyzing IT project risks?

2. What could be done so that CIOs and IT project managers would be more apt to use these tools?

3. Suppose you are the project manager for an ERP project. Provide an example of a situation where Monte Carlo simulation would be appropriate. Also provide an example of a situation where decision tree analysis would be appropriate.

SOURCE: Adapted from Scott Berinato, The Role of Risk Analysis in Project Portfolio Management, *Computerworld*, July 1, 2003.

Outsourcing—Big Savings, Big Risks

The top reason why organizations outsource services is to save money. However, many organizations are not saving as much money as they had hoped. According to Technology Partners International (TPI), the average savings from outsourcing is just less than 15 percent. Interestingly, a quarterly status report on outsourcing produced by TPI also stated that while the savings from outsourcing may not be what many organizations expect, outsourcing is still growing at a steady rate. The reason may not be the money an organization can save to reinvest into something else, but rather a shortage of experienced and skilled IT staff that can be hired. On the other hand, outsourcing has increasingly morphed from a cost savings strategy to a business strategy that can allow a company to enter new markets or consolidate several internal services to one provider. More organizations are finding out that saving money is only a small part of the overall picture.

However, outsourcing is not without risk. It's Tuesday morning at 8:30 and five members of a project team at Ondeo Nalco—a water treatment, chemical services company located in Naperville, Illinois—are gathered around a conference table while their project manager dials the speakerphone to call their counterparts in Manila. Meanwhile, it's 8:30 PM in Manila where three Filipino programmers from an outsourcing firm called Headstrong Corp. take the call after working a long day. Both teams know each other's faces behind the speakerphone because the three Filipino programmers spent two months in Naperville getting to know the Ondeo Nalco team. Although the Filipino's English is excellent, a Filipino project manager takes part in the conference to make sure that all instructions are understood.

This outsourcing partnership has been running smoothly for almost a year. Ondeo Nalco entered into this project with Headstrong to develop jointly a business intelligence warehouse. While Ondeo Nalco believed it could save money by scaling back and letting offshore programmers make smaller enhancements to the system, it soon learned that the Philippines was a good place for outsourcing many of its IT needs.

According to Atul Vahistha, CEO of NeoIT Inc., an offshore outsourcing advisory firm in San Ramon, California, "After India, the Philippines is probably the second most popular destination when it comes to pure offshore outsourcing." The popularity of the Philippines is due to its English proficiency, highly skilled workforce, developing telecommunications infrastructure, and low cost. For example, an experienced programmer in the Philippines earns between $6,000 and $12,000 a year.

The research firm Meta Group Inc. ranks the Philippines behind other Asia-Pacific countries because of its political instability and shortage of indigenous IT companies. The Philippines for the past decade has been dealing with militant Muslim insurgents. According to Howard Rubin, an executive vice president at Meta Group, "It has a destabilizing effect on the nation's ability to attract and sustain foreign capital investment, and thus poses serious threats to the economy." However, Vahistha counters that this threat is mainly limited to the southern islands and doesn't affect IT work in Manila. Yet he suggests that companies that offshore work to the Philippines should have a solid business continuity and disaster recovery plan.

Moreover, there appears to be a shortage of experienced project managers in the Philippines to oversee projects and more software developers are needed. While the Philippines with its large English-speaking population makes it a logical choice for software development, there are only about 10,000 software programmers nationwide and only 30 companies that focus on writing software. In contrast, Ireland has a population 20 times smaller than the Philippines and has over 800 indigenous software development firms.

Besides the time difference, Ondeo Nalco has found that a major challenge has been security. Paul Gould, an IT group leader for global development, explains "There's a perception that if you're going to open up your network to anybody on the other side of the world, you have to be extra secure because of the danger that they'll be contaminated by connections into their network." As a result, Ondeo Nalco and Headstrong spent a month determining which firewall ports should be open, what level of access people needed, and what work could be completed in Naperville, Illinois versus Manila.

1. Identify one technology risk and one non-technology risk an organization may encounter when outsourcing a component of an IT project to a foreign country. Develop a risk management plan to manage these risks.

SOURCE: Adapted from:

Stacy Collett, The Phillipines: Low Cost, but Higher Risk, *Computerworld*, September 15, 2003.

Jerri Ledford, Outsourcing to Save Money? Think Again! *Computerworld*, April 20, 2006.

BIBLIOGRAPHY

Choo, G. 2001. It's A Risky Business. www.systemcorp.com/framesite/downloads/choo_p.html

Delbecq, A. and A. H. Van de Van. 1971. A Group Process Model for Identification and Program Planning. *Journal of Applied Behavioral Sciences* 7: 466–492.

Jones, T. C. 1994. *Assessment and Control of Software Risks*. Upper Saddle River, NJ: Yourdon Press/Prentice Hall.

Kulik, P. 2000. What is Software Risk Management (And Why Should I Care)? www.klci.com

Lanza, R. B. 2001. Reviewing a Project Risk Management System. www.auditsoftware.net/infoarchive/articles/projmgmt/files/riskmgmt.htm

Tusler, R. 1998. An Overview of Project Risk Management. www.netcomuk.co.uk/~rtusler/project/elements.html

Wideman, R. M. 1992. *Project and Program Risk Management: A Guide to Managing Project Risks and Opportunities*. Newtown Square, PA: Project Management Institute.

Project Management Institute (PMI) 2004. *A Guide to the Project Management Body of Knowledge (PMBOK® Guide)*. Newtown Square, PA: PMI Publishing.

9

Project Communicaton, Tracking, and Reporting

CHAPTER OVERVIEW

In this chapter, you will learn about developing an effective communications plan to better track, monitor, and report the project's progress. After studying this chapter, you should understand and be able to:

■ Identify and describe the processes associated with the Project Management Body of Knowledge (PMBOK®) area called project communications management, which includes project communications planning, information distribution, performance reporting, and managing stakeholders.

■ Describe several types of reporting tools that support the communications plan.

■ Apply the concept of earned value and discuss how earned value provides a means of tracking and monitoring a project's scope, schedule, and budget.

■ Describe how information may be distributed to the project stakeholders and the role information technology plays to support project communication.

INTRODUCTION

Information technology projects historically have demonstrated a poor track record for a variety of reasons. Often unrealistic project plans are created from inaccurate estimates, and, as a result, projects have little chance of achieving their objectives. As you saw earlier, various tools and techniques for estimating IT projects exist; but consistently developing accurate and realistic estimates remains a challenge. Much of an organization's capability to consistently and accurately estimate IT projects lies with well defined processes, experience, and an information base of past projects.

Still, developing a realistic and effective project plan is only part of the solution. The project manager must also have a clear picture of how the actual progress or work compares to the original baseline plan. Seldom do things go according to plan, so the project manager must have the means to monitor and manage the project.

This will allow him or her to make well informed decisions, take appropriate actions when necessary, or make adjustments to the project plan.

Communication is important for successful project management. The PMBOK® area called project communications management includes:

- *Communications planning*—Communications planning attempts to answer the following questions:
  - How will information be stored?
  - How will knowledge be stored?
  - What information goes to whom, when, and how?
  - Who can access what information?
  - Who will update the information and knowledge?
  - What medium of communication is best?
- *Information distribution*—Focuses on getting the right information to the right people in the right format. Moreover, information distribution should also include organizing minutes from meetings and other project-related documents.
- *Performance reporting*—Focuses on the collection and dissemination of project information to the various project stakeholders. This should include status reports, progress reports, and forecast reports.
- *Managing stakeholders*—Ensuring that clear, consistent, and timely communication satisfies the information needs and resolves any issues of the project stakeholders.

A project communications plan should include not only the information content for each stakeholder, but the delivery of this information. Although a great deal of information can be obtained or distributed informally, the communications plan should detail the way data will be collected and the form in which information will be provided. Although an opportunity exists for capturing and disseminating data and information, an IT-based solution may not be practical or effective in all situations. For example, email is a powerful tool for communication; however, richer forms of communication, such as face-to-face meetings, may be more appropriate or effective in certain situations.

Various stakeholders have different roles and interests in the project. For example, the project client or sponsor may be interested in the overall performance of the project. More specifically, is the work defined in the project scope being completed on time and within budget? And what is the likelihood of the project achieving its MOV? On the other hand, members of the project team may be interested in knowing what tasks or activities they should be working on and how their work relates to the activities and tasks being performed by other members of the project team. It is important that the people doing the actual work be empowered to take corrective action so that problems and issues can be resolved sooner rather than later.

Therefore, it is important that everyone associated with the project know what is going on. A project manager can develop an accurate and realistic project plan, but that plan is useless unless it is executed effectively. And, because no project plan is perfect, communication allows timely and intelligent adjustments to be made so it can be executed effectively.

When it comes to projects, no one likes surprises. Nothing can diminish a project manager's credibility faster than the surfacing of unexpected situations that should have been identified some time before. The unexpected does, however, happen, and no one can anticipate every conceivable contingency in a project plan. Senior management or the client will feel much more comfortable with a project manager who identifies unexpected problems, challenges, or issues early on and then suggests various alternatives. The project manager's credibility will rise if the project sponsor is confident that someone knows what the problem is and knows how to fix it. Conversely, confidence will diminish if problems surface that should have been identified earlier.

MONITORING AND CONTROLLING THE PROJECT

Let's begin with a story about a project manager. This particular project manager developed a detailed project plan and had several experienced and skillful members on the project team. The estimates were realistic and reasonably accurate. About two months into the project, one of the key team members left the project to play lead guitar in a country-western band. Although the team member/lead guitarist gave the usual two weeks' notice, the project manager could only recruit and hire a less experienced replacement. The learning curve was steep. The other team members were asked to help this new person (in addition to doing their other work). As a result, many of the tasks and activities defined in the project plan took longer than expected. The schedule was in trouble. With a deadline looming in the near distance, the team began to take short cuts in an attempt to keep the project on track. The original project plan, for example, called for one month of testing. That seemed like a lot of time, so maybe the system could be tested in two weeks. As more and more tasks began to slip, testing was cut to one week, and then two days—okay, maybe the team could test the programs as they write them. Then they would just have to keep their fingers crossed and hope everything worked when the system was implemented!

On the day the system was supposed to be delivered, the project manager had to confess to senior management that the system was "not quite ready." Senior management then asked when the system *would* be ready. The project manager then sheepishly explained that there were a few *minor* setbacks due to unforeseen circumstances out of the project manager's control. Senior management once again asked when the system *would* be ready. After some hemming and hawing, the project manager explained that the project would take twice as long and cost twice as much to complete if the originally agreed-upon scope was maintained. Needless to say, the *new* project manager kept senior management informed about the project's progress.

The moral of this story is that project sponsors do not like surprises. Regardless of how well a project is planned, unexpected situations will arise. These unexpected events will require adjustments to the project schedule and budget. In fact, many cost overruns and schedule slippages can be attributed to poorly monitored projects (Van Genuchten 1991). The project plan gets thrown out the window as slippage in one task or activity causes a chain reaction among the other interdependent tasks. If that task is on the critical path, the problem can be especially serious. You know you're in trouble if a project sponsor asks, Why didn't you tell me about this earlier?

The problem may gain strength and momentum as the project manager attempts to react to these unexpected events. For example, resources may be reassigned to different tasks or processes and standards may be overlooked. The wiser project manager, on the other hand, will try to be more proactive and recognize the impact of these unexpected situations in order to plan and act in a definite and timely manner. As our story points out, many times things happen on projects that are out of our control. If the project manager had identified this problem earlier and analyzed its impact, he or she could have apprised senior management of the situation and then laid out several alternative courses of action and their estimated impact on the project's schedule and budget. Although senior management may not like the news, they probably would respect the project manager for providing an early warning. Moreover, having a feeling that someone is in control will give them a sense of security.

A project manager *will not* lose credibility because an unexpected event or situation arises. He or she *will*, however, lose (or gain) credibility in terms of how they handle a particular situation. By addressing the problem early, the chain reaction and impact on other project activities can be minimized. There will be less impact on the project's schedule and budget.

Therefore, planning and estimating are not sufficient. A project needs an early warning system to keep things on track. This early warning system allows the project manager to control and monitor the project's progress, identify problems early, and take appropriate corrective action.

The baseline plan acts as an anchor, allowing the project manager to gauge the project's performance against planned expectations. Once the baseline plan is approved, actual progress can be benchmarked to what was planned. This process is often referred to as comparing *actual to plan* performance, and the comparison is relatively easy and straightforward when using a project management software package.

Project control ensures that processes and resources are in place to help the project manager monitor the project. Although one might believe control has a negative connotation, it provides the capability to measure performance, alerts the project manager to problem situations, and holds people accountable. Controls also ensure that resources are being utilized efficiently and effectively while guiding the project toward its MOV. Controls can be either internal to the project (i.e., set by the project organization or methodology) or external (i.e., set by government or military standards). The control and monitoring activities of a project must be clearly communicated to all stakeholders. Everyone must be clear as to what controls will be in place and how data will be collected and information distributed.

THE PROJECT COMMUNICATIONS PLAN

The project communications plan can be formal or informal, depending on the needs of the project stakeholders and the size of the project. Regardless, communication is vital for a successful project. It is important that all of the project stakeholders know how their interests stand in relation to the project's progress.

Developing a communications plan starts with identifying the various stakeholders of the project and their information needs. Recall that stakeholder analysis helps the project manager and project team determine the different interests and roles of each of the stakeholders. Although some of the information contained in the stakeholder analysis may not be suitable for general dissemination, it provides a starting point for identifying who needs what information and when. Keep in mind that even stakeholders who may have a vested interest in the project *not* succeeding must be kept informed. Otherwise, a lack of communication and information can result in an attitude that "no news must be bad news," or speculation and frivolous assumptions that the project is in trouble.

Stakeholder	Reporting Requirements	Report/Metric	Reason
Sponsor or client	During periodic review meetings **Time Frame**: Considering projects with six months or more of duration, the project sponsor can be provided with this report monthly.	Project summary, budget, earned value	Sponsor or client will be concerned primarily with the strategic indicators including overall cost and value in the project. • Project summary report presents the overall cost that the project will incur. This report shows the baseline schedule and budget along with the actual schedule and budget and gives the project's overall status report. • The budget is also a top-of-view project summary of the cost for all tasks in the project. • Earned value report gives a top level summary of the project at a given status date. It also includes key metrics that monitor the health of the project
Project manager	At periodic intervals or even online **Time Frame**: This report can be sent to the project manager once in every two weeks for a typical six month or more project.	Earned value, project summary, slipping tasks, critical tasks, milestone, current activities reports, over budget tasks and resources	The project manager will be concerned with making both operational and strategic decisions. Therefore, reports that are primarily involved in tracking the current status of the project and its health are of utmost importance. The project manager would be required to be informed of the work progress compared to the baseline plan.
Project team	At periodic intervals **Time Frame**: Receiving this report weekly would help the team members benefit from it. They also need to get an updated copy in case of any changes in the schedule.	"Who Does What When" and "To Do List" reports	The project team would be concerned with day-to-day execution of the project. Issues like who does what and when, what is assigned to a team member would be key needs. In case of interdependent tasks, the team members can also see who performs preceding or succeeding tasks.

Figure 9.1 The Project Communications Plan

Figure 9.1 provides an example of a project communications plan. The idea behind this analysis is to determine:

- Who has specific information needs?
- What are those information needs?
- How will a particular stakeholder's information needs be met?
- When can a stakeholder expect to receive this information?
- How will this information be received?

This format helps clarify what all of the stakeholders know and what they will need to know. The following describes each of the areas for developing the communications plan:

- *Stakeholders*—Communication requires a sender, a message, and a receiver; however, we often focus mainly on the first two (Neuendorf 2002).

Stakeholders are individuals or groups who have a "stake" or claim in the project's outcome and, therefore, are the receivers of the project information we send. In general, this group would include the project sponsor or client, the project manager, and the project team because each would have a specific interest in the project's performance and progress. Other people, such as senior managers, financial and accounting people, customers, and suppliers, may have a special interest in the project as well. Therefore, it is important that we keep these special interests informed.

- *Information requirements*—A diverse group of stakeholders will result in diverse information requirements. Identifying the information requirements of the various stakeholders allows the project manager and project team to better determine the information reporting mechanisms, timings, and delivery medium for each stakeholder. Instead of a single report that may or may not meet the needs of each stakeholder, a particular report or metric can be designed to meet an individual stakeholder's needs and, therefore, improve communication with that stakeholder. In general, these information requirements will focus on scope, schedule, budget, quality, and risk. Depending on the needs of the stakeholder, the requirements and level of detail may be different.

- *Type of report or metric*—Depending on the information needs of a particular stakeholder, a specific report or reporting mechanism can be identified. These may include specific *canned*, or template, reports that are provided by a project management software tool or a custom report with specific metrics. In addition, reporting mechanisms may include formal or informal reviews of deliverables, milestones, or phases. Other reporting mechanisms, such as newsletters and other public relations tools, can serve a general population of stakeholders.

QUICK THINKING—POOR COMMUNICATION AND IT FAILURES

The Computer Technology Industry Association (CompTIA), a trade association located in Oakbrook, Illinois, conducted a survey of over 1,000 respondents and reported that poor communication is the reason most IT project fail. Insufficient resource planning and unrealistic deadlines were the second and third most cited reasons, respectively.

According to Kyle Gingrich, a director at CompTIA, "We wanted to run this poll specifically to find out what people perceived as pain points with relation to projects; what things really kept people up at night in relation to why their projects were failing." He adds that communication is a component at every project stage and that once managers understand the objectives of the project, the expected results, and budget restrictions, they need to communicate that information to everyone else. Gingrich also adds "You have to determine who you're going to communicate with, when you're going to communicate with the various people throughout the project, where you're going to be communicating with them. Are you going to be setting up meetings? Are you going to be just doing emails? How is that going to take place? What are you going to communicate?"

In addition, there are different ways and levels for communication depending on your audience. For example, executive-level managers need a high level of information to make decisions, but also need to tell their staff the reason for communication. For example, communication may be needed to resolve a conflict, to acquire more resources, or to keep people up to date on status of the project.

1. In the CompTIA survey almost 28 percent of the respondents said poor communication was the number one reason why projects failed, while about 18 percent attributed project failure to insufficient resource planning and 13 percent believed unrealistic deadlines were the cause. Could poor communication be an indirect result for insufficient resource planning and unrealistic deadlines? Why or why not?

SOURCE: Adapted from Linda Rosencrance, Survey: Poor Communication Causes Most IT Project Failures, *Computerworld*, March 9, 2007.

- *Timings/Availabilities*—The timing and availability of the reports set expectations for the stakeholder. Some stakeholders may feel they need up-to-the-minute or real time access to the project's performance and progress. Other stakeholders may have an almost casual interest. Set timing and availability to let people know when they will know. They also allow the project manager and team to stay focused by minimizing demands for ad hoc reports and status updates by powerful stakeholders.

- *Medium or format*—The medium or format defines how the information will be provided. Possible formats include paper reports, face-to-face, electronic files, email, or some other electronic format, such as the Web. Defining the format also sets expectations and allows the project manager to plan the resources needed to support the communications plan.

PROJECT METRICS

The communications plan described in the previous section is the output of the communications planning process. However, a project metric system must be in place to support the information requirements for all of the stakeholders. In general, project metrics should focus on the following key areas:

- Scope
- Schedule
- Budget
- Resources
- Quality
- Risk

Data to support these metric categories can be collected in a number of ways. For example, project team members may be asked to submit periodic reports or even time cards that describe what tasks they worked on, the time spent working on those tasks, and any other resources that they may have used on those tasks. In addition, the project team could report deliverables completed, function points, or even feature points. Data can be collected using expense reports, invoices, purchase orders, and so forth. Moreover, information can be provided informally through day-to-day contacts with various individuals or groups.

Collection of this data allows the project manager to compile a set of metrics that can be used to create the various reports for the stakeholders defined in the communications plan. A **project metric** may be defined as a qualitative measurement of some attribute of the project. This metric should be obtained from observable, quantifiable data (Edberg 1997). In addition, these metrics can be useful for developing a measurement program that allows the team and other stakeholders to gauge the efficiency and effectiveness of the work being done. Edberg suggests that a good project metric must be:

- *Understandable*—A metric should be intuitive and easy to understand; otherwise, the metric will be of little value and will most likely not be used.

- *Quantifiable*—A quantifiable metric is objective. A metric should have very little bias as a result of personal influence or subjectivity.

- *Cost effective*—Data must be collected in order to produce a metric. Subsequently, a metric should be relatively easy and inexpensive to create, and should not be viewed as a major disruption.

- *Proven*—A metric should be meaningful, accurate, and have a high degree of validity in order to be useful. The metric must measure exactly what one wants to measure. "What gets measured gets done!"

- *High impact*—Although the efficiency of computing a metric is important, the metric must be effective. Why measure something that has little impact on the project?

Meyer (1994) suggests that trying to run a team without a good measurement system is like trying to drive a car without a dashboard. He suggests the following principles as a guide:

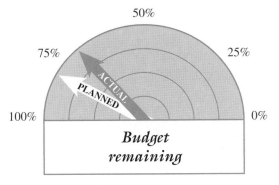

Figure 9.2   Dashboard Metric

- *A measurement system should allow the team to gauge its progress*—The project metrics should let the team know when to take corrective action rather than waiting for the project manager to intervene. Instead of using a measurement system to control a team, it should be used to empower the team to solve problems on its own.

- *The team should design its own measurement system*—The people actually doing the work know what metrics are best suited. However, a team should not develop project metrics or a measurement system without the aid of the project manager or other members of the organization because independent action could result in inconsistencies and parochial interests being served.

- *Adopt only a handful of measures*—The old saying "What gets measured gets done" can be an opportunity if the right metrics and measurement system are in place. Adding more and more measures as a means of encouraging team members to work harder can have the opposite effect. Collecting data to support a measurement system takes time and can interfere with the planned work. Having a few key measures keeps the team focused and creates minimal interference. In addition, these measures create a common language among team members and the other project stakeholders.

- *Measures should track results and progress*—Using the metaphor of a car's dashboard, Meyer suggests that an array of graphic indicators and easy-to-read gauges can be useful in helping a project team measure and track its own progress and in letting it know when to take corrective action. For example, a relative measure could be used to track the remaining project budget, as illustrated in Figure 9.2. As you can see, Figure 9.2 vividly shows that the project is consuming its budget faster than planned.

Earned Value

Suppose that we hired the infamous consulting firm Dewey, Cheatem, and Howe to develop an information system for your organization. The project is planned to cost $40,000 and take four months to complete. To keep things simple, let's also assume that the project requires 20 activities or tasks that are evenly divided over the four-month schedule. Since each task is expected to take the same amount of time, the expected cost per task is $2,000. This $2,000 is called the **planned value (PV)** because it is the planned or budgeted cost of work scheduled for an activity or component of the WBS. This information is summarized in Table 9.1.

Table 9.1   Planned Project Schedule and Budget

Task	Month 1	Month 2	Month 3	Month 4
1	$2,000			
2	$2,000			
3	$2,000			
4	$2,000			
5	$2,000			
6		$2,000		
7		$2,000		
8		$2,000		
9		$2,000		
10		$2,000		
11			$2,000	
12			$2,000	
13			$2,000	
14			$2,000	
15			$2,000	
16				$2,000
17				$2,000
18				$2,000
19				$2,000
20				$2,000
Total	**$10,000**	**$10,000**	**$10,000**	**$10,000**

However, the contract that we just signed stipulates that a payment of $10,000 must be made each month for four months. The total planned cost of our project is $40,000 and has a special name as well. It is called the **budget at completion (BAC)**. If we were to graph the planned expenditures for our project, the planned value for the cumulative cash flows would look like Figure 9.3.

At the end of the month, let's say that we receive the following invoice for $8,000:

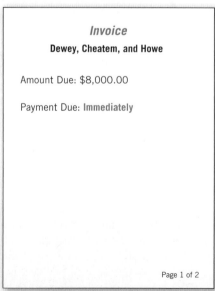

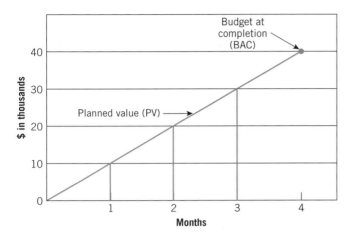

Figure 9.3   Planned Budget

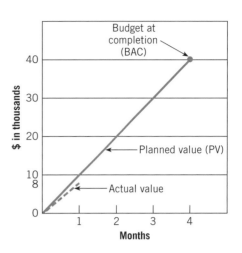

Figure 9.4   Planned Value versus Actual Cost

This actually sounds like good news! If you look at Figure 9.4, you will see that we planned to spend $10,000 at the end of the first month, but the invoice states that we only have to pay $8,000. It would appear that we are spending less money than planned. Since we will have to write a check to Dewey, Cheatem, and Howe for $8,000, we will call this the **actual cost (AC)**. It is the total cost incurred for completing a scheduled task or WBS component.

So is our project really $2,000 ahead of budget? Actually, all we are doing is staying within the budgeted or planned expenditures. To understand what's really going on, we need to look at the second page of the invoice.

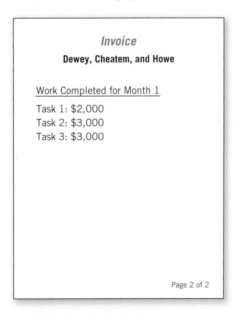

It looks like the consultants from Dewey, Cheatem, and Howe are only charging us $8,000, but they only completed three out of the five tasks that were expected to be completed by the end of the first month. As you can see in Table 9.2, we will have to pay $8,000 in actual costs for what we expected to achieve for $6,000.

Table 9.2   Planned, Actual, and Earned Values

Task	Month 1 Planned	Month 1 Actual	Month 1 Earned
1	$2,000	$2,000	$2,000
2	$2,000	$3,000	$2,000
3	$2,000	$3,000	$2,000
4	$2,000		-0-
5	$2,000		-0-
Cumulative	$10,000	$8,000	$6,000

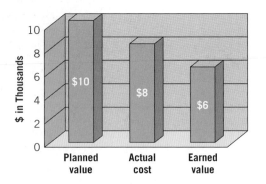

Figure 9.5   Comparison of Planned Value, Actual Cost, and Earned Value

This $6,000 is called the **earned value** (EV). EV provides a performance measurement that tells us how much of the budget we really should have spent for work completed so far. Figure 9.5 shows the relationship for planned value, actual costs, and earned value.

Using these basic values, we can extend our analysis and see how the earned value metric incorporates scope, budget, and schedule. For example, we can determine the **cost variance (CV)**, which is the difference between a WBS component's planned or estimated cost and its actual cost. The CV is computed by subtracting actual cost from earned value.

$$\text{Cost Variance (CV)} = \text{EV} - \text{AC}$$
$$= \$6,000 - \$8,000$$
$$= (-\$2,000)$$

A CV can be a positive or negative number. A negative $2,000 CV for our project is an important metric because it tells us that we have spent $8,000 in order to receive $6,000 worth of work. As you can see from our example, a negative CV indicates that the project is over budget. Unless appropriate action is taken to get the project back on track, we might have to increase the budget or reduce the project's scope. Conversely, a positive CV indicates that the project is under budget, while a CV of 0 would mean that the project is right on target.

In addition, we can also develop a performance metric for the project's schedule. The **schedule variance (SV)** shows the difference between the current progress of the project and its original or planned schedule. The SV is calculated by subtracting planned value from earned value.

$$\text{Schedule Variance (SV)} = \text{EV} - \text{PV}$$
$$= \$6,000 - \$10,000$$
$$= (-\$4,000)$$

As you can see, a negative SV indicates that the project is behind schedule. Conversely, a positive SV indicates that the project is ahead of schedule, and a SV of 0 would mean that the project is right on schedule.

The CV and SV performance metrics can be converted to efficiency indicators to reflect the cost and schedule performance of a project and as a basis for predicting the outcome.

A **cost performance index (CPI)** can be computed by taking the ratio of earned value to actual cost.

$$\text{Cost Performance Index (CPI)} = \text{EV}/\text{AC}$$
$$= \$6,000/\$8,000$$
$$= .75$$

A CPI of .75 tells us that for every $1.00 we spent so far on this project, only $0.75 was really being completed. A CPI greater than 1.0 indicates that we are ahead of our planned budget, while a CPI of less than 1.0 means we are encountering a cost overrun. It follows, then, that a CPI equal to 1.0 indicates that we are right on our planned budget.

We can also develop a schedule efficiency metric. A **schedule performance index (SPI)** is calculated by dividing earned value by planned value.

$$\text{Schedule Performance Index (SPI)} = \text{EV}/\text{PV}$$
$$= \$6,000/\$10,000$$
$$= .60$$

The SPI provides a ratio of the work performed to the work planned or scheduled. Therefore, for every $1.00 of work that was expected to be completed, only $0.60 was accomplished. A SPI greater than 1.0 indicates that the project is ahead of schedule, while a SPI of less than 1.0 means we are behind schedule. A SPI equal to 1.0 indicates that the project is right on schedule.

Table 9.3 summarizes the earned value performance metrics for our example. This analysis can be made for each task or for a larger component of the WBS.

We planned on spending $40,000 on this project, but is this total cumulative planned value at completion (i.e., the BAC) still realistic? Often cost and schedule overruns do not correct themselves and may become worse as the project progresses (Fleming and Koppelman 1996). In fact, if things continue as they are in our example, we can get a better feel for how much our project will end up costing us by using these performance metrics to forecast the project's final performance.

According to the *PMBOK® Guide*, we can compute the **expected time complete (ETC)**, which provides an estimate for completing the scheduled work that remains. The ETC can be just a revised schedule and budget if, for example, Dewey, Cheatem, and Howe informs us that the project work will take longer and cost more than we originally planned. On the other hand, we can calculate the ETC using one of the following formulas, depending whether the variances we encountered so far are typical of the variances we expect in the future.

Table 9.3   Summary of Project Performance Metrics

Task	Planned Value (PV)	Actual Cost (AC)	Earned Value (EV)	Cost Variance (CV)	Schedule Variance (SV)	Cost Performance Index (CPI)	Schedule Performance Index (SPI)
1	$2,000	$2,000	$2,000	-0-	-0-	1.00	1.00
2	$2,000	$3,000	$2,000	($1,000)	-0-	0.67	1.00
3	$2,000	$3,000	$2,000	($1,000)	-0-	0.67	1.00
4	$2,000			-0-	($2,000)	—	0.00
5	$2,000			-0-	($2,000)	—	0.00
Cumulative	$10,000	$8,000	$6,000	($2,000)	($4,000)	0.75	0.60

If we believe the variances encountered so far will most likely continue for the remainder of the project, then ETC is calculated by subtracting the cumulative earned value to date from the budget at completion and then dividing by the cumulative cost performance index. Although this may sound complicated, the formula is just:

$$\text{ETC (typical variances)} = (\text{BAC} - \text{Cumulative EV to date})/\text{Cumulative CPI}$$
$$= (\$40,000 - \$6,000)/.75$$
$$= \$45,333.33$$

Therefore, if things continue as they are, it appears that we will need just over $45,000 to complete the remainder of the project. On the other hand, if we believe that our consultants encountered some problems early in the project, and that the likelihood of encountering similar problems during the remainder of the project is low, we can use an alternative formula. In this case, a more appropriate formula for computing ETC is just subtracting the cumulative earned value to date from the budgeted cost of completion.

$$\text{ETC (atypical variances)} = \text{BAC} - \text{Cumulative EV to date}$$
$$= \$40,000 - \$6,000$$
$$= \$34,000$$

Therefore, the remaining funds to complete the remaining work on this project can range from $34,000 (as defined in our original planned budget) or more than $45,000. However, according to the *PMBOK® Guide*, we can calculate the **estimate at completion (EAC)** to estimate the most likely total or final value based on our project's performance and any risks that should be considered.

One way of estimating EAC is to develop a new estimate based on the actual costs incurred so far and a new estimate time to complete. So, for example, Dewey, Cheatem, and Howe might tell us that the new cost for our project might be the $8,000 in cumulative actual costs incurred so far plus a revised ETC of $38,000. In this case, the cost of our project will jump from $40,000 to $46,000.

However, if we are less willing to rely on guesstimates, we can use the project performance metrics to develop a more realistic picture for our project. There are two approaches for calculating EAC. The first approach is more appropriate when the variances encountered are viewed as being typical of future variances. EAC is computed by incorporating the CPI in the following formula:

$$\text{EAC (typical variances)} = \text{Cumulative AC} + (\text{BAC} - \text{Cumulative EV})/$$
$$\text{Cumulative CPI}$$
$$= \$8,000 + (\$40,000 - \$6,000)/.75$$
$$= \$53,333.33$$

As you can see, our total project budget will cost around $53,333 if things continue as they are. But what if these variances were atypical and we don't expect similar variances to occur in the future? Then a more appropriate formula would be to add cumulative actual costs and budget at completion and then subtract cumulative earned value.

$$\text{EAC (atypical variances)} = \text{Cumulative AC} + \text{BAC} - \text{Cumulative EV}$$
$$= \$8,000 + \$40,000 - \$6,000$$
$$= \$42,000$$

Table 9.4 Earned Value = PV × Percent Complete

Task	Planned Value	Percent Complete	Earned Value
A	$1,000	100%	$1,000
B	$1,500	100%	$1,500
C	$2,000	75%	$1,500
D	$800	50%	$400
E	$1,200	50%	$600
Cumulative	$6,500		$5,000

It appears that the final cost of our project will be somewhere between $42,000 and $53,333.

Earned value can also be calculated in terms of completion of the planned value. In this case, we just multiply the planned value of an activity, task, or WBS component by its percentage of completion. Table 9.4 provides an example of a project with five tasks. In this case, earned value is equal to planned value multiplied by its associated percent complete. An earned value analysis with the various project performance metrics described previously can then be used.

 ## REPORTING PERFORMANCE AND PROGRESS

Once the project data have been collected, the project manager can use it to update the project plan. An example of an updated project plan using Microsoft Project® is illustrated in Figure 9.6.

The project manager has a wide variety of software tools at his or her disposal, these include project management software, spreadsheets, databases, and so forth.

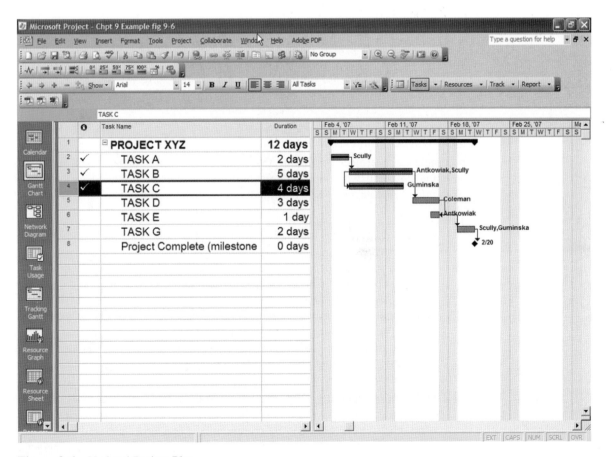

Figure 9.6 Updated Project Plan

In addition, project reporting tends to fall under one of the following categories:

- *Reviews*—Project reviews may be formal or informal meetings that include various project stakeholders. These reviews may focus on specific deliverables, milestones, or phases. The purpose of a review is to not only show evidence that the project work has been completed, but also that the work has been completed according to certain standards or agreed-upon requirements. For example, the project team may present the project plan to the project sponsor. If the scope, schedule, and budget are agreed upon, then the project plan is accepted and the project may proceed to the next phase. In addition, review meetings provide a forum for surfacing issues, problems, and even opportunities that may require stakeholders to negotiate or make decisions.

- *Status reporting*—A status report describes the present state of the project. In general, a status report compares the project's actual progress to the baseline plan. Analogous to a balance sheet used by accountants, a status report may include, for example, a variance analysis that compares actual schedule and cost information to the baseline schedule and budget.

- *Progress reporting*—A progress report tells us what the project team has accomplished. This report may compare the activities or tasks that were completed to the activities or tasks outlined in the original project network.

- *Forecast reporting*—A forecast report focuses on predicting the future status or progress of the project. For example, it may include a trend analysis that tells us when the project is most likely to finish and how much it will cost.

Many project management software tools, such as Microsoft Project®, provide a variety of *canned* reports or templates. The categories of reports found in Microsoft Project® are illustrated in Figure 9.7.

INFORMATION DISTRIBUTION

To complete the project communications plan, the project manager and team must determine how and when the required information will be provided to the various stakeholders. Although a variety of media exist, most communication will involve:

- *Face-to-face meetings*—A great deal can be learned from face-to-face meetings. Such meetings may range from informal conversations to more formal meetings and presentations. The advantage of face-to-face meetings is that one can see other people's expressions and body language. Sometimes the way someone says something can be more expressive than what they say. On the other hand, face-to-face meetings require arranging of schedules and additional costs if travel is involved. Certain issues and problems, of course, require people to meet face to face. For example, firing (or dehiring?) a person should only be done face to face. There are a number of war stories in the business world about people who found out they were let go by email. The general consensus is that this is an insensitive and tactless way to treat people.

- *Telephone, electronic mail, and other wireless devices*—It appears that we are in the midst of a wireless and mobile revolution. Cellular phones, pagers, and other wireless devices are commonplace and have increased our mobility and accessibility. Although these communication devices are not as personal as face-to-face meetings, they certainly make communication possible when

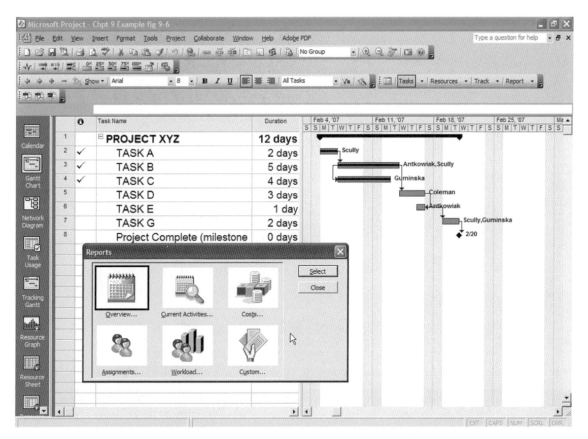

Figure 9.7   Project Report Categories

people cannot be at the same place at the same time. The communications plan (and project budget) should also include electronic means for the project team and other stakeholders to communicate.

- *Collaboration technology*—There are a variety of information technology tools to support communication and collaboration. For example, a project team could use Internet- or Web-based technologies to develop an Internet, intranet, or extranet application. The difference between Internet, intranet, or extranet really depends on who has access to the information stored on the server. For example, an Internet application would be available to anyone who has access to the World Wide Web or Internet. An intranet, on the other hand, may be developed using the same technology, but access is limited to the project team by means of passwords or firewalls. An extranet may include others outside the immediate project team or organization, such as the project sponsor or client. Similar to an intranet, access may be limited through the use of passwords or firewalls.

In summary, the sharing of information includes support for communication, collaboration, and the sharing of knowledge among the various project stakeholders. Then, the project communications plan must focus on supporting communication for people working in different places and at different times. Figure 9.8 provides an example of how people communicate and interact today and some examples of how they may be supported.

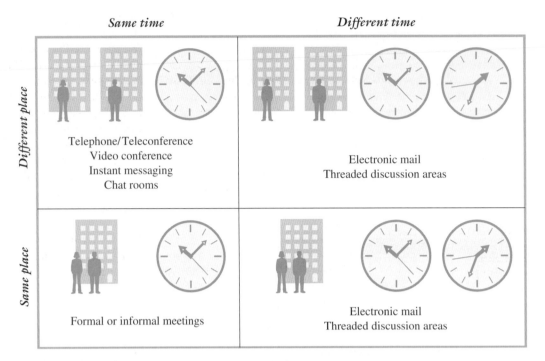

Figure 9.8   Communication and Collaboration Matrix

QUICK THINKING—COMMUNICATION AND MENTORING

Effective communication is one of the most important aspects of a project manager's job. Today, many project managers spend up to 90 percent of their time communicating with their project team, project sponsor, and other project stakeholders. However, up until about 20 years ago this wasn't the case. Back then the cornerstone of project management was scheduling. This involved a meticulous and complex process that often involved plotting and hanging large Gantt charts on walls. Today, anyone with access to a personal computer and project management software can "do" projects. However, this won't guarantee success unless you have the right "soft skills" that allow you to communicate effectively with people.

If communication is so important, then why is it so difficult to do well? Often project managers have been in an organization for some time and their familiarity with people, processes, and technology may create a "comfort zone" that is difficult to leave. Second, many times project managers are functional experts who rise through the ranks because of their expertise. Unfortunately, they may have limited or undeveloped communication skills and knowledge about project management processes. Lastly, communication issues often are a result of a person's personality. This may influence how they deal with other people and comfort in using a particular communication style. For

example, a person who does not like to deal with others face to face may prefer to rely on email as a primary way to communicate.

Since most project managers do not have a degree in project management or a PMP certification, mentoring can be a valuable means for teaching and learning project management. A project management mentor can play the role of advisor, coach, or teacher to work with a project manager in different ways.

1. How could a project mentor work with an inexperienced project manager in the following situations?

   a. A project manager who doesn't want to try a new approach because she is afraid that suggesting a change may be "rocking the boat"—i.e., disruptive change.

   b. A project manager who was a star programmer and is now leading her first software development project.

   c. A project manager who often screams at his project team when he feels that the team is not going to make a scheduled milestone.

SOURCE: Adapted from Bruce Anich, Talk to Me, *Projects@Work*, February 16, 2006.

CHAPTER SUMMARY

Project planning and estimation are critical processes. To be useful, the project plan must be accurate and realistic. But, even the best plans will fall short if the project manager and team do not follow the plan or know when to take corrective action. It is almost impossible to plan for all contingencies that may arise during a project, so the project plan should be revised and updated on an as-needed basis. For example, estimates made early in the project life cycle may be based on limited information. As new information comes to light, the project manager should revise estimates and project schedule and budget to ensure that the project plan is accurate and realistic. In addition, a project manager must be in control of the project and identify problems, issues, and situations that will impact the project schedule and budget. A measuring and reporting system allows the project manager to identify these situations early so that various alternative courses of action can be assessed and recommended. Although project sponsors may not like bad news, it is better for a project manager to deliver problematic news early than to have upper management unaware of the situation. Hoping that the problem will go away is not an effective action.

The Project Management Body of Knowledge defines a set of processes to support project communications management. This area of knowledge includes communications planning, information distribution, performance reporting, and administrative closure. The output of these processes is to develop a project communications plan. This plan may be formal or informal, depending on the size of the project and number of project stakeholders, but it must support an effective and efficient means of communication among the various project stakeholders. The development of this plan focuses on identifying the various stakeholders and their information requirements. In addition, the plan also sets expectations in terms of how and when this information will be made available.

The project communications plan must include a variety of ways for project stakeholders to communicate. More specifically, project stakeholders should be able to communicate:

- Same time–same place
- Same time–different places
- Different times–same place
- Different times–different places

Today, a number of IT-based tools and technologies are available to support the different needs of the project stakeholders; however, richer forms of communication, such as face-to-face meetings, are important and more appropriate in certain situations.

REVIEW QUESTIONS

1. Why should a project manager be concerned with monitoring a project's progress?

2. Describe the PMBOK® area called communications planning.

3. Compare the information requirements of a project sponsor to those of a project team member. How are they similar? How are they different?

4. What kinds of contingencies would be difficult for a project manager to anticipate when developing the project plan?

5. What is the purpose of a project communications plan? What kinds of things should this plan address?

6. Why is effective and efficient communication vital to a project?

7. What are project metrics?

8. Describe the qualities of a good project metric.

9. Why should a project have a good measurement system in place?

10. Discuss why a good measuring system should guide the progress of the project team rather than management alone.

11. What are the advantages of having the project team design its own metrics and measuring system?

12. If "what gets measured gets done," why should a project team not be accountable to numerous project metrics?

13. Describe the concept of earned value.

14. What is PV?

15. What is EV?

16. What is BAC?

17. Describe how the SPI and CPI can be used to forecast the final cost of a project.

18. What is a project review and what purpose does it serve?

19. What is a status report?
20. What is a progress report?
21. What is a forecast report?
22. When are face-to-face meetings more appropriate than phone calls or email?
23. Describe the role IT can play in supporting the project communications plan.
24. When are Internet, intranet, and extranet applications appropriate in supporting the project communications plan?

25. Give an example of a type of meeting project stakeholders may have under the following circumstances. Describe how IT might support their communication needs

   a. Same time–same place
   b. Same time–different places
   c. Different times–same place
   d. Different times–different places

EXTEND YOUR KNOWLEDGE

1. Using the WWW, visit each of the following Web sites:

   ■ www.lotus.com
   ■ www.microsoft.com/sharepoint
   ■ www.microsoft.com/groove

   Write a report that compares each specific tool. Be sure that the answers to the following questions are included:

   a. What technology platforms does each product require?
   b. Describe the functionality of each particular tool.
   c. Can you download and try each product before buying it?
   d. How well would each particular tool support communication and collaboration among project stakeholders?

   e. If you were a project manager interested in supporting communication and collaboration among the project's various stakeholders, which one of these tools might you choose? Why?

2. Given the following information, is this project in trouble? Explain.

Task	Planned Value	Earned Value	Actual Cost
A	$384.62	$384.62	$384.62
B	$576.92	$576.92	$576.92
C	$1,461.54	$1,461.54	$1,096.15
Total	$2,423.08	$2,423.08	$2,057.69

 GLOBAL TECHNOLOGY SOLUTIONS

Tim Williams stood in the doorway of Kellie Matthews' office. Kellie looked up from her notebook computer just as Tim was about to knock. "Hi, Tim. Come in and have a seat while I send off this email," Kellie said.

Tim took a seat at the small, round conference table next to the window. Kellie clicked the send button, then got up from her desk and took a seat at the table across from Tim.

"So how are things going?" Kellie asked.

Tim leaned back in his chair. "So far, I think we're doing fine," he said. "We still have to make a few more changes to our revised project plan, but the changes are minor and we should get the final approval from Husky Air's management later this week. Then we can start on the real work."

Kellie smiled, "That's great news, Tim! So what do we have to do before we start development?"

Tim chuckled. "I'm glad you asked. I remember working on a project a few years ago. Everything was going well—the project was achieving its goal and was right on schedule and budget. The problem was that the project sponsor didn't know it. In fact, he thought the project was in trouble and that no one wanted to deliver the bad news."

Kellie sat back in her chair. "I see how one could assume that no news is bad news. So what happened?" she asked.

Tim gazed out the window and said, "It took several meetings with the client to smooth things over. I remember we had to stop in the middle of development to gather all kinds of project information to document what was done, what we were working on currently, and what we had left to finish. It really slowed the project down and we almost missed an important milestone."

Kellie thought for a moment. Then she said, "It sounds like a communication problem—or rather a lack of communication that created a problem. Is there anything I can do to help?"

Tim gave Kellie a sly smile. "It's funny you should ask. I was just going to ask for your help in devising a way for tracking and reporting the progress of the project. Besides, you're great with numbers!"

Kellie laughed, "I just knew you were up to something the minute I saw you standing at my door. I would say the first thing we need to do is develop some kind of communications plan that outlines how we'll communicate with the client. The plan should include a list of the stakeholders and outline what information they will need and when they will need it."

Tim started writing the ideas in his PDA. "That's a great idea," he said. "The project management software package I'm using to create the plan will allow me to benchmark our actual progress to our baseline plan. In fact, there are several *canned* reports that I can create and give to the client and to the team. Perhaps we can even schedule some face-to-face meetings or reviews with the client to let them know not only how things are going, but to address any issues or problems that need to be resolved."

Kellie leaned forward to get a better look at what Tim was entering into his PDA. "I think we'll also have to set up some way for the team to communicate with each other and with us. I've been playing around with a couple of software collaboration tools. Maybe I can set something up for the team members to use. They will be able to have online discussions and share documents with each other. They can even use the collaboration tool as a repository to store their learning cycles and lessons learned."

Tim looked up from his PDA and said, "That sounds terrific. I can keep an updated copy of the project plan in the repository. In fact, team members can even put their status and progress reports in the repository so we'll all know how things are going at any given time. Everyone will have access to the same information. Thanks, Kellie, you've been a big help as always."

Kellie smiled and answered, "Why don't you get started on the communications plan, while I start putting together our collaboration and reporting system. I think it would be a good idea to get the team members' input since they're the ones who will be making the most use of this system."

Tim got up from his chair, still entering thoughts in his PDA. "Okay," he said, as he walked to the door. "Why don't we plan on meeting again tomorrow with the team to polish these ideas?"

Both Tim and Kellie said quick good-byes. Kellie returned to her computer.

Things to Think About

1. Why is communication among project stakeholders so important?

2. What kinds of information will the various stakeholders need?

3. What role does information technology play in supporting a communications plan?

4. When is face-to-face communication more appropriate than communication through email?

 # HUSKY AIR ASSIGNMENT—PILOT ANGELS

Earned Value Analysis

Suppose that the testing of the Pilot Angels system has been outsourced to another organization called Bug Busters. This company is located in another country and has marketed themselves as specialists in software testing. You have signed a contract and sent them a copy of all the code, database tables, and files they need to fulfill their end of the contract. The total expected cost or expected budget at completion for this "subproject" is $12,000. The contract stipulates that four payments must be made after completion of each of the four testing phases.

The first phase of testing went as planned, but, due to some problems encountered, the second payment that you authorized was more than planned. The project manager in charge of testing has assured you that the few problems they encountered could not be helped and that she does not expect them to continue in the remaining phases. As a smart project manager, you have asked Bug Busters for a work breakdown structure (WBS) and an update of their progress because you are not so sure that these problems are atypical and may continue throughout the testing process.

		Planned Value	Actual Cost	Percent Complete	Earned Value
Phase 1: Test Planning					
Develop unit test plan		$500	$500	100%	$500
Develop integration test plan		$600	$600	100%	$600
Develop acceptance test plan		$550	$550	100%	$550
	Payment 1:	$1,650	$1,650		$1,650
Phase 2: Unit Testing					
Code walkthrough with team		$600	$700	100%	$600
Test software units		$800	$1,200	100%	$800
Identify programs that do not meet specifications		$500	$500	100%	$500
Modify code		$1,200	$1,300	100%	$1,200
Retest units		$300	$400	100%	$300
Verify code meets standards		$200	$200	100%	$200
	Payment 2:	$3,600	$4,300		$3,600
Phase 3: Integration Testing					
Test integration of all modules		$600	$600	100%	$600
Identify components that do not meet specifications		$300	$500	75%	$225
Modify code		$1,400	$1,400	50%	$700
Retest integration of modules		$400	$400	75%	$300
Verify components meet standards		$200	$200	80%	$160
	Payment 3:	$2,900	$3,100		$1,985
Phase 4: Acceptance Testing					
Business review with client		$400		0%	
Client tests system		$800		0%	
Identify units and components that do not meet specifications		$550		0%	
Modify code		$800		0%	
Retest units and components		$700		0%	
Verify that system meets standards		$600		0%	
	Payment 4:	$3,850			

Using the following information, conduct an earned value analysis to determine whether you believe the project will remain within its original planned budget of $12,000.

Use a spreadsheet software package to determine the Estimate at Completion (EAC) for both typical and atypical variances.

 # CASE STUDIES

A Case of Collaborative Technologies and a Virtual Team

Jim Tisch, director of Knowledge Management Solutions for Robbins Gioia, LLC, describes a successful rollout of an enterprise content management system and portal platform to support an internal knowledge management initiative for more than 700 employees. The nine targeted outcomes of this project included:

- Improving the management of corporate knowledge
- Bringing together employee knowledge to create best practices for customer engagements

- Creating effective taxonomies and metadata to effectively search for knowledge artifacts
- Developing a rich online environment to promote employee community
- Integrating core business application systems to improve operational efficiencies
- Centralized reporting to provide access to key business intelligence
- Reducing operating costs
- Replacing paper-based processes with online forms and workflow
- Sharing intellectual capital

Aside from these aggressive requirements, the core team members were geographically dispersed among five states across the United States. As the project neared completion, the project team met at the company's headquarters for a final face-to-face review and decision to launch. This virtual project team met all of its deadlines and goals and made the decision to go live.

Tisch reflected how this was possible without the team relying on face-to-face conference room meetings. As Tisch believes, "The team succeeded by leveraging the use of collaborative technologies, following some online rules of engagement, having a strong virtual work ethic, and demonstrating good communication behaviors. It also succeeded because of trust, empowerment, management, and dedication to the program."

The virtual team relied on collaborative online workspaces to capture issues, schedules, tasks, and other key project information. Other collaboration tools, such as instant messaging, were useful for quick communication and discussion among team members. All of these online tools together provided an online virtual high performance team. However, some basic rules of engagement added to these technologies:

- Even though there were time zone differences, the team was online with presence technology at designated times during the day.

- Instant messaging tags such as "busy" or "on a call" were respected.

- Status reports were stored in a central workspace.

- Issues, risks, etc. were discussed during regularly scheduled conference calls.

- Documents and other files were tagged and stored in a central workspace.

- WebEx sessions allowed team members to share each other's desktops and allowed for program review sessions.

In addition, Tisch credits the success of the project to several additional factors. These include following a rapid applications development approach rather than a traditional "waterfall" approach and management's support in allowing the practice of telecommuting. As Tisch summarizes, "Businesses must embrace the Web as a platform and utilize its strengths for managing a geographically dispersed project team. If you have not looked at enterprise instant messaging, shared workspaces, Web conferencing, presence, etc., for how they can improve the collaboration and communication of your project teams, now is the time. The confinement of brick and mortar meetings has passed; today's workforce is more mobile and agile."

1. What is the importance of having rules of engagement to successfully support a virtual team when using collaborative technologies? Can you come up with any other rules that could be added?

2. Jim Tisch describes a number of advantages for using collaborative technologies. What resistance might be encountered if, for example, older workers were expected to use these technologies?

3. *Optional:* Using the Web as a resource, design a suite of available collaborative technologies that would support a geographically dispersed project team located in New York City, San Francisco, and Beijing. What specific communication needs would each technology support?

SOURCE: Adapted from Jim Tisch, Know-Go, *Projects@Work*, October 25, 2007.

Social Software for Project Management

Social software is an emerging technology that is being applied to a wide range of applications to support personal communication and relationships using an electronic network. Social networking Web sites such as Facebook® and MySpace® are examples of social software, as are blogs and wikis. Other types of social software such as virtual worlds—such as Second Life® or SimCity™—instant messaging, and email may fit into this category.

The term blog, short for Web log, focuses on a specific topic or interest. It is a Web site that allows people to post journal entries, with the most recent posting at the top. Many organizations are using blogs to communicate a corporate position or message to the public. People create and participate in blogs to chronicle their daily lives or to make their views and ideas public. Blogs can also include pictures or video clips that can be viewed by anyone on the Web or by a select few within an organization, if protected by a firewall. Readers can post comments that can evolve into a type of conversation.

Wiki is short for the Hawaiian term "wiki wiki," which means quick, and is a Web site that allows people to edit content collectively. The main difference between a blog and a wiki is that an author's post on a blog remains unaltered, while a wiki allows for shared authorship where people can add new content or change existing content without permission. Proponents of wikis believe that collaborative authorship provides a type of synergy that is greater than the sum of each individual author's contribution. Similar to blogs, a wiki can be open to the public or restricted within the organization. Blogs and wikis can also be combined into a hybrid technology that combines the best features of each tool. Articles, postings, or other content can be arranged in reverse chronological order on a main page like a blog, but allows for the content to be edited like a wiki.

Today, blogs and wikis are viewed as new types of organizational collaboration tools. While many people still rely on email as a primary source of communication, they are finding that email makes it difficult to find what they need or to manage documents effectively. Often important information is buried in an inbox, and searching for this information can be inefficient. Moreover, sharing information via email can be disorganized and haphazard because this information can be passed along largely on the prerogative of the sender. This can be in terms of the "to" or "cc" (carbon copy), or "bc" (blind copy) fields. As Chris Alden, vice president with an enterprise blogging company called Six Apart, suggests "If there is information in a cc storm and you're not on it, then you don't have any idea about what's going on. With blogs, information about specific topics lives on the intranet, and critical information can be broadcast to all who want to see it and who have permission to see it." In addition, another disadvantage of email is that when an individual leaves an organization their email account is deleted, along with any valuable information that was in that person's account. As Anil Dash, chief evangelist for Six Apart points out "It's forever lost. If it's a blog, it doesn't disappear when that person leaves."

Blogs and wikis are becoming more common in organizations because they are relatively inexpensive and easy to set up and maintain. Because these technologies are browser based, there is a short learning curve for the users. For example, Eugene Roman is a group president of systems and technology at Bell Canada and uses an enterprise blog as a forum where employees can discuss new product ideas, streamline processes, or even find new ways to cut energy costs. The blog effort was called "ID-ah" and first used by a few hundred employees in 2006. By the end of 2007, Bell Canada employees have submitted over 1,000 ideas with about 3,000 comments on those ideas. Of those 1,000 ideas, 27 have been culled for review and 12 have been implemented.

Interest in organizational wikis and blogs is growing as project teams are beginning to use them to improve communication, create a sense of community, and as a medium for collaboration and document management. They can provide a central location for meeting notes, files, calendars, ideas, and schedules.

1. Social software can provide a number of opportunities for managing projects. What are some challenges or issues that should be considered before a project team implements a blog or a wiki?

2. Jonathan Edwards, an analyst with the Yankee Group, states, "Some people clutch to their corporate email boxes as if they were cigarettes. They're hopelessly addicted. We're all so accustomed to it. You can't change the way people work overnight." Blogs and wikis have a number of advantages over email. As a project manager, how could you reduce your project team's resistance to rely less on email and embrace the use of social software?

3. Come up with an application specific to project management that uses social software. This could include a blog, wiki, instant messaging, or even a virtual world simulator.

SOURCE: Adapted from John K. Waters, ABC: An Introduction to Blogs and Wikis in the Business World, *CIO Magazine*, July 06, 2007; C. G. Lynch, How to Use Enterprise Blogs to Streamline Project Management, *CIO Magazine*, December 07, 2007; C. G. Lynch, Seven Reasons for Your Company to Start an Internal Blog, *CIO Magazine*, June 20, 2007.

 # BIBLIOGRAPHY

Edberg, D. T. 1997. Creating a Balanced Measurement Program. *Information Systems Management* (Spring): 32–40.

Fleming, Q. W. and J. M. Koppelman. 1996. *Earned Value Project Management*. Newtown Square, PA: Project Management Institute.

Meyer, C. 1994. How the Right Measures Help Teams Excel. *Harvard Business Review* (May–June): 95–103.

Neuendorf, S. 2002. *Project Measurement*. Vienna, VA: Management Concepts.

Project Management Institute (PMI) 2004. *A Guide to the Project Management Body of Knowledge (PMBOK® Guide)*. Newtown Square, PA: PMI Publishing.

Van Genuchten, M. 1991. Why is Software Late? An Empirical Study of Reasons for Delay in Software Development. *IEEE Transactions on Software Engineering* 17(6).

10

IT Project Quality Management

CHAPTER OVERVIEW

The focus of this chapter will be on several concepts and philosophies of quality management. By learning about the people who founded the quality movement over the last sixty years, we can better understand how to apply these philosophies and teachings to develop a project quality management plan. After studying this chapter, you should understand and be able to:

- Describe the Project Management Body of Knowledge (PMBOK®) area called project quality management (PQM) and how it supports quality planning, quality assurance, quality control, and continuous improvement of the project's products and supporting processes.

- Identify several quality gurus, or founders of the quality movement, and their role in shaping quality philosophies worldwide.

- Describe some of the more common quality initiatives and management systems that include ISO certification, Six Sigma, and the capability maturity model (CMM) for software engineering.

- Distinguish between verification and validation activities and how these activities support IT project quality management.

- Describe the software engineering discipline called configuration management and how it is used to manage the changes associated with all of the project's deliverables and work products.

- Apply the quality concepts, methods, and tools introduced in this chapter to develop a project quality plan.

INTRODUCTION

What is quality? Before answering that question, keep in mind that quality can mean different things to different people. For example, if we were comparing the quality of two cars—an expensive luxury car with leather seats and every possible option to a lower priced economy car that basically gets you where you want to go—many people might be inclined to say that the more expensive car has higher quality.

Although the more expensive car has more features, you might not consider it a bargain if you had to keep bringing it back to the shop for expensive repairs. The less expensive car might start looking much better to you if it were more dependable or met higher safety standards. On the other hand, why do car manufacturers build different models of cars with different price ranges? If everyone could afford luxury cars, then quality comparisons among different manufacturers' cars would be much easier. Although you might have your eyes on a luxury car, your current financial situation (and subsequent logic) might be a constraint. You might have to buy a car you could afford.

Therefore, it is important not to define quality only in terms of features or functionality. Other attributes such as dependability or safety may be just as important to the customer. Similarly in software development, we can build systems that have a great deal of functionality, but perform poorly. On the other hand, we can develop systems that have few features or limited functionality, but fewer defects.

However, we still need a working definition of quality. The dictionary defines quality as "an inherent or distinguishing characteristic; a property," or as something "having a high degree of excellence." In business, quality has been defined in terms of "fitness for use" and "conformance to requirements." "Fitness for use" concentrates on delivering a system that meets the customer's needs, while "conformance to requirements" centers more on meeting some predefined set of standards. Therefore, quality depends on the needs or expectations of the customer. It is up to the project manager and project team to define accurately those needs or expectations, while allowing the customer to remain within resource constraints.

Although the concepts and philosophies of quality have received a great deal of attention over the last 60 years in the manufacturing and service sectors, many of these same ideas have been integrated into a relatively new discipline or knowledge area called project quality management (PQM). The Project Management Body of Knowledge defines PQM as:

> PQM processes include all of the activities of the performing organization that determine quality policies, objectives, and responsibilities so that the project will satisfy the needs for which it was undertaken. It implements the quality management system through the policy procedures and processes of quality planning, quality assurance, and quality control with continuous process improvement activities conducted throughout, as appropriate. (*PMBOK® Guide*, 179)

Moreover, PMBOK® defines the major quality management processes as:

- *Quality planning*—Determining which quality standards are important to the project and deciding how these standards will be met.
- *Quality assurance*—Evaluating overall project performance regularly to ensure that the project team is meeting the specified quality standards.
- *Quality control*—Monitoring the activities and results of the project to ensure that the project complies with the quality standards. In addition, the project organization as a whole should use this information to eliminate causes of unsatisfactory performance and implement new processes and techniques to improve project quality throughout the project organization.

Therefore, PQM should focus on both the *product* and *process* of the project. From our point of view, the project's most important product is the information system solution that the project team must deliver. The system must be "fit for use" and "conform to specified requirements" outlined in both the project's scope and requirements definition. More importantly, the IT product must add measurable value to the sponsoring organization and meet the scope, schedule, and budget objectives. Quality can, however, also be built into the project management and software development processes. A **process** refers to the activities, methods, materials, and measurements used to produce the product or service. We can also view these processes as part of a quality chain where outputs of one process serve as inputs to other project management processes (Besterfield, Besterfield-Michna, et al. 1999).

By focusing on both the product and chain of project processes, the project organization can use its resources more efficiently and effectively, minimize errors, and meet or exceed project stakeholder expectations. The cost of quality, however, can be viewed as the cost of conforming to standards (i.e., building quality into the product and processes) as well as the cost of not conforming to the standards (i.e., rework). Substandard levels of quality can be viewed as waste, errors, or the failure to meet the project sponsor's or client's needs, expectations, or system requirements (Kloppenborg and Petrick 2002).

Failing to meet the quality requirements or standards can have negative consequences for all project stakeholders and impact the other project objectives. More specifically, adding additional work or repeating project activities will probably extend the project schedule and expand the project budget. According to Barry Boehm (1981), a software defect that takes one hour to fix when the systems requirements are being defined will end up taking 100 hours to correct if not discovered until the system is in production. Moreover, poor quality can be an embarrassment for the project manager, the project team, and the project organization. For example, one of the most widely publicized software defect stories was the faulty baggage-handling software at the Denver International Airport. Bugs in the software delayed the opening of the airport from October 1993 to February 1995 at an estimated cost of $1,000,000 a day! Newspaper accounts reported that bags were literally chewed up and contents of bags were flying through the air (Williamson 1997).

The concepts and philosophies of quality management have received a great deal of attention over the years. Although popularized by the Japanese, many organizations in different countries have initiated quality improvement programs. Such programs include ISO certification, six steps to Six Sigma initiatives, or awards such as the Deming Prize or the Malcolm Baldrige National Quality Award. More recently, the capability maturity model (CMM) has provided a framework for software quality that focuses on assessing the process maturity of software development within an organization. Based on writings and teachings of such quality gurus as Shewhart, Deming, Juran, Ishikawa, and Crosby, the core values of these quality programs have a central theme that includes a focus on the customer, incremental or continuous improvement, problem detection and correction, measurement, and the notion that prevention is less expensive than inspection. A commitment to these quality initiatives, however, often requires a substantial cultural change throughout the organization.

In this chapter, you will learn how the concepts of quality management can be applied to IT project management. We will also extend these concepts to include a broader view of PQM in order to support the overall project goal and objectives. As illustrated in Figure 10.1, PQM will not only include the concepts, teachings, tools, and methods of quality management, but verification/validation and change control.

Verification and validation (V&V) activities within PQM should be carried out throughout the project life cycle. They require the project team to ask continually, Are we building the right product? Are we building the product the right way? Therefore,

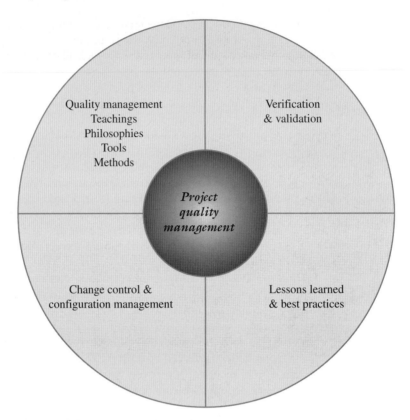

Figure 10.1 Project Quality Management

the project quality plan should not only focus on final testing of the system at the end of the project life cycle, but on all project deliverables. Finding and fixing problems earlier in the project life cycle is less costly than having to deal with them in the later stages of the project. Finding problems early not only leads to less rework later, but saves the project manager and project team from having to deal with embarrassing issues and problems once the project's product is in the hands of the project sponsor or end customer.

In addition, software development often requires a number of people to work on multi-versions of documents, programs, and database files that are shared and distributed among various project stakeholders. Change control in the form of configuration management, therefore, is a method of code and document management to track and organize the different versions of documents and files. It keeps the project team more focused and reduces the likelihood of errors.

In addition, knowledge management and the lessons learned can be implemented as best practices and incorporated in projects throughout the organization. Such changes lead to both continuous improvement and to a maturing of IT project management processes. Taken together, the concepts of quality management, V&V activities, change control, and knowledge management support the overall PQM plan. The plan not only helps improve the overall quality of the project's product and processes, but can lead to a competitive advantage for the project organization because the project will have a greater likelihood of achieving its expected organizational value and support the scope, schedule, and budget objectives.

QUICK THINKING—WHY DO WE ACCEPT LOW-QUALITY SOFTWARE?

Would you buy a car even if you had to agree to a contract not to hold the manufacturer liable for any damages or harm even if the car maker was negligent? Probably not, but many times that's exactly what you do when you mindlessly click the button to agree to an end user license agreement (EULA). Many EULAs today protect the software vendor from liability due to their negligence and only cover the cost of the CD on which the software is delivered. This can have a major impact as many organizations purchase software that becomes the backbone of their infrastructure. Unfortunately, as many organizations are under pressure to do more with fewer resources, so are software vendors. Pressure to get software out the door as quickly as possible often compromises the due diligence of quality and testing. While no one wants to deliver low-quality software, why does it still happen? One reason is history. Many software users have a history of expecting, accepting, and putting up with poor-quality software. In addition, the "historical" or traditional model of software development centers on software development teams following a serial or waterfall model where each step in the development process depends on the completion of a previous step or process. For example, requirements definition leads to design, coding, testing, and implementation. These processes are primarily the domain of the software developers and any quality assurance teams become

involved only later in the software development cycle. Subsequently, quality becomes an afterthought instead of being built in from the beginning. Deadlines and features or functionality take priority over quality. Lastly, the quality assurance team historically sits physically outside the development team and has less power or influence. That's too bad, because software vendors need to realize that proper software quality is critical and should not be undercut. Quality can be an important product feature and can be a powerful differentiator that can provide a competitive advantage.

1. Suppose an organization is considering the purchase of an enterprise software package that would be a mission critical application for that organization. How could the project manager ensure that her company does not purchase a low-quality software solution?

2. Choose a software package and find the EULA (usually you can find this under Help). What is the software vendor's liability for a defect in the software?

SOURCE: Adapted from Alberto Svoia, Click Here to Accept Poorly Tested, Low-Quality Software, *Computerworld*, February 10, 2006.

The remainder of this chapter will focus on introducing and delving into several PQM concepts. It includes an overview of the quality movement and a brief history of the people who provided the cornerstones for quality initiatives. It also provides an overview of several quality systems. Finally, it gives a framework to support PQM that integrates the concepts and philosophies of quality, as well as the concepts of software testing, configuration management, and knowledge management.

QUALITY TOOLS AND PHILOSOPHIES

In this section, we will focus on the concepts associated with quality management, a brief history and the people who helped shape this important area. This knowledge may help in giving us a better understanding of how to apply these concepts, ideas, and tools to IT projects.

Scientific Management

As a young man, Frederic W. Taylor (1856–1915) worked as an apprentice at the Enterprise Hydraulics Shop. Supposedly, he was told by the older workers how much he should produce each day—no more, no less (Woodall, Rebuck, et al. 1997). The workers were paid on a piece rate basis, and if they worked harder or smarter, management would change the production rates and the amount a worker would be paid. These arbitrary rates, or *rules of thumb*, restricted output, and workers produced well below their potential.

Later, as an engineer, Taylor became one of the first to study systematically the relationships between people and tasks. He believed that the production process could become more efficient by increasing the specialization and the division of labor. Using an approach called the **scientific management**, Taylor believed that a task could be broken down into smaller tasks and studied to identify the best and most efficient way of doing each subtask. In turn, a supervisor could then teach the worker and ensure that the worker did only those actions essential for completing the tasks, in order to remove human variability or errors. At that time, most workers in U.S. factories were immigrants, and language barriers created communication problems among the workers, their supervisors, and even with many coworkers. The use of a stopwatch as a basis for time-motion studies provided a more scientific approach. Workers could produce at their full potential, and arbitrary rates set by management would be removed. To be successful, Taylor also believed that the scientific management approach would require a spirit of cooperation between the workers and management.

Although the scientific management approach became quite popular, it was not without controversy. Many so-called efficiency experts ignored the human factors and tended to believe that profits could be increased by speeding up the workers. Dehumanizing the workers led to conflict between labor and management that eventually laid the foundation for labor unions. Just three years before Taylor died, he acknowledged that the motivation of a person can affect output more than just engineered improvements (Woodall, Rebuck, et al. 1997).

Control Charts

In 1918, Walter Shewhart (1891–1967) went to work at the Western Electric Company, a manufacturer of telephone equipment for Bell Telephone. At the time, engineers were working to improve the reliability of telephone equipment because it was expensive to repair amplifiers and other equipment after they were buried underground. Shewhart believed that efforts to control production processes were impeded by a lack of information.

Shewhart also believed that statistical theory could be used to help engineers and management control variation of processes. He also reasoned that the use of tolerance limits for judging quality was short sighted because it provided a method of judging quality for products only after they were produced (Woodall, Rebuck, et al. 1997). In 1924, Shewhart introduced the **control chart** as a tool better to understand variation and to allow management to shift its focus away from inspection and more toward the prevention of problems and the improvement of processes.

A control chart provides a picture of how a particular process is behaving over time. All control charts have a center line and control limits on either side of the center line. The center line represents the observed average, while the control limits on either side provide a measure of variability. In general, control limits are set at $\pm 3\sigma$ (i.e., ± 3 sigma) or $\pm 3s$, where σ represents the population standard deviation and s represents the sample standard deviation. If a process is normally distributed, control limits based on three standard deviations provides .001 probability limits.

Variation attributed to **common causes** is considered normal variation and exists as a result of normal interactions among the various components of the process—i.e., chance causes. These components include people, machines, material, environment,

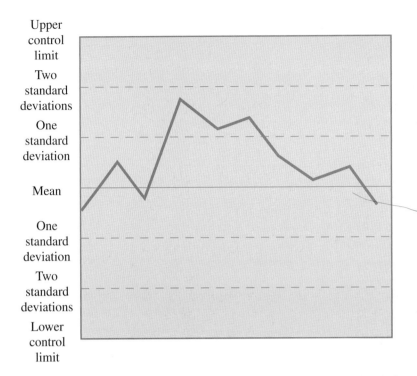

Upper control limit

Two standard deviations

One standard deviation

Mean

One standard deviation

Two standard deviations

Lower control limit

Figure 10.2 Control Chart for a Process within Statistical Control

and methods. As a result, common cause variation will remain stable and exhibit a consistent pattern over time. This type of variation will be random and vary within predictable bounds.

If chance causes are only present, the probability of an observation falling above the upper control limit would be one out of a thousand, and the probability of an observation falling below the lower control limit would be one out of a thousand as well. Since the probability is so small that an observation would fall outside either of the control limits by chance, we may assume that any observation that does fall outside of the control limits could be attributed to an **assignable cause**. Figure 10.2 provides an example of a control chart where a process is said to be stable or in **statistical control**.

Variations attributed to assignable causes can create significant changes in the variation patterns because they are due to phenomena not considered part of the normal process. An example of assignable cause variation can be seen by the pattern in Figure 10.3. This type of variation can arise because of changes in raw materials, poorly trained people, changes to the work environment, machine failures, inadequate methods, and so forth (Florac, Park, et al. 1997). Therefore, if all assignable causes are removed, the process will be stable because only chance factors remain.

To detect or test whether a process is not in a state of statistical control, one can examine the control chart for patterns that suggest nonrandom behavior. Florac and his colleagues suggest several tests that are useful for detecting these patterns:

- A single point falls outside the 3σ control limits.
- Although we won't get too bogged down in statistics, we can look for patterns that suggest that the observed data are not statistically independent. A process may not be in control if we observe:
  - At least two of three successive values that fall on the same side of and more than two standard deviations from the centerline.
  - At least four out of five successive values that fall on the same side of and more than one standard deviation away from the centerline.
  - At least eight successive values that fall on the same side of the centerline.

Control charts are a valuable tool for monitoring quality; however, it is important to keep in mind that one can see patterns where patterns may not exist (Florac, Park, et al. 1997).

The Total Quality Movement

While working at the Western Electric Hawthorne plant in Chicago, Illinois, during the 1920s, W. Edwards Deming (1900–1993) became aware of the extensive

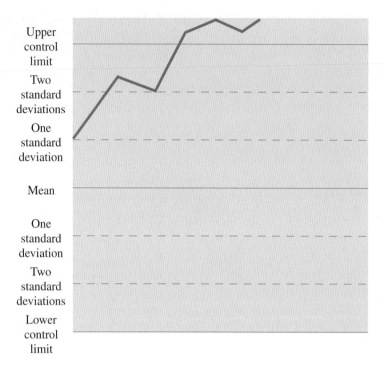

Figure 10.3   Control Chart for a Process Not in Statistical Control

division of labor. Management tended to treat the workers as just another cog in the machinery. Moreover, the workers were not directly responsible for the quality of the products they produced. Final inspection was used as a means to control quality and reductions in the per piece rate reflected scrap and rework.

Deming met Shewhart while working at Bell Laboratories in New Jersey in the 1930s and became interested in Shewhart's application of statistical theory. Deming realized that costly inspections could be eliminated if workers were properly trained and empowered to monitor and control the quality of the items they produced.

Deming and his teachings were relatively unnoticed in the United States. Soon after World War II, Japan was a country faced with the challenge of rebuilding itself after devastation and military defeat. Moreover, Japan had few natural resources so the export of manufactured goods was essential. Unfortunately, the goods that it produced were considered inferior in many world markets.

To help Japan rebuild, a group called the Union of Japanese Scientists and Engineers (JUSE) was formed to work with U.S. and allied experts to improve the quality of the products Japan produced. As part of this effort, in the 1950s Deming was invited to provide a series of day-long lectures to Japanese managers. The focus of these lectures was statistical control and quality. The Japanese embraced these principles, and the quality movement acquired a strong foothold in Japan. In tribute to Deming, the Japanese even named their most prestigious quality award the Deming Prize.

Until the 1970s, Deming was virtually unknown in the West. In 1980, an NBC documentary entitled *If Japan Can, Why Can't We* introduced him and his ideas to his own country and the rest of the world. Many of Deming's philosophies and teachings are summarized in his famous 14 points for quality that are outlined and discussed in his book *Out of the Crisis* (Deming 1982).

FOURTEEN POINTS FOR QUALITY

1. Create constancy of purpose toward improvement of products and services, with the aim to become competitive, and to stay in business, and to provide jobs.
2. Adopt the new philosophy. We are in a new economic arena. Western management must awaken to the challenge, must learn responsibilities, and take on leadership for change.
3. Cease dependencies on inspection to achieve quality. Eliminate the need for inspection on a mass basis by building quality into the product in the first place.
4. End the practice of awarding business on the basis of price tag. Instead, minimize total cost. Move toward a single supplier for any one item, on a long-term relationship of loyalty and trust.
5. Improve constantly and forever the system of production and service—to improve quality and productivity, and thus constantly decrease costs.
6. Institute training on the job.
7. Institute leadership.
8. Drive out fear, so that everyone may work effectively for the company.
9. Break down barriers between departments.
10. Eliminate slogans, exhortations, and targets for the workforce asking for zero defects and new levels of productivity.
11. (a) Eliminate work standards (quotas) on the factory floor. Substitute leadership. (b) Eliminate management by objective. Eliminate management by numbers, numerical goals. Substitute leadership.
12. Create pride in the job being done.
13. Institute a vigorous program of education and self-improvement.
14. Put everybody in the company to work to accomplish the transformation.

SOURCE: W. Edwards Deming, *Out of the Crisis*, Cambridge, MA: The MIT Press, 1982.

Quality Planning, Improvement, and Control

Joseph Juran's (1904–2008) philosophies and teachings have also had an important and significant impact on many organizations world wide. Like Deming, Juran started out as an engineer in the 1920s. In 1951 he published the *Quality Control Handbook*, which viewed quality as "fitness for use" as perceived by the customer. Like Deming, Juran was invited to Japan by JUSE in the early 1950s to conduct seminars and lectures on quality.

Juran's message on quality focuses on his belief that quality does not happen by accident—it must be planned. In addition, Juran distinguishes external customers from internal customers. Juran's view of quality consists of a quality trilogy—quality planning, quality control, and quality improvement—that can be combined with the steps that make up Juran's Quality Planning Road Map.

Quality Planning

1. Identify who the customers are.
2. Determine the needs of those customers.
3. Translate those needs into our language.
4. Develop a product that can respond to those needs.
5. Optimize the product features so as to meet our needs as well as customer needs.

Quality Improvement

6. Develop a process that is able to produce the product.
7. Optimize the process.

Quality Control

8. Prove that the process can produce the product under operating conditions.
9. Transfer the process to Operations.

Cause and Effect of Diagrams, Pareto Charts, and Flow Charts

Kaoru Ishikawa (1915–1989) studied under Deming and believed that quality improvement is a continuous process that depends heavily on all levels of the organization—from top management down to every worker performing the work. In Japan this belief led to the use of quality circles that engaged all members of the organization. In addition to the use of statistical methods for quality control, Ishikawa advocated the use of easy-to-use analytical tools that included cause-and-effect diagrams (called the Ishikawa diagram, or fishbone diagram, because it resembles the skeleton of a fish), the Pareto chart, and flow charts.

Although the Ishikawa, or fishbone, diagram was introduced in an earlier chapter, it can be used in a variety of situations to help understand various relationships between causes and effects. An example of an Ishikawa diagram is illustrated in Figure 10.4. The effect is the rightmost box and represents the problem or characteristic that requires improvement. A project team could begin by identifying the major causes, such as people, materials, management, equipment, measurements, and environment, that may influence the problem or quality characteristic in question. Each major cause can then be subdivided in potential subcauses. For example,

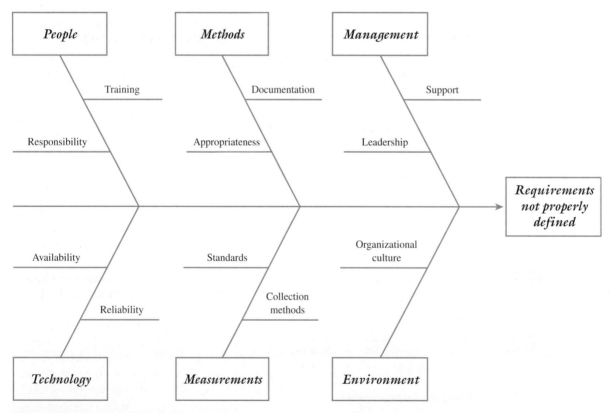

Figure 10.4   Ishikawa, or Fishbone, Diagram

causes associated with people may be lack of training or responsibility in identifying and correcting a particular problem. An Ishikawa diagram can be best developed by brainstorming or by using a learning cycle approach. Once the diagram is complete, the project team can investigate the possible causes and recommend solutions to correct the problems and improve the process.

Another useful tool is a **Pareto diagram**, which was developed by Alfred Pareto (1848–1923). Pareto studied the distribution of wealth in Europe and found that about 80 percent of the wealth was owned by 20 percent of the population. This idea has held in many different settings and has become known as the 80/20 rule. For example, 80 percent of the problems can be attributed to 20 percent of the causes.

Pareto diagrams can be constructed by (Besterfield, Besterfield-Michna, et al. 1999):

1. Determining how the data will be classified. It can be done by the nature of the problem, the cause, nonconformity, or defect or bug.
2. Determining whether frequency, dollar amount, or both should be used to rank the classifications.
3. Collecting the data for an appropriate time period.
4. Summarizing the data by rank order of the classifications from largest to smallest, from left to right.

Pareto diagrams are useful for identifying and investigating the most important problems by ranking problems in descending order from left to right. For example, let's say that we have tracked all the calls to a call center over a period of one week. If we were to classify the different types of problems and graph the frequency of each type of call, we would end up with a chart similar to Figure 10.5.

As you can see, the most frequent type of problem had to do with documentation questions. In terms of quality improvement, it may suggest that the user documentation needs to be updated.

In addition, **flow charts** can be useful for documenting a specific process in order to understand how products or services move through various functions or operations. A flow chart can help visualize a particular process and identify potential problems or bottlenecks. Standardized symbols can be used, but are not necessary. It is more important to be able to identify problems or bottlenecks, reduce complexity, and determine who is the next customer (Besterfield, Besterfield-Michna, et al. 1999). Figure 10.6, for example, documents the project management process for verifying a project's scope. The original customer who initiates the original project request might be the project's client or sponsor. The customer who receives the output of the scope verification process might be a specific member of the project team.

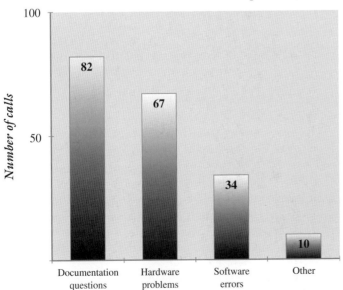

Figure 10.5 A Pareto Chart

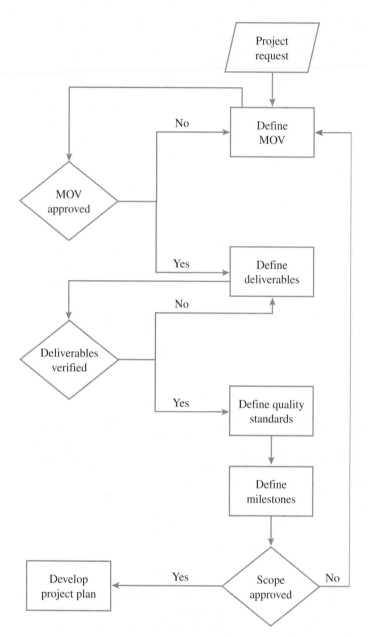

Figure 10.6 Flow Chart for Project Scope Verification

 QUALITY SYSTEMS

Although guilds were the first organizations to ensure quality standards, there are a number of different organizations and approaches for defining and implementing quality standards in organizations. **Standards** are documented agreements, protocols, or rules that outline the technical specifications or criteria to be used to ensure that products, services, processes, and materials meet their intended purpose. Standards also provide a basis for measurement because they provide a criterion, or basis, for comparison.

International Organization for Standardization (ISO)

One of the most widely known standards organizations is the International Organizations for Standardization (ISO). Although you may think the acronym should be IOS, the name for the organization is ISO and was derived from the Greek word *isos*, which means *equal*. The name avoids having different acronyms that would result from International Organization for Standardization being translated in different languages.

ISO was officially formed in 1947 after delegates from 25 countries had met in London the previous year with the intention of creating an international organization whose mission would be "to facilitate the international coordination and unification of industrial standards." ISO is not owned or managed by any national government, and today it has over 130 member organizations, with one member per country. Each participating member has one vote, regardless of its country's size or economic strength, to ensure that each member country's interests are represented fairly. As a result, each country has an equal say with respect to the standards that are adopted and published. Each member is then responsible for informing other interested organizations in his or her country of any relevant international standard opportunities and initiatives.

International standards are established for many technologies and industries. Countries that do business with each other need to have an agreed-upon set of standards to make the process of trade more logical and because a lack of standardization can create trade barriers. For example, credit cards adhere to a standard size and thickness so that they can be used world wide.

Although most of the ISO standards are specific to a particular product, material, or process, a set of standards make up the ISO 9000 and ISO 14000 families. These are known as "generic management system standards" in which the same standards can be applied to any size or type of organization in any industry. The term **management system** refers to the processes and activities that the organization performs. ISO 9000 was originally initiated in 1987 and focuses on quality management with respect to improved customer satisfaction and the continuous improvement of an organization's performance and processes. On the other hand, standards that fall under the ISO 14000 came about in 1997 and are concerned primarily with environmental management—that is, how an organization can minimize any harmful effects on the environment that may be caused by its activities and operations. Both the ISO 9000 and ISO 14000 families focus on continual process improvement.

To show that a product, service, or system meets the relevant standards, an organization may receive a certificate as proof. For example, many organizations have been issued ISO 9000 certificates as testaments that they have quality management systems in place and that their processes conform to the documented ISO standards. Again, keep in mind that these standards focus on processes, not products.

Today, two ISO standards pertain to software development: ISO 9001 and ISO/IEC 15504. One is ISO 9001 and is for organizations whose business processes range from design through development, as well as production, installation, and service. ISO 9001 consists of 20 standards, or requirements, that must be met for a quality system to be in compliance. Although ISO 9001 can be applied to all engineering disciplines, it is also relevant to software development.

If an organization decides that it would like to be ISO certified as meeting the ISO standards, it usually begins by studying the ISO guidelines and requirements. The organization then conducts an internal audit to make sure that every ISO requirement is met. After deficiencies or gaps are identified and corrected, the organization then has a third party called a **registrar** audit its quality management system. If the registrar finds that the organization meets the specified ISO standards and requirements, it will issue a certificate as a testament that the organization's products and services are managed and controlled by a quality management system that meets the requirements of ISO. ISO does not conduct the audits or issue certificates. In addition, an organization does not have to have a formal registration or certificate to be in compliance with the ISO standards; however, customers may be more likely to believe that an organization has a quality system if an independent third party attests to it.

Six Sigma (6σ)

The term *Six Sigma* was originated by Motorola (Schaumburg, Illinois) in the mid-1980s. The concept of Six Sigma came about as a result of competitive pressures by foreign firms that were able to produce higher quality products at a lower cost than Motorola. Even Motorola's own management at that time admitted that "our quality stinks" (Pyzdek 1999).

Sigma (σ) is a Greek letter and in statistics represents the standard deviation to measure variability from the mean or average. In organizations, variation is often the cause of defects or out-of-control processes and translates into products or services that do not meet customer needs or expectations. If a manufacturing process follows

Table 10.1 Sigma and Defects per Million

Sigma	Defects Per Million
1 σ	690,000
2 σ	308,537
3 σ	66,807
4 σ	6,210
5 σ	233
6 σ	3.4

a normal distribution, then the mean or average and the standard deviation can be used to provide probabilities for how the process can or should perform.

Six Sigma focuses on defects per opportunities (DPO) as a basis for measuring the quality of a process rather than products it produces, because products may vary in complexity. A defect may be thought of as anything that results in customer dissatisfaction. The sigma value, therefore, tells us how often defects are likely to occur. The higher the value of sigma, the lower the probability of a defect occurring. As illustrated in Table 10.1, a value of six sigma indicates that there will only be 3.4 defects per million, while three sigma quality translates to 66,807 defects per million. Table 10.2 provides several real-world examples that compare the differences between three sigma and six sigma quality.

Therefore, Six Sigma can be viewed as a quality objective whereby customer satisfaction will increase as a result of reducing defects; however, it is also a business-driven approach for improving processes, reducing costs, and increasing profits. The key steps in the Six Sigma improvement framework are the **D-M-A-I-C** cycle:

- *Define*—The first step is to define customer satisfaction goals and subgoals— for example, reduce cycle time, costs, or defects. These goals then provide a baseline or benchmark for the process improvement.

- *Measure*—The Six Sigma team is responsible for identifying a set of relevant metrics.

- *Analyze*—With data in hand, the team can analyze the data for trends, patterns, or relationships. Statistical analysis allows for testing hypotheses, modeling, or conducting experiments.

- *Improve*—Based on solid evidence, improvements can be proposed and implemented. The *Measure-Analyze-Improve* steps are generally iterative to achieve target levels of performance.

- *Control*—Once target levels of performance are achieved, control methods and tools are put into place in order to maintain performance.

To carry out a Six Sigma program in an organization, a significant investment in training and infrastructure may be required. Motorola adopted the following martial arts terminology to describe these various roles and responsibilities (Pyzdek 1999):

Table 10.2 Comparison of Three Sigma and Six Sigma

3σ	6σ
Five short or long landings at any major airport	One short or long landing in 10 years at all airports in the U.S.
Approximately 1,350 poorly performed surgical operations in one week	One incorrect surgical operation in 20 years
Over 40,500 newborn babies dropped by doctors or nurses each year	Three newborn babies dropped by doctors or nurses in 100 years
Drinking water unsafe to drink for about 2 hours each month	Water unsafe to drink for one second every six years

- *Master black belts*—Master black belts are people within the organization who have the highest level of technical and organizational experience and expertise. Master black belts train black belts and, therefore, must know everything a black belt knows. Subsequently, a master black belt must have technical competence, a solid foundation in statistical methods and tools, and the ability to teach and communicate.

- *Black belts*—Although black belts may come from various disciplines, they should be technically competent and held in high esteem by their peers. Black belts are actively involved in the Six Sigma change process.

- *Green belts*—Green belts are Six Sigma team leaders or project managers. Black belts generally help green belts choose their projects, attend training with them, and then assist them with their projects once the project begins.

- *Champions*—Many organizations have added the role of a Six Sigma champion. Champions are leaders who are committed to the success of the Six Sigma project and can ensure that barriers to the Six Sigma project are removed. Therefore, a champion is usually a high-level manager who can remove obstacles that may involve funding, support, bureaucracy, or other issues that black belts are unable to solve on their own

Although the concept of Six Sigma was initially used in a manufacturing environment, many of the techniques can be applied directly to software projects (Siviy 2001). The usefulness of Six Sigma lies in the conscious and methodical way of achieving customer satisfaction through the improvement of current processes and products and their design.

The Capability Maturity Model Integration (CMMI)

In 1986, the Software Engineering Institute (SEI), a federally funded research development center at Carnegie Mellon University, set out to help organizations improve their software development processes. With the help of the Mitre Corporation and Watts Humphrey, a framework was developed to assess and evaluate the capability of software processes and their maturity. This work evolved into the capability maturity model (CMM) (Humphrey 1988). The CMMI for Software version 1.0 was published in 1991 and provided an evolutionary path for organizations to improve their underlying software processes. Two years later, the CMMI was revised as version 1.1 with another revision planned for in 1997 as version 2.0. This planned version was never released, but it did serve as a basis for the Capability Maturity Model Integration (CMMI) initiative.

Since the original CMMI initiative in 1991, organizations have used a number of CMMs for different disciplines or areas. Although helpful, using several different models can be problematic because a particular model may limit process improvements to a specific area or discipline within the organization. Often these process improvements are not limited to a specific area but cut across different disciplines. As a result, the CMMI project was initiated to sort out the problem of using a number of CMMs (Chrissis, Konrad, and Shrum 2003). Currently, CMMI combined three models: The capability maturity model for software (SW-CMM), the system engineering capability model (SECM), and the integrated product development capability maturity model (IPD-CMM). The intent of CMMI was to combine these models into a single framework that could be used to improve processes across the organization. The CMMI framework was designed so that other disciplines could be integrated in the future. In this section, we will focus on how the CMMI can support software development.

The CMMI provides a set of recommended practices that define key process areas specific to software development. The objective of the CMMI is to offer guidance on how an organization can best control its processes for developing and maintaining software. In addition, the CMMI provides a path for helping organizations evolve their current software processes toward software engineering and management excellence (Paulk, Curtis, et al. 1993).

To understand how the CMMI may support an organization, several concepts must first be defined:

- *Software process*—A set of activities, methods, or practices and transformations used by people to develop and maintain software and the deliverables associated with software projects. Included are such things as project plans, design documents, code, test cases, user manuals, and so forth.

- *Software process capability*—The *expected* results that can be achieved by following a particular software process. More specifically, the capability of an organization's software processes provides a way of predicting the outcomes that can be expected if the same software processes are used from one software project to the next.

- *Software process performance*—The *actual* results that are achieved by following a particular software process. Therefore, the actual results achieved through software process performance can be compared to the expected results achieved through software process capability.

- *Software process maturity*—The extent to which a particular software process is explicitly and consistently defined, managed, measured, controlled, and effectively used throughout the organization.

One of the keys to the CMMI is using the idea of software process maturity to describe the difference between immature and mature software organizations. In an immature software organization, software processes are improvised or developed ad hoc. For example, a software project team may be faced with the task of defining user requirements. When it comes time to complete this task, the various members of the team may have different ideas concerning how to accomplish it. Several of the members may approach the task differently and, subsequently achieve different results. Even if a well defined process that specifies the steps, tools, resources, and deliverables required is in place, the team may not follow the specified process very closely or at all.

The immature software organization is characterized as being reactive; the project manager and project team spend a great deal of their time reacting to crises or find themselves in a perpetual state of *fire fighting*. Schedules and budgets are usually exceeded. As a result, the quality and functionality of the software system and the associated project deliverables are often compromised. Project success is determined largely by who is (or who is not) part of the project team. In addition, immature software organizations generally do not have a way of judging or predicting quality. Since these organizations operate in a perpetual crisis mode, there never seems to be enough time to address problem issues or improve the current processes.

Mature software organizations, on the other hand, provide a stark contrast to the immature software organization. More specifically, software processes and the roles of individuals are defined explicitly and communicated throughout the organization.

The software processes are consistent throughout the organization and improved continually based on experimentation or experiences. The quality of each software process is monitored so that the products and processes are predictable across different projects. Budgets and schedules are based on past projects so they are more realistic and the project goals and objectives are more likely to be achieved. Mature software organizations are proactive and they are able to follow a set of disciplined processes throughout the software project.

The CMMI defines five levels of process maturity, each requiring many small steps as a path of incremental and continuous process improvement. These stages are based on many of the quality concepts and philosophies of Shewhart, Deming, Juran, and Crosby (Paulk, Curtis, et al. 1993). Figure 10.7 illustrates the CMMI framework for software process maturity. These levels allow an organization to assess its current level of software process maturity and then help it prioritize the improvement efforts it needs to reach the next higher level (Caputo 1998).

Maturity levels provide a well defined evolutionary path for achieving a mature software process organization. With the exception of Level 1, each maturity level encompasses several key process areas that an organization must have in place in order to achieve a particular level of maturity. There are five levels of software process maturity.

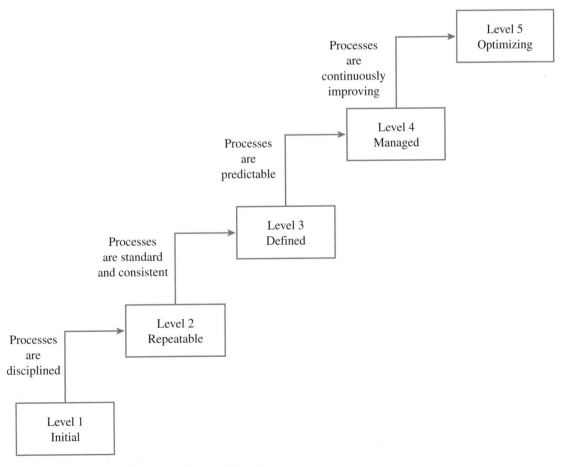

Figure 10.7 Levels of Software Process Maturity

Level 1: Initial   The initial level generally provides a starting point for many software organizations. This level is characterized by an immature software organization in which the software process is ad hoc and often reactive to crises. Few, if any, processes for developing and maintaining software are defined. The Level 1 software organization does not have a stable environment for software projects, and success of a project rests largely with the people on the project and not the processes that they follow. As a result, success is difficult to repeat across different projects throughout the organization.

Key Process Areas

■ No key process areas are in place.

Level 2: Repeatable   At this level, basic policies, processes, and controls for managing a software project are in place. Project schedules and budgets are more realistic because planning and managing new projects is based upon past experiences with similar projects. Although software processes between projects may be different at this level, the process capability of Level 2 organizations is more disciplined because software processes are more documented, enforced, and improving. As a result, many previous project successes can be repeated by other project teams on other projects.

Key Process Areas

■ *Software configuration management*—Supports the controlling and managing of changes to the various project deliverables and software products throughout the project and software life cycles.

■ *Software quality assurance*—Provides project stakeholders with an understanding of the processes and standards used to support the project quality plan.

■ *Software subcontract management*—Supports the selection and management of qualified software subcontractors.

■ *Software project tracking and oversight*—Ensures that adequate controls are in place to oversee and manage the software project so that effective decisions can be made and actions taken when the project's actual performance deviates from the project plan.

■ *Software project planning*—Establishes realistic plans for software development and managing the project.

■ *Requirements management*—Ensures that a common understanding of the user's requirements is established and becomes an agreement and basis for planning.

Level 3: Defined   At Level 3, software engineering and management processes are documented and standardized throughout the organization and become the organization's standard process. And, a group is established to oversee the organization's software processes and an organization-wide training program to support the standard process is implemented. Thus, activities, roles, and responsibilities are well defined and understood throughout the organization. The software process capability of this level is characterized as being standard, consistent, stable, and repeatable. However, this standard software process may be tailored to suit the individual characteristics or needs of an individual project.

Key Process Areas

- *Peer reviews*—Promotes the prevention and removal of software defects as early as possible and is implemented through code inspections, structured walkthroughs, and so forth.

- *Intergroup coordination*—Allows for an interdisciplinary approach where the software engineering group participates actively with other project groups in order to produce a more effective and efficient software product.

- *Software product engineering*—Defines a consistent and effective set of integrated software engineering activities and processes in order to produce a software product that meets the users' requirements.

- *Integrated software management*—Supports the integration of software engineering and management activities into a set of well-defined and understood software processes that are tailored to the organization.

- *Training programs*—Facilitates the development of individuals' skills and knowledge so that they may perform their roles and duties more effectively and efficiently.

- *Organization process definition*—Supports the identification and development of a usable set of software processes that improve the capability of the organization across all software projects.

- *Organization process focus*—Establishes organizational responsibility for implementing software processes that improve the organization's overall software process capability.

Level 4: Managed

At this level, quantitative metrics for measuring and assessing productivity and quality are established for both software products and processes. This information is collected and stored in an organization-wide repository that can be used to analyze and evaluate software processes and products. Control over projects is achieved by reducing the variability of project performance so that it falls within acceptable control boundaries. The software processes of software organizations at this level are characterized as being quantifiable and predictable because quantitative controls are in place to determine whether the process performs within operational limits. Moreover, these controls allow for predicting trends and identifying when assignable causes occur that require immediate attention.

Key Process Areas

- *Software quality management*—Establishes a set of processes to support the project's quality objectives and project quality management activities.

- *Quantitative process management*—Provides a set of quantitative or statistical control processes to manage and control the performance of the software project by identifying assignable cause variation.

Level 5: Optimizing

At the highest level of software process maturity, the whole organization is focused on continuous process improvement. These improvements come about as a result of innovations using new technology and methods and incremental process improvement. Moreover, the organization has the ability to identify its areas of strengths and weaknesses. Innovations and best practices based on lessons learned are identified and disseminated throughout the organization.

Key Process Areas

■ *Process change management*—Supports the continual and incremental improvement of the software processes used by the organization in order to improve quality, increase productivity, and decrease the cycle time of software development.

■ *Technology change management*—Supports the identification of new technologies (i.e., processes, methods, tools, best practices) that would be beneficial to the organization and ensures that they are integrated effectively and efficiently throughout the organization.

■ *Defect prevention*—Supports a proactive approach to identifying and preventing software defects.

As an organization's software process maturity increases, the difference between expected results and actual results narrows. In addition, performance can be expected to improve when maturity levels increase because costs and development time will decrease, while quality and productivity increase.

According to the SEI, skipping maturity levels is counter-productive. If an organization was evaluated at Level 1, for example, and wanted to skip to Level 3 or Level 4, it might be difficult because the CMMI identifies levels through which an organization must evolve in order to establish a culture and experiences.

Both the CMMI and ISO 9001 series of standards focus on quality and process improvement. A technical paper by Mark C. Paulk (1994) compares the similarities and differences between the CMMI and ISO 9001. His analysis indicates an ISO

QUICK THINKING—OPM3®

In 1998, the Project Management Institute (PMI) initiated a project to create the Project Management Maturity Model (OPM3®). While the traditional focus of the *Guide to the Project Management Body of Knowledge* (*PMBOK® Guide*) was the management of individual projects, the intent of OPM3® was to provide a global standard for managing projects across the organization. The OPM3® contains over 500 best practices. In addition to the capability maturity model (CMM), 26 other maturity models were reviewed during the research phase of the OPM3® project. OPM3® was originally published in 2003 and includes three interlocking elements:

■ *Knowledge*—Outlines project management and organizational maturity

■ *Assessment*—Describes the methods, processes, and procedures needed to assess maturity

■ *Improvement*—Presents a process for moving from a present maturity level to a higher maturity level

However, critics believe that the OPM3® is a fad exulted over by academics, management gurus, and

consultants. For example, Dhanu Kothari contends, "Ambiguities and uncertainties are part of project management. If a rational approach worked every time we wouldn't need project managers." Moreover, standard processes defined by maturity models can become overly bureaucratic, especially when strict adherence to a process is promoted over a simpler, more common sense approach. Organizations must also make a sizable commitment in terms of executive sponsorship, tools, training, and resources, so justifying the cost as well as the demonstrable progress can be tricky.

1. Why is it that a project team can follow a process and still fail?

2. Do maturity models neglect ambiguities and uncertainties of projects? Or do they do just the opposite?

SOURCE: Adapted from John L. Sullivan, Comparing CMMI® and OPM3®, AllPM.Com, http://www.allpm.com/modules.php?op=modload&name=News&file=article&sid=1659&mode=thread&order=0&thold=0; Abhay Padgaonkar, Assessing OPM3®, *Projects @Work*, January 15, 2007.

9001-compliant organization would satisfy most of the Level 2 and Level 3 goals. Although Level 1 organizations could be ISO 9001 compliant, it may be difficult for these organizations to remain compliant. In turn, there are many practices in the CMMI that are not addressed by ISO 9001, and it is, therefore, possible for a Level 1 organization to be ISO 9001 compliant. A Level 2 organization should have little difficulty in receiving ISO 9001 certification.

After reading this section, you may be wondering which quality system is best. Should an organization focus on ISO certification? Or, should it concentrate its efforts on the CMMI? Although the market may dictate a particular certification, an organization should be focused on continuous improvement that lead to competitive advantage and not necessarily on a certificate or maturity level (Paulk 1994).

THE IT PROJECT QUALITY PLAN

All project stakeholders want quality; unfortunately, there is no commonly accepted approach for PQM so many project managers approach it differently (Lewis 2000). Therefore, a basic framework will be introduced here to guide and integrate the knowledge areas of quality planning, quality assurance, quality control, and quality improvement. This framework provides a basic foundation for developing an IT project quality plan to support the project's quality objectives. This plan may be formal or informal, depending on the size of the project; however, the underlying philosophies, standards, and methods for defining and achieving quality should be well understood and communicated to all project stakeholders. Moreover, the project quality plan should support the project organization, regardless of whether it is attempting to meet ISO or CMMI requirements or self-imposed quality initiatives and objectives.

PQM also becomes a strategy for risk management. The objectives of PQM are achieved through a quality plan that outlines the goals, methods, standards, reviews, and documentation to ensure that all steps have been taken to ensure customer satisfaction by assuring them that a quality approach has been taken (Lewis 2000). Figure 10.8 provides a representation of the IT project quality plan discussed in this section.

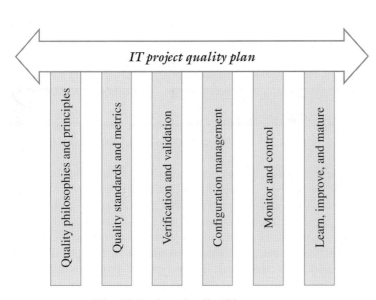

Figure 10.8   The IT Project Quality Plan

Quality Philosophies and Principles

Before setting out to develop an IT project quality plan, the project and project organization should define the direction and overall purpose for developing the project quality plan. This purpose should be grounded upon the quality philosophies, teachings, and principles that have evolved over the years. Although several different quality gurus and their teachings were introduced in this chapter, several common themes can provide the backbone for any organization's plan for ensuring quality of the project's processes and product. These ideas include: a focus on customer satisfaction, prevention of mistakes, improving the process to improve the product, making quality everyone's responsibility, and fact-based management.

Focus on Customer Satisfaction   Customer satisfaction is the foundation of quality philosophies and concepts. Customers have expectations and are the best judge of quality. Meeting or exceeding those expectations can lead to improved customer satisfaction. In addition, it is important to keep in mind that customers may be internal or external. The external customer is the ultimate customer—that is, the project sponsor or client. However, internal customers are just as important and may be thought of as an individual or group who are the receivers of some project deliverable or an output of a process.

For example, project team members may be assigned the task of defining the detailed user requirements for an application system. These requirements may be handed off to one or several systems analysts who will develop the design models and then hand these models off to the programmers. The quality of the requirements specifications, in terms of accuracy, completeness, and understandability, for example, will have a direct bearing on the quality of the models developed by the systems analysts. In turn, the quality of the models will impact the quality of the programs developed. Therefore, we can view the series of project and software development processes as a customer chain made up of both internal and external customers.

As you might expect, a chain is only as strong as its weakest link, and any quality problems that occur can impact the quality of the project's product downstream. The primary focus of the project team should be to meet or exceed the expectations and needs of their customer because the customer is the ultimate judge of quality (Ginac 1998).

Prevention, Not Inspection   One of Deming's most salient ideas is that quality cannot be inspected into a product. Quality is either built into the product or it is not. Therefore, the total cost of quality is equal to the sum of four components—prevention, inspection, internal failure, and external failure. The cost associated with prevention consists of all the actions a project team may take to prevent defects, mistakes, bugs, and so forth from occurring in the first place. The cost of inspection entails the costs associated with measuring, evaluating, and auditing the project processes and deliverables to ensure conformance to standards or requirement specifications. Costs of internal failure can be attributed to rework or fixing a defective product before it is delivered to the customer. These types of problems are, hopefully, found before the product is released. External failure costs entail the costs to fix problems or defects discovered after the product has been released. External failure costs can create the most damage for an organization because the customer's views and attitudes toward the organization may keep the customer from doing repeat business with the organization in the future. Thus, prevention is the least expensive cost and can reduce the likelihood of a defect or bug reaching the customer undetected. In turn, this will reduce the cost of developing the system and improve the overall quality of the product (Lewis 2000).

Improve the Process to Improve the Product   Processes are needed to create all of the project's deliverables and the final product—the information system. Subsequently, improving the process will improve the quality of the product. Project processes must be activities that add value to the overall customer chain. In addition, processes can be broken down into subprocesses and must be repeatable and measurable so that they can be controlled and improved. Improving any process, however, takes time because process improvement is often incremental. Most importantly, improvement should be continuous.

Quality Is Everyone's Responsibility Quality improvement requires time and resources. As many of the quality gurus point out, quality has to be more than just a slogan. It requires a commitment from management and the people who will do the work. Management must not only provide resources, but remove organizational barriers and provide leadership. On the other hand, those individuals who perform the work usually know their job better than their managers. These people are often the ones who have direct contact with the end customer. Therefore, they should be responsible and empowered for ensuring quality, and encouraged to take pride in their work. Quality improvement may not be all that easy to achieve because it may require an organization to change its culture and focus on long-term gains at the expense and pressure to deliver short-term results.

Fact-Based Management It is also important that a quality program and project quality plan be based on hard evidence. As Kloppenborg and Petrick (2002) point out, managing by facts requires that the organization (1) capture data and analyze trends that determine what is actually true about its process performance, (2) structure itself in such a way that it is more responsive to all stakeholders, and (3) collect and analyze data and trends that will provide a key foundation for evaluating and improving processes.

Quality Standards and Metrics

Standards provide the foundation for any quality plan; however, standards must be meaningful and clearly defined in order to be relevant and useful. As illustrated in Figure 10.9, the project's goal, defined in terms of the measurable organizational value or MOV, provides the basis for defining the project's standards. The MOV defines the project's ultimate goal in terms of the explicit value the project will bring to the organization. In turn, the MOV provides a basis for defining and managing the project's scope, which defines the high-level deliverables of the project as well as the general features and functionality to be provided by the IT solution. However, the scope of the project, in terms of the features and functionality of the information system, are often defined in greater detail as part of the requirements definition.

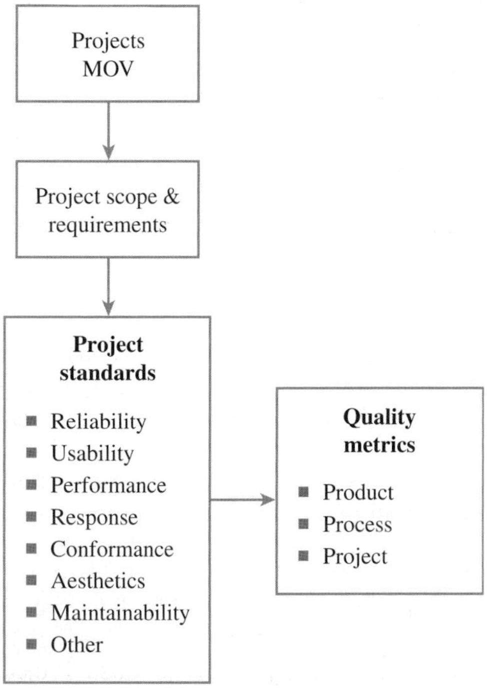

As Figure 10.9 demonstrates, the project's standards can be defined in terms of the project's deliverables and, most importantly, by the IT solution to be delivered. Once the features, functionality, or requirements are defined, the next step is to identify specific quality attributes or dimensions associated with each project deliverable. A customer-driven quality assurance plan first identifies each customer's requirements, represents them as quality attributes or dimensions, and then translates those dimensions into metrics (Ginac 1998). For example, Kan (1995) suggests

Figure 10.9 Developing Standards and Metrics

several dimensions that can serve as quality standards for the software product. These include the application's features, reliability, usability, performance, response, conformance, aesthetics, and maintainability. Although these dimensions focus on the application system, other dimensions can be identified for each of the project deliverables (e.g., business case, project charter and baseline project plan, project reporting, user documentation, etc.).

Metrics are vital for gauging quality by establishing tolerance limits and identifying defects. A **defect** is an undesirable behavior associated with the product or process (Ginac 1998). It is a failure to comply with a requirement (Lewis 2000). In software development, defects are often referred to as bugs.[1]

Once the quality dimensions are identified, the next step is to define a set of metrics that allow the project manager and team to monitor each of the project standards. There are two parts to a metric—the metric itself and an acceptable value or range of values for that metric (Ginac 1998). Metrics should focus on three categories (Kan 1995):

- *Process*—The control of defects introduced by the processes required to develop or create the project deliverables. Process metrics can be used to improve software development or maintenance processes. Process metrics should focus on the effectiveness of identifying and removing defects or bugs.

- *Product*—The intrinsic quality of the deliverables and the satisfaction of the customer with these deliverables. These metrics should attempt to describe the characteristics of the project's deliverables and final product. Examples of product metrics may focus on customer satisfaction, performance, reliability, and design features.

- *Project*—The control of the project management processes to ensure that the project meets its overall goal as well as its scope, schedule, and budget.

Metrics can be used to determine whether the software product and project deliverables meet requirements for "fitness for use" and "conformance to requirements" as defined by the internal or external customers. Many technical people, however, often feel that standards are restricting and only serve to stifle creativity. Although too many standards that are rigidly followed can lend support to that argument, well defined standards and procedures are necessary for ensuring quality. A quality approach can also decrease development costs because the sooner a defect or bug is found and corrected, the less costly it will be down the road (Lewis 2000). Table 10.3 provides a summary of some common process, product, and project metrics.

Verification and Validation

Verification and validation (V&V) are becoming increasingly important concepts in software engineering (Jarvis and Crandall 1997). V&V activities continually prompt us to ask whether we will deliver an IT solution that meets or exceeds our project sponsor's expectations.

The concept of **verification** emerged about 20 years ago in the aerospace industry, where it is important that software perform all of its intended functions correctly

---

[1] The term *bug* was introduced to the computer field by Dr. Grace Murray Hopper (1906–1992)—an extraordinary woman who retired as a Rear Admiral in the U.S. Navy. In 1946, while working on the Mark II and Mark III computers, she found that one of the computers had crashed as a result of a moth that had become trapped in one of the computer's relays. The moth was carefully removed and taped to the logbook, where an entry was made that the computer was debugged. For some reason the term stuck, and errors, or glitches, in a program or computer system are called *bugs*.

Table 10.3 Examples of Process, Product, and Project Metrics

Type	Metric	Description
Process	Defect arrival rate	The number of defects found over a specific period of time
	Defects by phase	The number of defects found during each phase of the project
	Defect backlog	The number of defects waiting to be fixed
	Fix response time	The average time it takes to fix a defect
	Defective fixes	The number of fixes that created new defects
Product	Mean time to failure	Average or mean time elapsed until a product fails
	Defect density	The number of defects per lines of code (LOC) or function points
	Customer found defects	The number of defects found by the customer
	Customer satisfaction	An index to measure customer satisfaction—e.g., scale from 1 (very unsatisfied) to 5 (very satisfied)
Project	Scope change requests	The number of scope changes requested by the client or sponsor
	Scope change approvals	The number of scope changes that were approved
	Overdue tasks	The number of tasks that were started but not finished by the expected date or time
	Tasks that should have started	The number of tasks that should have started but have been delayed
	Over budgeted tasks	The number of tasks (and dollar amount of tasks) that have cost more to complete than expected
	Earned value	Budgeted cost of work performed (BCWP)
	Over allocated resources	The number of resources assigned to more than one task
	Turnover	The number of project team members who quit or were terminated
	Training hours	The number of training hours per project team member

and reliably because any error in a software program could result in an expensive or disastrous mission failure (Lewis 2000). Verification focuses on the process-related activities of the project to ensure that the product or deliverable meets its specified requirements before final testing of the system begins.

Verification requires that the standards and metrics be defined clearly. Moreover, verification activities focus on asking the question of whether we followed the right procedures and processes. In general, verification includes three types of reviews (Ginac 1998):

- *Technical reviews*—A technical review ensures that the IT solution will conform to the specified requirements. This review may include conformance to graphical user interface (GUI) standards, programming and documentation standards, naming conventions, and so forth. Two common approaches to technical reviews include structured walkthroughs and inspections. A **walkthrough** is a review process in which the programmer or designer leads a group of programmers or designers through a program or technical design. The participants may ask questions, make comments, or point out errors or violations of standards (Ginac 1998). Similarly, **inspections** are peer reviews in which the key feature is the use of a checklist to help identify errors. The checklists are updated after data is collected and may suggest that certain types of errors are occurring more or less frequently than in the past (Lewis 2000). Although walkthroughs and inspections have generally focused on the development of programs, they can be used as a verification of all project deliverables throughout the project life cycle.

- *Business reviews*—A business review is designed to ensure that the IT solution provides the required functionality specified in the project scope and requirements definition. However, business reviews can include all project deliverables to ensure that each deliverable (1) is complete, (2) provides the necessary information required for the next phase or process, (3) meets predefined standards, and (4) conforms to the project methodology.

- *Management reviews*—A management review basically compares the project's actual progress against the baseline project plan. In general, the project manager is responsible for presenting the project's progress to provide a clear idea of the project's current status. Issues may need to be resolved, resources adjusted, or decisions made either to stay or alter the project's course. In addition, management may review the project to determine if it meets scope, schedule, budget, and quality objectives.

Validation, on the other hand, is a product-oriented activity that attempts to determine if the system or project deliverable meets the customer or client's expectations and ensures that the system performs as specified. Unlike verification, validation activities occur toward the end of the project or after the information system has been developed. Therefore, testing makes up the majority of validation activities. Table 10.4 provides a summary of the various types of tests that can be conducted for a software engineering project. Volumes and courses can be devoted to software testing, so just an overview (or refresher) can be provided in this text. However, understanding what needs to be tested, and how, is an important consideration for developing a quality strategy and plan for the IT project.

Testing provides a basis for ensuring that the system functions as intended and has all the capabilities and features that were defined in the project's scope and requirements. In addition, testing provides a formal, structured, and traceable process that gives management and the project sponsor confidence in the quality of the system (Lewis 2000). In addition, Lewis (2000) provides several suggestions for making software testing more effective:

- Testing should be conducted by someone who does not have a personal stake in the project. In other words, programmers should not test their own programs because it is difficult for people to be objective about their own work.

- Testing should be continuous and conducted throughout all the development phases.

- In order to determine whether the test met its objectives correctly, a test plan should outline what is to be tested, how it will be tested, when it will be tested, who will do the testing, and the expected results.

- A test plan should act as a service level agreement among the various project stakeholders and should encourage "quality before design and coding."

- A key to testing is having the right attitude. Testers should not be out to "break the code" or embarrass a project team member. A tester should evaluate a software product with the intent of helping the developers meet the customer's requirements and make the product even better.

Change Control and Configuration Management

Suppose you were developing a database application system for a client. After several weeks, you would undoubtedly make a number of changes to the tables, attributes, user interface, and reports as part of a natural evolution of the project. This

Table 10.4   Testing Approaches

Test	Description
Unit testing	Unit testing is done at the module, program, or object level and focuses on whether specific functions work properly. Unit testing can be accomplished via: ■ *Black box testing*—Tests the program code against specified requirements (i.e., functionality) ■ *White box testing*—Examines paths of logic inside the program (i.e., structure) ■ *Gray box testing*—Study the requirements and communicate with the developer to understand internal structure of the program (i.e., functionality and structure)
Integration testing	Tests whether a set of logically related units (e.g., functions, modules, programs, objects, etc.) work together properly after unit testing is complete
Systems testing	The system is tested as a whole in an operating environment to verify functionality and fitness for use. May include tests to verify usability, performance, stress, compatibility, and documentation
Acceptance testing	To certify that the system satisfies the end customer's scope and detailed requirement specifications after systems testing is complete. The end user or client is responsible for assuring that all specified functionality is included and will provide value to the organization as defined by the project's goal or MOV.

evolution is both normal and expected as you learn more about the technology and the requirements. In addition, the user/client may suggest changes or enhancements if the organizational environment changes.

If you are working alone, you may store all the products of the software development (i.e., reports, plans, design models, program and database files) on your computer. Change control may be nothing more than just keeping your documents and files organized. If, however, you need to share these files and documents with even one other person, controlling these changes becomes more problematic. You could all keep the files and documents being worked on at everyone's stand-alone workstation. Unfortunately, if you need to share or work on the same documents or files, this sharing can lead to several different versions of the same document or file distributed among several different computers. On the other hand, you may store all the work in a shared directory on a server. This solution would certainly allow everyone to share and use the same documents or files, but problems could occur if two or more people work on the same document or file at the same time. The changes one makes would be lost if someone else were to save a file after the first person saved it, thus replacing new file with a different new file. There could be a great deal of confusion and wasted time.

Change is inevitable throughout the life of the project. On any given project, each deliverable will progress through a series of stages from an initial conception through a final release. As the deliverable develops, changes will be made informally until it gets to a state of completeness, whereupon revision control is needed. At some point informal changes should be no longer permitted. After final acceptance, the deliverable should be frozen until it is released. An informal change control allows changes that can be traced and captured sequentially to be made to an evolving project deliverable. It provides for rapid development while allowing for backup and some measures of control. On the other hand, formal change control is a procedure in which changes to an accepted work are formally proposed and assessed and decisions to accept or reject proposed changes are documented to provide an element of stability beyond the informal change controls.

Configuration management is an important aspect of PQM that helps control and manage document and software product change (Jarvis and Crandall 1997). It provides the project team with an environment for efficiently accessing different versions of past documents or files. Its basic purpose is to establish and maintain the integrity of the various project work products and deliverables throughout the project life cycle. In short, configuration management attempts to answer the following basic questions (Ginac 1998):

■ What changes were made?

■ Who made the changes?

■ When were the changes made?

■ Why were the changes made?

Configuration management tools allow different project team members to work on a specific section of a document or file. The document or file can be checked out and checked back into a repository or library in order to maintain control. Software and the supporting project deliverables often go through an evolution of successive temporary states called *versions* (Lewis 2000). Configuration management, therefore, includes a set of processes and tools that allows the project team to manage its various documents and files as various configurations of IT solutions and project deliverables are derived. It may include specifying and enforcing various policies that restrict access to specific individuals or preventing two people from changing the same document or file at the same time (Ginac 1998).

Monitor and Control

Quality control focuses on monitoring the activities and results of the project to ensure that the project complies with the quality standards. Once the project's standards are in place, it is important to monitor them to ensure that the project quality objective is achieved. Moreover, control is essential for identifying problems in order to take corrective action and also to make improvements once a process is under control.

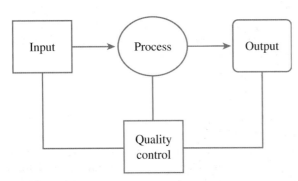

Figure 10.10   Quality Control Activities

Similar to the quality assurance activities, quality control should be ongoing throughout the life cycle of the project and only end when the customer or project sponsor accepts the final IT solution (Kloppenborg and Petrick 2002). Moreover, quality control includes monitoring and controlling activities concerning the product, processes, and project. Using the system concept as illustrated in Figure 10.10, quality control activities must focus on the inputs and outputs of each process. If inputs to a process are of poor quality, then the output of a particular process will be of poor quality as well because, in general, the process may not be capable of changing the inherent quality of the input. Moreover, even if the input to a process is of high quality, the process itself may create an output of lower quality. Finally, the input and process may not produce a quality output or product if the requirements are not properly defined.

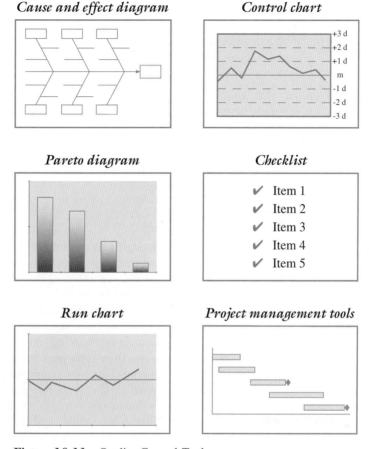

Figure 10.11   Quality Control Tools

To support the quality control activities, several tools and techniques were introduced in this chapter. Figure 10.11 provides a summary of those tools. As Besterfield, et al. (1999) point out, these tools can be used to monitor the process, product, and product metrics in order to:

Learn, Mature, and Improve

A central theme of this text has been the application of knowledge management as a tool for team learning and identifying best practices. Monitoring and controlling activities and tools can help point out problem areas, but the project team must solve these problems. Therefore, it is important that the lessons learned from a project team's experiences be documented so that best practices are identified and disseminated to other project teams. Continual, incremental improvements can make a process more efficient, effective, stable, mature, and adaptable (Besterfield, Besterfield-Michna, et al. 1999). A project quality plan should be more than an attempt to build a better IT solution, it should also support the organization in searching for ways to build a better product (Woodall, Rebuck, et al. 1997).

CHAPTER SUMMARY

Project quality management (PQM) is a knowledge area defined by the Project Management Body of Knowledge. It is defined as:

> the processes to ensure that the project will satisfy the needs for which it was undertaken. It includes all activities of the overall management function that determine the quality policy, objectives, and responsibility and implements them by means of quality planning, quality assurance, quality control, and quality improvement, within the quality system.

In this text, PQM has been expanded to include not only the quality management concepts, but verification and validation activities and change control to manage the various configurations of the project products throughout the project life cycle.

Although quality can mean different things to different people, quality in organizational settings has been traditionally defined as "fitness for use" and "conformance to requirements."

The scientific method put forth by F. W. Taylor attempted to define the best way for workers to perform tasks—allowing them to produce at their full potential while removing management's proclivity to set arbitrary production rates. Although the scientific method had the best of intentions, many managers used it as a way to speed up workers and increase profits. The work of Walter A. Shewhart and W. Edwards Deming attempted to change management's mindset by advocating leadership, prevention over inspection, and statistical control to improve productivity and quality. Because Japan faced the daunting task of rebuilding its economy after World War II with few natural resources and a reputation for inferior goods, a group called the Union of Japanese Scientists and Engineers (JUSE) was formed with the help of Japan's allies to help transform the nation. As part of this effort, Deming and Joseph Juran were invited to give lectures on statistical quality control. Japanese managers embraced these principles and ideas, and the quality movement officially was born. Many others, such as Kaoru Ishikawa and Philip Crosby, contributed to this worldwide movement, and proprietary and nonproprietary quality management systems have gained increasing popularity in many organizations.

As part of the quality movement, standards in the form of documented agreements, protocols, or rules that outline specific criteria for quality became the backbone for ensuring quality. Several organizations and quality initiatives have gained fame over the years. ISO, probably the most widely known standards organization, was formed in 1947 with the intention of creating and coordinating a set of international standards. While the ISO 14000 focus on environmental management, the ISO 9000 focus on eight quality management principles that provide a framework for different organizations. A third party, called a registrar, can audit an organization and issue a certification that the organization's processes conform to the ISO standards.

Other quality initiatives, such as Six Sigma, focus on variations in processes that may translate into products or services that do not meet customer needs and expectations. By improving the quality of its processes, an organization can achieve its Six Sigma goal of producing only 3.4 defects per million. More recently, the Software Engineering Institute at Carnegie Mellon University introduced capability maturity model integration (CMMI) that provides a set of recommended practices for a set of key process areas specific to software development. The CMMI also provides a path of five levels to help organizations determine their current maturity level and then take steps toward software engineering and management excellence. Although the competitive environment may dictate that an organization achieve or hold a particular certificate or level of maturity, an organization should be focused on continuous improvement. Continuous improvement leads to competitive advantage by incorporating the lessons learned from their experiences and then translating those experiences into best practices that can be repeated throughout the organization.

The concepts, tools, methods, and philosophies of the quality movement provide a foundation for developing the IT project quality plan. The plan should be based on the following:

- *Quality philosophies and principles*—To guide the plan's objective and mission.

- *Quality standards and metrics*—To define the quality objectives and expectations and to provide a baseline for benchmarking improvements.
- *Verification and validation activities*—To ensure a quality approach throughout the project. Verification activities, such as technical, business, and management reviews, determine whether the project team is building the system or producing project deliverables according to specified standards or requirements; validation activities, such as software testing, tend to focus on whether the project's products will meet customer expectations.
- *Change control and configuration management*—To support the natural evolution of the project's products. As these products evolve, change is inevitable. It is important that this change be managed effectively in order to reduce confusion and wasted effort. It includes a document repository library where files or documents can be checked out and checked in as needed. This process allows for versioning, backup, and safeguarding so that documents or files are not accidentally replaced by other project team members. Configuration

building also allows for identifying the correct component versions needed to execute build procedures. Configuration management also provides formal change control to ensure that changes to accepted work are formally proposed and assessed and any decisions to make the changes are documented.

- *Monitor and control*—To focus on monitoring the project activities to ensure that the project meets its quality standards. Once the project work begins, it is important that these activities be monitored and assessed so that appropriate corrective action can be taken when necessary. Quality control tools and techniques can be used to monitor each project or software development process and the inputs and outputs of the process, as well.
- *Learn, mature, and improve*—To focus on continuous quality improvement. As a project progresses, lessons learned can be documented from the project team's experiences. Recommendations, issues, challenges, and opportunities can be identified and shared with other project teams; and many of these experiences can provide the basis for best practices that can be implemented throughout the organization.

REVIEW QUESTIONS

1. Define quality in your own words. How would you define quality in a word processing, spreadsheet, or presentation software package?
2. Why is the number of features of a software system not necessarily the best measure of that system's quality?
3. How does "conformance to requirements" or "fitness for use" provide a definition of quality for an information system or software product?
4. What is PQM?
5. Define the following: (a) Quality planning; (b) quality assurance; (c) quality control.
6. Why should quality management include both the products and processes of a project?
7. What is scientific management? Why was it so popular? Why was it so controversial?
8. What is a control chart? When is a process said to be in statistical control? How would you know if it was not?
9. Why did the teachings of Deming and Juran have such an important impact on Japan just after World War II?
10. What is an Ishikawa diagram? How can it be used as a quality control tool for an IT project?
11. What is a Pareto diagram? How can it be used as a quality control tool for an IT project?
12. What is a flow chart? How can it be used as a quality control tool for an IT project?
13. What is a standard? What role do standards play in developing an information system?
14. What is ISO? Why would an organization wish to be ISO certified?

15. Briefly describe Six Sigma and its objectives.

16. How does achieving a Six Sigma objective improve quality?

17. What is process capability?

18. What is process maturity?

19. Describe an immature software organization.

20. Describe a mature software organization.

21. What is the relationship between standards and metrics?

22. What is a process metric? Give an example.

23. What is a product metric? Give an example.

24. What is a project metric? Give an example.

25. What is a defect? Give an example of a software defect.

26. Describe verification. What activities support verification?

27. Describe validation. What activities support validation?

28. Describe how technical, management, and business reviews are different.

29. What is the purpose of change control?

30. Why should some changes be allowed to be made informally, while other changes should be made formally?

31. What is configuration management? How does it support change control?

32. What role does knowledge management play in continuous quality improvement?

EXTEND YOUR KNOWLEDGE

1. Interview two or three people who regularly use an application software package. Examples of an application software package include an Internet browser, electronic spreadsheet package, or a word processing package. Summarize each interview in one or two pages based upon the following questions:

   a. What application software package do you use the most?

   b. How often do you use this particular software package?

   c. Which features or functions do you use the most? The least?

   d. How would you rate the overall quality of the software package on a scale from one to ten, where one indicates very low quality and ten indicates very high quality?

   e. Why did you give the software package this score?

   f. In your opinion, what are the three most important attributes of a high quality software package?

2. Contact someone in an organization who is willing to talk to you about her experiences implementing a quality program such as Six Sigma, ISO, or the CMMI. If this is not feasible, use the Internet or library to find an article. Prepare a short report that answers the following:

   a. What were the compelling reasons for initiating a quality program?

   b. What was the biggest challenge that the organization faced when trying to implement the quality program?

   c. How long did it take to implement the program? Or how far along are they?

   d. What lessons did the organization learn from its experience?

3. You and two other students have been hired by a local swim team to develop a Web site that will provide information about the team. The information on the Web site will be used to recruit new swimmers and will provide information to current members about upcoming meets and practices. In addition, team and individual statistics will be posted after each swim meet. Before you begin, you need to develop a quality plan. The plan should include:

   a. Your own quality philosophy

   b. Two metrics for ensuring that reliability standards are met

   c. Two metrics for ensuring that performance standards are met

   d. A means for validating and verifying that your client's needs and expectations will be met

GLOBAL TECHNOLOGY SOLUTIONS

It was mid-afternoon when Tim Williams walked into the GTS conference room. Two of the Husky Air team members, Sitaramin and Yan, were already seated at the conference table. Tim took his usual seat, and asked "So how did the demonstration of the user interface go this morning?"

Sitaramin glanced at Yan and then focused his attention on Tim's question. He replied, "Well, I guess we have some good news and some bad news. The good news is that our client was pleased with the work we've completed so far. The bad news, however, is that our prototype did not include several required management reports."

Yan looked at Tim and added, "It was a bit embarrassing because the CEO of the company pointed out our omission. It appears that those reports were specifically requested by him."

Tim looked a bit perplexed and asked, "So how did the client react?"

Sitaramin thought for a moment. "They were really expecting to see those reports," he replied, "but we promised that we would have them ready by next week. The CEO wasn't too happy to hear that it would take another week before we could add the reports and demonstrate the prototype again. However, everyone seemed pleased with what we were able to show them so far, and I think that helped buy us some time."

Tim took out his PDA and studied the calendar for a few minutes. Looking up, he asked, "So how will this impact our schedule?"

Yan opened the folder in front of her and found a copy of the project plan. She answered, "I wondered the same thing myself, and so I took a look at the original baseline project plan. The developers can begin working on what we've finished so far, but it looks like Sitaraman and I will have to work a few late nights this week and probably the weekend. That should get us back on track with minimal impact on the schedule."

Sitaramin sighed and said, "So much for going to the concert this evening. Do you know of anyone who would be interested in two tickets?" That brought a chuckle from the three team members.

Tim smiled and replied, "I'm glad to see that you both handled the situation fairly well and that you thought of a way to keep the project on track, even if it means some overtime for the two of you. However, I think we need to talk about why this problem

occurred in the first place and what we can do to reduce the likelihood of similar problems happening again in the future."

Yan gave Tim's words a few seconds to sink in. "After our meeting with the client I talked to a few of the other members of the team," she said. "It turns out that the reports Husky Air's management wanted to see were defined in the requirements document. Unfortunately, several people were working on the same document, and we were given an earlier version that didn't contain the entire specifications for the reports. As a result, we didn't even know the reports were part of the requirements and, therefore, didn't include them in the user interface prototype. I guess we should have checked with the other team members, but we were too busy just trying to get the prototype to work properly."

Tim stood up and walked over to the white board. He then wrote Quality, Verification/Validation, and Change Control on the board. Yan and Sitaramin gave Tim their full attention as he explained, "It seems that having several people work on the same documents, programs, or database files is a common problem. Often two people work on the same document or file at the same time without knowledge of what the other is doing. For example, let's say that person A is working on one section of a document or file, while person B is working on another. If person A saves the document or file to the server and then person B saves her or his document or file to the server afterwards, the changes to Person A's document or file are lost."

"That appears to be exactly what happened to the requirements document we used to develop the prototype!" exclaimed Yan.

"In fact," Sitaramin added, "Yan and I ran into a similar problem when we were working on the prototype. We had several versions of a program that we were developing, but it became confusing as to which version was the latest."

Tim turned to the two team members and said, "As I said before, this seems to be a common problem whenever several team members are working with the same files. What we need is a tool and a method for checking documents out and back in so that we reduce the likelihood of the errors we talked about."

Both Sitaramin and Yan agreed that this was a good idea. Sitaramin then interjected, "Tim, you have

'Verification and Validation' written on the board. Can you expand on your idea?"

Tim glanced at the board and then turned his attention back to Sitaramin and said, "Sure. We often think of testing as being one of the last activities in software development. But catching problems and errors earlier in the project life cycle are easier and less expensive to fix. Moreover, by the time those problems or errors reach the client, it's too late and can be somewhat embarrassing, as the two of you found out this morning. We need to ask two important questions with respect to each project deliverable, Are we building the right product? And are we building the product the right way? These two questions are the foundation for verification and validation and should be part of an overall quality plan for the project."

Yan thought for a moment and said, "I remember learning about total quality management when I was in school. From what I recall, a lot of this quality stuff really focuses on the customer. But I think we need to rethink our idea of who exactly is our customer."

Both Sitaramin and Tim looked confused. Sitaramin was the first to speak. "But isn't *Husky Air* our customer?"

Yan knew she would have to explain. "Yes, they are, but they are our *end* customer. The team members who carried out the requirements definition and wrote the requirements document didn't realize that you and I were *their* customers because we needed a complete and accurate set of requirements in order to develop the prototype. In turn, the prototype that we develop will be handed off to several other team members who will use it to develop the application system. Subsequently, they will be our customers. I guess we can view the whole project as a customer chain that includes all of the project stakeholders."

"That is a very interesting idea, Yan!" said Tim. "We can build the concepts of quality, verification/validation, and change control into each of the project activities as part of an overall quality plan." The three members of the team felt they had discovered something important that should be documented and shared with the other members of GTS.

Tim replaced the cap on the dry erase pen and said, "It looks like we all have our work cut out for us this next week. While the two of you are busy working on the prototype for your presentation next week, I'll be working late developing a project quality management plan. By the way, do you know of anyone who would be interested in two tickets to a hockey game?"

Things to Think About

1. What role does quality play in the IT project methodology?

2. How does verification/validation and change control support quality in an IT project?

3. Why should the project team focus on both internal and external customers?

 # HUSKY AIR ASSIGNMENT—PILOT ANGELS

The Quality Management Plan

In this assignment, you and your team will develop a quality management plan to support your project with Husky Air.

Please provide a professional-looking document that includes the following:

1. **Project name, project team name, and the names of the members of your project team**

2. **A brief project description** (This helps your instructor if different teams are working on different projects in your class.)

3. **The project's MOV** (This should be revised or refined if appropriate.)

4. **An IT quality management plan**—The plan should include the following:

   a. A short statement that reflects your team's philosophy or objective for ensuring that you deliver a quality system to your client.

   b. Other than the examples of quality based metrics found in Table 10.3, two process metrics, two product metrics, and two project metrics that can be used to monitor the quality of your project; develop and describe them.

   c. A set of verification activities that your project team could implement to ensure quality; develop and describe.

   d. A set of validation activities that your project team could implement to ensure quality; develop and describe.

CASE STUDIES

Speed vs. Quality

The mantra for many organizations today is "Do more with less." Often management is demanding that IT solutions be delivered within weeks instead of months, with key features and functions that are expected to provide immediate, bottom-line results. Unfortunately, this often means that quality and testing are sacrificed for speed. As Kevin Heard, a project manager at Clarkston Consulting in Durham, N.C., states "It's an uphill battle. Everyone realizes that if you sacrifice quality today, you're going to pay for it in the future."

The conflict between quality and speed becomes compounded when people are spread thin across several projects. Moreover, project managers must make sure that the project's scope is realistic and achievable, especially when the project's schedule is compressed. Too often management urges the project manager to "cut corners" in order to deliver an IT solution on time without reducing functionality. For example, Margo Visitación, an analyst at Forrester Research, tells of one instance where an IT manager was pressured by senior managers to expedite an ERP implementation by bypassing several important business processes. As Ken McLennan, a senior vice president at Fujitsu Consulting in Edison, N.J., adds "There's always a lot of pressure from executives to take shortcuts on IT projects." He believes that project managers must help executives understand the risks of taking shortcuts. McLennan says "If companies are seen making mistakes and that gets publicized, that could hurt their share price, so there's a tremendous balancing act going on."

1. Does there have to be a trade-off between the speed of delivery of an IT solution and quality?
2. If you were a project manager and senior management asked you to consider strongly taking a shortcut that could compromise quality, what argument could you make to convince them to not sacrifice quality over schedule?

SOURCE: Adapted from Thomas Hoffman, IT Project Management: Balancing Speed and Quality, *Computerworld*, February 14, 2004.

Pay to Play?

The capability maturity model (CMM) was born in the 1980s out of the U.S. Air Force and Department of Defense frustration with purchasing the right software. Carnegie Mellon University won the bid to create an organization called the Software Engineering Institute (SEI) to help improve the process of choosing the right software and vendor. In 1986, Watts Humphrey, a former software development chief at IBM, was brought in to lead this effort. As Humphrey explains, "We were focused on identifying competent people, but we saw that all of the projects the Air Force had were in trouble. It didn't matter who they had doing the work. So we said let's focus on improving the work rather than just the process."

The initial CMM developed in 1987 was a questionnaire designed to identify good software processes practiced by the software vendors bidding on the contracts. Unfortunately, many of these companies learned how to "work the system" in terms of filling out the questionnaire regardless of the quality of their software practices.

In 1991, the SEI refined the CMM to overcome these abuses. A more detailed model of software development best practices was created along with a group of lead appraisers trained and authorized by the SEI to audit and verify that the software vendors were following the practices that they said they were doing. The lead appraisers led a team within the organization being reviewed and would attempt to verify that the vendor was implementing the policies, procedures, and practices outlined in the CMM across a "representative" subgroup (about 10 percent to 30 percent) of all of the company's software projects. Over a period of one to three weeks, a number of confidential interviews with project managers and developers were conducted to confirm what was really going on. Since the lead appraiser led a team of the software vendor's own employees, there often could be a conflict of interest for these people to tell the truth. As one anonymous lead appraiser recalled, "It can be very stressful for the internal team. They have conflicting objectives. They need to be objective, but the organization wants to be assessed at a certain level."

Another lead appraiser, David Constant, also recalls a situation where the software developers were coached by management to say the right things. According to Constant "I had to stop the interviews and demand to see people on an ad hoc basis, telling the company who I wanted to speak to just before each interview began. And the sad part was that they didn't need to coach anybody. They would have easily gotten the level they were looking for anyway. They were very good."

As of 1994, the newer model became more difficult to exploit. Mark Martak of Westinghouse told his management that "This is a different ball game now. If you have a good lead appraiser, you can't fake it out." He was able to lead his group to a Level 4 assessment.

It is widely believed that moving up the CMM levels will allow an organization to better serve its customers. However, a higher CMM level does not guarantee the effectiveness of performance, only that the organization has processes in place for managing and monitoring software development that organizations on a lower level do not yet have. As Jay Douglas, director of business development at the SEI, points out "Having a higher maturity level significantly reduces the risk over hiring a company with a lower level, but it does not guarantee anything. You can be a Level 5 organization that produces software that might be garbage."

CMM can be costly and time consuming for an organization. On average it takes about seven years for an organization to move from Level 1 up to Level 5. The cost for a CMM assessment alone can be around $100,000, and doesn't even include the expense and disruption of developing repeatable software processes and the training needed to disseminate them throughout the organization.

Therefore, it's not uncommon for organizations to make false claims. Ron Radice, a lead appraiser and former SEI official, recalls a Chicago-based company that was deceived by an offshore company that falsely claimed to have a CMM rating. Not wanting to name the guilty party, Radice said "They said they were Level 4, but in fact they had never been assessed." In addition, some appraisers may feel pressured in their assessment. For example, Frank Koch, a lead appraiser with a software services consulting firm called Process Strategies, Inc., said that some Chinese consulting firms he worked with promised their clients that they had a certain CMM level and then expected that he would just give it to them. According to Koch, "We don't do work with certain [consultancies in China] because their motives are a whole lot less than wholesome. They'd say we're certain [certain clients] are a Level 2 or 3 and that's unreasonable, to say nothing of unethical. The term is called selling a rating."

Given the investment in time and resources to achieve a CMM rating, it's not uncommon for organizations "pay to play" or bribe appraisers for a particular rating. Many government agencies in the United States require companies who bid for their business to obtain at least a Level 3 rating, while many CIOs use a CMM in choosing an offshore provider. Will Hayes, a quality manager at SEI, acknowledged one case where an appraiser had his license revoked for improperly awarding a Level 4 rating.

The difficulty in knowing whether an organization's claim to a CMM rating is that the SEI does not monitor the organizations that claim to have a CMM rating, nor do they release any information regarding which organizations were assessed or the outcome of their assessment. As Hayes points out, "We weren't chartered to be policemen. We're a research and development group." Moreover, SEI does not have any intention of becoming a governing body like the American National Standards Institute (ANSI), which governs ISO certification in the United States. As Watts Humphrey contends, "No one has asked us to become a governing body, and that's not our mandate. And if we did, what would we solve? It wouldn't excuse anyone from doing their homework."

1. What is the value of having a CMM rating?
2. Do you think there should be a governing body to oversee CMM assessments?
3. As a project manger looking to outsource the programming of your project overseas to a software house claiming a Level 5 rating, what could you do as part of a due diligence to make sure that the claim is not false?

SOURCE: Adapted from Christopher Koch, Software Quality: Bursting the CMM Hype, *CIO Magazine*, March 1, 2004.

 # BIBLIOGRAPHY

Besterfield, D. H., C. Besterfield-Michna, et al. 1999. *Total Quality Management*. Upper Saddle River, NJ: Prentice Hall.

Boehm, B. W. 1981. *Software Engineering Economics*. Englewood Cliffs, NJ: Prentice Hall.

Caputo, K. 1998. *CMM Implementation Guide: Choreographing Software Process Development*. Reading, MA: Addison-Wesley.

Chrissis, M. B., M., Konrad, and S. Shrum. 2003. *CMMI®: Guidelines for Process Integration and Product Improvement. Addison-Wesley Professional Series: The SEI Series in Software Engineering*.

Deming, W. E. 1982. *Out of the Crisis*. Cambridge, MA: The MIT Press.

Florac, W. A., R. E. T. Park, et al. 1997. *Practical Software Measurement: Measuring for Process Management and Improvement*. Pittsburgh: Software Engineering Institute.

Ginac, F. P. 1998. *Customer Oriented Software Quality Assurance*. Upper Saddle River, NJ: Prentice Hall.

Humphrey, W. 1988. Characterizing the Software Process: A Maturity Framework. *IEEE Software* 5(3): 73–79.

Jarvis, A. and V. Crandall. 1997. *Inroads to Software Quality: How to Guide and Toolkit*. Upper Saddle River, NJ: Prentice Hall PTR.

Kan, S. H. 1995. *Metrics and Models in Software Quality Engineering*. Boston, MA: Addison-Wesley.

Kloppenborg, T. J. and J. A. Petrick. 2002. *Managing Project Quality*. Vienna, VA: Management Concepts.

Lewis, W. E. 2000. *Software Testing and Continuous Quality Improvement*. Boca Raton, FL: Auerbach.

Paulk, M. C. 1994. A Comparison of ISO 9001 and the Capability Maturity Model for Software. *Software Engineering Institute* CMU/SEI-94-TR-12.

Paulk, M. C., B., Curtis, et al. 1993. The Capability Maturity Model for Software. *IEEE Software* 10(4): 18–27.

Project Management Institute (PMI) 2004. *A Guide to the Project Management Body of Knowledge (PMBOK® Guide)*. Newtown Square, PA: PMI Publishing.

Pyzdek, T. 1999. *The Complete Guide to Six Sigma*. Quality Publishing.

Siviy, J. 2001. *Six Sigma*. The Software Engineering Institute (SEI).

Williamson, M. 1997. Quality Pays. *Computerworld* (August 18).

Woodall, J., D. K., Rebuck, et al. 1997. *Total Quality in Information Systems and Technology*. Delray Beach, FL: St. Lucie Press.

11

Managing Organizational Change, Resistance, and Conflict

CHAPTER OVERVIEW

Projects are planned organizational change. This chapter will focus on preparing the organization for change. After studying this chapter, you should understand and be able to:

■ Describe the discipline of organizational change management and its role in assessing the organization's readiness and capability to support and assimilate a change initiative.

■ Describe how change can be viewed as a process and identify the emotional responses people might have when faced with change.

■ Describe the framework for managing change that will be introduced in this chapter.

■ Apply the concepts and ideas in this chapter in order to develop a change management plan. This plan should focus on assessing the organization's willingness and ability to change, developing a change strategy, implementing and tracking the progress toward achieving the change and then evaluating whether the change was successful, and documenting the lessons learned from those experiences.

■ Discuss the nature of resistance and conflict and apply several techniques for dealing with conflict and resistance in an efficient and effective way.

INTRODUCTION

Most technical people tend to enjoy the challenges of setting up a network, writing snazzy code using the latest and hottest technology, or designing a solution to solve some organizational problem. After all, that is what they're trained to do, and most people who enter the IT profession enjoy new challenges and learning new things. Indeed, many IT professionals believe that given enough time, training, and resources just about any technical problem can be solved. Being stuck in a boring job with obsolete skills is not a condition for career longevity—people will either leave to find new challenges or find themselves looking for new jobs. It is important to keep pace with technological changes, and many of these changes are welcome.

IT projects are planned organizational change. Organizations are made up of people, and the implementation of the IT project's product can change the way people work, affect the way they share information, and alter their relationships. Whether you are an outside consultant or work for an internal IS department within the organization, your mere presence will often be met with suspicion and hostility because you will be viewed as a person who has the potential to disrupt their stability. You are an agent of change. As an old saying goes, the only people who like change are wet babies.

It is easy to concentrate on the hard side of IT project management. Dealing with the people issues, or soft side of technology, is an area that most technical people do not enjoy. It is human nature to focus on what we can accomplish with minimal conflict or on what we can control. Implementing a network of computers that communicate with each other or getting a program to work properly may be much easier and less stressful than dealing with resistance and conflict during systems development.

In addition, many technical people and managers naively believe that the users within the organization will gladly embrace a new system if it is built properly. Although a system may include the required features and functionality and perform as intended, this "build a better mousetrap and the world will beat a path to your door" mentality can still lead to a system that is a technical success but an organizational failure.

Implementation of the new system is a technical challenge. The system must be moved from the development environment to a production environment and properly tested before *going live*. The people within the organization, however, must be prepared for the impact that the new system will have on them. It is easy to underestimate this impact and, given human nature, downplay the response people will have. Managers and technical people may be given to false beliefs:

- "People want this change."
- "Monday morning we'll turn on the new system and they'll use it."
- "A good training program will answer all of their questions and then they'll love it."
- "Our people have been through a lot of change—what's one more change going to matter?"
- "We see the need for helping our people adjust, but we had to cut something. . ."
- "They have two choices: They can change or they can leave."

These statements reflect the view that it is easier to gain compliance than it is to gain acceptance. This supposition is faulty because it assumes that everyone will comply and that compliance will be long lasting. The results may be quite different:

- The change may not occur.
- People will comply for a time and then do things to get around the change.
- Users will accept only a portion of the change.

The full benefits of the project are never realized or are realized only after a great deal of time and resources have been expended.

The central theme of this text has been the concept of measurable organization value. The MOV is not only the overall goal of the project, but is also a measure

QUICK THINKING—IT'S NOT EASY GOING GREEN

WellPoint, a health benefits company in Indianapolis, Indiana is greening its IT users. The company was a founding partner in Dell's "Plant a Forest for Me" program where it pays an additional $40 when it purchases a server from Dell. Dell then gives the money to a conservation group to offset the carbon emissions produced by the server. In addition to recycling and using recycled paper, WellPoint has tried to become a better citizen by substituting videoconferencing for travel. In fact, employees will spend 25,000 hours videoconferencing a year that will save 4,500 tons of carbon dioxide emissions from cars and planes. Dave McDonald, vice president of infrastructure support services, says that WellPoint will also replace 900 older, inefficient computers with server consolidations, as well as most of its old CRTs with more energy efficient LCD monitors. However, there has been some resistance to WellPoint's green initiative. With respect to videoconferencing, McDonald said "People here were kind of scared of it. They didn't know if it was hard to do or how it worked.

But once they used it, it was an easy sell." Moreover, Mark Boxer, WellPoint's president and CEO, reflected "A lot of the improvements are about removing entitlements. Does everyone need a printer in their office? Does everyone need to travel to meetings? Moving away from these mind-sets requires very senior sponsorship."

1. Some people may believe that a green initiative would be an easy sell within an organization. Why would people be resistant to such a seemingly beneficial change?
2. Why is senior sponsorship so necessary for such a change initiative? What are some ways in which senior management could show implicit and explicit support for a green initiative?

SOURCE: Adapted from Gary Anthes, Top 12 Green-IT Users: No. 8 WellPoint Inc., *Computerworld*, February 15, 2008.

---

of the project's success. It is how we define the value our project will bring to the organization after the project is implemented as originally envisioned. It provides a means for determining which projects should be funded and drives many of the decisions associated with the project throughout its life cycle. If the project's MOV is not realized in its entirety, then only a portion of the project's value to the organization is realized. Organizations today cannot afford to mismanage change initiatives. Competitive pressures provide little room for error. There is also the potential for lawsuits arising from stress-related disabilities and wrongful discharge (Bridges 1991). Therefore, while it is important that we manage the development of our project well, we also need to ensure that the project's product is transferred successfully and accepted by the organization with minimal adverse impact.

Acceptance by the users of the system is much more powerful and longer lasting than compliance, which means we need to ensure that the people within the organization are prepared properly *before* the system is implemented. The discipline called **change management** is the area of IT project management that helps smooth the transition and implementation of the new IT solution. The Gartner Group defines change management as:

> The transforming of the organization so it is aligned with the execution of a chosen corporate business strategy. It is the management of the human element in a large-scale change project.

The remainder of this chapter will focus on how change may be viewed as a process and on the emotional aspects normally associated with change. A framework for developing a change management plan and several techniques for dealing with the resistance and conflict that are a natural part of the change initiative will be introduced. Although this chapter deals will the soft side of IT project management, it is an important foundation for planning the implementation of the IT solution that will be discussed in the last chapter.

 # THE NATURE OF CHANGE

In order to effectively plan and manage organizational change, it is important to understand the impact of change, how change may be viewed as a process, and the emotional behavioral patterns of change.

Change Has an Impact

At any given time we must deal with changes that affect us. These changes may result from world or local events, the organizations we are part of, or personal decisions and relationships (Conner 1995). Think about the changes that are going on in your life right now. You may be graduating soon, seeking employment, moving to a new residence, or scheduling root canal work with your dentist the day after tomorrow. The point is that there are a number of changes going on in our lives at any given moment. We may view these changes as being either positive or negative. As Jeanie Duck (2001) observes, nearly all change in our lives entails some amount of anxiety. Anxiety combined with hope is anticipation, while anxiety combined with apprehension is dread.

Whether we view change as positive (anticipation) or negative (dread), there is a certain amount of stress that accompanies each change. For example, let's say that you will graduate this semester and start a new job that requires you to move to a distant city. Although you may be looking forward to leaving school and earning some real money, you may still feel some apprehension. After all, you will have to leave your circle of family and/or friends and the familiarity of your present environment. Once you arrive in your new city, you will need to find a new place to live, make new friends, and become familiar with your new job, the company, and its people. Moving to a new city is relatively easy compared to the transition. The move itself is a change that will occur fairly quickly; the transition required to adjust to the change takes longer.

In *Managing at the Speed of Change*, Daryl Conner (1995) points out that an individual must deal with a variety of changes in his or her life and that we must assimilate these changes over time. **Assimilation** is the process of adapting to change and determines our ability to handle current and future change (Davidson 2002). For example, you may be dreading that root canal work next Wednesday, but once it's over you won't have the same level of anxiety that you are feeling right now. Or, you may be in the midst of planning a wedding. Most people view weddings as happy occasions, but anyone who has planned and gone through a wedding knows it can be stressful. The stress and anxiety felt before the ceremony, however, become a distant memory once the happy couple celebrates their first anniversary. It simply takes time to assimilate change because we must adjust to the transition. Major changes, whether positive or negative, will require more time to assimilate than small ones. But once change is assimilated, it no longer creates the same level of anxiety or stress.

Problems occur when we cannot assimilate change fast enough. Unfortunately, change tends to have a cumulative effect, and we can only assimilate change at a given pace. Different people will assimilate change at a different pace, and this ability to assimilate change becomes our resiliency to handle change. Figure 11.1 illustrates the cumulative effect of assimilating change over time.

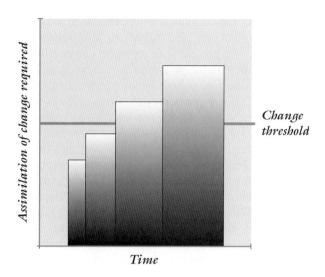

Figure 11.1 Assimilating Change

SOURCE: D. Conner, *Managing at the Change of Speed* (New York: Villard Books, 1995).

Problems occur when we have to deal with too many changes or when we cannot assimilate change fast enough. When an individual passes a certain threshold, he or she may become stressed out and exhibit dysfunctional behaviors. The behaviors depend largely on the person and may range from mild irritability to depression or dependence on alcohol or drugs. Therefore, it is important to manage the assimilation of change to keep things below the change threshold. In order to do this, an individual may try various tactics, such as exercising more regularly or postponing major life changes so as to deal more effectively with the present changes.

Organizations are made up of people and these people have any number of personal changes going on in their lives. Changes proposed by an organization (e.g., reorganization, downsizing, implementing a new information system) will certainly affect the way people work and the relationships that have become established. Although these organizational changes will have to be assimilated by each person, the organization must assimilate change similar to an individual. After all, organizations are made up of people. Therefore, each change adopted by an organization must be assimilated and managed within the change threshold. Just like people, organizations can exhibit dysfunctional behaviors. These behaviors may include an inability to take advantage of new opportunities or solve current problems. Eventually, an organization's inability to assimilate change will be reflected in the organization's ability to make a profit. Like an individual who cannot effectively deal with change and the associated stress, the long-term health and sustainability of the organization becomes questionable.

Change within an organization can affect different things in different ways. Leavitt's model, as illustrated in Figure 11.2, suggests that changes in people, technology, task, or organizational structure can influence or impact the other areas (Leavitt 1964). These four components are interdependent, where a change in one can result in a change in the others For example, a change in the organization's technology (e.g., implementing a new information system) can impact the people within the organization (e.g., new roles, responsibilities, etc.) as well as the tasks the individual's perform (i.e., the work they perform), and the organization's structure (i.e., formal or informal).

Change Is a Process

Although a great deal has been written about change management, one of the most useful models for understanding change was developed by Kurt Lewin (1951). Lewin developed the concept of force field analysis or change theory to help analyze and understand the forces for and against a particular plan or change initiative. A force field analysis is a technique for developing a big picture that involves all the forces in favor of or against a particular change. Forces that are viewed as facilitating the change are viewed as driving forces, while the forces that act as barriers or that work against the change are called resisting forces. By understanding all of the forces that act as aids or barriers to the change, one may enact strategies or decisions that take into account all of the various interests.

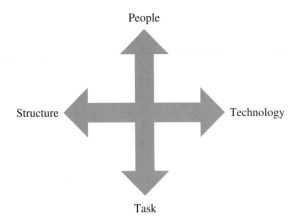

Figure 11.2 Leavitt's Model of Organizational Change

Lewin's basic model includes three concepts: unfreezing, changing, and refreezing as illustrated in Figure 11.3. The present state represents an equilibrium or status quo. To change from the current state, there must be driving forces both to initiate and to motivate the change. This requires an unfreezing, or an altering of the current state's habits, perceptions, and stability.

Figure 11.3 also depicts a transition from the present state to the desired state. This state is sometimes referred to as the neutral zone and can be a limbo or emotional wilderness for many individuals (Bridges 1991). Problems arise when managers do not understand, expect, or acknowledge the neutral zone. Those in the organization who act and support the driving forces for the change may be likely to rush individuals through the transition. This rushing often results in confusion on the part of those in the neutral zone, and the resisting forces (i.e., the emotional and psychological barriers) tend to push those individuals back to their present state. People do not like being caught in the neutral zone. They may try to revert to the original status quo or escape. Escape may mean leaving the organization or resistance to the change initiative altogether. In addition, individuals who find themselves in the neutral zone too long may attempt to create a compromise in which only a portion of the change is implemented. This compromise will only result in missed opportunities and sets a bad precedence for the next change initiative—if this one did not work, why should anyone believe the next one will?

People do not necessarily resist change; they resist losses and endings. Unfreezing, or moving from the current state, means letting go of something. Therefore, viewing change from Lewin's model suggests that beginning a change starts with an ending of the present state. Transition through the neutral zone also means a loss of equilibrium until an individual or organization moves to the desired state. Once there, it is important that the attitudes, behaviors, and perceptions be refrozen so that the desired state becomes the new status quo and equilibrium for the individuals involved.

Change Can Be Emotional

Until now, we have looked at change as a process and how change affects different areas of the organization. Change can also bring out emotional responses. An individual may have an emotional response to a change when the change is perceived as a significant loss or upsets a familiar or well established equilibrium. In her book *On Death and Dying*, Elizabeth Kübler-Ross (1969) provides insight into the range of emotions one may experience from the loss of a loved one. These same emotional responses can be applied to managing change whenever people experience the loss of something that matters to them.

The original model included five stages that we go through as part of a grieving process that leads to eventual healing. If

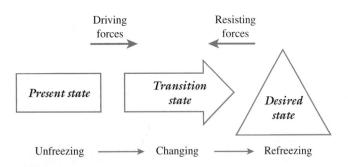

Figure 11.3 Change Process

SOURCE: Based on K. Lewin, *Field Theory in Social Science* (New York: Harper and Row, 1951).

people are not allowed to grieve and go through the first four stages, it becomes difficult to reach the last stage—acceptance. A person may have a number of emotions, such as sorrow, loneliness, guilt, and so forth, but the inability to work through these five stages can create more stress and difficulties than working through the stages. Although Kübler-Ross's model has been widely accepted, it has also been criticized as being oversimplified. However, it still provides some valuable insight for understanding how people may react to significant changes that affect their lives. The five stages include:

- *Denial*—The first stage is characterized by shock and denial. It is a common reaction when a person is given first notice of a change that will have significant impact. For example, when a person is informed that he or she is being fired by an organization, the initial response may be, Are you serious? This can't be true! The reality may be too overwhelming. Disbelief may be the immediate defense mechanism. The initial news, however, provides a beginning for understanding the full impact of the change that is about to take place.

- *Anger*—Once a person gets over the initial shock of the announcement, he or she may become angry toward others, or even the messenger. The reaction is to blame whoever is responsible for creating the change. Although anger is a more active emotional response, it can be a cathartic expression when people are allowed to vent their emotions. Keep in mind that there is a difference between feeling anger and acting out in anger. While having feelings is always acceptable, the latter never is.

- *Bargaining*—In the third stage, the person is no longer angry. In fact, he or she may be quite cooperative and may try to make deals in order to avoid the change. For example, the person who lost her job may begin making promises that she will "double my productivity" or "take a cut in pay" in order to avoid being let go. A person may look for ways to extend the status quo, or the present equilibrium, by trying to "work things out."

- *Depression*—Once a person admits that the change is inevitable, he or she may understand the full impact of the change and may enter the fourth stage—depression. This stage generally occurs when there is an overwhelming sense of the loss of the status quo. Although losing a job involves losing income, most people become depressed because they also lose the identity associated with their job.

- *Acceptance*—The last stage is when a person comes to grips with the change. A person does not have to like the change in order to accept it. This fifth stage has more to do with one's resolve that the change is inevitable and must be dealt with. Acceptance is an important part of ending the status quo and getting on with a new state.

These emotional responses can help us understand why people react the way they do when faced with organizational change. Because of these emotions, people may be drained and productivity in the organization will suffer. It is also important to understand that people will have different perceptions of change. But their perception is their reality. Often management and the project team will have known about and have had the time to prepare for an upcoming change. While they may be impatient for the change to occur, others in the organization will lag. Management and the project team may want to "get on with it," while the others are still dealing with their emotions during the transition. Instead of trying to suppress these individuals and their emotions, the leaders of change should accept them as a normal part of the change process and address them in the change management plan (Duck 2001).

THE CHANGE MANAGEMENT PLAN

The key to any organizational change is to plan for and manage the change and the associated transition effectively. This entails developing a change management plan that addresses the human side of change. The mere existence of such a plan can send an important message throughout the organization that management cares about the people in the organization and will listen and take their needs and issues seriously (Bridges 1991). Depending on the size and impact of the change initiative, the change management plan can be an informal or formal document; however, the project team and sponsor should address and be clear on several important areas. These areas are summarized in Figure 11.4, and provide a framework for developing a change management plan discussed in this section.

Assess Willingness, Readiness, and Ability to Change

The first step to developing a change management plan is to assess the organization's willingness, readiness, and ability to change. This assessment entails defining who the players or stakeholders involved in the change will be, their roles, and how they will interact with each other (Davidson 2002). Conner (1995) defines several roles or players involved in a change initiative: the sponsor, change agents, and targets.

Sponsor   The sponsor can be an individual or group that has the willingness and power, in terms of authority and making resources available, to support the project.

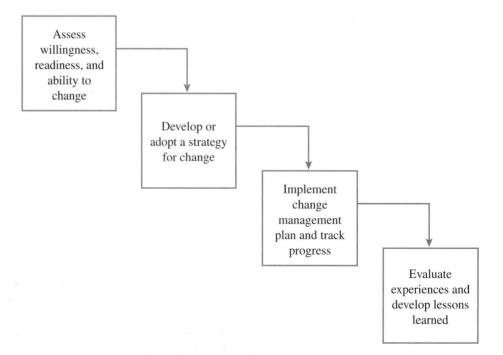

Figure 11.4   Change Management Plan

Although this person or group is often the project sponsor, an **initiating sponsor** may hand off the project to a **sustaining sponsor**. More specifically, after making the decision to fund and support the project, the initiating sponsor may become completely removed from the project. Without the support of a sustaining sponsor, the project will eventually lose steam and direction. Therefore, the sustaining sponsor must become the primary sponsor for the project. A major portion of the organization's ability and willingness to support the change rests with the sponsor's commitment to the project and the associated change that will impact the organization. This commitment may be in terms of how they communicate with the rest of the organization, how they deal with challenges and issues, and the amount and quality of resources made available. In addition, sponsors must be effective leaders. If the project fails because the organization cannot adapt to the change, the project's envisioned value to the organization is lost and the sponsor's credibility is diminished. As Conner points out, "they lose twice."

Change Agents   In the most basic terms, the change agents will be the project manager and team; however, others from inside or outside the organization may be involved as well. An agent may be an individual or group responsible for making the change happen in order to achieve the project's goal and objectives. Change agents report directly to the sponsor and must be able to diagnose problems, plan to deal with these issues and challenges effectively, and act as a conduit of communication between the sponsor and the targets of change. The ability to sustain the change associated with the IT project rests largely with the change agents. They must be ready and properly prepared to meet the challenges they face.

Targets   The target is the individual or group that must change. In general, these may be the users of the new system or those who will use or be directly involved with final product of the project. Conner uses the term "target" because these are the people who are the focus of the change effort and who play a critical role in the ultimate success of the project.

Although the project sponsors and change agents play important roles in supporting and carrying out the change effort, the dynamics associated with the targets of change become the most critical. Therefore, the willingness, ability, and readiness to change also rest largely with the change targets. This may require: (1) clarifying the real impacts of the change, (2) understanding the breadth of change, (3) defining what's over and what's not, and (4) determining whether the rules for success have changed.

The project team and sponsor often do not think about how the planned change and transition will really affect people within the organization. As described in the previous section, change often brings about endings and a sense of loss of control. The project team and sponsor should take the time to think about what various individuals or groups stand to lose. For example, perceptions of loss may include power, relationships with other people, stability, or even control. As a result, people may become confused and disoriented.

People also become confused and disoriented when the rules for success change or are no longer clearly defined. Let's say that you have been working at a company for several years. Over that time, you have come to understand and become part of that culture. You know from your own experience and from those around you that promotion is based solely on seniority. As long as you meet the minimum performance requirements of your job, you know that promotions and the pay raises that follow will come after working a specific amount of time in a particular job.

If the company ever has to lay off employees, you know that layoffs will begin with the employees with the least seniority. But what if the company you work for has been acquired by a larger organization? The acquiring company has decided to "make a few changes" and starts by downsizing the workforce in your company. But now each employee's performance will be reviewed and only the top performers will be invited to stay. You can only begin to imagine peoples' reactions. The rules for success have changed.

Develop or Adopt a Strategy for Change

Once the organization's capability to change is assessed, the next step involves developing or adopting a strategy for change. Davidson (2002) provides four approaches to change management.

Rational-Empirical Approach The rational-empirical approach to change management is based on the idea that people follow predictable patterns of behavior and that people will follow their own self-interests. Therefore, a change agent must be persuasive in convincing, explaining, and demonstrating how a particular change will benefit a particular person or group identified as a target of the change.

It is important that the individuals affected by the change be provided with consistent and timely information. Consistent information means that the project team and sponsor send the same message to all individuals and groups throughout the organization. Mixed messages can lead to confusion and suspicion. Credibility should not become suspect. In addition, each message must be accurate and timely. Often the excuse is, "It may be better to wait until we have all the details." But, saying nothing at all can send the wrong message.

When people are not given enough information, they tend to seek information from other sources. Often these sources rely on innuendos, misinformation, and opinions, which become gossip that spreads through the informal organization. Stress levels rise until a point is reached where the organization becomes dysfunctional. It is better to be honest and tell people that there is no news before the rumor mill goes into warp drive.

Many managers believe that it is better to spare people bad news until the very last moment. However, it may be better to give people enough advanced warning to allow them to prepare for any upcoming changes. Then they can deal effectively with the gamut of emotions that will be brought on by the change.

The change management plan based on this strategy should provide each individual with the purpose, a picture, and a part to play. Purpose is the reason for the change. Often individuals within the organization have a narrow view of their job and its relationship to the rest of the organization. It may be useful to provide people with a chance to see or experience the problem or opportunity first hand. For example, a person may be given the chance to witness how the current level of poor service is affecting the organization's customers. Then, it should be clear to that person that unless the organization does something (i.e., implement a new information system), it will continue losing customers to its competition. In time, the company will have to reduce its workforce or inevitably face bankruptcy.

A picture, on the other hand, provides a vision or a picture in the individual's mind as to how the organization will look or operate in the future. If done effectively, this procedure can help the individual buy into the proposed change.

A part to play can be very effective in helping the individual become involved in the proposed change. Although purpose and a picture of the proposed change are important, it is also important for the individual to understand and visualize the part he or she will play once the change is instituted. Having a part may provide the needed WIIFM (or, what's in it for me?) to help them through the transition.

Normative-Reeducation Approach The normative-reeducation strategy for change management is based on the work of Kurt Lewin. This approach takes the basic view that people are social beings and that human behavior can be changed by changing the social norms of a group. Instead of trying to change an individual, one must focus on the core values, beliefs, and established relationships that make up the culture of the group. For example, you may hear, "That's the way things are done around here." The targets of change in this case may be highly resistant to new ideas or new ways of doing things.

This approach can be very difficult and time consuming because the change agents and sponsor must study the existing values and beliefs of a group. It requires unfreezing the current norms so that the change can take place and so that a new set of norms can be refrozen in order to solidify the acceptance of the new way of doing things by the group. As a result, change becomes more effective when each person adopts the beliefs and values of the group. The focus for managing change under this strategy becomes helping people redefine their existing social norms into a new set that supports the change effort. Some key principles include:

- Capacity for change is directly related to a person's participation in a group. When we become part of a group, our views and beliefs and those of the group become interwoven with each other.

- Effective change requires changing something not only about the individual's values and beliefs, but also the values and beliefs that make up the existing group's culture.

- Bias and prejudice toward guarding one's closely held beliefs and values diminishes one's ability to think rationally. Even when presented with the facts, many people may not act upon them in a rational way.

Power-Coercive Approach The power-coercive approach to change management attempts to gain compliance from the change targets through the exercise of power, authority, rewards, or threat of punishment for nonconformance. Many managers may be lured into using this deceptively easy and straightforward approach, but there is a real risk when used in the wrong situation. People may comply (or at least go through the motions of compliance), but an approach based solely on rewards or punishment may have only a short-term effect. For example, a person may comply for the time being, until they can find new employment. On the other hand, a person may view the change as temporary and just "wait out the storm" until it is convenient or safe to go back to the old way of doing things.

There are, however, situations where the power-coercive approach is useful and effective. In such cases, the targets of change recognize the legitimate power or expertise of the change agent. For example, a person may not change his indolent lifestyle until the doctor cautions him that certain health problems will get worse unless he changes his diet and begins an exercise program. Similarly, an organization may be faced with a situation that requires immediate attention—that is, any inaction or time lost trying to get everyone "on board" would spell disaster for the company. In this case, the use of rewards and threats would be a rational approach. As Davidson observes:

> People's dependency on an organization largely dictates how effective the power-coercive approach and the use of sanctions can be. If people are highly dependent on the organization; live paycheck to paycheck; have few job alternatives; and are not financially, mentally, or emotionally prepared to walk, you are on relatively safe ground using the power-coercive approach judiciously (90–91).

The objective is to change the behaviors of the targets so that their new behavior supports the change effort. Davidson points out that sanctions should be imposed on an individual level and should focus on what an individual values and what they dread losing—perhaps a bonus, a paycheck, or a position within the organization. Sanctions can be imposed in ascending order to demonstrate a point in the beginning and to keep any target's losses at a minimum. A change agent or sponsor can lose credibility, however, if they issue a warning or sanction that they do not fully intend to carry out. Finally, the change agent or sponsor should never be abrasive or disrespectful and should not impose sanctions in a cruel or vindictive manner.

Environmental-Adaptive Approach   Like a pair of old, comfortable shoes, people often become attached to and comfortable with a certain way of doing things, perhaps an older system or established processes that have become part of the group's culture and norms. The premise of the environmental-adaptive approach is that although people avoid disruption and loss, they can still adapt to change.

Following this approach, the change agent attempts to make the change permanent by abolishing the old ways and instituting the new structure as soon as possible. Cortez, the explorer, probably displayed the most drastic form of this approach. After landing in the New World, many of his men began to grumble about the conditions and what lay ahead. In response, Cortez burned the boats so that there was no option other than pressing on. A much less drastic example would be upgrading everyone's word processing software over the weekend so that when everyone returned to work on Monday morning, they would have no choice but using the new software package. In both examples, the targets of change were given no choice but to change.

Although this approach may be effective in certain situations, it is still important that the targets of change assimilate the change as quickly as possible in order to adapt to the change as soon as possible. Some ways may include helping the targets of change see the benefits and showing them how the new way is similar to their old, familiar way of doing things.

The change management strategies introduced here are typical for many change initiatives. A single strategy or approach, however, may not be effective in every situation. A more useful approach may be to combine the different strategies, depending on the impact of the change and the organization.

Implement the Change Management Plan and Track Progress

Once the players and the strategy for the change management plan have been defined, the next step entails implementing the change management plan and tracking its progress. Although tracking progress should be integrated into the overall project plan and monitored using the various project tools, such as the Gantt chart, PERT chart, and so forth, introduced in an earlier chapter, milestones and other significant events should be identified and used to gauge how well the organization is adapting to the change.

In addition, one of the most critical issues for ensuring that the change takes place as planned is the establishment of effective lines of communication. At the very outset of any change initiative, gossip, rumors, and people's perceptions will find their way in both the formal and informal organizations. It is important that the project team and project sponsor create and open channels of communication.

The communication media can be important, especially when delivering certain types of news. For example, a richer media, such as face-to-face communication, is generally preferable when delivering important or bad news. There are a number of stories about people who realized that they were being let go when they found their phone line and network connections disconnected and security guards standing by their desk waiting to escort them out of the building. Delivering bad news is something that no one really enjoys, but must be done nonetheless. The point is that management can handle difficult situations with class or with very little class.

Finally, open channels of communication should be both ways. The project team and sponsor must communicate effectively with the various groups within the organization affected by the change, and these groups, in turn, must be able to communicate effectively with the project team and sponsor. In addition, Web sites, emails, memos, and newsletters can all be mediums for effective communication.

Evaluate Experience and Develop Lessons Learned

As the project team carries out the change management plan, they will, no doubt, learn from their experiences. These experiences should be documented and made available to other team members and other projects so that experiences can be shared and best practices can be identified. At the end of the project, it is important that the overall success of the change management plan be evaluated. This evaluation may help determine the effectiveness of the different players or a particular change management strategy. The important thing is to learn from experience and to share those experiences with others while adding new form and functionality to the project organization's IT project methodology.

DEALING WITH RESISTANCE AND CONFLICT

Resistance and conflict are a natural part of change (Davidson 2002). In this section, we will look at the nature of resistance and conflict and several approaches for dealing with these two issues. Keep in mind that the concept of conflict presented in this section can be applied to conflicts within the project team as well as external conflicts brought about by the change effort.

Resistance

Resistance should be anticipated from the outset of the project. Rumors and gossip will add fuel to the fire, and the change effort can easily run out of steam if those affected by the change begin to resist. Resistance can be either overt, in the form of memos, meetings, and so on, or covert, in the form of sabotage, foot dragging, politicking, etc. Once the change is compromised, management and the project team will lose credibility, and the organization may become resistant to all future changes.

Resistance can arise for many valid reasons. For example, someone may resist an information system because the response time is too slow or because it does not provide the features or functionality that were originally specified as part of the requirements. On the other hand, resistance due to cultural or behavioral reasons is harder to rationalize, but still can keep a project from reaching its intended goal. People may resist change even though they understand that the change will be beneficial (Davidson 2002). For example:

- Some people perceive the change as requiring more time and energy than they are willing to invest.

- Sometimes people feel that a change will mean giving up something that is familiar, comfortable, and predictable.

- People may be annoyed with the disruption caused by the change, even if they know that it will be beneficial in the long run.

- People may believe that the change is being imposed on them externally, and their egos will not tolerate being told what to do.

- In addition, people may resist because of the way the decision to change was announced or because it was forced on them.

Resistance is human nature and a natural part of any change process. Understanding what an individual or group perceives as a loss is the first step to dealing with resistance effectively. Because the project team and sponsor are the agents of change, it is easy to see those who resist as overreacting or not being logical. As the proponents of change, the project team and sponsor have had the luxury of knowing about the change early and, therefore, have had the time to become used to it. The rest of the organization, however, may learn about the change much later and, therefore, may not be at the same place for digesting the change. Subsequently, it is important that the project team and sponsor listen to what the rest of the organization is saying. Instead of arguing and trying to reason, it is better to allow people to vent their anger and frustration. Again, having defined a boundary of what is and what is not part of the change can help deal with stressful conflict situations. Keep in mind that empathizing or sympathizing with an individual is not the same as agreeing with them.

Conflict

Closely associated with resistance is the concept of conflict. Conflicts arise when people perceive that their interests and values are challenged or not being met. **Conflict management** focuses on preventing, managing, or resolving conflicts. Therefore, it is important to identify potential conflicts as early as possible so that the conflict can be addressed. Although conflict can be positive and help form new ideas and establish commitment, negative conflict left unresolved can lead to damaged relationships, mistrust, unresolved issues, continued stress, dysfunctional behavior, and low productivity and morale (Davidson 2002). As Verma (1998) suggests:

> Although conflict is one of the things most of us dislike intensely, it is inevitable. Most often when we try to avoid conflict, it will nevertheless seek us out. Some people wrongly hope that conflict will go away if it is ignored. In fact, conflict ignored is more likely to get worse, which can significantly reduce project performance. The best way to reduce conflict is to confront it (367).

QUICK THINKING—CROSS-FUNCTIONAL AND MULTICULTURAL TEAMS

Cross-functional projects are common in many organizations. Too often these project teams are composed of people who do not work together or even know one another. They may believe that they've been thrown together and are expected to produce something right away. Moreover, many projects may also be multicultural, either because of the organization's global reach or because many workers today have emigrated from another country. Unfortunately, cross-functional and multicultural projects almost always entail conflict because people often have different ideas of leadership, cultural backgrounds, language, or attitudes such as the importance of deadlines or the flexibility of rules. Cultural differences impeded the credit rating agency Moody's Investors Service's ability to conduct software testing and process audits. The organization's culture could be described as "a largely homogeneous American development environment" that encouraged independent thought and an open acknowledgement of defects. The quality assurance methodology depended upon democratic social discourse that supported freedom to express opinions, challenge others, and brainstorm solutions. Lastly, the organizational culture also encouraged a "tell it like it is" where everyone could express criticism without embarrassment or fear of reprisal. Many of these values and behaviors collided when the technical employees at Moody's became more multicultural. For some, a caste system or hierarchy established rules for social interaction, while others observed a strict obedience to authority. It became increasingly difficult to resolve conflict, as open disagreement and criticism could be viewed as a personal loss of face. More specifically, developers were perceived to have a higher level of status than the testers. Developers became less willing to collaborate with the testers, and the testers became less willing to criticize and potentially shame their betters. Since intellectual give-and-take might be perceived as a challenge to the developers, the testers began to show their productivity and worth by running a large series of easy, superficial tests that generated a mountain of documentation. While productivity appeared to be high, quality assurance in terms of testing and process audits were declining.

1. Often cross-cultural conflicts can be mistaken for personality or job performance issues. What signs might you look for to identify conflicts that result from cultural differences?

2. As a project manager, what would could you do to reduce conflict and bridge the communication differences between the testers and the developers?

SOURCE: Adapted from Deborah Barry, The People Side, *Projects@Work*, January 24, 2008; Deborah Barry, One on Ones, *Projects@Work*, January 15, 2008; Patricia Ensworth, Patricia Ensworh on Managing Multicultural Project Teams at Moody's, *Computerworld*, October 1, 2003.

There are three different views of conflict that have evolved from the late nineteenth century to today (Verma 1998). These views are (1) the traditional view (mid-nineteenth century to mid-1940s), (2) the contemporary view (mid-1940s to 1970s), and (3) the interactionist view (1970s to present).

- *Traditional view*—The traditional view considers conflict in a negative light and feels that conflict should be avoided. Conflict, according to this view, leads to poor performance, aggression, and devastation if left to escalate. Therefore, it is important to manage conflict by suppressing it before it occurs or eliminating it as soon as possible. Harmony can be achieved through authoritarian means, but the root causes of the conflict may not be adequately addressed.

- *Contemporary view*—The contemporary view, on the other hand, suggests that conflict is inevitable and natural. Depending on how conflict is handled, conflict can be either positive or negative. Positive conflict among people can stimulate ideas and creativity; however, negative conflict can have damaging effects if left unresolved. Therefore, positive conflict should be encouraged, while keeping negative conflict in check.

■ *Interactionist view*—Today, the interactionist view holds that conflict is an important and necessary ingredient for performance. Although the contemporary view accepts conflict, the interactionist view embraces it because teams can become stagnant and complacent if too harmonious or tranquil (Verma 1998). Subsequently, the project manager should occasionally stir the pot in order to encourage conflict to an appropriate level so that people engage in positive conflict. This may, however, be a fine line to walk for many project managers. Although someone who plays the role of the devil's advocate can be effective in many situations, people may become annoyed when it is used in every situation or used ineffectively.

To better understand the nature of conflict, Verma (1998) points out that conflict within projects can fit one, or a combination, of three categories:

1. Conflicts associated with the goals, objectives, or specifications of the project
2. Conflicts associated with the administration, management structures, or underlying philosophies of the project
3. Conflicts associated with the interpersonal relationships among people based on work ethics, styles, egos, or personalities

For the project manager and project team, the seeds of resistance can easily lead to negative conflicts. Subsequently, it is important to understand how to deal with conflict. Blake and Mouton (1964) and Verma (1998) describe five approaches for dealing with conflict. A project team member or project manager should choose an appropriate approach for managing conflict based on the situation.

■ *Avoidance*—Avoiding conflict focuses on retreating, withdrawing or ignoring conflict. Sometimes, a cooling-off period may be a wise choice, especially when emotions and tempers are high. Avoidance may be appropriate when you can't win, the stakes are low, or gaining time is important. However, it may not be useful when the immediate, successful resolution of an issue is required.

■ *Accommodation*—Accommodation, or smoothing, is an approach for appeasing the various parties in conflict. This approach may be useful when trying to reach an overall goal when the goal is more important than the personal interests of the parties involved. Smoothing may also be effective when dealing with an issue that has low risk and low return or when in a no-win situation. Because accommodation tends to work only in the short run, conflict may reappear in another form later on.

■ *Forcing*—When using this approach, a person uses his or her dominant authority to resolve the conflict. This approach often results in a one-sided or win-lose situation in which one party gains at the other's expense. This approach may be effective when no common ground exists, when you are sure you are right, when an emergency situation exists, or when time is of the essence. Forcing resolution may, however, cause the conflict to redevelop later because people dislike having a decision or someone else's views imposed on them.

■ *Compromise*—Compromise includes aspects of both forcing and accommodation; it gives up more than forcing and less than accommodation. Compromise is essentially bargaining—one person or group gives up something in exchange for gaining something else. In this case, no party actually wins and none actually loses, so that some satisfaction is gained from resolution of the conflict. This approach may be useful when attempting to resolve complex problems that must be settled in a short time and when the risks and rewards are moderately high. Unfortunately, important aspects of a project may be compromised as a means of achieving short-term results—for example, quality standards may be compromised in order to meet the project's schedule.

■ *Collaboration*—When the risks and benefits are high, collaboration may be the best approach for dealing with conflict. This approach requires confronting and attempting to solve the problem by incorporating different ideas, viewpoints, and perspectives. The focus of collaboration is learning from others and gaining commitment, trust, respect, and confidence from the various parties involved. Collaboration takes time and requires a sincere desire to work out a mutually acceptable solution. In addition, it requires a willingness to engage in a good-faith problem-solving process that facilitates open and honest communication.

Each conflict situation is unique and the choice of an approach to resolve conflict depends on:

■ Type of conflict and its relative importance to the project

■ Time pressure to resolve the conflict

■ Position of power or authority of the parties involved

■ Whether the emphasis is on maintaining the goals or objectives of the project or maintaining relationships

 # CHAPTER SUMMARY

Understanding organizational change is an important area for IT project management. IT professionals may concentrate exclusively on the technical, or hard, side of the project at the expense of the people, or soft, side. Unfortunately, this position often results in the implementation of information systems that are technical successes, but organizational failures. The system performs efficiently, but the people or users do not accept the system because of what the system represents.

Therefore, it is important the project sponsor, the IT project manager, and the project team help prepare the users, or targets, of the intended change before the system is implemented. Preparation requires that we first understand the nature of change when a change is introduced into the organization. Often change and peoples' reaction to change unfold in predictable patterns or behaviors.

In this chapter, we first looked at change as a process. Kurt Lewin introduced the concept of force field analysis, in which we try first to understand the driving and resisting forces that push and repel the change. In addition, Lewin's model of change helps us to

understand that we must unfreeze the current state, or status quo, and then move through a transitional state until the new or desired state is reached. Then, these new behaviors must be refrozen so that they become ingrained as the new status quo. It is important that those who sponsor and are responsible for implementing the change acknowledge and understand the transition state. Sometimes referred to as the neutral zone, the transition state can be frightening and frustrating for people who find themselves in a state of limbo. While the change is relatively easy, the transition can be a difficult time in which people may try to escape, or revert back to the more comfortable and familiar previous state. Moreover, initiating a change begins with an ending of the current equilibrium and may bring out a number of emotional responses as a result of a perceived loss. Since both people and organizations can only assimilate or process change at a given rate, the cumulative effect of change can result in stress and dysfunctional behavior if an individual's or organization's threshold for change is exceeded.

Understanding the effects of change on the organization allows us to develop a change management plan. This plan should first focus on assessing the organization's willingness, readiness, and ability to change. This assessment should focus on the change sponsor's commitment to supporting the change and associated transition and on the change agents' ability to facilitate the change. In addition, the sponsors and change agents should determine the impact the change will have on the targets. This assessment includes (1) clarifying the real impacts of the change, (2) understanding the breadth of change, (3) defining what's over and what's not, and (4) determining whether the rules for success have changed.

The next step of the change management plan should focus on adopting a strategy to support the change. Four approaches were outlined in the chapter: the (1) rational-empirical approach, (2) normative-reeducation approach, (3) power-coercive approach, and (4) environmental-adaptive approach. A change management plan could include one or a combination of approaches, depending on the situation.

The third component of the change management plan should center on implementing the plan and tracking its progress. Although several tools for tracking the project's progress were introduced in an earlier chapter (e.g., Gantt chart, PERT chart, etc.), several milestones and other significant events should be used to mark the organization's progress toward adapting and adopting the change.

The change management plan should also include the evaluation and documentation of lessons learned. It is important that the effectiveness of a given strategy be assessed and experiences be documented so that they may be shared and so that best practices can be identified.

Although a change management plan may send an important message to the organization that management cares about its people, resistance and conflict can still arise. Both resistance and conflict are a natural part of the change process and should be anticipated from the outset of the project. Resistance can arise for many reasons and take many forms. Although the traditional view of conflict suggests that all conflict is bad and should be avoided or resolved as soon as possible, the contemporary and interactionist views of conflict support the idea that positive conflict can stimulate new ideas and improve creativity.

In addition, several approaches to managing or dealing with conflict were introduced. These approaches include (1) avoidance, (2) accommodation, (3) forcing, (4) compromise, and (5) collaboration. Each approach has its advantages and disadvantages, and a project stakeholder should choose an appropriate approach based on the situation.

While this chapter focuses on the soft side of IT project management, it will provide an important foundation for understanding and supporting the operational objective of implementing the IT project's final product.

REVIEW QUESTIONS

1. As an IT professional, why does your mere existence in an organization suggest change?

2. Why is it just as important to deal with the people issues of an IT project as it is to deal with the technical issues?

3. Why do many IT professionals shy away from dealing with the people issues, the soft side of IT projects?

4. How can a system be a technical success, but an organizational failure?

5. How does change management fit with IT project management?

6. What is wrong with the idea of just expecting people to adapt to a new system by compliance?

7. Why is acceptance more powerful than compliance?

8. What are some down sides if an organization does not accept the project's final product as originally envisioned?

9. In your own words, define change management.

10. What is the difference between positive change and negative change? Do positive changes create stress for an individual? Why or why not?

11. Define assimilation and its importance to understanding how people deal with change.

12. What happens when an individual cannot assimilate change fast enough?

13. What happens when an organization cannot assimilate change fast enough?

14. Describe force field analysis.

15. Describe the three stages of Lewin's model for change.

16. Why is the transition state often referred to as the neutral zone?

17. What might happen if the project manager and sponsor do not understand, expect, or acknowledge the neutral zone?

18. What is the difference between a change and a transition? Give an example of each.

19. Why would a person have emotional responses when faced with doing her or his job differently or being forced to use and learn new technology?

20. Describe the emotional responses a person might go through when given the news that her job has been eliminated as a result of the implementation of a new accounts payable system.

21. Why is having a change management plan important?

22. Why should the project manager assess the willingness, readiness, and ability of the organization to change?

23. What is a change sponsor? What is the difference between an initiating sponsor and a sustaining sponsor?

24. What important criteria should be used to determine whether a sponsor can help the organization through the planned change?

25. What is a change agent? What role does a change agent play?

26. What is a target? Why are targets important to a change initiative?

27. Why should the real impacts of change be clarified in the change management plan?

28. Using Leavitt's model, provide an example of how an electronic commerce application would affect the organization's people, technology, task, and structure.

29. Why should the project team and sponsor be clear on defining what is over and what is not before a new system is implemented?

30. What are rules for success? Why is it important to determine whether the rules for success have changed in an organization before a new system is implemented?

31. Describe the rational-empirical approach to change. What things would a change management plan address under this approach?

32. Describe the normative-reeducation approach to change. What things would a change management plan address under this approach?

33. Describe the power-coercive approach to change. What things would a change management plan address under this approach?

34. Describe the environmental-adaptive approach to change. What things would a change management plan address under this approach?

35. How can you track the progress of your change management plan?

36. Why is it important to evaluate your change management experiences and document them as lessons learned?

37. What is resistance? How might an individual or group resist the implementation of a new information system?

38. Why would people resist change even if it were beneficial to them?

39. Why would a manager think that an individual or group is overreacting to a planned change?

40. What is conflict? Why should you anticipate conflict over the course of your project?

41. In your own words, define conflict management.

42. Why is it worse to try to ignore conflict than to deal with it?

43. Describe the traditional view of conflict.

44. Describe the contemporary view of conflict.

45. Describe the interactionist view of conflict.

46. What is the avoidance approach to dealing with conflict? When is it most useful? When is it not appropriate?

47. What is the accommodation approach to dealing with conflict? When is it most useful? When is it not appropriate?

48. What is the forcing approach to dealing with conflict? When is it most useful? When is it not appropriate?

49. What is the compromise approach to dealing with conflict? When is it most useful? When is it not appropriate?

50. What is the collaboration approach to dealing with conflict? When is it most useful? When is it not appropriate?

EXTEND YOUR KNOWLEDGE

1. Interview someone who has faced a major change. The change could be either positive or negative. Examples include someone moving to a new country, a new city, losing a job, or any major life event. Your questions should include, but should not be limited, to the following:

   a. Describe the change.

   b. What was the reason for the change?

   c. Describe the transition.

   d. How difficult was the transition?

   e. How did you adjust?

   f. What feelings or emotions did you feel over the course of the change?

   g. How long did it take before you finally accepted the change?

2. Suppose you were a project manager of an IT project and you hired a new college graduate. This person just graduated and has moved from a distant city to work for your firm. You are not only providing a decent salary and benefits package, but have paid for moving expenses and four weeks of IT boot camp training.

   a. What feelings or emotions might this person have?

   b. What could you do to help this person adjust and become a valued member of your team?

3. As a systems analyst, you have been assigned to interview a department supervisor. This supervisor has been with the company for almost 30 years and is known to be difficult to work with. However, his department's productivity and profitability have always been a model for the rest of the organization. Your task is to write up a report detailing the requirements and specifications for a new system. You arrive at this person's office on time for your meeting. You say hello in your most friendly voice, but he gruffly says, "What do you want? I'm really busy and don't have a lot of time for you right now. Besides, I can't understand why the company wants to throw away good money fixing something that isn't broke." How would you handle this situation?

4. Assume that three months ago you were hired as a project manager for a medium-size consulting firm. Shortly after arriving, you find out that one of your star network specialists and a senior manager of the company that hired your firm deeply dislike one another. Your network specialist is extremely knowledgeable and good at what she does, but, unfortunately, is not a really good people person. On the other hand, the manager thinks he knows everything, but he really doesn't know much about technology. That has never stopped him from giving out advice and trying to impress everyone with his limited knowledge—especially about networks. This behavior only makes the network specialist more resentful. How would you handle this conflict so that the project can continue as planned?

 GLOBAL TECHNOLOGY SOLUTIONS

Tim Williams could hear the drone of a single engine airplane as it flew overhead. He was sitting in the office of L.T. Scully, president and CEO of Husky Air. No one was really sure what the initials "L.T." represented; everyone just referred to Husky Air's top manager as "L.T." Tim could see by the pictures on the office walls that L.T. had begun his flying career in the military and then worked his way up to captain of a major airline. Five years ago L.T. left the airline and, along with several other investors, purchased Husky Air. Behind L.T.'s desk was a large window overlooking the ramp area and hangers where Husky Air's planes were kept. Tim watched as one of the service people towed a business charter jet from its hanger.

L.T. folded his hands on his tidy desk. "Tim, thanks for coming in on such short notice, but I think we might have a little problem."

Tim was a bit perplexed. Tim began, "L.T., testing is going as expected. Sure, we found a few problems, but the team is confident that the bugs will be fixed and implementation will go according to plan."

"No, no," L.T. responded. "I'm very happy with the work you all have done so far. In fact, I have every bit of confidence in you and your team. My degree was in engineering, so I understand that finding problems and fixing them is all part of the process. Heck, I'm just glad that you're finding them instead of us! No, it seems that the problem is one that I may have created."

Tim was intrigued, but confused, and urged L.T. to explain.

"I may have underestimated how the change of introducing a new system will affect my employees," L.T. said. "My vice president of operations, Richard Woodjack, told me that several of our employees are not happy about the new system. A few of them have even threatened to quit. I almost told those employees that they have a choice—they can like it or leave—even if it would mean a large disruption to our business. But then I calmed down and recalled how I grumbled along with my coworkers at the airline when management would try to get us to do something new. It became sort of a joke because management would make a big deal of some new way of doing things and then expect everyone just to jump on board. Things would change for a while but then people would revert to the old way of doing things. Soon, nobody took these announcements very seriously. It seemed that the more things changed, the more things stayed the same. I guess I thought my employees would see this new system as a positive change and that they would be open and welcome to it. I guess I was wrong."

Tim was impressed by L.T.'s candor. "I know what you mean. In fact, I've been on projects where the system ended up being a technical success, but an organizational failure. The system worked fine, but the people in the organization didn't accept it. It means missed opportunities because the system is never fully used as intended."

L.T. let out a deep sigh. "OK, you're my consultant. How should we handle this? We really need the new system, but it's important that we have everyone on board."

Tim thought for a moment. "The reason the employees are resistant to the new system is because they may be feeling that they have no control over the situation," he said. "Also, they may not understand the benefits of the new system or how they will fit into the new picture. We need to come up with a plan that communicates the benefits of the new system and why the company has to replace the old system."

"That's a good idea, Tim," reflected L.T. "However, I think it's important that we not only tell the employees, but listen to them and engage them in the process so that they become part of the change." L.T. sat back in his executive chair. "Would you be willing to work with Richard Woodjack on this, but keep me informed about your progress?" he asked. Before Tim could respond, L.T. smiled and said "I know what you're going to say. This is definitely scope creep. Why don't you get back to me as soon as you can with the schedule and budget increases so I know what my little mistake is going to cost?"

Tim laughed and said, "L.T., if you ever get tired of flying planes and running a company, you should get a job as a mind reader."

L.T. picked up his phone. "I'll let Richard know that you'll stop by and see him and explain to him what's going on. I know he'll be relieved."

Tim and L.T. shook hands, and Tim headed out the door and down the hallway to Richard Woodjack's office as L.T. picked up the phone and dialed Richard's extension.

Things to Think About

1. Why shouldn't managers expect people just to accept a new information system?

2. What impacts can implementing a new information system have on the people in an organization?

3. Why might people be resistant to a new information system?

4. How might people demonstrate this resistance?

5. What can the project team and organization do to help people adjust and accept the new information system?

 # HUSKY AIR ASSIGNMENT—PILOT ANGELS

The Change Management Plan

In this assignment, you and your team will develop a change management plan to support your project with Husky Air.

You and your team arrive on time for your meeting with Richard Woodjack, vice president of operations for Husky Air. The conference room has a finely polished oak table that can comfortably sit everyone. On the walls are pictures of older airplanes that epitomize a long-ago period. Richard greets you and the members of your team and then asks if anyone would care for a beverage before getting started.

As Richard takes a seat at the conference table, he smiles and says, "I want to thank you for coming in on such short notice. I know that the project has been progressing as planned, but I wanted to make all of you aware of a situation that may cause some problems going forward. We have two employees who have voiced several concerns with the new system that you will be implementing. One of the employees is Betty, who has been with the company for many years. Betty is close to retirement, but she knows more about the internal operations of this company than anyone else on my staff. In fact, most people around here say that if you have a question, go ask Betty. She's also well liked and respected by just about everyone. Some of the pilots and mechanics even call her Mom because she tends to look out for their best interests. The problem is that Betty does not like change. As a matter of fact, she came into my office yesterday and told me that the idea of learning how to use a computer system frightens her. She's thinking of taking an early retirement before the system is implemented so that she won't have to deal with all the stress. I was counting on her being here for a few more years, or at least until I could find someone to replace her. Her leaving before someone could transition into her job would have a major impact on company operations. Moreover, she is so popular that I think we would have a morale problem around here for a while. If at all possible, I would like to have Betty stay on and get someone up to speed to take over her job in the next couple of years."

Richard paused for a moment and then drew a deep breath before continuing. "And then there's Junior. Junior has been with Husky Air for about three years. He has an uncle who is on the airport's planning and control commission. Quite frankly, Junior is not one of our favorite employees, but every time we've tried to get rid of him, he threatens that he will sue for wrongful termination or use his uncle's connections to create all kinds of problems for us. Even though we have nothing to hide, the time and money to fight these little problems are a disruption we can do without. Although he can be a troublemaker, it's been easier for us to keep him around and let him do things that won't impact safety or quality. However, Junior has been spreading rumors about the new system to just about

anyone who will listen. The latest rumor is that the new system will allow the company to lay off half of our employees. That's totally untrue, as you know. In fact, our management team is predicting significant growth and planning on adding more planes, pilots, instructors, mechanics, and staff to support that growth."

A secretary knocks on the conference room door and tells Richard that he is needed in the hangar. Richard asks if you and your team have any questions. He then excuses himself and leaves the room.

Based on your conversation with Richard Woodjack, develop a change management plan to support the implementation of the new system.

Please provide a professional-looking document that includes the following:

1. **Project name, project team name, and the names of the members of your project team**
2. **A brief project description** (This helps your instructor if different teams are working on different projects in your class.)
3. **The project's MOV** (This should be revised or refined if appropriate.)
4. **A list that identifies the change sponsor(s), target(s), and agent(s) of change**
5. **A change assessment**—Assess the two employees' willingness, readiness, and ability to change.
6. **A change strategy**—Develop and discuss a strategy for change. Your strategy should be based on one or a combination of the following approaches:
   a. Rational-empirical
   b. Normative-reeducation
   c. Power-coercive
   d. Environmental-adaptive
7. **A process for monitoring the change initiative**—Develop a process for tracking the progress of your change management plan.

 CASE STUDIES

ERP and Change Management at Nestlé

A year after signing a $200 million contract with SAP and over $80 million for consulting services and maintenance, Anne Alexandre, an analyst for HSBC securities in London, downgraded her recommendation on Nestlé SA stock. Although the Enterprise Resource Planning (ERP) project will probably provide long-term benefits, she was concerned with what short-term effect the project will have on the company. She believes "It touches the corporate culture, which is decentralized, and tries to centralize it.

That's risky. It's always a risk when you touch the corporate culture."

Nestlé Company's goal is to build a business as the world's leading nutrition, health, and wellness company. The company was founded in 1867 when Henri Nestlé developed the first milk food for infants and saved the life of a neighbor's child. Nestlé is headquartered in Vevey, Switzerland with offices worldwide. Aside from chocolate and confectionaries, the company is widely known by its major brands, which include Purina®, Kit Kat®,

Stouffer's®, and Poland Spring®. Revenues reported in 2007 were 107,552 million Swiss francs with a net profit of 10,649 Swiss francs.

In the early 1990s, Nestlé was a decentralized company where each of the brands, such as Carnation® and Friskies®, operated independently. The brands were unified and reorganized under Nestlé USA, but the divisions still had geographically dispersed headquarters and made their own business decisions autonomously. Moreover, a team charged with examining the various systems and processes throughout the company found many problematic redundancies. For example, Nestlé USA brands were paying 29 different prices for vanilla to the same vendor. Jeri Dunn, vice president and CIO of Nestlé USA, said "Every plant would buy vanilla from the vendor, and the vendor would just get whatever it thought it could get. And the reason we couldn't check is because every division and every factory got to name vanilla whatever it wanted to. So you could call it 1234, and it might have a whole specification behind it, and I might call it 7778. We had no way of comparing." Dunn and her team recommended technology standards and common systems for each brand to follow that would provide for cost savings and group buying power. Dunn then went to Switzerland to facilitate the implementation of a common methodology for Nestlé projects worldwide, but when she returned stateside two years later as a CIO she found that only a few of her recommendations were being followed. As Dunn recalls, "My team could name the standards, but the implementation rollout was at the whim of the businesses."

Dunn's return to the states followed USA chairman and CEO Joe Weller's vision for uniting all of the individual brands into one tightly integrated company. Reflecting on the company's condition, Dunn said "I don't think they knew how ugly it was. We had nine different general ledgers and 28 points of customer entry. We had multiple purchasing systems. We had no clue how much volume we were doing with a particular vendor because every factory set up their oven vendor masters and purchased on their own." Dunn and a group of managers from finance, supply chain, distribution, and purchasing formed a key stakeholder team to study what Nestlé did right and what could be improved upon. They were given about two hours to present their findings to Joe Weller and other top executives, but the meeting ended up taking up the whole day.

The blueprint from the stakeholder team included SAP as a cornerstone project that would take three to five years to implement. As Dunn points out, "We made it very clear that this would be a business process reorganization and that you couldn't do it without changing the way you did business. There was going to be pain involved. It was going to be a slow process, and this was not a software project." Unfortunately, senior management did not take the key stakeholder team's recommendation to heart, nor did they understand the pain it would create. As Dunn said, "They still thought it was just about software."

In October a team of 50 senior business managers and 10 senior IT managers formed a team to carry out the SAP implementation. The team was responsible for defining a set of common processes for every division. More specifically, each divisional function, such as purchasing, manufacturing, inventory, accounting, and sales, would have to give up their old ways and start doing things the new Nestlé way.

Another team spent 18 months reviewing each piece of data in all the divisions in order to come up with a common data design across the entire business. For example, vanilla would now be coded as 1234 in every division so that the SAP system could be customized with uniform business processes and data. However, the team decided against using SAP's supply chain module, Advanced Planner and Optimizer (APO), because it was recently released and therefore viewed as too risky. Instead, the team recommended a supply chain module called Manugistics that was developed by an SAP partner.

By March the team had a project plan in place where Nestlé would implement five SAP modules: purchasing, financials, sales and distribution, accounts payable and receivable, and the Manugistics supply chain module across every Nestlé division. Implementation began in July with a deadline of approximately 18 months. The deadline was met, but just as many problems were created as were solved.

Before all of the modules were rolled out, there was a great deal employee resistance. It appears that the problem was that none of the groups affected by the new system and processes were represented on the key stakeholder team. Dunn recalls her near fatal mistake. "We were always surprising [the heads of sales and the divisions] because we would bring something up to the executive steering committee that they weren't privy to."

By the time of the expected rollout, the project had collapsed into chaos. Workers did not understand how to use the new system or the new processes. The divisional managers were just as confused as their employees and probably even a bit angrier. Dunn's help desk took 300 calls a day, and she admits "We were really naïve in the respect that these changes had to be managed."

Subsequently, morale deteriorated and nobody took an interest in doing things a new way. Turnover reached a new high of 77 percent. Supply chain planners were unable and unwilling to abandon their familiar spreadsheets in favor of the complex Manugistics system. Other technical problems began to arise due to the rush to make the project's deadline. Integration points between modules were overlooked. For example, although the purchasing departments now used common data conventions and followed the same processes, their systems could not integrate with the financial or sales groups.

The project was stopped in June. A coproject manager was reassigned and Dunn was given full responsibility. In October, Dunn invited 19 key stakeholders and business managers to a three-day offsite retreat. While the retreat started off as a gripe session, the members eventually made the decision that the project would have to be started over. The project team had lost sight of the big picture of how the various components would fit together. It was decided that the project would begin again with defining the business requirements before trying to fit the business into a mold that had to be completed by a predetermined deadline. Perhaps more importantly, they concluded that they required support from key divisional managers and that better communication was needed to tell all the employees when changes were taking place, when, why, and how.

By the following April, the project team had a well defined plan to follow. By May, Tom James was hired as director of process change and was responsible for acting as a liaison between the project team and the various divisions. James was shocked by the still poor relationships between the project team and divisions, so he and Dunn began meeting face to face with the division managers and started conducting regular surveys better to understand how the employees were affected by the new systems and how they were coping with the changes.

One difference was Dunn and the project team would act on what they found. For example, a rollout of a new comanufacturing package was delayed six months because feedback from the users suggested that they would not be prepared to make the process changes in time.

Although this project took much longer than expected, Dunn is not ashamed of the schedule overrun or the numerous deadends. She believes that slow and steady wins the race, and that the project has already achieved a significant return on investment, especially in terms of better demand forecasting. According to Dunn, "The old process involved a sales guy giving a number to the demand planner, who says 'Those guys don't know what the hell they are talking about; I'm going to give them this number.' The demand planner turns [that number] over to factory, and the factory says the demand planner doesn't know what the hell he's talking about. Then the factory changes that number again."

Now, SAP provides common databases and processes that allow for demand forecasts to be more accurate. Since all of Nestlé USA is using the same data, it can forecast down to the distribution center level. Subsequently, inventory levels and redistribution expenses can be reduced. The company reports that improvements in the supply chain alone have accounted for a major piece of the $325 million Nestlé has saved by implementing SAP.

Dunn reflects that if she had to do it over again, she would focus on changing the business processes, getting universal buy-in, and then and only then installing SAP. As she said, "If you try to do it with a system first, you will have an installation, not an implementation. And there is a big difference between installing software and implementing a solution."

1. What could Nestlé have done better in implementing SAP?

2. What did it do right?

3. What would have been the value of having a change management plan from the beginning?

4. The primary lesson that Dunn says she gained from this project is "No major software implementation is really about the software. It's about change management." Do you agree with her statement?

SOURCE: Adapted from Ben Worthen, Nestle's Enterprise Resource Planning (ERP) Odyssey, *Computerworld,* May 15, 2002; http://www.nestle.com.

From Ballpoints to Bits

An organization can develop or purchase an IT solution with the intent of adding value, but even the best solutions can fall short if the users do not accept the system. Projects are planned organizational change, so preparing the people within an organization is important to the success of the project.

Pfizer

Kolette is an epidemiologist at Pfizer who manages clinical trials for the treatment of metabolic diseases. She helped develop a data capture system called Investigator Net (I-Net) that automates data collection and analysis for drug development studies.

Pfizer recruited a university hospital to take part in a new study. Kolette met with the hospital's nursing coordinator to go over the program, but upon seeing the new computer being removed from the box the nursing coordinator exclaimed that computers were the "foot soldiers of the devil!"

Chicago Police Department

The Chicago Police Department is one of the largest police forces in the United States. The department began development of a relational database system called Citizen Law Enforcement Analysis and Reporting (CLEAR) to help the police sift through massive amounts of data to fight crime.

Joe is a 50-year-old veteran cop who has been working the streets of Chicago for decades. For his entire career he has filled out five-ply carbon forms to process his arrests and casework. On his first day of training on a PC, he picks up the mouse, points it at the screen, and starts clicking away. He then asks why the darn thing isn't working when nothing happens on the screen. Even the detectives who are computer literate grumble about the system. They claim that it isn't user friendly and getting approval from supervisors is cumbersome.

Procter & Gamble

Procter & Gamble encountered user resistance when it rolled out its Corporate Standards System (CSS)—a global, centralized system that manages all of the technical standards for each of the company's products to its 8,200 users. These technical standards are important in managing each product's life cycle and provide a communication link that connects R&D through the entire supply chain. For example, the beauty care group has an average of 125 standards for information regarding formulas, regulatory requirements, and packaging. Before CSS, people kept information about the technology standards in three-ring binders or on various computers.

Most complaints from the users were that the system was too slow, but it was discovered that the real reason wasn't the technology, but the process. For example, an employee may have been used to documenting last-minute change requests from a vendor on the back of an envelope, but now documenting those changes in CSS required more rigor and thus was more cumbersome for the employee.

1. Which change management strategy do you think would be the best approach for each of the above situations?

2. If you were a project manager, how would you implement your chosen strategy?

SOURCE: Adapted from Todd Datz, Change Management: Planning Is Crucial, *CIO Magazine*, February 15, 2004.

 # BIBLIOGRAPHY

Blake, R. R. and J. S. Mouton. 1964. *The Managerial Grid.* Houston, TX: Gulf Publishing.

Bridges, W. 1991. *Managing Transitions: Making the Most of Change.* Cambridge, MA: Perseus Books.

Conner, D. 1995. *Managing at the Change of Speed.* New York: Villard Books.

Davidson, J. 2002. *Change Management.* Indianapolis, IN: Alpha.

Duck, J. D. 2001. *The Change Monster: The Human Forces That Fuel or Foil Corporate Transformation and Change.* New York: Crown Business.

Kübler-Ross, E. 1969. *On Death and Dying.* New York: Macmillian.

Leavitt, H. J. 1964. Applied Organizational Change in Industry: Structural, Technical and Human Approaches. In *New Perspectives in Organizational Research*, edited by H. J. Leavitt. Chichester: John Wiley: 55–71.

Lewin, K. 1951. *Field Theory in Social Science.* New York: Harper and Row.

Verma, V. K. 1998. Conflict Management. In *Project Management Handbook,* edited by J. K. Pinto. San Francisco: Jossey-Bass.

CHAPTER

12

Project Procurement Management and Outsourcing

CHAPTER OVERVIEW

Chapter 12 focuses on project procurement management—one of the nine Project Management Body of Knowledge (PMBOK®) areas. Closely related to procurement is outsourcing or the subcontracting of organizational or project components to an external party. After studying this chapter, you should understand and be able to:

- Describe the PMBOK® area called project procurement management.
- Describe the six processes that make up project procurement management.
- Describe the three general categories for procurement-type contracts.
- Define outsourcing, business process outsourcing, and offshoring.
- Describe the reasons why organizations outsource projects and project components.
- Describe the advantages and disadvantages of outsourcing.
- Describe several ways to improve the likelihood of outsourcing success.

INTRODUCTION

Project procurement management is one of the nine Project Management Body of Knowledge (PMBOK®) areas and focuses on the acquisition and management of outside products and services. Project teams require resources, and many of these resources must be acquired externally from sellers such as vendors or suppliers. This may include technology such as hardware and software for systems development or office automation tools to support the project team. Other items, such as office supplies or the printing of support and training manuals, are often acquired from outside sources as well.

Physical items are not the only things a project may acquire from external sources. Often services and components of the project's scope are subcontracted to another firm. More specifically, the project's scope can be broken up into a number of subprojects. This idea is not new, since construction contractors often subcontract specific components of a building to other subcontractors such as framers, electricians, or plumbers. Today, however, the term "subcontracting" has been often substituted with the term "outsourcing." Outsourcing has become a strategic initiative for many organizations worldwide. It also has become a hot and controversial topic, especially when organizations look to fulfill their outsourcing needs overseas.

Outsourcing is a broad term that has different implications. For example, organizations can outsource entire functions and business processes (e.g., data centers, customer support, accounting, human resources). In this case, the outsourcing activities associated with selecting, negotiating, and transferring that particular function over to a third party would be a project in and of itself. On the other hand, a company may outsource a project (e.g., building an application system) or components of projects (e.g., programming, testing, training) to another organization such as a consulting firm. While outsourcing can make good business sense, it can be a complicated undertaking that requires a project management approach. For example, a survey of organizations that have contracted outsourcing services reports that 53 percent of the respondents have encountered outsourcing challenges because their organizations lack project management skills (Brown and Wilson 2005).

In the next section, we will take a closer look at project procurement management. This will entail understanding the various processes outlined in the *PMBOK®* *Guide* as well as the three general types of contract options available. The following section will delve into outsourcing, business process outsourcing, and offshoring. Although outsourcing presents many opportunities, a number of challenges must be addressed as well.

It is important for you to understand both sides of the procurement/outsourcing equation because it is very likely that you will be both a buyer and seller of outsourced products and services. For example, if you work as a consultant or for a software development house, you may not only be the seller of outsourcing services, but you might be a buyer of these services if you subcontract out any project components.

PROJECT PROCUREMENT MANAGEMENT

Projects generally require resources, products, or services that must be purchased or acquired externally. In this section, we will focus on another PMBOK® knowledge area called project procurement management.

According to the *PMBOK®* *Guide,* **project procurement management** is defined as:

> the contract management and change control processes required to administer contracts or purchase orders issued by authorized project team members. Project procurement management also includes administering any contract issued by an outside organization (the buyer) that is acquiring the project from the performing organization (the seller), and administering contractual obligations placed on the project team by the contract (269).

Again, it is important to keep in mind that the project team can be both a buyer and a seller of products and services. Even though we will mainly use the terms "buyer" and "seller" in this chapter, a buyer could be a client or a customer, while a seller could be a consultant, contractor, vendor, supplier, or a subcontractor.

For example, an organization may enter into a contract by outsourcing a specific project to a consulting firm. In this case, the organization would be the buyer of the consulting firm's (i.e., seller's) services. In turn, the consulting firm can also be a buyer of products (i.e., computers, software, paperclips) and services that could in turn be outsourced or subcontracted to other firms who specialize in a particular service (e.g., programming, system testing, printing of user manuals).

The Project Procurement Management Processes

The *PMBOK® Guide* outlines six processes to support project procurement management. These processes are summarized in Table 12.1 and are then discussed in more detail. These processes often interact with each other and with other processes from the other knowledge areas. It is also a good idea for the project manager and team to seek out the advice of specialists such as lawyers, accountants, or purchasing agents early in the project or as necessary to avoid potential problems and conflicts.

Plan Purchases and Acquisition

The first process, plan purchases and acquisition, begins by determining which project needs can be fulfilled internally by the project team and which can best be met externally. Moreover, the project manager and team must not only decide *what* project needs can be met internally or externally, but also *how, when, how many*, and *where* these products and services will be acquired.

The decision to go outside of the project team for products and services depends on several factors. First, the project manager and team may want to consider what products or services are available in the marketplace as well as the associated cost, quality, terms, and conditions. However, the most important consideration depends on the project's deliverables or scope. Often the project manager and team are faced with limited funds, resources, expertise, or tight delivery schedules and technology constraints. Given these factors, an external party may provide better opportunities to meet these challenges effectively and efficiently.

Table 12.1   Summary of Project Procurement Process

Plan purchases and acquisition	Making the decision as to what will be purchased or acquired as well as determining the logistics of when purchases will be made and how
Plan contracting	Documenting the product, services, or results needed as well as identifying potential sellers, vendors, suppliers, contractors, subcontractors, or other service providers
Request seller responses	Obtaining bids, quotes, proposals, literature, and other information from potential sellers or service providers
Select sellers	Negotiating, selecting, and contracting with a seller for a particular product or service
Contract administration	Managing the relationship and contract between the buyer and seller. This includes reviewing and documenting the seller's performance, contract changes, and taking corrective action when necessary
Contract closure	Completing and settling each contract after any open items or settlements are resolved

The decision whether to purchase or outsource specific project needs is similar to a "make or buy" decision that compares the total direct and indirect costs of "making" a particular product or performing a particular service internally to the total direct and indirect costs of "buying" or contracting externally. The same qualitative and quantitative tools for comparing various alternatives that were described in Chapter 2 to develop the business case can be used to make this decision. However, this decision can be viewed from a risk management perspective using the risk management framework presented in Chapter 8. For example, one reason for going to an outsider could be to transfer risk to the seller. In many respects, this may be a good idea if the seller has a particular expertise or more experience than the project team. Unfortunately, when you transfer control over to someone else, you may lose your control over the project schedule and budget if the external party cannot meet its promised obligations.

Depending on the needs of the project, the project manager and team may develop a formal or informal project procurement plan. This plan may be separate or it may become an integral part of the project's plan, scope, and work breakdown structure (WBS). In addition, the same or very similar project processes for managing scope changes, schedule, budget, quality, and communication must be in place and understood by all the project stakeholders.

Plan Contracting

The plan contracting process focuses on developing some type of procurement document, such as a request for proposal (RFP), that will be used to solicit bids, quotes, or proposals from prospective sellers. These documents are generally structured by the buyer so that a common means and set of measures can be used to compare and evaluate the responses from the different sellers. The complexity or rigor of these documents can be high when dealing with a government agency or if the product or service to be acquired is highly regulated.

The plan contracting process also includes the development of criteria for evaluating bids, proposals, and so forth after they are received from the sellers. While price might be one important factor, a seller or contractor may be chosen based on their experience, expertise, understanding of the seller's needs, management approach, financial strength, technical capability, or references from previous clients or customers.

Request Seller Responses

The general idea of the request seller responses is for the buyer to obtain a reasonable number of high-quality, competitive proposals. To achieve this objective, a buyer-organization may hold a conference with bidders, contractors, vendors, and so on. These preliminary meetings allow the sellers to have a better understanding of what products or services are needed and how to go about submitting the procurement document. Many times the governing policies and procedures for the buyer's organization entail a lengthy and public process to solicit bids from a number of prospective sellers. This may include advertising in newspapers, trade journals, or even the Web to let other parties know that requests for proposals, bids, or quotations are being sought. Alternatively, in many cases, the buyer may contact the seller directly for a bid, quotation, or request.

The proposal developed by the seller generally includes the price of the requested product or service as well as a description of the seller's ability and willingness to provide what was requested. Depending on the nature or the product or service requested, this could entail something as simple as a phone call or a lengthy, complex, and formal written document and a formal presentation to the buyer.

Select Sellers

Once the bids, proposals, or quotations are received, the buying organization begins the process of analyzing, evaluating, and selecting a seller. The criteria developed in the plan purchases and acquisition process are used as a basis. Again, price or cost may be an important consideration, but other factors should be considered because a decision on price or cost alone may prove moot if the seller is unable to provide a quality product or service in a timely manner.

A number of qualitative and quantitative approaches can be used to select a particular seller. For example, many of the tools and techniques for developing a business case in Chapter 2 or analyzing risk in Chapter 8 would be well suited for the task of choosing a seller. In general, a risk management approach for identifying and assessing risks, and then coming up with a risk strategy and response would be useful for not only selecting a seller but for managing the relationship as well.

Once a seller is selected, the buyer may enter into contract negotiations so that a mutual agreement can be reached. A **contract** is a document signed by the buyer and seller that defines the terms and conditions of the buyer–seller relationship. It serves as a legally binding agreement that obligates the seller to provide specific products, services, or even results, while obligating the buyer to provide specific monetary or other consideration. A contract defines the terms and conditions or such things as responsibilities and authorities, technical and project management approaches, proprietary rights, financing, schedule, payments, quality requirements, and price, as well as remedies and process for revisions to the contract. A contract can be simple or complex, informal or formal, depending on the nature of the relationship. For example, a purchase order would be an example of a simple contract, while an outsourcing agreement between two firms would require a more lengthy and detailed document.

Organizational policies and procedures usually govern how these relationships are created and who is authorized to enter into and manage these various agreements. Today, many projects also involve multiple contracts and subcontracts with many buyer and seller relationships that must be managed actively throughout the entire project life cycle.

Given that you may be the buyer or seller of procurement services, it is important that you understand types of contracts that exist and that one may be more appropriate for a given situation. The *PMBOK® Guide* outlines three general categories for procurement-type contracts:

1. *Fixed-price or lump-sum contracts*—A total or fixed price is negotiated or set as the final price for a specific product or service. For example, an organization may decide to outsource the development of an application system to a consulting firm. Based on the project's scope, the consulting firm will develop an estimated schedule and budget. Both firms may then negotiate a final cost of the project based on this triple constraint. On the other hand, the cost of a particular product or service may be fixed with little or no opportunity for negotiation. For example, let's say that a project team member requests a new laptop computer. Although policy and procedures vary greatly among organizations, usually some process is in place

for acquiring products or services and involves requests, authorizations, and purchase orders. This process could be simple and straightforward or an inefficient, bureaucratic mess. Fixed-price or lump-sum contracts may include incentives for meeting certain objects or penalties if those objectives are not met.

2. *Cost-reimbursable contracts*—For these types of contracts a payment or reimbursement is made to the seller to cover the seller's actual costs. These costs include direct costs (e.g., direct labor, materials) and indirect costs (e.g., administrative salaries, rent, utilities, insurance). However, an additional fee is added to the total direct and indirect costs as a profit to the seller. Cost-reimbursable contracts can also include incentives for meeting specific objectives or penalties if specific objectives are not met. In general, there are three types of cost-reimbursable projects:

   a. *Cost-plus-fee (CPF) or cost-plus-percentage of cost (CPPC)*—The seller is paid for the costs incurred in performing the work as well as a fee based on an agreed-upon percentage of the costs. For example, let's say that you take your car to a mechanic for a tune up. The mechanic might say that the cost of the tune up will include parts and labor plus a 20 percent fee. So if the mechanic charges $50 an hour to cover direct and indirect costs, works 2 hours on your car, and uses $100 worth of parts, the cost of parts and labor would be $200 (i.e., 2 × $50 + $100). Your bill would be $240 after the 20 percent fee is added on. Unless the mechanic is someone you can trust, you might want to take precautions such as getting an estimate in writing before the repair work begins; otherwise, an unscrupulous mechanic could increase the fee (i.e., profit) by driving up the costs of labor and/or parts.

   b. *Cost-plus-fixed-fee (CPFF)*—In this case, the seller is reimbursed for the total direct and indirect costs of performing the work, but receives a fixed amount. This fixed amount does not change unless the scope changes. For example, you may take your car to your friend who says that he will work on your car. In this case, the arrangement may be that you pay for all the parts needed for the tune up, but your friend will do the work for $20 as a favor. If your car needs $100 in parts, then the cost of having your friend work on your car will be $120. However, if you can find the same parts for $80 at an automotive superstore, then the cost of having your car tuned up will be $100, since your friend will receive $20 for his time regardless of the cost for the parts.

   c. *Cost-plus-incentive-fee (CPIF)*—Under this type of contract, the seller is reimbursed for the costs incurred in doing the work and receives a predetermined fee plus an incentive bonus for meeting certain objectives. In this case, let's say that while your friend is working on your car, you receive a call from another friend who offers you two free tickets to a concert that starts in a couple of hours. You might offer the extra ticket as an incentive to complete the repairs in an hour or less so that you can take your car to the concert and make it in time for the start of the show.

3. *Time and materials (T&M) contracts*—A T&M contract is a hybrid of cost-reimbursable and fixed-price contracts. Under a T&M contract, the buyer pays the seller for both the time and materials required to complete the work.

In this case, it resembles a cost-reimbursable contract because it is open-ended and the full cost of the project is not predetermined before the work begins. However, a T&M contract can resemble a fixed-price arrangement if unit rates are set. For example, let's say that you want to have your house painted. A painting contractor may tell you that the cost of painting your house will be $20 an hour plus the cost of paint. If a gallon of paint costs $10, the cost of painting your house will depend on how many gallons of paint are used and how long it takes. If one person works on your house for 20 hours and uses 5 gallons of paint, then the cost for the painter's time and the materials used will be $450.

Contract Administration

Once the contract is signed, both the buyer and seller enter into a relationship in which each must fulfill their contractual obligations. The contract administration process makes sure that both parties are performing in accordance to the terms of the contract. In general, contract administration includes:

- Authorizing and coordinating the contracted work at the appropriate time
- Monitoring the contractor's performance with respect to scope, schedule, budget, and quality
- Managing scope in terms of its definition and change control
- Risk identification, assessment, and control
- Monitoring that all payments, as stipulated in the contract, are made
- Reviewing and evaluating the seller's performance both in terms of fulfilling contract obligations but also the seller's response when problems arise and require corrective action
- Determining whether the contract needs to be amended
- Deciding if the contract should be terminated early for just cause, convenience, or when the seller is in default

Contract Closure

The process called contract closure centers on verifying that all of the work outlined in the contract is finished. Contract closure also includes updating records to reflect the final results, archiving information for future use, as well as other administrative activities.

Contract closure can result when the buyer and seller mutually agree that the obligations of the contract have been fulfilled. The seller may give the buyer a formal notice that all deliverables specified in the contract have been provided, and the buyer may provide the seller with a notice that the deliverables have been received and are acceptable. On the other hand, early termination of the project may occur when one party is unable to fulfill their rights and responsibilities. Based on the terms and conditions outlined in the contract, the other party may have the right to terminate the contract or seek punitive damages. Regardless of whether the contract was closed as planned or prematurely, the project manager and team should document any lessons learned so that best practices can be identified and made part of the organization's project methodology.

QUICK THINKING—THE EPA SUSPENDS IBM

International Business Machines (IBM) received about $1.4 billion in U.S. government contracts in 2007 from a variety of federal agencies. However, in April, 2008 the Environmental Protection Agency (EPA) suspended IBM from seeking new federal IT work as a result of an investigation of a 2006 contract bid that potentially violated federal procurement integrity rules. Although the suspension was lifted after a week, IBM's problems may not be over. According to IBM, the U.S. attorney's office had started a grand jury probe that was looking into "interactions between employees" between IBM and the EPA. The EPA has acknowledged that the suspension was "a temporary measure while the agency reviews concerns raised about potential activities involving EPA procurement." Moreover, a spokesperson for the U.S. General Services Administration, which administers all federal contracts and maintains a list of blacklisted contractors, said that suspensions are "not punitive in nature, but instead

are a prophylactic measure designed to protect the government." IBM has stated that it will "take all appropriate actions to challenge the suspension and limit its scope." Richard Colven, an analyst at Input—a market research firm—believes that there could be some negative issues for IBM, "But I would think that IBM's reputation across the government and in general will be able to overcome this."

1. Why would having "procurement integrity rules" be an important component of the project procurement processes?

2. How could "interactions between employees" give a contractor an unfair advantage?

SOURCE: Adapted from Patrick Thibodeau, Feds Remove IBM from IT Contractor Blacklist, *Computerworld*, April 4, 2008.

OUTSOURCING

Outsourcing can be defined as the procurement of products or services from an external vendor, supplier, or manufacturer. In this respect, outsourcing is analogous to procurement management. Perhaps one way to make a distinction is to view outsourcing as a strategic approach and regard the processes that make up project procurement management as a more tactical approach.

The Beginning of the Outsourcing Phenomenon

In 1989, the Eastman Kodak Company in Rochester, New York, was a leader in the photography industry. With annual revenues of $18.4 billion, Kodak was doing well as a company. However, Kodak was spending $250 million year on information technology, and management questioned why so much was being spent on IT when the company's mission was to be a leader in photography.

Kodak explored other options and eventually signed a 10-year, $250-million deal to outsource its entire IT function to IBM Corp., Digital Equipment Corporation (DEC), and Businessland, Inc. As part of the arrangement, DEC took over telecommunications, and Businessland handled all PC purchases and maintenance. IBM received the biggest share of the deal and assumed responsibility for data center operations. As part of the arrangement, 300 Kodak employees transferred to IBM, and 400 transferred to DEC and Businessland. Within the first year of the deal, Kodak's capital costs decreased almost 95 percent, while PC support costs dropped to about 5 to 10 percent. Mainframe costs also were reduced by 10 to 15 percent.

Kodak was not the first or the largest organization to turn to outsourcing, but it was the first well known and successful company to outsource an entire IT function. As a result, the perception that an organization had to provide its own IT support changed. Senior management began to talk about core competencies, cost savings, and strategic partnerships with IT vendors (Field 1999).

By the year 2000, the field of IT had come to a critical crossroads, when more than 54 percent of IT services purchased in North America were outsourced. Even today, the momentum for outsourcing has grown and it appears that Europe now exceeds the United States in terms of the value of major outsourcing deals (Pruitt 2005b).

Types of Outsourcing Relationships

Today, outsourcing has expanded to include **business process outsourcing** in which an organization turns over processes other than just IT (i.e., accounting, human resources management, research and development) to another organization that specializes in that process (Brown and Wilson 2005). In recent years, a great deal of attention has been given to the outsourcing of jobs overseas. This type of outsourcing, or **offshoring,** allows an organization to take advantage of labor arbitrage (i.e., cheap labor) by procuring a product or service from a supplier that operates in another country.

Outsourcing can be an organizational-level decision or a project-level decision. Just as an organization can pursue outsourcing as a strategic approach, so too can a project manager and team. Today, organizations and project teams have the opportunity to follow different approaches to outsourcing. This idea is illustrated in Figure 12.1, which shows that a continuum of outsourcing relationships can exist. For example, an organization or project could follow a **full-insourcing approach** in which all products and services would be retained internally. For a project, this would mean that the project team is responsible for all the project's processes and scope. On the other hand, a **full-outsourcing approach** would be followed if an organization or project acquires all products or services from external sources. In this case, we would have a virtual organization or project. However, the best approach for organizations and projects probably would be selective outsourcing. More specifically, **selective outsourcing** provides greater flexibility to choose which project processes deliverables should be outsourced and which should be kept internal. Although low cost is one advantage for outsourcing and offshoring, the objective should be to increase flexibility and quality (Lacity, Willcocks, and Feeny 1995).

The Realities of Outsourcing

Before the Kodak deal, outsourcing did not have many negative connotations, especially by IT professionals. Afterwards, however, a minority understood the virtues of outsourcing, while a vocal minority despised it (Field 1999). Today this debate continues, as many organizations view offshore outsourcing as an important organizational or project strategy.

The controversy over outsourcing, especially offshoring, centers on the perception that jobs within one country are replaced by lower wage jobs in another. Subsequently, domestic unemployment increases and thereby creates a negative impact on the nation's economy. A research company called Forrester predicts that, by 2015, U.S. companies will shift 3.3 million service jobs to lower wage countries; approximately 8 percent of these jobs will be in IT. Although over 3 million jobs will be displaced by offshore outsourcing, the total employment in the United States

Figure 12.1   Outsourcing Model

is about 130 million, and 22 million new jobs are expected to be created by 2010. This means that outsourcing would affect less than .2 percent of people employed in the United States (Drezner 2004). Moreover, this sounds even less ominous when you consider that more than 1 million people in the United States change jobs every month (Farrell 2004).

Although some people lose their jobs because of outsourcing, many new, higher paying jobs are often created. For example, in 2002, Delta Airlines had over 6,000 representatives in 20 call centers worldwide. The agents in these call centers interacted with customers through voice, fax, and email. Delta made the decision to offshore many of these activities and so 1,000 call center jobs were outsourced to India in 2003. This resulted in $25 million in savings that allowed Delta to add 1,200 reservation and sales positions in the United States (Robinson and Kalakota 2004).

Moreover, the McKinsey Global Institute estimates that the United States reaps between $1.12 and $1.14 for every dollar spent on outsourcing to India. In addition, Drezner also reports that although 70,000 computer programmers lost their jobs between 1999 and 2003, more than 115,000 software engineers found higher paying jobs (Drezner 2004).

Organizational change management plays an important role for outsourcing successfully. A poll conducted in Europe examined the opinions of 200 employees in large organizations before and after their positions were outsourced. Although this change can be unwelcome, the study found that, if done right, people may find that they have more opportunity to advance their careers and hone their skills (Pruitt 2005a). However, if the outsourcing decision is not handled properly, the remaining survivors can feel outrage or guilt, thus affecting the remaining employees' morale and motivation (Hamblen 2004). On the other hand, as Peter F. Drucker (2002) points out, developing people is the most important task in business. The trend toward outsourcing and relying on nontraditional employees can reduce an organization's ability to gain competitive advantage in a knowledge economy.

Managing the Outsourcing Relationship

Recently, a study was conducted by Deloitte Consulting. It surveyed 25 large organizations and reported that 70 percent have had negative experiences with outsourced projects and that a number of them are starting to bring projects back in house (Mears 2005). As an example, Sears, Roebuck and Co. recently ended a 10-year/$1.6 billion IT outsourcing agreement with Computer Sciences Corp., citing the vendor's failure to perform certain obligations.

So if outsourcing provides value to organizations and projects, how can we improve its likelihood of success? First, since outsourcing is a project, following a project management approach makes sense. However, Barthelemy (2003) provides some insight from a survey of just over 90 outsourcing efforts in Europe and the United States. These mistakes, termed the seven deadly sins of outsourcing, can be applied to the outsourcing of organizational activities and projects as well:

1. *Outsourcing activities that should not be outsourced*—Many believe that outsourcing results in an automatic reduction of costs and an increase in performance. However, this view is nonrealistic and many organizations outsource to mimic their competitors or success stories in trade journals. For outsourcing to be successful, an organization must understand where it gets its competitive advantage so that a decision can be made to determine what activities should be performed externally. This may not be that easy.

QUICK THINKING—SOCIALLY RESPONSIBLE OUTSOURCING

Ron Kifer is a CIO and group vice president at Applied Materials, Inc. in Santa Clara, California that creates and commercializes nanomanufacturing technology. In addition to believing in giving back to the community and green initiatives, Kifer looks closely at the outsourcing providers he hires to ensure that they are aligned with his company's values. He believes that socially responsible outsourcing is the next wave of the future and adds "We need to make sure that our suppliers are operating to the same high standards [as our company]."

Moreover, the International Association of Outsourcing Professionals (IAOP) predicts that socially responsible outsourcing will become an important trend in the future. A growing number of organizations will go beyond pure business objectives and will begin to set standards for ethical issues such as how an outsource provider treats its people and interacts with the environment. For example, Jagdish Dalal, the managing director of thought leadership at the IAOP, says "More people are looking at the ethics statements of the companies they do business with to make sure their statements are congruent." Much of this concern has come as a result of the bad publicity outsourcing and

offshoring has received. Some outsource providers—in particular, offshore providers—often pay their employees unfairly low wages while maintaining an environment that utilizes child labor and unsafe working conditions. As Dalal adds, "Sweatshops exist anywhere there is unethical practice. In the IT realm, companies that expect workers to be on call constantly or to always put in extra hours without additional compensation could be downgraded in the eyes of prospective partners. And companies that hire such outsourcing providers could face negative public pressure."

1. According to Ron Kifer, "Social responsibility is good business, besides being a good thing to do." Do you agree with this statement?

2. As a project manager looking to subcontract a WBS component of your project to an offshore provider, what types of questions would you ask if you wanted to be sure that a particular provider was socially responsible?

SOURCE: Adapted from Mary K. Pratt, Is Your Outsourcer an IT Sweatshop?, *Computerworld*, April 21, 2008.

For example, a car rental company outsourced its IT department to reduce costs, but found that applications development and maintenance should have remained in house because these activities were important to its core business. A loss of control and the risk of the vendor going out of business can have grave consequences for the company.

2. *Selecting the wrong vendor*—Although selecting a good vendor seems like common sense, vendors can be selected for the wrong reasons. It is important to note that not all organizations outsource to reduce costs. Some outsource because a vendor can do something better or faster. An organization looking to outsource should verify a prospective vendor's qualifications as well as their experience and financial strength. There should also be a good fit between the two organizations' cultures, as well as a commitment to continuous improvement, flexibility, and a long-term relationship.

3. *Writing a poor contract*—A good contract must be in place to establish a balance of power between client and vendor. Time must be invested to carefully negotiate the terms of the contract because this not only sets expectations but also creates a safety net in case the relationship breaks down. A well written contract should be precise, be complete, provide incentives for the right behavior, be balanced so that it does not become one-sided or in favor of one party, and be flexible so that changes in business conditions can allow for changes in the contract.

4. *Overlooking personnel issues*—Outsourcing, or even a rumor that an organization is contemplating outsourcing, can have a negative impact on employee

loyalty and sense of job security. In turn, this may lead to reduced productivity, dysfunctional behaviors, or a mass exodus of employees before the outsourcing decision is even made. Organizations must retain and motivate key employees since not all employees will be let go or transferred to the vendor. On the other hand, employees who will be transferred to the vendor may have concerns about their job security, pay, and benefits. Therefore, the retention of organizational-specific knowledge is important for those employees who will be retained and for those who will be transferred.

5. *Losing control over the outsourced activity*—An organization that outsources an activity can lose control if it does not manage the vendor actively. Often managers are tempted to outsource an activity that is performing poorly or is not well understood. Outsourcing does not mean full abdication of that activity. Even when an activity is outsourced, an individual or small group must still manage the vendor. A good contract is important, but good governance is essential.

6. *Overlooking the hidden costs of outsourcing*—Clients must take into account a number of hidden costs before they can be confident that an outsourced activity results in a cost savings. The main types of hidden costs include searching for vendors, negotiating and writing the contract, and managing the vendor relationship. These costs are an important consideration since they can turn a potentially attractive outsourcing arrangement into one that challenges the rationale for outsourcing.

7. *Failing to plan an exit strategy*—Some outsourcing relationships should be short term and others more long term. All outsourcing relationships should include an exit strategy that allows the client organization a means to switch vendors or reintegrate the outsourced activity later on. If an outsourced activity with a particular vendor is working, then the contract can be resigned with little renegotiation. However, an organization that outsources selectively should have options in the contract to buy premises and equipment, or hire employees back from the vendor.

 ## CHAPTER SUMMARY

Both organizations and projects often acquire products and services from external sources such as vendors, suppliers, or consultants. Project procurement management is one of the nine project management knowledge (PMBOK®) areas and is concerned with the contract management and change control processes required for administering contracts and purchase orders.

The *PMBOK® Guide* identifies six processes to support project procurement management. These include: (1) plan purchases and acquisition, (2) plan contracting, (3) request seller responses, (4) select sellers, (5) contract administration, and (6) contract closure. A contract provides a formal, binding agreement between the buyer and seller of products and services. It defines such things as price as well as responsibilities,

authorization, technical or management approaches, rights, financing, schedule payments, and quality requirements. In addition, the *PMBOK® Guide* outlines three general categories for procurement-type contracts. These include: (1) fixed-price or lump-sum contracts, (2) cost-reimbursable contracts that include cost-plus-fee or cost-plus-percentage-of-cost, plus-fixed-fee, and cost-plus-incentive-fee contracts, as well as (3) time and material contracts. Organizational policies and procedures often define how these buyer–seller relationships are created and who is authorized to enter into and manage the various agreements.

Outsourcing has received a great deal of attention since the late 1980s, and the growth of outsourcing is expected to continue. Outsourcing is defined as the procurement of products or services from an external vendor, supplier, or manufacturer and thus is analogous to procurement management. However, outsourcing has more of a strategic focus, while project procurement management may be viewed as a more tactical-level approach.

Various approaches to outsourcing were presented in this chapter. Business process outsourcing occurs when an organization turns over processes of functions such as IT, accounting, human resources, and so forth. Offshoring is a type of outsourcing when an organization takes advantage of lower wages in another country. Outsourcing decisions can be made at an organizational level, such as the outsourcing of a business process or function. In addition, an organization could make a decision to outsource the development of an application system or the implementation of a software package. In turn, a project manager could outsource specific project components such as programming, testing, or training as well. Subsequently, an organization or project could follow different approaches to outsourcing, such as full

insourcing, full outsourcing, or something in between called selective outsourcing. Selective outsourcing may allow the most flexibility since some activities would remain in house while others would be outsourced or subcontracted to external parties.

Offshoring or the outsourcing of organizational or project activities overseas has become a controversial topic. Some critics argue that IT work transferred overseas to lower wage countries has led to higher domestic unemployment and, in turn, a negative impact on the economy. Others have argued that while offshoring has negatively impacted some individuals, it has increased the number of higher value-adding and paying jobs. Regardless of which side of the debate you support, it appears that outsourcing and offshore outsourcing will remain viable options for both organizations and projects. However, for outsourcing to be successful, project management processes must be followed to ensure that effective decisions are made and that the outsourcing relationship is managed and controlled properly.

REVIEW QUESTIONS

1. Describe the Project Management Body of Knowledge (PMBOK®) area called project procurement management.
2. Describe the Project Management Body of Knowledge (PMBOK®) process called plan purchases and acquisition.
3. Describe the Project Management Body of Knowledge (PMBOK®) process called plan contracting.
4. Describe the Project Management Body of Knowledge (PMBOK®) process called request seller responses.
5. Describe the Project Management Body of Knowledge (PMBOK®) process called select sellers.
6. Describe the Project Management Body of Knowledge (PMBOK®) process called contract administration.
7. Describe the Project Management Body of Knowledge (PMBOK®) process called contract closure.
8. What is the purpose of a contract?
9. Describe how a fixed-price or lump-sum contract works. Give an example.
10. What are the three types of cost-reimbursable contracts?

11. Describe how a cost-plus-fee or cost-plus-percentage-of-cost contract works. Give an example.
12. Describe how a cost-plus-fixed-fee contract works. Give an example.
13. Describe how a cost-plus-incentive-fee contract works. Give an example.
14. Describe how a time and materials contract works. Give an example.
15. What is outsourcing? How does it relate to project procurement management?
16. What is business process outsourcing?
17. What is offshoring or offshore outsourcing?
18. What is meant by full insourcing?
19. What is meant by full outsourcing?
20. What is meant by selective outsourcing? Why might selective outsourcing be a better approach than full insourcing or full outsourcing?
21. Why is it important that organizations and project managers understand which activities should and should not be outsourced?
22. Why is selecting the right vendor important when considering an outsourcing agreement?

23. Why is writing a good contract important for an outsourcing relationship?

24. Why are personnel issues important when an organization or project manager is considering outsourcing activities?

25. Why is it not a good idea for a manger to consider outsourcing an activity that is not managed well or an activity that is not well understood?

26. What are some hidden costs of outsourcing? Why is it important to consider these costs?

27. What is the importance of having an exit strategy when entering into an outsourcing agreement?

 EXTEND YOUR KNOWLEDGE

1. Offshoring is a controversial topic. Using the World Wide Web (WWW), find three sources and summarize them in a short position paper (two to three pages) to support your view on offshore outsourcing.

2. A case study titled "One Outsources, the Other Doesn't" describes Huntington National Bank and Sears, Roebuck and Company's decision to outsource. This case can be found on the Web at http://www.cio.com/archive/110104/outsource html. Read the case and write a short analysis (two to three pages) that discusses whether you agree or disagree with the expert analyses in the case. Support your position. Also, provide a short summary of lessons that could be applied to other organizations that may be considering an outsourcing relationship.

3. Read the article "What It's Like to be the Last Man Standing," found on the Web at http://www.cio.com/archive/121504/cio_outsourcing.html. What feelings and emotions do you think you would have if you were in this person's position? How well was this situation handled? What lessons can we learn from this experience?

4. Using the Web, read the article "Security Risks in Outsourcing: No One in Asia Seems to Care" at http://www.computerworld.com/securitytopics/security/story/0,10801,101365,00.html. Do believe that security should be a major or a minor concern when outsourcing overseas?

 GLOBAL TECHNOLOGY SOLUTIONS

Since the beginning of the project, the Husky Air team has met every Wednesday morning in the GTS conference room for a status meeting. The weekly meeting provides an opportunity for the team to discuss challenges, risks, and ideas, and allows for an update of what each team member accomplished during the past week.

As usual, Tim Williams and the project team were holding their regularly scheduled meeting. After the last team member, Yan, concluded her status update, Tim drew a deep breath and reviewed his thoughts before speaking. He folded his hands on the conference table and began, "As you all know, Robert, our systems tester, has left the team and will be moving to Buffalo to help with the family business. Of course, we wish Robert well, but his departure could not have come at a worse time, since testing is scheduled to begin next month. It's going to be difficult to find someone qualified to take his place on such short notice and remain within our budget and on schedule. Anyone have any suggestions?"

The team members looked at each other. Yan suggested that the tasks for system testing could be shared by several of the team members. Tim thought about this for a moment and responded, "That's an interesting idea, Yan, but we're already a little behind schedule. The tasks for testing are on the critical path, so any delay will postpone our scheduled completion date. Besides, everyone is already working hard just to complete their assigned tasks."

Sitaramin was the next to offer a suggestion and said, "Tim, what if we outsource the testing of the system to another company? I have a cousin in India who owns a firm that specializes in programming and software testing. They've been in business a number of years and are CMMI certified at Level 5. They might be able to help."

Tim raised his eyebrows and said, "That sounds like a good idea. Our contract with Husky Air doesn't prohibit us from subcontracting out any of our work, but this would be something that I'd like to run by our client just the same. Many companies have turned to outsourcing overseas, but I'm not sure how we should get started. Given our schedule and budget constraints, this may be an alternative we need to consider. Sitaramin, can you contact your cousin and set up a conference call while the rest of us start thinking about how we might make this outsourcing arrangement work?" Sitaramin stood to leave and added, "It's still evening in Bangalore. I should be able to catch my cousin at home before he retires for the evening."

Things to Think About

1. Are there any other alternatives that GTS should consider so that the testing of the system can be completed as planned?

2. What are the advantages of outsourcing the testing of the system to a company overseas?

3. What risks or challenges could GTS encounter if Tim Williams decides to outsource overseas?

 ## HUSKY AIR ASSIGNMENT—PILOT ANGELS

Project Procurement Management Plan

For your next assignment, you and your team will develop a project procurement plan. Please provide a professional-looking document that includes the following:

1. **The project name, project team name, and the names of the members of your project team**

2. **A brief project description**

3. **The project's MOV** (This should be revised or refined if necessary.)

4. **Procurement strategy**—Based on the scope management plan you developed in Chapter 5, use the Deliverable Structure Chart to define which project and product deliverables should be developed in house by your project team, as well as which deliverables might be best outsourced to another organization. Be sure to select at least one deliverable to be outsourced.

5. **Outsourcing strategy**—Using only one deliverable that you've identified for outsourcing, use the Web or other sources to identify two or three organizations that could be candidates for outsourcing.

6. **Develop selection criteria**—Develop a template for a scoring model for comparing and selecting an outsourcing partner. See Chapter 2 for details on developing a scoring model. Your template should include just the criteria to be used, and not the scores.

7. **Managing the outsourcing relationship**—Discuss how you intend to manage the outsourced relationship. You could do this by identifying the various risks involved and then developing a plan for addressing and responding to those risks. On the other hand, you could take more of a process approach by identifying roles, responsibilities, and controls that must be in place.

 ## CASE STUDIES

Boeing's Risks and Challenges of Outsourcing

Over the past 50 years, Boeing has amassed knowledge of modern aircraft that is rivaled only by a few other companies in the world. Today, Boeing is outsourcing a large piece of that knowledge as it develops its new airplane—the 787 Dreamliner.

The 787 aircraft are actually a family of three aircraft that are designed to be super efficient. For example, the 787-8 Dreamliner will carry 210 to 250 passengers on flights up to 8,200 nautical miles (15,200 kilometers), while the 787-3 will carry 290 to 300 passengers on longer flights up to about 3,000 nautical miles (5,600 kilometers). The aircraft will use up to 20 percent less fuel than comparable airplanes flying today and will travel at speeds of mach 0.85. Passengers will also enjoy a better interior environment that includes increased comfort such as higher humidity.

The 787's performance is a result of a suite of new technologies by Boeing and an international team. For example, up to 50 percent of the plane's wing and fuselage will be made up of composite materials. Moreover, the aircraft will have a "health monitoring" system that will self-monitor and report maintenance requirements to a ground-based computer system.

Boeing started to take orders for the new plane in 2003, and by May 2008, 56 customers from six continents had placed orders for 857 airplanes. This has been the most successful launch for a commercial aircraft in Boeing's history. The first flight is expected to take place sometime in 2008. Depending on certification,

Boeing expects that the 787 will enter into service in 2009.

The 787 program is pushing the envelope for new technology, and Boeing has had few peers in terms of the art of making wings for commercial aircraft. However, Boeing is now outsourcing the wing and a section of the fuselage of the 787 to three Japanese companies: Mitsubishi, Fuji, and Kawasaki. Moreover, Boeing has also licensed the design and manufacturing technologies for the composite materials to the Japanese as well.

Although Boeing has always outsourced aircraft subcomponents and systems to other companies, many core technologies and competencies are now being acquired by the Japanese. According to Stan Sorscher, an engineer at Boeing, "The 787 composite wing and fuselage structure are new technologies—untried on this scale even by Boeing. Boeing developed much of the materials, manufacturing processes, tooling, tolerances, and allowances, and other design features, which are then transferred to suppliers in Japan, Italy, and elsewhere. Over time, institutional learning and forgetting will put the suppliers in control of the critical body of knowledge, and Boeing will steadily lose touch with key technical expertise."

However, outsourcing may be unavoidable for financial and political reasons. Boeing may use the threat of outsourcing to send a message to the unions—if you push too hard, your jobs can be outsourced overseas. On the other hand, outsourcing design and production work to other countries often provides aircraft sales to those countries. With the hosting of the Olympics in 2008, China has an immediate need for long-distance air travel; however, China demands access to technology in return for granting access to it. For example, ten Chinese companies are making components for the 787's main competitor, the Airbus aircraft.

1. Can Boeing and other companies put themselves out of business by outsourcing key technologies and core competencies?

2. Is outsourcing overseas an unavoidable political reality for global companies today? What do companies like Boeing gain? What do they give up?

SOURCE: Adapted from www.boeing.com; John Newhouse, Boeing Versus Airbus: Flight Risk, Outsourcing Challenges, *Computerworld*, March 1, 2007.

Outsourcing in a Flat World

Many organizations first considered offshore outsourcing as a way take advantage of cheaper labor. A salary survey conducted by the staffing firm Robert Half Technology reports that a skilled programmer in India costs about $30,000 a year, while a comparable programmer in the U.S. costs about $90,000.

Although many companies save money initially, they often find that outsourcing only hides long-term problems.

This is especially true if an organization outsources processes without understanding their quality and efficiency. Too often the outsource provider is expected or contractually demanded to fix problem areas. Moreover, a McKinsey report found that after the first year of a contractual engagement many organizations tend to focus more on flexibility and agility than saving money. Outsourcing is no longer about finding cheap labor, although taking something and shipping it offshore can probably still save some money. But as Tom Sanzone, CIO of Credit Suisse, points out "But cost in and of itself isn't going to get anyone a competitive advantage."

Nandan Nilekani is the CEO of the Indian firm called Infosys and is credited with the phrase "the world is flat." He believes that work will be done where it makes the most sense. For example, Nilekani offers that Infosys has offices in 39 countries, while Wipro, another large IT services company in India, has eight offices in Europe. Moreover, the large Indian consulting firm, Tata, has over 10,000 consultants in North America.

On the other hand, companies that often are identified as being American are becoming more global as well. For example, IBM now has approximately 53,000 employees in India, while Accenture will soon have more employees in India than the United States. As Ben Worthen of *CIO Magazine* explains, as "Sourcing has gone global; so have sourcing companies."

The new model for outsourcing is becoming more focused where IT work is broken down into pieces, and each piece is completed in a location that offers the best blend of experience, skill, cost, and quality. This can result in greater opportunity for organizations to tap into a global network of outsource providers that offer centers of excellence. For example, an outsourcing vendor may establish itself in Java programming, business intelligence, or testing. This requires that an organization understand its own internal model for delivering IT services or project processes and tasks. CIOs as well as project managers can then assess whether their IT staff or project team has the necessary skills and resources internally.

An organization may have a team of programmers that can turn out excellent applications that provide competitive advantage. In this case, it would not make sense to outsource this group just to save a few dollars. On the other hand, the team may not have the time, skill, or interest in testing, so finding an outsource provider domestically or internationally may be cheaper and more effective.

Ben Worthen believes that an organization can be a better outsourcing customer if it understands its true IT capabilities. Instead of outsourcing the entire IT function in one megadeal to a single vendor, CIO's and project managers can find the right partner for a particular process or task. Subdividing IT processes into distinct pieces allows an organization to better determine which components should be internal and which should be best performed by a partner. As a result, this may circumvent just shifting bad processes to someone else.

However, selective outsourcing increases complexity, and many organizations have created a high-level management position to deal with outsourcing partners and the projects they are working on. According to Louis Rosenthal, executive vice president of ABN Amro Services, "It's an emerging function that may not have existed at a global level before. Vendor management becomes much more important now. [Having that group] helps us facilitate business decisions in ways that we didn't have to before."

1. Do you agree with the statement, "If you are outsourcing a problem, it will still be a problem"? Why or why not?

2. Taking advantage of cheaper labor rates in other countries has been a main reason for many companies to outsource offshore. What do you think will happen to these labor rates as outsourcing providers become more global?

3. Provide an example or situation of an IT project process or task that would be a good candidate for being outsourced.

4. Provide an example or situation of an IT project process or task that should not be outsourced.

SOURCE: Adapted from Ben Worthen, What The World is Flat Means to Outsourcing, *CIO Magazine*, May 1, 2007.

BIBLIOGRAPHY

Barthelemy, J. (2003). The seven deadly sins of outsourcing. *Academy of Management Executive*. 17(2): 87–100.

Brown, D. and S. Wilson. (2005). *The Black Book of Outsourcing: How to Manage the Changes, Challenges, and Opportunities*. Hoboken, NJ: John Wiley.

Drezner, D. W. (2004). The Outsourcing Bogeyman. *Foreign Affairs*. May/June: 22–34.

Drucker, P. F. (2002). They're Not Employees, They're People. *Harvard Business Review*. February. Reprint R0202E.

Farrell, D. (2004). Beyond Offshoring. *Harvard Business Review*, December: 1–10. Reprint: R0412E. http://www.computerworld.com/printthis/2005/0,4814,101774,00.html

Field, T. (1999). 10 Years That Shook IT. *CIO Magazine*. October 1. http://www.cio.com/archive/100199/outsourcing.html.

Hamblen, M. (2004). Sidebar: After the Outsourcing. *Computerworld*. November 8. http://www.computerworld.com/printthis / 2004 / 0, 4814,97223,00.html

Lacity, M. C., L. P. Willcocks, and D. F. Feeny. (1995). IT Outsourcing: Maximize Flexibility and Control. *Harvard Business Review*. May–June: 84–93.

Mears, J. (2005). Study: Outsourcing Losing Luster. *Computerworld*. April 25. http://www.computerworld.com/printthis/2005/0,4814, 101380,00.html

Project Management Institute (PMI) 2004. *A Guide to the Project Management Body of Knowledge (PMBOK® Guide)*. Newtown Square, PA: PMI Publishing.

Pruitt, S. (2005a). Employees Can Benefit from Outsourcing, Poll Says. *Computerworld*. January 12. http://www.computerworld.com/printthis/2005/0,4814,98894,00.html

Pruitt, S. (2005b). Study: Europe Overtakes U.S. in Big Outsourcing Deals. *Computerworld*. January 14. http://www.computerworld.com/printthis/2005/0,4814,99086,00.html

Robinson, M. and R. Kalakota. (2004). *Offshore Outsourcing: Business Models, ROI, and Best Practices*. Suwanee, GA: Mivar Press.

13

Leadership and Ethics

CHAPTER OVERVIEW

Chapter 13 focuses on project leadership and two important related components—ethics and managing multicultural projects. After studying this chapter, you should understand and be able to:

- Define leadership and understand its role and importance in successfully managing IT projects.
- Describe the five approaches to exemplary leadership.
- Describe six leadership styles.
- Define the concept of emotional intelligence and how it can help one to become a more effective leader.
- Define ethics and understand its importance in project leadership.
- Understand some of the ethical challenges that you may face as a project leader or project team member.
- Describe a process for making ethical decisions.
- Understand culture and diversity as well as the some of the challenges of leading and managing a multicultural project.

INTRODUCTION

Up to this point, we have covered the important tools and processes needed to be an effective project manager. However, a successful project requires leadership. A project leader most certainly would be the project manager, but a project can also have other individuals who must assume leadership roles at different times over the course of the project life cycle. For example, a project team member may be called upon to provide leadership or guidance because of his or her experience or knowledge.

Although there is no dearth of books and articles on the topic of leadership, we will look at some commonsense approaches to leadership that can help you become an effective leader. In addition, we will discuss two important components of leadership. The first focuses on ethics, which has become an increasingly important topic for organizations as well as business programs in colleges and universities. The high-profile ethical meltdowns reported in the media are not limited to large organizations or senior managers. People at all levels in organizations of all sizes face ethical issues every day. No doubt you will often encounter ethical dilemmas throughout your career. Since only an overview of ethics can be covered in such a limited space and time, we will therefore take a more practical view to help you prepare for some of the common ethical dilemmas you may face in a project setting. These approaches are also important to project leaders in developing a culture that supports an ethical environment.

The second component of leadership discussed in this chapter focuses on managing multicultural projects. A multicultural project could include an international project or a domestic organization that would like to benefit from having a diverse workforce. Regardless, multicultural projects require an understanding of culture and diversity. Today, a successful project leader must also be able to effectively manage and lead projects that deal with multicultural clients and project team members.

PROJECT LEADERSHIP

What is a leader? Are leaders born? Or can one learn to become an effective leader? And how is leadership different from management? As John Kotter (2001) explains:

> Leadership is different from management, but not for the reasons most people think. Leadership isn't mystical and mysterious. It has nothing to do with having "charisma" or other exotic personality traits. It is not the province of a chosen few. Nor is leadership necessarily better than management or a replacement for it. Rather, leadership and management are two distinctive and complementary systems of action. Each has its own function and characteristic activities. Both are necessary for success in an increasingly complex and volatile business environment (3).

Management focuses on policies and procedures that bring order and predictability to complex organizational situations. Traditionally, management is defined within such activities as planning, organizing, controlling, staffing, evaluating, and monitoring (Shriberg, Shriberg, and Kumari 2005).

Although management and leadership tend to overlap, leadership centers on vision, change, and getting results. As Kouzes and Posner (2002) point out:

> Leaders inspire a shared vision. They gaze across the horizon of time, imagining the attractive opportunities that are in store when they and their constituents arrive at a distant destination. Leaders have a desire to make something happen, to change the way things are, to create something that no one else has ever created before. In some ways, leaders live their lives backward. They see pictures in their mind's eye of what the results will look like even before they've started their project, much as an architect draws a blueprint or an engineer builds a model. Their clear image of the future pulls them forward. Yet visions seen only by leaders are insufficient to create an organized movement or a significant change in a company. A person with no constituents is not a leader, and people will not follow until they accept a vision of their own. Leaders cannot command commitment, only inspire it (15).

Up to this point, we have concentrated on the planning activities and processes for *managing* projects. From earlier chapters, we defined project management as meeting or exceeding stakeholder expectations by applying and integrating the various project management processes. However, successful projects also require *leadership* that involves setting direction, aligning people, and motivating them. This requires understanding several approaches to leadership and appropriate leadership styles.

Some Modern Approaches to Leadership

Often when we hear the term "leader," we think of famous and powerful people in history. Some believe that certain individuals are born with traits that make them natural leaders. Others, however, believe that leadership is a function of the environment. Although we are born with certain traits, a person can develop leadership potential by developing or nurturing these traits. Personality, motivation, and intelligence are important traits, yet leadership, to a great degree, is about having the courage to do the right thing and being open minded (Shriberg, Shriberg, and Kumari 2005).

James Kouzes and Barry Posner (2002) conducted research for over 20 years on effective leadership experiences. They found that leaders are often ordinary people who help guide others along pioneering journeys rather than follow well worn paths. Based on this research, they defined five practices of exemplary leadership (see Figure 13.1) that can help you have a clearer direction to become a more effective and successful project leader:

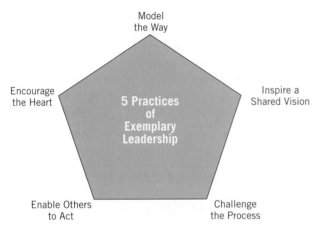

Figure 13.1 Five Practices of Exemplary Leadership

Source: Adapted from Kouzes and Posner, 2002.

1. *Model the way*—The most effective leaders lead by example. A leader's *behavior* wins respect, not his or her title or position within the organization. You must find your own voice based on your personal values and beliefs, but what you do in terms of your behavior and daily actions is often more important than what you say. Your words and deeds must be consistent so that you convey the right message. Leaders set an example of what they expect from others by modeling the way they want others to behave. This provides the leader with the respect and the right to lead others. People follow the person first, not the plan.

2. *Inspire a shared vision*—An exemplary leader has an exciting vision or dream that acts as a force for inventing the future. In turn, this vision should inspire people so they become committed to a purpose. This requires the leader to know their constituents so that they will believe the leader understands their needs, interests, and "speaks their language." A leader must engage in dialogue, not monologue, to understand the hopes and dreams of others and gain their support. A leader should try to ignite the passion in others through communication and enthusiasm of what the future *could be*.

3. *Challenge the process*—Exemplary leaders do not rely on fate or luck. They venture out and accept challenges. Leaders are pioneers who challenge the

status quo by seeking out new opportunities to innovate, grow, and improve. However, most leaders do not create, develop, or come up with new products, services, or processes. Often leaders are good listeners who recognize good ideas, support those ideas, and then challenge the process to make these new ideas happen. Leaders are also early adopters of innovation, but innovation and change require experimentation, risk, and failure. Although leaders accept risk and failure, they minimize it by taking and encouraging others to make incremental steps. They strive for small wins to boost confidence, commitment, and learning. However, people must feel safe and comfortable in taking risks so that both leaders and constituents learn from their failures and their successes.

4. *Enable others to act*—Visions and dreams do not just happen because of one person's actions. This requires a team effort so a leader's ability to get others to act is crucial. Exemplary leaders enable others to act by encouraging collaboration and building trust among all the project stakeholders. Leaders provide an environment that makes it possible for others to do good work. People should feel empowered and motivated to do their best, feel a sense of ownership, and take pride in what they do. A leader enables others to act by giving power away, not by hanging onto it. People should be made to feel strong and capable; otherwise, they will not give their best or stay around very long. In short, a leader must turn constituents into leaders themselves.

5. *Encourage the heart*—Often the project journey is long and difficult. People can become tired, disillusioned, frustrated, and willing to give up. Exemplary leaders rally others to carry on by encouraging the heart. Although this encouragement can be a simple gesture such as a thank-you note or something more dramatic like a marching band, the leader should show appreciation for people's contributions and create a culture of celebration that recognizes those accomplishments. Recognition and celebration should not be phony or lame. It is important to visibly link rewards with performance. Authentic rituals and celebrations that align with the team's values can build a strong collective identity and spirit that can carry the team through turbulent waters.

Leadership Styles

Although the five practices of exemplary leadership provide a model for effective leadership, research has also suggested that many effective leaders employ a collection of distinct leadership styles. Based on a sample of 3,871 executives worldwide, Daniel Goleman (2000) identified six distinct leadership styles. More important, Goleman found that the best leaders do not rely on only one leadership style, but tend to use several or a combination style, depending on the situation. The following summary of the six styles will help you understand how a particular leadership style influences performance and results. It can also offer guidance as to when you should use or change to another style.

1. *The coercive style*—The coercive style can be summarized as a "do as I say" approach to leading others. This style can be effective in a crisis, to kick-start a turnaround situation, when dealing with a problem employee, or when the leader is attempting to achieve immediate compliance. Although effective in

some situations, the coercive style can have a negative impact on the climate of the organization or project. For example, an extreme top-down approach to decision making and communication can often obstruct new ideas if people believe their ideas will be shot down or limit communication if people are apprehensive of being the bearer of bad news. Moreover, people will soon lose their initiative, motivation, commitment, and sense of ownership because the coercive style can make people resentful and disillusioned.

2. *The authoritative style*—The leader who follows the authoritative style takes a "come with me" approach in which the leader outlines a clearly defined goal but empowers people to choose their own means for achieving it. The authoritative leader provides vision and enthusiasm. He or she motivates people by making it clear as to how their work fits into the larger picture. People know that what they are doing has meaning and purpose. Standards for success and performance are clear to everyone. The authoritative style works well in most organizational and project situations, but is best suited for situations when the organization or project team is adrift. However, this approach may not be best for inexperienced leaders who are working with experts or a more experienced team. In this case, the leader can undermine an effective team if he or she appear pompous, out of touch, or overbearing.

3. *The affiliative style*—This style follows the attitude that "people come first." The affiliative style centers on the value of the individual rather than goals and tasks and attempts to keep people happy by creating harmony among them. The leader who uses this style attempts to build strong emotional bonds that translate into strong loyalty. Moreover, people who like each other tend to communicate more, share ideas and inspiration, and take risks. Flexibility is higher because the leader does not impose unnecessary rules and structures that define how the work must get done—that's up to those who must do the work. The affiliative style works well in situations that require building team harmony, morale, trust, or communication. However, often situations occur in which people need some structure or advice to navigate through complex tasks, and having little or no direction can leave them feeling rudderless. In addition, an overcaring and overnurturing approach that focuses exclusively on praise can create a perception that mediocrity is tolerated.

4. *The democratic style*—The democratic style attempts to develop consensus through participation by asking, "What do you think?" Using this style, the leader spends time getting other people's ideas, while building trust, respect, and commitment. People's flexibility and responsibility are increased because they have a greater say in the decisions that affect their goals and work. Subsequently, morale tends to be high, and everyone has a more realistic idea of what can or cannot be done. The democratic style works best when the leader needs to build buy-in or consensus, or to gain valuable input from others. For example, the leader may have a clear vision, but needs innovative ideas or guidance as to the best way to achieve that vision. However, this style can also lead to seemingly endless meetings in a vain attempt to gain group consensus. This can cause conflicts, confusion, and the perception that the group is leaderless. In addition, the democratic style would not be appropriate in a crisis or when the team does not have competence or experience to offer sound advice.

346 CHAPTER 13 / LEADERSHIP AND ETHICS

5. *The pacesetting style*—A leader who uses the pacesetting style sets high performance standards and has a "do as I do, now" attitude. This style exemplifies an obsession with doing things better and faster for him or herself and everyone else. Poor performers are quickly identified and replaced if standards are not met. Although the leader may try to get better results by setting an example for high performance, morale can deteriorate if people feel overwhelmed by the pacesetter's demands for excellence and performance. Often goals and expectations may be clear to the leader, but are poorly communicated to the rest of the team. An "if I have to tell you what to do, then you're the wrong person for this job," can turn into a situation in which people try to second-guess what the leader wants. People lose energy and enthusiasm if the work becomes task focused, routine, and boring. Subsequently, the pacesetting leader may micromanage by attempting to take over the work of others. As a result, people lose their direction or sense of how their work is part of a larger picture. Moreover, if the leader leaves, people will feel adrift since the pacesetting leader sets all direction. However, this style may be appropriate in situations that require quick results from a highly motivated, self-directed, and competent team. Given this situation, the pacesetter sets the pace for everyone else so that the work is completed on time or ahead of schedule.

6. *The coaching style*—The coaching style leader follows the "try this" approach to help people identify their unique strengths and weaknesses so that they can reach their personal and career goals. The leader who uses the coaching style encourages people to set long-term professional goals and then helps them develop a plan for achieving them. Coaching leaders are good at delegating and giving people challenging, but attainable, assignments. Even short-term or minor failures are acceptable and viewed as positive learning experiences. Goleman's research has found that the coaching style is the least often used, but can be a valuable and powerful tool for performance and for improving the climate of the organization or project. The coaching style works well in many situations, but is most effective when people are "up for it"—that is, people want to be coached. Consequently, this style is least effective when people are resistant to change or when the leader does not have the knowledge, capability, or desire to be a coach.

Emotional Intelligence

Goleman's study also suggests that leaders who have mastered the authoritative, democratic, affiliative, and coaching styles tend to create the best climate and have the highest performance. Moreover, the most effective leaders have the flexibility to switch among the leadership styles as needed. An individual can expand his or her repertoire by understanding their emotional intelligence competencies. **Emotional intelligence** can be defined as the ability to understand and manage our relationships and ourselves better. Although a person's intelligence quotient (IQ) is largely genetic, emotional intelligence can be learned at any age. Unfortunately, improving one's emotional intelligence is like changing a bad habit. It takes time, patience, and a great deal of effort. For example, as a leader you may follow a democratic style of leadership when things are going smoothly on a project, but may use a more coercive style when things don't go according to plan. As a result, you may tend to flare up and tune out other people's ideas and suggestions just when you need them the most.

Emotional intelligence includes four capabilities: self-awareness, self-management, social awareness, and social skills that comprise specific sets of competencies (Goleman 2000).

1. *Self-awareness*
   - *Emotional self-awareness*—Reading and understanding your emotions as well as how your emotions impact your job performance and those around you
   - *Accurate self-assessment*—Realistically evaluating your strengths and weaknesses
   - *Self-confidence*—Having a strong and positive sense of self-worth

2. *Self-management*
   - *Self-control*—Keeping your impulses and negative emotions in check
   - *Trustworthiness*—Maintaining a high level of honesty and integrity
   - *Conscientiousness*—Managing yourself and responsibilities effectively
   - *Adaptability*—Adjusting to new situations and overcoming challenges
   - *Achievement orientation*—Meeting high internal standards of excellence
   - *Initiative*—Seizing new opportunities

3. *Social awareness*
   - *Empathy*—Sensing and understanding other people's emotions, perspectives, and being genuinely concerned about their problems and interests
   - *Organizational awareness*—Being perceptive about the currents of everyday organizational life, building networks, and navigating through organizational politics
   - *Service orientation*—Recognizing and meeting customer needs

4. *Social skills*
   - *Visionary leadership*—Taking charge and inspiring others with a compelling vision
   - *Influence*—Having a wide range of persuasive tactics at your disposal
   - *Developing others*—Bolstering the abilities of others through feedback and guidance
   - *Communication*—Listening and sending clear, convincing, and well aimed messages
   - *Change catalyst*—Initiating new ideas and leading people in the right direction
   - *Conflict management*—Being able to deescalate disagreements and facilitate resolutions
   - *Building bonds*—Cultivating and maintaining a web of relationships inside and outside the organization
   - *Teamwork and collaboration*—Facilitating cooperation and building teams

Goleman, Boyatzis, and McKee (2001) suggest several ways to strengthen your emotional intelligence and emotional leadership. The first step entails asking two questions: "Who am I now?" and "Who do I want to be?" The idea is to make an honest assessment of how others view your leadership and how you would like to

QUICK THINKING—LEADERSHIP AND LISTENING

Project managers and other IT leaders tend to focus on sharpening their technical skills, but effective leaders need to work on their soft skills—and the ability to listen may be the most crucial soft skill for being an effective leader. Steven Covey, author of the bestselling book, *The 7 Habits of Highly Effective People*, writes "Seek first to understand, then to be understood." Moreover, former CEO of Chrysler Corporation Lee Iacocca once said "Business people need to listen at least as much as they talk. Too many people fail to realize that real communication goes in both directions." Being a good listener make you a better leader and your direct reports feeling appreciated. Consider the following example:

> You walk into your project manager's office with a problem that you hope he can help you work out. He invites you to take a seat and tell him about it, but as you begin to speak he turns his attention to his computer screen. He encourages you to tell him more about your problem as he reads and answers a list of new emails. Without turning your way, he nods and

grunts a couple of "uh-huhs." After you finish explaining your problem, he turns from the screen to face you and says, "I have the utmost faith that you'll handle this problem, and how you handle it is entirely up to you." The phone rings and your manager says that he's expecting an important call, which is an indication for you to leave. As you walk out of his office, he tells you to stop by any time you have a problem and that he's happy to help.

1. We've all experienced the above situation in some way. What effect would this have on your morale? Sense of value to the organization? Or your motivation?

2. As a project leader, what are some things you could do to become a better listener?

SOURCE: Adapted from Diann Daniel, Soft Skills: Listening for Better Leadership, *CIO Magazine*, September 4, 2007.

be viewed in the future. This may require gathering 360-degree feedback from your peers, subordinates, and superiors so that you can take stock of your strengths and weaknesses. The next step involves devising a plan for getting from where you are as a leader to where you want to be. This may mean having a trusted coach who can provide honest feedback and point out progress and relapses as you constantly rehearse new behaviors that lead you to improve specific emotional intelligence competencies. In time, this will allow you to learn new leadership styles.

ETHICS IN PROJECTS

Over the last several years, a great deal of attention has been given to organizations that have had ethical meltdowns. The questionable business dealings of Enron executives, for example, led to the largest corporate bankruptcy in U.S. history. This sinking ship also led to the demise of Arthur Andersen, LLP, which at one time was one of the Big Five international accounting firms. Although these are just two examples, the list of questionable ethical behaviors by organizational leaders is long and distinguished. Unfortunately, this list is getting longer.

As a result, many organizations are mandating and investing in ethical training for their employees. Over the last few years, many business programs in colleges and universities have added ethics courses or ethical components to courses to give students a sounder ethical foundation. From a philosophical view, **ethics** can be defined as a set of moral principles and values. Ethical dilemmas arise when our personal values come into conflict. However, Trevino and Nelson (2004) take a more practical view that can help you understand and apply several principles of ethics in a project setting:

> But our definition of ethics—the principles, norms, and standards of conduct governing an individual or group—focuses on conduct. We expect employers to establish guidelines for work-related conduct, including what time to arrive and leave the workplace, whether smoking is allowed on the premises, how customers are to be treated, and how quickly work should be done. Guidelines about ethical conduct aren't much different. Many employers spend a lot of time and money developing policies for a range of employee activities, from how to fill out expense reports to what kind of client gifts are acceptable, to what constitutes a conflict of interest or bribe. If we use this definition, ethics becomes an extension of good management. Leaders identify appropriate and inappropriate conduct, and they communicate their expectations to employees through ethics codes, training programs, and other communication channels (13).

You may be wondering whether this reaction is worth the time and effort. The answer is that unethical business behaviors cost organizations money and jobs. For example, at the end of 2000, Enron's stock was trading at over $80 a share. Less than a year later, it fell to less than a dollar a share. The dreams of many innocent investors went up in smoke. Even more disconcerting is the fact that over 20,000 employees lost their jobs.

In addition, acting unethically can also mean breaking a law. This can lead not only to financial penalties, but jail time. Moreover, acting ethically is just the right thing to do. It's not only in your best interest; it's in the best interest for people who are part of organizations and society. People want to work for and do business with organizations they can trust. Credibility and reputation take a great deal of effort and time to build, but can be ruined almost in an instant.

Unfortunately, ethical decisions are not always that clear cut. For example, Figure 13.2 shows that while some decisions (i.e., legal and ethical or illegal and unethical) are usually clear to us, we often have to make decisions that fall in the gray represented by the shaded quadrants. These types of decisions are more difficult because we may be torn by decisions or actions that may be legal but unethical, or illegal but ethical. To a large degree legality and the ethicalness of certain actions are governed by society and culture.

A project manager is a leader who can create, maintain, or change the culture of the project organization. **Culture** can be defined as the shared beliefs, assumptions, and values that we learn from society or a group that guides or influences our behavior (Trevino and Nelson 2004). More specifically, culture can be created, changed, or maintained in terms of formal systems that are in place. This would include such factors as the authoritative structure as well as policies and procedures for hiring, firing, rewarding performance, and training. However, culture can be influenced by informal systems such as the acceptable everyday norms and behaviors. These can be viewed in terms of how people associated with a particular group dress, as well as their

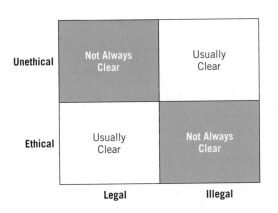

Figure 13.2 Ethics versus Legality

heroes, myths or stories, rituals, and language. For example, Microsoft's culture is still largely influenced by the legend of a young and brash group of technical wizards led by Bill Gates.

Ethical Leadership

People who are brought into an organization learn its culture through a process called **socialization**. This process of "learning the ropes" can occur through formal means such as training and mentoring or through less formal ones such as interaction with peers and superiors. New people not only learn such things as how to dress appropriately, they also learn what behaviors are acceptable and unacceptable. Subsequently, socialization can encourage or discourage ethical behavior (Trevino and Nelson 2004).

People look to their leaders for ethical guidance. If the leader does not provide this guidance, people may seek others who can. Often, this may allow them to be influenced by others who may intentionally or unintentionally lead them toward unethical behaviors. Therefore, a project manager must act as a moral individual and a moral manager. A moral individual is viewed as someone having certain personal traits such as integrity, honesty, and trustworthiness. A moral manager, on the other hand, is an individual who defines the right set of values and sends out the right message to shape an ethical culture. As Scriberg, Schriberg, and Kumari (2005) suggest, a leader can fall into one of the following categories:

- *Unethical leadership*—Unethical leaders are generally weak moral individuals and weak moral managers. For example, Al Dunlap was a senior executive who had a reputation for turning around struggling companies. His strategy usually included firing as many employees as possible to drastically reduce payroll. Dunlap was given the nickname "Chainsaw Al" for his slash-and-cut approach. Dunlap was successful, but he was also known for emotionally abusing his employees by being belligerent and condescending. Subordinates were expected to make the numbers at all costs. Those who did were rewarded. Those who didn't would suffer his wrath. Not surprisingly, people used questionable accounting and sales techniques, and, as CEO of Sunbeam, Chainsaw Al was caught lying and trying to cover up these questionable business practices. Sunbeam's board of directors fired Dunlap in 1998, but the company was near ruin. Dunlap paid $500,000 in a settlement with the SEC and agreed never to serve again as an officer of a publicly traded company.

- *Hypocritical leadership*—Probably the worst type of leader is the one who extols the virtues of integrity and ethical conduct, but then engages in unethical behavior, encourages others to do so, rewards bottom-line results by any means, or fails to discipline any wrongdoing. By standing on a pedestal of integrity and moral values, the leader may encourage people to place their trust in whatever the leader says or does. Sometimes they are led to believe that the ends justify the means and disregard ethical standards themselves or believe that it's fine for the leader to do so. On the other hand, many people can become cynical if they believe what the leader and his or her followers are doing is wrong. One example of a hypocritical leader is the reverend Jim Bakker. In the late 1970s and early 1980s, Bakker developed the PTL Ministries into the largest religious broadcasting empire. Bakker took in millions of dollars by convincing people to purchase a limited number of lifetime memberships for hotels that were part of a theme park. As part of the deal, only 25,000 memberships were to be made available and a membership would allow a family to stay free each year for four days and three nights. Unfortunately, over 66,000 memberships were sold, that would make it impossible for the hotels to support that many people. Moreover, a good portion of this money was diverted to supporting other PTL expenses such as large salaries and bonuses for Bakker and his wife Tammy Faye. Bakker resigned three months before the PTL filed for bankruptcy in 1987 and the IRS revoked the PTL's tax-exempt status. In 1989, Baker was convicted of fraud. He spent the next eight years in prison.

- *Ethically neutral leadership*—Many leaders tend to fall in a neutral zone where they are neither strong or weak ethical leaders. As a result, they do not provide clear ethical guidance because people do not know what the leader's ethical beliefs are or whether the leader cares. Unfortunately, no message often sends a message whereby people interpret silence to mean that the leader doesn't care how business goals are met—just that they are met. For example, in 2002, *Fortune* magazine described Citigroup as a money-making machine, but one that engaged in a number of questionable business practices such as allegedly helping Enron hide debt. Sandy Weill, chairman of the board and former CEO of Citicorp, told Citicorp's board of directors that his most important task would be to ensure that Citicorp now operated at the highest level of ethics and integrity. Weill can be viewed as a neutral ethical leader since he often looked the other way and seemed to take notice only after these problems became public.

- *Ethical leadership*—An ethical leader, then, is someone who makes it clear that bottom-line results are important, but only if they can be achieved in an ethical manner. Moreover, research suggests that when a culture is viewed as being ethical, employees tend to engage in fewer unethical behaviors, are more committed to the organization, and more willing to report problems to management (Trevino and Nelson 2004).

Common Ethical Dilemmas

There is no doubt that you will encounter ethical dilemmas when your values will be in conflict. Your career can be enhanced or be damaged depending on how you handle the situation. However, many ethical situations are predictable, so you can be prepared in advance to deal with them. Some of the more common ethical situations you might encounter include (Trevino and Nelson, 2004):

- *Human resource situations*—Project leaders must ensure that qualified team members are recruited and retained. This entails creating a project environment in which people feel safe and appreciated so that they want to put forth their best work. Issues that can lead to ethical situations include discrimination, privacy, sexual or other types of harassment, as well as appraisals, discipline, hiring, firing, and layoff policies and decisions. The key consideration should be fairness in terms of equity (only performance counts), reciprocity (expectations are understood and met), and impartiality (prejudice and bias are not factors).

- *Conflicts of interest*—Organizations and projects involve a number of relationships between people. These relationships can be professional and personal. Impartiality can come into question when these relationships overlap, and a conflict of interest can occur. For example, would a gift or favor from a vendor or a customer be viewed as having an influence on your judgment or a project-related decision? Trust is a key ingredient for personal and business relationships, and conflicts of interest can weaken trust if special favors are extended only to special friends at the expense of others. Many organizations have policies that define situations that are and are not acceptable. Conflict of interest issues can include such things as overt or subtle bribes or kickbacks as well as relationships that could question your impartiality. Moreover, as a project team member, you will gain access to confidential and private information that could be of value to you or someone else. When in doubt, it's best to provide full disclosure to mitigate any risk of impropriety.

■ *Confidence*—A project includes a number of stakeholders. Meeting or exceeding project stakeholder expectations, especially the client's, requires maintaining a strong sense of confidence with respect to such issues as confidentiality, product safety or reliability, truth in advertising, and special fiduciary responsibilities that require special commitments or obligations to the client or other project stakeholders. Although confidence issues can include a wide variety of issues, they can create special ethical considerations that can affect your relationship with project stakeholders. Trust can erode when your fairness, honesty, or respect come into question.

■ *Corporate resources*—As a project team member, you are a representation of both your team and your organization. This means that you are considered an agent of your organization and your actions can be considered the actions of your organization. For example, if you are a consultant working with a client, people will infer that you are representing and speaking on behalf of your company. In turn, your company may give you an email address with their domain, business cards, and stationery with the corporate letterhead. Therefore, your email and organizational stationery should only be used for business purposes. For example, writing a letter of recommendation for someone means that both you and your organization share the same opinion. Make sure that your personal opinion and corporate opinions are not in conflict. In addition, company equipment and services should only be used for business purposes. Often companies have policies about personal phone calls and email or the acceptable use of equipment. Another important issue concerns the truth. Many times people are asked to "fudge" the numbers by making things appear better than they are. Although many organizations now have procedures to follow if you're asked to engage in this type of behavior, you may want to consult with someone outside the chain of command such as someone in the legal department or human resources department if this type of situation arises and no policy exists. However, becoming a "whistle blower" can have its consequences—intended and unintended—and should be an option used with caution and as a last resort.

Making Sound Ethical Decisions

It appears that a single approach to dealing with ethical dilemmas does not exist. For example, let's say that you are working on an IT project and have just completed the testing of a system component. Let's also assume that the test results have shown that the system component does not meet certain performance and quality standards set by the client. The system component will require rework that will make an already late and over-budget project even later and more over budget. A superior has asked you to change the results so that they will meet the client's specification. The supervisor reasons with you that the results are "really not all that bad and that the component of the system can be fixed before going live." Trevino and Nelson (2004) provide a prescriptive approach for making sound ethical decisions in business that can be applied to a number of ethical dilemmas you may encounter in a project setting:

1. *Gather the facts*—It is easy to assume that you have all the facts, but we often jump to a conclusion without having enough relevant information. Begin by focusing on the historical facts that led to this situation and then what has happened since then. This can be difficult because the facts may not be that clear or readily available. However, you should also keep in mind that there are limitations if you do not have all the facts or information at hand. Given our example, the stress of dealing with a project that is going to be late and over budget may lead to situations in which people look to cut certain corners. Perhaps we are dealing with an inexperienced supervisor or a person who has gotten away with cutting corners in the past.

2. *Define the ethical issue*—Many people react impulsively to ethical dilemmas and jump to a conclusion without really understanding the underlying issues. We often stop at the first ethical issue we identify, but a number of related and interwoven issues may complicate things once we begin to realize them. Challenge yourself and others to see as many issues as you can so that you have a fuller understanding of the problem. The main ethical issue here deals with trust. The client expects to receive a system that meets or exceeds expectations. Is close enough good enough? Or will the system component really be fixed so that it meets those standards later on?

3. *Identify the affected stakeholders*—The next step involves identifying those who will be affected by the decision as well as any benefits or harm that will come to them. It is important to see things through the eyes of the visibly affected stakeholders and then consider those who are more indirectly affected. Obviously, the client is impacted directly. But what about the client's customers? The shareholders? Also, how will you and the rest of your project team be affected? If you're a consultant, how will your organization be affected? What about your family? Your team's families? And the families of your client?

4. *Identify the consequences*—Once you identify the affected stakeholders, the next step is to think about the potential consequences for each stakeholder. Although it may be impossible to identify every consequence, you can still get a good idea of whether the good of your decision or action outweighs the bad. In our example, the company's reputation and financial position could be damaged if the system component fails to perform as intended. In turn, this could have a negative impact on your project organization and your career. The idea is to think of your actions as having a number of impacts, much like the waves that are created when you toss a stone into still waters. The impact of your actions can be immediate and felt over time.

5. *Identify the obligations*—After you have identified the consequences of your action or decision, the next step involves identifying the obligations you have to the affected stakeholders. It may help to think of obligations in terms

of values, principles, character, and outcomes. For example, you may feel loyalty toward your supervisor because he or she hired you at a time when you were financially desperate or because you want to be viewed as a team player. On the other hand, you have an obligation to the client to tell the truth and report the results as they are.

6. *Consider your character and integrity*—Many people find the "sleep test" as a proxy for how the world would view their actions. Will your action or decision allow you to sleep restfully at night? Another way is to ask yourself, Would you feel comfortable if your action or decision were to appear on the news? Moreover, what would someone close to you (and whose opinion really matters) say if you told that person about your action or decision? In short, do you want people to say that you were a person of integrity or not?

7. *Think creatively about potential actions*—In coming up with a potential solution to an ethical dilemma, it is important that you do not "force yourself into a corner" by framing your decision in terms of two choices. In our example, this may mean either changing the test results as the supervisor wants or bypassing his or her authority and telling your boss's boss what your supervisor asked you to do. There may be a policy in your organization that outlines steps you could follow for blowing the whistle on your supervisor, but another option may be to talk with your supervisor and explain that you are uncomfortable with changing the results. Explaining the impact and consequences of the action may be enough to change the supervisor's mind. If that doesn't work, other options might include making sure that someone else knows what the original (and correct) test results report. Each situation is unique and therefore requires a unique and sometimes creative approach. Talking to someone outside the situation can be a great help.

8. *Check your gut*—Although the previous steps tend to follow a rational approach, you still need to check your gut or intuition. Empathy should not be discarded over logic because it can raise a warning flag that someone might be harmed. If your intuition is troubling you, then it may be time for more thought on the issue or situation. However, making a decision based solely on emotion is probably not a good idea either. Checking your gut should be a final stage of the process that provides you with confidence in your action or decision.

Codes of Ethics and Professional Practices

Professional associations tend to have codes of ethics that serve to define the ethical responsibilities for members of a particular field. Although there are a number of codes for ethics and professional practice, the two most common (and relevant to IT Project Management) are published by the Project Management Institute (PMI) and the Association for Computing Machinery (ACM). For example, although PMI's Member Code of Ethics[1] is a multipage document, it can be summarized as: **As a professional in the field of project management, PMI members pledge to uphold and abide by the following:**

- *I will maintain high standards of integrity and professional conduct.*

[1] Source: PMI Member Ethical Standards and http://www.acm.org/serving/se/code.htm#short.

- *I will accept responsibility for my actions.*
- *I will continually seek to enhance my professional capabilities.*
- *I will practice with fairness and honesty.*
- *I will encourage others in the profession to act in an ethical and professional manner.*

On the other hand, the ACM publishes a short and long version that outlines a Software Engineering Code of Ethics and Professional Practice. The code is summarized in terms of eight principles.

Software engineers shall commit themselves to making the analysis, specification, design, development, testing and maintenance of software a beneficial and respected profession. In accordance with their commitment to the health, safety and welfare of the public, software engineers shall adhere to the following Eight Principles:

1. *Public*—Software engineers shall act consistently with the public interest.
2. *Client and employer*—Software engineers shall act in a manner that is in the best interests of their client and employer consistent with the public interest.
3. *Product*—Software engineers shall ensure that their products and related modifications meet the highest professional standards possible.
4. *Judgment*—Software engineers shall maintain integrity and independence in their professional judgment.
5. *Management*—Software engineering managers and leaders shall subscribe to and promote an ethical approach to the management of software development and maintenance.
6. *Profession*—Software engineers shall advance the integrity and reputation of the profession consistent with the public interest.
7. *Colleagues*—Software engineers shall be fair to and supportive of their colleagues.
8. *Self*—Software engineers shall participate in lifelong learning regarding the practice of their profession and shall promote an ethical approach to the practice of the profession.

MULTICULTURAL PROJECTS

A common type of multicultural project would be an international one. However, domestic projects are becoming increasingly multicultural as many organizations attempt to diversify their workforce. Although ethics is an important component of leadership, the ability to lead and manage a multicultural team will become an increasingly more important skill for successful project leaders.

The Challenges of International Projects

The thought of being part of an international project can be exciting—travel, hotels, exotic food, and different customs. However, international projects also entail new challenges that can make or break your career depending on how well you handle these new and strange situations. International projects are more complex because

QUICK THINKING—SITTING DUCKS?

According to Bart Perkins of *Computerworld*, "Every organization has some 'ducks.' Ducks are employees who have a detrimental effect on productivity. Their work is consistently substandard, they rarely meet deadlines, and their skills are out of date. They hate change, resist taking responsibility and blame their failures on their co-workers. They constantly complain about their projects, their teammates, their workloads, and their managers. They stifle innovation by shooting down new proposals, claiming that changes 'just can't be done.'"

A "duck" can be brought into an organization in any number of ways. They can be hired in, or they can be acquired through mergers or acquisitions. It would make sense to limit the number of ducks in an organization by firing them, helping them gain new skills, by providing counseling, or by transferring them to a job that better meets their skills and experience.

Unfortunately, many ducks are not interested in change, and keeping them around can demotivate other employees. For example, high performers may become demoralized if their pay raises are only slightly higher than a nonperformer. Too often organizational policies or culture makes it difficult to get rid of the ducks.

A large organization hired a CIO with a mandate to improve IT services across the business units. He soon learned that there were many ducks among his staff. He needed to change the IT unit, but corporate policy made it difficult just to fire these nonperformers. With the knowledge and understanding of the executive team, the CIO created a "duck pond" that was a special, low priority project that included all of the nonperforming employees. Once the ducks were herded together, the project was cancelled and the nonperforming employees were let go.

1. Some may argue that an ineffective IT organization could be outsourced, so sacrificing the ducks to save the rest of the IT function was best for the better performing employees. Do you agree?

2. Was the action of the CIO ethical?

SOURCE: Adapted from Bart Perkins, IT Full of "Ducks"? Declare Open Season, *Computerworld*, April 28, 2008.

geographical, cultural, and social differences must be taken into account (Lientz and Rea 2003). These complexities include:

- *Number of locations*—Often international projects are located in several different countries, cities, or regions. Travel time and costs must be taken into account as well as differences in time zones.

- *Currency exchange*—Most countries today still have their own unique currency. These currencies are subject to fluctuations in exchange rates and inflation. Moreover, some currencies are not valued outside the issuing country.

- *Regulations and laws*—Each country has its own regulations and laws, but laws can be local and interpreted differently.

- *Political instability*—Doing a project in a politically unstable country can create interesting challenges that can endanger the safety and welfare of the project team.

- *Attitude toward work and time*—Different cultures can have different attitudes toward work and time. For example, in some cultures work is perceived as something not that critical. People do what they have to do, and getting ahead is not important. On the other hand, work for some becomes an obsession and their job and title define who they are. For these individuals, competition to be the best is important because it can lead to promotion and more pay. In addition, people in some cultures feel less pressure to be regulated by a clock and may not even own one. As a result, a project leader who attempts to make people work harder or adhere to time pressure will meet resistance.

- *Religion*—Although religion has an important influence in all societies, some societies are more affected in terms of how they go about their daily life and their work. For example, in many Islamic countries the weekend is on Thursday and Friday, while in other countries the weekend is on Saturday and Sunday. In such cases, offices in two different countries may be able to communicate only on Mondays, Tuesdays, and Wednesdays (Murphy 2005).

- *Language*—Not everyone speaks the same language you do. Although English has become the international language of business, not everyone can speak it fluently and words can have different meanings. Careful selection of words and phrases is important to reduce the likelihood that they are misunderstood or misinterpreted.

- *Food*—Some people have different tastes and are more willing to try new things. Each country has its own cuisine that may seem strange, but don't forget that what seems normal to you can be strange or even disgusting to someone from somewhere else.

Understanding and Managing Diversity

As discussed earlier, culture is a set of social lessons of behaviors that we learn over time. For example, these behaviors influence our language and customs in terms of how we eat, sleep, or conduct business. Often we become emotionally attached to our cultural beliefs. We then try to preserve them rather than learn from other cultures. **Diversity** is defined as differences in culture as well as nationality, ethnicity, religion, gender, or generation. To a great degree, the ability to lead an international project successfully requires understanding and managing diversity. As a project leader, you may encounter diversity in terms of your client or sponsor, as well as within the project team.

To be an effective leader, it is important that you develop an awareness of the different dimensions of culture that make up the various project stakeholder groups. Shriberg, Schriberg, and Kumari (2005) developed a diversity wheel that is illustrated in Figure 13.3 to help us better understand individual differences. The diversity wheel is composed of four circles representing different dimensions for each individual. The first dimension, or the inner circle, signifies a person's personality—the internal aspects that define us (e.g., introvert versus extrovert, hard-charging Type A versus laidback Type B, etc.). Moving outward from the center, the second circle represents individual characteristics that are often visible to others. The third dimension includes a set of social characteristics such as education, marital status, economic status, and religion that tend to shape our beliefs and behaviors. The outer circle represents several organizational aspects that also help to shape our identity. These include such factors as seniority, formal position within the organization, and the physical location where we work.

The value of the diversity wheel is that it can remind us that even though some individuals may appear to look like us, they may represent a different culture even within our own country or region. As a result, we can then begin to understand how each dimension of the diversity wheel influences attitudes, motivations, and behaviors as well as social and business customs. This may allow us to see not only how people are different, but also how we might be similar.

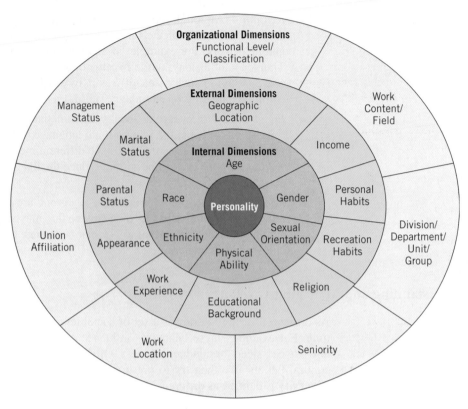

Figure 13.3   The Diversity Wheel

SOURCE: Adapted from Shriberg, Shriberg, and Kumari (2005).

CHAPTER SUMMARY

This chapter focuses on three key areas: leadership, ethics, and effectively managing a multicultural project. Although leadership and management are closely related and complementary, leadership focuses on the relationship between people. More specifically, leadership concentrates on inspiring a vision, creating change, and getting results. On the other hand, management emphasizes the processes and activities associated with planning, organizing, controlling, staffing, evaluating, and monitoring.

Although some are born with certain traits that make them natural leaders, a person can still develop leadership potential by having the courage to do the right thing and by being an active learner. Based on the work of Kouzes and Posner, five practices for exemplary leadership were presented. These practices include: (1) model the way, (2) inspire a shared vision, (3) challenge the process, (4) enable others to act, and (5) encourage the heart.

In addition, six leadership styles were discussed based on the research of Daniel Goleman. These styles include: (1) the coercive style, (2) the authoritative style, (3) the affiliative style, (4) the democratic style, (5) the pacesetting style, and (6) the coaching style. Goleman's study also suggests that each style has its own place when it is most effective as well as situations when it is least effective. Moreover, effective leaders have the flexibility to switch among the different styles as needed. The concept of emotional intelligence (i.e., the ability to understand our relationships and ourselves) is an important element for learning a new leadership style. Emotional intelligence is composed of four capabilities: (1) self-awareness, (2) self-management, (3) social awareness, and (4) social skills.

Ethics has received a great deal of attention in the media because of the ethical transgressions of a number of high-profile leaders. From a philosophical view, ethics can be viewed as a set of moral principles and values. Ethical dilemmas arise when these values come into conflict. However, ethical decisions and actions are not always clear cut, especially when some actions or decisions may be ethical but illegal, or unethical but legal. Subsequently, our ethical decisions and actions are often influenced by societal norms as well as culture.

Culture is defined as the shared beliefs, assumptions, and values that we learn from society or a group. In a project setting, a project leader can create, change, or maintain a particular culture in terms of the formal and informal systems that are in place. Formal systems include policies and procedures as well as reporting or authoritative structures. Information systems include the acceptable norms and behaviors are passed on to group members through a process called socialization.

People look to their leaders for ethical guidance. Leaders can be considered (1) unethical, (2) hypocritical, (3) ethically neutral, or (4) ethical. An ethical leader is someone who makes it clear that bottom-line results are important, but only if they can be achieved in an ethical manner.

Some common ethical situations you may face in a project setting include those involving human resources, conflicts of interest, confidence issues, or corporate resources. It is important that policies and procedure be in place to guide ethical behavior so that people understand what is and is not acceptable.

Although no single approach to dealing with ethical dilemmas exists, Trevino and Nelson have provided a process for making sound ethical decisions. The process includes: (1) gather the facts, (2) define the ethical issue, (3) identify the affected stakeholders, (4) identify the consequences, (5) identify the obligations, (6) consider your character and integrity, (7) think creatively about potential actions, and (8) check your gut.

Multicultural projects can be international projects or domestic projects whereby an organization is attempting to diversify its workforce. Just as ethics is an important component of leadership, the ability to manage a multicultural team is becoming an increasingly important skill for successful project leaders. To be effective, a project leader must understand and be able to manage diversity, which is defined as the differences between cultures, nationality, ethnicity, religion, gender, or generation. The diversity wheel was developed by Shriberg, Shriberg, and Kumari and provides a useful tool for understanding diversity. Using this device, one can better understand how the different dimensions of diversity influence attitudes, motivations, behaviors, and so forth.

REVIEW QUESTIONS

1. Develop your own definition of leadership.
2. What is the relationship between leadership and management?
3. What role does leadership play in project management?
4. What does a leader do?
5. Describe the five practices for exemplary leadership.
6. Describe the coercive leadership style.
7. Describe the authoritative leadership style.
8. Describe the affiliative leadership style.
9. Describe the democratic leadership style.
10. Describe the pacesetting leadership style
11. Describe the coaching leadership style.
12. What is emotional intelligence?
13. Describe the emotional intelligence competency called self-awareness.
14. Describe the emotional intelligence competency called self-management.
15. Describe the emotional intelligence competency called social awareness.
16. Describe the emotional intelligence competency called social skills.
17. What is the definition of ethics?
18. Why is the application of ethics to business settings important?
19. What is the difference between ethical and legal? Can something be ethical but illegal? Unethical but legal?
20. Define culture.
21. How can a project leader change, maintain, or create culture?
22. What is the difference between a formal system and an informal system with respect to culture?
23. What is socialization?
24. Describe unethical leadership.

25. Describe hypocritical leadership.
26. Describe ethically neutral leadership.
27. Describe ethical leadership.
28. What is an ethical dilemma? Give an example.
29. Develop a hypothetical ethical dilemma for a human resource situation.
30. Develop a hypothetical ethical dilemma for a conflict-of-interest situation.
31. Develop a hypothetical ethical dilemma for a confidence situation.
32. Develop a hypothetical ethical dilemma for a corporate resource situation.
33. For a hypothetical ethical dilemma you develop, use the eight-stage process for making a sound ethical decision.
34. Why are international projects more complex than domestic projects?
35. What is diversity?
36. Why is understanding diversity important when managing a multicultural project?

EXTEND YOUR KNOWLEDGE

1. Most of us think we are unbiased, but the truth is that we may not be as ethical and unbiased as we think. For example, we may believe that we will act objectively when hiring a new candidate or that biases will not influence our decisions or inhibit us from collaborating with people who are different from us. We may also know that such actions and stereotyping can erode team performance and lead to an exodus of talented people. Although most people consider themselves fair minded and try to judge others on their merits, research shows that people still view others according to unconscious stereotypes or implicit prejudice. Tony Greenwald at the University of Washington developed an experimental tool called the Implicit Association Test (IAT) in the mid-1990s. The purpose of the IAT is to study unconscious bias when subjects rapidly classify words and images as "good" or "bad." The computerized test requires the subject to make split-second decisions based on images of faces that are old or young, black or white, fat or thin, and so forth. Using the Web, visit the site of the Implicit Association Test (IAT) at https://implicit.harvard.edu/implicit/. Select and take one of the online tests. Do the results of the test match your expectations?

SOURCE: Adapted from "How (Un)ethical Are You?" by Mahzarin R. Banaji, Max H. Bazerman, and Dolly Chuh. *Harvard Business Review*, December, 2003. Product 5526.

2. Choose a foreign country that you've never visited before. Suppose you are part of a multicultural team and you have been asked travel to the capital of that country for one week on business. Using the Web, find an airfare that will allow you to leave next Wednesday and return the follow Wednesday. Also, use the Web to find the daily rate for a moderately priced hotel. Next, check the Web or another resource to determine the currency and current exchange rate for that country. Last, use the Web or another resource to find out more about the business culture of the country you will supposedly visit. List three things that make this culture unique to yours when conducting business.

   ■ Some suggested Web sites include www.travelocity.com, www.orbitz.com, www.executiveplanet.com, http://www.cyborlink.com/

3. Using the Web or another resource, prepare a short presentation on a successful leader in world history. Provide a brief background of this person and explain why you chose this particular leader. What made or makes this leader effective? What lessons can we learn from this person's leadership?

GLOBAL TECHNOLOGY SOLUTIONS

It had been a few months since Tim Williams had gotten together with his old college friend, Peter F. Hay. Pete had been working for a large software development company since he and Tim graduated. Pete had started as a programmer and over the years worked his way up to project manager. Pete suggested that they meet at a local coffee shop after work to relax and catch up. Tim arrived a few minutes after six o'clock and saw his good friend seated at a table next to the window. Tim and Pete shook hands, and Tim sat down across from his friend. They talked about family, mutual friends, until finally the subject of work came up. "So," Tim began, "what's new at Megasoft?" Pete chuckled, took a sip of coffee, and said, "Well, it seems that I have an interesting dilemma and could use your advice. I've been managing a project with a large overseas client. It's an interesting project, and my company expects to make several million dollars just from this one installation. The client has expressed an interest in purchasing several more of our products depending on how well this project goes. The travel and coordination between a geographically dispersed team located in different time zones have been a real challenge, but we seem to be making progress." Tim nodded and added, "Sounds like a real career enhancer, Pete. So what's your dilemma?" Pete's face became more serious as he contemplated the question. Pete placed both hands around his coffee cup and began, "This project is really important to my company. We not only stand to do well financially, but we'll also have the opportunity to sell several more of our products to this particular client. That should certainly help our stock price. And, quite honestly, I have a nice bonus riding on the outcome. It would certainly come in handy in making a down payment on a house." Pete stopped for a moment, and Tim urged him to continue. Pete began again and said, "The dilemma is that I have a terrific member on my project team. She's bright, experienced, and a cornerstone to the team." "So what's the problem," Tim asked. "Well, the problem is

that the client is in a country whose culture does not look favorably on women in positions of authority. She just returned from a two-week trip to the client's site and things did not go all that well. She complained that the client's management tended to ignore her and treated her coolly. Just before she got back, I received a call from the client, who complained that she was incompetent and they wanted her replaced. They didn't say "Anyone but a woman," but it was obvious that's what they meant. The project is now two weeks behind schedule. This employee is one of our rising stars and an international project would be a great boost for her career. I'm afraid that she might leave if I pull her off this project—she could find a new job with another organization in a second. Needless to say, this problem has been keeping me up at night. So, good buddy, what would you do if you were in my position?" Before Tim could answer, Pete's cell phone rang. From the caller ID Pete could see that the caller was someone from work. He excused himself and told Tim that he had to take this call. Tim welcomed the interruption because it gave him a chance to think before responding to Pete's question.

Things to Think About

1. What advice should Tim give to Pete?

2. Why is this situation a dilemma for Pete?

3. What makes managing an international project more complex than a domestic project?

 # HUSKY AIR ASSIGNMENT—PILOT ANGELS

Multicultural Projects

Please provide a professional-looking document that includes the following:

1. **The project name, project team name, and the names of the members of your project team**

2. **A brief project description**

3. **The project's MOV** (This should be revised or refined if necessary.)

4. **Personality analysis**

   a. Start by having each member of your team take an online personality test at http://www.keirsey.com. The results of the test will tell you your basic temperament and explain what it means. Although you have to register with the Web site to take the temperament test, you do not have to purchase anything to get a basic personality pro-

   file. Summarize the personality temperaments for each member of your team.

5. **Team analysis**—This section of the assignment will provide more insight if your team has worked together for a while. However, even if your team does not have much of a history, you can still discuss how your different personalities can impact how you will work together.

   a. Based on your personality test results, describe how the different personality temperaments interacted well with each other.

   b. In addition, describe any challenges that you may have encountered due to personality differences.

   c. Now that you know your personality temperament and those of your team members, what new insights does this provide in terms of any future interactions as a team?

CASE STUDIES

Don't Tell Anyone or You're Fired!

The CIO of your organization walks into your office one Friday afternoon. As she closes the door behind her she says that "If you say anything to anyone concerning what I'm about to tell you, you're fired." She then explains that the team of programmers that you supervise will be "released to seek other options" and that all of your project's programming tasks will be outsourced to a country in Eastern Europe. Your job is to coordinate with this new outsource provider so that all programming work can be scheduled and transferred over in less than three months. In addition, you're not to let on to any of the company's programmers that they will soon be replaced. She instructs you to carry on as nothing has changed. In fact, the company will give them a bonus if they can complete their current work assignment in three months rather than the scheduled four months.

As the project manager of this team, you've gotten to know each of the programmers fairly well. For example, one of the programmers has just signed a mortgage to purchase her first house. Another is a single mother with her oldest child just entering college, and another has confided in you that he has been experiencing some health problems lately.

1. What would you do?
   a. Follow your CIO's orders because that is what you're expected to do.
   b. Update your resume and start looking for a new job.
   c. Pretend to comply with the CIO's orders, but tell the programmers anyway.
   d. Wait until Monday and then go talk with your CIO to try and convince her that telling them is the right thing to do. (What will you do if the CIO rejects your suggestion?)
   e. Do something else? If so, what?

Source: Adapted from Esther Schindler, a blog posted on *CIO Magazine*, Advice & Opinion: You're the Boss, November 13, 2006.

A Failed ERP Implementation Results in a Lawsuit

Waste Management provides trash and waste removal, recycling, and environmentally safe waste management services in the United States and Canada. Recently, Waste Management has filed a lawsuit against the SAP AG for a fraudulent sales scheme that resulted in a failed ERP project. The legal action is an attempt by Waste Management to recover over $100 million in project costs as well as the savings and benefits that SAP promised to Waste Management.

About three years before, Waste Management was interested in a new revenue management system. According to a Waste Management statement, "SAP proposed its Waste and Recycling product and claimed it was a tested, working solution that had been developed with the needs of Waste Management in mind." In addition, the statement also states that SAP promised that the ERP system could be implemented throughout Waste Management within 18 months.

Waste Management also claims that SAP assured them from the outset that their system was an "out of the box" solution that would not require any customization or improvements. However, Waste Management soon discovered that these assertions were not true and that SAP conducted product demonstration in a contrived software environment that did not represent the actual ERP system. A court document filed by Waste Management states that the demos were "rigged and manipulated." The complaint also states SAP executives and engineers represented that the software was a mature solution and conducted a demonstration that turned out to be a "mockup" version intended to deceive Waste Management.

Waste Management signed a contract with SAP in October 2005, but the SAP implementation team quickly discovered gaps between the ERP system's functionality and Waste Management's business requirements. Waste Management contends that SAP's development team in Germany knew before the sales contract was signed that the software lacked the basic functionality to run Waste Management's business. On the other hand, SAP's implementation team countered and blamed Waste Management for the gap in business requirements and for submitting change requests.

The complaint also states that SAP promised that a pilot implementation would be completed in New Mexico by December 2006, but it appears that the implementation still had not been completed even after 18 months past the promised date. SAP conducted a Solutions Review in the summer of 2007 and concluded that the ERP system was not an enterprise solution that would meet Waste Management's needs. Moreover, the complaint contends that SAP said that Waste Management would have to start over and allow SAP to develop a new version of the system if it wanted to have the software implemented across the business. According to Waste Management, SAP's new proposal was exactly the kind of risky and costly project they wanted to stay away from when they reviewed proposals from other ERP vendors. The complaint states "Indeed, the development project that SAP proposed would drastically lengthen the implementation timetable from the original December 2007 end-date to an end-date sometime in 2010 without any assurance of success."

1. If you were the project manager at Waste Management, what would be your recommendation to senior management?
2. Why might this be an ethical issue?
3. Do you think the blame lies with SAP only? Or should Waste Management share in the blame?

4. If you were a project manager of an ERP project, what are some things you could do to lessen the chances of a misunderstanding?

SOURCE: Adapted from Chris Kanaracus, Waste Management Sues SAP over ERP Implementation, *Computerworld*, March 27, 2008.

BIBLIOGRAPHY

Banaji, M. R., M. H. Bazerman, and D. Chugh. (2003). How (Un)ethical Are You? *Harvard Business Review.* December: 1–10. Product 5526.

Goleman, D. (2000). Leadership That Gets Results. *Harvard Business Review.* March–April: 79–90.

Goleman, D. (2004). What Makes a Leader? *Harvard Business Review.* January. Reprint RO401H. 1–11.

Goleman, D., R. Boyatzis, and A. McKee. (2001). Primal Leadership: The Hidden Driver of Great Performance. *Harvard Business Review.* December: 42–51.

Kotter, J. P. (2001). What Leaders Really Do. *Harvard Business Review.* December: 3–11.

Kouzes, J. and B. Posner. (2002). *The leadership challenge,* third ed. San Franciso, CA: Jossey-Bass.

Lientz, B. P. and K. P. Rea. (2003). *International Project Management.* San Diego, CA: Academic Press.

Murphy, O. J. (2005). *International Project Management.* Mason, OH: Thompson.

Project Management Institute (PMI) 2004. *A Guide to the Project Management Body of Knowledge (PMBOK® Guide).* Newtown Square, PA: PMI Publishing.

Shriberg, A., D. L. Shriberg, and R. Kumari. (2005). *Practicing Leadership: Principles and Applications*, third ed. Hoboken, NJ: John Wiley.

Trevino, L. K. and K. A. Nelson. (2004). *Managing Business Ethics,* third edition, Hoboken, NJ: John Wiley.

Project Implementation, Closure, and Evaluation

CHAPTER OVERVIEW

In this chapter, we will focus on three important areas: project implementation, closure, and evaluation. After studying this chapter, you should understand and be able to:

- Describe the three tactical approaches to information system implementation and installation: (1) direct cutover, (2) parallel, and (3) phased, as well as compare the advantages and disadvantages of each approach.
- Describe the processes associated with project closure to ensure that the project is closed in an orderly manner.
- Identify four different types of project evaluations or reviews: (1) individual performance review, (2) postmortem review, (3) project audit, and (4) evaluation of the project's MOV.

INTRODUCTION

The topic of change management was introduced in Chapter 11 and focused on preparing the people within the organization for the upcoming change and, more importantly, the transition that will occur as a result of the change. Understanding the human element or the "soft side" of IT project management is critical for ensuring that the individuals or groups within the organization will accept and adapt to the new information system implemented by the project team.

In this final chapter we will concentrate on three important areas—project implementation, closure, and evaluation. **Project implementation** focuses on installing or delivering the project's major deliverable in the organization—the information system that was built or purchased. The implementation of the information system requires a tactical plan that allows the project team to move the IT solution from a development and test environment to the day-to-day operations of the organization.

In general, implementing the product of an IT project can follow one of three approaches. These approaches are (1) direct cutover, (2) parallel, or (3) phased. Each approach has unique advantages and disadvantages that make a particular approach appropriate for a given situation. Subsequently, understanding and choosing an appropriate approach can have a profound impact on the success or failure of the project.

As discussed in Chapter 1, a project is a temporary endeavor undertaken to accomplish a unique purpose. This means that a project has a definite beginning and a definite end. Once the information system is implemented, the project manager and team must prepare for terminating, or closing, the project. Closing a project includes organizing and archiving project documents and deliverables, performing an audit and assessment of the project, documenting lessons learned, evaluating the performance of the project manager and team, releasing project resources, and closing all project-related accounts.

For a project to be closed successfully, the product of the project must be formally accepted by the project sponsor or customer. Not all projects, of course, are successful; however, a number of administrative tasks must still be completed. In such cases, it is necessary to assess whether any salvage value exists, and, more importantly, to understand the reasons why the project was not successful.

Once the project is closed, the project manager should evaluate each project team member individually in order to assess and provide feedback to the individual about his or her performance on the project. In addition, the project manager and project team should meet to conduct a postmortem review of the project. The outcome of this review should be a set of documented lessons learned and best practices that can be shared throughout the organization.

In addition, the project should be reviewed by an impartial outside party. An audit or outside review can provide valuable insight on how well the project was managed and on how well the project members functioned as a team. The auditor or audit team should also determine whether the project manager and team acted professionally and ethically.

The project's real success will be determined by the project sponsor or customer. In this text, the project's overall goal was defined as the MOV, or measurable organizational value. The MOV must be clearly defined and agreed upon in the early stages of the project. Unfortunately, the project's true value to the organization may not be discernable immediately following implementation. It may take weeks or even months after the information system is implemented, but an evaluation must be made to determine whether the project was successful, as defined by its MOV.

PROJECT IMPLEMENTATION

At some point, testing is complete and the project team and project manager then become responsible for ensuring that the information system is transferred successfully from the development and test environment to the operational environment of the sponsor or customer's organization. This transfer requires a tactical approach, and it can be a stressful time for all the stakeholders involved. Choosing an inappropriate implementation approach can negatively impact the project's remaining schedule and budget. In general, the project team can take one of three approaches for implementing the information system. These approaches include (1) direct cutover, (2) parallel, and (3) phased.

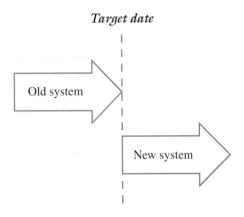

Figure 14.1 Direct Cutover

Direct Cutover

The direct cutover approach, as illustrated in Figure 14.1 is an approach where the old system is shut down and the new system is turned on. In general, a target, or *go live,* date is agreed upon, and the new system simply replaces the old.

This approach can be effective when quick delivery of the new system is critical or when the existing system is so poor that it must be replaced as soon as possible. Direct cutover may also be appropriate when the system is not mission critical—i.e., the system's failure will not have a major impact on the organization. It is important, however, that the new system be thoroughly tested so everyone is confident that few, if any, major problems will arise.

Although there are some advantages to using the direct cutover approach, there are also a number of risks involved that generally make this the least favored approach except in a few, carefully planned situations. Although the direct cutover approach can be quick, it may not always be painless. You might think of this approach as walking a tightrope without a safety net. You may get from one end of the tightrope to other quickly, but not without a great deal of risk. Subsequently, there may be no going back once the old system is turned off and the new system is turned on. As a result, the organization could experience major delays, frustrated users and customers, lost revenues, and missed deadlines. The pressure of ensuring that everything is right or having to deal with problems and irate users or project stakeholders can create a great deal of stress for the project team.

Parallel

As Figure 14.2 illustrates, the parallel approach to implementation allows the old and the new systems to run concurrently for a time. At some point, the organization switches entirely from the old system to the new.

The parallel approach is appropriate when problems or the failure of the system can have a major impact on the organization. For example, an organization may be implementing a new accounts receivable package. Before switching over completely to the new system, the organization may run both systems concurrently in order to compare the outputs of both systems. This approach provides confidence that the new system is functioning and performing properly before relying on it entirely.

Although the parallel approach may not be as stressful for the project team as the direct cutover approach, it can create more stress for the users of the system. The users will probably have to enter data into both systems and even be responsible for comparing the outputs. If the new system performs as expected, they may be willing to put up with the extra workload until the scheduled target date when the new system stands alone. If, however, unexpected problems are

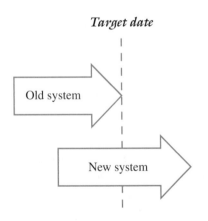

Figure 14.2 Parallel

encountered, the target date for switching from the old to the new system may be pushed back. The extra workload and overtime hours may begin to take their toll and pressure for the project team to "get on with it" may create a stressful environment for everyone involved.

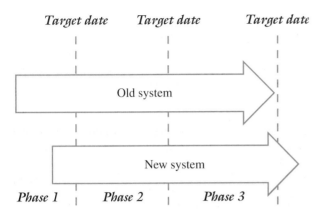

Target date   Target date   Target date

Old system

New system

Phase 1 | *Phase 2* | *Phase 3*

Figure 14.3   Phased

Phased

Following the phased approach, the system is introduced in modules or in different parts of the organization incrementally as illustrated in Figure 14.3. For example, an organization may implement an accounting information system package by first implementing the general ledger component, then accounts payable and accounts receivable, and finally payroll.

The phased approach may be appropriate when introducing a software system to different areas of the organization. When upgrading an operating system, for example, the IT department may perform the upgrade on a department-by-department basis according to a published schedule. In this case, a target date for each department would be set to allow each department to plan for the upgrade accordingly. A phased approach may also allow the project team to learn from its experiences during the initial implementation so that later implementations run more smoothly.

Although the phased approach may take more time than the direct cutover approach, it may be less risky and much more manageable. Also, overly optimistic target dates or problems experienced during the early phases of implementation may create a chain reaction that pushes back the scheduled dates of the remaining planned implementations.

Table 14.1 provides a summary of each of the three implementation approaches discussed.

As the end of the project draws near, everyone may become anxious to finish the project and move onto other things. Unfortunately, there is often a great deal of work that still needs to be completed. Delays or unanticipated problems may require additional time and unbudgeted resources, leading to cost and schedule overruns or extra unpaid effort, especially if an implied warranty exists (Rosenau 1998).

During the final stages of the project, the project team may be faced with both time and performance pressures as the project's deadline looms in the near future. On the other hand, the sponsor or client may become more concerned about whether the time and money spent on the project will reap the envisioned benefits. The project

Table 14.1   Comparison of Implementation Approaches

Direct Cutover	*Parallel*	*Phased*
■ Implementation can be quick ■ Can be risky if system is not fully tested ■ Places more pressure on the project team	■ Provides a safety net or backup in case problems are encountered with the implementation of the new system ■ Can increase confidence in the new system when output of old system and new system is compared ■ Takes longer and may cost more than direct cutover approach ■ Places more pressure on the users of the system	■ Allows for an organized and managed approach for implementing system modules of system upgrades in different departments or geographical locations ■ Experience with early implementation can guide and make later implementations go more smoothly ■ Takes longer and may cost more than the direct cutover approach ■ Problems encountered during early phases can impact the overall implementation schedule

manager is often caught in the middle attempting to keep the project team happy and on track, while assuring the project sponsor that all is well.

ADMINISTRATIVE CLOSURE

Although all projects must come to an end, a project can be terminated for any number of reasons. Gray and Larson (2000) define five circumstances for ending a project: normal, premature, perpetual, failed, and changed priorities.

- *Normal*—A project that ends normally is one that is completed as planned. The project scope is achieved within the cost, quality, and schedule objectives, although there probably was some variation and modification along the way. The project is transferred to the project sponsor, and the end of the project is marked with a celebration, awards, and recognition for a good job well done by those involved. As you might suspect, this is an ideal situation.

- *Premature*—Occasionally, a project team may be pushed to complete a project early even though the system may not include all of the envisioned features or functionality. For example, an organization may need to have a new system operational—with only a core set of original requirements—to respond to a competitor's actions, to enter a new market early, or as a result of a legal or governmental requirement. Although there is pressure to finish the project early, the risks of this decision should be carefully thought through by all the project stakeholders.

- *Perpetual*—Some projects seem to take on a "life of their own" and are known as runaway, or perpetual, projects. These projects never seem to end. Perpetual projects may result from delays or a scope or MOV that was never clearly defined or agreed upon. Then, the project sponsor (or even the team) may attempt to add on various features or functionality to the system, which results in added time and resources that increase the project schedule and drain the project budget. Some runaway projects result from an organization not making the appropriate decision to "pull the plug" on an unsuccessful project. The decision to terminate a project is not an easy one if egos and perhaps even careers or jobs are on the line. This phenomenon may also occur when the project has a high payoff to the organization and when admitting to failure is strongly against the corporate culture (Keil 1995). No matter what the cause, project resources are eventually drained to a point where a potentially successful project becomes unsuccessful (Nicholas 1990). Attention to defining and agreeing to the project's MOV, the project scope processes, and timely project reviews can reduce the risk of perpetual projects.

- *Failed*—Sometimes projects are just unsuccessful. In general, an IT project fails if insufficient attention is paid to the people, processes, or technology. Even though the project's MOV may define the project's value to the organization, cost and schedule overruns may drain the project's value to a point where the costs of completing the project outweigh the benefits.

- *Changed priorities*—In some circumstances, a project may be terminated as a result of a change in priorities. Financial or economic reasons may dictate that resources are no longer available to the project. Or, management may decide to divert resources to higher priority projects. This change can happen when the original importance or value of the project was misjudged or

QUICK THINKING—KILLING A PROJECT

The decision to cancel a project that has little or no chance of meeting its envisioned benefits or meeting its objectives can be a difficult and complex decision. According to Bart Perkins, euthanizing these projects is important to the health of the organization. However, before "pulling the plug," it's important to understand and plan for a number of important issues. For example, large projects can have political ramifications, especially if powerful stakeholders have a vested interest in the project. This can lead to finger pointing and looking for someone to blame for the project's failure. Moreover, a cancelled project can be expensive if cancelling a project includes severance packages, contractual agreements (i.e., early termination penalties), litigation, writing off sunk costs, or missed business opportunities. Failed projects can also impact relationships. This may include damaged working relationships with suppliers who may refuse to work with your organization in the future. Lastly, killing a project can also affect the

project team. Project team members' morale may suffer if they have an emotional attachment to the project's failure. Disillusioned employees may become unproductive or those with highly marketable skills may leave, often making it difficult to attract or retain other valuable project team members.

1. What criteria should be used to cancel a project?
2. Who should make the decision to kill a project?
3. How can an organization ensure that a doomed project is euthanized as early as possible?
4. As a project manager of a doomed project, what would be your top three priorities for planning the cancellation of the project?

SOURCE: Adapted from Bart Perkins, Opinion: Before You Kill That Project..., *Computerworld*, March 10, 2008.

---

misrepresented or when organizational needs or technology change over the course of a long-term project. Some projects are "terminated by starvation." As Meredith and Mantel (2000) describe it, successive budget cuts over time can slowly starve a project budget to the point where it is ended but the termination is masked. Senior management may not want to admit that it had championed a failed project or that a project will be unsuccessful in meeting its goals. The project budget receives a large cut or a series of smaller cuts. The result is that the project will die eventually and the project resources will be reassigned, even though the project is never officially closed.

Ideally, a project is closed or terminated under normal circumstances. The project achieves its desired goal and objectives. The project sponsor is delighted with the project's product and shows his or her delight by paying for the invoiced project work on time and contracts for more work in the future. Unfortunately, closing a project does not often happen this way. As J. Davidson Frame (1998) points out, the project manager and team should be prepared to deal with the following realities:

- *Team members are concerned about future jobs.* Often the members of the project team are borrowed from different departments or functional areas of the organization. Once the project is finished, they will return to their previous jobs. For consulting firms, the project team members will move from one project to the next as part of their career path. Regardless, as the project nears its end, these project team members may begin to wonder what they will do next. For some, there will be a rewarding life after the project—for others it may mean looking for new jobs. For many it may mean disrupting a close-knit relationship with other members of the project team (Meredith and Mantel 2000). Therefore, project team members may become preoccupied with moving on with their lives and the project at hand may become a lesser priority. As a result, the project team members may not focus on what has to be done to close the project, and wrapping up the project may be a challenge.

■ *Bugs still exist.* Testing the information system is an important process of systems development. However, software quality testing may not find all the defects, and certain bugs may not become known until after the system has been implemented. The appearance of these problems can be frustrating and stressful to all the project stakeholders. Unless these defects and bugs are promptly addressed and fixed, the project sponsor's satisfaction with the project team and the information system may become an issue.

■ *Resources are running out.* Resources and the project schedule are consumed from the project's earliest inception. At the end of the project, both resources and time remaining are usually depleted. As unanticipated issues, problems, or challenges arise, the project manager may find that adequate resources to deal with these events effectively are not available. The project manager may find his or her situation aggravated if management decides to cut or control the project's budget.

■ *Documentation attains paramount importance.* Information technology projects have numerous documentation requirements. They require project, system, training, and user documentation. Under ideal circumstances, the time to write documentation is built into the project plan and completed throughout the project. Many times, however, documentation is put off until the end of the project. As the end draws near, documentation becomes increasingly important. As a result, documentation may require more time and resources to complete, or shortcuts are taken to remain within the current project constraints.

■ *Promised delivery dates may not be met.* Most projects experience schedule slippage. This slippage may be due to poor project management, implementation risks, competitive requirements, or overly optimistic estimates. A project will require a certain amount of resources and a certain amount of time to complete. Any misjudgment concerning what has to be done, what is needed to complete the job, and how long it will take will result in a variance between the planned and actual schedule and budget.

■ *The players may possess a sense of panic.* As schedules begin to slip and project resources become depleted, various project stakeholders may experience a sense of alarm. The managers or partners of a consulting firm may worry that the project will not be profitable or satisfactory to the customer. The sponsor or customer may worry that the information system will not be delivered on time and within budget or provide the expected value to the organization. Moreover, the project manager and team may also be worried that the project will not be successful and the blame will rest squarely on their shoulders. As the sense of panic increases, the chances for an orderly closeout grow dim.

Regardless of whether a project ends normally or prematurely, it is important that an orderly set of processes be followed in order to bring it to closure. A good closeout allows the team to wrap up the project in a neat, logical manner. From an administrative view, this procedure allows for all loose ends to be tied up. From a psychological perspective, it provides all of the project stakeholders with a sense that the project was under control from the beginning through to its end (Frame 1998).

Project Sponsor Acceptance

The most important requirement for closure under normal circumstances is obtaining the project sponsor's acceptance of the project. Delivery, installation, and implementation of the information system do not necessarily mean that the project sponsor or client will accept the project's product. Since acceptance depends heavily on the fulfillment of the project's scope, the project manager becomes responsible for demonstrating that all project deliverables have been completed according to specifications (Wysocki, Beck, et al. 1995). Ancillary items, such as documentation, training, and ongoing support, should not be afterthoughts. These items should have been included in the original scope of the project. Any attempt to renegotiate what is and what is not part of the project work at this late stage of the project can create ill feelings or hold up payment by the client (Rosenau 1998).

There are two basic types of project sponsors. *Shortsighted* sponsors tend to view the project as a short-term buyer–seller relationship in which getting the most for their money is the most important criteria for accepting the project. This view often leads to an adversarial relationship if the sponsor attempts to renegotiate the project scope or price at the end of the project.

Knowledgeable sponsors realize that they have an important stake in the outcome of the project. As a result, they will be actively involved throughout the project in a constructive manner. Knowledgeable sponsors may ask tough questions during project reviews, but their objective is not to embarrass the project team or manager, but to ensure the success of the project. Instead of an adversary trying to get the most in a "win-lose" situation, the knowledgeable sponsor will negotiate intelligently and in good faith.

Regardless of whether the sponsor is shortsighted or knowledgeable, the project manager and team can improve the likelihood that the project will be accepted if they (1) clearly define the acceptance criteria for the project at the early stages of the project, and (2) document the completion of all project deliverables and milestones.

A clear definition of the project deliverables is an important concern for project scope management (discussed in an earlier chapter). Yet, defining and verifying that the project scope and system requirements are accurate and complete is only one component. Having scope change procedures in place that are understood by all the project stakeholders also ensures that everyone has the same expectations concerning what will and what won't be delivered at the end of the project.

The IT project methodology incorporated in this text also focused on managing the project based on phases that focus on specific deliverables. Project milestones ensure that the deliverables are not only complete, but completed right. Documenting each deliverable and milestone throughout the project provides confidence to the project sponsor that the project has been completed fully.

The Final Project Report

In general, the project manager and team should develop a final report and presentation for the project sponsor and other key stakeholders. The objective of the report and presentation should be to give the project sponsor confidence that the project has been completed as outlined in the business case, project charter, and project plan. By gaining this confidence, the sponsor or client will be more likely to formally accept the project that will allow for a smooth termination of the project.

The report may be circulated to key stakeholders before the presentation in order to get feedback and to identify any open or unfinished items that need to be scheduled for completion (Rosenau 1998; Buttrick 2000). Once finalized, the final project report provides a background and history of the project. The report should include and discuss the following areas at a minimum:

- Project summary
  - Project description
  - Project MOV
  - Scope, schedule, budget, and quality objectives
- Comparison of planned versus actual
  - Original scope and history of any approved changes
  - Original scheduled deadline versus actual completion date
  - Original budget versus actual cost of completing the project
  - Test plans and test results
- Outstanding issues
  - Itemized list and expected completion
  - Any ongoing support required and duration
- Project documentation list
  - Systems documentation
  - User manuals
  - Training materials
  - Maintenance documentation

The Final Meeting and Presentation

If the project manager has been diligent in gaining the confidence of the project sponsor, the final meeting and presentation should be a simple, straightforward affair. Buttrick (2000) suggests that the final meeting is useful for:

- *Communicating that the project is over.* By inviting key stakeholders to the meeting, the project manager is formally announcing that the project is over. This action not only provides a sense of closure for those close to the project, but also for the organization, as well.
- *Transferring the information system from the project team to the organization.* Although the information system may have been implemented and is being used by the organization, the final meeting provides a formal exchange of the project's product from the project team to the organization. Unless some type of ongoing support is part of the contractual agreement, this transfer signals that the project team will not be at the client or sponsor's site much longer.
- *Acknowledging contributions.* The meeting provides a forum for the project manager to acknowledge the hard work and contributions of the project team and other key stakeholders.
- *Getting formal signoff.* Finally, the meeting can provide a ceremony for the sponsor or client to formally accept the information system by signing off on the project. A space for signatures could be part of the final project report or part of some other contractual document.

Closing the Project

Once the project is accepted by the sponsor or customer, a number of administrative closure processes remain. These last items can be difficult because the project manager or team may view these administrative items as boring or because they are already looking forward to and thinking about their next assignment (Gray and Larson 2000). Unfortunately, administrative closure is a necessity because once the project manager and team are officially released from the current project, getting them to wrap up the last of the details will be difficult. The requirements for administrative closure include:

1. Verifying that all deliverables and open items are complete
2. Verifying the project sponsor or customer's formal acceptance of the project
3. Organizing and archiving all project deliverables and documentation
4. Planning for the release of all project resources (i.e., project team members, technology, equipment, facilities)
5. Planning for the evaluations and reviews of the project team members and the project itself
6. Closing of all project accounts
7. Planning a celebration to mark the end of a (successful) project

PROJECT EVALUATION

The question on everyone's mind throughout the project is, Will this project be successful? Different stakeholders will have different views of success. For the project team members, it may be gaining valuable experience and feeling that their work will have a positive impact on the organization. For the project manager, it may be leading a project that will be profitable to the firm or a promotion to a larger and more visible project. On the other hand, the client or sponsor may view project success in terms of organizational value received after the project is implemented.

Therefore, four types of project evaluations should be conducted. There should be (1) an individual review of each team member's performance, (2) a postmortem review by the project manager and project team, (3) an audit of the project by an objective and respected outside party, and (4) an evaluation sometime after the project is implemented to determine whether the project achieved its envisioned MOV.

Individual Performance Review

The project manager should conduct an individual performance review with each project team member. Although the project organization may have its own process and procedure for conducting reviews, the project manager should focus on the following points:

- *Begin with the individual evaluating his/her performance.* Evaluating someone's performance can be an emotional experience. Even with the best intentions, being critical of someone can put her or him on the defensive. Instead of beginning an evaluation with a critique of the individual's performance, it is usually more effective to begin by asking how *that person* would evaluate her or his performance. Surprisingly, most people are more critical of themselves. This opening provides an opportunity for the person doing the evaluation either to agree or to disagree with the individual's self-evaluation and to point out several positive aspects of the person's performance. This system creates a useful dialog that provides the individual with more useful feedback.

■ *Avoid "why can't you be more like...?"* It's easy to compare individuals. Unfortunately, comparisons can have a counter effect. First, the person you exalt may not be the shining star you think. Second, others may become jealous and look for ways to discredit or disparage the individual. Keep in mind that people are different and should be evaluated as individuals.

■ *Focus on specific behaviors, not the individual.* When discussing opportunities for improvement with a person, it is important to focus on specific behaviors. For example, if a project team member has a habit of consistently showing up late and disrupting team meetings, it is important not to focus on the individual (i.e., Why are you so lazy and disrespectful?), but on how showing up late to team meetings is disruptive. Often people do not realize how their behaviors affect others.

■ *Be consistent and fair.* Being consistent and fair to everyone is easier said than done. The person conducting the evaluation should be aware of how decisions concerning one person may affect the entire group. Also, be aware that people talk to one another and often compare notes. Therefore, making a decision concerning one person may set a precedent for others. Having policies and procedures in place and sticking to them can mitigate the potential for inconsistency and the perception that the evaluator is not fair with everyone.

■ *Reviews should provide a consensus on improving performance.* The purpose of conducting a review or evaluation with each project team member is to provide constructive feedback for individuals. No one is perfect, so understanding where an individual can improve and how they might go about improving is important. The individual and the evaluator should agree on what areas the individual needs to improve upon and how the organization can support this endeavor. For example, the individual and the evaluator may agree that the team member should improve his or her communication skills. The evaluator may then recommend and provide support for the person to attend a particular training class.

The meeting can serve to help prepare the individual to move on and accept the psychological fact that the project will end (Gray and Larson 2000). And, in most cases, the project manager could use this meeting to discuss the project team member's next assignment.

Postmortem Review

Shortly after the final project report and presentation are completed, the project manager and project team should conduct a postmortem review of the project. This should be done before the project team is released from the current project. It is more difficult to get people to participate once they are busy working on other projects or if they no longer work for the project organization. Moreover, memories tend to become clouded as time passes. Thoroughness and clarity are critical (Nicholas 1990). The formal project summary report should focus on the project's MOV and the project management knowledge areas. The focus of this review should include the following:

- *Review the initial project's MOV.* Was the project's MOV clearly defined and agreed upon? Did it change over the course of the project? What is the probability that it will be achieved?

- *Review the project scope, schedule, budget, and quality objectives.* How well was the scope defined? Did it change? How effective were the scope management processes? How close were the project schedule and budget estimates to the actual deadline and cost of the project? Were the quality objectives met? How well did the quality management processes and standards support the project processes?

- *Review each of the project deliverables.* How effective were the business case, the project charter, the project plan, and so forth? How could these deliverables be improved?

- *Review the various project plans and Project Management Body of Knowledge (PMBOK®) areas.* The team should review its effectiveness in the following areas:
  - Project integration management
  - Project scope management
  - Project time management
  - Project cost management
  - Project quality management
  - Project human resources management
  - Project communications management
  - Project risk management
  - Project procurement management
  - Organizational change management
  - Project implementation

- *How well did the project team perform?* Were conflicts handled effectively? Did the team suffer any morale problems? What main challenges did the team face? How well did they handle these challenges? How well did the members function as a cohesive team?

The discussion and recommendations from the postmortem review should be documented. In particular, the project manager and team should identify what they did right and what they could have done better. These lessons learned should be documented so that they can be shared with others in the organization. Moreover, best practices should be identified and become part of the organization's IT project methodology.

Project Audit

The individual performance and postmortem reviews provide an important view of the internal workings of the project. In general, these reviews are conducted between the project manager and the project team. To provide a more objective view of the project, an audit or review by an outside party may be beneficial for uncovering problems, issues, or opportunities for improvement. Similar to the postmortem

376 CHAPTER 14 / PROJECT IMPLEMENTATION, CLOSURE, AND EVALUATION

QUICK THINKING—THE POST-IMPLEMENTATION AUDIT

Once an off-the-shelf Web-based procurement system was implemented, Bruce Higgins, the CIO of a $405 million engineering and construction company called Michael Baker Corp., was inundated by questions regarding the system's effectiveness. Unfortunately, he didn't have any concrete proof that the system improved efficiency. As a result, he decided to conduct the company's first post-implementation audit that included a thorough evaluation of the system's benefits, security, and project management processes. Although Higgins found out that the system's return on investment was lower than originally envisioned due to a miscalculation of the number of user licenses needed, the audit uncovered that the company was saving over $150,000 a year. He also learned several valuable lessons on what not to do on future projects. While post-implementation audits are a useful tool to show the value of projects, Gartner's research director Barbara Gomolski estimates that only 20 percent of organizations conduct one. Many organizations are reluctant to make a post-implementation audit a standard

process for three main reasons. First, they may take too much time, which adds to a project's cost and schedule. Second, post-implementation audits often require massive amounts of documentation to validate results. Last, uncovering unfavorable results may lead to a fear that someone will be blamed. However, post-implementation audits serve an important role. According to Jim Smith, CIO of Sun Life Financial, "With [the] pressure on business today and the responsibility of IT to help the business units understand where their dollars are being spent, I really have trouble with anyone saying you shouldn't be doing [post-implementation audits] in this [hard economic] time."

1. As a consultant, how could you convince your client that conducting a post-implementation audit is worth the added time and cost?

SOURCE: Adapted from Meridith Levinson, How to Conduct Post-Implementation Audits, *CIO Magazine*, October 1, 2003.

review, the auditor or audit team should focus on how well the project was managed and executed. This may include the project plans and Project Management Body of Knowledge areas described in the previous section, as well as the underlying project management and systems development processes outlined in the organization's IT project methodology. In addition, the auditor or audit team should assess whether the project manager and team acted in a professional and ethical manner.

As Gray and Larson (2000) suggest, the depth of the audit depends on the organization's size, the importance and size of the project, the risks involved, and the problems encountered. The audit may involve the project manager and the project team, as well as the project sponsor and other key project stakeholders. In addition, the third party auditor or audit team should:

- Have no direct involvement or interest in the project
- Be respected and viewed as impartial and fair
- Be willing to listen
- Present no fear of recrimination from special interests
- Act in the organization's best interest
- Have broad base of project and/or industry experience

The findings or results of the project audit should be documented, as well as any lessons learned and best practices.

Evaluating Project Success—The MOV

The MOV, or measurable organization value, was defined at the beginning of the project. It provided the basis for taking on the project and supported many of the decision points throughout the project life cycle. Often, the MOV cannot be readily determined at the close of the project. Many of the benefits envisioned by the implemented system may require weeks or even months before they are realized.

Although the different project stakeholders and players may have different views as to whether the project was a success, it is important to assess the value that the project provides the organization. This review may be conducted by several people from both the project sponsor or client's organization and the organization or area responsible for carrying out the project. In particular, this review should focus on answering and documenting the following questions:

- Did the project achieve its MOV?
- Was the sponsor/customer satisfied?
- Was the project managed well?
- Did the project manager and team act in a professional and ethical manner?
- What was done right?
- What can be done better next time?

Before conducting this evaluation, the consulting firm or individuals representing the project should be sure that the information system delivered has not been changed. Often when an information system is handed over to the project sponsor, the users or support staff may make changes. It is not uncommon for these changes to have unintended adverse affects. Care should be taken to ensure that the system being evaluated is the system that was delivered (Nicholas 1990).

The evaluation of the project's MOV may be intimidating—it can be the moment of truth as to whether the project was really a success. However, a successful IT project that brings measurable value to an organization provides a foundation for organizational success.

 ## CHAPTER SUMMARY

This chapter provides closure for both this text and for managing an IT project. Throughout the project life cycle, processes to support both the project and development of the project's product—the information system—have been discussed. These processes are important for managing the project from its inception through to its conclusion.

Once the information system has been built or purchased, it must be tested adequately in order to make installation of the system go more smoothly. However, implementation requires a tactical approach for ensuring that the information system is transferred efficiently and effectively from the project environment to the day-to-day operations of the organization.

Three approaches to implementation were discussed in this chapter. The first approach, called direct cutover, provides the quickest means for implementing the system. In general, the old system is turned off and the new system is turned on. This approach can be risky if the system has not been thoroughly tested. As a result,

it can put a great deal of pressure on the project team to "get it right" the first time, especially if the system supports a mission-critical function of the organization.

The parallel and phased approaches are less risky alternatives, although implementation may take longer. The parallel approach requires that both the old system and new system run concurrently for a time until there is enough confidence that the new system is working properly. At some point, a switch is made from the old system to the new system. The parallel approach can be stressful for the users of the system because they may be required to provide input for both systems and then compare the outputs.

The phased approach may be appropriate when implementing an upgrade or modular system in different departments or at different geographical locations. Under this approach, implementation takes place over phases according to a published schedule. Experience gained from early implementations can make later implementations go more smoothly; on the other hand, any unanticipated problems can create a chain reaction that pushes back the entire implementation schedule. Choosing and implementing the correct implementation approach can have a significant impact on the project schedule and budget.

Once the information system has been implemented, the project manager and team must plan for an orderly end to the project. Projects can be terminated for a variety of reasons, but a project must be properly closed, regardless of whether the project ends successfully or unsuccessfully. Ideally, the project is closed under normal conditions—that is, the project scope is completed within reasonable modifications to the original schedule, budget, and quality objectives. Delivery or installation of the information system does not necessarily mean that the project's sponsor or customer will accept the project. Therefore, closure must focus on providing both proof and confidence that the project team has delivered everything according to the original business case, project charter, and project plan.

A useful way to gain acceptance is the development of a final project report. This report provides a history of the project and outlines how each deliverable was completed and meets the standards of the client or sponsor. The report should also address any open items or issues so that they can be completed within a reasonable time. This report can serve as a foundation for the project team's final meeting with and presentation to the key stakeholders of the project. This meeting not only provides closure for the project, but also serves as a communication tool for informing the stakeholders that the project has been formally accepted and, therefore, is coming to an end.

Several processes for closing a project were discussed in this chapter. They include closing the project accounts, releasing or transferring project resources, documenting lessons learned, and archiving all project documents and deliverables.

Before a project is completely terminated, it is important that several reviews or evaluations be conducted. These evaluations include a performance review between the project manager and each project team member. A postmortem review with the project manager and the entire team should include all of the project deliverables, project plans, and, in general, the various project management body of knowledge areas. Lessons learned should be documented and best practices identified.

The performance reviews and postmortem should provide preparation for the project audit. In this case, a respected and objective third party should review all of the project deliverables and processes to assess how well the project was managed. The auditor or audit team should also focus on the specific challenges the project manager and team faced and how well they addressed these challenges. The professional and ethical behavior of the project manager and project team should be examined as well.

The concept of a project's measurable organization value (MOV) has been a central theme in this text. The MOV provided a basis for deciding whether to invest in the project and guided many of the project decisions throughout the project life cycle. Although different stakeholders may have different views of project success, the overall guiding mechanism for determining whether the project was a success is the project's MOV. Unfortunately, the organizational value that a project provides may not be readily discernible immediately after the information system is implemented. Even if it takes place weeks or months after the project is officially closed, an evaluation as to whether the project has met its MOV must still be conducted. This evaluation should involve various key stakeholders. This moment of truth may make some people anxious, but it provides the necessary means for determining whether the project has brought any real value to the organization.

REVIEW QUESTIONS

1. What is implementation?
2. Describe the three approaches to implementing an information system.
3. What are the advantages and disadvantages of the direct cutover approach?
4. What are the advantages and disadvantages of the parallel approach?
5. What are the advantages and disadvantages of the phased approach?
6. Describe the various scenarios for project termination.
7. Why might an organization terminate a project prematurely? What are the risks?
8. What is a perpetual project? Why might an organization be reluctant to terminate a project that many would consider unsuccessful?
9. Why would senior management cut a project's budget without officially terminating the project?

10. Why might some project team members be reluctant to see the end of a project?

11. Why can the end of a project be stressful for many of the project stakeholders?

12. Why is the sponsor's acceptance of the project important to project closure?

13. How can the project manager and project team facilitate the project sponsor's acceptance of the project?

14. What is the difference between a *shortsighted* and a *knowledgeable* project sponsor? How can making this distinction help the project manager during project closure?

15. What is the purpose of the final project report?

16. What is the purpose of the final meeting and presentation?

17. Describe some of the steps for administrative closure.

18. What is the purpose of the project manager conducting a performance review with each member of the project team?

19. What is the purpose of conducting a postmortem review?

20. What is the purpose of a project audit?

21. What criteria should be used to choose a project auditor or auditing team?

22. What is the purpose of evaluating the project's MOV?

23. Why would it be difficult to evaluate whether or not a project achieved its MOV shortly after the information system is implemented?

24. Why should any lessons learned from project evaluations be documented?

25. Why would evaluating whether a project achieved its MOV make many project managers and teams anxious? Why should it still be done?

EXTEND YOUR KNOWLEDGE

1. Suppose you are the project manager for a mid-sized consulting firm. You have been leading a team of twelve consultants who have been working three months on a six-month project for your firm's largest client. You have managed two projects in the past for this client, and both of these projects were successful. In fact, the client has asked that you personally lead the current project. Your relationship with the client's Chief Information Officer (CIO) has been excellent. Unfortunately, that CIO left the company two weeks ago to start a blues band. Her replacement has just been hired, and your meeting with the new CIO this morning did not go well at all. The new CIO figuratively shredded a status report that you had prepared. Moreover, the CIO seemed to have little understanding of the technology being used to develop the system and complained that the prototypes of the user interface that your team had developed were "too hard to understand and use." Just before leaving his office, the new CIO mentioned that this project was costing way too much money and taking too long to complete. Given the state of the economy, some cuts to the project's budget and schedule may be forthcoming.

   a. Given the situation, do you think this project will survive?

   b. Terminating this project prematurely would have a major impact on the profitability of your firm. What could you do to save either the project or the long-term relationship with this client?

2. Suppose that a client has complained that your organization has allegedly acted in a manner both unprofessional and unethical. While investigating these allegations, senior management has asked you to draft a one-page statement to guide your organization's behavior. How could this code be monitored to ensure that all employees comply? You may use the World Wide Web (WWW) or any other resources as reference, but be sure to cite your references.

3. Using the WWW or any other resources (e.g., you could interview a project manager), write a summary of a company's experience implementing an Enterprise Resource Planning (ERP) system. Was this implementation successful? Why or why not? What were the major challenges? Did the implementation go according to plan? What lessons did the organization learn from this experience? Be sure to include your references.

GLOBAL TECHNOLOGY SOLUTIONS

The party was winding down as Tim Williams and Kellie Matthews sat alone at a table and watched the band pack up its instruments and sound system. It was getting late and only a few other GTS employees and their guests remained. The company had rented a stylish banquet room in a local hotel to mark the conclusion of the Husky Air project. The event allowed Tim and Kellie the opportunity to formally recognize and thank each member of the team for their hard work over the last several months. During a ceremony before dinner, Tim gave each member of the project team a small gift to commemorate Global Technology Solutions' first successful project. In addition, several humorous certificates were given out to keep the occasion fun and lively. The dinner and the band were excellent, and everyone had a great time.

As Tim and Kellie sat at the table, Kellie raised her glass in the air, "Well, here's to the first of many successful projects."

Tim raised his glass as well, "And here's to a great party."

GTS was growing. The company had successfully completed its first project and now two new projects were scheduled to start in a few weeks. Moreover, one of the Husky Air team members, Yan, had been promoted to project manager for one of the upcoming projects. To support this growth, three new employees had been hired and were scheduled to start the next week.

The glasses clinked, then both Kellie and Tim sipped from their glasses. "It was a lot of work, but a lot of fun," reflected Tim.

Kellie smiled, "Don't forget, we still have a few things to wrap up before it's really over. I have to meet with each member of the team next week to make sure that all of the project documents and deliverables are organized and archived. You'll be pretty busy finishing up each team member's evaluation. Then there are these two new projects that we have to start thinking about. And, we still have to meet with Husky Air's

management in a couple of weeks to assess how well the project met its MOV."

"Okay, okay!" laughed Tim. "I didn't want to turn this into a business meeting. For once, let's leave work at the office."

"You're right," laughed Kellie. "Let's leave it at the office. However, I think our little party was a success. We may have even started a new tradition for GTS."

Tim smiled, "I could get used to this. It was kind of stressful at times, especially toward the end, but completing the project and having this party has helped everyone feel good about themselves and the work they did."

By this time the band had carried away the last amplifier, and one could sense that the waitstaff wanted to clear the last of the remaining tables and go home. It was clearly time to leave. Kellie and Tim stood and started walking toward the door. As they put their coats on, Kellie turned to Tim and gave him a quick hug. "It has been a real pleasure starting this company and working so closely with you," she said. "No one in our family would have thought when we were kids that we'd work this well together."

Tim returned the hug. "I never thought that we'd ever get along this well either."

As they headed toward the elevator, Kellie reminded Tim, "Don't forget about dinner at Mom and Dad's house tomorrow night. Mom expects us around six, so don't be late again."

Tim shook his head as the elevator door opened. "Geez, do you always have to act like my older sister?"

Things to Think About

1. What is the purpose of bringing closure to a project?

2. Why is it important to evaluate the project and the team's performance?

3. Why should the project's MOV be evaluated some time after the project is implemented and some time has passed?

HUSKY AIR ASSIGNMENT—PILOT ANGELS

The Implementation and Project Closure Plan

The testing of the application system is now close to being complete. In this assignment, you and your team will develop an implementation and project closure plan to support your project with Husky Air.

Please provide a professional-looking document that includes the following:

1. **Project name, project team name, and the names of the members of your project team**

2. **A brief project description** (This helps your instructor if different teams are working on different projects in your class.)

3. **The project's MOV** (This should be revised or refined if appropriate.)

4. **A conversion strategy**—Develop a strategy for converting Husky Air's current system to the new application system your consulting firm has developed. Be sure to explain why you have chosen one of the following conversion strategies, as well as why you didn't select one of the other two strategies:
   a. Direct cutover
   b. Parallel
   c. Phased

5. **A closure checklist**—Develop a checklist that the project team will use to ensure that the project has been closed properly.

6. **A project evaluation**—Prepare an outline and discussion of how your project's MOV will be evaluated.

 # CASE STUDIES

Kaiser e-Health Records Management System Implementation

Kaiser Foundation Health Plan/Hospitals' implementation of HealthConnect, a $4 billion electronic health records management system from Epic Systems Corp., received media attention as another IT project in serious trouble. As the project drew public attention, Kaiser's CIO, Cliff Dodd, resigned while another Kaiser employee, Justen Deal, sent a memo to all fellow employees detailing the project's financial and technological problems. Deal, a publication project supervisor in the Health Education and Training Department, stated that he also made his concerns known to Kaiser management, but company officials reported that Deal's concerns were looked into and that the HealthConnect project's implementation was not a failure. One of Kaiser's attorneys replied in a letter to Deal that "in the implementation of a new, large and complex system such as KP HealthConnect, various technical problems are likely to arise, but none that you mention are unknown to KP-IT nor were as insurmountable as you imply."

Kaiser did not offer any details regarding Cliff Dodd's departure, and Justen Deal was placed on administrative leave.

The HealthConnect system was expected to provide more than 100,000 of Kaiser's doctors and employees with immediate access to almost 9 million patient medical records. In addition, the system would provide e-messaging, online order entry and filling of prescriptions that would also integrate with appointment scheduling, registration and billing, as well as other functionality that would be available to Kaiser members through its Web site.

However, a 722-page internal report obtained by *Computerworld* listed hundreds of technical problems, some that impacted patient care. Deal's memo stated that reliability and scalability were the main issues because the Citrix Application Delivery infrastructure implemented by Kaiser could not handle the load of the Epic system. According to Deal, "We're the largest Citrix deployment in the world. We're using it in a way that's quite different from the way most organizations are using it. A lot of users use it to allow remote users to connect to the network. But

we actually use it from inside the network. For every user who connects to HealthConnect, they connect via Citrix, and we're running into monumental problems in scaling the Citrix servers. Epic simply cannot scale to meet the size and needs of Kaiser Permanente. And we're wasting billions of dollars trying to make it. The issues for me are the financial repercussions of trying to launch such an ineffective and inefficient and unreliable system across the organization. Using Citrix is something that defies common sense. It would be like trying to use a dial-up modem for thousands of users. It's just not going to work, and it's not something anyone would tell you a dial-up modem should work for." Deal also stated that Kaiser is wasting more than $1.5 billion a year on HealthConnect as well as other troubled IT projects.

Some problems described in the Kaiser report include:

Date	Impact	Description
March 26	3 hours 51 minutes	Users across several locations have intermittent access to HealthConnect, receive Citrix error messages and are unable to access patient records.
April 10	1 hour 23 minutes	Users in Baldwin Park Medical Facility are unable to place new orders for in-patients.
May 9	55 hours 7 minutes	Due to a power outage at Kaiser's data center in Corona, CA, users at numerous health care facilities are unable to access medical information to treat members, process lab and pharmacy requests, or access current medical information for decision making.
October 10	3 hours 24 minutes	Doctors and nurses in several facilities are unable to retrieve critical medical information to treat patients.

Scott Herren, a group vice president and general manager at Citrix Systems Inc., believes the problem isn't scalability but the overall architecture that is being used to support loads this large. Moreover, he states that Health-Connect's problems do not have anything to do with the Citrix product: "In fact, we have many very large successful Epic deployments around the world. However, in order to support large deployments, the Citrix implementation must be architected accordingly."

Matthew Schiffgens, a spokesperson for Kaiser, said "As you move out with a very large deployment like this, you encounter challenges along the way, and we have a process to systematically address challenges as they arise. The problem at the Corona data center was a good one. It came up, we addressed it, and we feel confident that we made the proper infrastructure to manage that. That is a fundamental practice of running a good business. Does that mean there are systematic and ongoing problems? No. You identify issues and address them as they go along."

However, a number of Kaiser employees are still concerned. As one Kaiser IT employee, who wished to remain anonymous, stated: "People out in the field are frustrated, and the people in IT are just as frustrated because this was a solution forced upon us and was not an IT solution. I know in conversations I've had with my superiors there was a big push back in selecting Epic, and it was not a choice made by IT simply because of the large infrastructure needed to support it."

1. In your opinion, do you think that by "blowing the whistle" Justen Deal was a troublemaker, or a concerned employee who did the right thing by detailing the project's problems to all employees across the organization?

2. Compare the views of Justen Deal, Scott Herren, and Matthew Schiffgens. Why would these individuals have such different views of this project's implementation?

3. Should Kaiser terminate this project? Or should they continue with the implementation? What are the ramifications for terminating the project, or continuing?

SOURCE: Adapted from Linda Rosencrance, Problems Abound for Kaiser e-Health Records Management System, *Computerworld*, November 13, 2006.

Project Ocean—Part 2[1]

Project Ocean was a new water billing system that the city of Philadelphia initiated in 2002. By 2006, the city had

[1] A description of Project Ocean can be found in Chapter 1.

spent over $18 million (twice what it expected to spend), the project was two years late, and the system still had not been deployed. The project suffered from a number of problems that included software vendor problems, turnover of key employees, poor project management, and weak governance. However, when Michael Nutter was sworn in as mayor in January 2008, the city had a new and functional water billing system.

Although Oracle was the original software provider, the final implementation of the system was provided by a new off-the-shelf billing system from Prophecy International PTY in Adelaide, Australia. According to the city's CIO, Terry Phillis, the Prophecy billing system was implemented one month ahead of schedule and 25 percent under budget. The Prophecy system was chosen after Phillis and the city of Philadelphia decided to scrap most of the original Oracle applications chosen by Dianah Neff, Phillis' predecessor. The new system replaces a 30-year-old mainframe legacy system that still relied on punch cards. Changes to the old system required writing new Cobol programs, which could take up to a year. The new system now allows the city to make changes in a matter of days and allows customers to track their water conservation efforts. According to Phillis, "Converting this thing over was a huge effort. We had to deal with 30 years of garbage data in the old system." After taking over as the city's new CIO, Phillis led an implementation team of managers from three city agencies. The implementation of the project comes with the hefty price tag of $47 million. However, according to Phillis, this estimate includes many years of costs associated with changing the system prior to starting Project Ocean in 2002. Phillis believes that the biggest lesson learned from this experience is that "technology is not the prime concern in being successful in a project of this size. Instead success is a matter of process, collaboration, and leadership, although the technology has to work and it has to match your skill sets. We had to spend a lot of time upfront deciding how to run this and how to collaborate between three departments."

1. Although Philadelphia's new water billing system was implemented, would you consider this project a success?

SOURCE: Adapted from Matt Hamblen, Philadelphia Bouyant after Completing Water Billing System, *Computerworld*, January 18, 2008.

BIBLIOGRAPHY

Buttrick, R. 2000. *The Interactive Project Workout.* London: Prentice Hall/Financial Times.

Frame, J. D. 1998. Closing Out the Project. In *Project Management Handbook*, edited by J. K. Pinto. San Francisco, CA: Jossey-Bass: 237–246.

Gray, C. F. and E. W. Larson. 2000. *Project Management: The Managerial Process.* Boston: Irwin McGraw-Hill.

Keil, M. 1995. Pulling the Plug: Software Project Management and the Problem of Project Escalation. *MIS Quarterly* (December): 421–447.

Meredith, J. R. and S. J. Mantel, Jr. 2000. *Project Management: A Managerial Approach.* New York: John Wiley.

Nicholas, J. M. 1990. *Managing Business and Engineering Projects: Concepts and Implementation*. Upper Saddle River, NJ: Prentice Hall.

Project Management Institute (PMI) 2004. *A Guide to the Project Management Body of Knowledge (PMBOK® Guide).* Newtown Square, PA: PMI Publishing.

Rosenau, M. D. J. 1998. *Successful Project Management*. New York: John Wiley.

Wysocki, R. K., R. J. Beck, et al. 1995. *Effective Project Management.* New York: John Wiley.

An Introduction to Function Point Analysis

This appendix provides more information about function point analysis. Keep in mind that even this discussion will provide you with only a basic understanding. Although function point analysis is not difficult, the rules for counting function points can be complex for the novice. Resources, such as books, Web sites, training, and certification, are widely available if you are interested in learning more.

BACKGROUND

Lines of code (LOC) or source lines of code (SLOC) have been the traditional way of estimating the size of an application. Although intuitively appealing, estimating or counting lines of code have several disadvantages. First, many organizations develop applications using different programming languages, platforms, tools, and so on. An IT project developed in Visual Studio® and SQL Server® will be difficult to compare to a mainframe-based COBOL application. Moreover, experienced and talented programmers tend to write more efficient code than novice programmers. As a result, experienced programmers may write fewer lines of code than novices and still accomplish the same thing. In addition, no set standard exists for determining what exactly should be counted. For example, should remarks or documentation lines be counted? What about the initialization of variables? Although counting lines of code seems fairly straightforward, the actual implementation becomes problematic.

To overcome many of the inherent problems with counting LOC, Allan Albrecht (1979, 1983) proposed the idea of function points at a conference sponsored by IBM in 1979. The basic concept behind function points is to focus on the *functionality* of the application. After all, the size and complexity of an application (and subsequently the number of lines of code to be written) are based upon what the application must do. Function points provide a synthetic metric, similar to hours, kilos, and degrees Celsius, for software engineering that gives consistent results, regardless of the technology or programming language used.

In the early 1980s, statistical analysis provided the means for refining the function point technique. Since 1986, function point analysis rules and guidelines have been overseen by a nonprofit organization called the International Function Point Users Group (IFPUG). The IFPUG maintains the *Counting Practices Manual* that contains all the current guidelines and certification for counting function points under the IFPUG standard. The material in this appendix will be based upon the latest counting practices by IFPUG.

You should know, however, that there is an alternative way of counting function points. In 1983, Charles Symons, working for Nolan, Norton, and Company (later acquired by KPMG Consulting) critiqued Albrecht's proposed function point technique and argued the existence of several flaws. As a result, Symons proposed an alternative function point technique called the Mark II approach. The Mark II technique has become popular primarily in the United Kingdom and is overseen by the United Kingdom Function Point Users Group (UFPUG).

WHAT PRECISELY IS A FUNCTION POINT?

Function point analysis is a structured technique for breaking up or modularizing an application by categories or classes based on functionality. A function point is a software metric. Similar to the many metrics you use each day, a function point provides an idea of the size and complexity of a particular application or module of that application. For example, it should be pretty straightforward that a 4,000-square-foot home is larger than a 2,000-square-foot home. But will a 4,000-square-foot house take twice as long and cost twice as much to build as a 2,000-square-foot house? It depends. What if the larger house uses stock material and includes only the basic amenities, while the 2,000-square-foot house has many custom features? The custom features may include a handcrafted staircase, exotic wood, imported marble, and other very expensive items. As you can see, depending on the features or requirements of each house, the time to build and the cost for each house can differ radically (Dekker 1999).

Similarly, an application that has 4,000 LOC has twice as many lines of code as a 2,000 LOC application. But will a 4,000 LOC application take twice as long and cost twice as much to build as a 2,000 LOC application? Again, the answer is that it depends. In this case, it depends more on the features or required functionality of the system and the complexity of those required features. Function points provide a useful metric that combines both functionality and complexity. For example, a 4,000 function point application will, in fact, be larger, have more functionality, and be more complex than a 2,000 function point application. Since function points are independent of the technology, we can compare these two applications regardless of the fact that one application is written in Java and the other in COBOL. More specifically, the size of the application is based upon functionality in terms of:

- Inputs
- Outputs
- Inquiries
- Internal files
- External files
- The complexity of the general characteristics of the system

Therefore, the key to function point analysis is having a good understanding of the system's requirements (Jones 1998). Often at the outset of a project, the requirements may not be clear. A function point analysis can still be conducted and then updated throughout the project life cycle as these requirements become more clearly defined. For example, a function point analysis can be conducted based upon the definition of the project's scope. This analysis will provide a solid definition of the application's boundary and will provide a starting point for defining and subsequently estimating the size and complexity of the application deliverable (McConnell 1996). A clearer picture of the features and functionality of the application will follow during the analysis and design phases of the project. Later on, a function point analysis can be conducted when the project application is delivered, in order to compare the agreed-upon requirements to what was delivered. In general, function points can be useful for:

- *Managing scope*—Scope changes will change an application's total function point count. As a result, the project manager and project sponsor/client may use function point analysis to determine the impact of a proposed scope change in terms of the project's schedule and budget.

- *Benchmarking*—The value of function point analysis is that data can be collected and compared to other projects. For example, the true value of counting function points is to compare a project to past projects and to other projects throughout the organization. This comparison allows an organization to identify challenges and opportunities in order to take corrective action when necessary. In addition, estimation becomes more meaningful and accurate when similar methods, tools, and resources are part of the data analysis. An organization can inventory its application portfolio to understand cost structures and the impact of new best practices. Function points by themselves do not provide much information without the use of other metrics, such as time, cost, and quality.

- *Reliability*—Once knowledgeable and experienced in function point counting, different people can count function points for the same application and obtain the same measure within an acceptable margin of error.

HOW TO CONDUCT A FUNCTION POINT ANALYSIS

The process of conducting a function point analysis can be summarized in seven steps (Longstreet 2002):

- Determine the function type count to be conducted.
- Define the boundary of the application.
- Define all data functions and their degree of complexity.
- Define all transactional functions and their complexity.
- Calculate the unadjusted function point count.
- Calculate the value adjustment factor based on a set of general system characteristics.
- Calculate the final adjusted function point count.

Step 1: Determine the Function Type Count to Be Conducted

The first step in conducting a function point analysis is to determine the type of function count to be conducted. Function points can be counted by an individual or a small team, and the type of function point count will help the counters plan their strategy and determine what documents and resources will be required. A function type count can be one of three types:

- *Development*—A development function type count would be made for a new project. These types of counts would be based initially on the scope definition of the project and would be updated throughout the project life cycle as requirements and functionality are more clearly defined. The basic purpose of development function type counts is estimating the size and effort of the application.

- *Enhancement*—Enhancement focuses more on maintenance projects, or projects that attempt to modify or enhance existing applications. These projects may include deleting, changing, or adding functionality to the existing application.

- *Application*—An application function type count may be viewed as an inventorying of an existing application in the IT project portfolio in order to create a baseline or benchmark. Combined with other metrics, a database can be created to support analysis and estimation.

Step 2: Define the Boundary of the Application

The application boundary defines the border for the user, the application itself, and any other external application. The boundary should be based upon the user's view of the domain and not technology partitions or platforms. Often applications today must interface or integrate with each other, so it is important that the boundary be defined clearly. Scope management is concerned with defining, managing, and controlling the project's scope. More specifically, tools such as data flow diagrams and use case diagrams are useful for defining the project's scope and the boundary for the application.

Step 3: Define All Data Functions and Their Degree of Complexity

Data function types may be thought of as data at rest; they are the logical data that can be updated and queried. The transactional functions, such as external inputs (EI), external outputs (EO), and external inquiries (EQ), are processes that set the data in motion. These processes act directly on the logical data to perform the updates and queries. In particular, data functions can be either internal logical files (ILF) or external interface files (EIF). As their names imply, ILFs are maintained within the application boundary and EIFs are maintained by an external application but available to the application being counted. For example, a sales application might keep track of customers and the products they purchase, but customer balances and other credit-related information may be maintained by a separate accounts receivable application.

Once the ILFs and EIFs are identified and counted, they are scored or rated based on their functional complexity in terms of their number of record type elements (RETs) and data element types (DETs). A record type element, or RET, is a recognizable subgroup of data elements contained within the ILF or EIF. These are one of the more difficult concepts in function point analysis, but you can think of them as representing a parent–child relationship. In object-oriented terms, you can think of this as a subclass and a superclass. On the other hand, a data element type, or DET, is defined as a unique, nonrecursive field recognized by the user. For example, let's say that an entity called student has a student identification number, name, address, and a cumulative number of credit hours. In addition, there are two types of students—undergraduate and graduate. If the data about students were stored, updated, retrieved, and queried by our application, we would count this as 1 ILF with 6 DETs and 2 RETs as illustrated in Table A.1.

Once the ILFs and EIFs and their associated RETs and DETs have been identified and counted, their complexity can

Table A.1 Data Function Count

	Count as
Superclass: Student	ILF
Student ID number	DET
Name	DET
Address	DET
Cumulative credit hours	DET
Subclass: Graduate	RET
Graduate assistantship	DET
Subclass: Undergraduate	RET
Class Standing	DET

Table A.2   Complexity for ILFs and EIFs

	DET: Data Element Type		
RET: Record Element Type	*1–19*	*20–50*	*51 or More*
Less than 2	Low	Low	Average
2–5	Low	Average	High
More than 5	Average	High	High

be determined using the matrix shown in Table A.2. For example, the student ILF would have a complexity score of Low because the number of RETs is less than 2 and the number of DETs is between 1 and 19.

Step 4: Define all Transactional Functions and Their Complexity

Transactional functional types focus on the processing of data between the user and the application and between the application and any external applications. Therefore, transactional functions, called external inputs (EIs), external outputs (EOs), and external inquiries (EQs), perform updates, retrievals, and queries on the data contained within the ILFs and EIFs.

An external input (EI) is defined as an elementary process that processes data or control information that originates from outside the application boundary. An elementary process is defined as the smallest unit of activity that is meaningful to the user. The elementary process must be viewed from the user's perspective (i.e., not a technical perspective) and must leave the application in a consistent state after performing its function. Data refers to the actual data processed by the transaction, while control information refers to such things as rules or parameters passed to the application. An example of an EI would be an input screen to add new students to the student ILF. The elementary process would require that all required fields be filled before adding the new student's information to the student ILF in order to leave the application in a consistent state.

Once the EIs have been identified and counted, their complexity can be determined using the following matrix based on the file types referenced (FTR) and data element types. An FTR is just the number of ILF and EIF files referenced. For example, if an input screen to add new students only accessed the student ILF and included only 6 DETs, the complexity rating for this particular EI would be Low. See Table A.3.

Similarly, an external output (EO) is an elementary process that allows data or control information to exit the application boundary. Examples of EOs would include reports, receipts, confirmation messages, derived or calculated totals, and graphs or charts. Once the EOs are identified and counted, their relative functional complexity can be determined based on the FTRs and DETs. Continuing with our example,

Table A.3   Complexity for External Inputs (EI)

	DET: Data Element Type		
FTR: File Types Referenced	*1–4*	*5–15*	*16 or More*
Less than 2	Low	Low	Average
2	Low	Average	High
More than 2	Average	High	High

Table A.4   Complexity for External Outputs (EO)

	DET: Data Element Type		
FTR: File Types Referenced	1–5	6–19	20 or More
Less than 2	Low	Low	Average
2–3	Low	Average	High
More than 3	Average	High	High

suppose that the student application printed two reports, one report listing all the students alphabetically and the other grouping by graduate and undergraduate. If all data fields were included in each report, the complexity rating for the application's EOs would be Low. See Table A.4.

An external inquiry (EQ) is defined as an elementary process that includes both a combination of inputs and outputs for retrieving data from one or more ILFs and/or EIFs. Unlike an EI, the EQ input process does not update any internal or external files, and the output of the EQ transaction does not calculate or derive any data. Once the EQs have been identified and counted, a relative complexity score can be made. For example, let's suppose our student application allows searching by student number. This query would count as one EQ. In addition, let's suppose that an error message is displayed if no matching student numbers are found. The number of DETs would include the 6 data fields plus an additional DET for the error message. Therefore, the complexity rating for the application's EQ would be Low. See Table A.5.

Step 5: Calculate the Unadjusted Function Point Count

Using the counts for each ILF, EIF, EI, EO, and EQ, an unadjusted function point count can be computed using Table A.6 (Dennis and Haley 2000).

Table A.5   Complexity for External Inquiries (EQ)

	DET: Data Element Type		
FTR: File Types Referenced	1–5	6–19	20 or More
Less than 2	Low	Low	Average
2–3	Low	Average	High
More than 3	Average	High	High

Table A.6   Computing UAF

	Complexity			Total
	Low	Average	High	
Internal Logical Files (ILF)	___×7 = ___	___×10 = ___	___×15 = ___	
External Interface Files (EIF)	___×5 = ___	___×7 = ___	___×10 = ___	
External Input (EI)	___×3 = ___	___×4 = ___	___×6 = ___	
External Output (EO)	___×4 = ___	___×5 = ___	___×7 = ___	
External Inquiry (EQ)	___×3 = ___	___×4 = ___	___×6 = ___	

Total Unadjusted Function Points (UAF)

To find the total unadjusted function point total (UAF), multiply the number of low, average, and high ILFs, EIFs, EIs, EOs, and EQs by the appropriate number in each cell. These values are then summed across the rows for each function type. The grand total is just a summation of these row totals.

Step 6: Calculate the VAF Based on a Set of General System Characteristics

The value adjustment factor (VAF) is multiplied by the unadjusted function point (UAF) calculated in step 5 to come up with a final adjusted function point total. In identifying each ILF, EIF, EO, EI, and EQ, a complexity matrix was used to determine the complexity for each data and transactional function type in terms of low, average, or high complexity. However, at this time a set of 14 general system characteristics (GSC) are used to compute a total degree of influence. This degree of influence will be used to compute the VAF.

To determine the total degree of influence, each GSC is rated based on its degree of influence using the following 0 to 5 scale:

0. Not present or no influence

1. Incidental influence

2. Moderate influence

3. Average influence

4. Significant influence

5. Strong influence throughout

Following is information about each GSC that can be used to rate it.

1. ***Data communications***—A communication facility is required to send data and control information via teleprocessing (TP). These links require protocols that allow for the exchange of data between a sender and receiver. Examples include TCP/IP, Ethernet, AppleTalk, and so on.

   Degree of Influence
   0. Pure batch or stand-alone PC
   1. Batch but with remote data entry or printing
   2. Batch but with remote data entry and remote printing
   3. Online data collection or TP on the front end to a batch processing or query system
   4. More than a front end, but only one type of TP protocol supported
   5. More than a front end with more than one type of TP protocol supported

2. ***Distributed data processing***—Distributed data processing is a characteristic of the application.

   Degree of Influence
   0. Does not aid the transfer of data or processing function between components of the system
   1. Prepares data for end user processing or another component of the system (e.g., spreadsheet, DBMS, etc.)
   2. Data prepared for transfer, then transferred and processed by another component

3. Distributed processing and data transfer are online but only in one direction

4. Distributed processing and data transfer are online and in both directions

5. Processing of functions is dynamic and performed by the most appropriate component of the system

3. *Performance*—Performance in terms of response time or throughput. It will greatly influence the design, development, implementation, support, and maintenance of the application.

Degree of Influence

0. No special performance requirements stated

1. Performance and design requirements stated and reviewed, but no special attention needed

2. Response time or throughput critical at peak times. No special design required and processing deadline is the next business day

3. Response time and throughput are critical during all business hours. Although no special design for CPU utilization is required, the processing deadline requirements with interfacing systems pose constraints

4. Stated user performance requirements are stringent and require a performance analysis in the design phase

5. Performance analysis tools needed in the design, development, and/or implementation phases to meet stated user performance requirements

4. *Heavily used configuration*—The volume of data and transactions placed on a particular hardware platform.

Degree of Influence

0. No operational restrictions

1. Operational restrictions exist, but are not overly restrictive and no special attention is needed

2. Some security and timing considerations are needed

3. Specific processor requirements for a specific component of the application exist

4. Stated operational restrictions exist and require special attention

5. There are special constraints with respect to the distributed components of the system

5. *Transaction rate*—Similar to GSC 3, the number of transactions handled by the application will be a performance consideration with respect to the design, development, implementation, and maintenance of the system.

Degree of Influence

0. No peak transaction period is anticipated

1. A single peak transaction period (i.e., daily, weekly, monthly, etc.) is anticipated.

2. A peak transaction period will occur weekly

3. A peak transaction period will occur daily

4. Transaction rates are high enough that a performance analysis is required during the design phase

5. Transaction rates are high enough to require performance analysis and, in addition, the use of performance analysis tools during the design, development, and/or implementation phases

6. ***Online data entry***—The amount of data entered online will influence the design development, implementation, and maintenance of the application. *Note:* these guidelines may not be realistic since they have not been updated to reflect most systems today.

Degree of Influence

0. All transactions are processed in batch mode

1. 1–7% of transactions are done interactively

2. 8–15% of transactions are done interactively

3. 16–23% of transactions are done interactively

4. 24–30% of transactions are done interactively

5. Over 30% of transactions are done interactively

7. ***End user efficiency***—The functions provided by the application may emphasize user efficiency. This may include

- Navigational aids
- Menus
- Online help/documentation
- Automated cursor movement
- Scrolling
- Remote printing
- Preassigned function keys
- Submission of batch jobs from online transactions
- Cursor selection of screen data
- Heavy use of reverse video, highlighting, colors, etc.
- Hard copy user documentation of online transactions
- Mouse interface
- Pop up windows
- As few screens as possible to accomplish a business function
- Bilingual support
- Multilingual support

Degree of Influence

0. None

1. 1–3

2. 4–5

3. Six or more but with no specific user requirements in terms of efficiency

4. Six or more and stated user requirements are strong enough to require design tasks for human factors to be included (e.g., minimize keystrokes)

5. Six or more and stated user requirements are strong enough to require special tools and processes to demonstrate that requirements have been achieved

8. *Online update*—Related to the number of ILFs updated by the application.

Degree of Influence

0. None
1. Online update of one to three files, but volume of updating is low and recovery is easy
2. Online update of four or more files, but volume is low and recovery is easy
3. Online update of major internal files internal logical files (ILF)
4. In addition, protection from data loss is critical and must be specially designed and built into the system
5. In addition, high volumes lead to high recovery cost considerations, whereby recovery procedures must be automated and cause minimal operator intervention

9. *Complex processing*—Complex processing is a characteristic of the application and includes:

- Sensitive control and/or application specific security processing
- Extensive logical processing
- Extensive mathematical processing
- A great deal of exception processing whereby incomplete transactions that may be caused by such things as TP interruption, missing data values, or failed edits must be processed again
- Complex processing to handle multiple input/output possibilities (e.g., multimedia or device dependence)

Degree of Influence

0. None
1. Any one
2. Any two
3. Any three
4. Any four
5. All five

10. *Reusability*—The degree to which the application will be usable in other applications.

Degree of Influence

0. There is no reusable code
1. Reusable code is used within the application
2. Less than ten percent of the application considers more than one user's needs
3. Ten percent or more of the application considered more than one user's needs

4. The application was specially developed to ease reuse. The application is customizable to the user at the source code level

5. The application was specifically designed to ease reuse. The application is customizable to use at source code level by means of user parameter maintenance

11. *Installation ease*—The ease or degree of difficulty during conversion and installation.

Degree of Influence

0. No special considerations stated by the user. No special setup required

1. No special considerations stated by the user. However, special setup required for installation

2. Conversion and installation requirements stated by the user. Conversion and installation guides provided and tested, but impact of conversion is not considered important

3. Conversion and installation requirements stated by the user. Conversion and installation guides provided and tested, but impact of conversion is considered important

4. In addition to 2, automated conversion and installation tools were provided and tested

5. In addition to 3, automated conversion tools were provided and tested

12. *Operational ease*—The efficiency and effectiveness of startup, backup, and recovery procedures that were provided and tested during the system testing phase.

Degree of Influence

0. No special considerations were stated by the user other than normal backup procedures

1–4. Select the following items that apply to the application. Each item has a value of one unless noted otherwise:

  ■ Effective startup, backup, and recovery processes were provided, but operator intervention is required

  ■ Effective startup, backup, and recovery processes were provided, but no operator intervention is required (count as 2 items)

  ■ The application minimizes the need for tape mounts

  ■ The application minimizes the need for paper handling

5. The application is designed for unattended operation—that is, no operator intervention is needed other than to start or shut down the application. Automatic error recovery is a feature of the application

13. *Multiple sites*—The degree to which the application has been designed specifically to be installed and operated at multiple sites and/or for multiple organizations.

Degree of Influence

0. Only one user/installation site is required

1. Needs of multiple sites were considered and the application is designed to operate only under identical hardware and software environments

2. Needs of multiple sites were considered and the application is designed to operate only under similar hardware and software environments

3. Needs of multiple sites were considered and the application is designed to operate only under different hardware and software environments

4. Documentation and a support plan are provided and tested to support the application at multiple sites as described in 1 or 2

5. Documentation and a support plan are provided and tested to support the application at multiple sites as described in 3

14. *Facilitate change*—The degree to which the application was developed to facilitate change.

Degree of Influence

0. No special user requirements were stated to minimize or facilitate change

1–5. Select the items that apply to the application:

- Flexible query/report facility is provided to handle simple requests— i.e., and/or logic is applied to only one ILF (count as 1)

- Flexible query/report facility is provided that can handle requests of average complexity—i.e., and/or logic applied to more than one ILF (count as 2 items)

- Flexible query/report facility is provide that can handle complex requests—i.e., and/or logic combinations on one or more ILFs (count as 3 items)

- Control data is kept in tables and maintained by the user online. Changes take effect next business day

- Control data kept in tables and maintained by the user online. Changes take effect immediately (count as 2 items)

Once each of the fourteen general systems characteristics (GSCs) is evaluated on a scale of one to five, the fourteen scores are summed to compute the total degrees of influence.

$$TDI = \sum_{i=1}^{14} \text{Degrees of Influence}$$

The TDI is then used to determine the value added adjustment factor (VAF) using the following equation:

$$VAF = (TDI \times 0.01) + .65$$

Note that if all the degrees of influence for each of the GSCs are scored as zero, the VAF will be equal to. 65. On the other hand, if all of the GSCs are scored as five, the VAF will be equal to 1.35. Therefore, simpler systems will score closer to .65, while more complex systems will score closer to 1.35. Subsequently, an application of average complexity will score close to 1.00. Therefore, the VAF can be used as a reality check for assessing the overall complexity of the application.

Step 7: Calculate the Final Adjusted Function Point Count

The final adjusted function point count is readily found by multiplying the unadjusted function point (UAF) by the value added adjustment factor (VAF).

$$FP = UAF \times VAF$$

The project team should then review the function point analysis for completeness and accuracy. Errors usually are the result of forgetting or missing something; therefore, the person or small group in charge of the function point analysis should be certified and use the most current standards as published in the IFPUG *Counting Practices Manual*. As with most things in life, function point analysis becomes easier and more meaningful with experience. If a function point analysis is conducted for each application, the function point information can be integrated with other financial and nonfinancial metrics to improve estimating and understanding of the development process.

BIBLIOGRAPHY

Albrecht, Allan J. 1979. Measuring Application Development Productivity. Proceedings SHARE/GUIDE IBM Applications Development Symposium, Monterey, Calif., Oct 14–17, 1979.

Albrecht, A. J. and J. E. Gaffney. 1983. Software Function, Source Lines of Code and Development Effort Prediction: A Software Science Validation. *IEEE Transactions Software Engineering*, SE-9(6): 639–647.

Dekker, C. A. 1999. Managing (the size of) your projects: A project management look at function points. *Crosstalk: The Journal of Defense Software Engineering*, February: 24–26.

Dennis, A. and W. B. Haley. 2000. *Systems Analysis and Design: An Applied Approach*. New York: John Wiley.

Jones, T. C. 1998. *Estimating Software Costs*. New York: McGraw-Hill.

Longstreet, David. *Function Point Training and Analysis Manual*. Longstreet Consulting Inc, Revision Dates: Feb. 2001, 30 Aug. 2001, 1 March 2002. <http://www.SoftwareMetrics.Com/freemanual.htm>.

McConnell, S. 1996. *Rapid Development: Taming Wild Software Schedules*. Redmond, WA: Microsoft Press.

INDEX

Interpersonal skills, of team, 114
Interviewing, 216
Intranets, 12
Ishikawa diagram, 272
ISO certification, 263
Isolation, project, 107
Iterative systems development,
22–23
  agile, 23
  prototyping, 22
  rapid applications
   development, 22
  spiral development, 22

J

Joint applications development
(JAD), 20, 142
Juran, Joseph, 271

K

Kick-off meeting, 93
Kill points, 16
Knowledge, in organizations, 104
Knowledgeable sponsors, 371
Knowledge management, 12
  project quality management
   and, 291
  project teams and, 117–18
Knowledge-management
  approach, 12–13
Knowledge Plan, 171
Known risks, 213
Known-unknown risks, 213

L

Lag time, 189
Language, international projects
and, 357
Leadership, 341–63
  affiliative style, 345
  approaches to, 343–44
  authoritative style, 345
  coaching style, 346
  coercive style, 344–45
  defined, 342
  democratic style, 345
  emotional intelligence and,
   346–48
  ethical, 350–51
  ethically neutral, 351

hypocritical, 350–51
listening and, 348
pacesetting style, 346
styles, 344–46
unethical, 350
visionary, 347
Lead time, 189
Learning curve, 197
Learning cycles
  concepts of, 118
  risk and, 215
  work breakdown structure
   and, 159
Learning cycle theory, 118
Leavitt's model of organizational
  change, 304
Legality, ethics *versus*, 349
Lessons learned, 12, 121
  change, 311
  work breakdown structure
   and, 159
Lines of code (LOC), 153,
164–65
  function point analysis
   and, 384
  function point conversion
   to, 168
Listening, leadership and, 348
Low-quality software, acceptance
  of, 267
Lump-sum contracts, 328–29

M

Malcolm Baldridge National
  Quality Award, 265
Management
  change, 88, 301
  configuration, 288–90
  conflict, 312
  crisis, 206
  fact-based, 284
  fire fighting, 206, 278
  productivity, 78
  project integration, 81–83
  requirements, 280
  reserves, 229
  reviews, 288
Management information systems
  (MIS)
Management plan
  quality, 88

scope, 88, 135
Management system, 275
Managers
  project, 78, 111–13
  study of, 7
Managing at the Speed of Change
  (Conner), 302
Managing stakeholders, 241
Matrix
  balanced, 107
  functional, 108
  project, 108
Matrix organization, 107–9
  advantages of, 108–9
  disadvantages of, 109
  structure, 101
Measurable organizational value
  (MOV), 44–50
  evaluation of, 375, 376–77
  as goal of project, 212
  project charter and, 86
  project planning framework
   and, 90
  sample, 50
  scope and, 144
  scorecard and, 63
  summarizing, 50
  time frame for, 49
  work breakdown structure
   and, 158–59
Meetings
  face-to-face, 254
  final, 372–73
Mentoring, communication and,
256
Methodology
  defined, 35
  information technology project,
   11
Metrics
  cost effectiveness of, 246
  dashboard, 247
  developing, 47–48
  earned value, 247–53
  high impact of, 247
  process, 286
  product, 286
  project, 246–53, 286
  project performance, 251
  proven, 247
  quality, 285–86